Complete Computer Concepts and Programming in QuickBASIC

GARY B. SHELLY
THOMAS J. CASHMAN
GLORIA A. WAGGONER

Contributing Authors

James S. Quasney
Misty E. Vermaat
William C. Waggoner

boyd & fraser publishing company

bf

© 1994 by boyd & fraser publishing company
One Corporate Place • Ferncroft Village
Danvers, Massachusetts 01923

ITP International Thomson Publishing
boyd & fraser publishing company is an ITP Company.
The ITP trademark is used under license

2 3 4 5 6 7 BC 9 8 7 6 5

Manufactured in the United States of America ISBN 0-87709-655-4

PHOTO CREDITS

CHAPTER 1 *Opening Page*, ©Robert Holmgren; *Figure 1-1*, Texas Instruments; *Figure 1-2*, (pc) International Business Machines Corp.; (printer) Panasonic Communications and Systems Co.; *Figure 1-3*, International Business Machines Corp.; *Figure 1-4*, International Business Machines Corp.; *Figure 1-7*, (pc) Dell Computer Corp.; (palmtop) Hewlett-Packard Co.; (laptop) International Business Machines Corp.; (supercomputer) Paul Shambroom, courtesy of Cray Research, Inc.; *Figure 1-9*, Curtis Fukuda; *Figure 1-15*, Hewlett-Packard Co.; *Figure 1-16*, International Business Machines Corp.; *Figure 1-17*, International Business Machines Corp.; *Figure 1-18*, UNISYS Corp.; *Figure 1-19*, Lockheed Corp.; *Figure 1-20*, NCR Corp.; *Figure 1-21*, UNISYS Corp.; *Figure 1-22*, Hewlett-Packard Co.; *Figure 1-23*, Intertec Diversified Systems; *Figure 1-24*, International Business Machines Corp.; *Figure 1-25*, (1) Compaq Computer Corp. All rights reserved.; (2) International Business Machines Corp.; (3) UNISYS Corp.; (4) Compaq Computer Corp. All rights reserved.; (5) International Business Machines Corp.; (6) Zenith Data Systems; (7) International Business Machines Corp.; (8) International Business Machines Corp.; (9) Hewlett-Packard Co. **TIMELINE** *Page 1 (1937–52)*, (top left three photos of Atanasoff, Berry, ABC) Iowa State University, News Service, Photo Dept.; (top right) Princeton University; (bottom three photos) UNISYS Corp.; *Page 2 (1952–60)*, (top three photos of Dr. Hopper, COBOL, FORTRAN) U.S. Department of the Navy; (top-IBM 650) International Business Machines Corp.; (bottom-core memory) M.I.T.; (bottom two photos of transistors) International Business Machines Corp.; *Page 3 (1964–69)*, (top left-IBM 360) International Business Machines Corp.; (top right-DEC) Digital Equipment Corp.; (bottom left-Kemeny) Dartmouth College News Service; (bottom right-Hoff) Intel Corp.; (bottom right-4004) Intel Corp.; *Page 4 (1970–80)*, (top two photos on the left-LSI) International Business Machines Corp.; (top right-MITS) The Computer Museum; (bottom-Wozniak) Apple Computer, Inc.; (bottom-first Apple) Apple Computer, Inc.; (bottom right-VisiCalc) ©Ira Wyman; *Page 5 (1981–84)*, (top left-Gates) Microsoft Corp.; (top right-IBM) International Business Machines Corp.; (bottom left-Lotus) Lotus Development Corp.; (bottom left-Kapor) Lotus Development Corp.; (bottom right-Apple) Apple Computer, Inc.; *Page 6 (1987–90)*, (top left-Compaq) Compaq Computer Corp. All rights reserved.; (top right-Intel) Intel Corp.; (bottom left-NeXT) NeXT Computer, Inc.; (bottom right-Windows) Microsoft Corp. **CHAPTER 2** *Opening Page*, Stan Musilek Photography; *Figure 2-1*, (far left) Curtis Fukuda; *2-1*, (icons) Microsoft Corp.; *2-1*, (mouse) Apple Computer, Inc.; *Figure 2-2*, (left) Curtis Fukuda; (right) Hewlett-Packard Co.; *Figure 2-3*, Reference Software Intl.; *Figure 2-14*, Dubl-Click Software, Inc.; *Figure 2-15*, Lotus Development Corp.; *Figure 2-23*, Hewlett-Packard Co.; *Figure 2-25*, Curtis Fukuda; *Figure 2-35*, International Business Machines Corp.; *Figure 2-36*, Business & Professional Software, Inc. Image created with BPS's 35mm Express Software; *Figure 2-37*, Compaq Computer Corp. All rights reserved.; *Figure 2-38*, Prodigy; *Figure 2-39*, Microsoft Corp.; *Figure 2-40*, Borland International ©1991; *Figure 2-41*, Symantic Corp.; *Figure 2-42*, The Aldridge Co.; *Figure 2-43*, Curtis Fukuda; *2-44*, (bottom left) Curtis Fukuda; *2-44*, (bottom right) Wink Data Products **CHAPTER 3** *Opening Page*, Hank Morgan/Rainbow; *Figure 3-6*, International Business Machines Corp.; *Figure 3-7*, (left) Applied Data Signs; *3-7*, (right) Hewlett-Packard Co.; *Figure 3-8*, Compaq Computer Corp. All rights reserved.; *Figure 3-9*, International Business Machines Corp.; *Figure 3-10*, (top) Microsoft Corporation; (bottom) Curtis Fukuda; *Figure 3-11*, Logitech, Inc.; *Figure 3-12*, Hewlett-Packard Co.; *Figure 3-13*, Kensington Microware; *Figure 3-14*, International Business Machines Corp.; *Figure 3-15*, Design Technology; *Figure 3-16*, Summagraphics Corp.; *Figure 3-17*, CalComp Digitizer Products Group; *Figure 3-18*, Compaq Computer Corp. All rights reserved.; *Figure 3-19*, GRID Systems Corp.; *Figure 3-20*, Texas Instruments; *Figure 3-21*, Hewlett-Packard Co.; *Figure 3-22*, Logitech, Inc.; *Figure 3-23*, Wang Laboratories, Inc.; *Figure 3-24*, (both) Spectra-Physics Scanning Systems, Inc.; *Figure 3-25*, (close-up) Soricon Corp.; (less close) International Business Machines Corp.; *Figure 3-28*, Caere Corp.; *Figure 3-29*, Scantron Corp.; *Figure 3-30*, NCR Corp.; *Figure 3-31*, International Business Machines Corp.; *Figure 3-32*, Symbol Technologies, Inc.; *Figure 3-33*, Photo courtesy of Intermec Corp.; *Figure 3-34*, International Business Machines Corp.; *Figure 3-41*, Microsoft Corp.; *Figure 3-47*, Acme Visible Records **CHAPTER 4** *Opening Page*, Chuck O'Rear/West Light; *Figure 4-19*, Intel Corp.; *Figure 4-20*, International Business Machines Corp.; *Figure 4-22*, International Business Machines Corp.; *Figure 4-23*, International Business Machines Corp.; *Making a Chip*: (1) Intel Corp.; (2) Intel Corp.; (3) AT&T; (4) Siltec Corp.; (5) Siltec Corp.; (6) Micron Technology, Inc.; (7) Intel Corp.; (8) Micron Technology, Inc.; (9) Intel Corp.; (10) National Semiconductor Corp.; (11) International Business Machines Corp.; (12) AT&T Bell Laboratories; (13) 3M Corp. **CHAPTER 5** *Opening Page*, ©Robert Holmgren; *Figure 5-1*, Hewlett-Packard Co.; *Figure 5-7*, Britannica Software Inc.; *Figure 5-8*, Owens-Corning Fiberglas Corp.; *Figure 5-11*, Panasonic Communications and Systems Co.; *Figure 5-12*, (both) Printronix, Inc.; *Figure 5-13*, Dataproducts Corp.; *Figure 5-18*, (left) Storage Technology Corp.; (right) Atchison, Topeka and Santa Fe Railway Co.; *Figure 5-19*, Epson America, Inc.; *Figure 5-20*, Dataproducts Corp.; *Figure 5-22*, McDonnell Douglas Automation Co.; *Figure 5-23*, Dataproducts Corp.; *Figure 5-25*, International Business Machines Corp.; *Figure 5-26*, NEC Technologies, Inc.; *Figure 5-28*, Hewlett-Packard Co.; *Figure 5-29*, Xerox Corp.; *Figure 5-31*, Radius, Inc.; *Figure 5-33*, (left) Ramtek Corp.; (right) Evans & Southerland; *Figure 5-35*, International Business Machines Corp.; *Figure 5-36*, Toshiba America Information Systems, Inc.; *Figure 5-39*, Proxima Corp.; *Figure 5-40*, Electrohome Ltd.; *Figure 5-41*, Hewlett-Packard Co.; *Figure 5-42*, (both) CalComp Digitizer Products Group. **CHAPTER 6** *Opening Page*, Stan Musilek Photography; *Figure 6-2*, Gregg Hadel; *Figure 6-3*, Jerry Spagnoli; *Figure 6-10*, Seagate Technology, Inc.; *Figure 6-11*, Amdahl Corp.; *Figure 6-12*, International Business Machines Corp.; *Figure 6-13*, Microscience International Corp.; *Figure 6-14*, ©Robert Holmgren; *Figure 6-18*, Control Data Corp.; *Figure 6-19*, Plus Development Corp.; *Figure 6-20*, Plus Development Corp.; *Figure 6-21*, Jerry Spagnoli; *Figure 6-22*, Hewlett-Packard Co.; *Figure 6-24*, International Business Machines Corp.; *Figure 6-25*, Hewlett-Packard Co.; *Figure 6-26*, Everex System, Inc.; *Figure 6-30*, Plasmon Data Systems, Inc.; *Figure 6-32*, 3M Corp.; *Figure 6-33*, EMC Corp.; *Figure 6-34*, Storage Technology Corp.; *Figure 6-35*, Applied Systems Institute, Inc.; *Figure 6-36*, Canon **CHAPTER 7** *Opening Page*, Charles Thatcher/Tony Stone; *Figure 7-20*, UNISYS Corp.; *Figure 7-21*, (left) Borland International, Inc.; (right) Ashton-Tate Corp. **CHAPTER 8** *Opening Page*, A. Tennenbaum/Sygma; *Figure 8-2*, Inmac; *Figure 8-3*, Inmac; *Figure 8-4*, Siecor Corporation of America; *Figure 8-6*, Hewlett-Packard Co.; *Figure 8-7*, NASA; *Figure 8-8*, Photonics Corp.; *Figure 8-9*, Motorola Mobile Data Division; *Figure 8-18*, (left) Hayes Microcomputer Products, Inc.; (right) Hayes Microcomputer Products, Inc. ©1991 Hayes Microcomputer Products, Inc.; *Figure 8-19*, Hayes Microcomputer Products, Inc. ©1991 Hayes Microcomputer Products, Inc.; *Figure 8-20*, Panasonic Industrial Co.; *Figure 8-22*, International Business Machines Corp.; *Figure 8-23*, (left) Hayes Microcomputer Products, Inc. ©1991 Hayes Microcomputer Products, Inc.; (right) Hayes Microcomputer Products, Inc. ©1991 Hayes Microcomputer Products, Inc.; *Figure 8-24*, Digital Communications Associates, Inc.; *Figure 8-27*, EDS Corp. **CHAPTER 9** *Opening Page*, Steve Smith/West Light; *Figure 9-9*, UIS, Inc.; *Figure 9-11*, Apple Computer, Inc.; *Figure 9-12*, International Business Machines Corp.; *Figure 9-13*, Microsoft Corp. **CHAPTER 10** *Opening Page*, New York Stock Exchange; *Figure 10-4*, International Business Machines Corp.; *Figure 10-5*, Zenith Data Systems; *Figure 10-6*, (both) COMSHARE Incorporated; *Figure 10-7*, Frito-Lay, Inc.; *Figure 10-8*, Neuron Data; *Figure 10-10*, Ford Motor Co. **CHAPTER 11** *Opening Page*, Hewlett-Packard Co.; *Figure 11-14*, *PC* Magazine, Sept. 26, 1989 Copyright ©1989, Ziff Communications Co.; *Figure 11-15*, International Business Machines Corp.; *Figure 11-16*, Curtis Fukuda; *Figure 11-22*, Hewlett-Packard Co.; *Figure 11-23*, Intersolv, Inc.; *Figure 11-24*, International Business Machines Corp.; *Figure 11-25*, Curtis Fukuda **CHAPTER 12** *Opening Page*, ©Robert Holmgren; *Figure 12-27*, (both) Oracle Corp.; *Figure 12-28*, Oracle Corp. **CHAPTER 13** *Opening Page*, Lannie Duka/Tony Stone; *Figure 13-1*, Tandy Corp.; *Figure 13-2*, Hewlett-Packard Co.; *Figure 13-4*, Egghead Software; *Figure 13-5*, Tandy Corp.; *Figure 13-6*, International Business Machines Corp.; *Figure 13-12*, The Interface Group; *Figure 13-13*, Jerry Spagnoli **CHAPTER 14** *Opening Page*, R. Ian Lloyd Singapore/West Light; *Figure 14-1(a), Compaq Computer Corp. All rights reserved.; 14-1(b), Microsoft Corp.; 14-1(c), Macromind, Inc.; 14-1(d), International Business Machines Corp.; 14-1(e), Hewlett-Packard Co.;* *Figure 14-2*, NEC Technologies, Inc.; *Figure 14-3*, Compression Labs, Inc.; *Figure 14-4*, (both) Computervision, A Prime Company; *Figure 14-5*, NASA; *Figure 14-6*, Ford Motor Co.; *Figure 14-8*, Prodigy; *Figure 14-9*, *ComputorEdge* Magazine; *Figure 14-10*, (both) Broderbund Software; *Figure 14-11*, Electronic Arts; *Figure 14-12*, Quicksoft, Inc.; *Figure 14-13*, (Eyedentify) Eyedentify, Inc.; (Identix) Identix, Inc.

CONTENTS

CHAPTER 3 Input to the Computer 3.1

CHAPTER 4 The Processor Unit 4.1

CHAPTER 5 Output from the Computer 5.1

CHAPTER 6 Auxiliary Storage 6.1

CHAPTER 7 File and Database Management 7.1

CHAPTER 8 Communications 8.1

CHAPTER 9 Operating Systems and Systems Software 9.1

CHAPTER 10 Management Information Systems 10.1

CHAPTER 11 The Information System Life Cycle 11.1

CHAPTER 12 Program Development 12.1

CHAPTER 13 Career Opportunities in Information Processing 13.1

CHAPTER 14 Trends and Issues in the Information Age 14.1

INTRODUCTION TO DOS

PROJECT 1 Working with Files on Disks DOS2

PROJECT 2 Managing and Organizing Files on Disks DOS41

PROGRAMMING IN QuickBASIC

PROJECT 1 An Introduction to Programming in QuickBASIC QB1

PROJECT 2 Basic Arithmetic Operations and Accumulating Totals QB25

PROJECT 3 Decisions QB42

PROJECT 4 Interactive Programming, For Loops, and an Introduction to the Top-Down Approach QB62

PROJECT 5 Sequential File Processing QB83

PROJECT 6 Arrays and Functions QB99

APPENDIX QuickBASIC Debugging Techniques QB115

◆ PREFACE

SHELLY CASHMAN SERIES

◆ The Shelly Cashman Series offers superior materials from which to learn about computers. In addition to computer concepts and programming, the Shelly Cashman Series is proud to present both Windows- and DOS-based personal computer applications in a variety of traditionally bound textbooks. The table on page xv shows the available books in the Shelly Cashman Series.

If you do not find the exact Shelly Cashman Series book to fit your needs, boyd & fraser's unique **Custom Edition**™ program allows you to choose from a number of options and create a textbook perfectly suited to your course. This exciting program is explained and summarized in the table on page xvi.

CONTENT

◆ The Shelly Cashman Series textbooks assume no previous experience with computers and are written with continuity, simplicity, and practicality in mind. The Shelly Cashman Series presents materials using a unique step-by-step screen-intensive pedagogy to guide students as they learn important concepts and techniques.

Computer Concepts

The Shelly Cashman Series computer concepts textbooks offer up-to-date coverage to fit every need. *Essential Computer Concepts, Second Edition* is a brief concepts textbook that covers the topics most commonly found in short courses on computer concepts. *Complete Computer Concepts* offers a more comprehensive treatment of computer concepts.

All Shelly Cashman Series computer concepts textbooks are lavishly illustrated with hundreds of photographs and carefully developed illustrations—features that have become a hallmark of the Shelly Cashman Series. The impact of personal computers and the user's point of view are consistently addressed throughout these books. In addition, they include coverage of important topics to help students understand today's rapidly changing technology:

- A chapter on Management Information Systems that presents information as an asset to organizations, discusses how computer-based systems effectively manage information, and addresses recent trends in decision support and expert systems.
- An innovative approach to the phases of the Information System Life Cycle.
- Up-to-date coverage of local area networks, pen-based and notebook computers, graphical user interfaces, multimedia, object-oriented programming, page printers, and desktop publishing.

Each concepts chapter concludes with:

- A Chapter Summary to help students recall and comprehend key concepts.
- Key Terms to reinforce terminology introduced in the chapter.
- Review Questions to test students' mastery of the chapter content.
- Controversial Issues to stimulate classroom discussion and critical thinking.
- Research Projects to provide opportunity for in-depth investigation of chapter content.

Windows Applications

The Shelly Cashman Series Windows Applications textbooks present word processing, spreadsheet, database, presentation graphics, and Windows itself by showing the actual screens displayed by Windows and the applications software. Because the student interacts with pictorial displays when using Windows, written words in a textbook substituting for the actual displays the student will see does not suffice. For this reason, the Shelly Cashman Series emphasizes screen displays as the primary means of teaching Windows applications software. Every screen shown in the Shelly Cashman Series Windows Applications textbooks appears in color, because the student views color on the screen. In addition, the screens appear exactly as the student will see them—the screens in the books were captured while using the software. Nothing has been altered or changed except to highlight portions of the screen when appropriate.

With this unique approach, the Shelly Cashman Series once again sets the standard for teaching applications software.

DOS Applications

The Shelly Cashman Series DOS Applications textbooks include projects on DOS, word processing, spreadsheet, database management, and integrated software. In each project, students learn by way of a unique and time-tested problem-solving approach, in which problems are presented and then thoroughly solved in a step-by-step manner. The steps, along with carefully labeled screens, illustrate the exact order of operations. Using this approach, students are visually guided as they perform the various commands and quickly come up to speed.

Each DOS Application textbook begins with an introduction to computers and two projects on DOS. The first DOS project covers the concepts of a disk operating system and the essential commands on file management. The second DOS project presents directory and subdirectory file management concepts.

The Word Processing Applications textbooks contain five word processing projects. After an introduction to the keyboard, students are guided through the word processing cycle—starting the software, creating a document, editing a document, spell checking, printing the document, saving the document, and exiting to DOS. In subsequent projects, students learn to create a business letter and resume; learn how to enter a research report with headers and footnotes; learn how to complete a merge operation; and use the fundamentals of desktop publishing.

The Spreadsheet Applications textbooks contain six spreadsheet projects. In Project 1, students learn spreadsheet terminology and basic spreadsheet characteristics and apply this information to create a company's first quarter sales report. In Project 2, students continue to use this sales report, learning such skills as adding summary totals, formatting, changing column widths, replication, debugging, and printing. In Project 3, students create a more complex quarterly report and then apply what-if analysis to evaluate new data. They also learn about inserting and deleting rows and columns, how to change default settings, and how to copy absolute cell addresses. Later projects cover functions and macros, graphing, and the database capabilities of the spreadsheet package.

The Database Applications textbooks contain five database projects where students learn to design and create a database of employee records, which they use as an example throughout the remainder of the projects. Students learn to query a database, use compound conditions, and use sorting and joins. Students are taught how to maintain a database by adding, deleting, and changing the contents of the records in a table. Later projects show students how to present data in reports and forms and finally how to graph.

The Integrated Applications textbook contains twelve projects. The first three projects cover the Word Processor tool. Projects 4 through 7 cover the Spreadsheet tool and graphing. Projects 8 through 10 present the Database tool. Project 11 describes the Calendar, Calculator, Address Book, Wizards, and Communications tool. Project 12 presents integration of the Word Processor, Spreadsheet, and Database tools.

In all the Shelly Cashman Series DOS Applications textbooks, the key terms are presented at the end of each project along with a Quick Reference providing a guide to each task presented in the project with its available options for accomplishing the task. The Quick Reference is divided into four parts—the Task, Mouse, Menu, and Keyboard Shortcuts.

Finally, each project concludes with a wealth of assignments including Short Answer Assignments, Hands-On Exercises, and Laboratory Assignments. The Hands-On Exercises require that the student load files from the Student Diskette that accompanies the textbook.

Visual Basic Programming

The Shelly Cashman Series Microsoft Visual Basic for Windows textbook introduces the student to the development of Windows-based applications using the three-step approach of creating the interface, setting properties, and writing code. This textbook includes an introduction to computers, two projects that introduce the student to Microsoft Windows 3.1, and five Visual Basic projects. The Visual Basic projects step the student through the most often used controls and properties in the Visual Basic Standard Edition, and introduce both event-driven programming and the use of structured programming within subroutines. The projects are sequenced to build increasingly sophisticated applications that include menus, dialog boxes, the use of color, database access, and common Windows graphical user interactions, such as dragging and dropping of objects.

BASIC Programming

The Shelly Cashman Series includes QuickBASIC and Microsoft BASIC programming textbooks. They are divided into six projects that provide students with knowledge that is central to a real programming environment. They present the essentials of the language as well as structured and top-down programming techniques. In each project, a problem is presented and then thoroughly solved step-by-step with a program.

In Project 1, students learn the program development cycle, the basic characteristics of the programming language, and the operating environment. Project 2 presents computations, summary tools, report editing, and report printing. In Project 3, students learn about decision making. Topics include implementing If-Then-Else and Case structures, and the use of logical operators. Unlike the first three projects, which use the READ and DATA statements to integrate data into a program, Project 4 shows students how to use the INPUT statement to accomplish this task. Also included is coverage of how to use For loops to implement counter-controlled loops, and how to design top-down programs. Project 5 introduces students to creating and processing a sequential data file. In Project 6, students learn how to write programs that can look up information in tables; they are then acquainted with the most often used built-in functions and, if applicable, special variables, of the language. Finally, an appendix on debugging techniques introduces students to debugging features that are built into the language.

Each programming project includes one or more sets of Try It Yourself Exercises, paper-and-pencil practice exercises to help master the concepts presented. Each project concludes with challenging and field-tested Student Assignments. All programming assignments contain a problem statement, sample input data, and sample output results. Also included is a Reference Card that lists all statements, functions, and features of the language.

SUPPLEMENTS

Ten available supplements complement the various textbooks in the Shelly Cashman Series.

Workbook and Study Guide with Computer Lab Software Projects

This highly popular supplement contains completely new activities to enhance the concepts chapters and to simulate computer applications that are not usually available to beginning students. Included for each chapter are:

- Chapter Objectives that help students measure their mastery of the chapter content
- A Chapter Outline that guides students through the organization of the chapter
- A Chapter Summary that helps students recall and comprehend key concepts
- Key Terms with definitions that reinforce terminology introduced in the chapter
- Six projects which range from self-testing on paper and communications skills activities to on-line computerized testing with self-scoring. Answers are included for all projects and exercises

The Computer Lab Software Projects simulate the following applications in an interactive environment:

- Home banking
- Airline reservations
- On-line information services
- Electronic mail
- Desktop publishing
- Presentation graphics

Instructor's Manual to accompany the Workbook and Study Guide with Computer Lab Software Projects

The Instructor's Manual to accompany the workbook includes answers and solutions for the entire workbook, and the software for the on-line, self-testing projects as well as for the Computer Lab Software Projects.

Educational Versions of Applications Software

Free educational versions of WordPerfect 4.2, WordStar 6.0, Quattro 1.01, Paradox 2.04, and dBASE III PLUS are available to adopting institutions. This software is available for IBM and IBM compatible systems.

Instructor's Guide Including Answer Manual and Test Bank

The Instructor's Guide and Answer Manual includes Lesson Plans for each chapter or project. The Lesson Plans begin with behavioral objectives and an overview of each chapter or project to help instructors quickly review the purpose and key concepts. Detailed outlines of each chapter and/or project follow. These outlines are annotated with the page number of the book on which the outlined material is covered; notes, teaching tips, and additional activities that the instructor might use to embellish the lesson; and a key for using the Transparency Masters and/or Color Transparencies. Complete answers and solutions for all Exercises, Discussion Questions, Projects, Controversial Issues, Student Assignments, and Try It Yourself Exercises are also included.

This manual also contains three types of test questions with answers and is a hard copy version of MicroExam 4.0 (see below). The three types of questions are—true/false, multiple choice, and fill-in. Each chapter or project has approximately 50 true/false, 25 multiple choice, and 35 fill ins.

MicroExam 4.0

MicroExam 4.0, a personal computer based test-generating system, is available free to adopters. It includes all of the questions from the Test Bank in an easy-to-use, menu-driven package that allows testing flexibility and customization of testing documents. For example, with MicroExam 4.0, a user can enter his or her own questions and can generate review sheets and answer keys. MicroExam 4.0 will run on any IBM and IBM compatible system with two diskette drives or a hard disk.

Transparency Masters

Transparency Masters are available for every illustration in all of the Shelly Cashman Series textbooks. The transparency masters are conveniently bound in a perforated volume; they have been photographically enlarged for clearer projection.

Color Transparencies

One hundred high-quality, full-color acetates contain key illustrations found in *Complete Computer Concepts*. Each transparency is accompanied by interleaved lecture notes.

Instructor's Diskette

The Instructor's Diskette contains the files used in the DOS projects; the letters and memos, and the final versions of documents used to teach the word processing projects; the project worksheets and Laboratory Assignment worksheet solutions for the spreadsheet projects; the databases that students will create and use; the data for the employee database example, and program solutions to all of the programming assignments.

HyperGraphics® for Computer Concepts

HyperGraphics®, a software-based, instructor-led classroom presentation system, is available to assist adopters in delivering top-notch computer concepts lectures. It allows instructors to present much of the textbook's content using graphics, color, animation, and instructor-led interactivity. It requires an LCD projection panel, a microcomputer, and an overhead projector.

Lecture Success System

The Shelly Cashman Series Windows Applications textbooks are supported by the finest LCD learning material available in textbook publishing. The Lecture Success System is a series of files on a diskette that relate to figures in the book. To lecture on a project, the instructor loads the files that relate to figures in the project and then moves from one to the next using the Window menu. This support package has been field tested with great success. The Lecture Success System eliminates the need to type large amounts of data while lecturing to the students.

ACKNOWLEDGMENTS

◆ The Shelly Cashman Series would not be the success it is without the contributions of outstanding publishing professionals. First, and foremost, among them is Becky Herrington, director of production and designer of this book. She is the heart and soul of the Shelly Cashman Series, and it is only through her leadership, dedication, and untiring efforts that superior products are produced.

Under Becky's direction, the following individuals made significant contributions to these books; Ginny Harvey, style coordinator and manuscript editor; Ken Russo, senior illustrator; Anne Craig, Mike Bodnar, John Craig, Greg Herrington, and Greg Archambault, illustrators; Jeanne Black, Betty Hopkins, and Rebecca Evans, typographers; Sue Sebok, copy editor; Marilyn Martin and Nancy Lamm, proofreaders; Dave Wyer, program design consultant; and Tracy Murphy, manufacturing coordinator.

Special recognition for a job well done must go to James Quasney, who, together with writing, assumed the responsibilities as series editor. Particular thanks go to Thomas K. Walker, president and CEO of boyd & fraser publishing company.

We hope you will find using the book an enriching and rewarding experience.

Gary B. Shelly
Thomas J. Cashman

SHELLY CASHMAN SERIES—TRADITIONALLY BOUND TEXTBOOKS

The Shelly Cashman Series presents both Windows- and DOS-based personal computer applications in a variety of traditionally bound textbooks, as shown in the table below. For more information, see your South-Western/boyd & fraser representative or call 1-800-543-8444.

COMPUTER CONCEPTS	
Computer Concepts	*Complete Computer Concepts* *Essential Computer Concepts, Second Edition*
Computer Concepts Workbook and Study Guide	*Workbook and Study Guide with Computer Lab Software Projects to accompany Complete Computer Concepts*
Computer Concepts and Windows Applications	*Complete Computer Concepts and Microsoft Works 2.0 for Windows* (also available in spiral bound) *Complete Computer Concepts and Microsoft Word 2.0 for Windows, Microsoft Excel 4 for Windows, and Paradox 1.0 for Windows* (also available in spiral bound)
Computer Concepts and DOS Applications	*Complete Computer Concepts and WordPerfect 5.1, Lotus 1-2-3 Release 2.2, and dBASE IV Version 1.1* (also available in spiral bound) *Complete Computer Concepts and WordPerfect 5.1, Lotus 1-2-3 Release 2.2, and dBASE III PLUS* (also available in spiral bound)
Computer Concepts and Programming	*Complete Computer Concepts and Programming in QuickBASIC* *Complete Computer Concepts and Programming in Microsoft BASIC*
WINDOWS APPLICATIONS	
Integrated Package	*Microsoft Works 2.0 for Windows* (also available in spiral bound) *Microsoft Works 3.0 for Windows* (also available in spiral bound) (Summer 1994)
Graphical User Interface	*Microsoft Windows 3.1 Introductory Concepts and Techniques* *Microsoft Windows 3.1 Concepts and Techniques* (Spring 1994)
Windows Applications	*Microsoft Word 2.0 for Windows, Microsoft Excel 4 for Windows, and Paradox 1.0 for Windows* (also available in spiral bound)
Word Processing	*Microsoft Word 2.0 for Windows* *Microsoft Word 6.0 for Windows* (Summer 1994) *WordPerfect 5.2 for Windows* *WordPerfect 6.0 for Windows* (Summer 1994)
Spreadsheets	*Microsoft Excel 4 for Windows* *Microsoft Excel 5 for Windows* (Summer 1994) *Lotus 1-2-3 Release 4.0 for Windows* (Summer 1994)
Database Management	*Paradox 1.0 for Windows* *Paradox 4.5 for Windows* *Microsoft Access 2.0 for Windows* (Summer 1994)
Presentation Graphics	*Microsoft PowerPoint 4.0 for Windows* (Summer 1994)
DOS APPLICATIONS	
Operating Systems	*DOS 6 Introductory Concepts and Techniques* *DOS 6 and Microsoft Windows 3.1 Introductory Concepts and Techniques*
Integrated Package	*Microsoft Works 3.0* (also available in spiral bound)
DOS Applications	*WordPerfect 5.1, Lotus 1-2-3 Release 2.2, and dBASE IV Version 1.1* (also available in spiral bound) *WordPerfect 5.1, Lotus 1-2-3 Release 2.2, and dBASE III PLUS* (also available in spiral bound)
Word Processing	*WordPerfect 6.0* *WordPerfect 5.1* *WordPerfect 5.1, Function Key Edition* *WordPerfect 4.2* (with Educational Software) *Microsoft Word 5.0* *WordStar 6.0* (with Educational Software)
Spreadsheets	*Lotus 1-2-3 Release 2.4* *Lotus 1-2-3 Release 2.3* *Lotus 1-2-3 Release 2.2* *Lotus 1-2-3 Release 2.01* *Quattro Pro 3.0* *Quattro with 1-2-3 Menus* (with Educational Software)
Database Management	*dBASE IV Version 1.1* *dBASE III PLUS* (with Educational Software) *Paradox 4.5* *Paradox 3.5* (with Educational Software)
PROGRAMMING	
Programming	*Microsoft BASIC* *QuickBASIC* *Microsoft Visual Basic 3.0 for Windows*

SHELLY CASHMAN SERIES—Custom Edition™ PROGRAM

If you do not find a Shelly Cashman Series traditionally bound textbook to fit your needs, boyd & fraser's unique **Custom Edition** program allows you to choose from a number of options and create a textbook perfectly suited to your course. The customized materials are available in a variety of binding styles, including boyd & fraser's patented **Custom Edition** kit, spiral bound, and notebook bound. Features of the **Custom Edition** program are:

- Textbooks that match the content of your course
- Windows- and DOS-based materials for the latest versions of personal computer applications software
- Shelly Cashman Series quality, with the same full-color materials and Shelly Cashman Series pedagogy found in the traditionally bound books
- Affordable pricing so your students receive the **Custom Edition** at a cost similar to that of traditionally bound books

The table on the right summarizes the available materials. For more information, see your South-Western/boyd & fraser representative or call 1-800-543-8444.

COMPUTER CONCEPTS	
Computer Concepts	*Complete Computer Concepts* *Essential Computer Concepts, Second Edition* *Introduction to Computers*
OPERATING SYSTEMS	
Graphical User Interface	*Microsoft Windows 3.1 Introductory Concepts and Techniques* *Microsoft Windows 3.1 Concepts and Techniques* (Spring 1994) *DOS 6 and Microsoft Windows 3.1 Introductory Concepts and Techniques*
Operating Systems	*Introduction to DOS 6* (using DOS prompt) *Introduction to DOS 5.0* (using DOS shell) *Introduction to DOS 5.0 or earlier* (using DOS prompt)
WINDOWS APPLICATIONS	
Integrated Package	*Microsoft Works 2.0 for Windows* *Microsoft Works 3.0 for Windows* (Summer 1994)
Word Processing	*Microsoft Word 2.0 for Windows* *Microsoft Word 6.0 for Windows* (Summer 1994) *WordPerfect 5.2 for Windows* *WordPerfect 6.0 for Windows* (Summer 1994)
Spreadsheets	*Microsoft Excel 4 for Windows* *Microsoft Excel 5 for Windows* (Summer 1994) *Lotus 1-2-3 Release 4.0 for Windows* (Summer 1994)
Database Management	*Paradox 1.0 for Windows* *Paradox 4.5 for Windows* *Microsoft Access 2.0 for Windows* (Summer 1994)
Presentation Graphics	*Microsoft PowerPoint 4.0 for Windows* (Summer 1994)
DOS APPLICATIONS	
Integrated Package	*Microsoft Works 3.0*
Word Processing	*WordPerfect 6.0* *WordPerfect 5.1* *WordPerfect 5.1, Function Key Edition* *Microsoft Word 5.0* *WordPerfect 4.2* *WordStar 6.0*
Spreadsheets	*Lotus 1-2-3 Release 2.4* *Lotus 1-2-3 Release 2.3* *Lotus 1-2-3 Release 2.2* *Lotus 1-2-3 Release 2.01* *Quattro Pro 3.0* *Quattro with 1-2-3 Menus*
Database Management	*dBASE IV Version 1.1* *dBASE III PLUS* *Paradox 4.5* *Paradox 3.5*
PROGRAMMING	
Programming	*Microsoft BASIC* *QuickBASIC* *Microsoft Visual Basic 3.0 for Windows*

An Overview of Computer Concepts

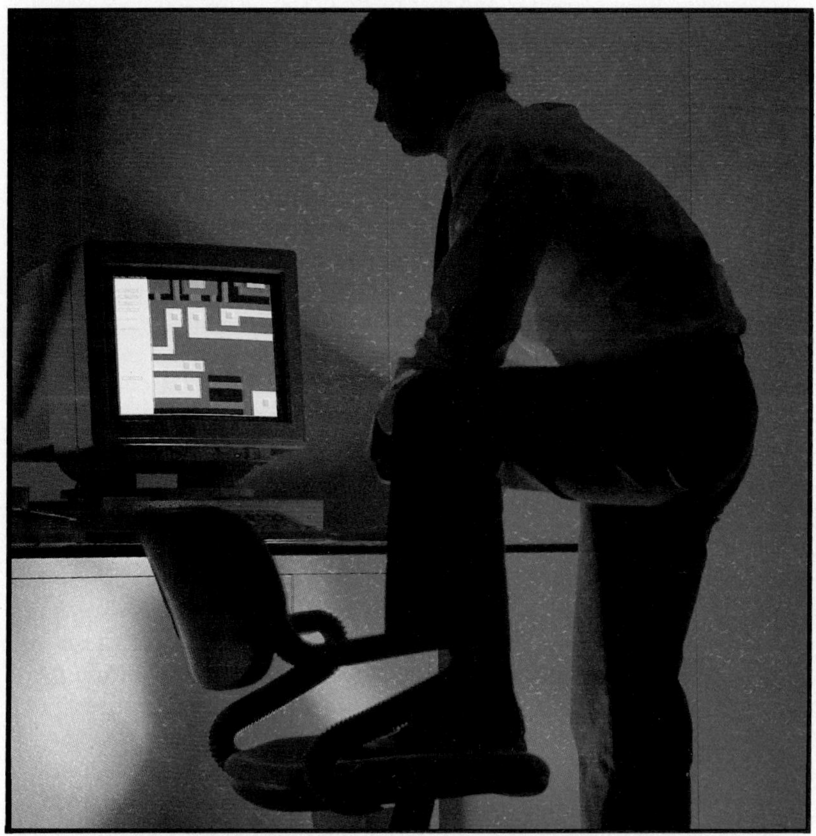

OBJECTIVES

- Explain what a computer is and how it processes data to produce information
- Identify the four operations of the information processing cycle: input, process, output, and storage
- Explain how the operations of the information processing cycle are performed by computer hardware and software
- Identify the major categories of computers
- Describe the six elements of an information system: equipment, software, data, personnel, users, and procedures
- Explain the responsibilities of information system personnel
- Explain the use of computers in our world
- Describe the evolution of the computer industry

Every day computers play a key role in how we work and how we live. Today, even the smallest organizations usually have computers to help them operate more efficiently. Computers also affect our lives in many unseen ways. When we buy groceries at the supermarket, use an automatic teller machine, or make a long-distance phone call, we are also using computers.

As they have for a number or years, personal computers continue to make an increasing impact on our lives. Both at home and at work, these small desktop systems help us do our work faster, more accurately, and in some cases, in ways that previously would not have been possible.

Today, many people believe that knowing how to use a computer, especially a personal computer, is a basic skill necessary to succeed in business or to function effectively in society. Given the increasing use and availability of computer systems, such knowledge will continue to be an essential skill. The purpose of this book is to give you this knowledge so that you will understand how computers are used today and so that you can adapt to how computers will be used in the future.

In this first chapter we will give you an overview of computer concepts. You will begin to learn what a computer is, how it processes data into information, and what elements are necessary for a successful information system. While you are reading, remember that this chapter is an overview and that many of the terms and concepts that are introduced will be discussed in more detail in later chapters.

WHAT IS A COMPUTER?

The most obvious question related to understanding computers and their impact on our lives is, "What is a computer?". A **computer** is an electronic device, operating under the control of instructions stored in its own memory unit, that can accept data (input), process data arithmetically and logically, produce output from the processing, and store the results for future use. While broader definitions of a computer exist, this definition includes a wide range of devices with various capabilities. For example, the tiny microcomputer chip shown in Figure 1-1 can be called a computer. Generally the term is used to describe a collection of devices that function together to process data. An example of the devices that make up a computer is shown in Figure 1-2.

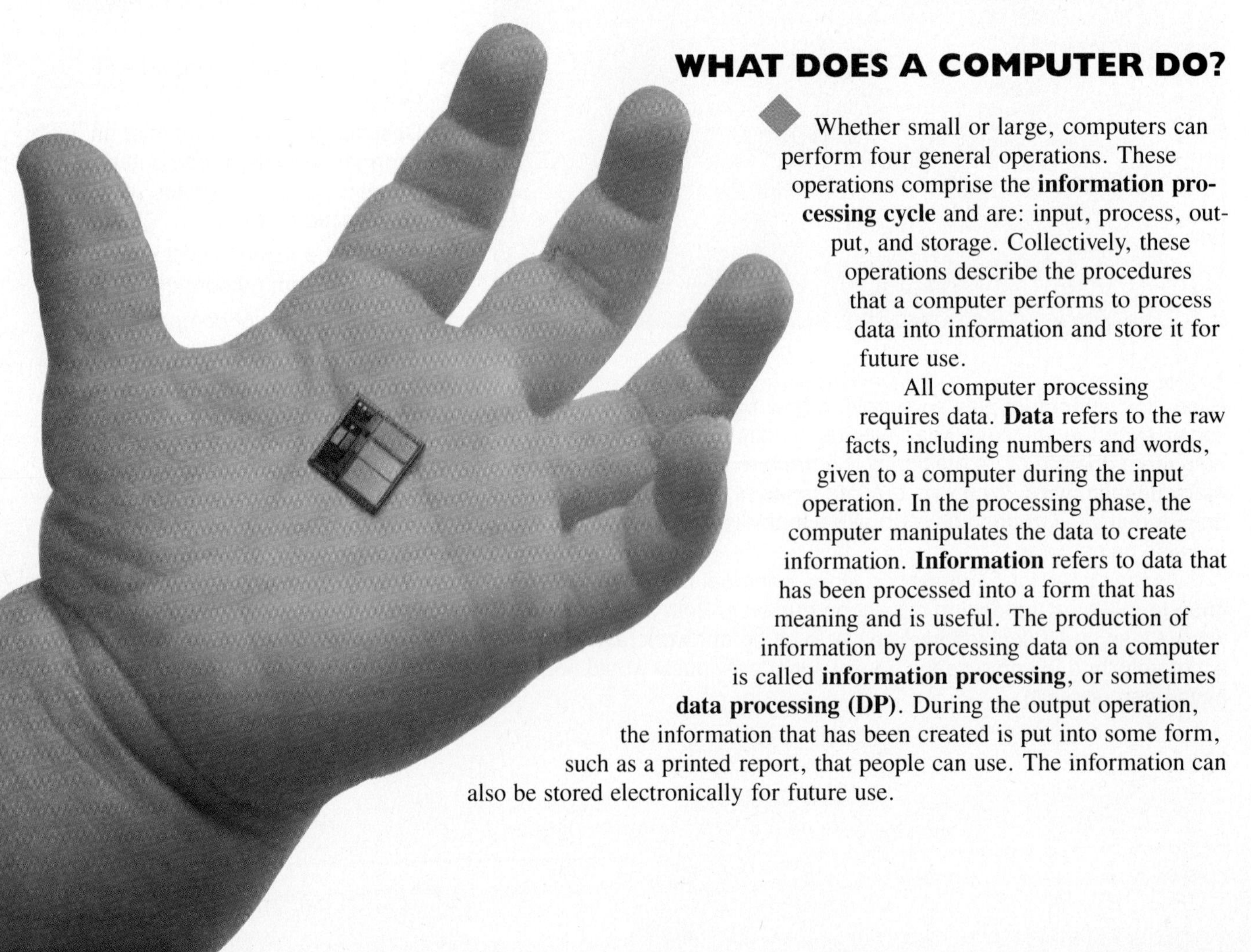

FIGURE 1-1
Small enough to fit in the palm of a baby's hand, this microcomputer chip contains the electronic circuits that perform the operations of a computer.

WHAT DOES A COMPUTER DO?

Whether small or large, computers can perform four general operations. These operations comprise the **information processing cycle** and are: input, process, output, and storage. Collectively, these operations describe the procedures that a computer performs to process data into information and store it for future use.

All computer processing requires data. **Data** refers to the raw facts, including numbers and words, given to a computer during the input operation. In the processing phase, the computer manipulates the data to create information. **Information** refers to data that has been processed into a form that has meaning and is useful. The production of information by processing data on a computer is called **information processing**, or sometimes **data processing (DP)**. During the output operation, the information that has been created is put into some form, such as a printed report, that people can use. The information can also be stored electronically for future use.

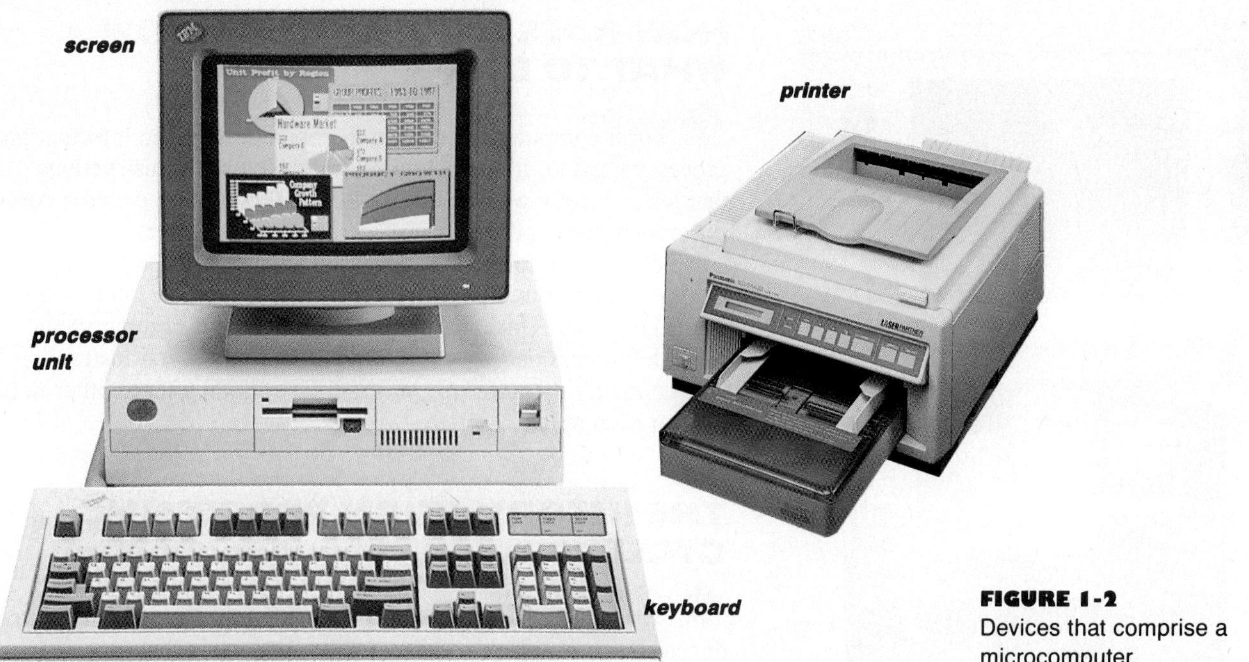

FIGURE 1-2
Devices that comprise a microcomputer.

The people who either use the computer directly or use the information it provides are called **computer users**, **end users**, or sometimes just simply **users**. Figure 1-3 shows a computer user and demonstrates how the four operations of the information processing cycle can occur on a personal computer. ① The computer user inputs data by pressing the keys on the keyboard. ② The data is then processed by the unit called the processor. ③ The output, or results, from the processing are displayed on the screen or printed on the printer, providing information to the user. ④ Finally, the output may be stored on a disk for future reference.

WHY IS A COMPUTER SO POWERFUL?

The input, process, output, and storage operations that a computer performs may seem very basic and simple. However, the computer's power derives from its capability to perform these operations very quickly, accurately, and reliably. In a computer, operations occur through the use of electronic circuits contained on small chips as shown on the next page in Figure 1-4. When data flows along these circuits it travels at close to the speed of light. This allows processing to be accomplished in billionths of a second. The electronic circuits in modern computers are very reliable and seldom fail. Storage capability is another reason why computers are so powerful. They can store enormous amounts of data and keep that data readily available for processing. This capability combined with the factors of speed, accuracy, and reliability are why a computer is considered to be such a powerful tool for information processing.

FIGURE 1-3
The use of this personal computer illustrates the four operations of the information processing cycle: input, process, output, and storage.

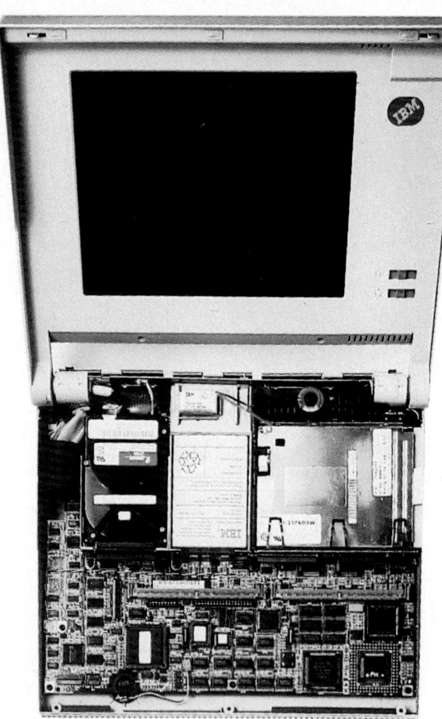

FIGURE 1-4
Inside a computer are chips and other electronic components that process data in billionths of a second.

HOW DOES A COMPUTER KNOW WHAT TO DO?

For a computer to perform the operations in the information processing cycle, it must be given a detailed set of instructions that tell it exactly what to do. These instructions are called a **computer program**, **program instructions**, or **software**.

Before the information processing cycle for a specific job begins, the computer program corresponding to that job is stored in the computer. Once the program is stored, the computer can begin to process data by executing the program's first instruction. The computer executes one program instruction after another until the job is complete.

THE INFORMATION PROCESSING CYCLE

Your understanding of the information processing cycle introduced in this chapter is fundamental to understanding computers and how they process data into information. To review, the information processing cycle consists of four operations. They are: input, process, output, storage.

The first three of these operations, **input**, **process**, and **output**, describe the procedures that a computer performs to process data into information. The fourth operation, **storage**, describes a computer's electronic storage capability. As you learn more about computers, you will see that these four operations apply to both the computer equipment and the computer software. The equipment, or devices, of a computer are classified according to the operations that they perform. Computer software is made up of instructions that describe how the operations are to be performed.

WHAT ARE THE COMPONENTS OF A COMPUTER?

Data is processed by specific equipment that is often called computer **hardware** (Figure 1-5). This equipment consists of: input devices, a processor unit, output devices, and auxiliary storage units.

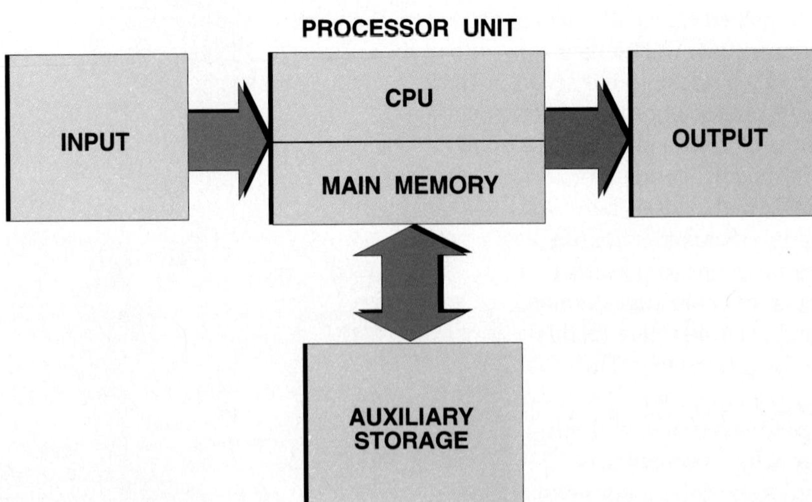

FIGURE 1-5
A computer is composed of input devices through which data is entered into the computer; the processor that processes data stored in main memory; output devices on which the results of the processing are made available; and auxiliary storage units that store data for future processing.

Input Devices

Input devices are used to enter data into a computer. A common input device is the **keyboard**, shown in Figure 1-6⟨a⟩. As the data is entered, or keyed, it is stored in the computer and displayed on a screen.

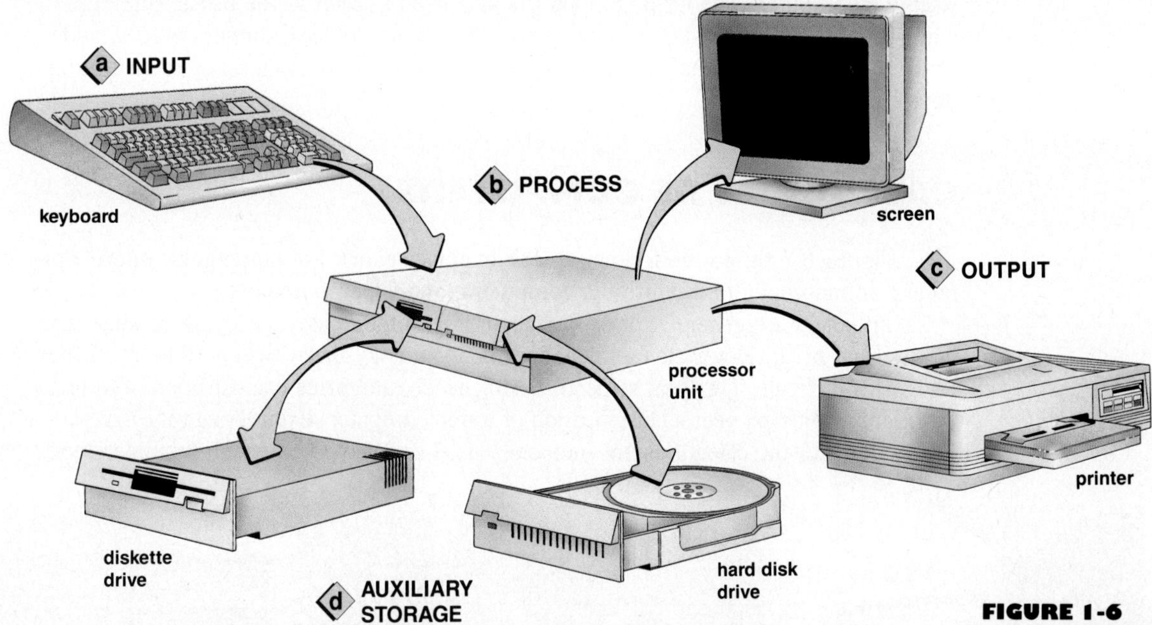

FIGURE 1-6
The components of a computer perform the four operations of the information processing cycle.

Processor Unit

Figure 1-6⟨b⟩ shows the **processor unit** of a computer, which contains the electronic circuits that actually cause the processing of data to occur. The processor unit is divided into two parts, the central processing unit and main memory. The **central processing unit (CPU)** contains a **control unit** that executes the program instructions and an **arithmetic/logic unit (ALU)** that performs math and logic operations. **Arithmetic operations** include numeric calculations such as addition, subtraction, multiplication, and division. Comparisons of data to see if one value is greater than, equal to, or less than another are called **logical operations**.

Main memory, also called **primary storage**, is a part of the processor unit. Main memory electronically stores data and program instructions when they are being processed.

Output Devices

Output from a computer can be presented in many forms. The two most commonly used **output devices** are the **printer** and the computer **screen** shown in Figure 1-6⟨c⟩. Other frequently used names for the screen are the **monitor**, or the **CRT**, which stands for **cathode ray tube**.

Auxiliary Storage Units

Auxiliary storage units, shown in Figure 1-6⟨d⟩, store instructions and data when they are not being used by the processor unit. A common auxiliary storage device on personal computers is a diskette drive, which stores data as magnetic spots on a small plastic disk called a **diskette**. Another auxiliary storage device is called a hard disk drive. **Hard disk** drives contain nonremovable metal disks and provide larger storage capacities than diskettes.

As you can see, each component shown in Figure 1-6 plays an important role in information processing. Collectively, this equipment is called a **computer system**, or simply a computer. The term computer is also used to refer to the processing unit where the actual processing of data occurs. The input devices, output devices, and auxiliary storage units that surround the processing unit are sometimes referred to as **peripheral devices**.

CATEGORIES OF COMPUTERS

Figure 1-7 shows the following four major categories of computers: microcomputers, minicomputers, mainframe computers, and supercomputers.

Computers are generally classified according to their size, speed, processing capabilities, and price. However, rapid changes in technology make firm definitions of these categories difficult. This year's speed, performance, and price classification of a mainframe might fit next year's classification of a minicomputer. Even though they are not firmly defined, the categories are frequently used and should be generally understood.

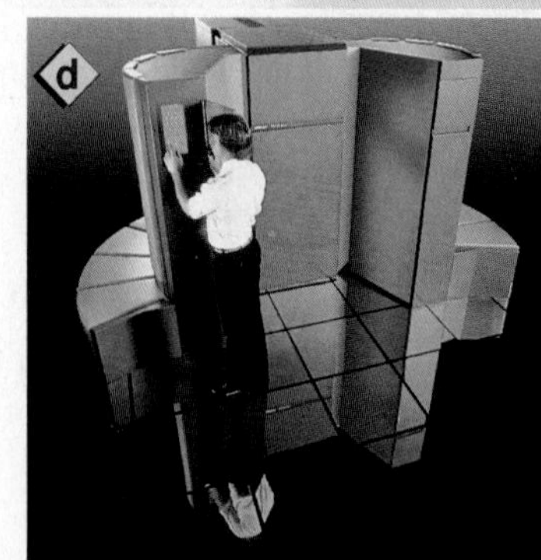

FIGURE 1-7
(a) Microcomputers are small desktop-sized computers. These machines have become so widely used that they are sometimes called desktop appliances. (b) Minicomputers can perform many of the functions of a mainframe computer, but on a smaller scale. (c) Mainframe computers are large, powerful machines that can handle many users concurrently and process large volumes of data. (d) Supercomputers are the most powerful and expensive computers.

Microcomputers, shown in Figure 1-7⟨a⟩, also called **personal computers** or **micros**, are the small desktop-sized systems that have become so widely used in recent years. These machines are generally priced under $10,000. This category also includes hand-held, notebook, laptop, portable, and supermicrocomputers.

Minicomputers, shown in Figure 1-7⟨b⟩, are more powerful than microcomputers and can support a number of users performing different tasks. Originally developed to perform specific tasks such as engineering calculations, their use grew rapidly as their performance and capabilities increased. These systems can cost from approximately $15,000 up to several hundred thousand dollars. The most powerful minis are called superminicomputers.

Mainframe computers, shown in Figure 1-7⟨c⟩, are large systems that can handle hundreds of users, store large amounts of data, and process transactions at a very high rate. Mainframes usually require a specialized environment including separate air conditioning, cooling, and electrical power. Raised flooring is often built to accommodate the many cables connecting the system components underneath. The price range for mainframes is from several hundred thousand dollars to several million dollars.

Supercomputers, shown in Figure 1-7⟨d⟩, are the most powerful category of computers and, accordingly, the most expensive. The capability of these systems to process hundreds of millions of instructions per second is used for such applications as weather forecasting, engineering design and testing, space exploration, and other jobs requiring long, complex calculations. These machines cost several million dollars.

Computers of all categories, especially microcomputers, are sometimes wired together to form networks that allow users to share data and computing resources.

COMPUTER SOFTWARE

As we mentioned previously, a computer is directed by a series of instructions called a computer program (Figure 1-8), which specifies the sequence of operations the computer will perform. To do this, the program must be stored in the main memory of the computer. Computer programs are commonly referred to as **computer software**. Many instructions can be used to direct a computer to perform a specific task. For example, some instructions allow data to be entered from a keyboard and stored in main memory; some instructions allow data in main memory to be used in calculations such as adding a series of numbers to obtain a total; some instructions compare two values stored in main memory and direct the computer to perform alternative operations based on the results of the comparison; and some instructions direct the computer to print a report, display information on the screen, draw a color graph on a screen, or store data on a disk.

FIGURE 1-8

A computer program contains instructions that specify the sequence of operations to be performed. This program is written in a language called BASIC. It allows the user to generate a telephone directory of names, area codes, and telephone numbers.

COMPUTER PROGRAM LISTING

```
100 REM TELLIST              SEPTEMBER 22            SHELLY CASHMAN
110                                                             REM
120 REM THIS PROGRAM DISPLAYS THE NAME, TELEPHONE AREA CODE
130 REM AND PHONE NUMBER OF INDIVIDUALS.
140                                                             REM
150 REM VARIABLE NAMES:
160 REM    A.....AREA CODE
170 REM    T$....TELEPHONE NUMBER
180 REM    N$....NAME
190                                                             REM
200 REM ····· DATA TO BE PROCESSED ·····
210                                                             REM
220 DATA 714, "749-2138", "SAM HORN"
230 DATA 213, "663-1271", "SUE NUNN"
240 DATA 212, "999-1193", "BOB PELE"
250 DATA 312, "979-4418", "ANN SITZ"
260 DATA 999, "999-9999", "END OF FILE"
270                                                             REM
280 REM ····· PROCESSING ·····                                  REM
290
300 READ A, T$, N$                                              REM
310                                                             REM
320 WHILE N$ <> "END OF FILE"
330   PRINT N$, A, T$
340   READ A, T$, N$
350 WEND
360                                                             REM
370 PRINT " "
380 PRINT "END OF TELEPHONE LISTING"
390 END
```

Most computer programs are written by people with specialized training. They determine the instructions necessary to process the data and place the instructions in the correct sequence so that the desired results will occur. Complex programs may require hundreds or even thousands of program instructions.

Computer software is the key to productive use of computers. With the correct software, a computer can become a valuable tool. Software can be categorized into two types: system software and application software.

System Software and Application Software

System software consists of programs that are related to controlling the actual operations of the computer equipment. An important part of the system software is a set of programs called the operating system. The instructions in the **operating system** tell the computer how to perform functions such as how to load, store, and execute an application program and how to transfer data between the input/output devices and main memory. For a computer to operate, an operating system must be stored in the main memory of the computer. Each time a computer is started, or turned on, the operating system is loaded into the computer and stored in the computer's main memory. Many different operating systems are available for computers. An operating system commonly used on many microcomputers is called DOS. The letters stand for Disk Operating System.

Application software consists of programs that tell a computer how to produce information. When you think of the different ways that people use computers in their careers or in their personal lives, you are thinking of examples of application software. Business, scientific, and educational programs are all examples of application software.

Application Software Packages

Most end users do not write their own programs. In large corporations, the information processing department develops programs for unique company applications. Programs required for common business and personal applications can be purchased from software vendors or stores that sell computer products (Figure 1-9). We often refer to purchased programs as **application software packages**, or simply **software packages**.

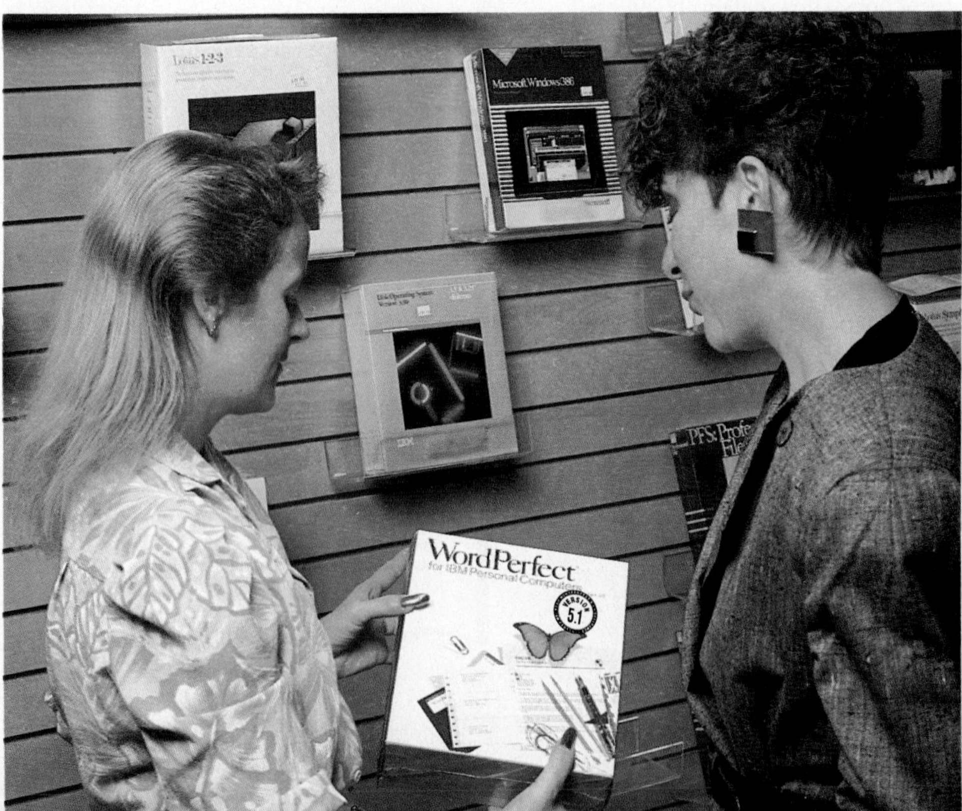

FIGURE 1-9
Many programs commonly required for business and personal applications can be purchased from computer stores.

Microcomputer Applications Software Packages

Personal computer users often use applications software packages. Some of the most commonly used packages, shown in Figure 1-10, are: word processing software, electronic spreadsheet software, computer graphics software, and database software.

FIGURE 1-10 Commonly used microcomputer applications software packages.

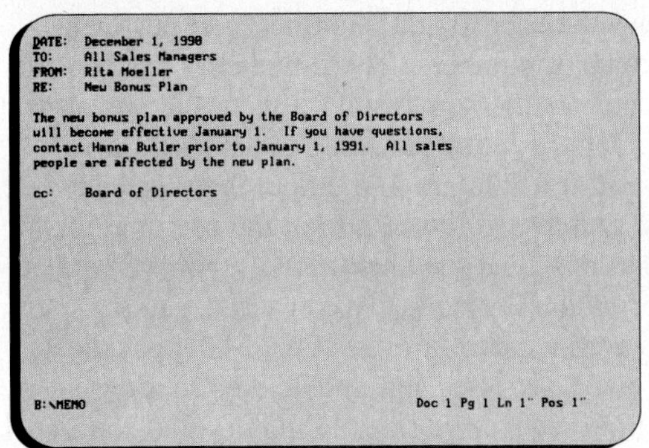

word processing

Word processing is used to write letters, memos, and other documents. As the user keys in words and letters, they display on the screen. The user can easily add, delete, and change any text entered until the document is exactly what he or she wants. The user can then save the document on auxiliary storage and can also print it on a printer.

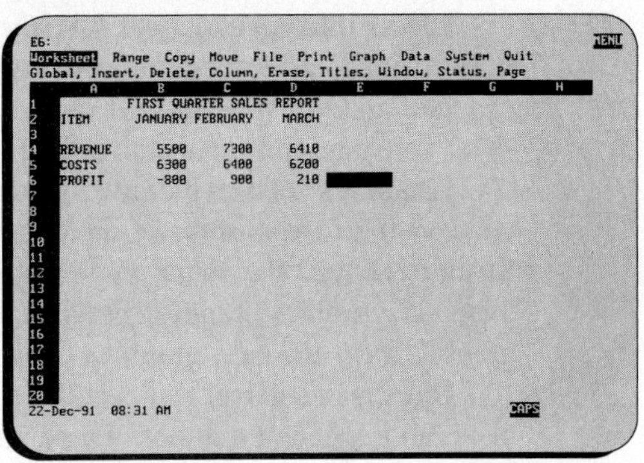

electronic spreadsheet

Electronic spreadsheet software is frequently used by people who work with numbers. The user enters the data and the formulas to be used on the data; then the program applies the formulas to the data and calculates the results. A powerful feature of electronic spreadsheet software is the capability to ask what-if questions by changing the data and quickly recalculating the new results. For example, the user could direct the software to recalculate the total sales based on a percentage increase in the second quarter sales.

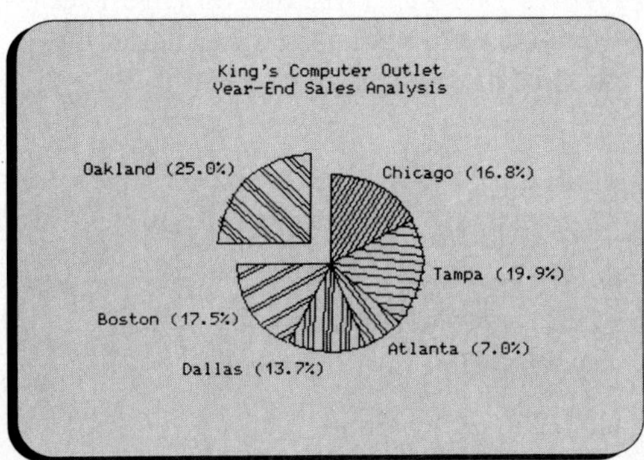

computer graphics

Computer graphics software provides the capability to transform a series of numeric values into graphic form for easier analysis and interpretation. In this example, the sales values from an electronic spreadsheet have been transformed into a pie chart. Using graphics software, these graphs can be produced in seconds instead of the hours that were required for a graphic artist to hand draw each graph.

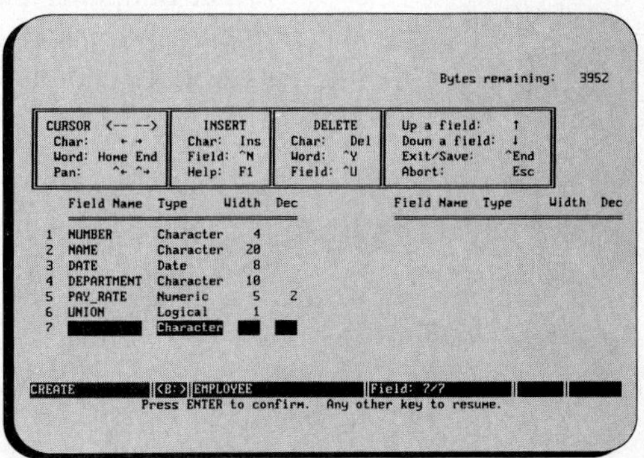

database

Database software allows the user to enter, retrieve, and update data in an organized and efficient manner. This screen shows how a database is created by defining the information that can be stored in each database record. After the database is defined, the user can add, delete, change, display, print, or reorganize the database records.

Word processing software is used to create and print documents that would otherwise be prepared on a typewriter. A key advantage of word processing software is its capability to make changes easily in documents, such as correcting spelling, changing margins, and adding, deleting, or relocating entire paragraphs. These changes would be difficult and time consuming to make on a typewriter. With a word processor, documents can be printed quickly and accurately and easily stored on a disk for future use.

Electronic spreadsheet software allows the user to add, subtract, and perform user-defined calculations on rows and columns of numbers. These numbers can be changed and the **spreadsheet** quickly recalculates the new results. Electronic spreadsheet software eliminates the tedious recalculations required with manual methods.

Graphics software converts numbers and text into graphic output that visually conveys the relationships of the data. Some graphics software allows the use of color to further enhance the visual presentation. Line, bar, and pie charts are the most frequent forms of graphics output. Spreadsheet information is frequently converted into a graphic form. In fact, graphics capabilities are included in most spreadsheet packages.

Database software allows the user to enter, retrieve, and update data in an organized and efficient manner. These software packages have flexible inquiry and reporting capabilities that allow users to access the data in different ways and create custom reports.

A TYPICAL BUSINESS APPLICATION

Electronic spreadsheets are one of the most widely used software applications. In the following example, a user develops a budget spreadsheet for the first quarter of a year. After loading the operating system and spreadsheet program, the user enters the revenues and the costs for the first three months of the year. The spreadsheet program then calculates the total revenues and total costs, the profit for each month (determined by subtracting costs from revenues), and the profit percentage (obtained by dividing the profit by the revenues). In addition, the spreadsheet program calculates the total profit and the total profit percentage.

The diagrams shown in Figures 1-11 and 1-12, and on page 1.12 in Figure 1-13 show the steps that occur to obtain the spreadsheet output. A more complete description of these steps follows.

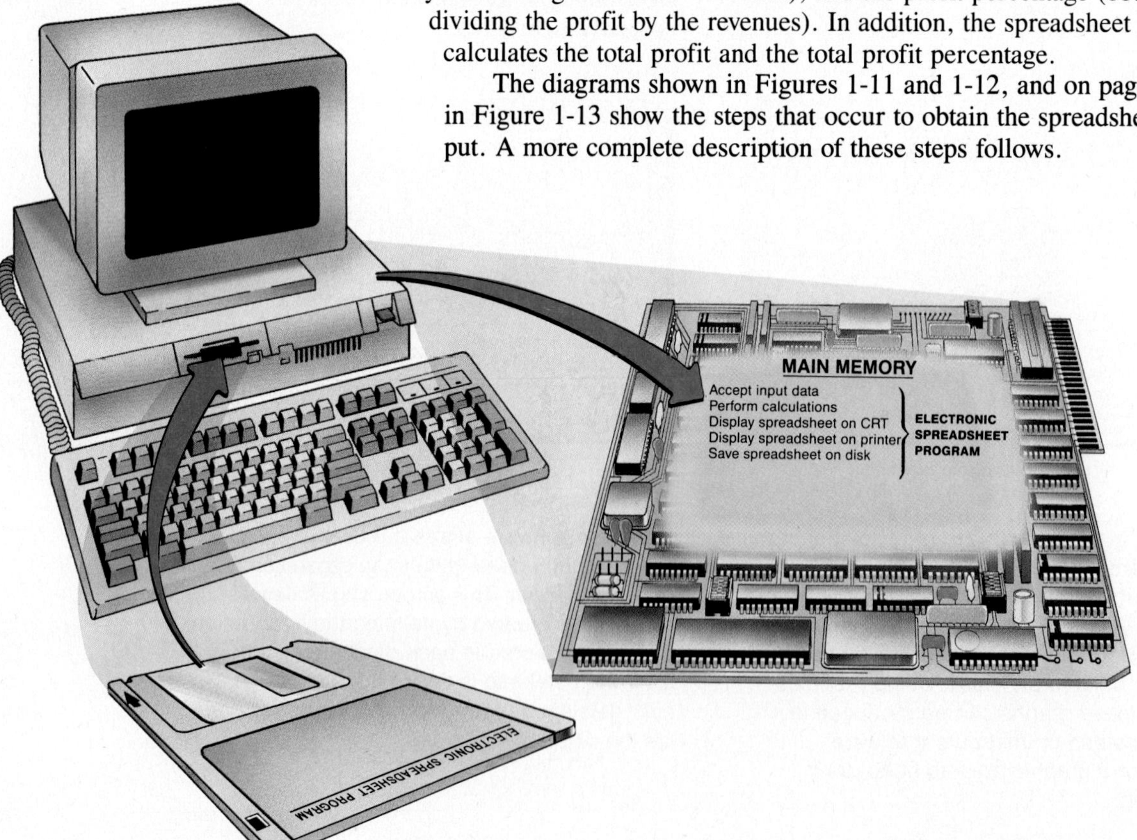

FIGURE 1-11
After the diskette is inserted in the disk drive, the spreadsheet program is copied into main memory. In this example we use English statements for ease of understanding.

Load the Operating System

When the user turns on the power to the computer, a copy of the operating system is transferred from the hard disk into the main memory of the computer. When this process is complete, the computer is ready to load the application software.

Loading the Application Software

For processing to occur, the application software must also be stored in the main memory of the computer. In this example, the application software is a spreadsheet program that is stored on a diskette. The process of getting the program into the main memory is called loading the program.

In Figure 1-11 the diskette on which the program is stored is inserted into the disk drive. The user then issues a command that instructs the operating system to load a copy of the program from the diskette into main memory. After loading the program, the operating system instructs the computer to begin executing the program.

Input: Enter the Data

The next step is to input the data (Figure 1-12). The user does this by using a keyboard. As the user enters the data on the keyboard ⟨1⟩, the data displays on the screen ⟨2⟩, and it is stored in main memory ⟨3⟩.

The data in this example consists of the words indicating the contents of each of the columns and rows on the screen and the numbers on which the calculations are to be performed.

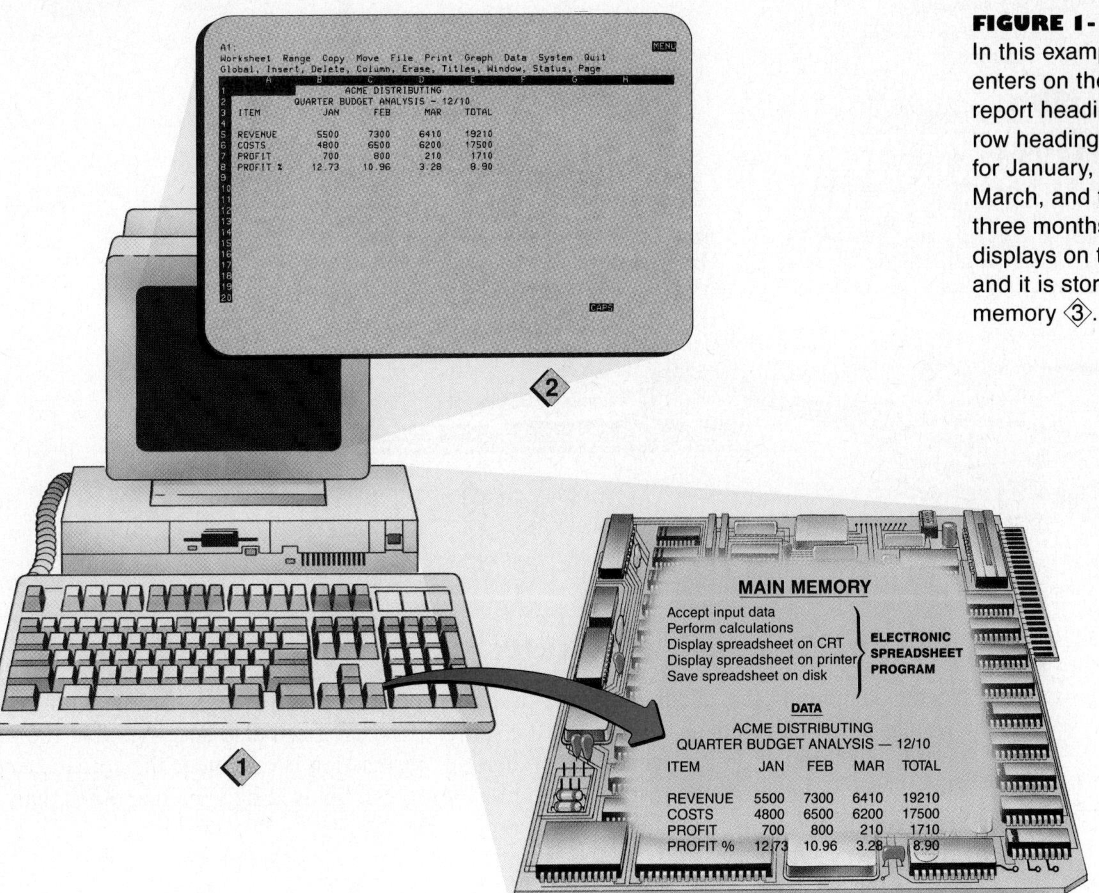

FIGURE 1-12
In this example, the user enters on the keyboard a report heading, column and row headings, the revenues for January, February, and March, and the costs for the three months ⟨1⟩, the data displays on the screen ⟨2⟩, and it is stored in main memory ⟨3⟩.

Process: Perform the Calculations

As Figure 1-13 shows, the user has entered the data ①, and the program will direct the processor to perform the required calculations ②. In this example, the program calculates the profit for each month, the total revenue, costs, and profit for the quarter, the profit percent for each month, and the total profit percent.

The preceding operations illustrate the calculating capability of computers. Whenever any calculations are performed on data, the data must be stored in main memory. The results of the calculations are also stored in main memory. If you desire, the program can issue instructions to store the results on an auxiliary storage device such as a hard disk or diskette.

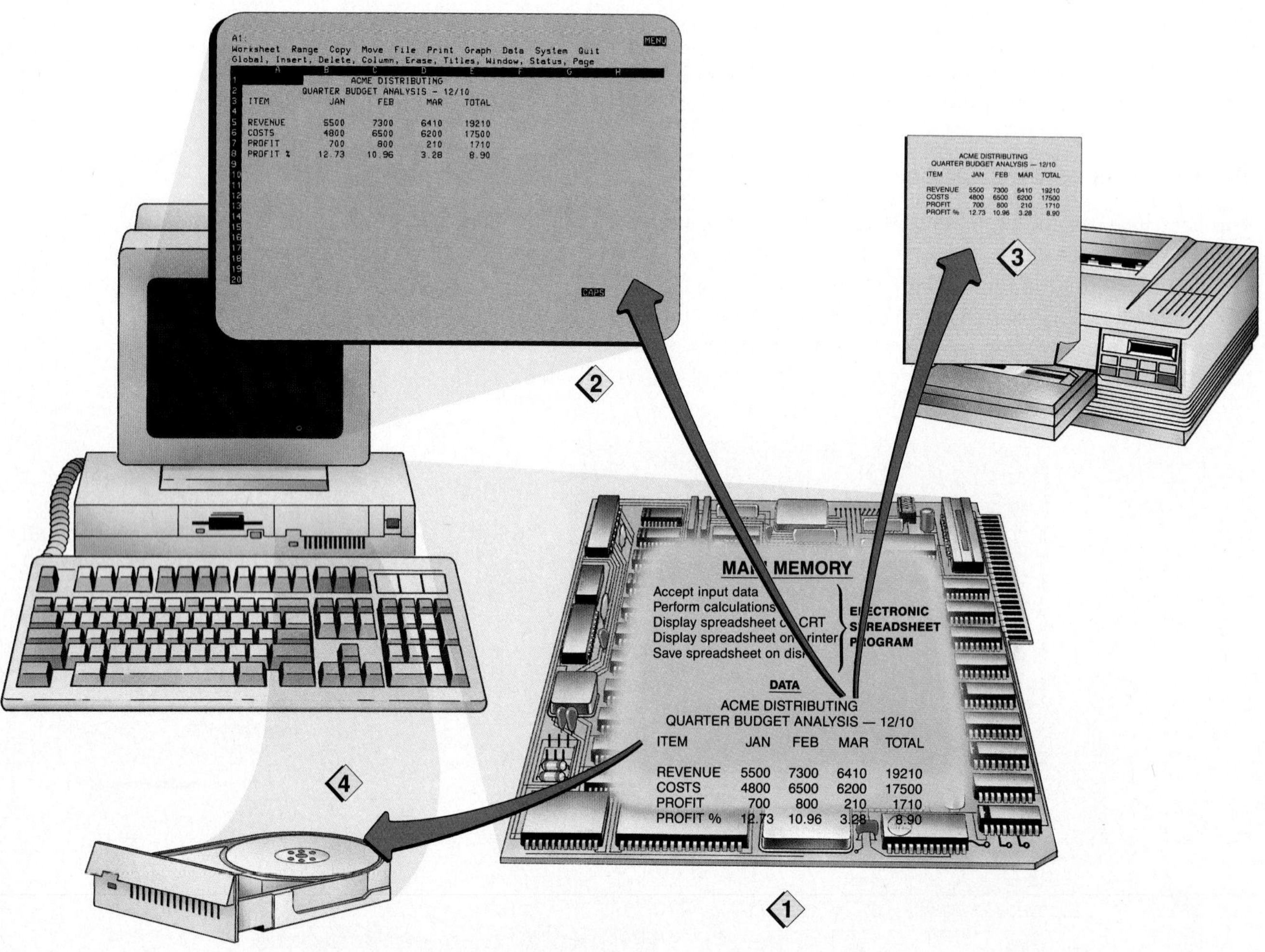

FIGURE 1-13
After the data has been entered, the program specifies the following processing steps: ① Perform calculations. ② Display the entire spreadsheet, with the calculation results, on the screen. ③ Print the spreadsheet. ④ Store the spreadsheet data and results on auxiliary storage.

Output: Display the Results

After completing the calculations, the program specifies that the spreadsheet, with the results of the calculations, display on the screen. The program also specifies that the results are printed on the printer ③. When this instruction is executed, the spreadsheet is printed on paper so the results of the processing can be used by someone other than the computer user.

Storage: Save the Results

The spreadsheet is also stored on a disk, in this example a hard disk, so that at a later time it can be retrieved and used again ④.

WHAT ARE THE ELEMENTS OF AN INFORMATION SYSTEM?

◆ Obtaining useful and timely information from computer processing requires more than just the equipment and software we have described so far. Other elements required for successful information processing include accurate data, trained information systems personnel, knowledgeable users, and documented procedures. Together these elements are referred to as an **information system** (Figure 1-14).

FIGURE 1-14
An information system requires computer equipment; software, which runs the equipment; data, which the computer manipulates; people, including both computer personnel who manage the equipment and users who use the information that the equipment produces; and finally procedures, which help the entire system run efficiently.

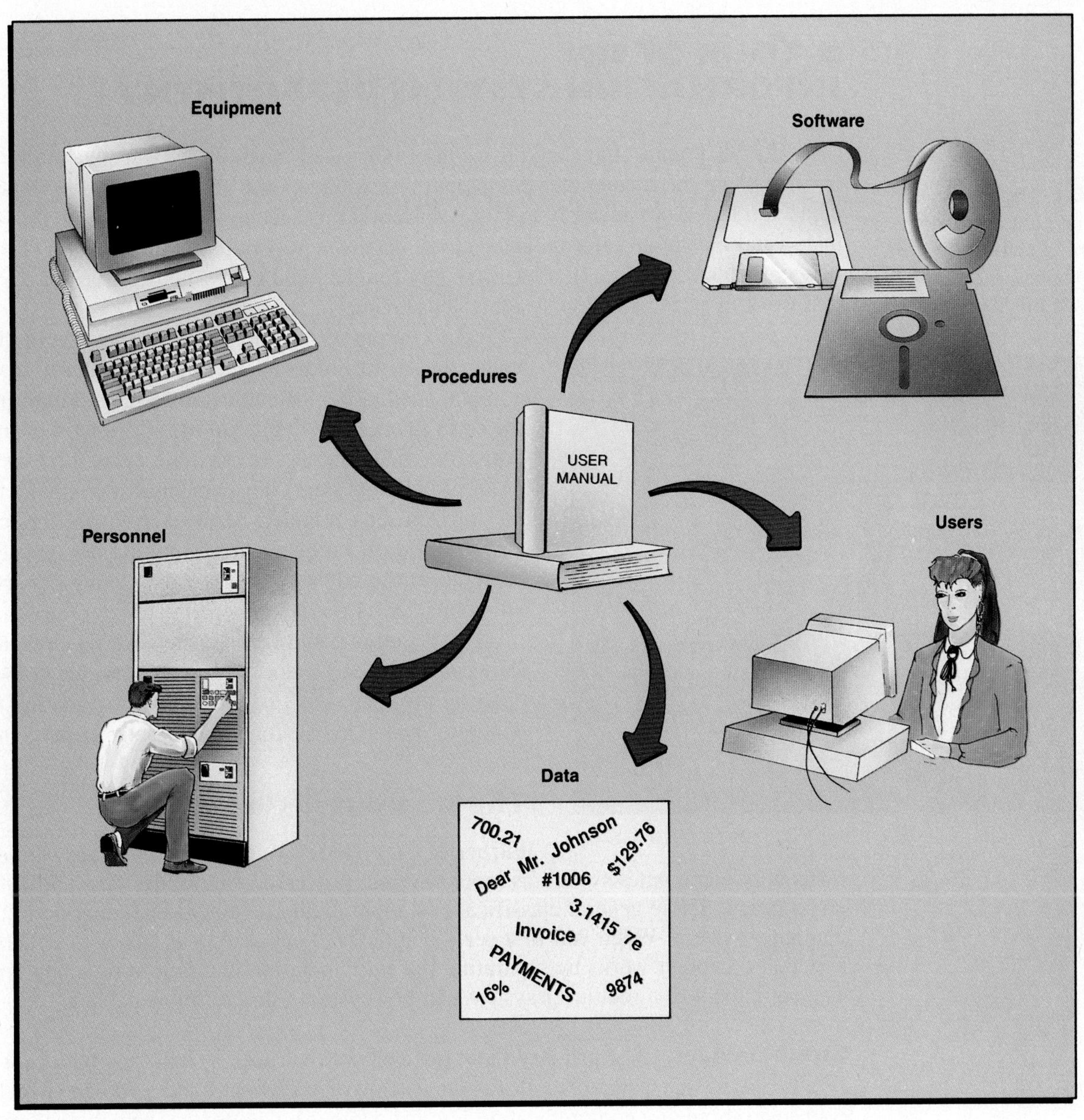

For an information system to provide accurate, timely, and useful information, each element in the system must be strong and all of the elements must work together. The equipment must be reliable and capable of handling the expected work load. The software must have been carefully developed and tested, and the data entered to be processed must be accurate. If the data is incorrect, the resulting information produced from it will be incorrect. Properly trained data processing personnel are required to run most medium and large computer systems. Users are sometimes overlooked as an important element of an information system, but with expanding computer use, users are taking increasing responsibility for the successful operation of information systems. This includes responsibility for the accuracy of both the input and output. In addition, users are taking a more active role in the development of computer applications. They work closely with information systems department personnel in the development of computer applications that relate to their areas of expertise. Finally, all information processing applications should have documented procedures covering not only the computer operations but any other related procedures as well.

A TOUR OF AN INFORMATION SYSTEMS DEPARTMENT

To this point in the chapter, we have illustrated most of the concepts you have learned using microcomputer equipment and applications. To show you how the concepts you have learned apply to larger systems, this section will take you on a narrative and visual tour of an information systems department. In this section we also discuss how computers are used in a business environment and the responsibilities of personnel that work in an information systems department.

FIGURE 1-15
A terminal contains a keyboard and a screen. The screen displays the data entered via the keyboard.

The computers used in a business are generally under the control of a separate department within the company called the **information systems department**, the **data processing department**, or sometimes just the **computer department**. In our tour we will be visiting an information systems department of a company that has a multiuser computer. **Multiuser computers** concurrently process requests from more than one user. For example, if the employees in the accounting department are connected to the computer, one or more accounts receivable clerks could be entering cash receipts at the same time that one or more accounts payable clerks are entering invoices. Let's begin our tour by visiting the computer room and seeing the computer equipment.

The Computer Room

Earlier in the chapter, we identified the hardware components of a computer system as input devices, processor, output devices, and auxiliary storage. These general classifications apply to all computers including a multiuser computer system. When you first see a computer of any size, it is easier to understand how that computer works by separating the equipment into the four component areas. The equipment of a multiuser system can be separated in the following way.

Input Devices The primary input device on a multiuser system is a **terminal** (Figure 1-15). A terminal is a device consisting of a keyboard and a screen, which is connected through a communication line, or cable, to a computer. Sometimes personal computers are used as terminals. While there may be a few terminals in the computer room, most of the terminals are located on the desktops of employees throughout the organization.

FIGURE 1-16
This mainframe computer processes data for hundreds of users. Such a computer is usually placed in a room designed specifically for the machine. Special air conditioning, humidity control, electrical wiring, and flooring are required for many of these installations.

Processor One of the main pieces of equipment in the computer room is the processor unit (Figure 1-16). The processor unit of a multiuser computer allocates computer resources to the programs that are being processed. Modern computer processors are so fast that they can usually handle numerous users and still provide very quick response time.

Output Devices The most commonly used output devices for a multiuser computer are a printer (Figure 1-17) and a terminal (Figure 1-18). When large volumes of printed output must be produced, high-speed printers are used. Some terminals can display both text material and graphics in either monochrome or color.

Auxiliary Storage The two major types of auxiliary storage for a multiuser computer are magnetic disk and magnetic tape.

Magnetic disk is the most widely used auxiliary storage on multiuser computers. When using magnetic disk, data is recorded on an oxide coated metal platter (the disk) as a series of magnetic spots. Disk drives can store data on either removable disks or hard disks, sometimes called fixed disks. **Removable disks** refer to disk packs that can be taken out of the disk drive. In Figure 1-19, the containers for the removable disk packs can be seen sitting on the disk drives. Most hard disks contain platters that are enclosed in sealed units to prevent contamination of the disk surface.

FIGURE 1-17
High-speed printers are necessary to print the large volume of reports generated by a multiuser computer system.

FIGURE 1-18
A terminal is both an input and an output device. Here, the user is viewing a color graphics display.

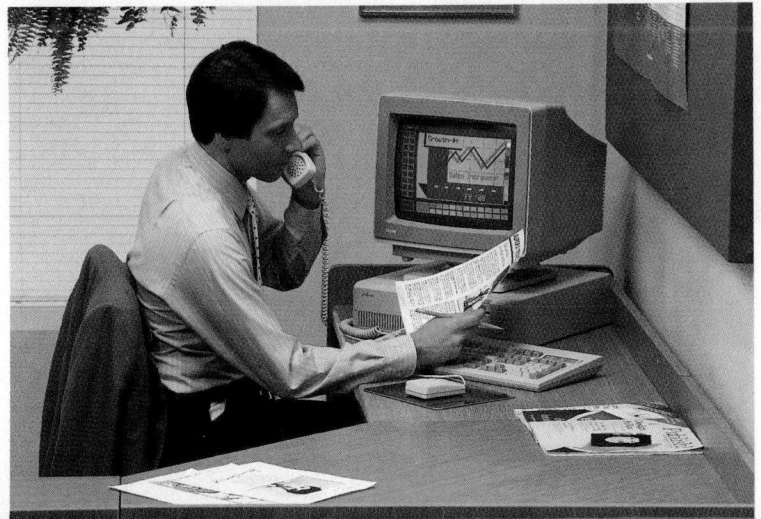

FIGURE 1-19
Removable disk packs are mounted on the disk drives. The multiple disk drives shown here are common in large computer installations.

FIGURE 1-20
This magnetic tape drive uses reels of one-half-inch tape. Tape is often used to backup the data stored on disk drives.

Magnetic tape (Figure 1-20) stores data as magnetic spots on one-quarter- to one-half-inch tape on cartridges or reels. On systems with disk drives, tape is most often used to store data that does not have to be accessed frequently. Another common use of tape is for backup storage. The contents of the disk drives are regularly copied to tape to provide protection against data loss.

FIGURE 1-21
The console allows the computer operator to monitor the processing.

Computer Operators The **computer operator** works in the computer room and is responsible for a number of different tasks. When the computer is running, the operator's console displays messages that indicate the status of the system (Figure 1-21). For example, a message may indicate that a special form, such as a check, must be placed in a printer. The operator responds to these messages to keep the computer running. In many instances, more than one operator is required to run a large computer.

The Data Library

The information systems department keeps its software and data on either disks or tapes. When a disk pack or tape is not in use, it is stored in a **data library** (Figure 1-22). The data library is usually located close to the computer room and is usually staffed by a **data librarian**. The disk packs and tapes in the library must be catalogued so that when they are required, they can be located quickly and taken to the computer room for use.

FIGURE 1-22
The data library stores disk packs and tapes when they are not in use.

Depending on the amount of disk storage available and how frequently it is used, some software applications and data are always available for processing. An example would be order processing software that enters orders into the computer while the sales clerk is on the phone with the customer. Because a phone call can come in at any time, this software application and the data associated with it must always be available for processing.

Offices of Information Systems Personnel

To implement applications on a computer, the information systems department usually employs people who have specialized training in computers and information processing. These employees may include computer operators who work in the computer room and run the equipment; data entry personnel who prepare and enter data into the computer; systems analysts who design the software applications; programmers who write specialized programs; a database administrator who controls and manages data; and managers who oversee the use of the computer.

Data Entry Personnel **Data entry personnel** (Figure 1-23) are responsible for entering large volumes of data into the computer system. Data is usually entered on terminals from **source documents**, which are original documents such as sales invoices. The accuracy of the data is important because it will affect the usefulness of the resulting information.

Mirror Catalogue Sales

Order Form

Customer Name: FELICIA DEVRY

Transaction Number: VPR 1257 Date: 10/10/93

Ship to: 4137 MARINA BLVD. MONTE NM 88100
No. Street City State ZIP

Bill to:
(if different) No. Street City State ZIP

Catalogue No.	Item/Description	Quantity	Unit Price	Total Price
7512367	SLIPPERS/BLUE	1	17.90	17.90
7512569	SLIPPERS/PINK	2	17.90	35.80
P619220	OAK TABLE/RD.	1	47.70	47.70
F523981	TABLE LAMP	1	26.90	26.90

Subtotal:	128.30
Shipping:	9.50
Tax:	7.70
Total invoice amount:	145.50

FIGURE 1-23
Data entry personnel specialize in entering large amounts of data from source documents.

Systems Analysts **Systems analysts** review current or proposed applications within a company to determine if the applications should be implemented using a computer. The systems analyst would consider applications for computer implementation if, among other things, productivity can be increased or more timely information can be generated to aid in the management of the company. If an application is to be *computerized*, the systems analyst studies the application to identify what data is used, how the data is processed, and other aspects of the application that are pertinent to the new system. The systems analyst then designs the new system by defining the data required for the computer application, developing the manner in which the data will be processed in the new system, and specifying the associated activities and procedures necessary to implement the application using the computer. Systems analysts work closely with both the people who will be using and benefiting from the new system and the programmers in the information systems department who will be writing the computer programs (Figure 1-24).

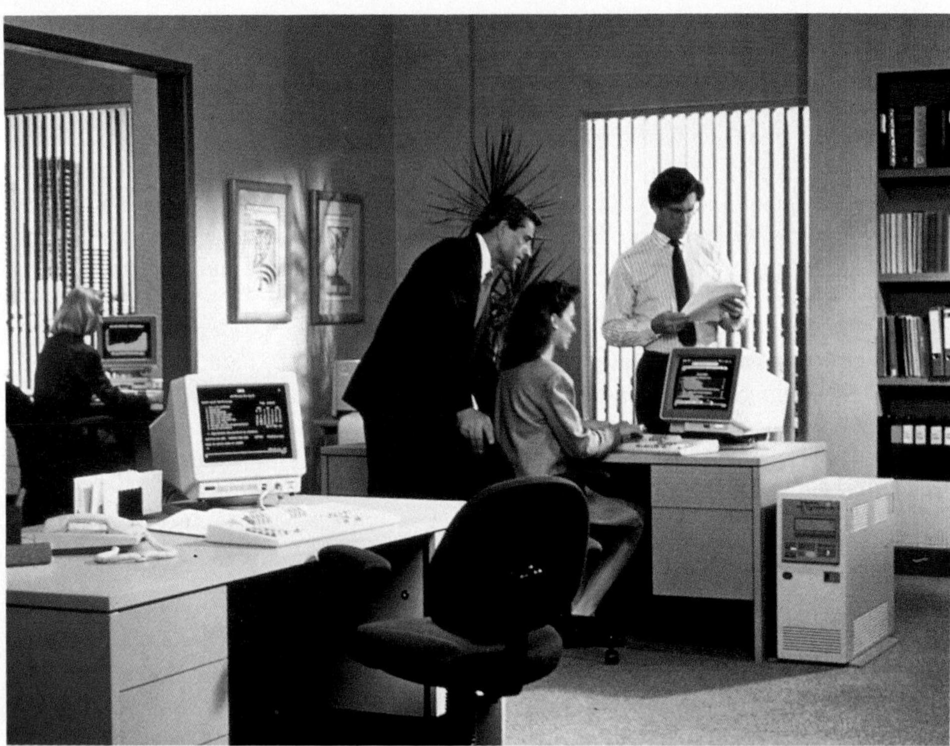

FIGURE 1-24
Programmers, systems analysts, and users all work closely in developing new computer applications.

Computer Programmers **Computer programmers** design, write, test, and implement specialized programs that process data on a computer. The design specifications from the systems analyst tell the programmer what processing needs to be accomplished. The programmer develops the specific programs of computer instructions that process the data and create the required information. The systems analyst specifies *what* is to be done; the programmer decides *how* to do it.

Database Administrator An important function within the information systems department is the management of data. In many companies, this task is the responsibility of the **database administrator**. Among other things, the database administrator must develop procedures to ensure that correct data is entered into the system, that confidential company data is not lost or stolen, that access to company data is restricted to those who need the data, and that data is available when it is needed. Data administration is very important. In a business, billions of pieces of data are processed on the computer, and the loss or misappropriation of that data could be extremely detrimental.

Information Systems Department Management Management within an information systems department varies depending on the size and complexity of the department. Most information systems departments have an operations manager, a systems manager, a programming manager, and a manager of the entire department. The **systems manager** oversees the activities in the systems analysis and design area of the department. The **programming manager** is in charge of all programmers within the department. Each of the managers we previously mentioned may also have project managers within their own areas. The **operations manager** oversees the operational aspects of the department such as the scheduling, maintenance, and operation of the equipment. The information systems department manager is in charge of the entire department and may have the title **vice president of information systems**, or **chief information officer (CIO)**.

Summary of the Tour of an Information Systems Department

During the tour of the information systems department we have seen the computer room, data library, and the offices of information systems personnel. You should know more about an information systems department and how a multiuser computer is used in a business.

HOW COMPUTERS ARE USED TODAY

In addition to business, the use of computer technology is widespread in our world. Figure 1-25 shows a variety of computers and their applications. New uses for computers and improvements to existing technology are continually being developed. How do computers affect your life? How will you use computers in the future?

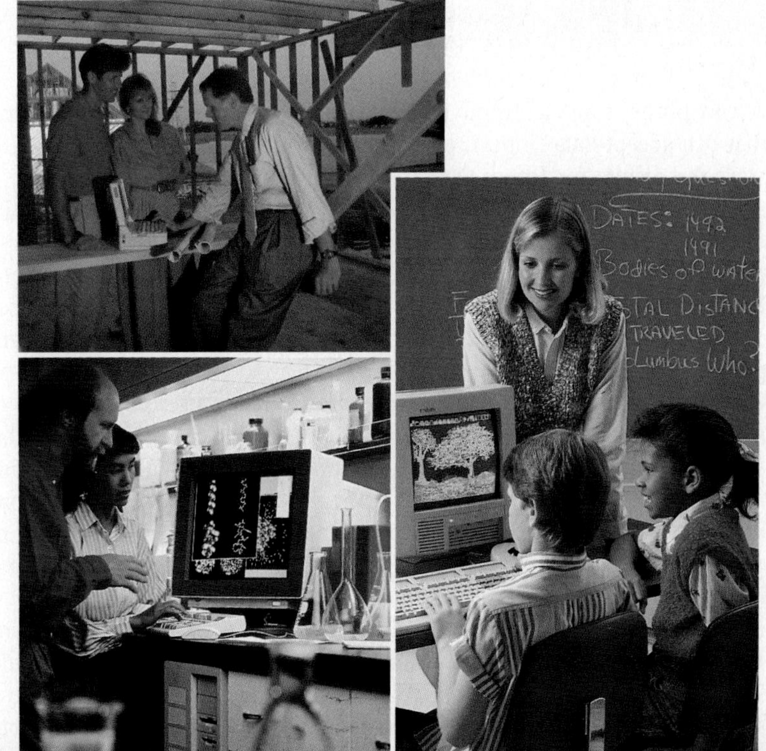

FIGURE 1-25
Here we see computers being used in a wide variety of applications and professions. New applications are being developed every day.

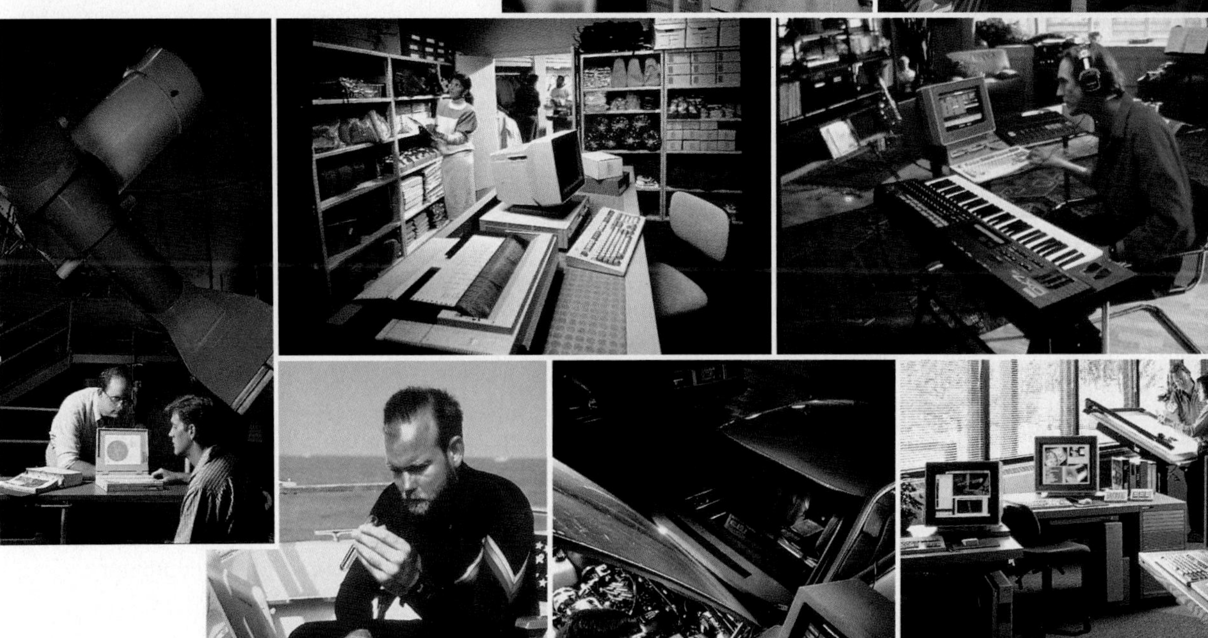

SUMMARY OF AN INTRODUCTION TO COMPUTERS

In this chapter we presented a broad introduction to concepts and terminology that are related to computers. You now have a basic understanding of what a computer is, how it processes data into information, and what elements are necessary for a successful information system. You have also seen some examples of different types of computers and how they are used. The photo essay at the end of the chapter is a time line that shows the evolution of modern computers.

CHAPTER SUMMARY

1. A **computer** is an electronic device, operating under the control of instructions stored in its own memory unit, that can accept data (input), process data arithmetically and logically, produce output from the processing, and store the results for future use.
2. A computer can perform **input**, **process**, **output**, and **storage** operations. These operations are called the **information processing cycle**.
3. **Data** refers to the raw facts, including numbers and words, that are processed on a computer.
4. **Information** is data that has been processed into a meaningful and useful form.
5. The production of information by processing data on a computer is called **information processing**, or **data processing (DP)**.
6. **Computer users** are the people who either directly use the computer or utilize the information it provides.
7. A computer is a powerful tool because it is reliable and can process data quickly and accurately.
8. A **computer program** is a detailed set of instructions that tells the computer exactly what to do.
9. Computer processing can produce many different forms of information from a single set of data.
10. Processing data on a computer is performed by computer equipment including input devices, the processor unit, output devices, and auxiliary storage units. Computer equipment is often referred to as **hardware**.
11. **Input devices** are used to enter data into a computer.
12. The **processor unit** contains the electronic circuits that cause processing to take place.
13. The processor unit contains the central processing unit (CPU) and main memory.
14. The **central processing unit (CPU)** contains the **control unit** and the **arithmetic and logic unit (ALU)**.
15. **Arithmetic operations** are numeric calculations such as addition, subtraction, multiplication, and division that take place in the processor.
16. **Logical operations** are comparisons of data in the processor to see if one value is greater than, equal to, or less than another value.
17. **Main memory** electronically stores data and program instructions.
18. **Output devices** are used to print or display data and information.
19. **Auxiliary storage units** are used to store program instructions and data when they are not being used in the main memory of the computer.
20. The four major categories of computers are microcomputers, minicomputers, mainframes, and supercomputers.
21. Types of **microcomputers** include hand-held, notebook, laptop, portable, desktop, and supermicrocomputers.
22. **Minicomputers** address the needs of users who want more processing power than a microcomputer but do not need the power of a mainframe. Minicomputers can support a number of users performing different tasks.
23. **Mainframe** computers are large systems that can handle hundreds of users, store large amounts of data, and process transactions at a very high rate.
24. **Supercomputers**, the most powerful and expensive category of computers, can process hundreds of millions of instructions per second and perform long, complex calculations.
25. **Computer software** is another name for computer programs.
26. A computer program must first be loaded into main memory before it can be executed.
27. **System software** consists of programs that are related to controlling the actual operations of the computer equipment.

28. An important part of the system software is a set of programs called the **operating system**, which tells the computer how to perform its various functions.
29. **Application software** consists of programs that tell a computer how to produce information.
30. Programs purchased from computer stores or software vendors are called **application software packages**.
31. Commonly used personal computer software packages are word processing, electronic spreadsheet, graphics, and database software.
32. **Word processing software** is used to create and print documents.
33. **Electronic spreadsheet software** performs calculations on rows and columns of numeric data based on formulas entered by the user.
34. **Graphics software** provides the capability to transform numbers and text into a graphic format.
35. **Database software** allows the user to enter, retrieve, and update data efficiently.
36. The elements of an information system are equipment, software, data, personnel, users, and procedures.
37. **Multiuser computers** can concurrently process requests from more than one user.
38. A **terminal**, consisting of a keyboard and screen, is the most commonly used input device for a large computer.
39. Modern computer processors are so fast that they can usually handle numerous users and still provide very quick response time.
40. The most commonly used output devices for large computers are terminals and high-speed printers.
41. Auxiliary storage devices used on a large computer include magnetic disk and magnetic tape.
42. **Computer operators** run the computer equipment and monitor processing operations.
43. A **data library** stores disk packs and tapes when they are not in use.
44. **Source documents** are original documents, such as sales invoices, from which data can be entered.
45. **Data entry personnel** prepare and enter data into the computer.
46. **Systems analysts** review and design computer applications. Systems analysts work closely with users and programmers.
47. **Computer programmers** design, write, test, and implement programs, that process data on a computer.
48. A **database administrator** is responsible for managing an organization's computerized data.
49. Management within an information systems department includes a **systems manager**, **programming manager**, **operations manager**, and a department manager, who is sometimes called the **vice president of information systems**, or **chief information officer (CIO)**.
50. The use of computer technology is widespread in our world.

KEY TERMS

ALU (Arithmetic/Logic Unit) *1.5*
Application software *1.8*
Application software package *1.8*
Arithmetic/Logic Unit (ALU) *1.5*
Arithmetic operation *1.5*
Auxiliary storage unit *1.5*
Cathode ray tube (CRT) *1.5*
Central processing unit (CPU) *1.5*
Chief information officer (CIO) *1.19*
Computer *1.2*
Computer department *1.14*
Computer operator *1.16*
Computer program *1.4*
Computer programmer *1.18*
Computer software *1.7*
Computer system *1.6*
Computer users *1.3*
Control unit *1.5*
CPU (central processing unit) *1.5*
CRT (cathode ray tube) *1.5*
Data *1.2*
Data entry personnel *1.17*
Data librarian *1.16*
Data library *1.16*
Data processing (DP) *1.2*
Data processing department *1.14*
Database administrator *1.18*
Database software *1.10*
Diskette *1.6*
Electronic spreadsheet software *1.10*
End users *1.3*
Graphics software *1.10*
Hard disk *1.6*
Hardware *1.4*
Information *1.2*
Information processing *1.2*
Information processing cycle *1.2*
Information system *1.13*
Information systems department *1.14*
Input *1.4*
Input device *1.5*
Keyboard *1.5*
Logical operation *1.5*
Magnetic disk *1.15*
Magnetic tape *1.16*
Main memory *1.5*
Mainframe *1.7*
Micro *1.7*
Microcomputer *1.7*
Minicomputer *1.7*
Monitor *1.5*
Multiuser computer *1.14*

Operating system *1.8*
Operations manager *1.18*
Output *1.4*
Output device *1.5*
Peripheral device *1.6*
Personal computer *1.7*
Primary storage *1.5*
Printer *1.5*
Process *1.4*
Processor unit *1.5*
Program instruction *1.4*
Programming manager *1.18*
Removable disk *1.15*
Screen *1.5*
Software *1.4*
Software package *1.8*
Source document *1.17*
Spreadsheet *1.10*
Storage *1.4*
Supercomputer *1.7*
Systems analyst *1.17*
Systems manager *1.18*
System software *1.8*
Users *1.3*
Vice president of information systems *1.19*
Word processing software *1.10*

REVIEW QUESTIONS

1. What is the definition of a computer?
2. Define the term computer user.
3. What is the difference between data and information? How is information derived from data?
4. What is the information processing cycle?
5. Describe the four hardware units found on a microcomputer.
6. What is the difference between main memory and auxiliary storage? Why are both necessary?
7. Identify some of the differences among microcomputers, minicomputers, mainframe computers, and supercomputers.
8. What is computer software? How does a computer use software?
9. What is system software? List two functions that the operating system performs.
10. Identify four application software packages often used with personal computers.
11. What are the six elements of an information system?
12. What is the user's role in an information system?
13. Who are some of the personnel who work in an information systems department?
14. What is the role of a systems analyst? How does that position differ from the job of a computer programmer?
15. Describe the key developments in the evolution of the modern computer during the 1960s.

CONTROVERSIAL ISSUES

1. At what grade level should computers be introduced to students? Should all high school or college graduates have a minimum computer skill level? If yes, what should the minimum skill level include?
2. Do computers make mistakes, or is it the humans that program and operate the computers who make the mistakes? Discuss what you think caused recent *computer errors* that you experienced or read about.

RESEARCH PROJECTS

1. Write or call a manufacturer of a minicomputer or mainframe, such as IBM, Bull, DEC, or HP, and ask for a brochure describing one of its popular models. Prepare a report for your class based on what you learned.
2. Prepare a report for your class describing the use of computers at your school. You may focus on a single department or prepare a general report about computer use throughout the school.
3. Prepare a detailed report on an individual who made a contribution to the history of computing.

The Evolution of the Computer Industry

The electronic computer industry began about fifty years ago. This time line summarizes the major events in the evolution of the computer industry.

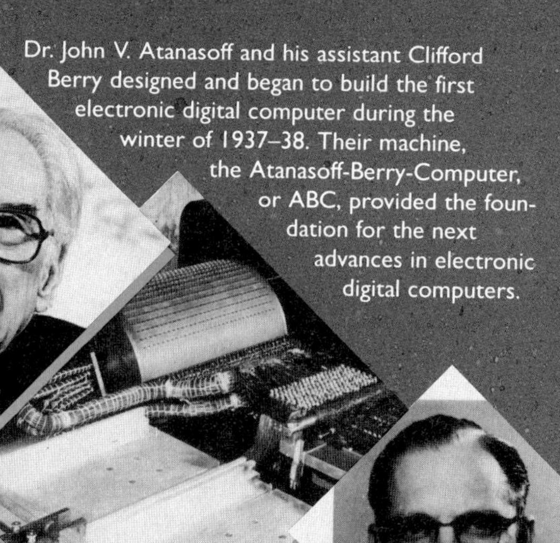

Dr. John V. Atanasoff and his assistant Clifford Berry designed and began to build the first electronic digital computer during the winter of 1937–38. Their machine, the Atanasoff-Berry-Computer, or ABC, provided the foundation for the next advances in electronic digital computers.

Dr. John von Neumann is credited with writing a brilliant report in 1945 describing several new hardware concepts and the use of stored programs. His breakthrough laid the foundation for the digital computers that have since been built.

1937

1945

1951

1952

During the years 1943 to 1946, Dr. John W. Mauchly and J. Presper Eckert, Jr. completed the ENIAC (Electronic Numerical Integrator and Computer), the first large-scale electronic digital computer. The ENIAC weighed thirty tons, contained 18,000 vacuum tubes, and occupied a thirty-by-fifty-foot space.

In 1951–52, after much discussion, IBM decided to add computers to their line of business equipment products. This led IBM to become a dominant force in the computer industry.

J. Presper Eckert, Jr., standing left, explains the operations of the UNIVAC I, to newsman Walter Cronkite, right. This machine was the first commercially available electronic digital computer.

8:30 PM

UNIVAC on Election Night

IT'S AWFULLY EARLY, BUT I'LL GO OUT ON A LIMB.

UNIVAC PREDICTS—with 3,398,745 votes in—

	STEVENSON	EISENHOWER
STATES	5	43
ELECTORAL	93	438
POPULAR	18,986,436	32,915,049

THE CHANCES ARE NOW 00 to 1 IN FAVOR OF THE ELECTION OF EISENHOWER.

Public awareness of computers increased when in 1951 the UNIVAC I, after analyzing only 5% of the tallied vote, correctly predicted that Dwight D. Eisenhower would win the presidential election.

In 1952, Dr. Grace Hopper, a mathematician and commodore in the U.S. Navy, wrote a paper describing how to program a computer with symbolic notation instead of the detailed machine language that had been used.

Dr. Hopper was instrumental in developing high-level languages such as COBOL, a business applications language introduced in 1960. COBOL uses English-like phrases and can be run on most computers, making it one of the most widely used languages in the world.

The IBM model 650 was one of the first widely used computer systems. Originally IBM planned to produce only 50 machines, but the system was so successful that eventually they manufactured over 1,000.

FORTRAN (FORmula TRANslator) was introduced in 1957 proving that efficient, easy-to-use programming languages could be developed. FORTRAN is still in use.

1952 1953 1957 1958 1959 1960

By 1959 over 200 programming languages had been created.

Core memory, developed in the early 1950s, provided much larger storage capacities and greater reliability than vacuum tube memory.

In 1958, computers built with transistors marked the beginning of the second generation of computer hardware. Previous computers built with vacuum tubes were first-generation machines.

From 1958 to 1964, it is estimated, the number of computers in the U.S. grew from 2,500 to 18,000.

Third-generation computers, with their controlling circuitry stored on chips, were introduced in 1964. The IBM System/360 computers were the first third-generation machines.

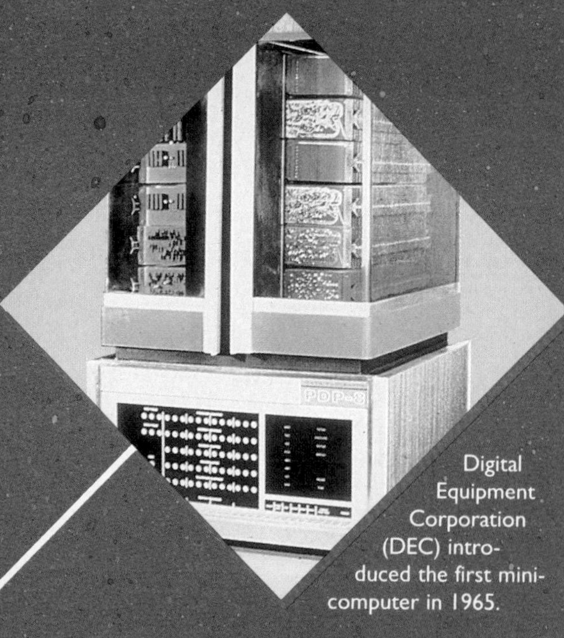

Digital Equipment Corporation (DEC) introduced the first minicomputer in 1965.

1964

1965

1968

1969

In 1965, Dr. John Kemeny of Dartmouth led the development of the BASIC programming language. BASIC is the language most commonly used on microcomputers. More people program in BASIC than any other language.

The software industry emerged in the 1960s. In 1968, Computer Science Corporation became the first software company to be listed on the New York Stock Exchange.

In 1969, under pressure from the industry, IBM announced that some of its software would be priced separately from the computer hardware. This "unbundling" allowed software firms to emerge in the industry.

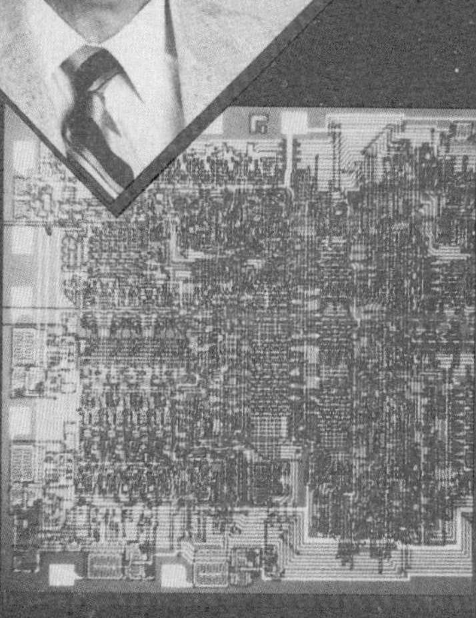

In 1969, Dr. Ted Hoff of Intel Corporation developed a microprocessor, or microprogrammable computer chip, the Intel 4004.

The MITS, Inc. Altair computer, sold in kits for less than $400, was the first commercially successful microcomputer.

The fourth-generation computers built with chips that used LSI (large-scale integration) arrived in 1970. The chips used in 1965 contained as many as 1,000 circuits. By 1970, the LSI chip contained as many as 15,000.

1970 1975 1976 1979 1980

In 1976, Steve Wozniak and Steve Jobs built the first Apple computer.

The VisiCalc spreadsheet program written by Bob Frankston and Dan Bricklin was introduced in 1979. This product was originally written to run on Apple II computers. Together, VisiCalc and Apple II computers rapidly became successful. Most people consider VisiCalc to be the singlemost important reason why microcomputers gained acceptance in the business world.

In 1980, IBM offered Microsoft Corporation's founder Bill Gates the opportunity to develop the operating system for the soon-to-be-announced IBM personal computer. With the development of MS-DOS, Microsoft achieved tremendous growth and success.

The IBM PC was introduced in 1981, signaling IBM's entrance into the microcomputer marketplace. The IBM PC quickly garnered the largest share of the personal computer market and became the personal computer of choice in business.

It is estimated that 313,000 microcomputers were sold in 1981. In 1982, the number jumped to 3,275,000.

1981 1982 1983 1984

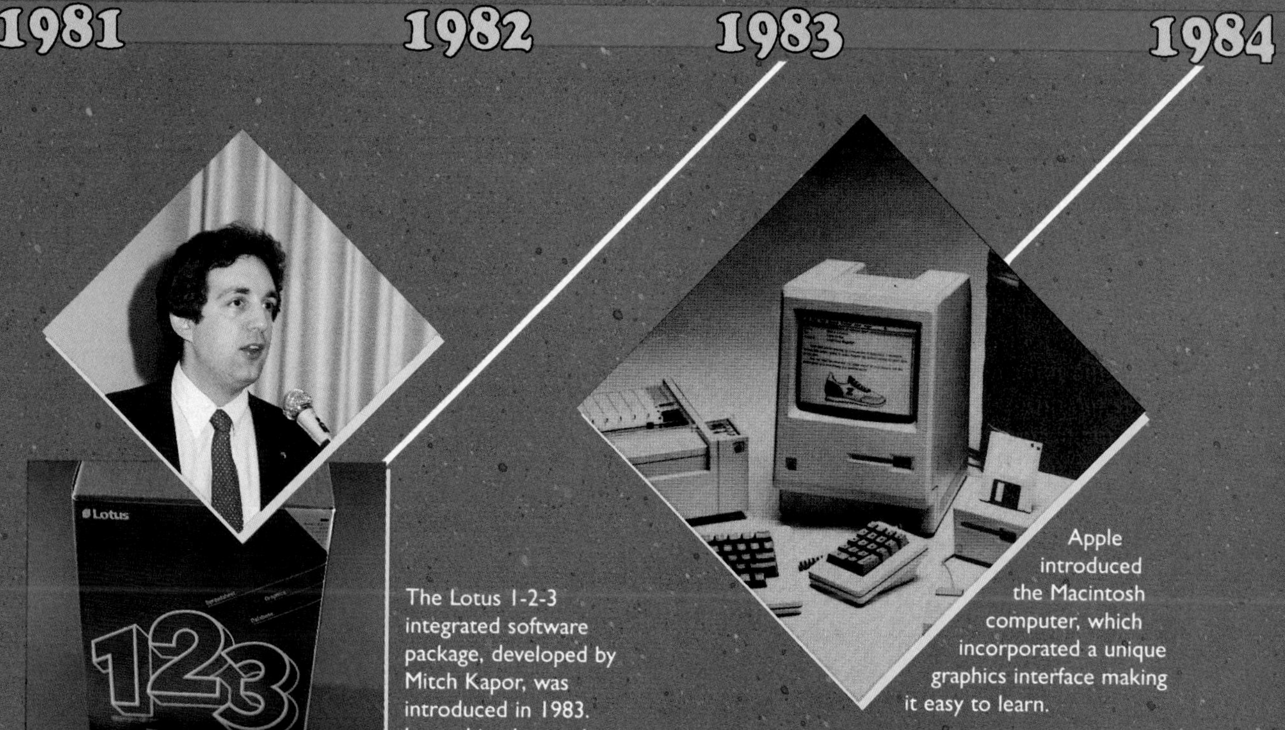

The Lotus 1-2-3 integrated software package, developed by Mitch Kapor, was introduced in 1983. It combined spreadsheet,graphics, and database programs in one package.

Apple introduced the Macintosh computer, which incorporated a unique graphics interface making it easy to learn.

Several microcomputers using the powerful Intel 80386 microprocessor were introduced in 1987. These machines could handle processing performed previously only by large systems.

The Intel 80486 became the world's first 1,000,000-transistor microprocessor. It crammed 1.2 million transistors on a sliver of silicon that measured .4" × .6" and executed instructions at 15 MIPS (million instructions per second)—four times as fast as its predecessor, the 80386.

In early 1990, estimates indicated that over 54 million computers were in use in the United States.

1987 1988 1989 1990

In October of 1988, former Apple founder Steve Jobs announced his long-awaited NeXT computer. Innovative features included the capability to record and process sound and the use of erasable optical disk storage.

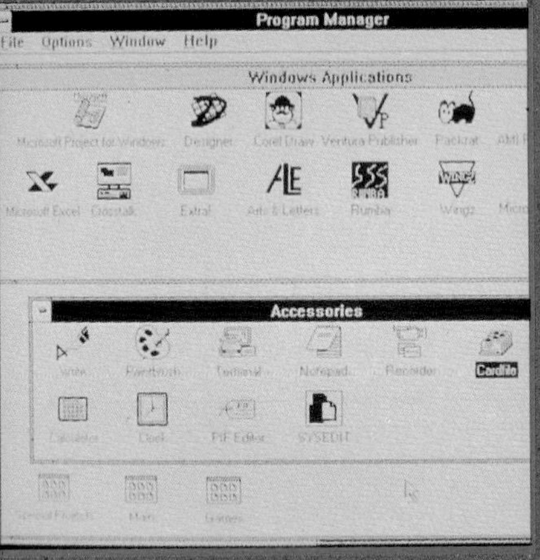

Microsoft released Windows 3.0, a substantially enhanced version of its Windows graphics user interface first introduced in 1985. The software allows users to run multiple applications on a personal computer and more easily move data from one application to another. The package became an instant success selling hundreds of thousands of copies.

The computer industry will continue to evolve as improved technology and innovation lead to a variety of new computer applications.

Microcomputer Applications: User Tools

OBJECTIVES

- Identify the most widely used general microcomputer software applications
- Describe how each of the applications can help users
- Explain the key features of each of the major microcomputer applications
- Explain integrated software and its advantages
- List and describe six guidelines for purchasing software application packages
- List and describe learning aids and support tools that help users to use microcomputer applications

Today, understanding the applications commonly used on microcomputers is considered a part of being computer literate. In fact, a knowledge of these applications is now considered by many educators and employers to be more important than a knowledge of programming. Because of this, we introduce microcomputer applications, focusing on the most widely used applications early in this book. Learning about each application will help you understand how people use microcomputers in our modern world.

AN INTRODUCTION TO GENERAL MICROCOMPUTER APPLICATIONS

The applications discussed in this chapter are usually called **general microcomputer applications**. This software is called *general* because it is useful to a broad range of users. Word processing is a good example of a general application. Regardless of the type of business a company does, word processing can be used as a tool to help employees generate documents.

An important advantage of general applications is that you do not need any special technical skills or ability to use them. These programs are designed to be **user friendly**, in other words, easy to use. You do not need detailed computer instructions. Instead, you use the software through simple commands. **Commands** are instructions that tell the software what you want to do. For example, when you are finished using an application and you want to save your work, you issue an instruction called a SAVE command. In some applications you must type the command, in other applications the command is entered through a user interface.

User interfaces (Figure 2-1) are methods and techniques that make using an application simpler. They include function keys, screen prompts, menus, icons, and a device called a mouse. To help you understand how to use the software, we include an introduction to these features in this chapter. We present a more thorough discussion in Chapter 3.

FIGURE 2-1
User interfaces.

▲ Function keys — programmed to execute commonly used instructions.

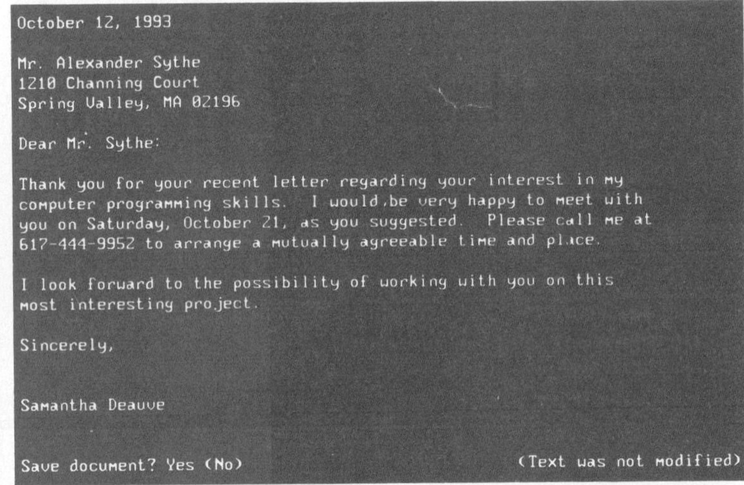

▲ Screen prompts — such as the question in the lower left of this screen — indicate that the software is waiting for the user to respond.

Menus — such as this "pull-down" menu — offer a list of possible processing selections. ▶

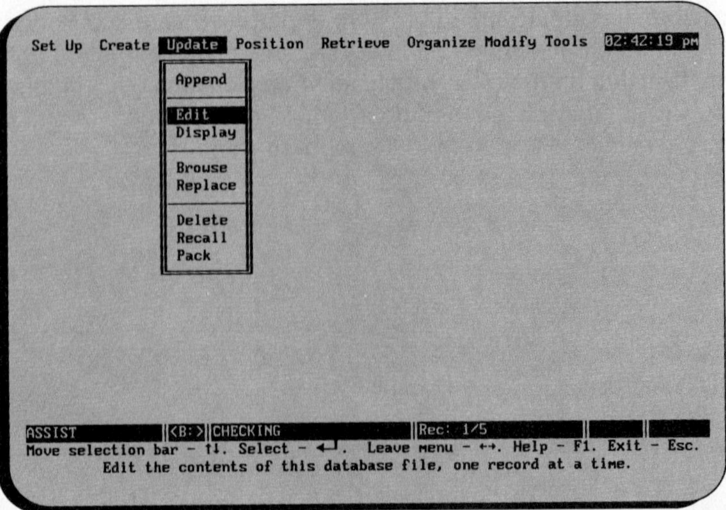

The **function keys** that are included on computer keyboards are a type of user interface. Pressing a function key in an applications program is a shortcut that takes the place of entering a command. The software defines exactly what the function key causes to happen. If you used a function key to save your work as we discussed in the previous example, pressing one key instead of several could issue the entire command.

Screen **prompts** are the messages that the program displays to help you while you are using an application. **Menus**, a special kind of screen prompt, are used in applications to provide a list of processing options. You make a selection from the menu by pressing the number or letter key that corresponds with the option you desire. Some applications use a menu called a **pull-down menu**. In this menu style the selections are displayed across the top of the screen. As you use the arrow keys to move from one selection to the next, the options associated with that selection appear to be *pulled down* from the top of the screen like a window shade. **Icons** refer to pictures instead of words that are displayed on the screen to show you various program options. A user interface that extensively uses icons to graphically represent files and processing options is called a **graphic user interface (GUI)**.

A **mouse** is a small input device that is used to move the cursor and input commands. The **cursor** is a symbol, such as an underline character or an arrow, that indicates where you are working on the screen. Many applications require you to move the cursor around on the screen. You do this by using the arrow keys on the keyboard or by moving the mouse. For example, a mouse could be used to move the cursor so that it is pointing to a selection you want to make on a menu. You can then press a button on the mouse to select that menu option.

These are some of the user interfaces that help to make application packages user friendly. User interfaces help minimize the technical computer knowledge you need when you are using general applications packages.

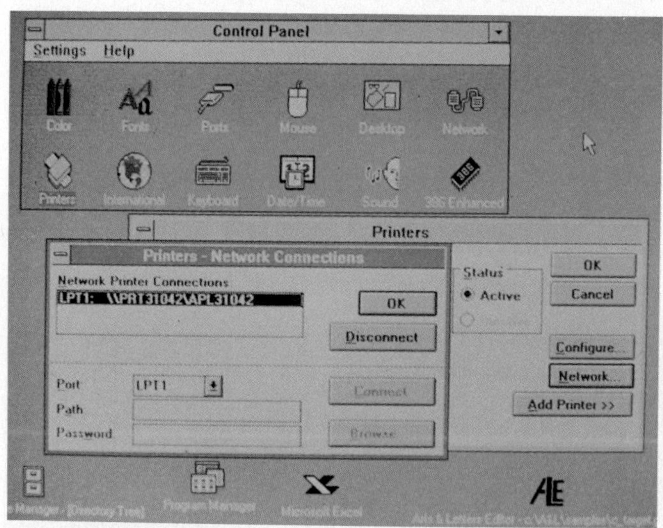

▲ Icons — symbols that represent program options.

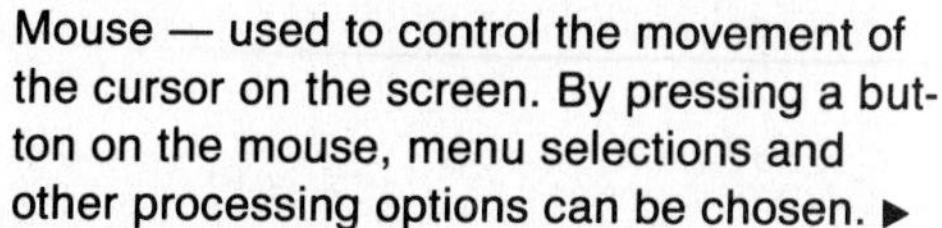

Mouse — used to control the movement of the cursor on the screen. By pressing a button on the mouse, menu selections and other processing options can be chosen. ▶

Many kinds of general applications are available. Some of the most widely used software includes:

- Word processing
- Desktop publishing
- Electronic spreadsheet
- Database
- Graphics
- Data communications

Although we will discuss these applications as they are used on microcomputers, they are actually available on computers of all sizes. The concepts you will learn about each application package on microcomputers will also apply if you are working on a larger system.

WORD PROCESSING SOFTWARE: A DOCUMENT PRODUCTIVITY TOOL

The most widely used general application is word processing. If you need to create **documents**, such as letters or memos, you can increase your productivity by learning to use this software tool. Some of the popular packages used today include WordPerfect, Microsoft Word, and WordStar. This section discusses using a word processor to create a document.

Word processing software is used to prepare documents electronically (Figure 2-2). It allows you to enter text on the computer keyboard in the same manner as you create documents on a typewriter. As you enter the characters, they are displayed on the screen and stored in the computer's main memory. Because the document is in an electronic format, you can easily **edit** it by making changes and corrections to the text. You can correct errors and add, move, or delete characters, words, sentences, paragraphs, and large blocks of text. When the document is complete, you enter a command and have the computer send the document to the printer. The document's format is also under your control. You can specify the margins, define the page length, and select the print style. The document can be printed as many times as you like. Each copy is an original and looks the same as the other copies. The computer's storage capability allows you to store your documents so they can be used again. It is an efficient way to file documents because many documents can fit on one disk. If you wish, previously stored documents can be combined to make new documents, and you do not have to reenter the text as you would on a typewriter.

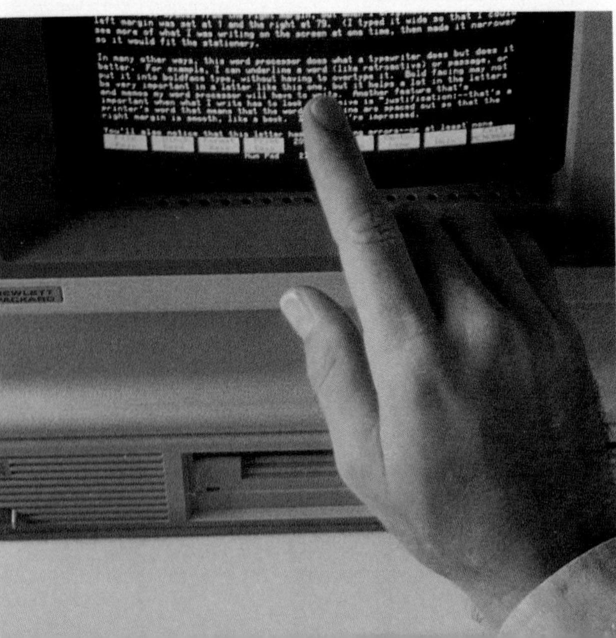

FIGURE 2-2
Word processing using a computer is faster, more accurate, and less tedious than using a typewriter.

The value of word processing is that it reduces the time required to prepare and produce written documents. Any editing you want to do in the document is easy because the software allows you to make changes quickly and efficiently. In addition, you can eliminate the tedious task of typing a final draft.

Most word processing packages include additional support features such as a spelling checker and a thesaurus. In addition, software may be purchased for grammar checking that is designed to work with word processors.

Spelling Checker

Spelling checker software allows you to check individual words or the entire document for correct spelling. To check a document for misspelled words, you enter a command that instructs the software to check the spelling. The words in the text will then be checked against an electronic dictionary stored on a disk that is part of the spelling checker software. If an exact match is not found, the word is highlighted. A menu is then superimposed on the screen, giving you a list of similar words that may be the correct spelling. You can select one of the words displayed on the menu, edit the highlighted word, leave the word unchanged, or add the word to the dictionary.

Some spelling checker dictionaries contain over 120,000 words. Many users customize their software dictionaries by adding company, street, city, and personal names so that the software can check the correct spelling of those words.

While spelling checkers can catch misspelled words and words that are repeated such as the the, they cannot identify words that are used incorrectly. A thesaurus and grammar checker will help you to choose proper words and use them in a correct manner.

Thesaurus

Thesaurus software allows you to look up synonyms for words in a document while you are using your word processor. Using a thesaurus is similar to using a spelling checker. When you want to look up a synonym for a word, you place the cursor on the word that you want to check, enter a command through the keyboard, and the thesaurus software displays a menu of possible synonyms. If you find a word you want to use, you select the desired word from the list and the software automatically incorporates it in the document by replacing the previous word.

Grammar Checker

Grammar checker software is used to check for grammar, writing style, and sentence structure errors (Figure 2-3). This software can check documents for excessive use of a word or phrase, identify sentences that are too long, and find words that are used out of context such as four example.

Whereas many word processors include a spelling checker and a thesaurus, grammar checkers are usually purchased separately. A popular grammar checker that is compatible with many word processing packages is Grammatik.

FIGURE 2-3
This grammar checker software is named Grammatik. It can proofread a document for mistakes in grammar, usage, punctuation, and spelling. The document being proofread is shown in the top portion of the screen. The possible problem identified by the software is displayed in the lower portion of the screen.

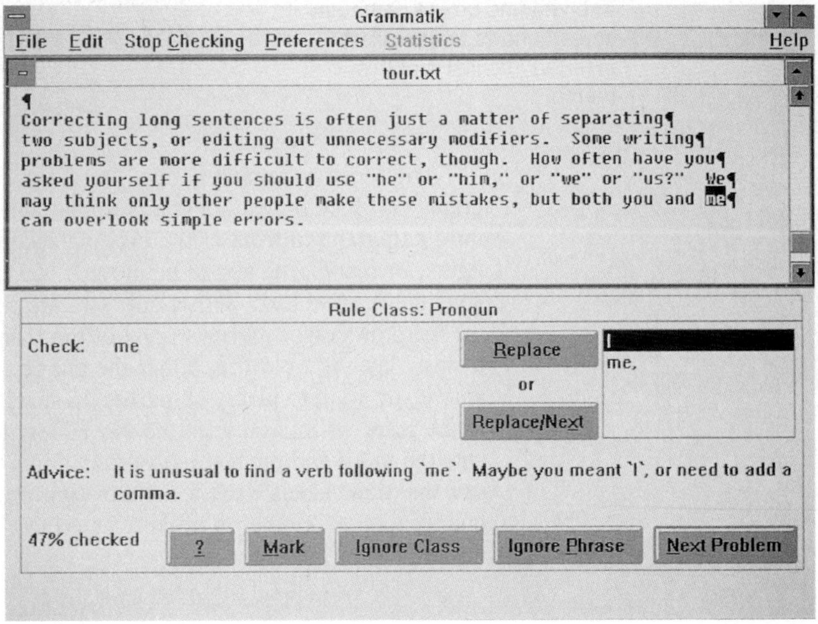

A Word Processing Example

Figures 2-4 through 2-11 illustrate the following word processing example. Let's say that Julia Broderick, Vice President of Sales of a company, wants to send a memo announcing a meeting of all sales personnel. She remembers that last month she sent a similar memo to just the sales managers. Thus, the first thing she does is load last month's memo into main memory so it will appear on the screen (Figure 2-4). This memo might be stored on a hard disk or on a diskette.

Word processing changes are usually one of three types: inserting text, deleting text, or moving text. When you **insert**, you add characters and words to the existing text in your document. When you **delete**, text is removed from your document. Often it makes sense to do your insertions and deletions at the same time; as you edit your document, you delete the existing word or phrase and insert the new one. Figure 2-5 shows the document with the text to be deleted. Figure 2-6 shows the document after she enters the new text.

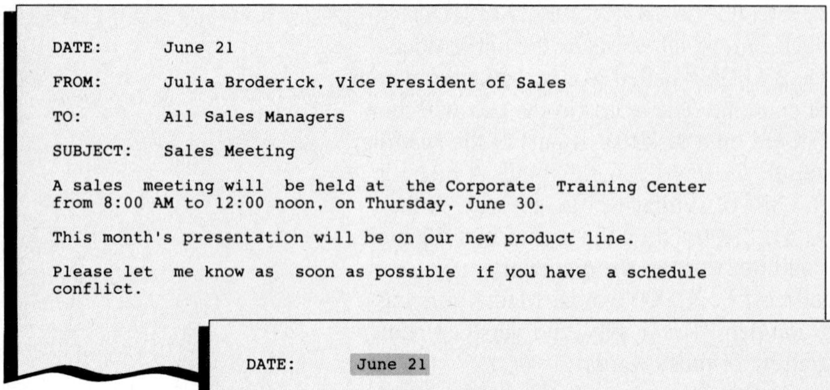

```
DATE:      June 21
FROM:      Julia Broderick, Vice President of Sales
TO:        All Sales Managers
SUBJECT:   Sales Meeting

A sales  meeting will  be held at  the Corporate  Training Center
from 8:00 AM to 12:00 noon, on Thursday, June 30.

This month's presentation will be on our new product line.

Please let  me know as  soon as possible  if you have  a schedule
conflict.
```

FIGURE 2-4
Last month's memo that will be changed for this month's meeting.

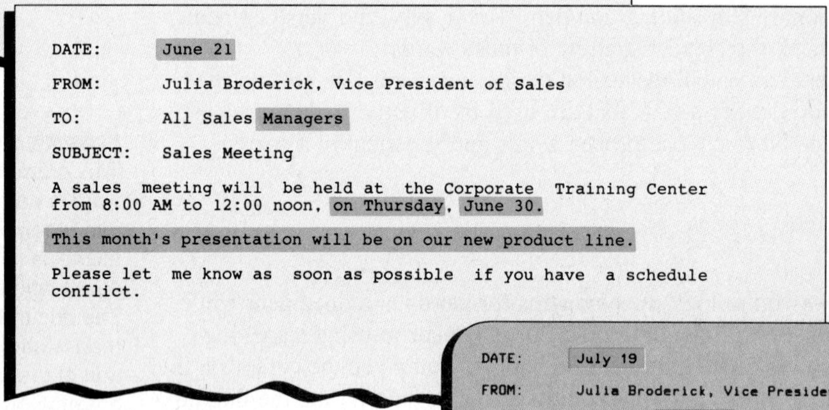

```
DATE:      June 21
FROM:      Julia Broderick, Vice President of Sales
TO:        All Sales Managers
SUBJECT:   Sales Meeting

A sales  meeting will  be held at  the Corporate  Training Center
from 8:00 AM to 12:00 noon, on Thursday, June 30.

This month's presentation will be on our new product line.

Please let  me know as  soon as possible  if you have  a schedule
conflict.
```

= Items to be deleted

FIGURE 2-5
The shaded areas indicate text to be deleted.

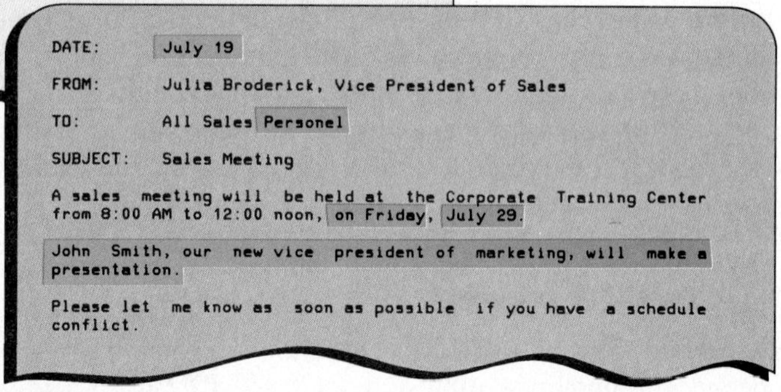

```
DATE:      July 19
FROM:      Julia Broderick, Vice President of Sales
TO:        All Sales Personel
SUBJECT:   Sales Meeting

A sales  meeting will  be held at  the Corporate  Training Center
from 8:00 AM to 12:00 noon, on Friday, July 29.

John  Smith, our  new vice  president of  marketing, will  make a
presentation.

Please let  me know as  soon as possible  if you have  a schedule
conflict.
```

= Inserted information

FIGURE 2-6
The shading on the computer screen shows the new text inserted into last month's memo.

The Move command allows you to either cut (remove) or copy a sentence, paragraph, or block of text. In our example, Julia decides she wants to **move** the existing third paragraph in front of the existing second paragraph (Figure 2-7). First, she highlights, or marks, the text to be moved. Next, she indicates that she wants to *cut* and not *copy* the marked text. With a **cut**, you are removing text from an area. With a **copy**, the word processor makes a copy of the marked text but leaves the marked text where it was. After you perform either the cut or the copy, the word processor needs to know where you want to place, or **paste**, the text. This is usually done by moving the cursor to the point where you want the moved text to begin. You then give a command to execute the move and the text is inserted. Figure 2-8 shows the cut text *pasted* into a position that now makes it the second paragraph. This capability to easily move text from one location to another is often referred to as *cut and paste*.

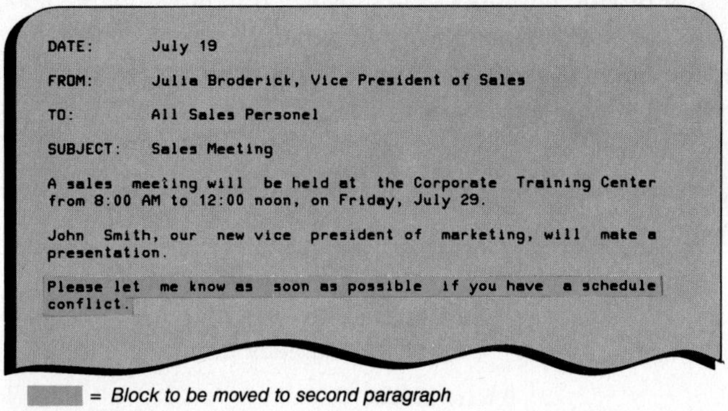

DATE: July 19
FROM: Julia Broderick, Vice President of Sales
TO: All Sales Personel
SUBJECT: Sales Meeting

A sales meeting will be held at the Corporate Training Center from 8:00 AM to 12:00 noon, on Friday, July 29.

John Smith, our new vice president of marketing, will make a presentation.

Please let me know as soon as possible if you have a schedule conflict.

= *Block to be moved to second paragraph*

FIGURE 2-7
The shading shows the text to be moved from the third to the second paragraph.

DATE: July 19
FROM: Julia Broderick, Vice President of Sales
TO: All Sales Personel
SUBJECT: Sales Meeting

A sales meeting will be held at the Corporate Training Center from 8:00 AM to 12:00 noon, on Friday, July 29.

Please let me know as soon as possible if you have a schedule conflict.

John Smith, our new vice president of marketing, will make a presentation.

= *Block that was moved*

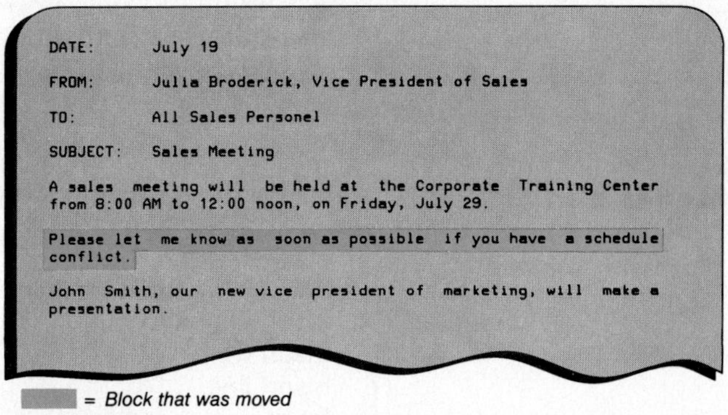

FIGURE 2-8
Memo after the third paragraph was moved to the second paragraph.

After the text changes are made, Julia runs a spelling checker. The spelling checker matches each word in the document against its spelling dictionary and discovers an unrecognized word: personel. Figure 2-9 shows how a spelling checker might present two alternatives for the correct spelling of the word. Julia merely has to enter the letter B and the word processor changes personel to personnel (Figure 2-10).

Before printing the memo, Julia reviews its format. She decides that the length of the lines in the document are too wide and she increases the margins. Figure 2-11 shows the document with the wider, 1 1/2-inch margins.

Now that the text and format are correct, Julia saves the document before printing it in case a system or power failure occurs during printing. Once she saves it, she can print the document as often as necessary. With the document saved, it is readily available to be retrieved by the word processor at any time.

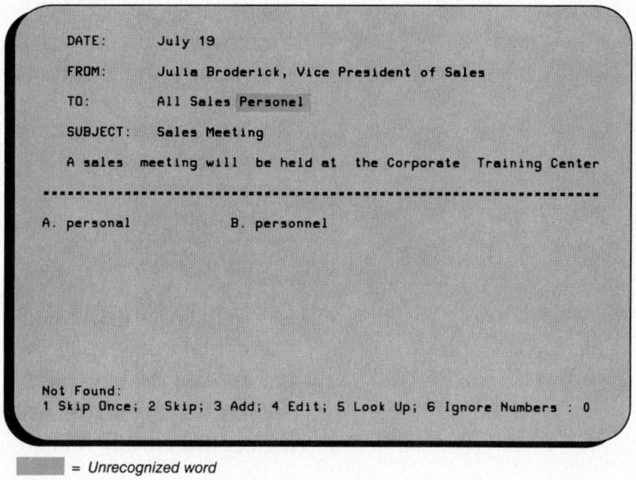

FIGURE 2-9
Spelling checker highlighting unrecognized word and showing two possible spellings.

DATE: July 19
FROM: Julia Broderick, Vice President of Sales
TO: All Sales Personel
SUBJECT: Sales Meeting

A sales meeting will be held at the Corporate Training Center

A. personal B. personnel

Not Found:
1 Skip Once; 2 Skip; 3 Add; 4 Edit; 5 Look Up; 6 Ignore Numbers : 0

= *Unrecognized word*

FIGURE 2-10
Correct spelling of personnel inserted into text by spelling checker.

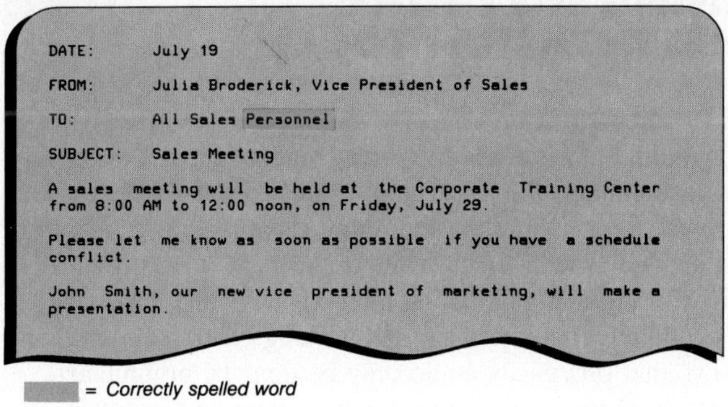

DATE: July 19
FROM: Julia Broderick, Vice President of Sales
TO: All Sales Personnel
SUBJECT: Sales Meeting

A sales meeting will be held at the Corporate Training Center from 8:00 AM to 12:00 noon, on Friday, July 29.

Please let me know as soon as possible if you have a schedule conflict.

John Smith, our new vice president of marketing, will make a presentation.

= *Correctly spelled word*

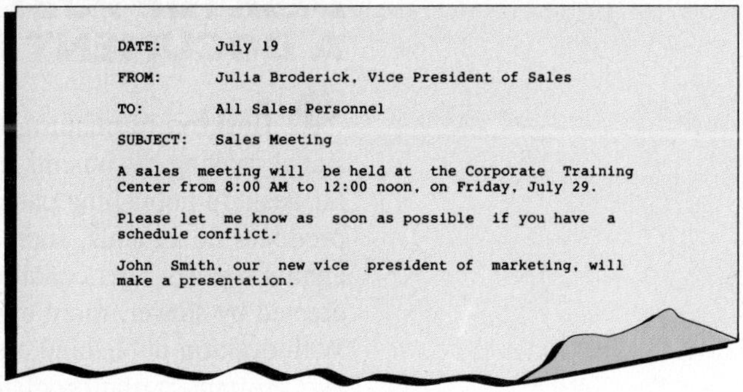

DATE: July 19
FROM: Julia Broderick, Vice President of Sales
TO: All Sales Personnel
SUBJECT: Sales Meeting

A sales meeting will be held at the Corporate Training Center from 8:00 AM to 12:00 noon, on Friday, July 29.

Please let me know as soon as possible if you have a schedule conflict.

John Smith, our new vice president of marketing, will make a presentation.

FIGURE 2-11
Memo after margins are changed.

Word processing software is a productivity tool that allows you to create, edit, format, print, and store documents. Each of the many word processing packages available may have slightly different capabilities, but most have the features summarized in Figure 2-12.

FIGURE 2-12
Common features of word processing software.

WORD PROCESSING FEATURES	
INSERTION AND MOVING Insert character Insert word Insert line Move sentences Move paragraphs Move blocks Merge text **DELETE FEATURES** Delete character Delete word Delete sentence Delete paragraph Delete entire text **SCREEN CONTROL** Scroll up and down by line Scroll by page Word wrap Uppercase and lowercase display Underline display Screen display according to defined format Bold display Superscript display Subscript display	**SEARCH AND REPLACE** Search and replace word Search and replace character strings **PRINTING** Set top and bottom margins Set left and right margins Set tab stops Print columns Single, double, triple space control Variable space control within text Right, left, full justification Center lines Subscripts Superscripts Underline Boldface Condense print Enlarge print Special type fonts Proportional spacing Headers Footers Page numbering Print any page from file

While our discussion of word processing has focused on the creation of documents that contain only text, you should know that some word processing packages now incorporate desktop publishing features that allow graphics to be included with the text. As you will see in the next discussion, the areas of word processing and desktop publishing are closely related.

DESKTOP PUBLISHING SOFTWARE: A DOCUMENT PRESENTATION TOOL

◆ **Desktop publishing (DTP) software** allows users to design and produce professional looking documents that contain both text and graphics (Figure 2-13). Two popular desktop publishing packages are Ventura Publisher and PageMaker. This software produces documents, such as newsletters, marketing literature, technical manuals, and annual reports, that contain art as well as text. Documents of this type were previously created by slower, more expensive traditional publishing methods such as typesetting. With desktop publishing, users can now create professional looking documents on their own computers and produce work that previously could only be done by graphic artists. By using desktop publishing, both the cost and time of producing quality documents is significantly decreased.

As we previously mentioned, some word processing packages now have desktop publishing capabilities. Packages such as WordPerfect and Microsoft Word contain enough features to satisfy the needs of many users. However, most desktop publishing packages still exceed the capabilities of word processing software. On the other hand, the word processing features of many desktop publishing packages are not as complete as those offered by word processing packages. Therefore, text is usually created with a word processor and then transferred into the desktop publishing package.

The graphic art used in the documents created with desktop publishing usually comes from one of three sources:

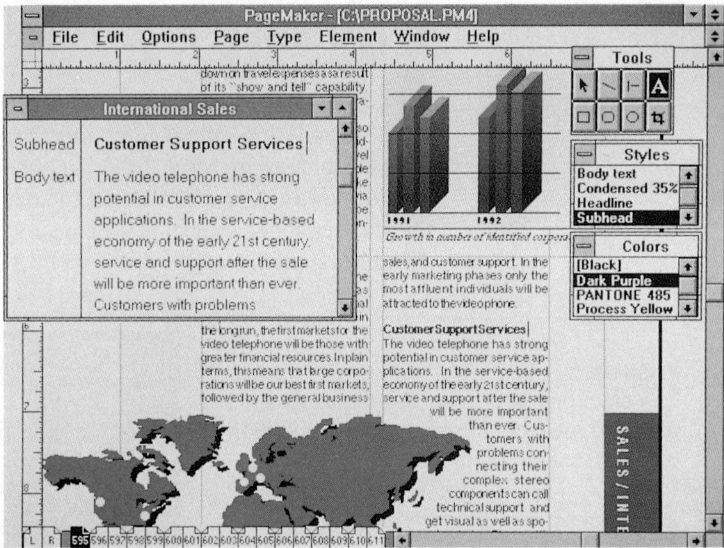

FIGURE 2-13
High-quality printed documents can be produced with desktop publishing software.

1. Art can be selected from clip art collections. **Clip art** refers to collections of art that are stored on disks and are designed for use with popular desktop publishing packages (Figure 2-14).
2. Art can be created on the computer with software packages that are specifically designed to create graphics, or through software such as spreadsheet packages that can create pie, line, and bar charts.
3. An input device called a scanner can be connected to the computer and used to electronically capture copies of pictures, photographs, and drawings and store them on a disk for use with desktop publishing software.

FIGURE 2-14
Clip art consists of previously created figures, shapes, and symbols that can be added to documents.

An important feature of desktop publishing is page composition. This means that a user is able to design on the screen an exact image of what a printed page will look like. This capability is called WYSIWYG. **WYSIWYG** is an acronym for What You See Is What You Get. Some of the page composition or layout features that are available include the use of columns for text, the choice of different type sizes and font (type) styles, and the capability to place, edit, enlarge, and reduce the size of charts, pictures, and illustrations in the document. Also, numerous special effects such as borders and backgrounds can be used to enhance the appearance of a document.

As new versions of word processing and desktop publishing software are introduced, the capabilities of both applications will increase and the differences between the two applications will decrease.

ELECTRONIC SPREADSHEET SOFTWARE: A NUMBER PRODUCTIVITY TOOL

Electronic spreadsheet software allows you to organize numeric data in a worksheet or table format called an **electronic spreadsheet** or **spreadsheet**. Manual methods, those done by hand, have long been used to organize numeric data in this manner (Figure 2-15). You will see that the data in an electronic spreadsheet is organized in the same manner as it is in a manual spreadsheet. Within a spreadsheet, data is organized horizontally in **rows** and vertically in **columns**.

FIGURE 2-15
The electronic spreadsheet on the right still uses the row-and-column format of the manual spreadsheet on the left.

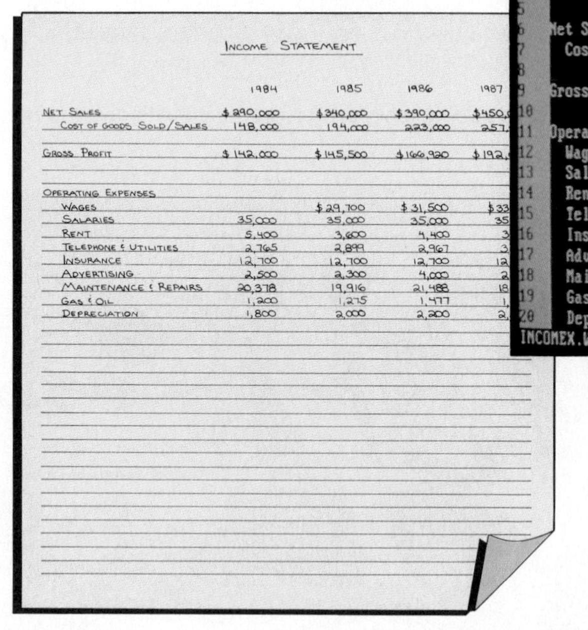

B12: (C0) U +<<SALARIES.WK1>>1984_WAGES READY

INCOME STATEMENT

	A	B	C	D	E
4		1984	1985	1986	1987
6	Net Sales	$290,000	$340,000	$390,000	$450,000
7	Cost of Goods Sold / Sales	148,000	194,500	223,080	257,400
9	Gross Profit	$142,000	$145,500	$166,920	$192,600
11	Operating Expenses				
12	Wages	[illegible]	$29,700	$31,500	$33,400
13	Salaries	35,000	35,000	35,000	35,000
14	Rent	5,400	3,600	4,400	3,800
15	Telephone & Utilities	2,765	2,899	2,967	3,098
16	Insurance	12,700	12,700	12,700	12,700
17	Advertising	2,500	2,300	4,000	2,200
18	Maintenance & Repairs	20,378	19,916	21,488	18,555
19	Gas & Oil	1,200	1,275	1,477	1,659
20	Depreciation	1,800	2,000	2,200	2,400

INCOMEX.WK1 UNDO

The intersection where a row and column meet is called a **cell** (Figure 2-16). Cells are named by their location in the spreadsheet. In Figure 2-16, the cursor is on cell C2, the intersection of column C and row 2.

Cells may contain three types of data: labels (text), values (numbers), and formulas. The text, or **labels**, as they are called, identify the data and document the worksheet. Good spreadsheets contain descriptive titles. The rest of the cells in a spreadsheet may appear to contain numbers, or **values**. However, some of the cells actually contain formulas. The **formulas** perform calculations on the data in the spreadsheet and display the resulting value in the cell containing the formula.

FIGURE 2-16
In a spreadsheet, rows refer to the horizontal lines of data and columns refer to the vertical lines of data. Rows are identified by numbers and columns are identified by letters. The intersection of a row and column is called a cell. The highlighted cell is the cursor. You can move the cursor by pressing the arrow keys on the keyboard.

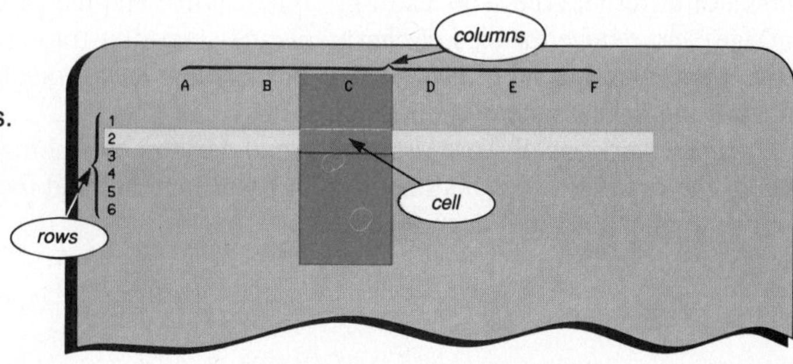

To illustrate this powerful tool, we will show you how to develop the spreadsheet that we used as an example in Chapter 1. Recall that the completed spreadsheet contains revenues, costs, profit, and profit percentage for three months and the totals for the three months. By looking at Figure 2-17, you can see that the first step in creating the spreadsheet is to enter the labels or titles. These should be short but descriptive, to help you organize the layout of the data in your spreadsheet.

The next step is to enter the data or numbers in the body of the spreadsheet (Figure 2-18). The final step is to enter the formulas that calculate the totals. (Some users enter the formulas before they enter the data.)

In a manual spreadsheet, you would have to calculate each of the totals by hand or with your calculator. In an electronic spreadsheet, you simply enter a formula into the cell where the total is to appear. The total is calculated and displayed automatically (Figure 2-19).

Once a formula is entered into a cell, it can be copied to any other cell that requires a similar formula. As the formula is copied, the formula calculations are performed automatically (Figure 2-20). After entering the remaining formulas, the spreadsheet is complete (shown on the next page in Figure 2-21). You can now give the commands to print the spreadsheet and to store it on a disk.

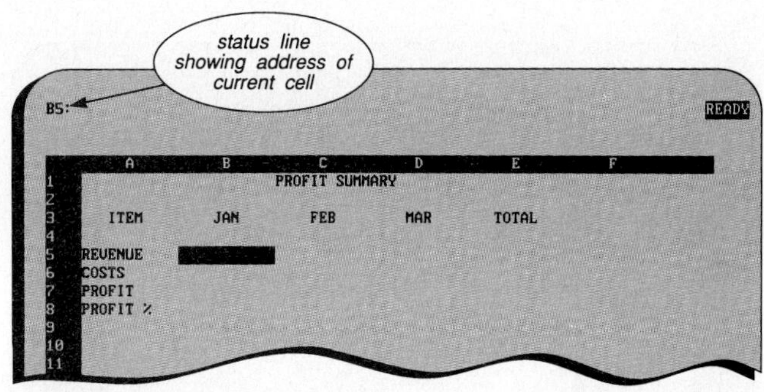

FIGURE 2-17
Labels such as JAN, FEB, REVENUE, and COSTS are entered in the spreadsheet to identify columns and rows of data. The status line shows the address and contents of the current cell. The address of a cell is the intersection of the column letter and row number. Here, the current cell is B5 (column B, row 5). Nothing has been entered for this cell, so the status line shows only the cell address.

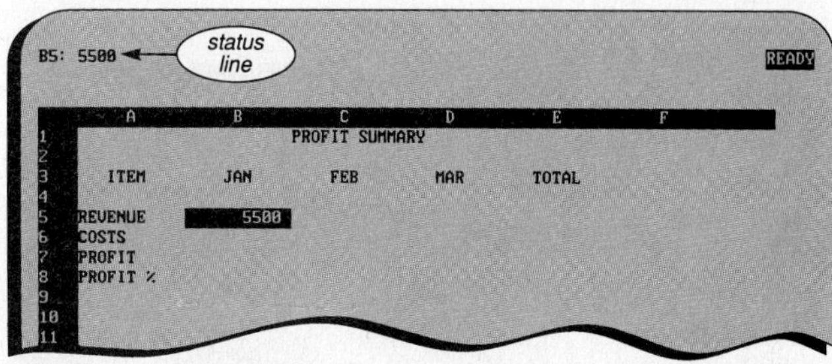

FIGURE 2-18
The value 5500 is entered and stored in cell B5. The status line now displays both the cell address and the cell value.

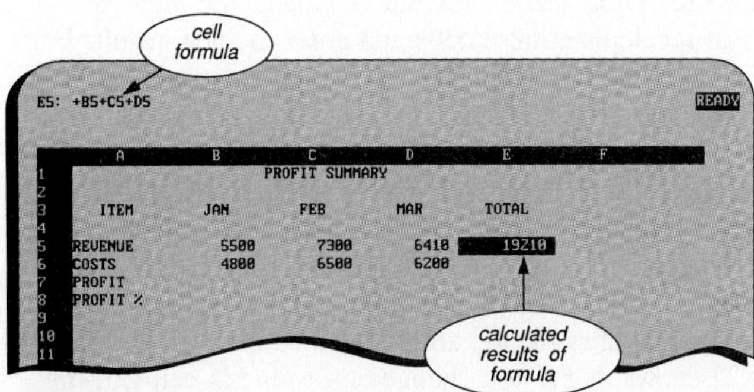

FIGURE 2-19
The remaining values are entered in cells C5, D5, B6, C6, and D6. A formula is entered in cell E5. The formula specifies that cell E5 is to be the sum of the values in cells B5, C5, and D5. Cell E5 displays the numeric sum. The status line at the top of the screen, however, shows the formula that calculates the value in that cell.

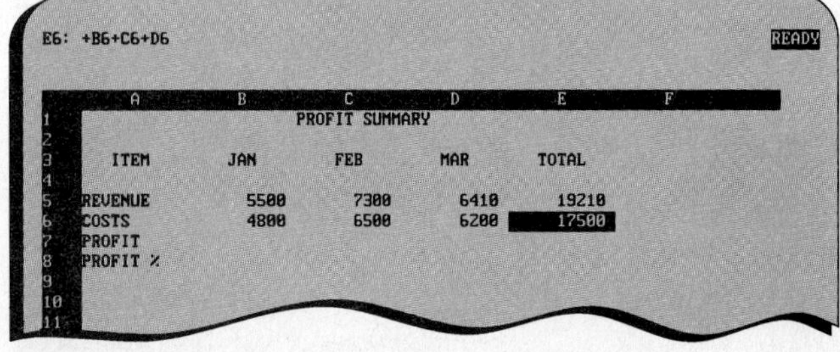

FIGURE 2-20
The formula required for cell E6 is similar to the one for cell E5; it totals the amounts in the three previous columns. When we copy the formula from E5 into E6, the software automatically changes the cell references from B5, C5, and D5 to B6, C6, and D6.

E8: (P1) +E7/E5 READY

	A	B	C	D	E	F
1			PROFIT SUMMARY			
2						
3	ITEM	JAN	FEB	MAR	TOTAL	
4						
5	REVENUE	5500	7300	6410	19210	
6	COSTS	4800	6500	6200	17500	
7	PROFIT	700	800	210	1710	
8	PROFIT %	12.7%	11.0%	3.3%	8.9%	
9						
10						
11						
12						
13						
14						
15						

FIGURE 2-21
This screen shows the completed spreadsheet. The value in cell E8 is derived from the formula on the status line, which specifies that the value in cell E7 is to be divided by the value in cell E5 (the slash character indicates division). Since the value in E7 is the total profit and the value in E5 is the total revenue, the result of the division operation is the profit percentage.

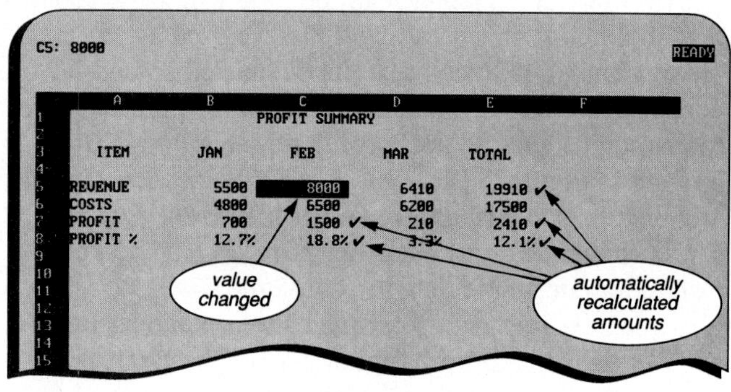

FIGURE 2-22
This screen shows the capability of a spreadsheet to recalculate totals when data is changed. This capability gives the user the ability to quickly see the total impact of changing one or more numbers in a spreadsheet. Using the spreadsheet shown in FIGURE 2-21, one number was changed; the REVENUE amount for February. This one change results in five numbers automatically recalculating in the spreadsheet (the recalculated numbers are shown with a check mark). In a manual spreadsheet, each of these five numbers would have to be recalculated separately.

FIGURE 2-23
The what-if testing capability of electronic spreadsheets is a powerful feature used to aid managers in making decisions.

One of the most powerful features of the electronic spreadsheet occurs when the data in a spreadsheet changes. To appreciate the capabilities of spreadsheet software, let's discuss how a change is handled in a manual system. When a value in a manual spreadsheet changes, you must erase it and write a new value into the cell. You must also erase all cells that contain calculations referring to the value that changed and then you must recalculate these cells and enter the new result. For example, the row totals and column totals would be updated to reflect changes to any values within their areas. In large manual spreadsheets, accurately posting changes and updating the values affected can be time consuming and new errors can be introduced. But posting changes on an electronic spreadsheet is easy. You change data in a cell by simply typing in the new value. All other values that are affected are updated automatically. Figure 2-22 shows that if you changed the value in cell C5, the column and row totals that use the value in C5 will automatically change. All other values and totals in the spreadsheet remain unchanged. On a computer, the updating happens very quickly. As row and column totals are recalculated, the changes are said to *ripple* through the spreadsheet.

An electronic spreadsheet's capability to recalculate when data is changed makes it a valuable tool for decision making. This capability allows people to perform what-if testing by changing the numbers in a spreadsheet (Figure 2-23). The resulting values that are calculated by the spreadsheet software provide valuable decision support information based on the alternatives tested.

An electronic spreadsheet is a productivity tool that organizes and performs calculations on numeric data. Spreadsheets are one of the most popular software applications. They have been adapted to a wide range of business and nonbusiness applications. Some of the popular packages used today are Lotus 1-2-3, Excel, and Quattro. Most spreadsheet software has the features shown in Figure 2-24.

SPREADSHEET FEATURES	
WORKSHEET Global format Insert column Insert row Delete column Delete row Set up titles Set up windows **RANGE** Format range of data Erase cells **COPY** Copy from cells Copy to cells	**MOVE** Move from cells Move to cells **FILE** Save Retrieve Erase List **PRINT** Set up margins Define header Define footer Specify range to print Define page length Condense print

FIGURE 2-24
Common features of spreadsheet software.

DATABASE SOFTWARE: A DATA MANAGEMENT TOOL

A **database** refers to a collection of data that is stored in files. **Database software** allows you to create a database and to retrieve, manipulate, and update the data that you store in it. In a manual system (Figure 2-25), data might be recorded on paper and stored in a filing cabinet. In a database on the computer, the data will be stored in an electronic format on an auxiliary storage device such as a disk.

FIGURE 2-25
An electronic database is similar to a manual system; related data items are stored in files.

When you use a database, you need to be familiar with the terms file, record, and field. Just as in a manual system, the word **file** is a collection of related data that is organized in records. Each **record** contains a collection of related facts called **fields**. For example, a file might consist of records containing information about a checking account. All the data that relates to one check would be considered a record. Each fact, such as the check number or amount, is called a field.

The screens in Figures 2-26 through 2-32 present the development of a database containing personal checking account information using the popular database program dBASE III PLUS. To begin creating the database, you would select the Create menu by moving the cursor until Create was highlighted, as shown in Figure 2-26.

FIGURE 2-26
A menu used to create a file in the popular database program dBASE III PLUS.

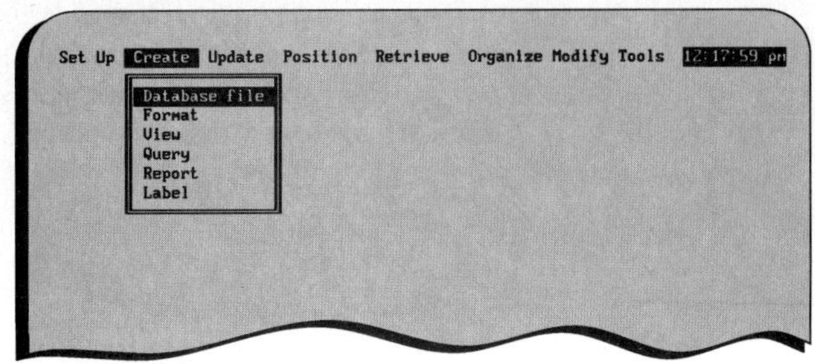

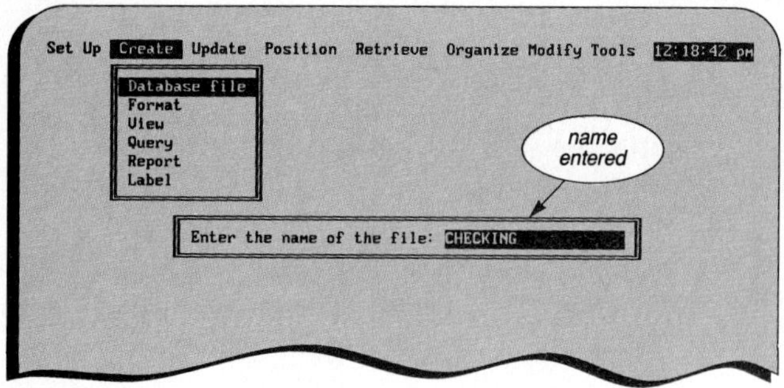

FIGURE 2-27
Screen used to enter the name of the file.

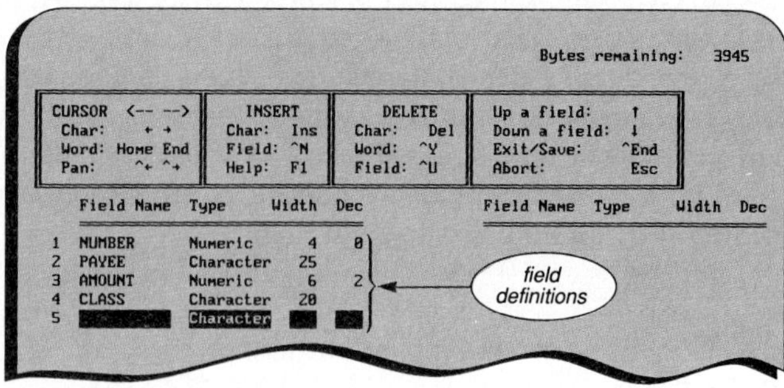

FIGURE 2-28
CREATE FILE screen showing definition of fields for records in the CHECKING file.

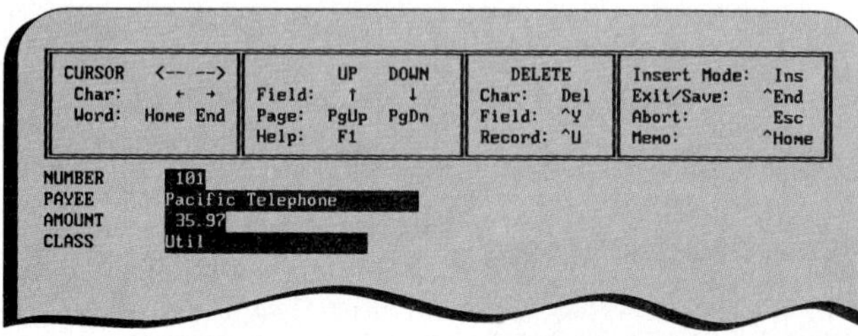

FIGURE 2-29
Data entry screen with the word Utility partially entered.

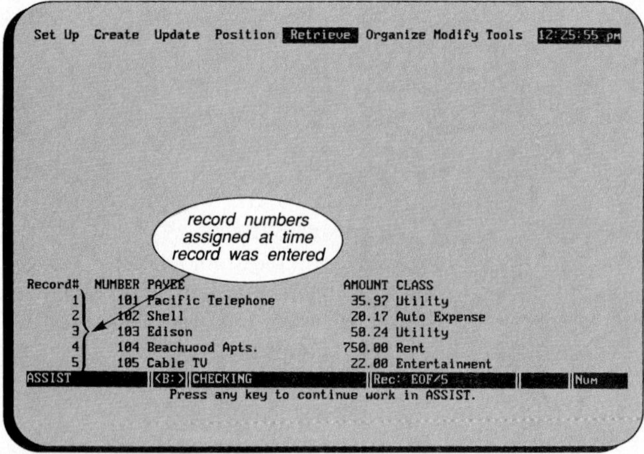

FIGURE 2-30
Display of all records sorted by record number.

Using the pull-down menu displayed under Create, you would select the "Database file" option. After identifying the disk drive to use, the screen would look like Figure 2-27. A prompt asks you to enter a file name, the name under which the file being created will be stored on disk. In this example, you would enter the name "CHECKING".

You are then asked to enter descriptions for each field (Figure 2-28). A field description consists of a field name, the type of data to be stored in the field (C for character, N for numeric data), and the number of characters in the field. In a numeric field, if you want to put digits to the right of the decimal point, you must specify the number of digits to the right. Thus, for the amount field, the designation 6.2 means that the field is six characters wide with two digits to the right of the decimal point. Because the decimal point takes one of the positions, the largest number that can be displayed in this field is 999.99.

Once you have defined the fields in the records, you enter data into the records (Figure 2-29). The software prompts you to enter data for each record. As you type the data into each field it is stored. Thus, after the field name NUMBER, you enter the check number. You complete each field in the same manner, and continue to enter data until all data is entered for the checking account file.

After the file has data stored in it, you can use the file to produce information. For example, suppose you want to display the checks in order by check number. You can use the "Organize" and "Retrieve" options on the menu to enter commands that sort all records by NUMBER and display the sorted list on the screen. Figure 2-30 shows a display of the sorted list. Suppose you also want to display your utility expenses.

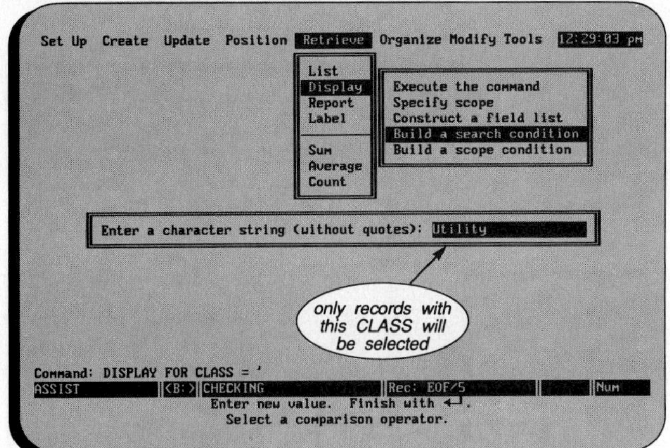

FIGURE 2-31
The software is directed to display only records with a CLASS equal to Utility.

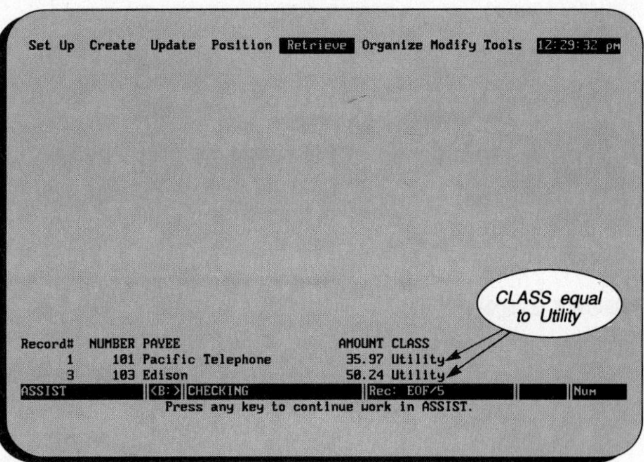

FIGURE 2-32
Display of only the Utility CLASS records.

In Figure 2-31, you direct the system to display only those records where the class is equal to Utility. As a result, only those records for which the classification is Utility are retrieved and displayed (Figure 2-32).

As shown in our checkbook example, database software assists users in creating files and storing, manipulating, and retrieving data. Popular software packages that perform these functions include dBASE III PLUS, dBASE IV, R:Base, and Paradox. Figure 2-33 lists some of the common features of these packages.

Recall that when you use a microcomputer database software application, you do not need to have any special technical knowledge. Database software is a general application tool that is designed to help you easily and efficiently manage data electronically.

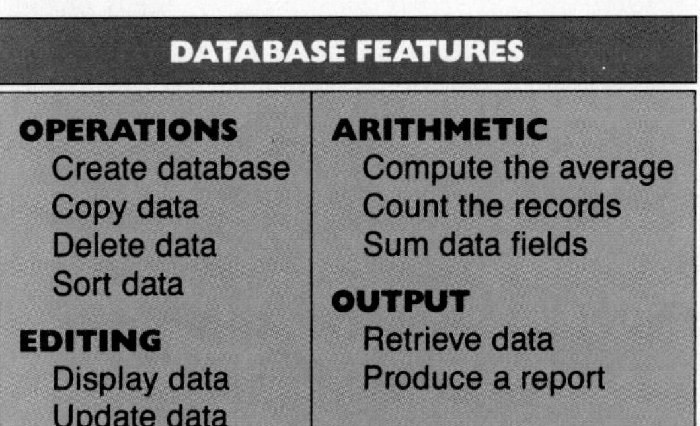

FIGURE 2-33
Common features of database software.

GRAPHICS SOFTWARE: A DATA PRESENTATION TOOL

Information presented in the form of a graph or a chart is commonly referred to as **graphics**. Studies have shown that information presented as graphics can be understood much faster than information presented in writing. Three common forms of graphics are **pie charts**, **bar charts**, and **line charts** (on the next page in Figure 2-34).

Today, many software packages can create graphics, including most spreadsheet packages. The graphics capabilities of these packages can be grouped into two categories: analytical graphics and presentation graphics.

FIGURE 2-34

Bar charts display blocks, or bars, to show relationships among data clearly.

Pie charts, so called because they look like pies cut into pieces, are particularly effective for showing the relationship of parts to a whole.

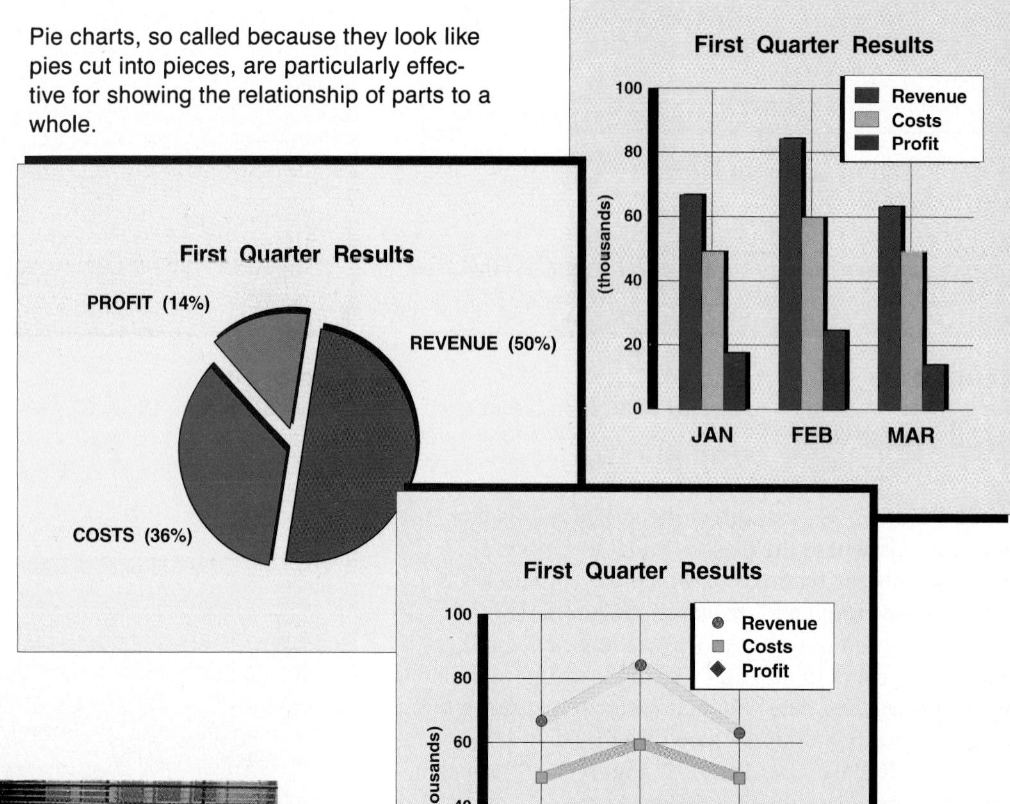

Line charts are effective for showing a trend as indicated by a rising or falling line.

FIGURE 2-35
Color can enhance the presentation of graphic information.

Analytical graphics is widely used by management personnel when they analyze information and when they communicate information to others within their organization (Figure 2-35). For example, a production manager who is planning a meeting with the president of the company may use color graphics to show him the expenses of the production department. This graphic display would have more impact and lead to better understanding than would a printed column of numbers.

To create analytical graphics on your computer, you must follow the directions that apply to your graphics software package. Most packages will prompt you to enter the data the graph will represent, and then ask you to select the type of graph you would like. After entering the data, you can select several different graphic forms to see which one will best convey your message. When you decide on a graph, you can print it and also store it for future reference.

As its name implies, **presentation graphics** goes beyond analytical graphics by offering the user a wide choice of presentation effects. These include three-dimensional displays, background patterns, multiple text fonts, and image libraries that contain illustrations of factories, people, coins, dollar signs, and other symbols that can be incorporated into the graphic (Figure 2-36). Figure 2-37 shows an example of presentation graphics projected.

Using graphics software as a presentation tool allows you to efficiently create professional quality graphics that can help you communicate information more effectively. Persuasion and Harvard Graphics are two popular presentation graphics packages.

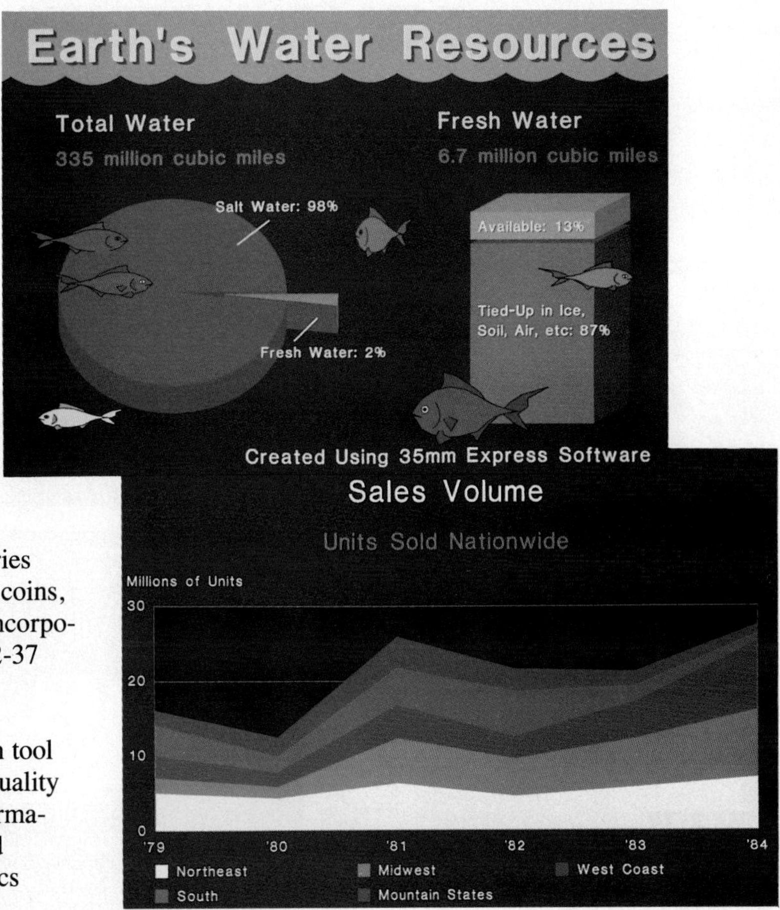

FIGURE 2-36
Examples of presentation graphics.

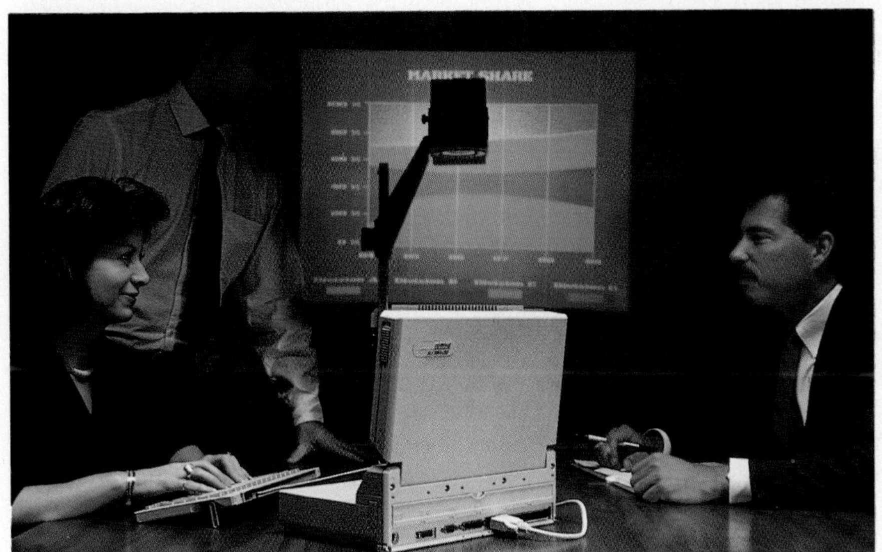

FIGURE 2-37
Presentation graphics can be an effective way to communicate information to a large group. Presenters can use devices such as the computer projection device shown. When this device is connected to a microcomputer, it can project everything on the microcomputer screen onto a large screen.

DATA COMMUNICATIONS SOFTWARE: A CONNECTIVITY TOOL

Data communications software is used to transmit data from one computer to another. It gives users access to databases such as stock prices and airline schedules, and services such as home banking and shopping (Figure 2-38).

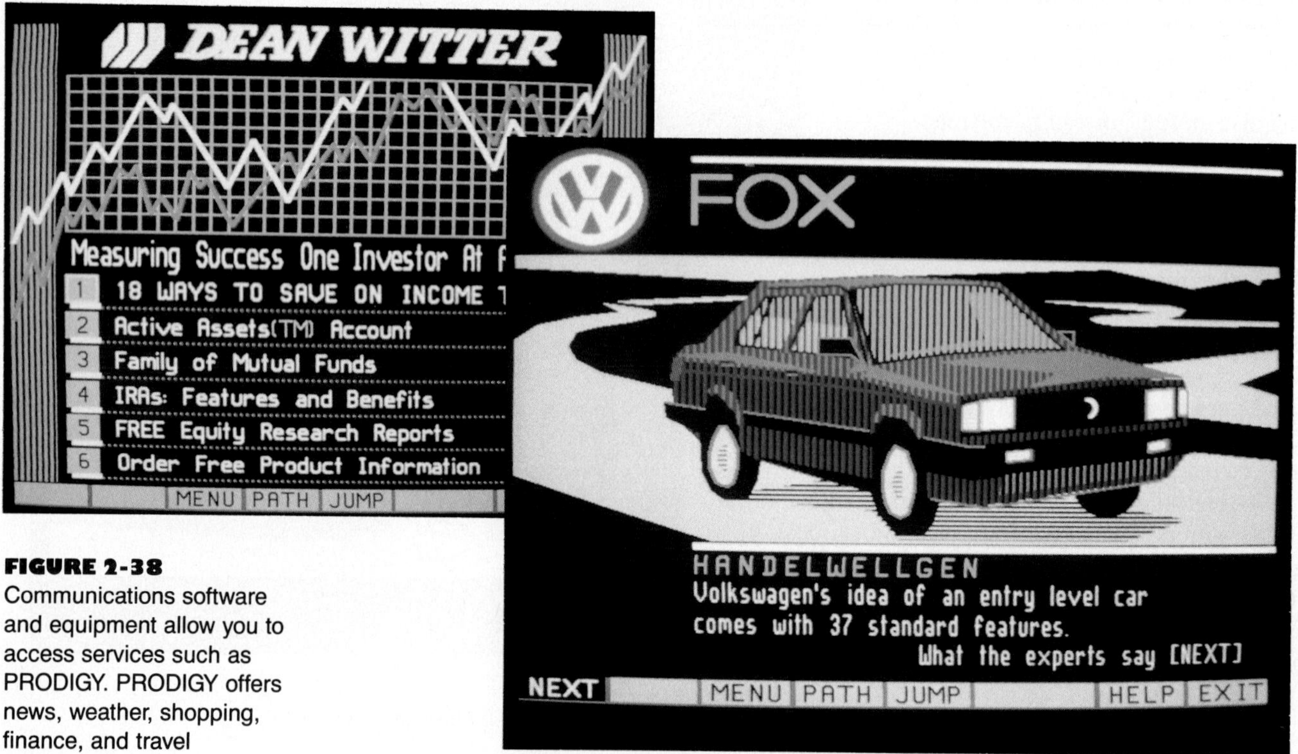

FIGURE 2-38
Communications software and equipment allow you to access services such as PRODIGY. PRODIGY offers news, weather, shopping, finance, and travel information.

For two computers to communicate, they each must have data communications software, data communications equipment, and be connected to a telephone line. To establish a communications link, you would use the data communications software to dial the phone number of the computer you want to call. Once the connection is established, you would enter commands and answer responses to control the transmission of data between the computers. Popular communication software packages include CROSSTALK Communicator and PROCOMM PLUS.

INTEGRATED SOFTWARE: A COMBINATION PRODUCTIVITY TOOL

Software packages such as databases and electronic spreadsheets are generally used independently of each other. But what if you wanted to place information from a database into a spreadsheet? The data in the database would have to be reentered in the spreadsheet. This would be time consuming and errors could be introduced as you reentered the data. The inability of separate programs to communicate with one another and use a common set of data has been overcome through the use of integrated software.

Integrated software refers to packages that combine applications such as word processing, electronic spreadsheet, database, graphics, and data communications into a single, easy-to-use set of programs. The applications that are included in integrated packages are designed to have a consistent command structure; that is, the user can use the same set of common commands such as SAVE or LOAD in all the applications in the package. Besides these consistent commands, a key feature of integrated packages is their capability to pass data quickly and easily from one application to another. For example, revenue and cost information from a database on daily sales could be quickly loaded into a spreadsheet. The spreadsheet could be used to calculate gross profits. Once the calculations are completed, all or a portion of the spreadsheet data can be passed to the graphics program to create pie, bar, line, or other graphs. Finally, the graphic (or the spreadsheet) can be transferred to word processing to create a printed report. A possible disadvantage of an integrated package is that individual integrated programs may not have all the features that are available in nonintegrated packages. Two popular integrated software packages are Microsoft Works and Lotus Works.

Integrated programs frequently use windows. A **window** is a rectangular portion of the screen that is used to display information. They are called *windows* because of their capability to *see* into another part of a program. Many people consider windows to be like multiple sheets of paper on top of a desk. In the same way that each piece of paper on the desk contains different information, each window on the screen contains different information. And just as papers can be moved from the bottom of a pile to the top of the desk when they are needed, windows can be created on a screen and used to show information when it is needed. Windows are used to display a variety of information including: help information about the commands of the program you are using; text from different documents in a word processor and; different parts of a large spreadsheet. With some integrated packages, windows can be used to display data from separate applications such as a spreadsheet and a word processing document. Many programs today use windows and can display multiple windows on the screen at the same time (Figure 2-39). These programs allow you to easily move between applications by moving from one window to another.

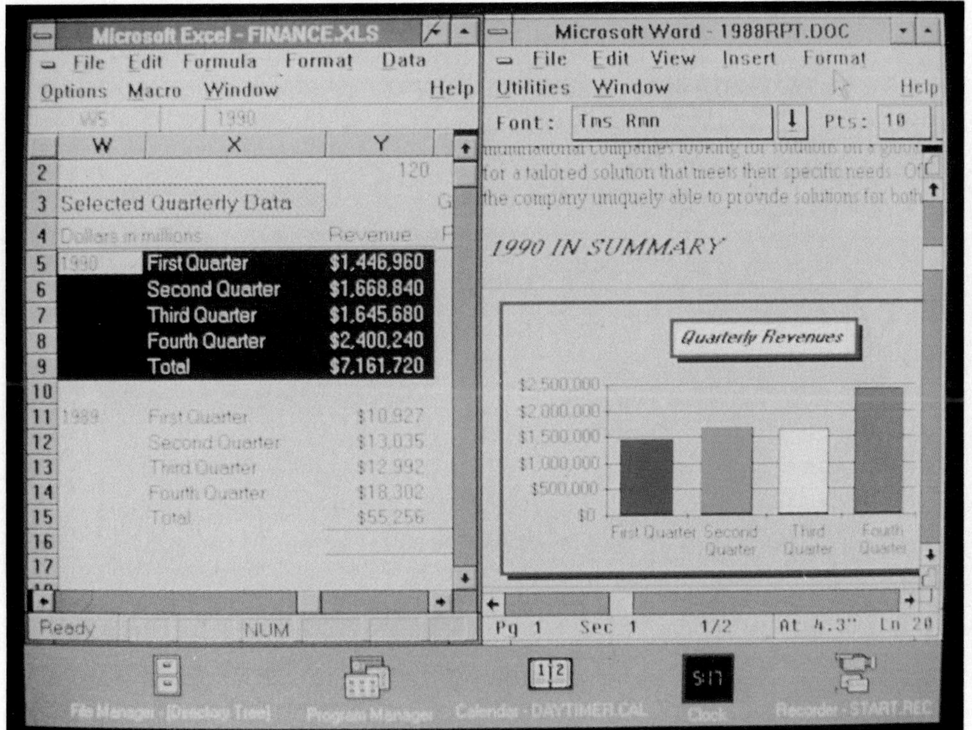

FIGURE 2-39
This screen shows two windows. The window on the left shows a spreadsheet, whereas the window on the right displays a word processing document. The user can work on information displayed in either application.

OTHER POPULAR MICROCOMPUTER APPLICATIONS

The applications we have discussed so far are the most widely used microcomputer applications. Three other application areas that are becoming increasingly popular are software for personal information management, project management, and utilities.

Personal Information Management

Personal information management (PIM) software helps users keep track of the miscellaneous bits of personal information that each of us deals with every day. This information can take many forms: notes to ourselves or from others, phone messages, notes about a current or future project, appointments, and so on. Programs that keep track of this type of information, such as electronic calendars, have been around for some time. In recent years, however, such programs have been combined, or integrated, so that one package can keep track of all of a user's personal information.

Because of the many types of information that these programs can manage, it is difficult to precisely define personal information software. However, the category can be applied to programs that offer any of the following capabilities: appointment calendars, outliners, electronic notepads, data managers, and text retrieval. Some personal information software packages also include communications software capabilities such as phone dialers and electronic mail. Appointment calendars allow you to schedule activities for a particular day and time (Figure 2-40). Most of them will warn you if two activities are scheduled for the same time. Outliners allow you to *rough out* an idea by constructing and reorganizing an outline of important points and subpoints. Electronic notepads allow the user to record comments and assign them to one or more categories that can be used to retrieve the comments. Data managers are simple file management systems that allow the input, update, and retrieval of related records such as name and address lists or phone numbers. Text retrieval provides the capability to search files for specific words or phrases such as Sales Meeting. Two popular personal information management packages are Lotus Agenda and GrandView.

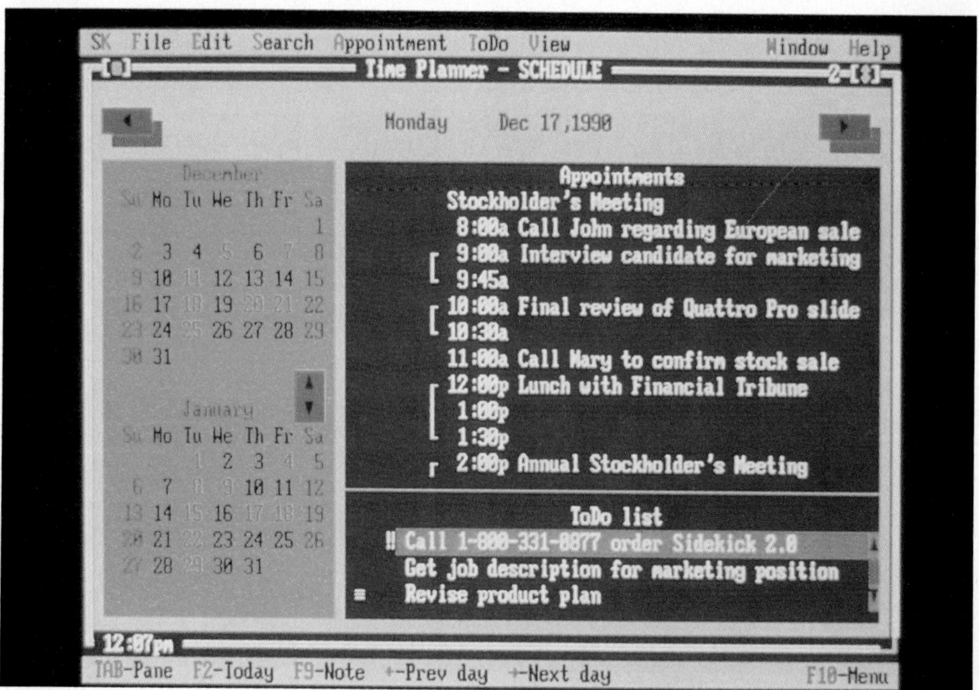

FIGURE 2-40
Personal information management software packages include calendars that help the user schedule and keep track of appointments.

Project Management

Project management software allows users to plan, schedule, track, and analyze the events, resources, and costs of a project (Figure 2-41). For example, a construction company might use this type of software to manage the building of an apartment complex or a campaign manager might use it to coordinate the many activities of a politician running for office. The value of project management software is that it provides a method for managers to control and manage the variables of a project to help ensure that the project will be completed on time and within budget. Popular project management packages include Timeline and Microsoft Project.

FIGURE 2-41
This output was prepared using project management software. It shows the individual tasks that make up the project and the elapsed time that each task is scheduled to take.

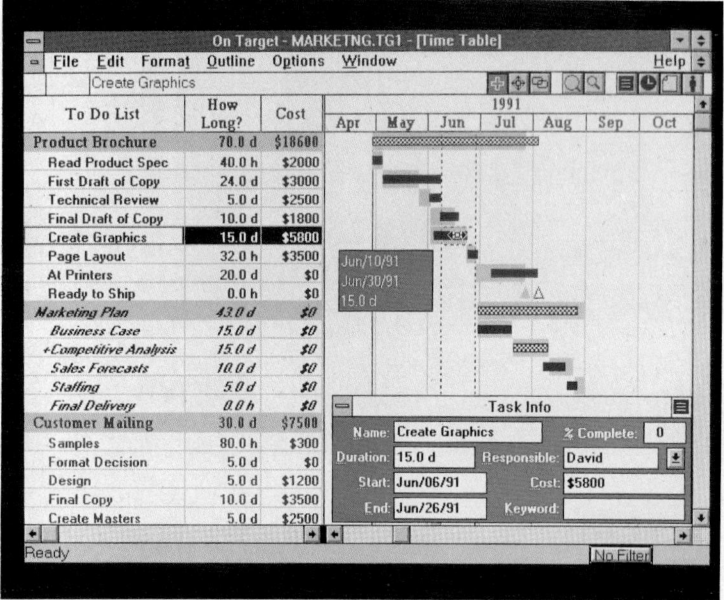

Utilities

As its name implies, **utility software** includes a variety of programs to help you manage and maintain the data on your computer system. One of the more valuable utility features is the ability to recover *deleted* files. This is made possible by the fact that when a file is deleted, the data is still on the disk. The process of deletion only modifies the disk directory to indicate that the area of the disk that contains the file information is now available for new data. The disk directory is a special file on a disk that is used to keep track of which files are stored on the disk and where each file is located. If the data has not been overwritten, the utility software can rebuild the disk directory to allow access to the previously deleted file. Another common utility software feature is a defragmenter. When a file is written to the disk it sometimes has to be stored in separate areas because no one area is large enough to hold it all. In such cases, the file is said to be *fragmented*. The **defragmenter** analyzes and reorganizes the disk so that related file information is stored in one continuous area. Other common utility software features include visual directory listings (Figure 2-42), file management capabilities, and disk defect analysis. Popular utility software packages include the Norton Utilities (Advanced Edition), PC Tools Deluxe, and Mace Utilities.

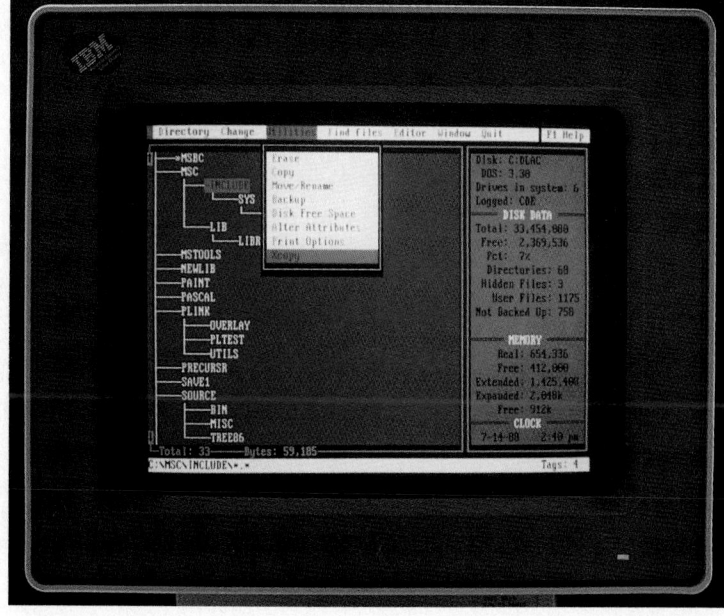

FIGURE 2-42
This visual directory listing, sometimes called a directory tree, makes it easier to see the relationship of the files that are on a disk.

GUIDELINES FOR PURCHASING MICROCOMPUTER APPLICATIONS SOFTWARE

To ensure that applications software will meet your needs, you should follow these six steps when you purchase the software (Figure 2-43).

FIGURE 2-43
Shop carefully for software, evaluating the available packages and suppliers. Many people spend more on software than they do on their computer equipment.

1. **Read software product reviews.** A good place to start shopping for microcomputer applications software is in computer magazines such as *PC Magazine* and *MACWORLD*. These magazines regularly review applications packages and publish articles and charts to help you choose the package best suited to your needs.
2. **Verify that the software performs the task you desire.** In some cases, software that is supposed to perform particular functions either does not perform the functions or performs them in a manner that will be unacceptable to you. The best method of verifying that the software performs satisfactorily is to try it out prior to purchase. Many computer stores and software vendors will allow you to try software to see if it meets your needs before you purchase it. Some software developers even have special demonstration versions that allow you to try package features on a limited-use basis.
3. **Verify that the software will run on your computer.** The best way to verify this is to run the software on a computer that is the same as yours. Such factors as the number of disk drives, whether the software can run on a computer without a hard disk, main memory requirements, and graphics capabilities or requirements must be evaluated before you buy. For example, it would be unwise to purchase a package that is incompatible with your printer or one with graphics capabilities that your computer cannot handle.
4. **Make sure that the software is adequately documented.** The written material that accompanies the software is known as documentation. Even the best software may be unusable if the documentation does not clearly and completely describe what the software does, how it does it, how to recover from processing errors, and how to back up data.
5. **Purchase software from a reputable software developer or software publisher.** Regardless of the care taken, software sometimes contains errors. A reputable software developer or publisher will correct those errors or replace your software.
6. **Obtain the best value, but keep in mind that value might not mean the lowest price.** Different stores or distributors will sell the same software package for different prices. Be sure to compare prices, but also ask about product support. Sometimes a store will offer training on products that you buy from them; other vendors, such as mail order houses, provide no support or training but offer discount prices. Also, some vendors offer telephone service so that you can call to ask questions about the software.

If you keep these factors in mind when buying application software packages, you are likely to be pleased with the software you buy.

LEARNING AIDS AND SUPPORT TOOLS FOR APPLICATION USERS

◆ Learning to use an application software package involves time and practice. In addition to taking a class to learn how to use a software application, several learning aids and support tools are available to help you including: tutorials, online help, trade books, and keyboard templates (Figure 2-44).

FIGURE 2-44
Four ways to learn application software packages are shown here.

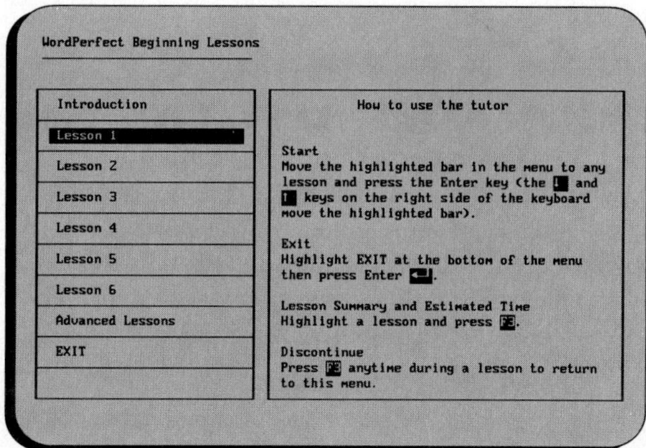

Software tutorials help you learn an application while using the actual software on your computer.

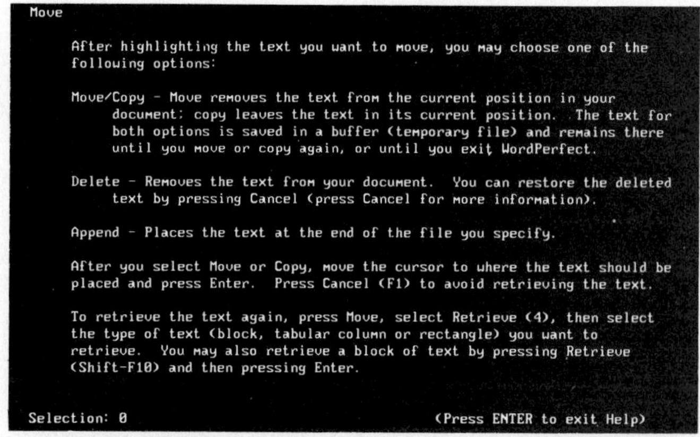

Online help gives you assistance without your having to leave the application.

Trade books are available for the popular software applications.

Keyboard templates give you quick reference to software commands.

Tutorials are step-by-step instructions using real examples that show you how to use an application. Some tutorials are written manuals, but more and more, tutorials are in the software form, allowing you to use your computer to learn about a package.

Online help refers to additional instructions that are available within the application. In most packages, a function key or special combination of keys are reserved for the help feature. When you are using an application and have a question, pressing the designated *help* key will temporarily overlay your work on the screen with information on how to use the package. When you are finished using the help feature, pressing another key allows you to return to your work.

The documentation that accompanies software packages is frequently organized as reference material. This makes it very useful once you know how to use a package, but difficult to use when you are first learning it. For this reason, many **trade books** are available to help users learn to use the features of microcomputer application packages. These books can usually be found where software is sold and are frequently carried in regular bookstores.

Keyboard templates are plastic sheets that fit around a portion of your keyboard. The keyboard commands to select the various features of the application programs are printed on the template. Having a guide to the commands readily available is helpful for both beginners and experienced users.

SUMMARY OF MICROCOMPUTER APPLICATIONS

By reading this chapter, you have learned about several of the commonly used microcomputer applications. You have also learned some guidelines for purchasing microcomputer software and seen some of the learning aids and support tools that are available for applications software. Knowledge about these topics increases your computer literacy and helps you to understand how microcomputers are being used.

CHAPTER SUMMARY

1. Understanding the software applications commonly used on microcomputers is considered a part of being computer literate.
2. Software that is useful to a broad range of users is sometimes referred to as **general microcomputer applications** software.
3. **User interfaces** are methods and techniques including **function keys**, screen **prompts**, **menus**, **icons**, and a device called a **mouse** that make using an application simpler.
4. A **graphic user interface (GUI)** makes extensive use of icons to graphically represent files and processing options.
5. The most widely used microcomputer software applications are word processing, desktop publishing, electronic spreadsheet, database, graphics, and data communications.
6. **Word processing software** is used to prepare documents electronically. With word processing software you **insert**, **delete**, and **move** text.
7. The MOVE command allows you to **cut**, **copy**, and **paste** text.
8. Additional support for a word processing application can include a spelling checker, thesaurus, and grammar checker.
9. **Spelling checker software** allows you to check individual words or an entire document for correct spelling.
10. **Thesaurus software** allows you to look up synonyms for words in a document while you are using your word processor.
11. **Grammar checker software** is usually purchased separately from a word processing package and is used to identify possible grammar, writing style, and sentence structure errors.
12. Word processing software is a document productivity tool that allows you to create, edit, format, print, and store documents.
13. **Desktop publishing software** allows you to design and produce professional looking documents that contain both text and graphics.
14. **WYSIWYG** is an acronym for What You See Is What You Get and describes the capability of a desktop publishing package to display on the screen an exact image of what the printed page will look like.
15. **Electronic spreadsheet software** allows you to organize numeric data in a worksheet or table format.
16. A **spreadsheet** is composed of **rows** and **columns**. Each intersection of a row and column is a **cell**.
17. A spreadsheet cell can contain one of the following: a **label**, a **value**, or a **formula**.

18. The what-if capability of electronic spreadsheet software is a powerful feature that is widely used by management personnel for decision support information.
19. A **database** refers to a collection of data that is stored in files. **Database software** allows you to create a database and to retrieve, manipulate, and update data that you store in it.
20. Just as in a manual system, the word **file** is a collection of related data that is organized in records. Each **record** contains a collection of related facts called **fields**.
21. Information presented in the form of a graph or a chart is commonly referred to as **graphics**. Three popular graphics used to present information include **pie charts**, **bar charts**, and **line charts**.
22. **Analytical graphics** is widely used by management personnel when analyzing information and when communicating information to others within their organization.
23. **Presentation graphics** allows you to create professional quality graphics that can be used to communicate information more effectively.
24. **Data communications software** allows you to transmit data from one computer to another.
25. **Integrated software** packages combine several applications in one package and allow data to be shared between the applications.
26. **Personal information management (PIM) software** packages include capabilities such as appointment calendars, outliners, electronic notepads, data managers, and text retrieval.
27. **Project management software** allows users to plan, schedule, track, and analyze the events, resources, and costs of a project.
28. **Utility software** includes a variety of programs to help you manage and maintain the data on your computer system.
29. When you purchase software, you should follow these six steps: (1) Read software product reviews. (2) Verify that the software performs the task desired. (3) Verify that the software runs on your computer. (4) Make sure the software documentation is adequate. (5) Purchase software from a reputable developer or publisher. (6) Obtain the best value.
30. Aids such as tutorials, online help, trade books, and keyboard templates are useful in learning and using microcomputer applications.

KEY TERMS

REVIEW QUESTIONS

1. What is a user interface? List five examples.
2. What is general microcomputer applications software?
3. List six of the most widely used microcomputer application packages and describe how each application helps users.
4. What is a grammar checker? Give three examples of how a grammar checker works.
5. Describe three sources for art that is used in desktop publishing.
6. What are the three types of data that can be entered into a spreadsheet cell? Explain the purpose of each type of data.
7. Write a definition of the terms database and database software.
8. List the three most commonly used computer graphics. Draw an example of each.
9. Describe the advantage of using integrated software. What is a possible disadvantage? What are windows and how are they used in integrated software packages?
10. Describe how you would make a communications link between your microcomputer and another computer.
11. What is project management software and how is it used?
12. Explain why data files that have been deleted can sometimes be recovered by using a utility software application.
13. List the six steps that should be performed when purchasing software.
14. List and describe four learning aids that can help you use general microcomputer application packages.

CONTROVERSIAL ISSUES

1. As the owner of a small business you are trying to decide whether to purchase a word processor, a desktop publishing software package, or both. Some people have advised you that a word processor is all you need. Other people say you will be disappointed unless you have a desktop publishing package. Discuss the advantages and disadvantages of each option.
2. Some organizations insist that their employees use an integrated package so that data can be easily transferred between users. Other organizations let their users make individual decisions on which package they want to use for a particular application. Discuss the advantages and disadvantages of both policies.

RESEARCH PROJECTS

1. Interview a person who uses a desktop publishing package on a regular basis. Write a report on the types of documents he or she prepares. Include the person's comments on the different desktop publishing features.
2. Find someone who has developed an electronic spreadsheet. Ask him or her to review with you the formulas that he or she used in the spreadsheet.
3. Assume that you have decided to use a database package to keep track of all the members of a ski club. Define the fields that would make up your database record.

Input to the Computer

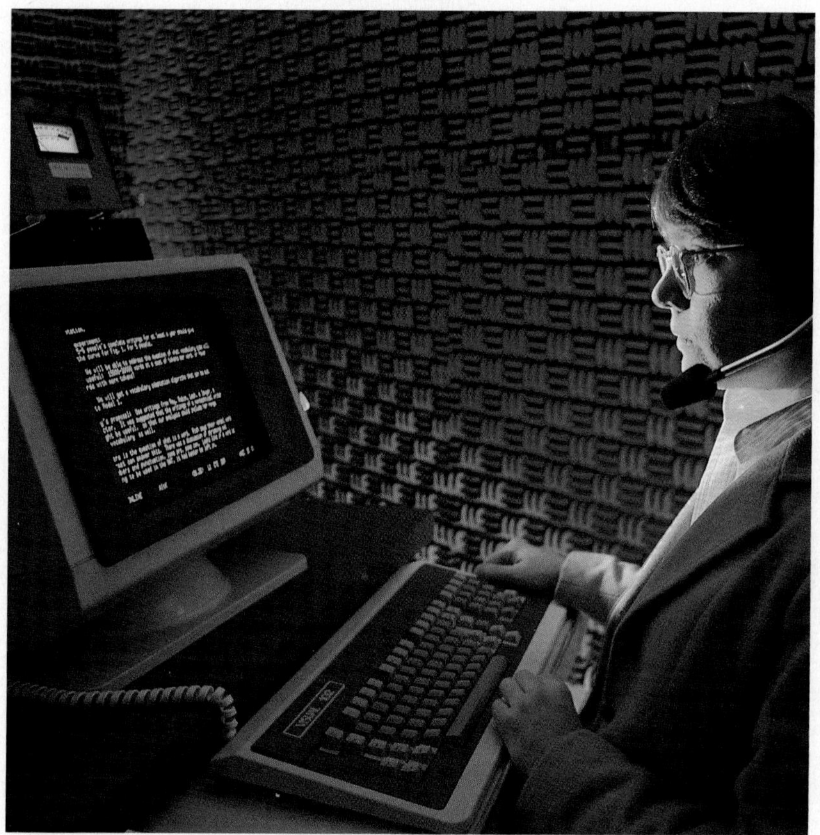

The information processing cycle is basic to all computers, large or small. It is important that you understand this cycle, for much of your success in understanding computers and what they do depends on having an understanding or *feeling* for the movement of data as it flows through the information processing cycle and becomes information. In this chapter we discuss the information processing cycle focusing on input operations. We examine the nature of data and how it is organized, describe some of the devices used for input, and explain the ways that both hardware and software are designed to make input operations easier for the user. We also discuss data entry methods and the design, arrangement, and usage of equipment.

OBJECTIVES

- Review the four operations of the information processing cycle: input, process, output, and storage
- Define the four types of input and how the computer uses each type
- Define data and explain the terms used to describe data: field, record, file, database
- Describe the standard features of keyboards, and explain how to use the cursor control and function keys
- Explain the three types of terminals and how they are used
- Describe several input devices other than the keyboard and terminal
- Explain user interfaces and list the features that a good user interface should have
- Discuss how data entry differs in interactive and batch processing
- List and explain the systems and procedures associated with data entry
- Explain the term ergonomics and describe some of the important features of good equipment design

OVERVIEW OF THE INFORMATION PROCESSING CYCLE

As we saw in Chapter 1, the information processing cycle consists of four operations: input, processing, output, and storage (Figure 3-1). Regardless of the size and type of computer, these operations process data into a meaningful form called information.

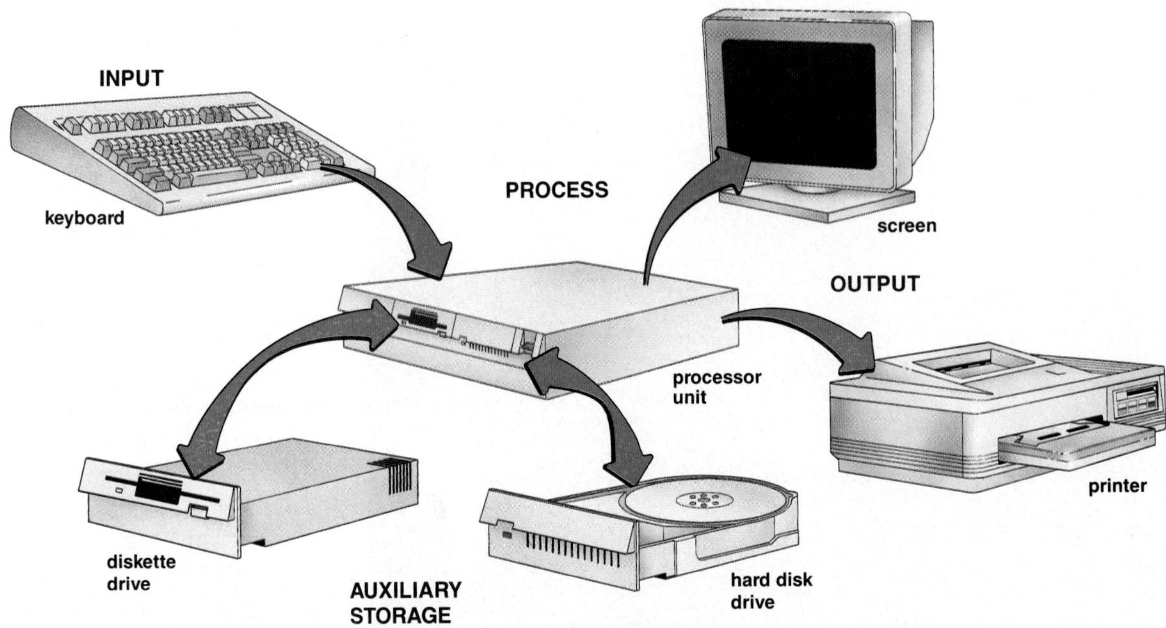

FIGURE 3-1
A computer consists of input devices, the processor unit, output devices, and auxiliary storage units. This equipment, or hardware, is used to perform the operations of the information processing cycle.

The operations in the information processing cycle are carried out through the combined use of computer equipment, also called computer hardware, and computer software. The computer software, or programs, contain instructions that direct the computer equipment to perform the tasks necessary to process data into information. In the information processing cycle, the input operation must take place before any data can be processed and any information produced and stored.

WHAT IS INPUT?

Input refers to the process of entering programs, commands, user responses, and data into main memory. Input can also refer to the media (e.g., disks, tapes, documents) that contain these input types. These four types of input are used by a computer in the following ways:

- **Programs** are instructions that direct the computer to perform the necessary operations to process data into information. The program that is loaded and stored in main memory determines the processing that the computer will perform. When a program is first created it is input by using a keyboard. Once the program has been entered and stored on auxiliary storage, it can be transferred to main memory by a command.
- **Commands** are key words and phrases that the user inputs to direct the computer to perform certain activities. For example, if you wanted to use a payroll program, you might issue a command such as LOAD "PAYROLL" to load the program named

PAYROLL into main memory from auxiliary storage. To begin the execution of the program you would enter another command such as RUN (Figure 3-2).

- **User responses** refer to the data that a user inputs to respond to a question or message from the software. Usually these messages appear on a screen and the user responds through a keyboard. One of the most common responses is to answer "Yes" or "No" to a question. Based on the answer, the computer program will perform specific actions. For example, typing the letter Y in response to the message "Do you want to save this file?" will result in the file being saved (written) to the auxiliary storage device.
- **Data** refers to the raw facts, including numbers and words, that a computer receives during the input operation and processes to produce information. Data must be entered and stored in main memory for processing to occur. For example, data entered from sales orders can be processed by a computer program to produce sales reports useful to management. Data is the most common type of input.

Because data is such an important part of the input operation it is important for you to understand what data is and how it is organized.

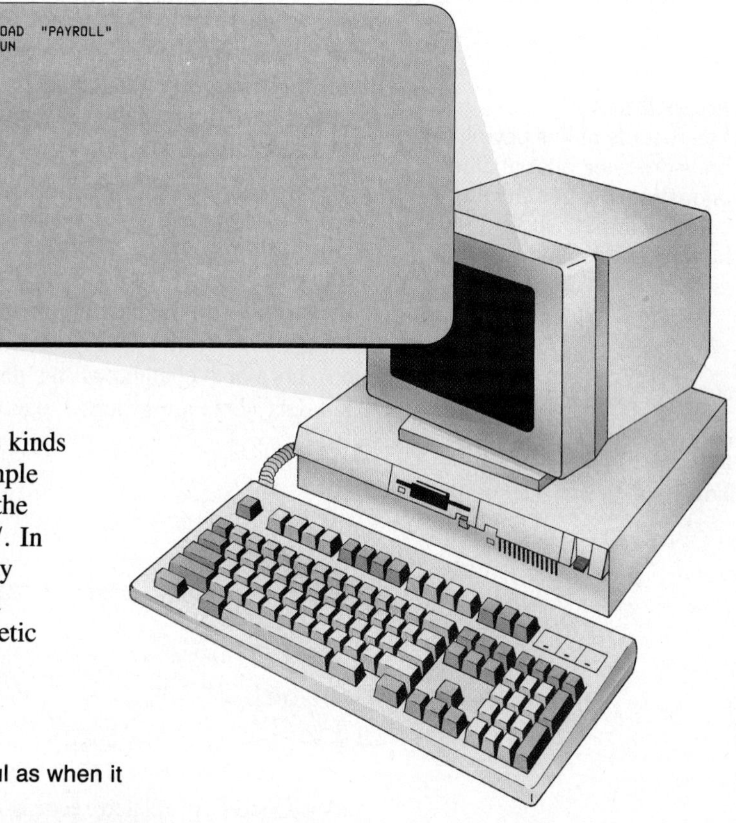

FIGURE 3-2
In this example, the computer user first entered a command to load the program called "PAYROLL" and then issued the command RUN, which will execute the program.

HOW IS DATA ORGANIZED?

Data is comprised of **characters**. These characters are classified as **alphabetic** (A–Z), **numeric** (0–9), or **special** (all characters other than A–Z and 0–9 such as ()*&%#@,). The raw facts that we refer to as data are made up of a combination of these three kinds of characters. In the monthly sales application example shown in Figure 3-3, the date 01/31 is made up of the numeric characters 0 1 3 and the special character /. In the payroll example (Figure 3-4), the Social Security number contains numeric characters and the special character -. The name Haynes contains only alphabetic characters.

FIGURE 3-3
By itself, the month-ending date, 01/31, is not as useful as when it is related to the monthly sales amount.

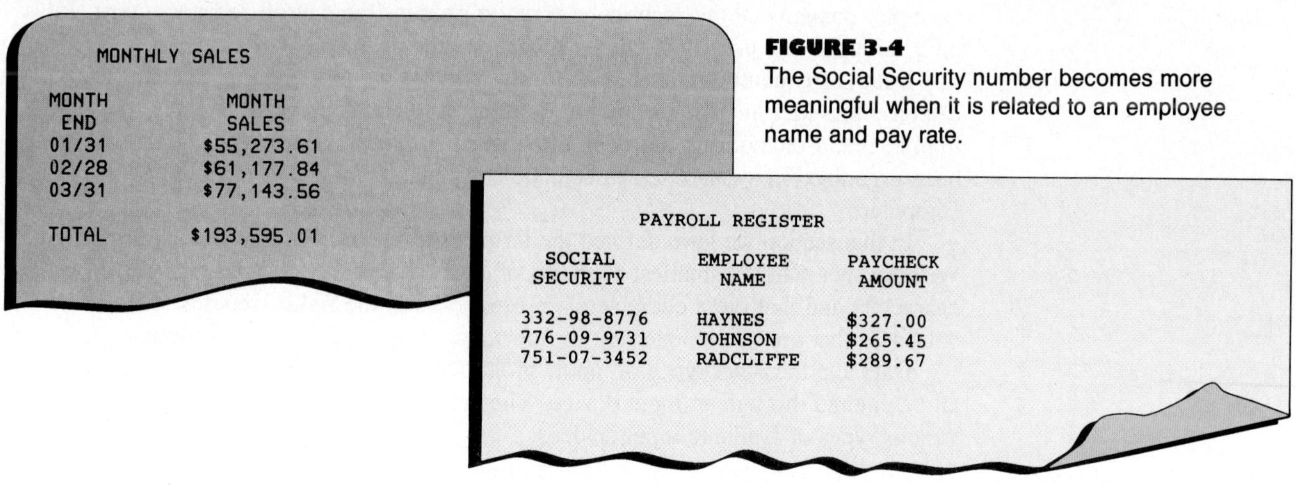

MONTHLY SALES

MONTH END	MONTH SALES
01/31	$55,273.61
02/28	$61,177.84
03/31	$77,143.56
TOTAL	$193,595.01

PAYROLL REGISTER

SOCIAL SECURITY	EMPLOYEE NAME	PAYCHECK AMOUNT
332-98-8776	HAYNES	$327.00
776-09-9731	JOHNSON	$265.45
751-07-3452	RADCLIFFE	$289.67

FIGURE 3-4
The Social Security number becomes more meaningful when it is related to an employee name and pay rate.

Each fact or unique piece of data is referred to as a **data item**, **data field**, or simply a **field**. Fields are classified by the characters that they contain. For example, a field that contains only alphabetic characters, such as the name field which contains Haynes, is called an **alphabetic field**. A field that contains numeric characters is called a **numeric field**. Numeric fields may also contain some special characters that are commonly used with numbers such as a decimal point (.) and the plus (+) and minus (–) signs. Even with the plus sign (+) and decimal point (.), the number +500.00 is still called a numeric field. Fields that contain a combination of character types, such as the date 01/31 (numeric and special characters), are called **alphanumeric fields**. Although the word *alphanumeric* implies only alphabetic and numeric characters, it also includes fields that contain special characters. The term alphanumeric is used to describe all fields that do not fall into the alphabetic or numeric classifications.

A field is normally most meaningful when it is combined with related fields. To illustrate, the month and day 01/31 by itself is not as useful as when it is related to monthly sales (Figure 3-3). Also, the Social Security number 332-98-8776 is more useful when it is related to the name HAYNES and to the paycheck amount $327.00 (Figure 3-4). Because related fields are more meaningful if they are together, fields are organized into groups called records.

A **record** is a collection of related fields. Each record normally corresponds to a specific unit of information. For example, a record that could be used to produce the payroll report in Figure 3-4 is illustrated in Figure 3-5. The fields in the record are the Social Security number, employee name, and paycheck amount. This example shows that the data in each record is used to produce a line on the payroll report. The first record contains all the data concerning the employee named HAYNES. The second record contains all the data concerning the employee named JOHNSTON. Each subsequent record also contains all the data for a given employee. Thus, you can see how related data items are grouped together to form a record.

FIGURE 3-5
The records of this payroll file are stored one after another on magnetic tape. The file contains the Social Security number, name, and paycheck amount for all employees.

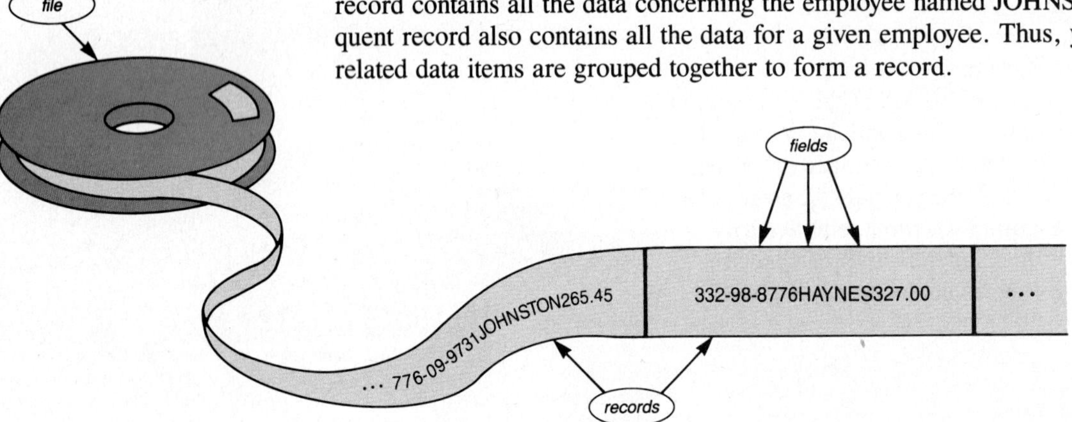

A collection of related records is called a **file**. The payroll file in Figure 3-5, for example, contains all the records required to produce the payroll register report. Files on a computer are usually stored on magnetic tape or magnetic disk.

Data is frequently organized in a **database**. As we discussed in Chapter 2, a database provides an efficient way to establish a relationship between data items and implies that a relationship has been established between multiple files. Data that has been organized in a database can be efficiently manipulated and retrieved by a computer.

In this section we have defined the terms used to describe how data is organized. We have seen that the smallest elements of data are alphabetic, numeric, and special characters and that these characters are used to build the fields, records, files, and databases that are manipulated by an information system to create information.

Data and the other types of input, programs, commands and user responses, will all be entered through an input device. The next section of this chapter discusses the various types of available input devices.

THE KEYBOARD

The **keyboard** is the most commonly used input device. Users input data to a computer by pressing the keys on the keyboard. Keyboards are connected to other devices that have screens, such as a personal computer or a terminal. As the user enters data through the keyboard, the data appears on the screen.

The keyboards used for computer input are very similar to the keyboards used on the familiar office machine, the typewriter. They contain numbers, letters of the alphabet, and some special characters (Figure 3-6). In addition, many computer keyboards are equipped with a **numeric keypad** on the right-hand side of the keyboard. These numeric keys are arranged in an adding machine or calculator format and aid the user with numeric data entry.

Keyboards also contain keys that can be used to position the cursor on the screen. A **cursor** is a symbol, such as an underline character or an arrow, that indicates where on the screen the next character entered will appear. The keys that move the cursor are called **arrow keys** or **cursor control keys**. Cursor control keys have an up arrow, a down arrow, a left arrow, and a right arrow. When you press any of these keys, the cursor moves one space in the same direction as the arrow. In addition, many keyboards contain other cursor control keys such as the Home key, which when you press it can send the cursor to a beginning position such as the upper left position of the screen or document.

Some computer keyboards also contain keys that can alter or edit the text displayed on the screen. For example, the Insert and Delete keys allow characters to be inserted into or deleted from data that appears on the screen.

Function keys are keys that can be programmed to accomplish certain tasks that will assist the user. For example, a function key might be programmed for use as a help key when a terminal is used for word processing. Whenever the key is pressed, messages will appear that give helpful information about how to use the word processing software. Function keys can also save keystrokes. Sometimes several keystrokes

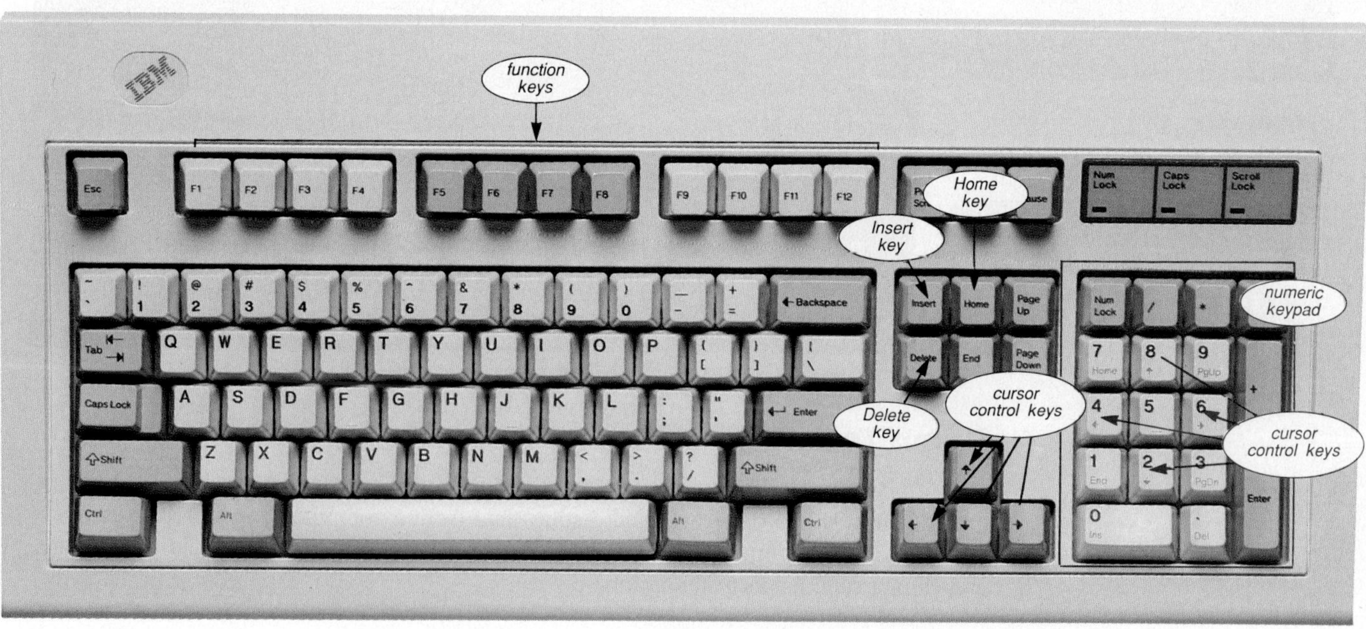

FIGURE 3-6
The IBM PS/2 Model 30 keyboard contains a numeric keypad, cursor control keys, and function keys. The keys on the numeric keypad are arranged in the same order as the keys on an adding machine or a calculator. This arrangement allows people who are skilled in entering numbers to input numeric data at a much faster rate than if the number keys were positioned across the top of the keyboard as they are on a typewriter. The four cursor control keys are identified by up ↑, down ↓, left ←, and right → arrows. When the user presses one of these keys, the cursor moves one position in the direction indicated by the arrow. Function keys are used for specific commands that are either programmed by the user or determined by the application software. Function keys can be in different places, but on most keyboards they are either on the left side or along the top.

are required to accomplish a certain task, for example, printing a document. Some application software packages are written so that the user can either enter the individual keystrokes or press a function key and obtain the same result.

The disadvantage of using a keyboard as an input device is that training is required to use it efficiently. Users who do not know how to type are at a disadvantage because of the time they spend looking for the appropriate keys. While other input devices are appropriate in some situations, users should be encouraged to develop their keyboard skills.

TERMINALS

Terminals, sometimes called **display terminals** or **video display terminals (VDTs)**, consist of a keyboard and a screen. They fall into three basic categories: dumb terminals, intelligent terminals (sometimes called programmable terminals) and special-purpose terminals. We explain the features of each type in the following sections. Figure 3-7 shows a dumb and an intelligent terminal.

FIGURE 3-7
A dumb terminal (left) and a group of intelligent terminals (right). From appearance alone, it is often difficult to tell in which category a terminal belongs. Intelligent terminals have built-in processing capabilities.

Dumb Terminals

A **dumb terminal** consists of a keyboard and a display screen that can be used to enter and transmit data to or receive and display data from a computer to which it is connected. A dumb terminal has no independent processing capability or auxiliary storage and cannot function as a stand-alone device.

Intelligent Terminals

Intelligent terminals have built-in processing capabilities and often contain not only the keyboard and screen, but also disk drives and printers. Because of their built-in capabilities, these terminals can perform limited processing tasks when they are not communicating directly with the central computer. Intelligent terminals are also known as **programmable terminals** or **smart terminals** because they can be programmed by the user to perform many basic tasks, including arithmetic and logic operations. Personal computers are frequently used as intelligent terminals (Figure 3-8).

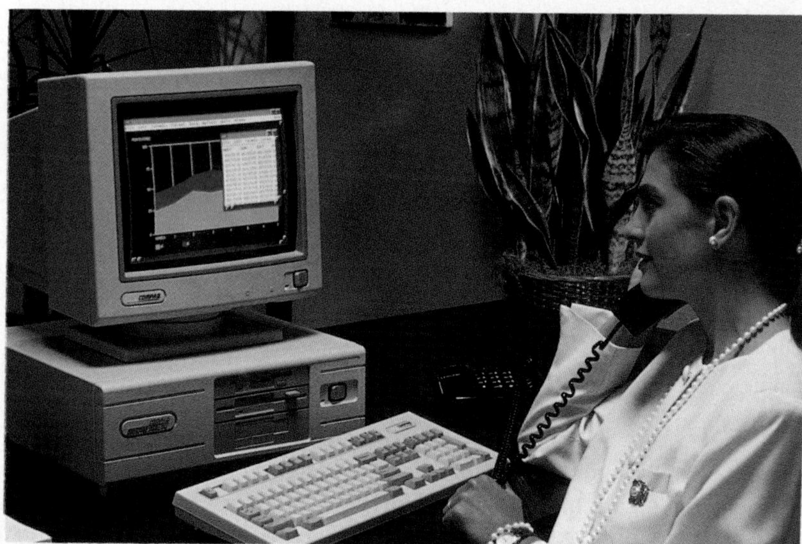

FIGURE 3-8
This personal computer can function as both a stand-alone computer or as a terminal when it is connected to another computer system.

As the amount of processing power that is incorporated into intelligent terminals increases, more processing can occur at the site of the terminal. This means that the large minicomputer or mainframe at the central site can perform the main processing and serve multiple users faster, rather than having to use its resources to perform tasks that can be performed by the intelligent terminal.

Special-Purpose Terminals

Terminals are found in virtually every environment that generates data for processing on a computer. While many are general terminals like those we previously described, others are designed to perform specific jobs and contain features uniquely designed for use in a particular industry.

The terminal shown in Figure 3-9 is called a point-of-sale terminal. **Point-of-sale (POS) terminals** allow data to be entered at the time and place where the transaction with a customer occurs, such as in fast-food restaurants or hotels, for example. Point-of-sale terminals serve as input to either minicomputers located at the place of business or larger computers located elsewhere. The data entered is used to maintain sales records, update inventory, make automatic calculations such as sales tax, verify credit, and perform other activities associated with the sales transactions and critical to running the business. Point-of-sale terminals are designed to be easy to operate, requiring little technical knowledge. As shown in Figure 3-9, the keys are labeled to assist the user.

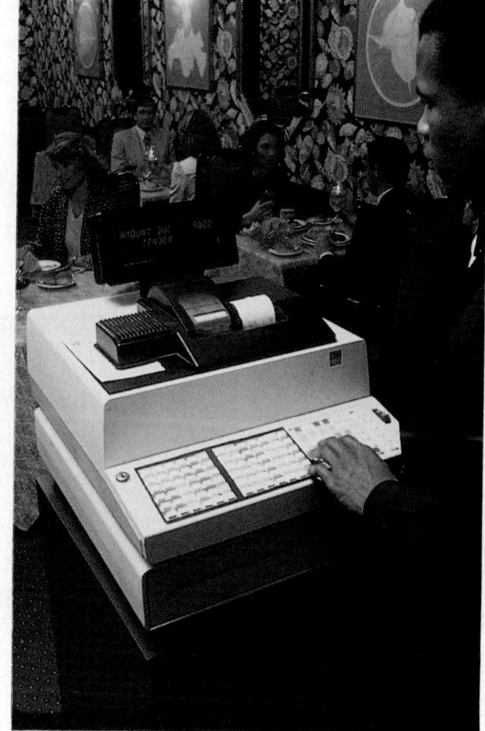

FIGURE 3-9
This point-of-sale terminal has been specifically designed for use in a restaurant. The operator can press separate keys to enter the prices of certain menu items.

OTHER INPUT DEVICES

Besides keyboards and terminals, there is an increasing variety of other input devices. This section describes some of the devices used for general-purpose applications.

Mouse

The mouse is a unique device used with personal computers and some computer terminals. A **mouse** is a small, lightweight device that easily fits in the palm of your hand. You move it across a flat surface such as a desktop (Figure 3-10) to control the movement of the cursor on a screen.

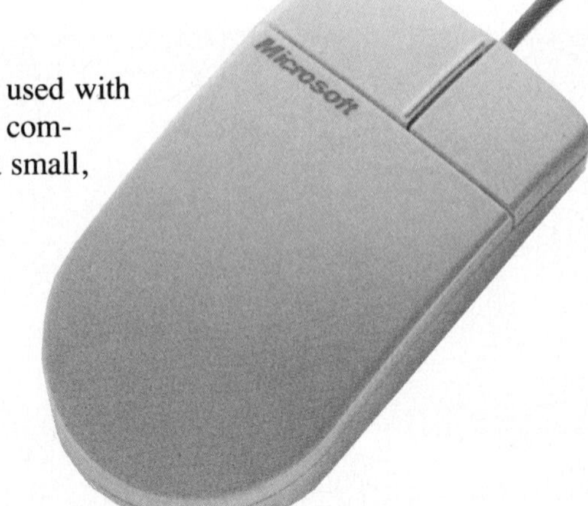

FIGURE 3-10
The mouse can be moved to control the cursor on the screen. You press the button on the top of the mouse to make selections or perform functions, depending on the software you are using. The ball on the underside of the mouse moves as you push the mouse around on a hard, flat surface. The movement of the ball causes the cursor to move correspondingly on the screen.

The mouse is attached to the computer by a cable. On the bottom of the device is a small ball. As the mouse moves across the flat surface, the computer electronically senses the movement of the ball. The movement of the cursor on the screen corresponds to the movement of the mouse (Figure 3-11). When you move the mouse left on the surface of the table or desk, the cursor moves left on the screen. When you move the mouse right, the cursor moves right, and so on.

On top of the mouse are one or more buttons. By using the mouse to move the cursor on the screen and pressing the buttons on the mouse, you can perform many actions such as making menu selections, editing a word processing document, and moving data from one point on the screen to another.

The primary advantage of a mouse is that it is easy to use. Proponents of the mouse say that with a little practice, a person can use a mouse to point to locations on the screen just as easily as using a finger.

There are two major disadvantages of the mouse. The first is that it requires empty desk space where it can be moved about (Figure 3-12). The second disadvantage is that the user must remove a hand from the keyboard and place it on the mouse whenever the cursor is to be moved or a command is to be given. Some keyboard experts have noted that taking hands from the keyboard slows the speed of data entry considerably.

FIGURE 3-11
Here, a mouse is being moved from one side to another. This action will result in the cursor moving from one side of the screen to the other. The buttons on top of the mouse can be used instead of keys on the keyboard.

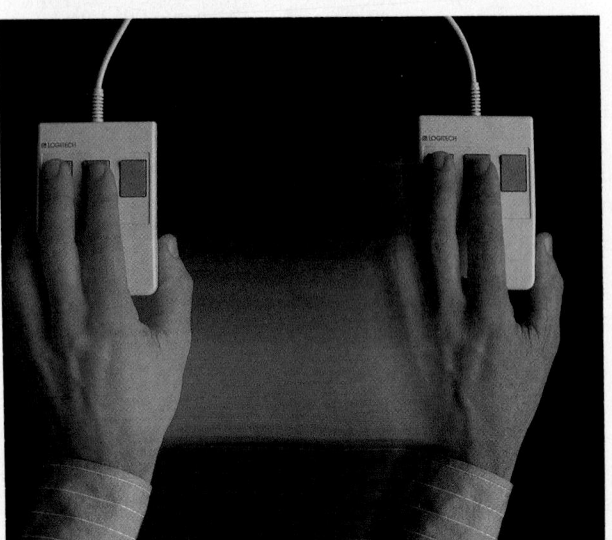

FIGURE 3-12
Notice that some amount of clear desk space is required for moving the mouse.

Thus, some people have said the mouse is not an effective tool in those environments where keying must be performed rapidly, such as in word processing applications. Others, however, say that using a mouse is far superior to using the cursor control keys on a keyboard.

Trackball

A **trackball** is a graphic pointing device like a mouse only with the ball on the top of the device instead of the bottom (Figure 3-13). To move the cursor with a trackball, all you have to do is rotate the ball in the desired direction. With a mouse, you have to move the entire device. To accommodate movement with both the fingers and palms of a hand, the ball on top of a trackball is larger than the ball on the bottom of a mouse. The main advantage of a trackball over a mouse is that it doesn't require the clear desk space.

FIGURE 3-13
The trackball is similar to the mouse but does not require the same amount of clear desk space. The user rotates the ball to move the cursor and then presses one of the keys shown at the top of this trackball device.

Touch Screens

Touch screens allow users to touch areas of the screen to enter data. They let the user interact with a computer by the touch of a finger rather than typing on a keyboard or moving a mouse. The user enters data by touching words or numbers or locations identified on the screen (Figure 3-14).

Several electronic techniques change a touch on the screen into electronic impulses that can be interpreted by the computer software. One of the most common techniques uses beams of infrared light that are projected across the surface of the screen. A finger or other object touching the screen interrupts the beams, generating an electronic signal. This signal identifies the location on the screen where the touch occurred. The software interprets the signal and performs the required function.

Touch screens are not used to enter large amounts of data. They are used, however, for applications where the user must issue a command to the software to perform a particular task or must choose from a list of options to be performed.

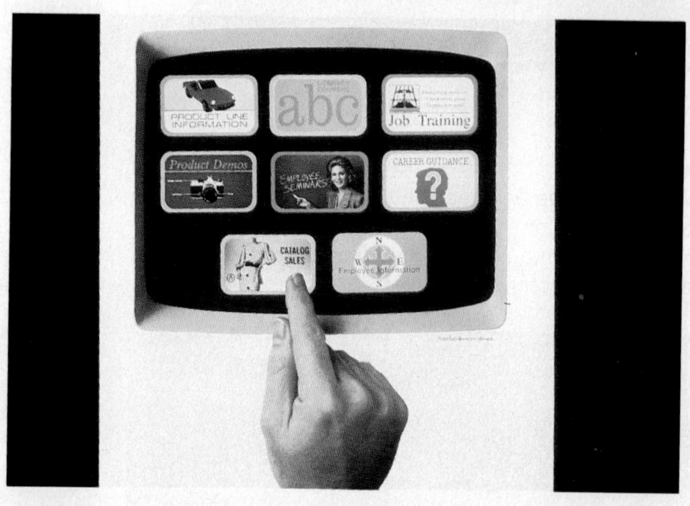

FIGURE 3-14
Touch screens allow the user to make choices and execute commands by actually touching areas of the screen. Touch screens require special software that determines where the user touched the screen and what action should be taken.

There are both advantages and disadvantages to touch screens. A significant advantage is that they are very *natural* to use; that is, people are used to pointing to things. With touch screens, users can point to indicate the processing they want performed by the computer. In addition, touch screens are usually easy for the user to learn. As quickly as pointing a finger, the user's request is processed. This is considerably faster than repeatedly pressing arrow keys to move the cursor from one location on the screen to another.

There are some disadvantages to touch screens. First, the resolution of the touching area is not precise. Thus, while a user can point to a box or a fairly large area on the screen and the electronics can determine the location of the touch, it is difficult to point to a single character in a word processing application, for example, and indicate that the character should be deleted. In cases such as these, a keyboard is easier to use. A second disadvantage is that after a period of reaching for the screen, the user's arm might become tired.

Graphic Input Devices

Graphic input devices are used to translate graphic input data, such as photos or drawings, into a form that can be processed on a computer. Three devices that are often used for graphic input are light pens, digitizers, and graphics tablets. A **light pen** is used by touching it on the display screen to create or modify graphics (Figure 3-15). An electronic grid on the screen senses the light generated at the tip of the light pen when it is touched to the screen. A **digitizer** converts points, lines, and curves from a sketch, drawing, or photograph to digital impulses and transmits them to a computer (Figures 3-16 and 3-17). The user indicates the data to be input by pressing one or more buttons on the hand-held digitizer device. A **graphics tablet** works in a manner similar to a digitizer, but it also contains unique characters and commands that can be automatically generated by the person using the tablet (Figure 3-18).

FIGURE 3-15
Placing the light pen at a point on the screen activates a sensing device within the pen. The activated pen transmits the location of the light to the computer, where the program can perform the desired tasks.

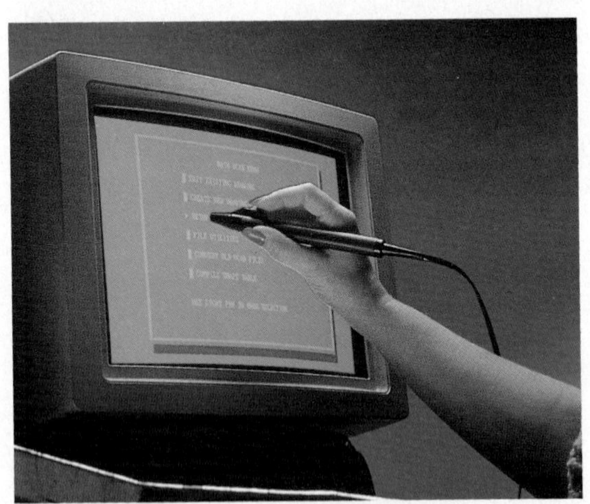

Pen Input Devices

Pen input devices allow the user to input hand-printed letters and numbers to record information. These devices work with a type of hand-held computer sometimes called *scratchpad computers*. These systems consist of a flat screen and the pen device (Figure 3-19). As the characters are printed, special circuitry records the movement of the pen on the screen.

FIGURE 3-16
The device in the engineer's hand reads and translates the coordinates on the drawing into data that can be stored in the computer and later used to reproduce the drawing on a screen or a printer.

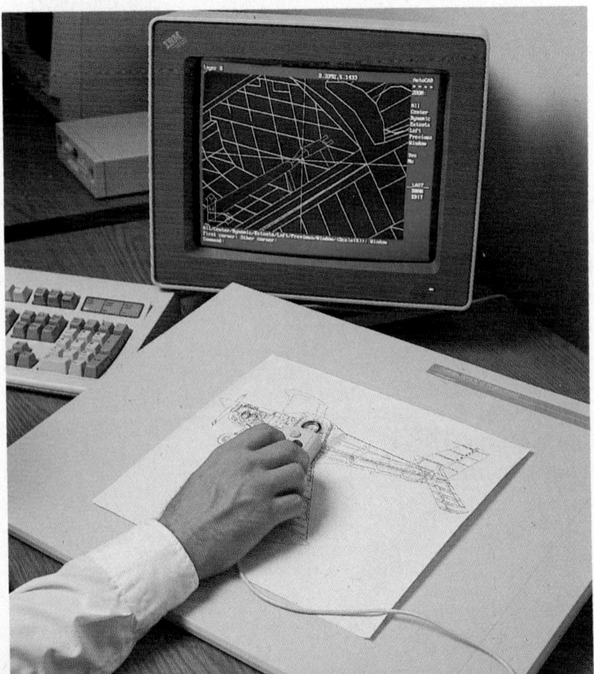

FIGURE 3-17
Digitizers are used to create original drawings or to trace and reproduce existing drawings quickly and accurately.

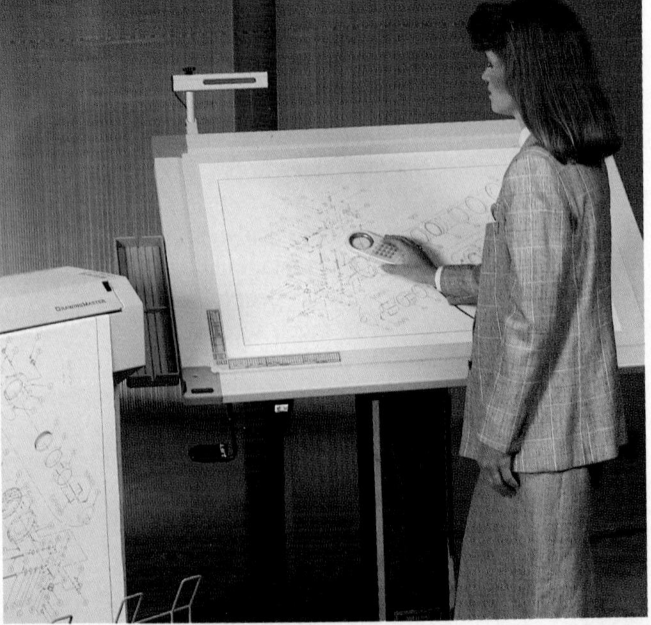

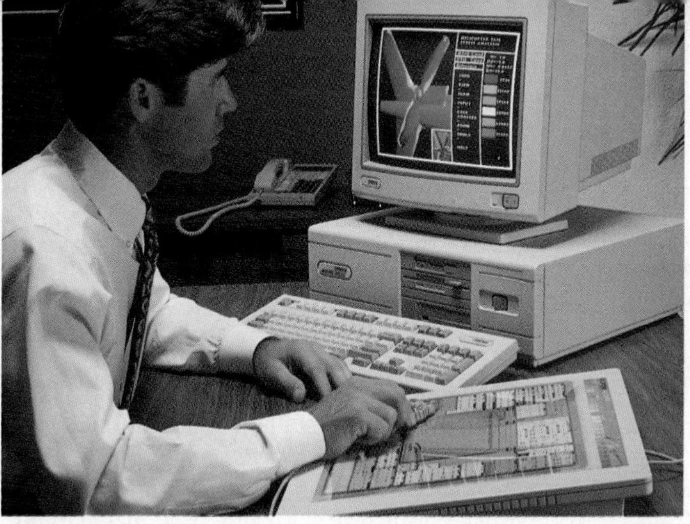

FIGURE 3-18
The color template on the graphics tablet allows the user to select processing options by placing a hand-held device over the appropriate location on the tablet and pressing a button.

FIGURE 3-19
Pen input systems allow the user to use an electronic pen to enter data or select processing options without using a keyboard. This method is easy to learn by individuals who have worked with a pencil and paper.

The computer translates the pen strokes into characters. The characters are then processed as text or as a user response to a message displayed on the screen. The advantage of pen input systems is that many workers who may have a difficult time using a keyboard can use the more familiar pen to enter data.

Voice Input

One of the more exciting recent developments is the use of voice input, sometimes referred to as voice or speech recognition. As the name implies, **voice input** allows the user to enter data and issue commands to the computer with spoken words (Figure 3-20).

Most systems require the user to *train* the system to recognize their voice by first speaking the words that will be used a number of times. As the words are spoken, they are digitized by the system; that is, they are broken down into digital components that the computer can recognize. After each word has been spoken several times, the system develops a digital pattern for the word that can be stored on auxiliary storage. When the user later speaks a word to the system to request a particular action, the system compares the word to words that were previously entered and that it is trained to *understand.* When it finds a match, the software performs the activity associated with the word. For example, in voice-controlled word processing systems, spoken words can control such functions as single- and double-spacing, choosing type styles, and centering text. The major advantage of voice input is that the user does not have to key, move, or touch anything to enter data into the computer. Many experts believe that voice input will be used extensively in the years to come.

FIGURE 3-20
Voice input systems allow the user to enter data without using the keyboard. The microphone headset is attached to the personal computer. Special software and hardware are used to interpret the voice commands.

INPUT DEVICES DESIGNED FOR SPECIFIC PURPOSES

◆ Some input devices are designed to perform specific tasks. Examples are scanners, MICR readers, and data collection devices.

Scanners

Scanners include a variety of devices that *read* printed codes, characters, or images and convert them into a form that can be processed by the computer. This section describes several different types of scanning devices.

Page Scanners A **page scanner** is an input device that can electronically capture an entire page of text or images such as photographs or art work (Figure 3-21). The scanner converts the text or image on the original document into digital information that can be stored on a disk and processed by the computer. The digitized information can be printed or displayed separately or merged into another document such as a newsletter. Hand-held devices that can scan a portion of a page are also available (Figure 3-22) as well as color scanners.

FIGURE 3-21
This scanner can input text, graphics, or photographs for use in word processing or desktop publishing applications.

Image Processing Much of the data input to a computer is taken from source documents. Usually, you input only a portion of the data on the source document, but sometimes you might find it necessary to store the entire source document, such as legal document with a signature or a drawing. In these situations, organizations often implement image processing systems. **Image processing systems** use software and special equipment, including scanners, to input and store an actual image of the source document. These systems are like electronic filing cabinets that allow users to rapidly access and review exact reproductions of the original documents (Figure 3-23).

FIGURE 3-22
A hand-held scanner can enter text or graphics less than a page wide. Software allows you to join separately scanned items to make up a complete page.

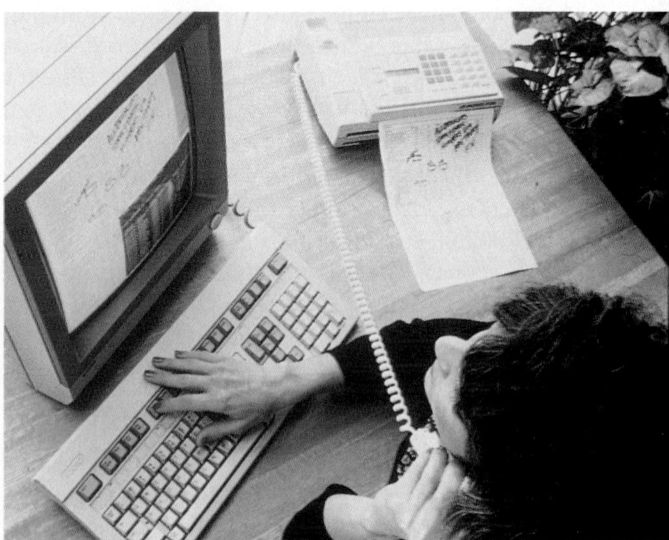

FIGURE 3-23
Image processing systems record and store an exact copy of a document. These systems are often used by insurance companies that may need to refer to any of hundreds of thousands of documents.

FIGURE 3-24
Most modern grocery stores use optical scanning devices such as the one shown here. A laser beam, emitted from the opening on the counter, reads the bar code on the product package. Most retail products have the Universal Product Code (UPC) imprinted somewhere on the label or package (located at the bottom of the can in the photo below). The UPC code uniquely identifies both the manufacturer and the product. The scanning device is connected to a computer system that uses the UPC code to look up the price of the product and add the price into the total sale. A keyboard above the scanner is used to code the numbers for items such as fruit, which do not have UPC labels.

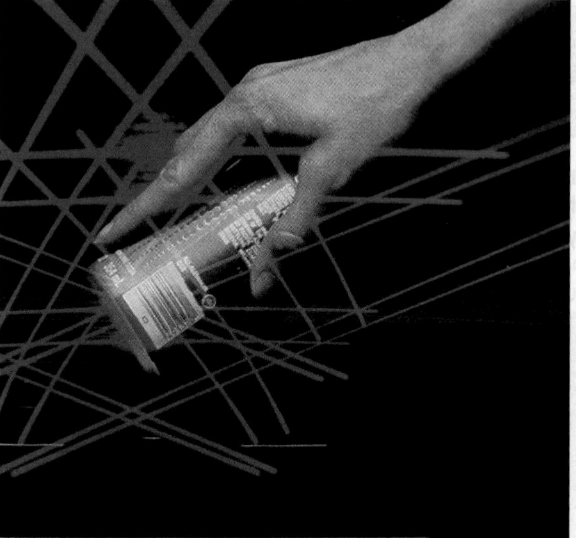

Laser Scanners A scanning device often used by modern grocery stores at checkout counters is a **laser scanner**, also called a **bar code reader** (Figure 3-24). These devices use a laser beam to scan and read the special bar code printed on the products.

Optical Character Readers **Optical character recognition (OCR)** devices are scanners that read typewritten, computer-printed, and in some cases hand-printed characters from ordinary documents. OCR devices range from large machines that can automatically read thousands of documents per minute to hand-held wands (Figure 3-25).

FIGURE 3-25
This hand-held optical character recognition device is being used to read a typed document one line at a time. Other OCR devices can scan an entire page at one time.

Data Collection Devices

Many **data collection devices** are designed and used for obtaining data at the site where the transaction or event being reported takes place. For example, in Figure 3-32, a man is taking inventory in a warehouse. Rather than write down the number and type of items and then enter this data, he uses a portable data collection device to record the inventory count in the device's memory. After he takes the inventory, he can transmit the data to a computer for processing.

FIGURE 3-32
This portable data collection device is being used to take an inventory in a warehouse. The data is stored in memory and can later be transferred to a computer system for processing.

Sometimes data collection equipment is needed in environments where heat, humidity, and cleanliness are difficult or impossible to control (Figure 3-33). In addition, these devices are often used by people whose primary task is not entering the data. Entering the data is only a small portion of their job duties. Data collection devices used in this manner must be designed and built for use in uncontrolled environments and they must be easy to operate.

Using data collection devices can provide important advantages over alternative methods of input. Because the data is entered as it is collected, clerical costs and transcription errors are reduced or eliminated. If the data collection devices can be connected directly to the computer, the data is immediately available for processing.

FIGURE 3-33
This data collection terminal has been designed to accommodate the user. Data collection devices should be simple and quick to operate, so that entering the data does not interfere with the main job of the person using the terminal.

Data collection devices range from portable devices that can be carried throughout a store or factory to sophisticated terminal systems with multiple input stations that feed directly into a central computer (Figure 3-34). These devices will continue to improve and find increased use in data entry applications.

FIGURE 3-34
A data collection device located in a production area. Data collected at this station is transferred to the main computer that keeps track of total production.

Figure 3-35 summarizes the most commonly used input devices. Although each device has advantages and disadvantages, each is appropriate for specific applications.

DEVICE	DESCRIPTION
Keyboard	Most commonly used input device. Special keys may include numeric keypad, cursor control keys, and function keys.
Terminal	Can be dumb, intelligent, or special-purpose.
Mouse or Trackball	Input devices used to move the cursor on a screen and select options.
Touch screens	User interacts with the computer by touching the screen.
Graphic input	Light pens, digitizers, and graphics tablets translate graphic data into a form that can be processed by a computer.
Pen	Allows input or hand-printed characters.
Voice input	User enters data and issues commands with spoken words.
MICR reader	Used primarily in banking to read the magnetic ink characters printed on checks.
Scanner	A variety of devices that read printed codes, characters, or images.
Data collection	Used to input data where it is generated.

FIGURE 3-35
This table summarizes some of the more common input devices.

With the widespread use of terminals, personal computers, and other input devices, input operations are performed by many types of users whose computer knowledge and experience varies greatly. Some users have a limited knowledge of computers and others have many years of experience. In addition, some users interact with computers daily, while others use them only occasionally. Information systems need to provide all users with a means of interacting with the computer efficiently. This is accomplished through user interfaces.

USER INTERFACES

A **user interface** is the combination of hardware and software that allows a user to communicate with a computer system. Through a user interface, users are able to input values that (1) respond to messages presented by the computer, (2) control the computer, and (3) request information from the computer. Thus, a user interface provides the means for communication between an information system and the user.

Both the hardware and software working together form a user interface. A terminal is an example of hardware that is frequently part of a user interface. The screen on the terminal displays messages to the user. The devices used for responding to the messages and controlling the computer include the keyboard, the mouse, and other types of input devices. The software associated with an interface are the programs. These programs determine the messages that are given to the user, the manner in which the user can respond, and the actions that will take place based on the user's responses.

In the following sections we discuss two of the most commonly found user interface techniques—prompts and menus—and describe how these interface techniques have improved communication between the user and the computer.

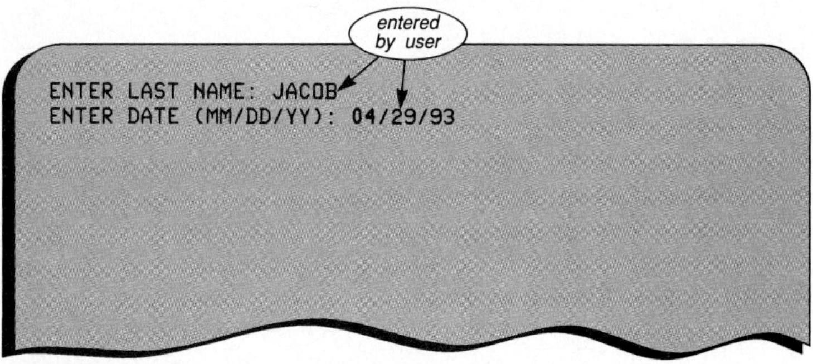

FIGURE 3-36
Prompts aid the user in entering data. They can tell the user what data to enter as well as the required format (as shown for the date entry). Prompts were one of the first types of interfaces designed to assist the user in utilizing the computer.

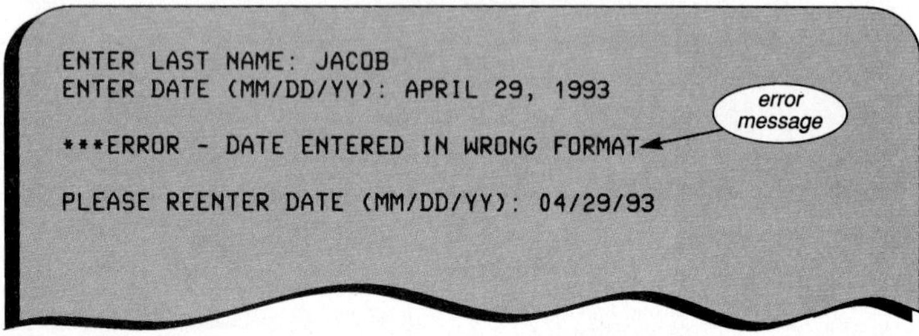

FIGURE 3-37
The software used for this screen checks the date entered and gives an error message if the date is entered in the wrong format.

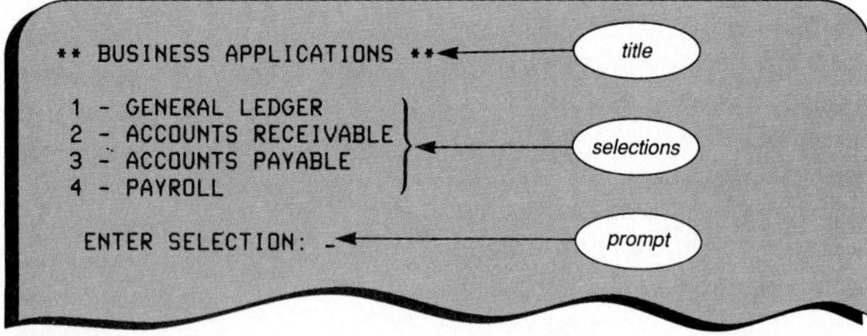

FIGURE 3-38
A menu consists of a title, the selections that can be made, and a prompt for the user to make an entry.

Prompts

A **prompt** is a message to the user that appears on the screen and provides helpful information or instructions regarding an entry to be made or action to be taken. The example in Figure 3-36 illustrates the use of prompts.

On the first line, the prompt "ENTER LAST NAME:" appears on the screen. This message tells the user to enter his or her last name. After the user enters the last name, a second prompt displays. This prompt, "ENTER DATE (MM/DD/YY):", indicates not only what the user is to enter but also exactly how the user should enter it. MM/DD/YY means to enter the date as a two-digit month number followed by a slash (/), a two-digit day number followed by a slash, and a two-digit year number. Thus, the entry 04/05/93 is valid, but 4/5/93 is not.

To help ensure that the user inputs valid data, the software should use **data editing**, the capability to check the data for proper format and acceptable values. When data is entered incorrectly, a message should appear to identify the error so the user can enter the correct data. The example in Figure 3-37 illustrates what might occur if a user does not enter data in the correct format. An error message appears and requests the user to reenter the date.

Menus

A **menu** is a screen display that provides a list of processing options for the user and allows the user to make a selection. A menu generally consists of three parts: a title, the selections, and a prompt (Figure 3-38). The title identifies the menu and orients the user to the choices that can be made. The selections consist of the words that describe each selection. The prompt asks the user to choose one of the selections.

The user can choose a menu selection in several ways. Figure 3-39 illustrates four common techniques, each of which is described as follows.

1. **Sequential Number**. Numbers are used to identify each of the selections. The user enters the number that corresponds to his or her selection and then presses the Enter key.
2. **Alphabetic Selection**. Letters of the alphabet identify the various processing options. The user enters the letter or letters that correspond to the selection and then presses the Enter key.
3. **Cursor Positioning**. The user presses the arrow or cursor control keys to position the cursor adjacent to the desired selection and then presses the Enter key.

4. **Reverse Video**. **Reverse video**, also called **inverse video**, means that the normal screen display, such as amber characters on a black background, is reversed to black characters on an amber background to highlight and draw attention to a certain character, word, or section on the screen. The directions instruct the user to move the reverse video from one selection to another by pressing the Spacebar (or arrow keys). Pressing the Spacebar once moves the reverse video from word processing to graphics; pressing it again highlights the database selection. When the desired selection is highlighted the user presses the Enter key to make that selection.

FIGURE 3-39
This example illustrates four different types of menus and menu selection methods.

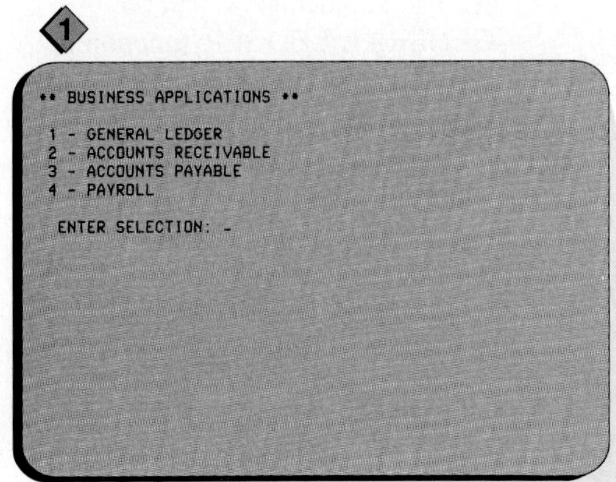

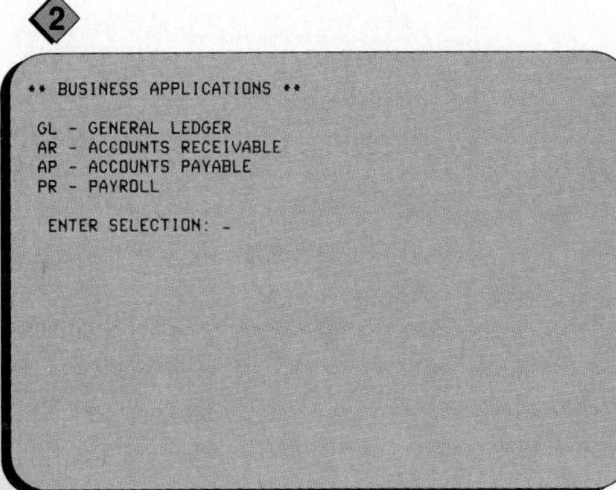

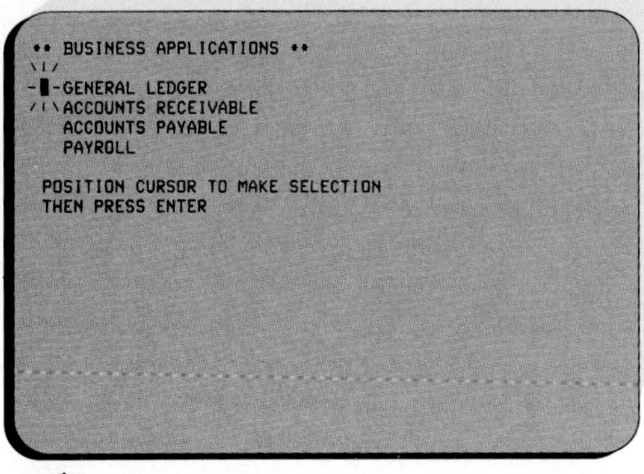

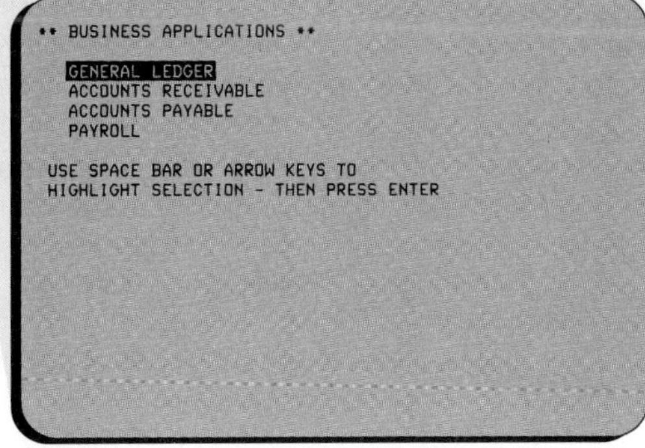

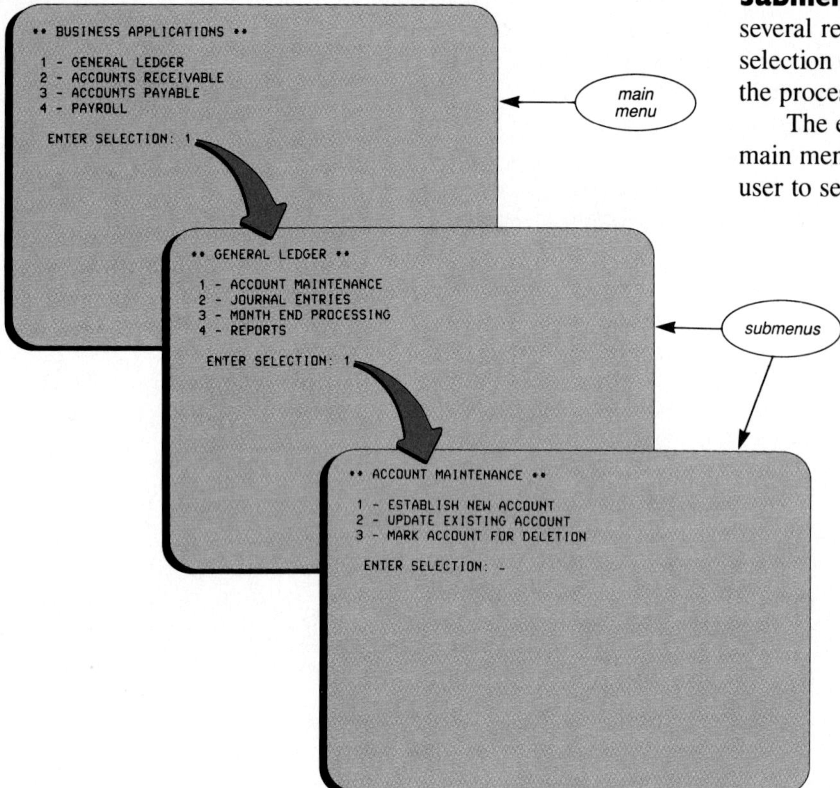

FIGURE 3-40
A submenu is used when additional selections can be made within an application. In this example, the first submenu shows additional General Ledger selections. The second submenu shows General Ledger Account Maintenance options.

Submenus Some applications require the use of several related menus. When a user chooses a selection on a menu, a **submenu** further defines the processing options that are available.

The example in Figure 3-40 illustrates the main menu from Figure 3-38, which allows the user to select GENERAL LEDGER, ACCOUNTS RECEIVABLE, ACCOUNTS PAYABLE, or PAYROLL. Also shown are two submenus. When the GENERAL LEDGER function is selected, a submenu appears. This submenu contains more detailed functions. Depending on the submenu selection, additional menus could be displayed. For example, if the user selected option 1, ACCOUNT MAINTENANCE, a third menu would appear that displays selections relative to establishing a new account, updating an existing account, or marking an existing account for deletion.

Menus: Advantages and Disadvantages Menus are a type of user interface that is used with all sizes and types of computers. There are both advantages and disadvantages to menus. Some of the advantages are:

- The user does not have to remember special commands. He or she merely chooses a selection from a list of possible operations that appear on the menu.
- The user can become productive with minimum training. Instead of having to learn a lot of technical computer information, he or she needs only to learn the application and the results of choosing a particular selection from the menu.
- The user is guided through the application because the selections that are available appear on the menus.

The disadvantage most often associated with menus, according to some experienced users, is that they can be slow and restrictive. For example, the menus illustrated in Figure 3-40 are good for the novice or infrequent computer user because they take him or her step by step through the possible operations that can be performed. The experienced user, however, knows which operations to perform. Therefore, he or she may prefer to enter a few quick commands and immediately begin work instead of having to view and respond to two or more menus. Some menus allow users to go directly to a processing option by entering a code such as the first one or two letters of the processing option name. For example, the user could enter AM to go directly to the Account Maintenance menu.

GRAPHIC USER INTERFACE

A **graphic user interface (GUI)** uses on-screen pictures, called **icons** to represent data or processing options (Figure 3-41). Rather than typing a command to open a file or start a program, with a GUI, the user uses a mouse to select one of the graphic images on the screen. Although they were first developed in the early 1970s by Xerox, GUIs did not become popular until the mid 1980s when Apple introduced the Macintosh computer. Today, many software products offer a GUI. The advantages of a GUI include ease of use, a shorter learning time, and quicker execution of commands.

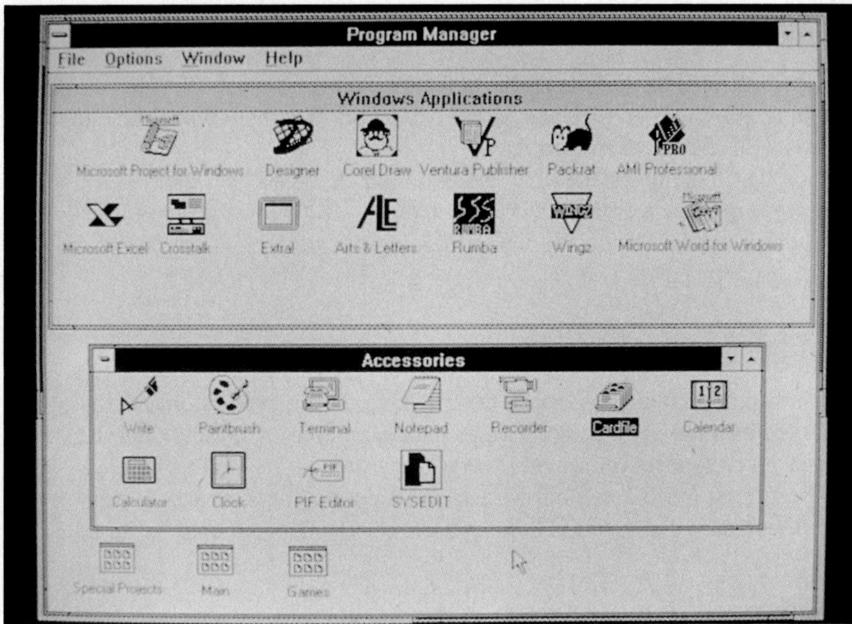

FIGURE 3-41
A graphic user interface (GUI) uses pictures (called icons) to represent data or functions that the user can select. The user selects an icon by using a mouse or similar device to place the cursor on top of the picture and then pressing a button.

FEATURES OF A USER INTERFACE

The following list identifies some features that should be included in a good user interface.

1. Meaningful responses to the user—System responses are the messages a computer displays and the actions the computer takes when a user enters data into the computer. In a well-designed system, the user receives a response for every action he or she takes. Without a response, the user does not know if the computer accepted the input. A system response from the computer avoids user confusion.
2. Good screen design—The design of the messages and pictures that appear on the screen can have a significant impact on the usability of the system. The most important rule is to keep the screen uncluttered and simple. Each message and each action that a user must take should be clear and easily understood. All messages, menus, and prompts within a system should follow a consistent format. This reduces the time needed for users to learn how to use a system and increases ease of use for experienced users.
3. Simple user responses—In general, the simpler the response required from the user, the better the user interface. If the user does not have to enter a large number of characters, data entry will be faster and fewer errors will occur.

4. Error recovery procedures—Errors are inevitable, thus users should be able to easily recover from them. Whenever the user makes an error, three user interface activities should take place: (1) the user should be alerted that an error has been made; (2) the error should be identified as specifically as possible; and (3) the user should be told how to recover from the error.

5. Control and security—Many multiuser computer systems require users to *sign on* to the computer by entering identification such as a name or account number followed by a password. A **password** is a value, such as a word or number, which identifies the user. The computer will only allow a user to sign on if he or she enters the correct password. These procedures help to ensure that only authorized users obtain access to the computer.

Computer professionals should keep these features in mind when they are designing and developing user interfaces. Users should also consider them when they are evaluating software or hardware for purchase.

The question that must be asked when designing or deciding on a user interface is, *Who will be using it and what is their level of computer experience?* A good user interface must be appropriate for the people who are going to use it.

DATA ENTRY

◆ Of the four types of input—program, commands, user responses, and data—the most common type of input is data. Sometimes data is entered by professional data entry operators who are specially trained in data entry procedures and techniques. However, it is becoming more common for data to be entered at its source by users working where the data is generated. The next section explains data entry techniques.

DATA ENTRY FOR INTERACTIVE AND BATCH PROCESSING

◆ Two methods of processing data on a computer are interactive processing and batch processing. **Interactive processing** means that data is processed immediately as it is entered. In **batch processing**, data is collected and, at some later time, all the data that has been gathered is processed as a group or *batch*. As you will see in the following sections, the methods used to enter data for interactive and batch processing differ.

Data Entry for Interactive Processing

Data entered in the interactive processing mode generates immediate output. In most interactive data entry, the person entering the data is communicating directly with the computer that will process the data. Therefore, data entry for interactive processing is said to be **online data entry**, meaning that the device from which the data is being entered is connected directly to the computer.

The output generated from interactive data entry processing is not always produced at the location where the data was entered. In Figure 3-42, for example, the data is entered from a terminal located in the order entry department. The data entered concerns a purchase by a customer. After the data is entered, a picking slip is printed in the warehouse. The worker in the warehouse then retrieves the item purchased (in this case, a lawn mower) and packages it for shipping. The terminal operator in the order entry department never sees the output generated, yet this is interactive processing because the data entered is processed immediately.

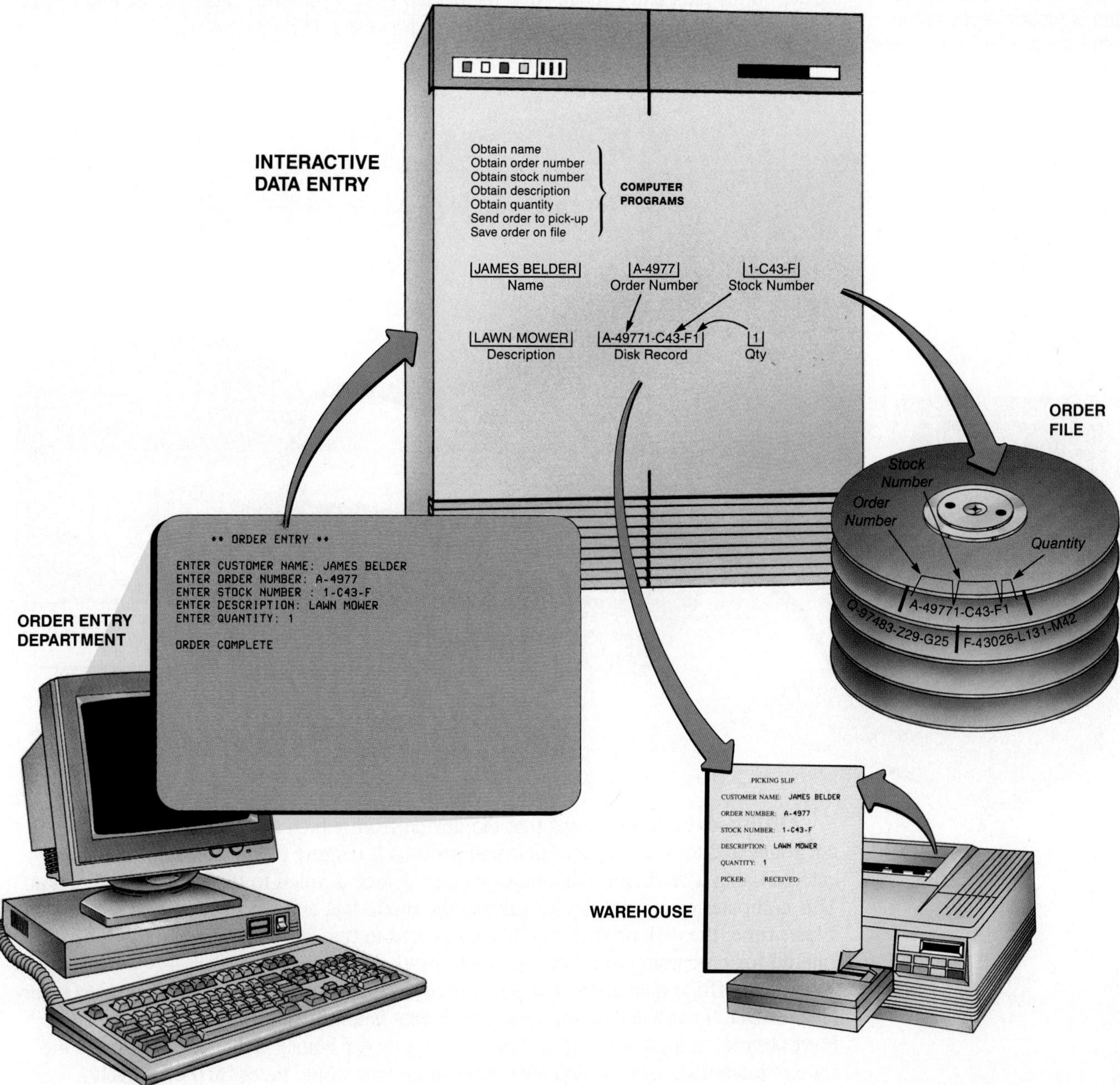

FIGURE 3-42
In this example of data entry for interactive processing, the data is entered by a terminal operator in the order entry department. The output generated, a picking slip, is printed in the warehouse. In addition, a record of the order is stored on disk.

The person entering the order in the order entry department may enter hundreds of such orders each day. When large amounts of data are entered by a terminal operator whose only job is to enter the data, the data entry function is called **production data entry**.

Data Entry for Batch Processing

When data is entered for processing in the batch processing mode, it is stored on a storage medium (usually tape or disk) for processing at a later time. Data for batch processing can be entered in either an online or offline manner. As we noted previously, online data entry means that the device from which the data is being entered is connected directly to the computer that will process it (Figure 3-43).

data is accumulated
in a batch and processed
as a group

FIGURE 3-43
In online batch data entry, data is input directly to the computer and stored on disk or tape. At a later time, the stored data will be processed as a group by the computer.

Offline data entry means that the device from which the data is being entered is not connected to the computer that will process it (Figure 3-44). Instead, the data is entered using a dedicated computer or other device devoted to the data entry function. This computer or special device accepts the input data and stores it on disk or tape. At a later time, the disk or tape can be transported to the site where the data will be entered for processing in a batch mode to produce information.

When offline data entry is used, source documents are accumulated prior to entering the data. Then the data on these documents is entered into the computer system. For example, in a payroll application, time cards for hourly employees would be the source documents from which data entry operators would enter the hours each employee worked.

To ensure that data is entered and processed accurately, controls are established within applications. Controls are the methods and procedures that ensure the accuracy and reliability of data and processing techniques. In a credit card payment application, for example, payments are usually divided into batches for processing. The payments for each batch are added manually and recorded prior to data entry. When the payment batches are processed on the computer, the total amount of the payments calculated by the computer for each batch is compared to the total determined from the manual addition performed prior to data entry. If the totals are the same, the data was input to the computer accurately. If the totals are not the same, then either the data was entered incorrectly or the manually determined batch total was calculated incorrectly. This technique of balancing to a predetermined total is called a **batch control**.

Summary of Interactive and Batch Data Entry

Entering data to produce information can take place online or offline. Online data entry is always used for interactive processing and often for batch processing as well. Offline data entry is used for batch processing. When using offline data entry, source documents from which the data is obtained must be gathered prior to the data being entered. Regardless of the processing method, producing information often requires a large amount of data entry.

FIGURE 3-44
In offline data entry, the data is input to a computer other than the one that will eventually process it. Often computers used for offline data entry are dedicated to data input functions and perform little if any processing. The data entered is later transferred to another computer for processing.

DATA ENTRY PROCEDURES

The procedures developed for the data entry function are important because accurate data must be entered into a computer to ensure data integrity. In addition, since users are interacting directly with the computer during the data entry function, procedures and documentation must be quite clear. The following questions must be answered in order to implement a data entry application successfully:

- *Who originates the data?* Data entered for processing on a computer is generated from many sources. It is important to identify which people and operations will generate the data so that appropriate procedures can be written to specify what data is to be gathered, how it is to be gathered, and who is to gather it.
- *Where will the data be entered?* Data is generally entered either from the centralized data entry section of the information systems department or from various locations throughout an organization. The hardware, software, and personnel needs vary depending upon which of these two methods is used. In a **centralized data entry** operation, the data is keyed by trained operators from source documents. When data is entered in the centralized data entry section, it is usually processed in a batch processing mode.

  Entering data from various locations in an organization is called **distributed data entry**. Quite often the data entry takes place at the site where the data is generated, for example, sales orders being entered by the sales department. Often, data entered using distributed data entry is processed in an interactive processing mode.
- *How soon will the data be entered?* The amount of time that can elapse between when the event being reported takes place and when the data about that event must be entered should be specified. In some applications, an event can occur but the data need not be entered until hours or even days later. For example, in the payroll application, the time cards are retrieved by a clerk on Monday at 4:00 p.m. These time cards record the workers' time for the previous week. Data entry personnel might not enter this data until Tuesday. Therefore, more than a week might elapse between when the event occurred and when the data about the event was entered. In most cases when entry time is not a critical factor, the data is recorded on source documents and given to data entry personnel to enter at either a centralized or distributed location. In other applications, however, the data must be entered as the event or transaction is occurring and at the location where it is occurring. This process is sometimes called **source data collection**. For example, when a retail sale is made using a point-of-sale terminal, the data must be entered at the moment the sale is made so that the sale can be completed with the customer. Therefore, the documentation for the data entry system should specify the timing requirements for entering data.
- *How will the data be entered?* Based on many of the factors discussed in the first three questions, the procedures must specify how the data will be entered, identifying devices and methods. For example, data will be entered from source documents using terminals in an online, centralized environment.
- *How much data will be entered?* The amount of data entered for a given time period and location must be estimated. Any particularly high or low volumes may require special procedures.
- *How will data errors be identified and corrected?* The documentation must specify the editing for the entered data and the steps to take if the data is not valid. Although different applications will have specific criteria for validating input data, several tests can be performed on input data before the data is processed in a computer. Some of these tests are:
  - Tests for numeric or alphabetic data—For example, in the United States a ZIP code must always be numeric. Therefore, the program performing the editing can

check the values in the ZIP code field. If they are not numeric, the data is incorrect (Figure 3-45).

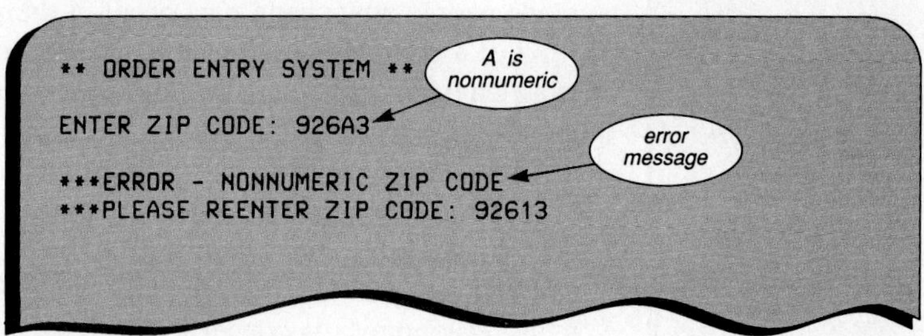

FIGURE 3-45
In this example, a nonnumeric ZIP code is entered and an error message displays. When a numeric ZIP code is entered, the data is accepted and no error message displays. An additional test could be performed to match the entry against a file of valid ZIP codes.

- Tests for data reasonableness—A reasonableness check ensures that the data entered is within normal or accepted boundaries. For example, suppose no employee within a company is authorized to work more than 80 hours per week. If the value entered in the hours worked field is greater than 80, the value in the field would be indicated as a probable error.
- Tests for data consistency—In some cases, data entered cannot, by itself, be found to be invalid. If, however, the data is examined in the context of other data entered for the same record or group of fields, discrepancies might be found. For example, in an airline reservation system, passengers often purchase round-trip tickets (Figure 3-46). If the terminal operator enters the date on which the passenger is leaving, the editing program can only check whether the date entered is valid. Similarly, when the return date is entered, the program can again make sure it is a valid date. The return date can also be compared to the departure date. If the return date is earlier than the departure date, it is likely that an error has been made when entering one of the dates.
- Tests for transcription and transposition errors—There is always a possibility that an operator will make an error when entering data. A **transcription error** occurs when an error is made in copying the values from a source document. For example, if the operator keys the customer number 7165 when the proper number is 7765, the operator has made a transcription error. A **transposition error** happens when the operator switches two numbers. Such an error has occurred when the number 7765 is entered as 7756.

- *How will data be controlled?* The controls and security that will be applied to the data must be defined. This includes what the controls and security measures are, how they are to be implemented, and what action is to be taken if the security of the data is compromised in any way.
- *How many people are needed?* Specifying personnel requirements includes defining who will gather the data, who will enter it, and how many people will be required. Personnel must be educated about gathering and entering the data. They must be trained in using the equipment and software, ensuring reliable data entry, entering the data according to specified procedures, and interpreting any output received from the computer during interactive processing.

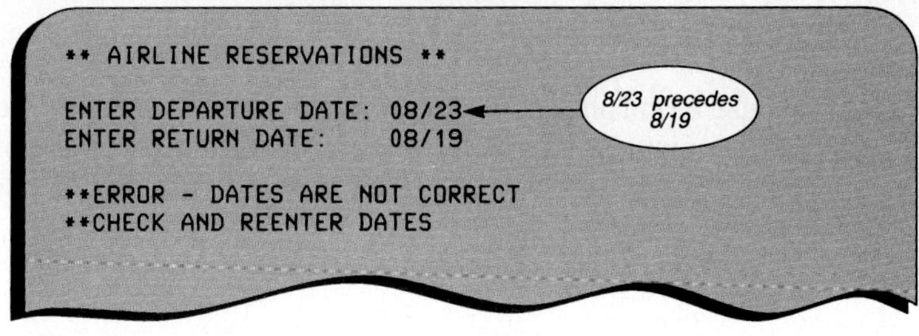

FIGURE 3-46
On this airline reservation screen, the user entered a return date earlier than the departure date and the system displayed an error message.

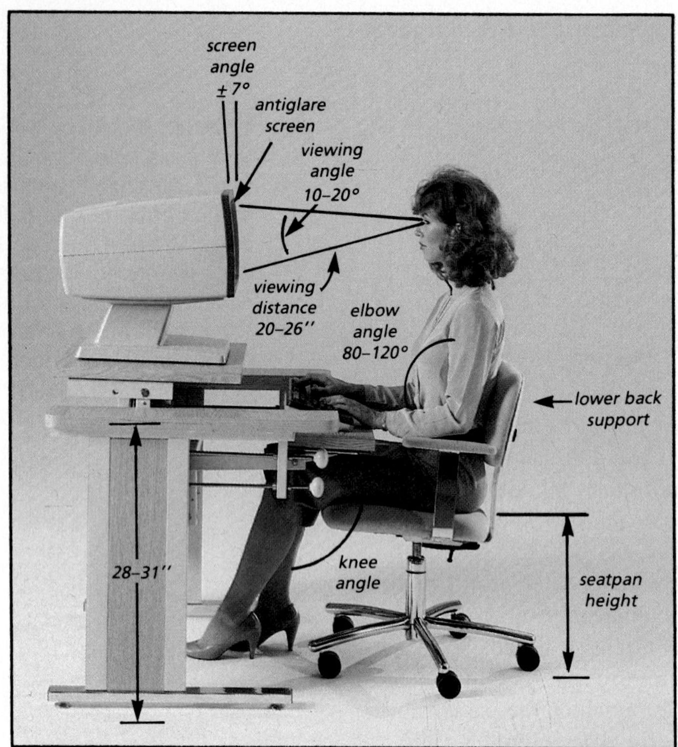

FIGURE 3-47
Here, we see some of the ergonomic factors that should be considered when using a terminal for an extended period of time.

ERGONOMICS

Because of the increased use of computers, many people now spend part or all of their day in front of a computer terminal. In order to make this work environment more comfortable, many equipment manufacturers and users have turned to ergonomics. **Ergonomics** is the study of the design and arrangement of equipment so that people will interact with the equipment in a healthy, comfortable, and efficient manner. As related to computer equipment, ergonomics is concerned with such factors as the physical design of the keyboard, screens, related hardware, computer furniture, and the manner in which people interact with this equipment.

The first computer terminals contained the keyboard and screen as a single unit. The screen frequently displayed white characters on a black background. Early studies found significant user dissatisfaction with these terminals. One study reported that many of the people who used them complained of health problems, including eye fatigue, blurred vision, itching and burning eyes, and back problems. As a result of these and other studies, a number of design recommendations have been made, including the following:

1. Computer keyboards should be detached from the screen so that they can be positioned on a desk for the convenience and comfort of the user.
2. The screen should be movable, and the angle at which the user views the contents of the screen should be adjustable.
3. The screen should be high quality to eliminate any flickering of the image and characters on the screen. The characters displayed on the screen should appear as solid as possible and the images on the screen should be in sharp focus over the entire screen area.
4. The screen should have brightness and contrast adjustments.
5. The screen should have an antiglare coating. Screen glare has been a common complaint of many terminal users, and it is known that glare can be harmful to eyes. A flat screen, now used on some terminals, can also reduce glare.
6. Terminals with screens that display amber or green characters on a black background are preferable to those that display black characters on a white background or white characters on a black background.
7. The screen and keyboard should be positioned at an appropriate height for the user.
8. Users should sit directly in front of the screen and keyboard and use an adjustable chair that has a lower-back support.

Figure 3-47 illustrates some of these recommendations. The keyboard is detachable, the screen is adjustable and has an antiglare coating. The illustration also shows the use of a chair with a lower-back support. Notice the position of the user's body in relation to the terminal.

As more workers use terminals and personal computers, the importance of ergonomically designed equipment increases. Manufacturers are now aware of the importance of ergonomic design and, as a result, are designing and building terminals and personal computers that incorporate ergonomic design for the health and comfort of users.

SUMMARY OF INPUT TO THE COMPUTER

In this chapter we presented an overview of the information processing cycle and discussed how data is organized. We also discussed the four types of input, a variety of input devices, user interfaces, data entry, and ergonomics. After reading this chapter you should have a better overall understanding of computer input.

CHAPTER SUMMARY

1. In the **information processing cycle** (input, processing, output, and storage), the input operation must take place before any data can be processed and any information produced and stored.
2. **Input** refers to the process of entering programs, commands, user responses, and data into main memory.
3. **Data** refers to the raw facts and consists of the numbers and words that a computer receives and processes to produce information.
4. Data is composed of **characters**. These include **alphabetic** (A–Z), **numeric** (0–9), and **special** characters, such as ()*&%#@,.
5. Individual facts are referred to as **data items**, **data fields**, or **fields**.
6. Fields may be classified as **numeric**, **alphabetic**, or **alphanumeric**.
7. A **record** is a collection of related fields.
8. A collection of related records is called a **file**.
9. Files on a computer are usually stored on magnetic tape or magnetic disk.
10. A **database** provides an efficient way to establish a relationship between data items and implies that a relationship has been established between multiple files.
11. A **cursor** is a symbol, such as an underline character or an arrow, that indicates where on the screen the next character entered will appear.
12. The **keyboard** is the most commonly used input device. Special keys may include the **numeric keypads**, **cursor control keys**, and **function keys**.
13. Terminals may be classified as **dumb terminals**, **intelligent terminals**, and **special-purpose terminals**.
14. A **mouse** is a small input device used to control the movement of the cursor and to select options displayed on the screen.
15. A **trackball** is a graphic pointing device like a mouse only with the ball on the top of the device instead of on the bottom.
16. **Touch screens** allow the user to interact with a computer by merely touching the screen.
17. **Light pens**, **digitizers**, and **graphics tablets** are **graphic input devices** used to translate graphic input data into a form that can be processed by the computer.
18. **Pen input devices** allow the user to input hand-printed letters and numbers to record information.
19. **Voice input** allows the user to enter data and issue commands to a computer with spoken words.
20. **Scanners** are devices that read printed codes, characters, or images and convert them into a form that can be processed by the computer.
21. A **page scanner** is an input device that can electronically capture an entire page of text or images such as photos and art work.
22. **Image processing systems** use software and special equipment, including scanners, to input and store an actual image of a source document.
23. A scanning device called a **laser scanner**, or a **bar code reader**, uses a laser beam to scan and read the special bar code printed on products.

24. **Optical character recognition (OCR)** devices are scanners that read typewritten, computer-printed, and in some cases hand-printed characters from ordinary documents.
25. An **Optical mark reader (OMR)** is a scanning device that can read carefully placed pencil marks on a specially designed form.
26. **Magnetic ink character recognition (MICR)** is a type of machine-readable data. **MICR readers**, used almost exclusively in the banking industry, are a type of input device used to process checks.
27. **Data collection devices** are designed and used for obtaining data at the site where the transaction or event being reported takes place.
28. A **user interface** is the combination of hardware and software that allows a user to communicate with a computer system.
29. A **prompt** is a message to the user that is displayed on the screen and provides information or instructions regarding some entry to be made or action to be taken.
30. **Data editing** is used to check input data for proper format and acceptable values. It helps to ensure that valid data is entered by the user.
31. A **menu** is a screen display that provides a list of processing options for the user and allows the user to make a selection. There are several types of menu-selection techniques including sequential number, alphabetic selection, cursor positioning, and reverse video.
32. **Submenus** are used to further define the processing options that are available.
33. A **graphic user interface (GUI)** uses on-screen pictures, called **icons** to represent data or processing options.
34. Features that relate to good interfaces include: system responses, screen design, user responses, error recovery, and control and security.
35. A **password** is a value, such as a word or number, which identifies the user.
36. **Interactive processing** means that data is processed immediately as it is entered.
37. In **batch processing**, data is collected and, at some later time, all the data that has been gathered is processed as a group or *batch*.
38. Data entry for interactive processing is said to be **online data entry**, meaning that the device from which the data is being entered is connected directly to the computer.
39. Data for batch processing can be entered in either an online or offline manner. **Offline data entry** means that the device from which the data is being entered is not connected to the computer that will process it.
40. Controls are the methods and procedures that ensure the accuracy and reliability of data and processing techniques. For example, balancing to a predetermined total is called a **batch control**.
41. Data entry procedures are important because accurate data must be entered into a computer to ensure data integrity.
42. **Centralized data entry** is performed by trained operators from source documents.
43. **Distributed data entry** often takes place at the site where the data is generated and is input to the computer by a variety of users.
44. **Source data collection** refers to data that is entered as the event or transaction is occurring and at the location where it is occurring.
45. Several tests can be performed on the input prior to processing. Some of these are numeric and alphabetic testing, tests for reasonableness and consistency, and transcription and transposition tests.
46. **Transcription errors** refer to operator errors made at the time of input, such as entering 7165 instead of 7665.
47. **Transposition errors** refer to operator errors where two characters are switched, such as entering 7756 instead of 7765.
48. **Ergonomics** is the study of the design and arrangement of equipment so that people will interact with the equipment in a healthy, comfortable, and efficient manner.

KEY TERMS

Alphabetic character *3.3*
Alphabetic field *3.4*
Alphanumeric field *3.4*
Arrow keys *3.5*
Bar code reader *3.13*
Batch control *3.25*
Batch processing *3.22*
Centralized data entry *3.26*
Character *3.3*
Command *3.2*
Cursor *3.5*
Cursor control keys *3.5*
Data *3.3*
Database *3.4*
Data collection device *3.16*
Data editing *3.18*
Data field *3.4*
Data item *3.4*
Digitizer *3.10*
Display terminal *3.6*
Distributed data entry *3.26*
Dumb terminal *3.6*
Ergonomics *3.28*
Field *3.4*
File *3.4*
Function keys *3.5*
Graphic input device *3.10*
Graphic user interface (GUI) *3.21*
Graphics tablet *3.10*
Icon *3.21*
Image processing system *3.12*
Input *3.2*
Intelligent terminal *3.6*
Interactive processing *3.22*
Inverse video *3.19*
Keyboard *3.5*
Laser scanner *3.13*
Light pen *3.10*
Magnetic ink character recognition (MICR) *3.15*
Menu *3.18*
MICR reader *3.15*
Mouse *3.8*
Numeric character *3.3*
Numeric field *3.4*
Numeric keypad *3.5*
Offline data entry *3.24*
Online data entry *3.22*
Optical character recognition (OCR) *3.13*
Optical mark reader (OMR) *3.14*
Page scanner *3.12*
Password *3.22*
Pen input device *3.10*
Point-of-sale (POS) terminal *3.7*
Production data entry *3.23*
Programmable terminal *3.7*
Program *3.2*
Prompt *3.18*
Record *3.4*
Reverse video *3.19*
Scanners *3.12*
Smart terminal *3.7*
Source data collection *3.26*
Special character *3.3*
Submenu *3.20*
Touch screen *3.9*
Trackball *3.9*
Transcription error *3.27*
Transposition error *3.27*
Turn-around document *3.14*
User interface *3.17*
User response *3.3*
Video display terminal (VDT) *3.6*
Voice input *3.13*

REVIEW QUESTIONS

1. List the four operations of the information processing cycle. What types and sizes of computers use the information processing cycle?
2. What is input? What are the four types of input used by a computer?
3. What is data? What terms are used to describe how data is organized for processing?
4. Describe the different types of keys on a keyboard and how they are used.
5. Name three types of terminals. Describe how they are different.
6. How is a mouse used? Describe the advantages and disadvantages of using a mouse. How is a trackball different from a mouse?
7. How does a touch screen work? What are the advantages and disadvantages of a touch screen?
8. Describe three different types of graphic input devices.
9. Describe several applications that use scanners.
10. What types of applications use data collection devices? How do they differ from other input devices?
11. What is the purpose of a user interface?
12. Describe several commonly used user interface techniques.
13. How is a graphic user interface (GUI) different from other interface techniques?
14. Name several features that a good user interface should have.
15. What are the differences between data entry for interactive and batch processing?
16. What are some of the questions that should be answered in order to implement a data entry application?
17. What is ergonomics? Describe several ergonomic features that a terminal or personal computer workplace should have.

CONTROVERSIAL ISSUES

1. Some people believe that the keyboard and the mouse are difficult to learn and use. They believe that voice and pen input systems will someday be the most widely used input devices. Discuss the advantages and disadvantages of each type of device.
2. Some local governments have passed laws regulating the work environment of people who work with terminals. The laws address such issues as proper lighting, furniture, and the amount of time that workers can spend in front of a screen. Other organizations have passed voluntary guidelines. Do you believe that such issues should be regulated?

RESEARCH PROJECTS

1. At school or a local computer store, use a program that allows the use of both function keys and a mouse. Perform several operations using only the function keys or only the mouse. Report on which method you liked best and why.
2. Visit a retail or grocery store in your area that uses laser scanners to check out the merchandise. Ask the clerks what they like and dislike about the system they use. Report back to your class. (You may need to obtain the store manager's approval.)
3. Find a document that is used for input to the computer. Examples might be school registration forms, job applications, or membership applications. Does it appear to be well designed to help both the person completing the document as well as the person who inputs the data to the computer?
4. Visit a fast food franchise that uses point-of-sale terminals. Write a report on how orders are taken, reported to the cooks, and eventually cleared from the system.

The Processor Unit

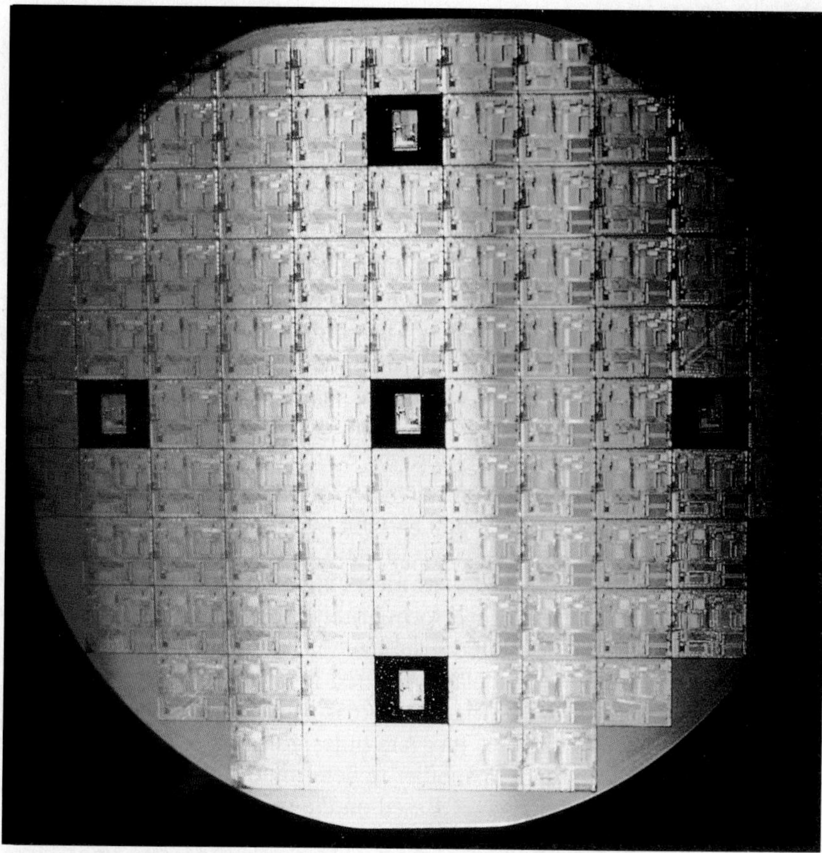

The information processing cycle consists of input, processing, output, and storage operations. When an input operation is completed and both a program and data are stored in main memory, processing operations can begin. During these operations, the processor unit executes, or performs, the program instructions and processes the data into information.

In this chapter we examine the components of the processor unit, describe how main memory stores programs and data, and discuss the sequence of operations that occurs when instructions are executed on a computer.

OBJECTIVES

- Identify the components of the processor unit and describe their use
- Define a bit and describe how a series of bits in a byte is used to represent characters
- Discuss how the ASCII and EBCDIC codes represent characters
- Describe why the binary and hexadecimal numbering systems are used with computer systems
- List and describe the four steps in a machine cycle
- Discuss the three primary factors that affect the speed of the processor unit
- Describe the characteristics of RAM and ROM memory, and list several other types of memory
- Describe the process of manufacturing integrated circuits

THE PROCESSOR UNIT

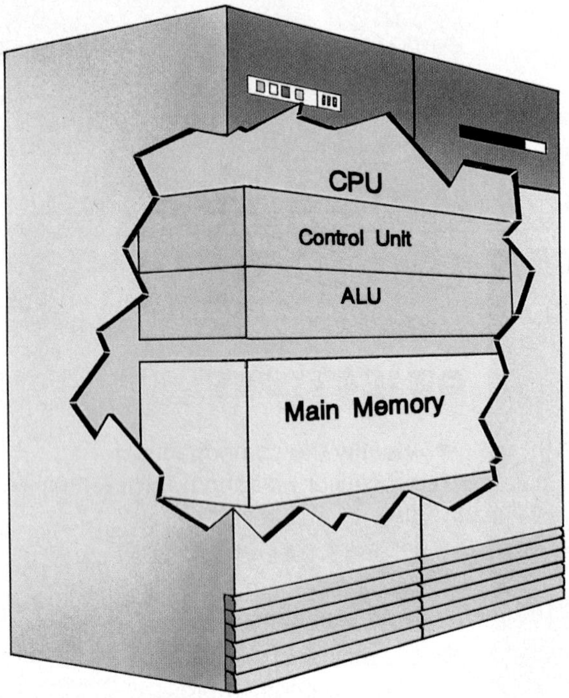

CPU

Control Unit

ALU

Main Memory

FIGURE 4-1
The processor unit of a computer contains two components: the central processing unit (CPU) and main memory. The CPU includes the control unit and the arithmetic/logic unit.

WHAT IS THE PROCESSOR UNIT?

The term computer is usually used to describe the collection of devices that perform the information processing cycle. This term is also used more specifically to describe the processor unit, because this is where the *computing* actually occurs. It is in the processor unit that the computer programs are executed and the data is manipulated. The main components of the processor unit are the central processing unit, or CPU, and the main memory (Figure 4-1).

The Central Processing Unit

The central processing unit (CPU) contains the control unit and the arithmetic/logic unit. These two components work together using the program and data stored in main memory to perform the processing operations.

The control unit can be thought of as the *brain* of the computer. Just as the human brain controls the body, the control unit *controls* the computer. The **control unit** operates by repeating the following four operations: fetching, decoding, executing, and storing. **Fetching** means obtaining the next program instruction from main memory. **Decoding** is translating the program instruction into the commands that the computer can process. **Executing** refers to the actual processing of the computer commands, and **storing** takes place when the result of the instruction is written to main memory.

The second component of the CPU is the **arithmetic/logic unit (ALU)**. This unit contains the electronic circuitry necessary to perform arithmetic and logical operations on data. **Arithmetic operations** include addition, subtraction, multiplication, and division. Often, the result of one arithmetic calculation is used in a subsequent operation. An example would be a payroll calculation where the gross pay (hours worked times pay rate) is used to calculate the payroll taxes (tax rate times gross pay). **Logical operations** consist of comparing one data item to another to determine if the first data item is *greater than*, *equal to*, or *less than* the other. Based on the result of the comparison, different processing may occur. For example, two part numbers in different records can be compared. If they are equal, the part quantity in one record can be added to the quantity in the other record. If they are not equal, the quantities would not be added.

Both the control unit and the ALU contain **registers**, temporary storage locations for specific types of data. Separate registers exist for the current program instruction, the address of the next instruction, and the values of data being processed.

Main Memory

In addition to the CPU, **main memory**, or **primary storage**, is also contained in the processor unit of the computer. Main memory (Figure 4-2) stores three items: the *operating system* that directs and coordinates the computer equipment; the *application programs* containing the instructions that will direct the work to be done; and the *data* currently being processed by the application programs. Data is stored in areas of main memory referred to as input and output areas and working storage.

The input and output areas receive and send data to the input and output devices. *Working storage* is used to store any other data that is needed for processing.

Within main memory, each storage location is called a **byte**. Just as a house on a street has a unique address that indicates its location on the street, each byte in the main memory of a computer has an address that indicates its location in memory (Figure 4-3). The number that indicates the location of a byte in memory is called a **memory address**. Whenever the computer references a byte, it does so by using the memory address, or location, of that byte.

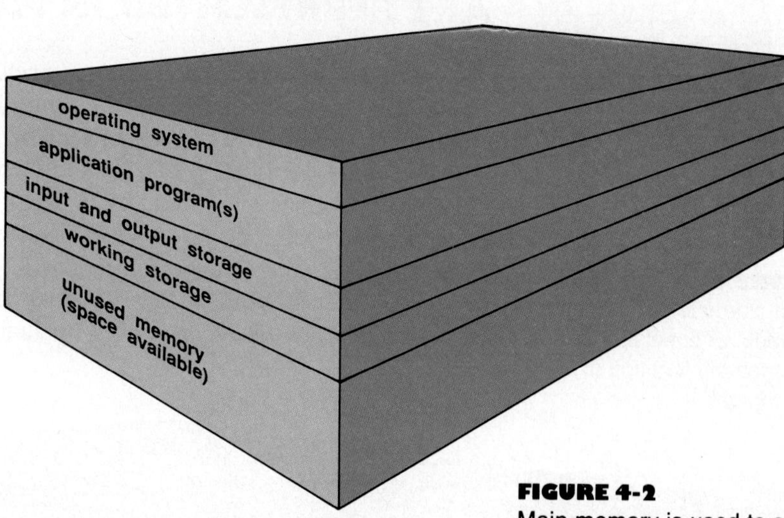

FIGURE 4-2
Main memory is used to store several types of data and programs. The amount of memory space in use changes as program instructions are executed and data is input and output.

The size of main memory is normally measured in kilobytes. A **kilobyte** (abbreviated as **K** or **KB**) is equal to 1,024 bytes. Often, memory is referred to as if a kilobyte contained only 1,000 bytes. The difference between the actual and the approximate size of memory is usually unimportant and if the exact size of memory is needed, it can be calculated by using the value 1,024. For example, 640K is approximately 640,000 bytes (640 × 1,000). The exact size of 640K is 655,360 bytes (640 × 1,024). When memory exceeds 1,000K or one million bytes, it is referred to in **megabytes**, abbreviated **MB**.

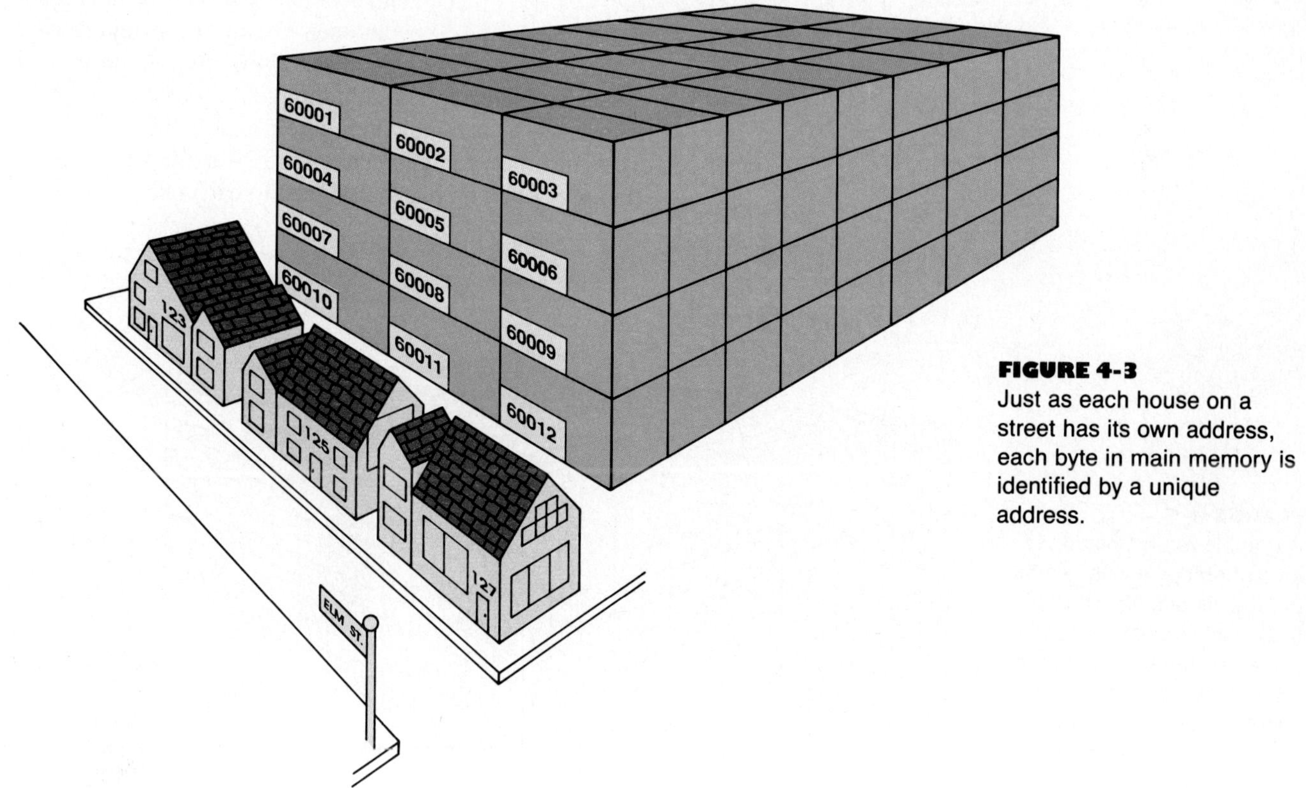

FIGURE 4-3
Just as each house on a street has its own address, each byte in main memory is identified by a unique address.

HOW PROGRAMS AND DATA ARE REPRESENTED IN MEMORY

Program instructions and data are made up of a combination of the three types of characters: alphabetic (A through Z), numeric (0 through 9) and special (all other characters such as *,?/&). To understand how program instructions and data are stored in main memory, it is helpful to think of them as being stored character by character. Generally speaking, when we think of characters being stored in main memory, we think of one character being stored in one memory location, or byte. Thus, the name TOM would take three memory locations, or bytes, because there are three letters in that name. The address 125 Elm St. would take eleven memory locations, or bytes, because it contains eleven characters (including the spaces and .) (Figure 4-4).

FIGURE 4-4
Each character (alphabetic, numeric, or special) requires one memory location (byte) for storage.

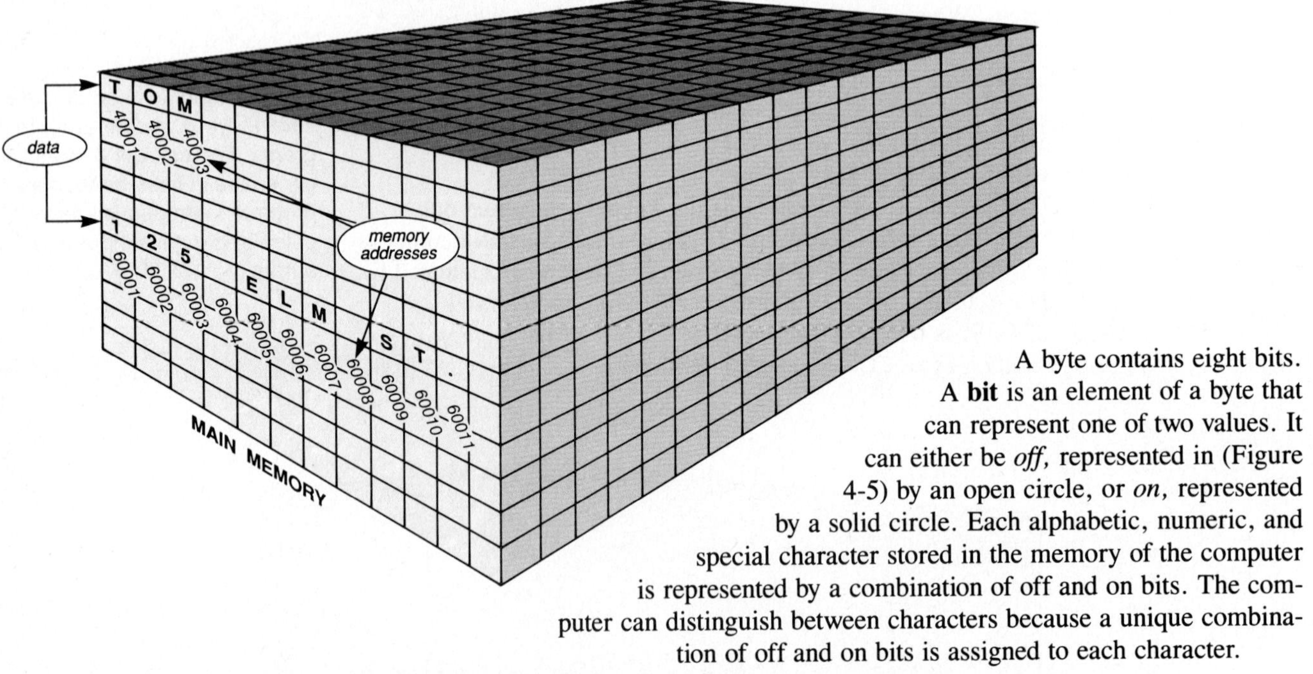

A byte contains eight bits. A **bit** is an element of a byte that can represent one of two values. It can either be *off,* represented in (Figure 4-5) by an open circle, or *on,* represented by a solid circle. Each alphabetic, numeric, and special character stored in the memory of the computer is represented by a combination of off and on bits. The computer can distinguish between characters because a unique combination of off and on bits is assigned to each character.

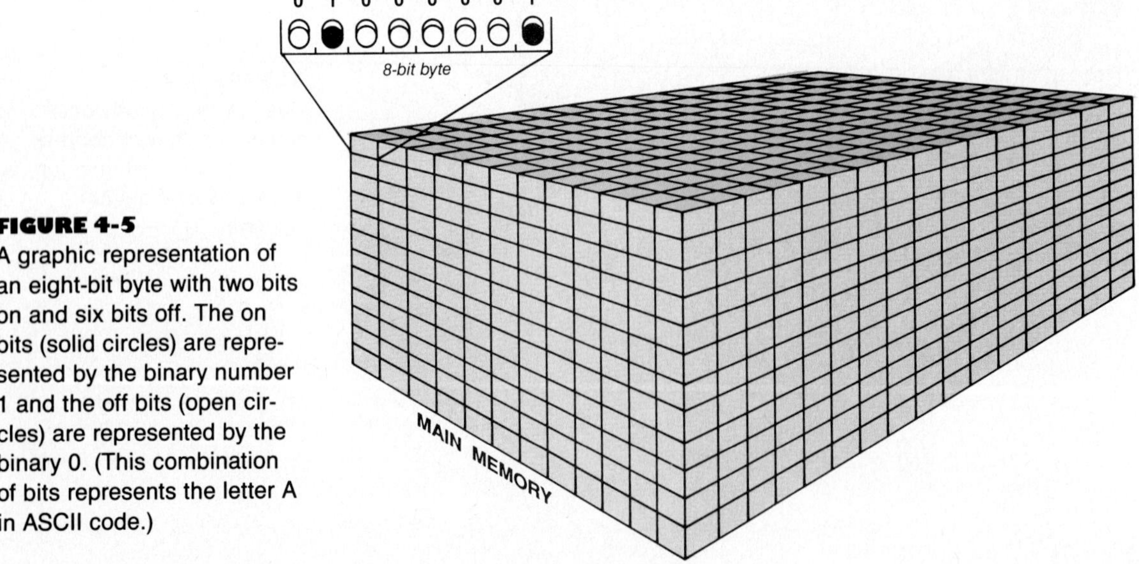

FIGURE 4-5
A graphic representation of an eight-bit byte with two bits on and six bits off. The on bits (solid circles) are represented by the binary number 1 and the off bits (open circles) are represented by the binary 0. (This combination of bits represents the letter A in ASCII code.)

A mathematical way of representing the off and on conditions of a bit is to use 0 to represent off and 1 to represent on. The **binary** number system (base 2) represents quantities by using only two symbols, 0 and 1. For this reason, binary is used to represent the electronic status of the bits inside the processor unit. The term bit was derived from the a combination of words *b*inary dig*it*.

Two popular codes that use combinations of zeros and ones to represent characters in memory and on auxiliary storage are the ASCII and EBCDIC codes. Figure 4-6 summarizes these codes. Notice how the combination of bits, represented in binary, is unique for each character.

SYMBOL	ASCII	EBCDIC	SYMBOL	ASCII	EBCDIC	SYMBOL	ASCII	EBCDIC
(space)	0100000	01000000	?	0111111	01101111	^	1011110	
!	0100001	01011010	@	1000000	01111100	_	1011111	
"	0100010	01111111	A	1000001	11000001	a	1100001	10000001
#	0100011	01111011	B	1000010	11000010	b	1100010	10000010
$	0100100	01011011	C	1000011	11000011	c	1100011	10000011
%	0100101	01101100	D	1000100	11000100	d	1100100	10000100
&	0100110	01010000	E	1000101	11000101	e	1100101	10000101
'	0100111	01111101	F	1000110	11000110	f	1100110	10000110
(	0101000	01001101	G	1000111	11000111	g	1100111	10000111
)	0101001	01011101	H	1001000	11001000	h	1101000	10001000
*	0101010	01011100	I	1001001	11001001	i	1101001	10001001
+	0101011	01001110	J	1001010	11010001	j	1101010	10010001
,	0101100	01101011	K	1001011	11010010	k	1101011	10010010
–	0101101	01100000	L	1001100	11010011	l	1101100	10010011
.	0101110	01001011	M	1001101	11010100	m	1101101	10010100
/	0101111	01100001	N	1001110	11010101	n	1101110	10010101
0	0110000	11110000	O	1001111	11010110	o	1101111	10010110
1	0110001	11110001	P	1010000	11010111	p	1110000	10010111
2	0110010	11110010	Q	1010001	11011000	q	1110001	10011000
3	0110011	11110011	R	1010010	11011001	r	1110010	10011001
4	0110100	11110100	S	1010011	11100010	s	1110011	10100010
5	0110101	11110101	T	1010100	11100011	t	1110100	10100011
6	0110110	11110110	U	1010101	11100100	u	1110101	10100100
7	0110111	11110111	V	1010110	11100101	v	1110110	10100101
8	0111000	11111000	W	1010111	11100110	w	1110111	10100110
9	0111001	11111001	X	1011000	11100111	x	1111000	10100111
:	0111010	01111010	Y	1011001	11101000	y	1111001	10101000
;	0111011	01011110	Z	1011010	11101001	z	1111010	10101001
<	0111100	01001100	[	1011011	01001010	{	1111011	
=	0111101	01111110	\	1011100		}	1111101	
>	0111110	01101110	]	1011101	01011010			

FIGURE 4-6
This chart shows alphabetic, numeric, and special characters as they are represented in the ASCII and EBCDIC codes. Each character is represented in binary using a unique ordering of zeros and ones.

The ASCII Code

The **American Standard Code for Information Interchange**, called **ASCII** (pronounced ask-ee), is the most widely used coding system to represent data. Figure 4-7 illustrates the letter A stored in an eight-bit byte in main memory using the ASCII code. When you type the letter A on the keyboard, the electronic circuitry of the computer interprets the character and stores it in main memory as a series of off and on bits. When the character A appears on the screen or is printed, the ASCII code is converted back into the alphabetic symbol A.

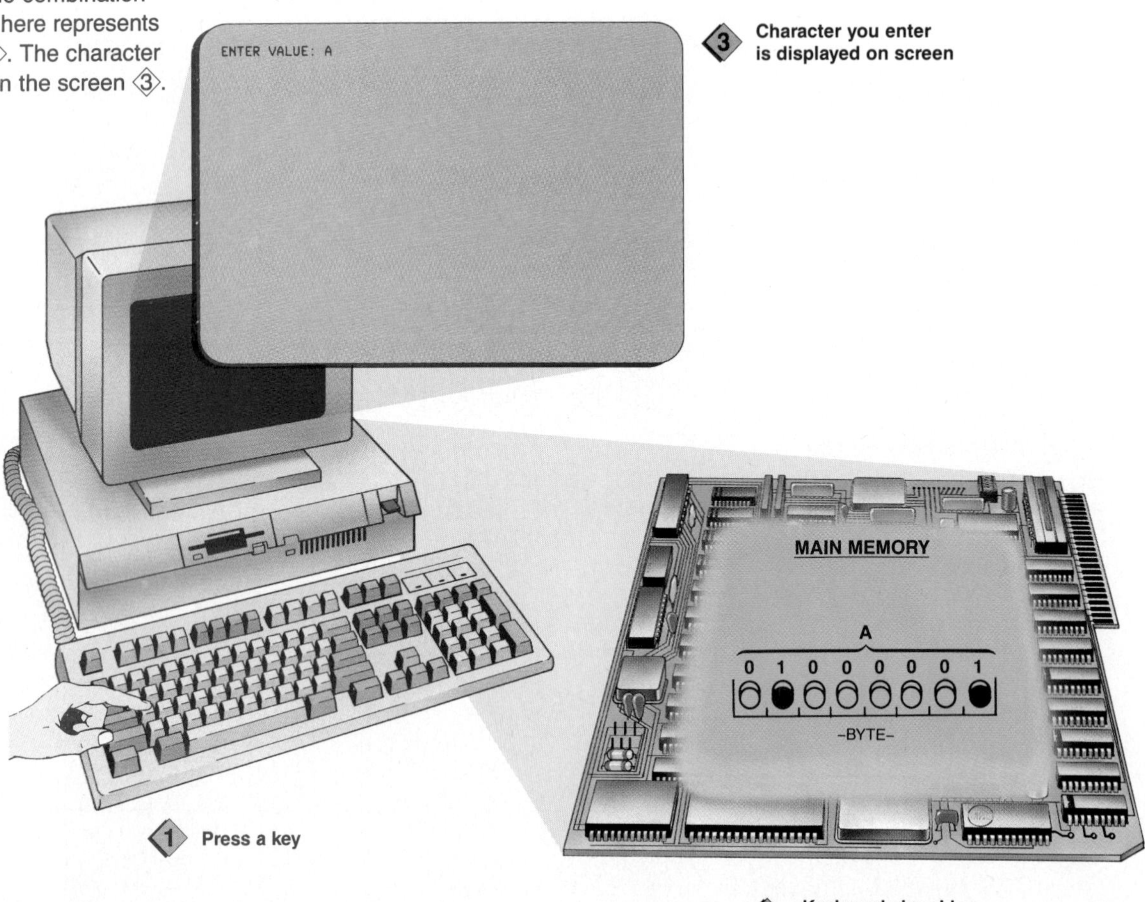
ENTER VALUE: A
3 Character you enter is displayed on screen
MAIN MEMORY
A
0 1 0 0 0 0 0 1
-BYTE-
1 Press a key
2 Keyboard signal is converted to character

FIGURE 4-7
Pressing the letter A key on the keyboard sends an electronic signal to the computer ①. Computer circuts convert the signal into a particular combination of bits that are on and off. The combination of bits shown here represents the letter A ②. The character is displayed on the screen ③.

As you can see by looking at Figure 4-6, the ASCII code uses only the rightmost seven bits of the eight bits in a byte to represent characters. These seven bits provide 128 orderings of zeros and ones, enough to represent all the standard characters including numeric, uppercase and lowercase alphabetic, and special. An extended version of the ASCII code has been developed that allows certain foreign alphabetic letters and additional special characters to be stored. This extended version makes use of the eighth bit.

The EBCDIC Code

The ASCII code is widely used on personal computers and many minicomputers. Another common coding scheme used primarily on mainframes is called the **Extended Binary Coded Decimal Interchange Code**, or **EBCDIC** (pronounced eb-see-dick).

Binary Representation of Numbers

When the ASCII or EBCDIC code is used, each character that is represented is stored in one byte of memory. There are other binary formats, however, that the computer sometimes uses to represent numeric data. For example, a computer may store, or *pack* two numeric characters in one byte of memory. These binary formats are used by the computer to increase storage and processing efficiency.

FIGURE 4-8
In a computer with odd parity, the parity bit is turned on or off in order to make the total number of on bits (including the parity bit) an odd number. Here, the letters T and O have an odd number of bits and the parity bit is left off. However, the number of bits for the letter M is even, so in order to achieve odd parity, the parity bit is turned on. Turning on the parity bit makes the total number of bits in the byte an odd number (five).

PARITY

◆ Regardless of whether ASCII, EBCDIC, or other binary methods are used to represent characters in main memory, it is important that the characters be stored accurately. For each byte of memory, most computers have at least one extra bit, called a **parity bit**, that is used by the computer for error checking. A parity bit can detect if one of the bits in a byte has been inadvertently changed. Such an error could occur because of voltage fluctuations, static electricity, or a memory chip failure.

T O M

parity T 3 bits on parity off

parity O 5 bits on parity off

parity M 4 bits on parity on

Computers are either odd or even parity machines. In computers with **odd parity**, the total number of *on* bits in the byte (including the parity bit) must be an odd number (Figure 4-8). In computers with **even parity**, the total number of on bits must be an even number. Parity is checked by the computer each time a memory location is used. When data is moved from one location to another in main memory, the parity bits of both the sending and receiving locations are compared to see if they are the same. If the system detects a difference or if the wrong number of bits is on (e.g., an even number in a system with odd parity), an error message displays. Some computers use multiple parity bits that enable them to detect and correct a single-bit error and detect multiple-bit errors.

FIGURE 4-9
The chart shows the binary and hexadecimal representation of decimal numbers 0 through 15. Notice how letters represent the numbers 10 through 15.

DECIMAL	BINARY	HEXADECIMAL
0	0000	0
1	0001	1
2	0010	2
3	0011	3
4	0100	4
5	0101	5
6	0110	6
7	0111	7
8	1000	8
9	1001	9
10	1010	A
11	1011	B
12	1100	C
13	1101	D
14	1110	E
15	1111	F

NUMBER SYSTEMS

◆ This section describes the number systems that are used with computers. Whereas thorough knowledge of this subject is required for technical computer personnel, a general understanding of number systems and how they relate to computers is all most users need.

As you have seen, the binary (base 2) number system is used to represent the electronic status of the bits in main memory. It is also used for other purposes such as addressing the memory locations. Another number system that is commonly used with computers is **hexadecimal** (base 16). Figure 4-9 shows how the decimal values 0 through 15 are represented in binary and hexadecimal.

The mathematical principles that apply to the binary and hexadecimal number systems are the same as those that apply to the decimal number system. To help you better understand these principles, we will start with the familiar decimal system, then progress to the binary and hexadecimal number systems.

The Decimal Number System

The decimal number system is a base 10 number system (*deci* means ten). The *base* of a number system indicates how many symbols are used in it. Decimal uses 10 symbols, 0 through 9. Each of the symbols in the number system has a value associated with it. For example, you know that 3 represents a quantity of three and 5 represents a quantity of five. The decimal number system is also a *positional* number system. This means that in a number such as 143, each position in the number has a value associated with it. When you look at the decimal number 143, you know that the 3 is in the ones, or units, position and represents three ones or (3 × 1); the 4 is in the tens position and represents four tens or (4 × 10); and the 1 is in the hundreds position and represents one hundred or (1 × 100). The number 143 is the sum of the values in each position of the number (100 + 40 + 3 = 143). The chart in Figure 4-10 shows how the positional values (hundreds, tens, and units) for a number system can be calculated. Starting on the right and working to the left, we raise the base of the number system, in this case 10, to consecutive powers (10^2, 10^1, 10^0). These calculations are a mathematical way of determining the place values in a number system.

FIGURE 4-10
This chart shows the positional values in the decimal number 143.

power of 10	10^2	10^1	10^0
positional value	100	10	1
number	1	4	3

$$(1 \times 10^2) + (4 \times 10^1) + (3 \times 10^0) =$$
$$(1 \times 100) + (4 \times 10) + (3 \times 1) =$$
$$100 + 40 + 3 = 143$$

When you use number systems other than decimal, the same principles apply. The base of the number system indicates the number of symbols that are used, and each position in a number system has a value associated with it. The positional value can be calculated by raising the base of the number system to consecutive powers beginning with zero.

The Binary Number System

As we have discussed, binary is a base 2 number system (*bi* means two), and the symbols that are used are 0 and 1. Just as each position in a decimal number has a place value associated with it, so does each position in a binary number. In binary, the place values are successive powers of two (2^3, 2^2, 2^1, 2^0) or (8 4 2 1). To construct a binary number, you place ones in the positions where the corresponding values add up to the quantity you want to represent; you place zeros in the other positions. For example, the binary place values are 8, 4, 2, and 1, and the binary number 1001 has ones in the positions for the values 8 and 1 and zeros in the positions for 4 and 2. Therefore, the quantity represented by binary 1001 is 9 (8 + 0 + 0 + 1) (Figure 4-11).

power of 2	2^3	2^2	2^1	2^0
positional value	8	4	2	1
binary	1	0	0	1

$$(1 \times 2^3) + (0 \times 2^2) + (0 \times 2^1) + (1 \times 2^0) =$$
$$(1 \times 8) + (0 \times 4) + (0 \times 2) + (1 \times 1) =$$
$$8 + 0 + 0 + 1 = 9$$

FIGURE 4-11
This chart shows how to convert the binary number 1001 to the decimal number 9. Each place in the binary number represents a successive power of 2.

The Hexadecimal Number System

Many computers use a base 16 number system called hexadecimal. The hexadecimal number system uses 16 symbols to represent values. These include the symbols 0 through 9 and A through F (Figure 4-9). The mathematical principles we previously discussed also apply to hexadecimal (Figure 4-12).

power of 16	16^1	16^0
positional value	16	1
hexadecimal	A	5

$$(10 \times 16^1) + (5 \times 16^0) =$$
$$(10 \times 16) + (5 \times 1) =$$
$$160 + 5 = 165$$

FIGURE 4-12
This chart shows how the hexadecimal number A5 is converted into the decimal number 165. Notice that the value 10 is substituted for the A during calculations.

The primary reason why the hexadecimal number system is used with computers is because it can represent binary values in a more compact form and because the conversion between the binary and the hexadecimal number systems is very efficient. An eight-digit binary number can be represented by a two-digit hexadecimal number. For example, in the EBCDIC code, the decimal number 5 is represented as 11110101. This value can be represented in hexadecimal as F5.

One way to convert a binary number to a hexadecimal number is to divide the binary number (from right to left) into groups of four digits; calculate the value of each group; and then change any two-digit values (10 through 15) into the symbols A through F that are used in hexadecimal (Figure 4-13).

positional value	**8421**	**8421**
binary	1111	0101
decimal	15	5
hexadecimal	F	5

FIGURE 4-13
This chart shows how the EBCDIC code 11110101 for the value 5 is converted into the hexadecimal value F5. Each group of four binary digits is converted to a hexidecimal symbol.

Summary of Number Systems

As we mentioned at the beginning of the section on number systems, binary and hexadecimal are used primarily by technical computer personnel. A general user does not need a complete understanding of numbering systems. The concepts that you should remember about number systems are that binary is used to represent the electronic status of the bits in main memory and auxiliary storage. Hexadecimal is used to represent binary in a more compact form.

HOW THE PROCESSOR UNIT EXECUTES PROGRAMS AND MANIPULATES DATA

The program instructions that users write are usually in a form similar to English. Before these instructions can be executed, they must be translated by the computer into a form called machine language instructions. A **machine language instruction** is one that the electronic circuits in the CPU can interpret and convert into one or more of the commands in the computer's instruction set. The **instruction set** contains commands, such as ADD or MOVE, that the computer's circuits can directly perform. To help you understand how the processor unit works, let's look at an example of a machine language instruction.

Machine Language Instructions

FIGURE 4-14
A machine language instruction consists of an operation code, the lengths of the field to be processed, and the main memory addresses of the field.

A machine language instruction is usually composed of three parts: an operation code; values that indicate the number of characters to be processed by the instruction; and the addresses in main memory of the data to be used in the execution of the instruction (Figure 4-14).

The **operation code** is a unique value that is typically stored in the first byte in the instruction. This unique value indicates which operation is to be performed. For example, the letter A stored as the operation code might mean *addition*. The letter M might mean *move*.

The number of characters to be processed is included in the machine language instruction so the CPU will manipulate the proper number of bytes. For example, if a four-digit field were to be added to another four-digit field, the number of characters specified in the instruction for each field would be four. The main memory addresses of the fields involved in the operation are also specified in the instruction. This specification of the main memory address enables the CPU to locate where in main memory the data to be processed is stored. The steps involved in executing a computer instruction are illustrated in Figure 4-15. The instruction A44 7000 9000 indicates that the four-digit fields that begin in locations 7000 and 9000 are to be added together. When this instruction is executed, the following steps occur:

1. The instruction is fetched from main memory and placed in an instruction register. An **instruction register** is an area of memory within the control unit of the CPU that can store a single instruction at a time.
2. The control unit decodes the instruction, and then fetches the data specified by the two addresses in the instruction from main memory.
3. The arithmetic/logic unit executes the instruction by adding the two numbers.
4. The control unit then stores the result of the processing by moving the sum to main memory. This basic sequence of fetch the instruction, decode the instruction, execute the instruction, and store the results, is the way most computers process instructions.

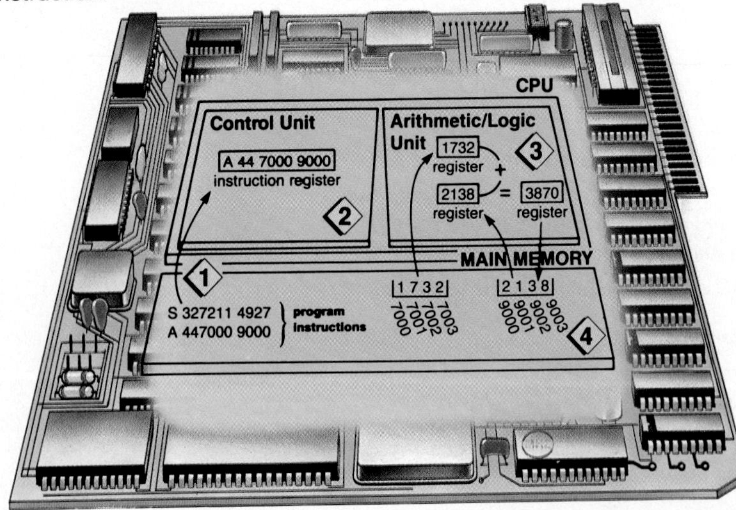

FIGURE 4-15
The four steps involved in executing a program instruction.

The Machine Cycle

These four steps—fetch, decode, execute, and store—are called the **machine cycle**. As shown in Figure 4-16, the machine cycle is made up of the instruction cycle and the execution cycle. The **instruction cycle** refers to the fetching of the next program instruction and the decoding of that instruction. The **execution cycle** includes the execution of the instruction and the storage of the processing results. One machine cycle is completed when the computer is again ready to fetch the next program instruction.

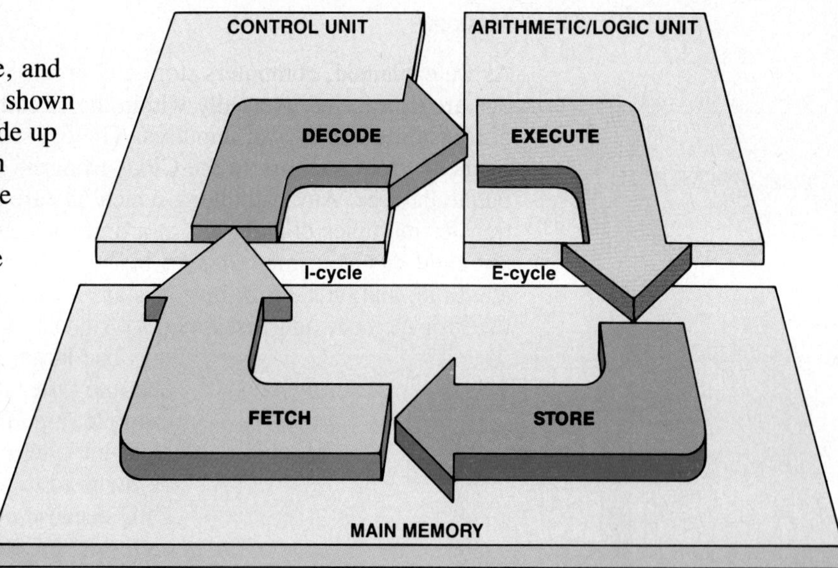

FIGURE 4-16
The machine cycle consists of four steps: fetching the next instruction, decoding the instruction, executing the instruction, and storing the result. Fetching and decoding are part of the instruction, or I-cycle. Executing and storing are part of the execution, or E-cycle.

PROCESSOR SPEEDS

Although the machine cycle may appear to be cumbersome and time consuming, computers can perform millions of machine cycles in one second. In fact, the processing speed of computers is often measured in **MIPS**—million instructions per second. A computer with a rating of 1 MIPS can process one million instructions per second. The most powerful personal computers today are rated at between 10 and 15 MIPS. Larger computers can process 75 to 100 MIPS and supercomputers are capable of over 200 MIPS. The speed at which a computer can execute the machine cycle is influenced by three factors: the system clock, the buses, and the word size (Figure 4-17).

FACTOR	AFFECT ON SPEED
System clock	The system clock generates electronic pulses used to synchronize processing. Faster clock speed results in more operations in a given amount of time.
Bus width	Bus width determines how much data can be transferred at any one time. A 32-bit bus can transfer twice as much data at one time as a 16-bit bus.
Word size	Word size is the number of bits that can be manipulated at any one time. A computer with a 32-bit word size can manipulate twice as much data at one time as a system with a 16-bit word size.

FIGURE 4-17
Factors affecting computer speed.

System Clock

The control unit utilizes the **system clock** to synchronize, or control the timing of, all computer operations. The system clock generates electronic pulses at a fixed rate, measured in **megahertz**. One megahertz equals one million pulses per second. The speed of the system clock varies among computers. Some personal computers can operate at speeds in excess of 30 megahertz.

Buses

As we explained, computers store and process data as a series of electronic bits. These bits are transferred internally within the circuitry of the computer along paths capable of transmitting electrical impulses. The bits must be transferred from input devices to memory, from memory to the CPU, from the CPU to memory, and from memory to output devices. Any path along which bits are transmitted is called a **bus**. Buses can transfer multiples of eight bits at a time. An eight-bit bus has eight lines and can transmit eight bits at a time. On a 16-bit bus, bits can be moved from place to place 16 bits at a time, and on a 32-bit bus, bits are moved 32 bits at a time. Separate buses are used for memory addresses, control signals, and data (Figure 4-18).

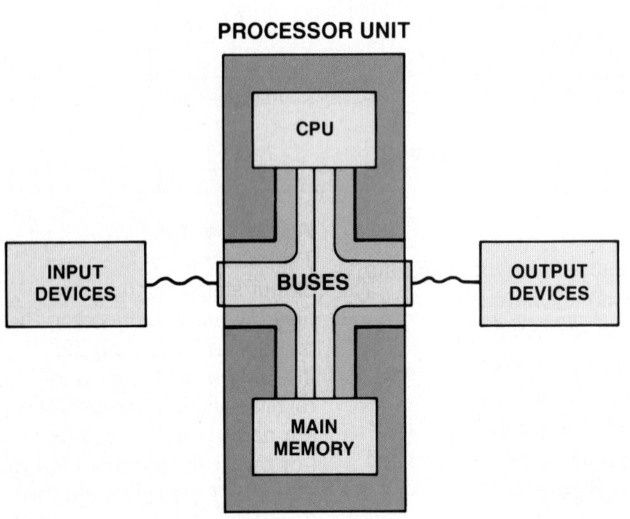

FIGURE 4-18
Data is transmitted between computer components via electrical pathways called buses. Separate buses exist for memory addresses, control signals, and data. Input and output devices are connected to the buses by electrical cables.

The larger the number of bits that are handled by a bus, the faster the computer can transfer data. For example, assume a number in memory occupies four eight-bit bytes. With an eight-bit bus, four steps would be required to transfer the data from memory to the CPU because on the eight-bit bus, the data in each eight-bit byte would be transferred in an individual step. A 16-bit bus has 16 lines in the bus, so only two transfers would be necessary to move the data in four bytes. And on a 32-bit bus, the entire four bytes could be transferred at one time. The fewer number of transfer steps required, the faster the transfer of data occurs.

Word Size

Another factor that affects the speed of a computer is the word size. The **word size** is the number of bits that the CPU can *process* at one time, as opposed to the bus size, which is the number of bits the computer can *transmit* at one time. Like a bus, the word size of a machine is measured in bits. Processors can have 8-bit, 16-bit, 32-bit, or 64-bit word sizes. A processor with an eight-bit word size can manipulate eight bits at a time. If two four-digit numbers are to be added in the ALU of an eight-bit processor, it will take four operations because a separate operation will be required to add each of the four digits. With a 16-bit processor, the addition will take two operations; with a 32-bit processor, only one operation would be required to add the numbers together. Sometimes the word size of a computer is given in bytes instead of bits. For example, a word size of 16 bits may be expressed as a word size of two bytes because there are eight bits in a byte. The larger the word size of the processor, the faster the capability of the computer to process data.

In summary, the speed of a computer is influenced by the system clock, the size of the buses, and the word size. When you purchase a computer, the speed requirements you want should be based on your intended use of the computer. Sixteen-bit computers are widely used today for applications such as word processing, electronic spreadsheets, or database. Thirty-two-bit computers are considered powerful and are useful for applications that require complex and time-consuming calculations such as graphics. The more powerful personal computers, many minicomputers, and most mainframes are 32-bit computers. Most supercomputers are 64-bit computers.

ARCHITECTURE OF PROCESSOR UNITS

The processor unit of a computer can be designed and built in many different ways. For example, the processor for a personal computer may be housed on a single printed circuit board while a larger machine may require a number of circuit boards for the CPU, main memory, and the related electronic circuitry.

Microprocessors

The smallest processor, called a **microprocessor** (Figure 4-19), is a single integrated circuit that contains the CPU and sometimes memory. An **integrated circuit**, also called an **IC**, **chip**, or **microchip**, is a complete electronic circuit that has been etched on a small chip of nonconducting material such as silicon. Microcomputers are built using microprocessors for their CPU.

Figure 4-20 shows the location of the microprocessor chip in the main circuit board, called a **motherboard**, of a personal computer. Some of the microprocessors commonly used in personal computers today are listed on the next page in Figure 4-21.

FIGURE 4-19
The Intel 80486 microprocessor has a word size and bus width of 32 bits and can operate at between 25 and 33 megahertz.

FIGURE 4-20
The main circuit board (motherboard) of an IBM PS/2 personal computer. The microprocessor is shown in the lower left corner.

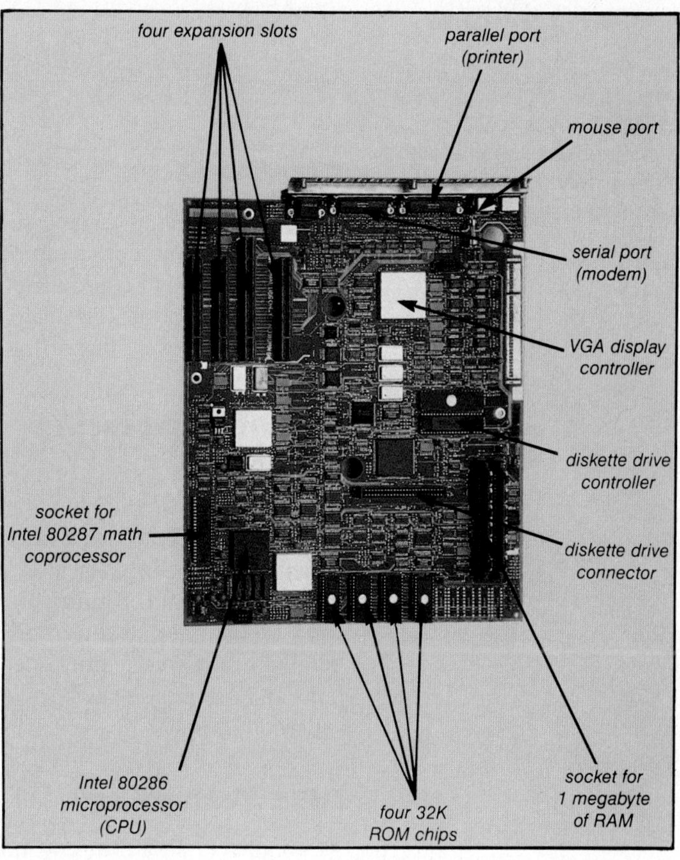

MICROPROCESSOR	MANUFACTURER	WORD SIZE (BITS)	I/O BUS WIDTH (BITS)	CLOCK SPEED (MHz)	MICROCOMPUTERS USING THIS CHIP
6502	MOS Technology	8	8	4	Apple IIe Atari 800
8088	Intel	16	8	8	IBM PC and XT HP 150 Compaq Portable
8086	Intel	16	16	8	Compaq Deskpro Many IBM compatibles
80286	Intel	16	16	8–12	IBM PC/AT Compaq Deskpro 286
68000	Motorola	32	16	12–20	Apple Macintosh SE Commodore Amiga
68020	Motorola	32	32	12–33	Apple Macintosh II
80386	Intel	32	32	16–33	Compaq Deskpro 386 IBM PS/2
68030	Motorola	32	32	16–40	Apple Macintosh SE/30 Apple Macintosh IIfx
68040	Motorola	32	32	25–33	Engineering Workstations
80486	Intel	32	32	25–33	IBM PS/2 Model 70 Compaq Systempro

FIGURE 4-21
A comparison of some of the more widely used microprocessor chips.

Coprocessors

One way computers can increase their productivity is through the use of a **coprocessor**, a special microprocessor chip or circuit board designed to perform a specific task. For example, math coprocessors are commonly added to computers to greatly speed up the processing of numeric calculations. Other types of coprocessors extend the capability of a computer by increasing the amount of software that will run on the computer.

Parallel Processing

Most computers contain one central processing unit (CPU) that processes a single instruction at a time. When one instruction is finished, the CPU begins execution of the next instruction, and so on until the program is completed. This method is known as **serial processing**. **Parallel processing** involves the use of multiple CPUs, each with their own memory. Parallel processors divide up a problem so that multiple CPUs can work on their assigned portion of the problem simultaneously. As you might expect, parallel processors require special software that can recognize how to divide up problems and bring the results back together again. Parallel processors are often used in supercomputers.

RISC Technology

As computers have evolved, more and more commands have been added to hardware instruction sets. In recent years, however, computer designers have reevaluated the need for so many instructions and have developed systems based on RISC technology.

RISC, which stands for reduced instruction set computing (or computers), involves reducing the instructions to only those that are most frequently used. Without the burden of the occasionally used instructions, the most frequently used instructions operate faster and overall processing capability, or throughput, of the system is increased (Figure 4-22).

In summary, you can see that computers have many different types of processor architecture. Regardless of the architecture used, the important concept to remember is that the processor units on all computers perform essentially the same functions.

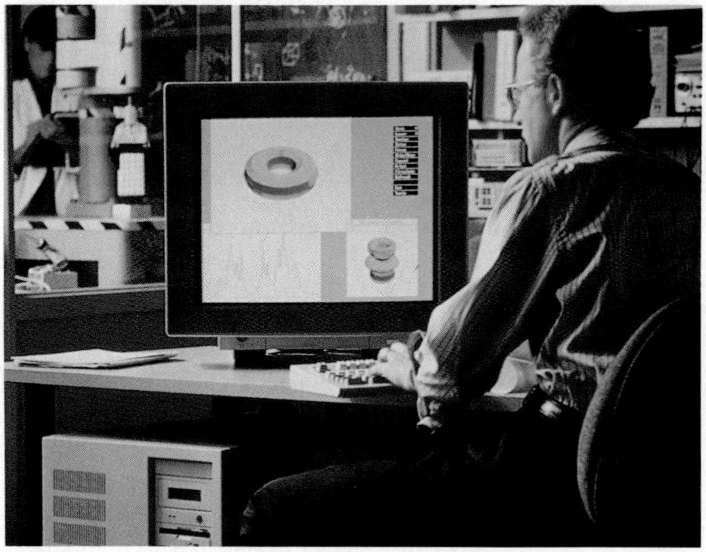

FIGURE 4-22
This IBM computer uses reduced instruction set computer (RISC) technology to obtain performance of over 27 million instructions per second. This level of processing power is best used in applications that require numerous calculations such as computer-aided design (CAD).

TYPES OF MEMORY

◆ Recall that electronic components are used to store data in computer memory. The actual materials and devices used for memory have changed throughout the years. The first device used for storing data was the vacuum tube. After the vacuum tube, core memory was used. **Core memory** consisted of small, ring-shaped pieces of material that could be magnetized, or polarized, in one of two directions. The polarity indicated whether the core was on or off. Today, semiconductor memory is used in virtually all computers (Figure 4-23). **Semiconductor memory** is an integrated circuit containing thousands of transistors. A **transistor** is an electronic component that can be either on or off and represents a bit in memory.

When core memory was used as main memory, the time required to access data stored in the memory was measured in microseconds. A **microsecond** is one millionth of a second. Access to data stored in semiconductor memory is measured in nanoseconds. A **nanosecond** is one billionth of a second. In addition, the cost of semiconductor memory is just a fraction of the cost for core memory. Figure 4-24 shows how the storage capacity of semiconductor memory has increased over recent years, while the cost of semiconductor memory has decreased. The trend is expected to continue.

FIGURE 4-23
This semiconductor memory chip can store one million bits of information. Memory chips that can store up to 64 million bits are also available.

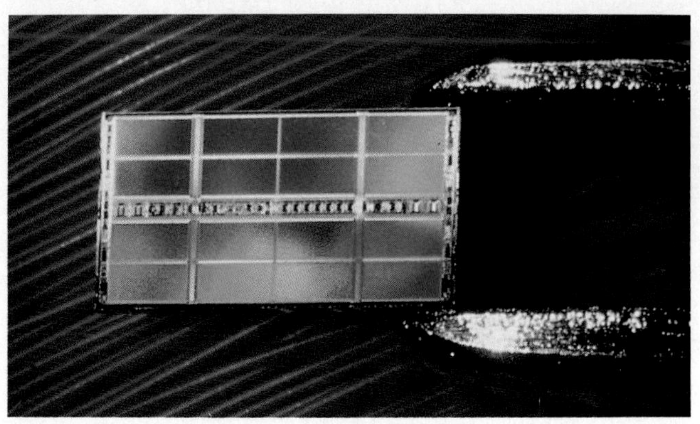

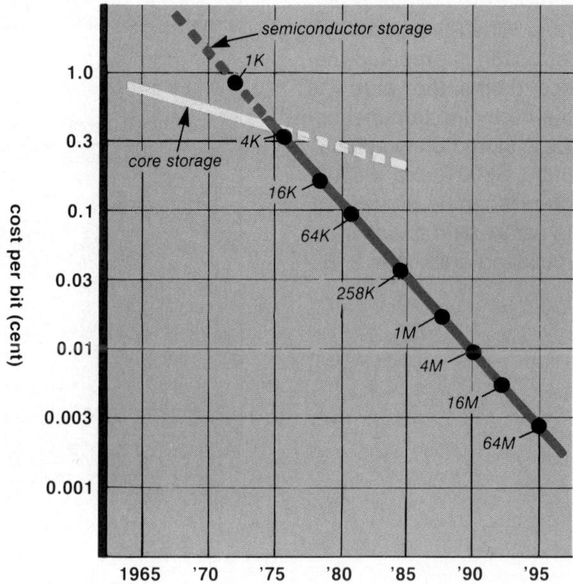

FIGURE 4-24
The declining cost and increased storage capacity of semiconductor storage are shown here.

Chip manufacturers say that by the end of the century it will be possible to store over a billion components on a chip. As you can see, semiconductor memory is compact, fast, and inexpensive. Several different types of semiconductor memory chips are used in computers. They are RAM, ROM, PROM, EPROM, and EEPROM chips.

RAM Memory

Random access memory, or **RAM**, is the name given to the integrated circuits, or chips, that are used for main memory. This is the type of memory we have discussed so far in this chapter. Data and programs are transferred into and out of RAM, and data stored in RAM is manipulated by computer program instructions.

There are two types of RAM memory chips: dynamic RAM and static RAM. **Dynamic RAM (DRAM)** chips are smaller and simpler in design than static RAM chips. With dynamic RAM, the current, or charge, on the chip is periodically regenerated by special regenerator circuits, which allow the chip to retain the stored data. **Static RAM** chips are larger and more complicated than dynamic RAM and do not require the current to be periodically regenerated. The main memory of most computers uses dynamic RAM chips.

Figure 4-25 illustrates the processing that could occur as a series of area codes are entered into RAM (computer memory) from a terminal. The first area code, 212, is entered from the keyboard and stored at memory locations 66000, 66001, and 66002. Once in memory, this field can be processed as it is required.

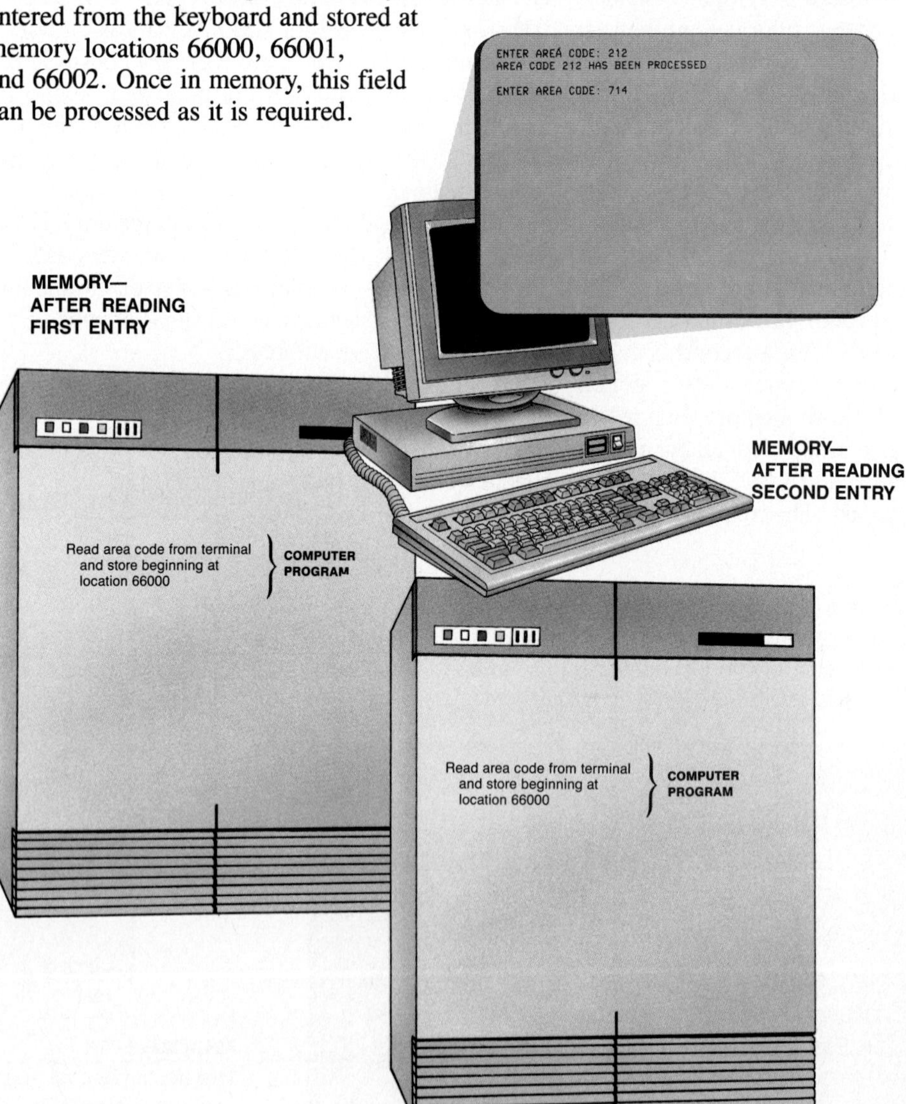
ENTER AREA CODE: 212
AREA CODE 212 HAS BEEN PROCESSED
ENTER AREA CODE: 714
MEMORY—
AFTER READING
FIRST ENTRY
Read area code from terminal and store beginning at location 66000
COMPUTER PROGRAM
MEMORY—
AFTER READING
SECOND ENTRY
Read area code from terminal and store beginning at location 66000
COMPUTER PROGRAM

FIGURE 4-25
The instruction in the program specifies that the telephone area code is to be read into adjacent memory locations beginning with location 66000. After the data is placed in the locations, it can be processed by the program. When the same instruction is executed the second time, the value 714 entered by the terminal operator is stored on locations 66000, 66001, and 66002, where it can be processed by the same instructions that processed area code 212.

When the instruction to read (input) data into memory from the keyboard is executed again, the second area code entered from the keyboard, area code 714, would replace the previous value (212) at locations 66000, 66001, and 66002 in memory. Area code 714 could then be processed by the same instructions that processed area code 212.

Some computers improve their processing efficiency by using a limited amount of high-speed RAM memory between the CPU and main memory (Figure 4-26). High-speed memory used in this manner is called **cache memory** (pronounced cash). When the processor needs the next program instruction or data, it first checks the cache memory. If the required instruction or data is present in cache, the processor will execute faster than if the instruction or data had to be retrieved from the slower main memory. Cache memory is used to store the most frequently used instructions and data.

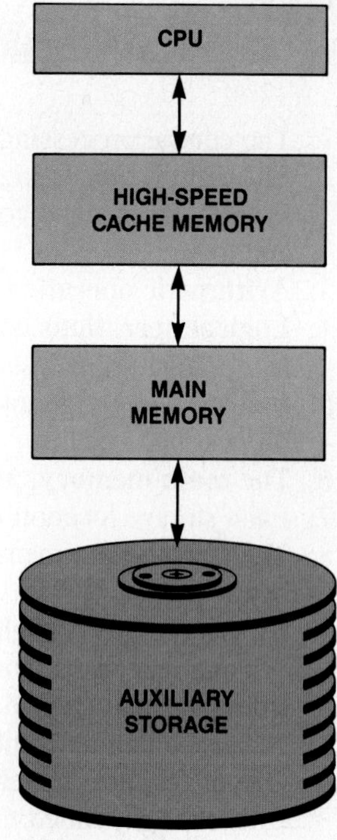

FIGURE 4-26
Some computers use an area of high-speed RAM memory, called cache memory, between the CPU and main memory. If the required data or instruction is found in cache, a program will run faster than if the information has to be retrieved from main memory or auxiliary storage.

RAM memory is said to be **volatile** because the programs and data stored in RAM are erased when the power to the computer is turned off. As long as the power remains on, the programs and data stored in RAM will remain intact until they are replaced by other programs and data. Programs and data that are needed for future use must be transferred from RAM to auxiliary storage before the power is turned off.

ROM Memory

ROM stands for **read only memory**. With ROM, data is permanently recorded in the memory when it is manufactured. ROM memory retains its contents even when the power is turned off. The data or programs that are stored in ROM can be read and used, but cannot be altered, hence the name *read only*. ROM is used to store items such as the instruction set of the computer. In addition, many of the special-purpose computers used in automobiles, appliances, and so on use small amounts of ROM to store instructions that will be executed repeatedly. Instructions that are stored in ROM memory are called **firmware** or **microcode**.

Other Types of Memory

PROM means **programmable read only memory**. PROM acts the same as ROM when it is part of the computer; that is, it can only be read, and its contents cannot be altered. With PROM, however, the data or programs are not stored in the memory when they are manufactured. Instead, PROM can be loaded with specially selected data or programs prior to installing it in a computer. A variation of PROM is **EPROM** (pronounced ee-prom), which means **erasable programmable read only memory**. In addition to being used in the same way as PROM, EPROM allows the user to erase the data stored in the memory and to store new data or programs in the memory. EPROM is erased through the use of special ultraviolet light devices that destroy the bit settings within the memory.

EEPROM (pronounced double-ee-prom), or **electronically erasable programmable read only memory**, allows the stored data or programs to be erased electronically. The advantage of EEPROM is that it does not have to be removed from the computer to be changed.

SUMMARY

In this chapter we examined various aspects of the processor unit including its components, how programs and data are stored, and how the processor executes program instructions to process data into information. Although a detailed understanding of this material is not a prerequisite for computer literacy, understanding these principles will increase your overall comprehension of how processing occurs on a computer.

CHAPTER SUMMARY

1. The central processing unit and the main memory are contained in the processor unit.
2. The central processing unit, or CPU, contains the **control unit** and the **arithmetic/logic unit (ALU)**. The control unit directs and coordinates all the activities on the computer. The arithmetic/logic unit performs arithmetic and logic operations.
3. **Arithmetic operations** consist of adding, subtracting, multiplying, and dividing.
4. **Logical operations** consist of comparing one data item to another to determine if the first data item is greater than, equal to, or less than the other.
5. **Registers** are temporary storage locations in the CPU that store specific data such as the address of the next instruction.
6. The **main memory**, also called **primary storage**, stores the operating system, application programs, and data.
7. Each storage location in main memory is called a **byte** and is identified by a **memory address**.
8. The size of main memory is normally expressed in terms of **kilobytes (KB)**. Each kilobyte is equal to 1,024 bytes.
9. A byte consists of eight **bits**. A bit can represent one of two values—off and on.
10. When a letter is entered into main memory from a keyboard, the electronic circuitry interprets the character and stores the character in memory as a series of off and on bits. The computer can distinguish between characters because a unique combination of off and on bits are assigned to each character.
11. One of the most widely used codes to represent characters is the **American Standard Code for Information Interchange**, called the **ASCII code**.
12. A code used for mainframes is the **Extended Binary Coded Decimal Interchange Code (EBCDIC)**.
13. Computers use **parity bits** for error checking.
14. The **binary** (base 2) number system is used by the computer for purposes such as representing memory addresses and the electronic status of the bits in main memory. **Hexadecimal** (base 16) is used to represent binary in a more compact form.
15. A **machine language instruction** can be decoded and executed by the CPU.
16. A machine language instruction is usually composed of an **operation code**; values indicating the number of characters to be processed; and main memory addresses of the data to be processed.
17. Steps in the **machine cycle** consist of: fetch the next instruction; decode the instruction; execute the instruction; and store the results.
18. The speed of a computer is influenced by the system clock, the bus size, and the word size.
19. The **system clock** is used by the control unit to synchronize all computer operations.
20. A **bus** is any line that transmits bits between memory and the input/output devices, and between memory and the CPU.
21. The number of bits that the CPU can process at one time is called the **word size**.
22. Computers can be 8-bit, 16-bit, 32-bit, or 64-bit machines.
23. **Microprocessors** are used for the CPU in microcomputers.
24. **Coprocessors** can be used to enhance and expand the capabilities of a computer.
25. Parallel processors divide up a problem so that multiple CPUs can work on their assigned portion of the problem simultaneously.
26. **RISC** technology involves reducing a computer's instruction set to only those instructions that are the most frequently used.
27. **Core memory** consisted of small, ring-shaped pieces of material that could be magnetized, or polarized, in one of two directions.
28. **Semiconductor memory** is now used in most computers. It consists of transistors etched into a semiconductor material such as silicon.
29. A **microsecond** is a millionth of a second. A **nanosecond** is a billionth of a second. Access to data stored in semiconductor memory is measured in nanoseconds.
30. **RAM**, which stands for **random access memory**, is used for main memory.

31. Some computers improve their processing efficiency by using a limited amount of high-speed memory, called **cache memory**, between the CPU and main memory.
32. RAM memory is said to be **volatile** because the programs and data stored in RAM are erased when the power to the computer is turned off.
33. **ROM** stands for **read only memory**. Data or programs are stored in ROM when the memory is manufactured, and they cannot be altered.
34. **PROM** means **programmable read only memory**. PROM acts the same as ROM except data can be stored into the PROM memory prior to being installed in the computer.
35. **EPROM**, or **erasable programmable read only memory**, can be erased through the use of special ultraviolet devices.
36. **EEPROM**, or **electronically erasable programmable read only memory**, can be electronically erased without being removed from the computer.

KEY TERMS

American Standard Code for Information Interchange (ASCII) *4.6*
Arithmetic/logic unit (ALU) *4.2*
Arithmetic operations *4.2*
ASCII code *4.6*
Binary *4.5*
Bit *4.4*
Bus *4.12*
Byte *4.3*
Cache memory *4.17*
Chip *4.13*
Control unit *4.2*
Coprocessor *4.14*
Core memory *4.15*
Decoding *4.2*
Dynamic RAM (DRAM) *4.16*
EBCDIC *4.6*
EEPROM *4.17*
Electronically erasable programmable read only memory (EEPROM) *4.17*
EPROM *4.17*
Erasable programmable read only memory (EPROM) *4.17*
Even parity *4.7*
Executing *4.2*
Execution cycle *4.11*
Extended Binary Coded Decimal Interchange Code (EBCDIC) *4.6*
Fetching *4.2*
Firmware *4.17*
Hexadecimal *4.7*
IC *4.13*
Instruction cycle *4.11*
Instruction register *4.10*
Instruction set *4.10*
Integrated circuit (IC) *4.13*
K *4.3*
KB *4.3*
Kilobyte (K or KB) *4.3*
Logical operations *4.2*
Machine cycle *4.11*
Machine language instruction *4.10*
Main memory *4.2*
MB *4.3*
Megabyte (MB) *4.3*
Megahertz *4.11*
Memory address *4.3*
Microchip *4.13*
Microcode *4.17*
Microprocessor *4.13*
Microsecond *4.15*
MIPS *4.11*
Motherboard *4.13*
Nanosecond *4.15*
Odd parity *4.7*
Operation code *4.10*
Parallel processing *4.14*
Parity bit *4.7*
Primary storage *4.2*
Programmable read only memory (PROM) *4.17*
PROM *4.17*
RAM *4.16*
Random access memory (RAM) *4.16*
Read only memory (ROM) *4.17*
Registers *4.2*
RISC (reduced instruction set computing) *4.15*
ROM *4.17*
Semiconductor memory *4.15*
Serial processing *4.14*
Static RAM *4.16*
Storing *4.2*
System clock *4.11*
Transistor *4.15*
Volatile *4.17*
Word size *4.12*

REVIEW QUESTIONS

1. Identify the components of the processor unit and describe the functions of each.
2. What are the three items that are stored in main memory? Draw a diagram of main memory and label each of the areas.
3. Define the terms bit and byte. Illustrate how the number 12 is represented in binary, hexadecimal, ASCII, and EBCDIC.
4. What do the letters KB and MB stand for when referring to main memory? What quantity does each represent?
5. Describe how a group of characters entered into the computer as a field are stored in main memory. Draw a diagram to illustrate how the letters in your last name would be stored using the ASCII code. Begin at main memory address 55231.
6. What is parity and how is it used?
7. Why are the binary and hexadecimal number systems used with computers?
8. List and describe the four steps of the machine cycle.
9. What are the three factors that influence the speed of a processor?
10. What is parallel processing and how is it used?
11. Define RAM memory. How is cache memory used by the computer?
12. Describe the process of manufacturing integrated circuits.

CONTROVERSIAL ISSUES

1. Some people feel that industry standards should be set to eliminate the problems caused by incompatibility. For example, unless special enhancements are made, software that is written for an IBM personal computer system will not run on an Apple Macintosh computer. Others feel that standards would restrict competition and product development. Write a paper to discuss your opinions on this topic.
2. The importation of computer goods from foreign manufacturers has affected the computer industry in this country. In addition, the lower cost of producing electronic components outside the United States has caused many U.S. companies to become involved in offshore manufacturing. Discuss whether restrictions should be placed on integrated circuits and other computer goods that are imported or manufactured offshore.

RESEARCH PROJECTS

1. The semiconductor industry continues to develop and introduce new microprocessor and memory chips. Prepare a report on the latest microprocessor and memory chips that are available. Include information on speed and storage capabilities.
2. Research the history of main memory and prepare a report. Include information on the way the data was stored, the speed of the memory, any limitations of the method, the amount of memory that could be used, and the cost of the memory.

MAKING A CHIP

◆ A chip is made by building layers of electronic pathways and connections by using conducting and nonconducting materials on a surface of silicon. The combination of these materials into specific patterns forms microscopic electronic components such as transistors, diodes, and capacitors that make up the integrated chip circuit. The application of the materials to the silicon is done through a series of technically sophisticated chemical and photographic processes. Some of the manufacturing steps are shown in the following photographs.

A chip begins with a design developed by an engineer using a computer-aided circuit design program. Some circuits take only a month or two to design, whereas others may take a year or more. The computer-aided design system allows the engineer to rearrange the design of the circuit pathways and then see them displayed on the screen ⟨1⟩. Most chips have at least four to six layers, but some have up to fifteen. A separate design is required for each layer of the chip circuit. To better review the design, greatly enlarged printouts are prepared ⟨2⟩. After the design is finalized, a glass photo mask is prepared for each layer ⟨3⟩. To provide for mass production of the chips, the design is reduced to the actual size of the circuit, approximately 1/4-inch square, and duplicated over one hundred times on the surface of the photo mask. In a process similar to printing a picture from a negative, the photo mask will be used to project the circuit design onto the material used to make the chips.

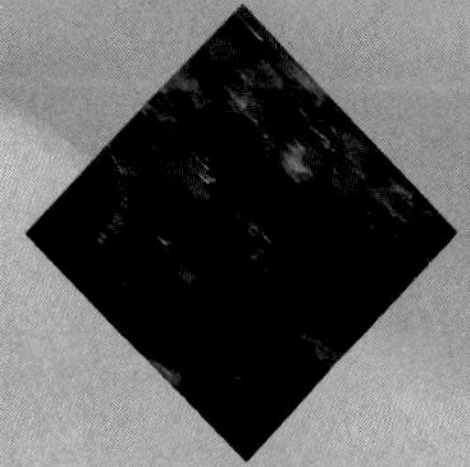

Although other materials can be used, the most common raw material used to make chips is silicon crystals that have been refined from quartz rocks ⟨4⟩. The silicon crystals are melted and *grown* into a cylinder, called an ingot, two to three feet long and eight inches in diameter ⟨5⟩. After being smoothed, the silicon ingot is sliced into wafers four to eight inches in diameter and 4/1000 of one inch thick. Much of the chip manufacturing process is performed in special laboratories called clean rooms. Because even the smallest particle of dust can ruin a chip, rooms are kept 1,000 times cleaner than a hospital operating room. People who work in these facilities must wear special protective clothing called bunny suits ⟨6⟩. After the wafer has been polished and sterilized, it is placed in a diffusion oven where the first layer of material is added to the wafer surface ⟨7⟩. These layers of materials will be etched away to form the circuits.

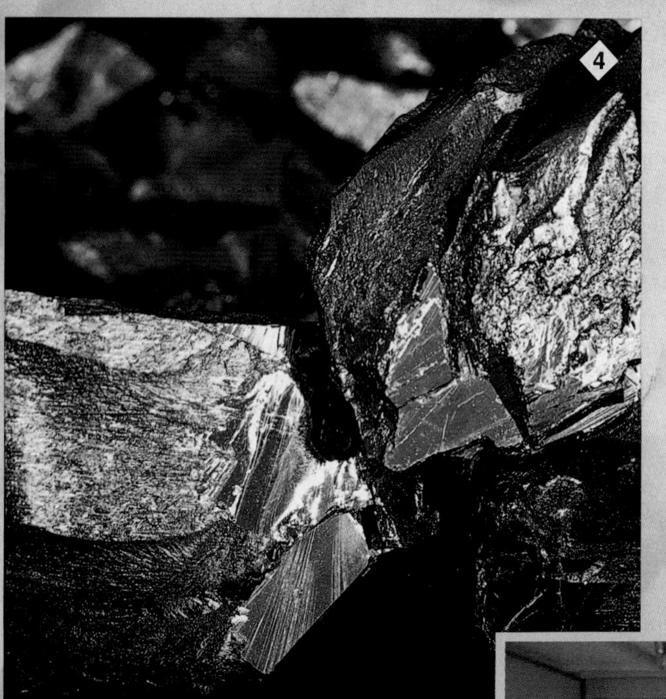

Before etching, a soft gelatin-like emulsion called photoresist is added to the wafer. During lithography ⟨8⟩, the photoresist is covered by a photo mask and exposed to ultraviolet light. The exposed photoresist becomes hard and the covered photoresist remains soft. The soft photoresist and some of the surface materials are etched away with chemicals or hot gases leaving what will become the circuit pathways. In some facilities, the etching process is done by a robot ⟨9⟩.

The process of adding material and photoresist to the wafer, exposing it to ultraviolet light, and etching away the unexposed surface, is repeated using a different photo mask for each layer of the circuit. After the circuits are tested on the wafer, they are cut into pieces called die by the use of a diamond saw ⟨10⟩ or a laser.

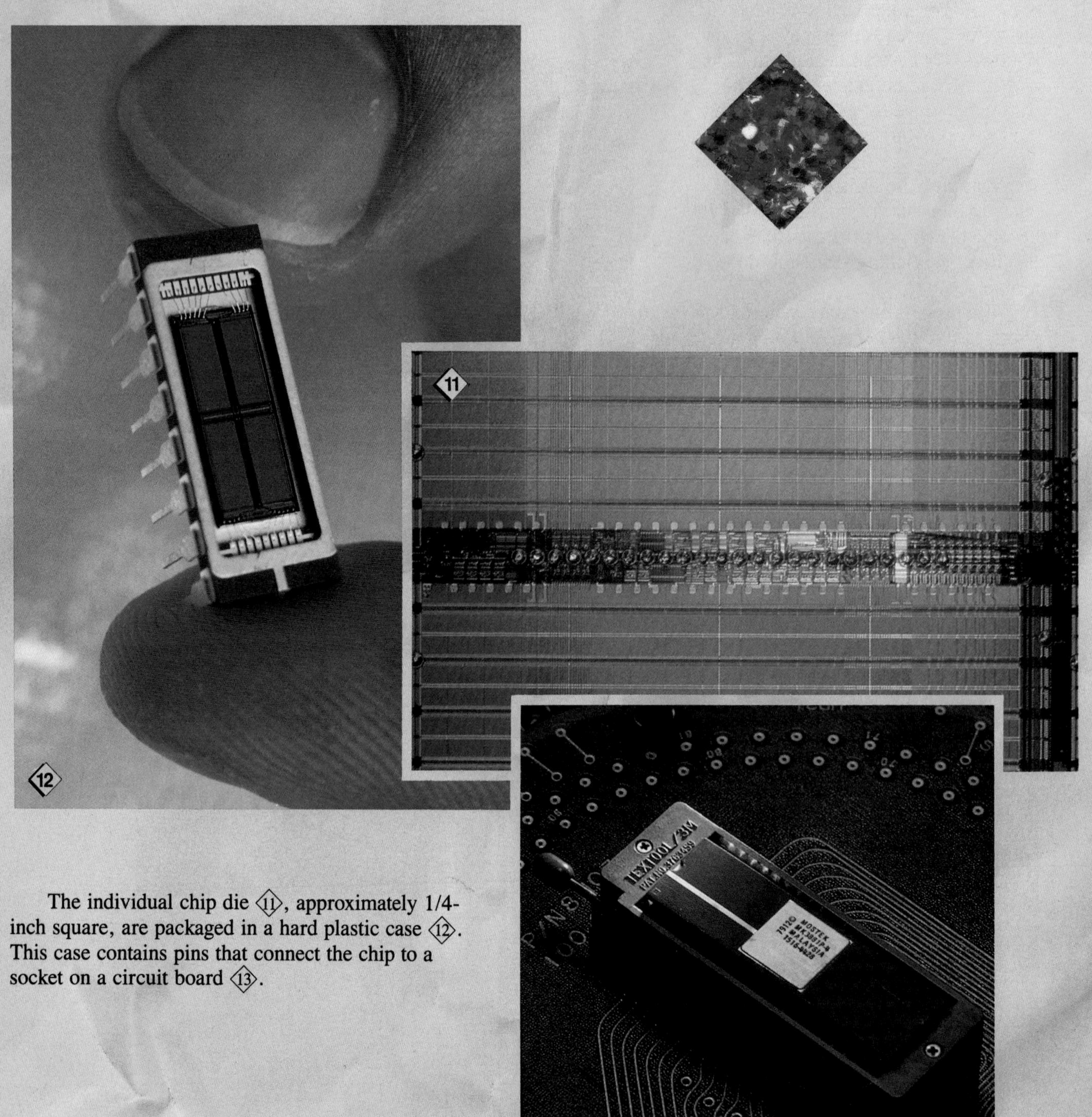

The individual chip die ⟨11⟩, approximately 1/4-inch square, are packaged in a hard plastic case ⟨12⟩. This case contains pins that connect the chip to a socket on a circuit board ⟨13⟩.

Output from the Computer

OBJECTIVES

- Define the term output
- List the common types of reports that are used for output
- Describe multimedia
- Describe the features and classification of printers
- Identify and explain impact printers
- Identify and explain nonimpact printers
- Describe the types of screens available and list common screen features
- List and describe other types of output devices used with computers

Output is the way the computer communicates with the user; therefore, it is important to know the many forms output can take. In this chapter we discuss the types of output and the devices computers use to produce output.

WHAT IS OUTPUT?

Output is data that has been processed into a useful form called information that can be used by a person or a machine. Output that is used by a machine, such as a disk or tape file, is usually an intermediate result that eventually will be processed into output that can be used by people.

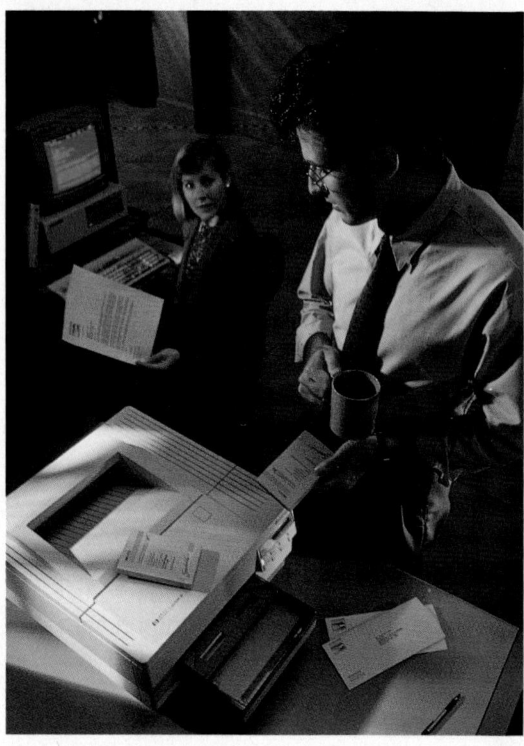

FIGURE 5-1
Here, you see the same output in hard-copy and soft-copy form. An advantage of hard copy is that the user can write comments on it and route it to other users.

TYPES OF OUTPUT

The type of output generated from the computer depends on the needs of the user and the hardware and software that are used. Two common types of output are reports and graphics. These types of output can be printed on a printer or displayed on a screen. Output that is printed is called **hard copy** and output that is displayed on a screen is called **soft copy** (Figure 5-1). An exciting method of displaying information, called multimedia, combines several types of output on a single screen.

Reports

A **report** is information presented in an organized form. Most people think of reports as items printed on paper or displayed on a screen. For example, word processing documents can be considered reports. Information printed on forms such as invoices or payroll checks can also be considered types of reports. One way to classify reports is by who uses them. An **internal report** is used by individuals in the performance of their jobs. For example, a daily sales report that is distributed to sales personnel is an internal report because it is used only by personnel within the organization. An **external report** is used outside the organization. Sales invoices that are printed and mailed to customers are external reports.

Reports can also be classified by the way they present information. The four types of common reports are: narrative reports, detail reports, summary reports, and exception reports.

Narrative reports may contain some graphic or numeric information, but are primarily text-based reports. These reports, usually prepared with word processing software, include the various types of correspondence commonly used in business such as memos, letters, and sales proposals (Figure 5-2). Detail, summary, and exception reports are primarily used to organize and present numeric-based information.

FIGURE 5-2 ▼
A word processing document is an example of a narrative report.

```
Date:     March 10

To:       Gloria Gilbert

From:     Charlene Kim

Subject:  Electronics Trade Show

The recent Electronics Trade Show was a great success!

At the show, we booked orders of over $2 million.  Most of the
orders were for our new computer product line that was introduced
in January.

In addition to the actual orders, we obtained the names of over
two hundred businesses that are interested in our products.  We
have already added these names to the prospect database and will
be following up with literature and direct phone calls in the
next two weeks.  These names will also be passed along to our
dealers where appropriate.

Based on these successful results, I strongly recommend that we
attend the Computer Products Show next September.  I will obtain
the necessary information and forward it to you as soon as I
receive it.
```

In a **detail report**, each line on the report usually corresponds to one input record that has been read and processed. Detail reports contain a great deal of information and can be quite lengthy. They are usually required by individuals who need access to the day-to-day information that reflects the operating status of the organization. For example, people in the warehouse of a hardware distributor should have access to the location and number of units on hand for each product. The Detail Inventory Report in Figure 5-3 contains a line for each warehouse location for each part number. Separate inventory records exist for each line on the report.

Detail Inventory Report
By Part Number

Part #	Description	Location	Quantity On Hand
1001	claw hammer	W1	1,000
1001	claw hammer	W2	420
1001	claw hammer	W3	75
1049	pipe wrench	W2	725
1075	gas welder	W1	13
1075	gas welder	W2	7
1075	gas welder	W4	11

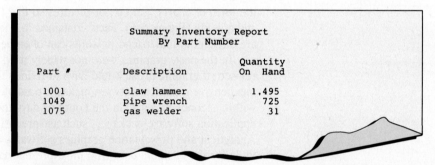

FIGURE 5-3
The data for this detail report was obtained from each input record that was read and processed. A line was printed for each record.

As the name implies, a **summary report** summarizes data. It contains totals for certain values found in the input records. The report shown in Figure 5-4 contains a summary of the total quantity on hand for each part. The information on the summary report consists of totals for each part from the information contained in the detail report in Figure 5-3. Detail reports frequently contain more information than most managers have time to review. With a summary report, however, a manager can quickly review information in summarized form.

Summary Inventory Report
By Part Number

Part #	Description	Quantity On Hand
1001	claw hammer	1,495
1049	pipe wrench	725
1075	gas welder	31

FIGURE 5-4
This summary report contains the total on-hand quantity for each part. The report can be prepared using the same data that prepared the report in Figure 5-3.

An **exception report** contains information that is outside of *normal* user-specified values or conditions, called the exception criteria. Records meeting this criteria are an *exception* to the majority of the data. For example, if an organization wants to know when to reorder inventory items to avoid running out of stock, it would design an exception report. The report would tell which inventory items fell below the reorder points and therefore need to be ordered. An example of such a report is shown in Figure 5-5.

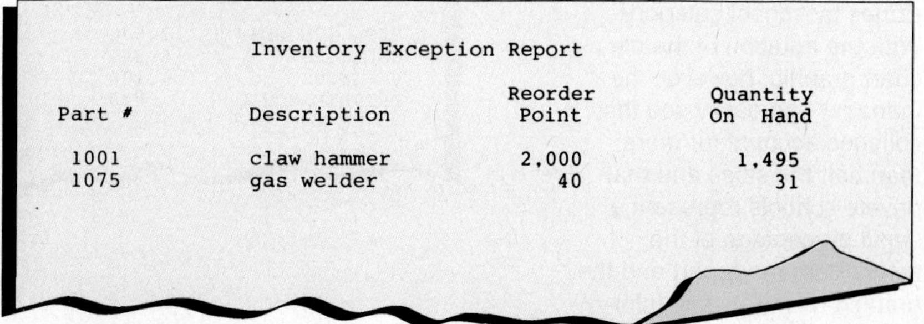

Inventory Exception Report

Part #	Description	Reorder Point	Quantity On Hand
1001	claw hammer	2,000	1,495
1075	gas welder	40	31

FIGURE 5-5
This exception report lists inventory items with an on-hand quantity below their reorder points. These parts could have been selected from thousands of inventory records. Only these items met the user's exception criteria.

Exception reports help users focus on situations that may require immediate decisions or specific actions. The advantage of exception reports is that they save time and money. In a large department store, for example, there may be over 100,000 inventory items. A detail report containing all inventory items could be longer than 2,000 pages. To search through the report to determine the items whose on-hand quantity was less than the reorder point would be a difficult and time-consuming task. The exception report, however, could select these items, which might number 100 to 200, and place them on a two- to four-page report that could be reviewed in just a few minutes.

Reports are also sometimes classified by how often they are produced. **Periodic reports**, also called **scheduled reports**, are produced on a regular basis such as daily, weekly, or monthly. **On-demand reports** are created for information that is not required on a scheduled basis, but only when it is requested.

Graphics

Another common type of output is computer graphics. In business, **computer graphics** are often used to assist in analyzing data. Computer graphics display information in the form of charts, graphs, or pictures so that the information can be understood easily and quickly (Figure 5-6). Facts contained in a lengthy report and data relationships that are difficult to understand in words can often be summarized in a single chart or graph.

In the past, graphics were not widely used in business because each time data was revised, a graphic artist would have to redraw the chart or graph. Today, relatively inexpensive graphics software makes it possible to redraw a chart, graph, or picture within seconds rather than the hours or days that were previously required. Many application software packages, such as spreadsheets, include graphics capabilities. Analytical and presentation graphics software, discussed in Chapter 2, offer powerful tools for the business user who must present data in a meaningful manner or for the manager who must review, analyze, and make decisions based on data relationships.

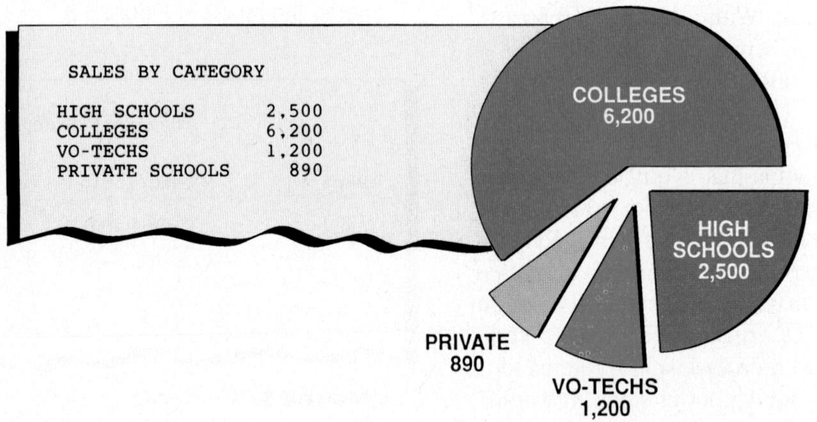

FIGURE 5-6
This report lists sales of magazines by school category. With the addition of the pie chart graphic, however, the manager can easily see that colleges account for more than half the sales and that private schools represent a small percentage of the sales. Both the report and the graphic use the same information, but the graphic helps the manager to understand the information more quickly.

Multimedia

Multimedia is the mixing of text, graphics, video (pictures) and audio (sound) output on a screen. An example would be a multimedia encyclopedia where in addition to the standard text, an animated image with sound is displayed (Figure 5-7).

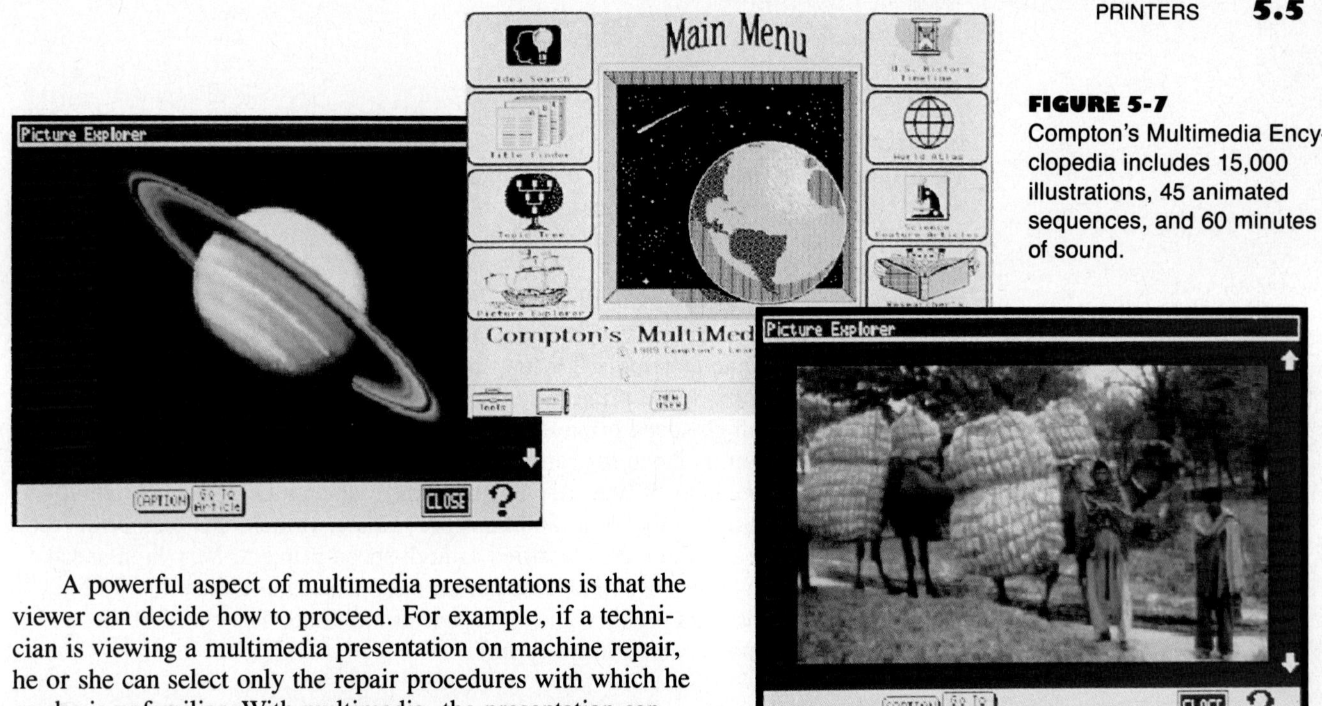

FIGURE 5-7
Compton's Multimedia Encyclopedia includes 15,000 illustrations, 45 animated sequences, and 60 minutes of sound.

A powerful aspect of multimedia presentations is that the viewer can decide how to proceed. For example, if a technician is viewing a multimedia presentation on machine repair, he or she can select only the repair procedures with which he or she is unfamiliar. With multimedia, the presentation can also include sounds that can help the technician identify a specific problem (Figure 5-8).

One of the technical issues that multimedia developers are working on is the tremendous amount of storage required by full-motion video. One minute of full-motion video requires over two billion bytes of storage. Because of this requirement, most multimedia presentations use animation instead of TV-quality video. The key to more widespread use of full motion is **video compression**, making the large amounts of data take up less storage space. One compression technique currently being developed is **digital video interactive (DVI)**. This technique can reduce storage requirements by a factor of 100 or more.

A variety of devices produce the output created in the information processing cycle. The following sections describe the devices most commonly used.

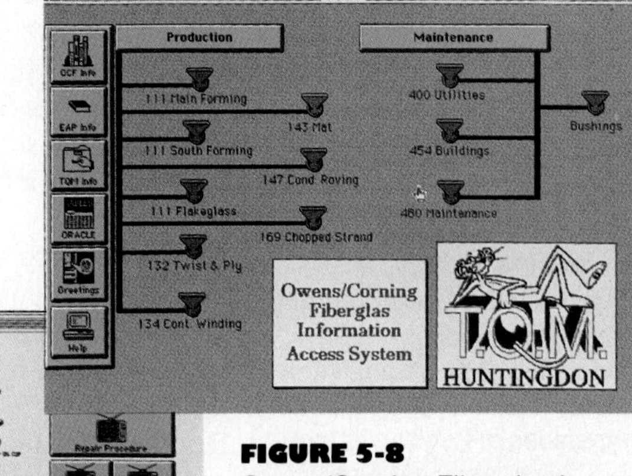

FIGURE 5-8
Owens/Corning Fiberglas has a multimedia equipment maintenance system that provides general and specific information on pieces of equipment. The multimedia presentation includes sounds that can be used to identify a specific repair problem.

PRINTERS

Printing requirements vary greatly among computer users. For example, the user of a personal computer generally uses a printer capable of printing 100 to 200 lines per minute. Users of mainframe computers, such as large utility companies that send printed bills to hundreds of thousands of customers each month, need printers that are capable of printing thousands of lines per minute. These different needs have resulted in the development of printers with varying capabilities. Due to the many choices available and because printed output is so widely used, users must be familiar with printer features and printer technology when choosing a printer.

Printer Features

To decide which printer to choose for a particular application, it is important to know the different features that a printer might have. The main feature choices include speed, paper types and sizes, print quality, and typefaces. Other features include the capability to print color, printer size, and the type of printer interface.

Speed Printers can be rated as low speed, medium speed, high speed, and very high speed. Low-speed printers print one character at a time and are sometimes called character printers. The rate of printing for low-speed printers is expressed in **characters per second (cps)**. Low-speed printers can print from 50 to 400 characters per second. Medium-speed and high-speed printers are called **line printers** because they can print multiple characters on a line at the same time. The rate of printing for these machines is expressed in the number of **lines per minute (lpm)** that can be printed. Medium-speed printers can print from 300 to 600 lines per minute. Printers that can print from 600 to 3,000 lines per minute are classified as high-speed printers. Very high-speed printers can print in excess of 3,000 lines per minute; some, more than 20,000 lines per minute. Some printers produce an entire page at one time. The speed of these printers is rated in **pages per minute (ppm)**.

Paper Types and Sizes Most printers use either continuous-form or single-sheet paper. Some printers can use both. The pages of **continuous-form paper** are connected together for a continuous flow through the printer. The advantage of continuous-form paper is that it doesn't need to be changed frequently; thousands of pages come connected together. A disadvantage of continuous-form paper is that sometimes the individual pages of the report have to be separated. The advantage of using single-sheet printers is that different types of paper, such as letterhead, can be changed quickly.

Continuous-form paper usually has a page size of 8 1/2 by 11 inches or 11 by 14 inches. Single-sheet paper is usually either standard letter size (8 1/2 by 11 inches) or legal size (8 1/2 by 14 inches). Numerous variations on these sizes are available.

Print Quality When users require high-quality printed output, such as for business or legal correspondence, a printer that provides letter-quality output is chosen. The term **letter quality (LQ)** means that the printed character is a fully formed, solid character like those made by a typewriter. Printers that cannot make fully formed characters, but still offer good print quality are said to provide **near letter quality (NLQ)**. **Draft-quality** printers provide output that a business would use for internal purposes and not for correspondence.

FIGURE 5-9
Many printers can now print different typefaces. Here, examples of the Avant Garde, Helvetica, and Times Roman typefaces are shown in regular, italics, and bold type.

REGULAR	ITALIC	BOLD
Avant Garde	*Avant Garde*	**Avant Garde**
Helvetica	*Helvetica*	**Helvetica**
Times Roman	*Times Roman*	**Times Roman**

Typefaces A **typeface** is a set of letters, numbers, and special characters that have a similar design. Commonly used typefaces include Avant Garde, Helvetica, and Times Roman. Each typeface can be printed in a variety of styles and sizes. An example of a different style is *italics* where the characters are slanted or **bold** where the characters are darker (Figure 5-9). Character size is measured in points. A **point** is 1/72 of an inch. Common point sizes for text used in the body of a document are 10 or 12 points. A complete set of characters in the same typeface, style, and size is called a **font**. One feature you should consider when evaluating a printer is the number of fonts it can print. Some printers can print only a limited number of fonts, whereas others are capable of printing numerous fonts.

Other Printer Features Other features that you should consider when you evaluate a printer include color output, the amount of desk space the printer requires (referred to as the *footprint*) and the printer interface, which is the way the printer electronically communicates with the computer to which it is attached. With a **serial interface**, data is sent to the printer a single bit at a time. With a **parallel interface**, an entire byte (eight bits) is sent at the same time. Printers with a parallel interface must be located close to the computer, generally within fifty feet. Serial interface printers can be located up to 1,000 feet away from the computer and can even be used at remote locations where the printed information is transmitted over a communication link such as a phone line.

How Are Printers Classified?

Printers can be classified by how they transfer characters from the printer to the paper, either by impact or nonimpact.

Impact printers transfer the image onto paper by some type of printing mechanism striking the paper, ribbon, and character together. One technique is front striking in which the printing mechanism that forms the character strikes a ribbon against the paper from the front to form an image. This is similar to the method used on typewriters. The second technique utilizes a hammer striking device. The ribbon and paper are struck against the character from the back by a hammer to form the image on the paper (Figure 5-10).

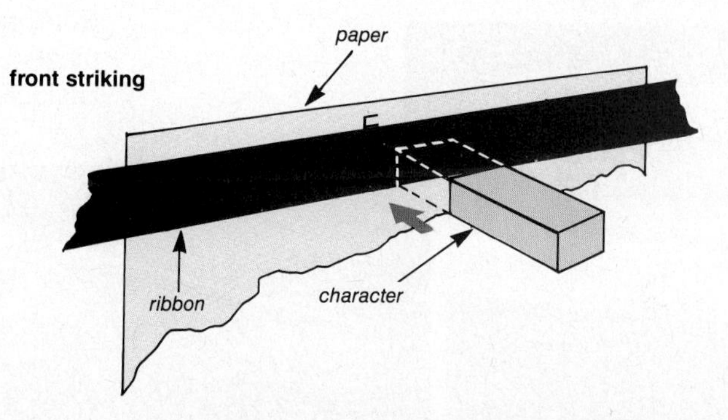

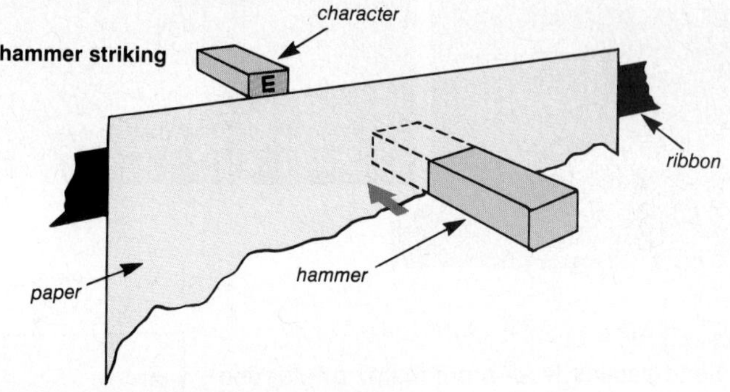

FIGURE 5-10
Impact printers operate in one of two ways: front striking or hammer striking.

Nonimpact printing means that printing occurs without having a mechanism striking against a sheet of paper. For example, ink is sprayed against the paper or heat is used to fuse a fine black powder into the shape of a character.

Impact and nonimpact methods of printing each have advantages and disadvantages. Impact printing can be noisy because the paper is struck when printing occurs. But because the paper is struck, specially treated multipart paper can be used to create multiple copies of a report at one time, such as an invoice, that is routed to different people. Nonimpact printers are quiet and produce high-quality output. However, they do not strike the paper and can therefore only create one printed copy at a time. If additional copies are needed, they must each be printed separately.

IMPACT PRINTERS

◆ The increased use of computers has resulted in the development of a variety of impact printers that vary significantly in speed, quality, and price. Some of these printers, such as dot matrix, daisy wheel, and small page printers, are commonly used on microcomputers or small minicomputers. As the demand for printing information from a computer increases, the use of higher speed printers is required. In industry, minicomputers and mainframes are frequently used to process and print large volumes of data. The two types of impact printers often used to print large volumes of data are chain printers and band printers. The following sections describe the various types of impact printers.

FIGURE 5-11 ▼
This Panasonic dot matrix printer is popular for use with personal computers.

Dot Matrix Printers

Dot matrix printers are used extensively because they are versatile and relatively inexpensive. The Panasonic printer shown in Figure 5-11 is a well-known dot matrix printer that is used with personal computers. Figure 5-12 shows a popular Printronix dot matrix printer that is frequently used with minicomputers. A **dot matrix printer** is an impact printer. Its print head consists of a series of small tubes containing pins that, when pressed against a ribbon and paper, print small dots. The pins are activated by electromagnets that are arranged in a radial pattern. The combination of small dots printed closely together forms the character (Figure 5-13).

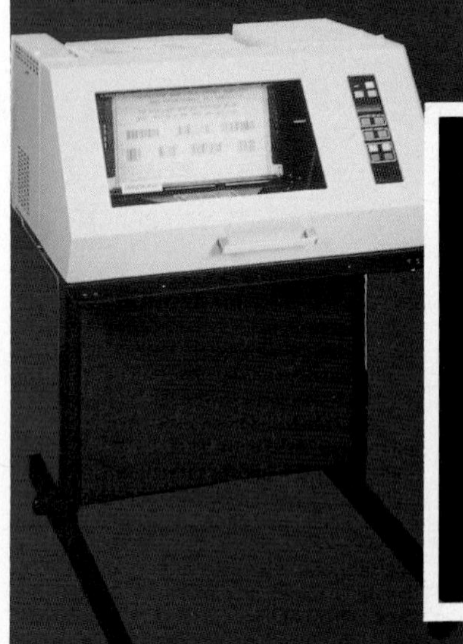

◄ FIGURE 5-12
This dot matrix line printer can print up to 800 lines per minute and is used in many business applications. Print heads at each print position allow this device to print an entire line at one time.

FIGURE 5-13 ▼
The print head assembly for a dot matrix printer consists of a series of pins that are fired at the paper by electromagnets. When activated, the pins strike the ribbon that strikes the paper, creating a dot on the paper.

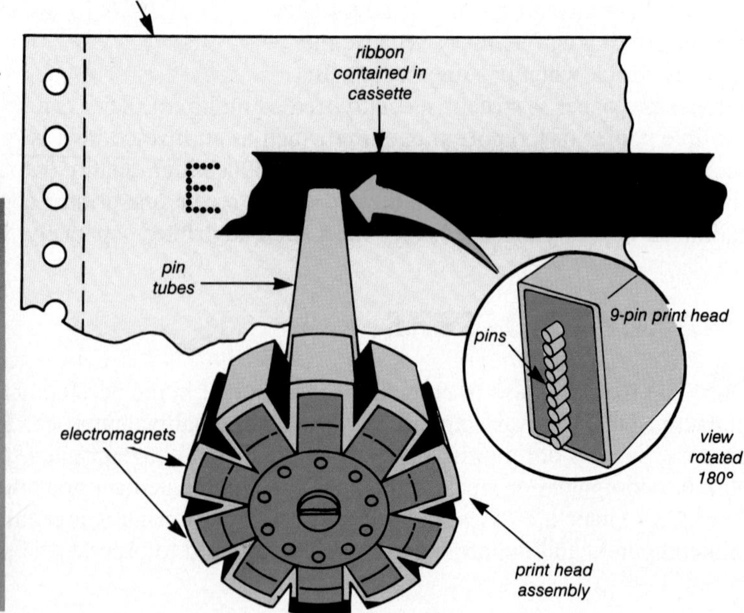

To print a character using a dot matrix printer, the character stored in main memory is sent to the printer's electronic circuitry. The printer circuitry activates the pins in the print head that correspond to the pattern of the character to be printed. The selected pins strike the ribbon and paper and print the character. Most dot matrix printers used with personal computers have a single print head that moves across the page. Dot matrix printers used with larger computers usually have fixed print mechanisms at each print position and can print an entire line at one time.

Dot matrix printers can contain a varying number of pins, depending on the manufacturer and the printer model. Print heads consisting of 9, 18 (two vertical rows of 9), and 24 pins (two vertical rows of 12) are most common. Figure 5-14 illustrates the formation of the letter E using a nine-pin dot matrix printer.

The print quality of dot matrix printers can be improved by overlapping the printed dots. Nine-pin print heads accomplish the overlapping by printing the line twice. The character is slightly offset during the second printing. This results in the appearance of solid characters (Figure 5-15).

Eighteen-pin and 24-pin printers can accomplish the overlapping on a single pass because their multiple rows of pins are slightly offset (Figure 5-16).

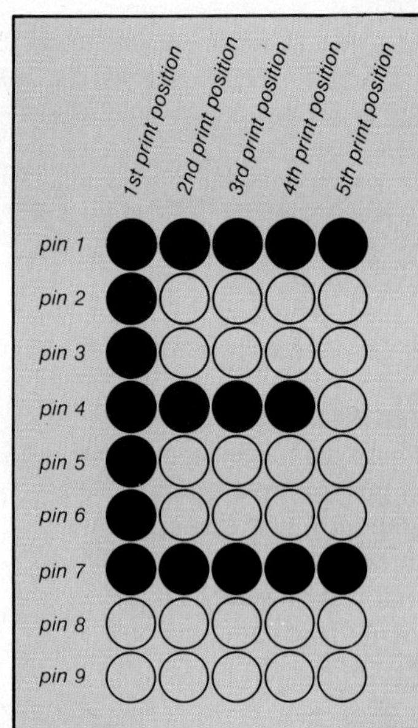

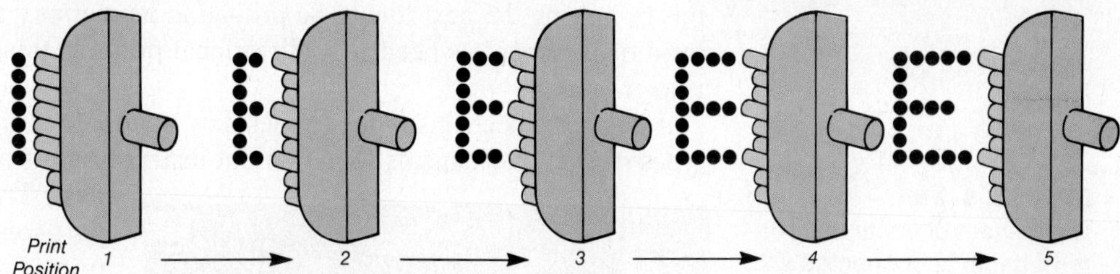

FIGURE 5-14
The letter E is formed with seven vertical and five horizontal dots. As the nine-pin print head moves from left to right, it fires one or more pins into the ribbon, which makes a dot on the paper. At print position 1, it fires pins 1 through 7. At print positions 2 through 4, it fires pins 1, 4, and 7. At print position 5, it fires pins 1 and 7. Pins 8 and 9 are used for lowercase characters such as p, q, y, g, and j that extend below the line.

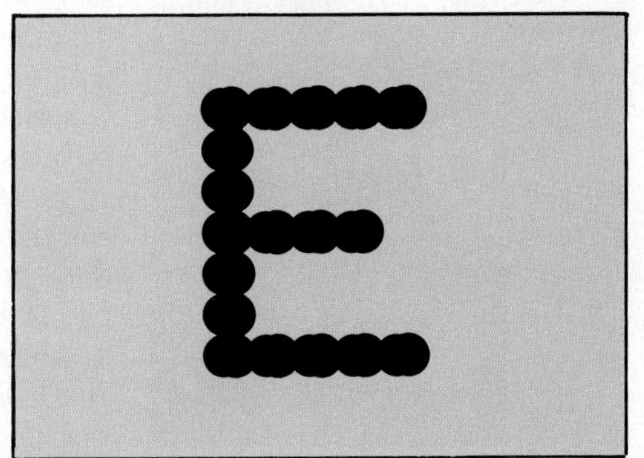

FIGURE 5-15
The letter E in this example is formed by overlapping, or printing the character twice. When it is printed the second time, the character is printed slightly offset so that much of the space between the dots is filled in. This gives the character a better appearance and makes it easer to read.

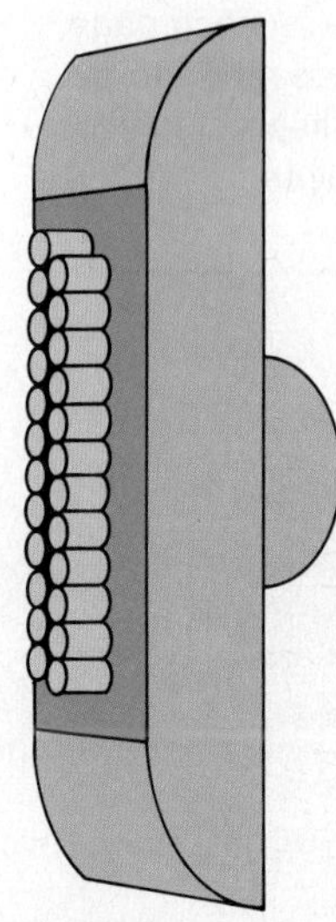

FIGURE 5-16
The two rows of pins on this 24-pin print head are slightly offset (one is higher than the other) so that they will overlap and produce a more solid looking character or a smoother line.

CONDENSED PRINT - NORMAL CHARACTERS
CONDENSED PRINT - EMPHASIZED CHARACTERS

STANDARD PRINT - NORMAL CHARACTERS
STANDARD PRINT - EMPHASIZED CHARACTERS

ENLARGED PRINT - NORMAL CHARACTERS
ENLARGED PRINT - EMPHASIZED CHARACTERS

FIGURE 5-17
Three type sizes are shown in this example—condensed, standard, and enlarged. All three are printed using normal and emphasized (also called bold) print density.

Many dot matrix printers can also print characters in a variety of sizes and densities. Typical sizes include condensed print, standard print, and enlarged print. In addition, each of these print sizes can be printed with increased density or darkness, called bold, or emphasized, print. Figure 5-17 illustrates condensed, condensed bold, standard, standard bold, enlarged, and enlarged bold print.

Dot matrix printers are designed to print in a **bidirectional** manner. That is, the print head, the device that contains the mechanism for transferring the character to the paper, can print as it moves from left to right, and from right to left. The printer does this by storing the next line to be printed in its memory and then printing the line forward or backward as needed. Bidirectional printing greatly increases the speed of the printer.

The feed mechanism determines how the paper moves through the printer. Two types of feed mechanisms found on dot matrix printers are tractor feed and friction feed. **Tractor feed mechanisms** transport continuous-form paper through the printer by using sprockets, small protruding prongs of plastic or metal, which fit into holes on each side of the paper (Figure 5-18). Where it is necessary to feed single sheets of paper into the printer, **friction feed mechanisms** are used. As the name implies, paper is moved through friction feed printers by pressure on the paper and the carriage, as it is on a typewriter. As the carriage rotates, the paper moves through the printer.

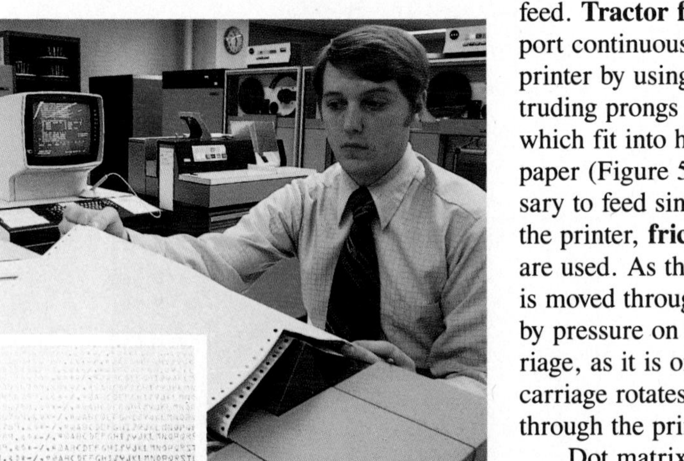

FIGURE 5-18
Each sheet of continuous-form paper is connected with the next. A feed mechanism pulls the paper through the printer using the holes on each side of the form. Perforations between each page allow a printed report to be folded to be separated into individual pages.

Dot matrix printers are built with a standard, medium, or wide carriage. A standard carriage printer can accommodate paper up to 8 1/2 inches wide. A medium carriage can accommodate paper up to 11 inches wide, and a wide carriage printer can accommodate paper up to 14 inches wide. Using a normal character size, most printers can print from 80 characters per line on a standard carriage to 132 characters per line on a wide carriage.

Some dot matrix printers can print in multiple colors using ribbons that contain the colors red, yellow, and blue in addition to the standard black. Color output is obtained by repeated printing and repositioning of the paper, print head, and ribbon.

Such printers can be useful in printing graphs and charts, but other types of color printers offer a higher quality of color output.

Most dot matrix printers have a graphics mode that enables them to print pictures and graphs (Figure 5-19). In graphics mode, the individual print head pins can be activated separately or in combination to form unique shapes or continuous lines. The flexibility of the dot matrix printer has resulted in widespread use of this type of printer by all types of computer users.

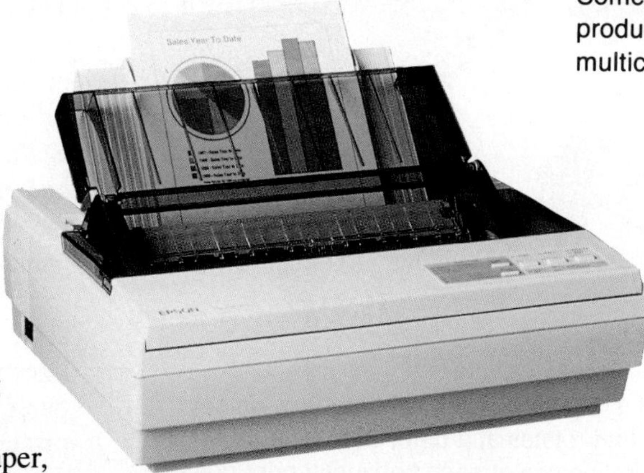

FIGURE 5-19
Some dot matrix printers can produce color output using multicolor ribbons.

Daisy Wheel Printers

The **daisy wheel printer** is an impact printer. The daisy wheel type element resembles the structure of a flower, with many long, thin petals (Figure 5-20). Each *petal* has a raised character at the tip. When printing occurs, the type element (daisy wheel) rotates so that the character to be printed is in the printing position. A hammer extends, striking the selected character against the ribbon and paper, printing the character. Because of the time required to rotate the daisy wheel, the daisy wheel printer is normally slower than a dot matrix printer; however, the print quality is higher because fully formed characters are printed. Printing speeds vary from 20 to 80 characters per second.

An additional feature of the daisy wheel printer is that the daisy wheel can be easily replaced. Daisy wheels come in a variety of sizes and fonts. Therefore, whenever the user wants to change fonts, he or she can remove one daisy wheel and put another wheel on the printer.

The disadvantage of a daisy wheel printer is that it is capable of printing only the characters that are on the wheel. It cannot, therefore, print graphic output. Although daisy wheel printers are still used, they are being replaced by other letter-quality printers.

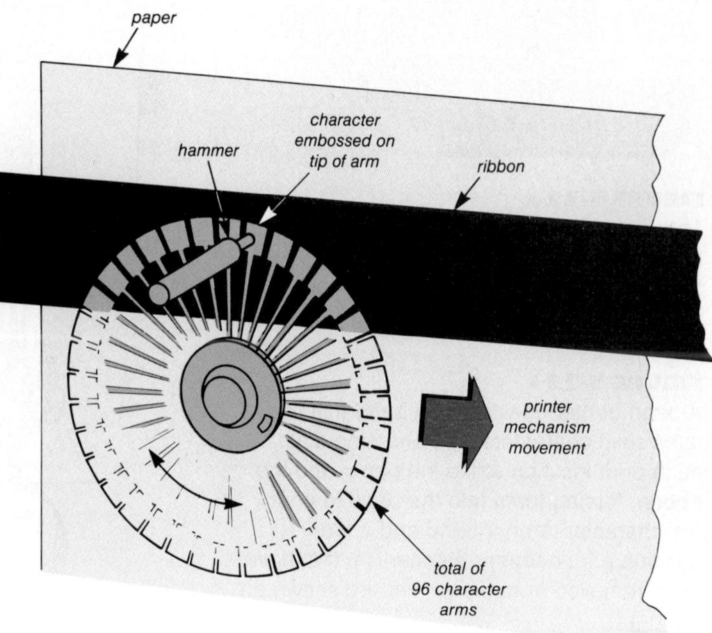

FIGURE 5-20
The daisy wheel print element consists of a number of arms, each with a character at the end. When the printer is running, the wheel spins until the desired character is lined up with the hammer. The hammer then strikes against the ribbon and paper, printing the character.

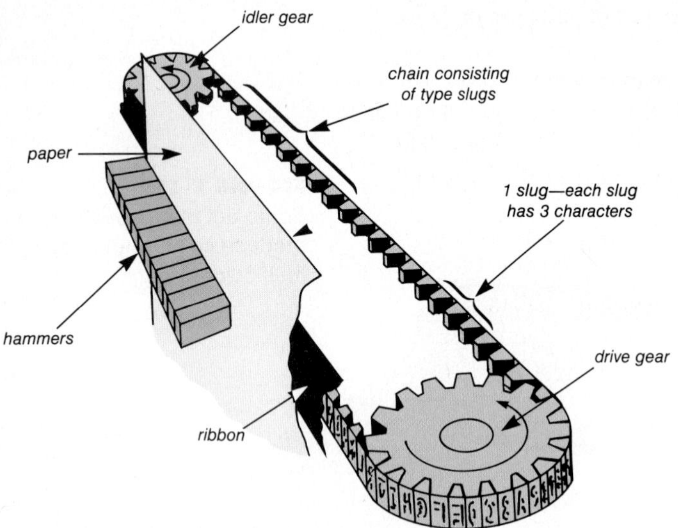

FIGURE 5-21 ▲
The chain printer contains a complete set of characters on several sections of a chain that rotates at a high, constant rate of speed. Print hammers are located at each horizontal print position. The paper and ribbon are placed between the hammers and the chain. As the chain rotates, the hammers fire when the proper characters are in front of their print positions.

Chain Printers

The **chain printer** is a widely used high-speed printer. It contains numbers, letters of the alphabet, and selected special characters on a rotating chain (Figure 5-21). The chain consists of a series of type slugs that contain the character set. The character set on the type slugs is repeated two or more times on the chain mechanism. The chain rotates at a very high speed. Each possible print position has a hammer that can strike against the back of the paper, forcing the paper and ribbon against the character on the chain. As the chain rotates, the hammer strikes when the character to be printed is in the proper position.

The chain printer has proven to be very reliable. It produces good print quality up to 3,000 lines per minute. The printers in the large computer installation in Figure 5-22 are chain printers.

Band Printers

Band printers, similar to chain printers, use a horizontal, rotating band containing characters. The characters are struck by hammers located at each print position behind the paper and ribbon to create a line of print on the paper (Figure 5-23).

FIGURE 5-22 ▲
These high-speed chain printers are used in a large computer installation to produce thousands of lines of printed output per minute.

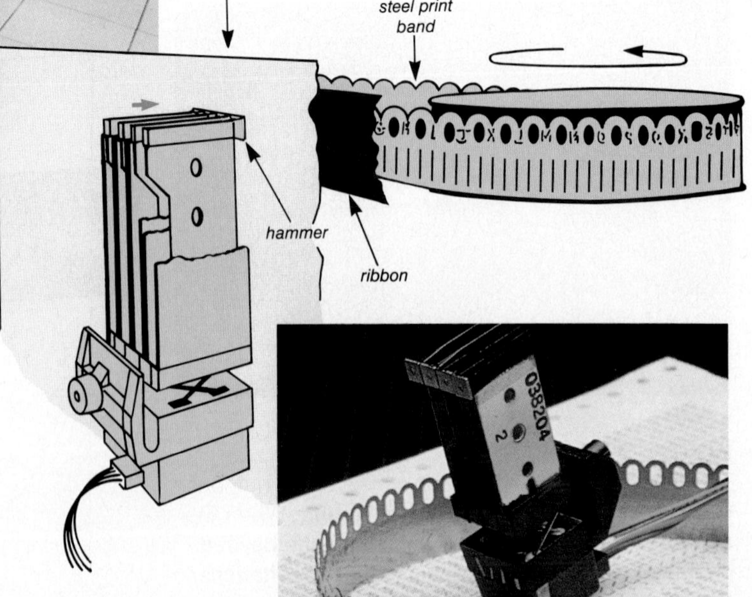

FIGURE 5-23 ▶
A band printer uses a metal band that contains solid characters. Print hammers at each print location strike the paper and the ribbon, forcing them into the band to print the character. A print band and a four-position print hammer mechanism that have been removed from the printer are shown on the right.

Interchangeable type bands can be used on band printers. The different type bands contain many different fonts, or print styles. A band printer can produce up to six carbon copies, has good print quality, high reliability, and depending on the manufacturer and model of the printer, can print in the range of 300 to 2,000 lines per minute.

NONIMPACT PRINTERS

Just as there are a variety of impact printers, there are also a variety of nonimpact printers. Ink jet, thermal, and small page printers are frequently used on microcomputers and small minicomputers. Medium- and high-speed page printers are used on minicomputers, mainframes, and supercomputers. The following sections discuss the various types of nonimpact printers.

Ink Jet Printers

A popular type of nonimpact printer is an **ink jet printer**. To form a character, an ink jet printer uses a nozzle that shoots electronically charged droplets of ink onto the page. The droplets pass between electrically charged deflection plates that guide the droplets to the correct position on the paper (Figure 5-24). Ink jet printers produce high-quality print and graphics and are quiet because the paper is not struck as it is by dot matrix or daisy wheel printers. Disadvantages are that ink jet printers cannot use multipart paper, and the ink sometimes smears on soft, porous paper. Ink jet printers that produce color output are also available (Figure 5-25).

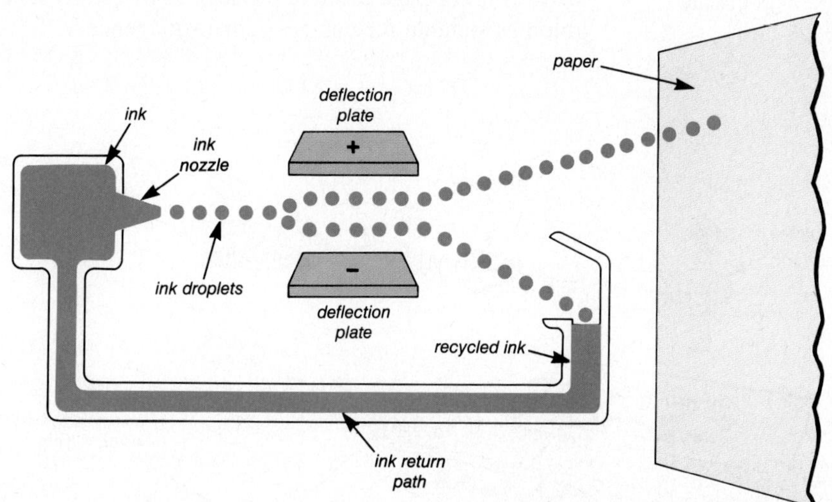

◄ **FIGURE 5-24**
Ink jet printers spray thousands of tiny ink drops toward the paper. The drops are directed to form characters or images by electrically charged deflection plates.

FIGURE 5-25 ▼
An IBM color ink jet printer.

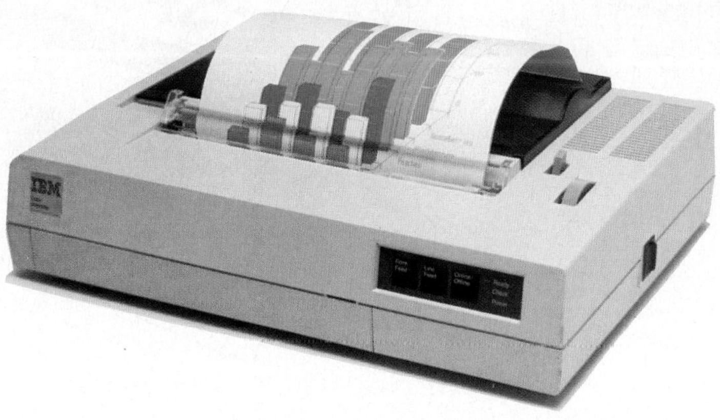

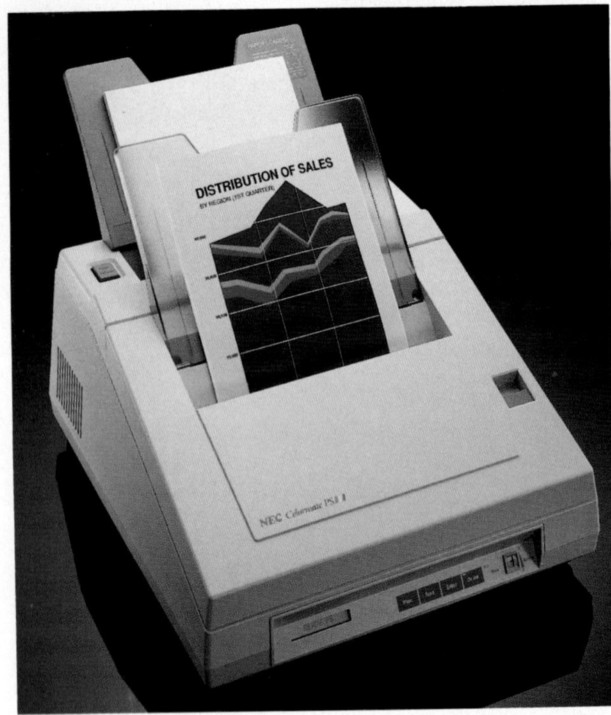

FIGURE 5-26
This thermal transfer printer can produce high-quality color output.

Thermal Printers

Thermal printers use heat to produce fully formed characters and graphic images on special chemically treated paper. Disadvantages of thermal printers are their use of special paper and their relatively slow printing speed. A category of thermal printers called **thermal transfer printers** are used for color printing (Figure 5-26).

Page Printers

The **page printer** is a nonimpact printer that operates similar to a copying machine. The page printer converts data from the computer into light that is directed to a positively charged revolving drum. Each position on the drum touched by the light becomes negatively charged and attracts the toner (powdered ink). The toner is transferred onto the paper and then fused to the paper by heat and pressure. Several methods are used to direct light to the photosensitive drum and create the text or image that will be transferred to the paper. **Laser printers** use a laser beam aimed at the drum by a spinning mirror (Figure 5-27). Other page printers use light emitting diode (LED) arrays or liquid crystal shutters (LCS). With these methods, the light can expose thousands of individual points on the drum. All page printers produce high-quality text and graphics suitable for business correspondence.

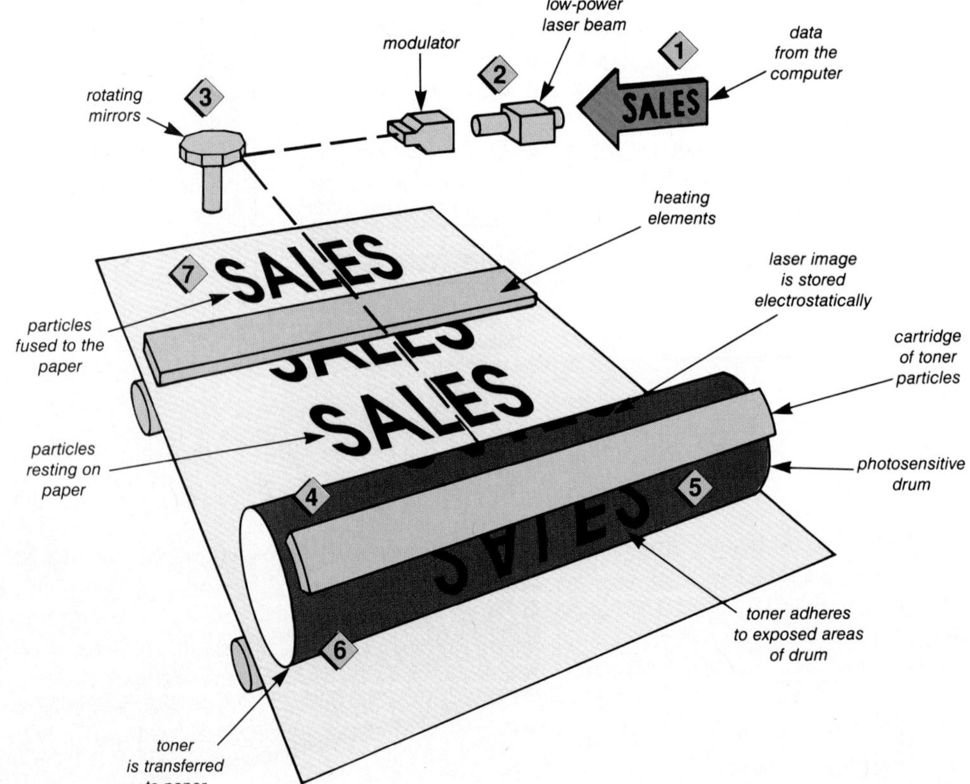

FIGURE 5-27
Laser printers use a process similar to a copying machine. Data from the computer, such as the word SALES ①, is converted into a laser beam ② that is directed by a mirror ③ to a photosensitive drum ④. The sensitized drum attracts toner particles ⑤ that are transferred to the paper ⑥. The toner is fused to the paper with heat and pressure ⑦.

A wide range of page printers are available. Page printers commonly used with personal computers are capable of printing from 4 to 16 pages a minute (Figure 5-28).

Various page printers used with larger computers can print from 20 to 100 pages a minute. **High-speed page printers** can produce printed output at the rate of several hundred pages per minute. As shown in Figure 5-29, these high-speed printers usually consist of a dedicated computer and tape drive to maximize the printing speed.

FIGURE 5-28
The output shown here was produced by a laser printer. Notice that the output contains a mixture of different sizes and styles of print.

CONSIDERATIONS IN CHOOSING A PRINTER

In addition to understanding the features and capabilities of the various types of printers that are available, you must consider several other factors before choosing a printer. These include factors such as how much output will be produced and who will use the output. Considering these and the other factors stated in Figure 5-30 will help you to choose a printer that will meet your needs.

FIGURE 5-29
This laser printer can operate at speeds up to 120 pages per minute. On the left is a tape drive that is used as an input device.

QUESTION	EXPLANATION
How much output will be produced?	Desktop printers are not designed for continuous use. High volume (more than several hundred pages a day) requires a heavy-duty printer.
Who will use the output?	Most organizations want external reports to be prepared on a high-quality printer.
Where will the output be produced?	If the output will be produced at the user's desk, a sound enclosure may be required to reduce the noise of some printers to an acceptable level.
Are multiple copies required?	Some printers cannot use multipart paper.

FIGURE 5-30 Factors that affect the choice of a printer.

SCREENS

The **screen**, also called the **monitor**, **CRT (cathode ray tube)**, or **VDT (video display terminal)**, is another important output device. Screens are used on both personal computers and terminals to display many different types of output. For example, when a user queries a database, the resulting information is frequently displayed on a screen. A screen can also be used to display electronic spreadsheets, electronic mail, and graphs.

Screen Features

Some of the features that should be considered when selecting a screen include size, resolution, and color. A discussion of these and other features follows.

Size The most widely used screens are equivalent in size to a 12- to 16-inch television screen. Although there is no standard number of displayed characters, screens are usually designed to display 80 characters on a line with a maximum of 25 lines displayed at one time. The twenty-fifth line is often reserved for messages or system status reports, not for data. By reducing the character size, some terminals can display up to 132 characters on a single horizontal line. Screens designed for use with desktop publishing or engineering applications come in even larger sizes that can display one or sometimes two 8 1/2 by 11 inch pages of data. One company even makes a screen that can be tilted 90 degrees to display either a long or wide page (Figure 5-31).

FIGURE 5-31
Radius manufactures a screen that can be tilted 90 degrees to display the equivalent of one long or two wide pages.

Resolution The **resolution**, or clarity, of the image on the screen depends on the number of individual dots that are displayed on the screen. Each dot that can be illuminated is called a **picture element**, or **pixel** (Figure 5-32). The greater the number of pixels, the better the screen resolution. The resolution of a screen is important, especially when the screen will be used to display graphics or other nontext information.

Screens used for graphics are called **dot-addressable displays**, or sometimes **bit-mapped displays**. On these monitors, the number of addressable locations on the screen corresponds to the number of pixels, or dots, that can be illuminated. The number of pixels on a screen is determined through a combination of the software in the computer, the graphics capability of the computer, and the screen itself.

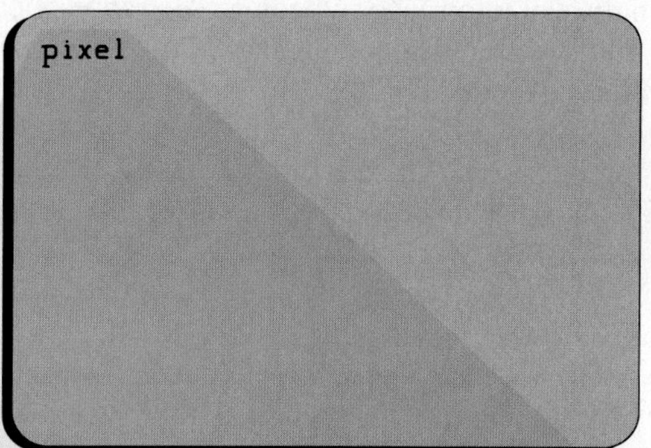

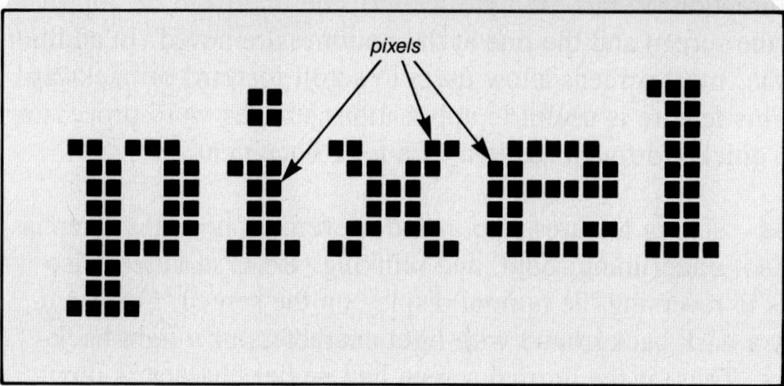

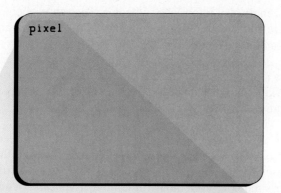

◂ FIGURE 5-32
The word pixel shown here is made up of pixels as they would be displayed on a dot-addressable or bit-mapped screen. Each pixel is a small spot of light that appears on the screen at the point where it is activated by an electron beam.

FIGURE 5-33 ▴
Very high-resolution graphics can depict features such as shading, reflections, and highlights as shown in the top photo. Very high-resolution graphics can also be used for simulation exercises; in this case, a flying situation as shown in the bottom photo. Through the use of the computer, this simulation could be changed quickly to show the plane taking off and landing.

Devices are currently available that offer very high-resolution graphics. The resolution of these devices is high enough to provide an image that is almost equivalent to the quality of a photograph (Figure 5-33). High-resolution graphics require a great deal of storage and are more difficult electronically to maintain as a steady image on the screen. In the past few years, however, picture resolutions have greatly improved. In addition, costs have been reduced so that high-resolution graphics are now widely used.

Several graphics standards have been developed, including CGA (Color Graphics Adapter), EGA (Enhanced Graphics Adapter), VGA (Video Graphics Array), super VGA, and 1024. As shown in Figure 5-34, each standard provides for a different number of pixels and colors. Some manufacturers offer even higher resolution screens.

FIGURE 5-34
A summary of the graphics resolution standards for display screens.

STANDARD	CGA	HERCULES	EGA	VGA	SUPER VGA	1024
Year	1981	1982	1984	1986	1988	1989
Resolution (W × H)	640 × 200	720 × 348	640 × 350	640 × 480	800 × 600	1024 × 768
Available Colors	16	None	64	262,144	256	262,144
Maximum Displayed Colors	4	None	16	256	16	256

Color Some screens can display information in color. The range of colors available depends on what software and hardware is being used. Microcomputers are available with screens that can simultaneously display 256 colors.

Cursor A **cursor** is a symbol such as an underline character or an arrow that indicates where you are working on the screen. Most cursors blink when they are on the screen so the user can quickly find their location.

Scrolling **Scrolling** is a method of moving lines displayed on the screen up or down one line at a time. For example, as a new line is added to the bottom of the screen, an existing one, from the top of the screen, is removed. The line removed from the screen remains in the computer's memory even though it no longer appears. When the screen is scrolled in the opposite direction (in this example, down), the line from the top that was removed reappears on the screen and the line at the bottom is removed. In addition to scrolling one line at a time, most screens allow users to scroll forward or backward one full screen at a time. This feature is useful in applications such as word processing when a user wants to move quickly through sections of a long document.

Other Screen Features Screen features also include several options that emphasize characters: reverse video, underlining, bold, and blinking. **Reverse video**, also called **inverse video**, refers to reversing the normal display on the screen. For example, it is possible to display a dark background with light characters or a light background with dark characters. Thus, if the normal screen had amber characters on a black background, reverse video shows black characters on an amber background. This feature permits single characters, whole words or lines, and even the entire screen to be reversed. The **underlining** feature allows characters, words, lines, or paragraphs to be underlined. Another feature used for emphasis is bold. **Bold** means that characters are displayed at a greater brightness level than the surrounding text. The **blinking** feature makes characters or words on a screen blink, thus drawing attention to them.

Types of Screens

Several types of screens are used with computers. The most common types are monochrome screens, color screens, plasma screens, and LCD screens. Plasma and LCD screens, which do not use the conventional cathode ray tube technology, are sometimes called **flat panel display screens** because of their relatively flat screens.

Monochrome screens designed for use with personal computers or as computer terminals usually display a single color such as white, green, or amber characters on a black background (Figure 5-35) or black characters on a white background.

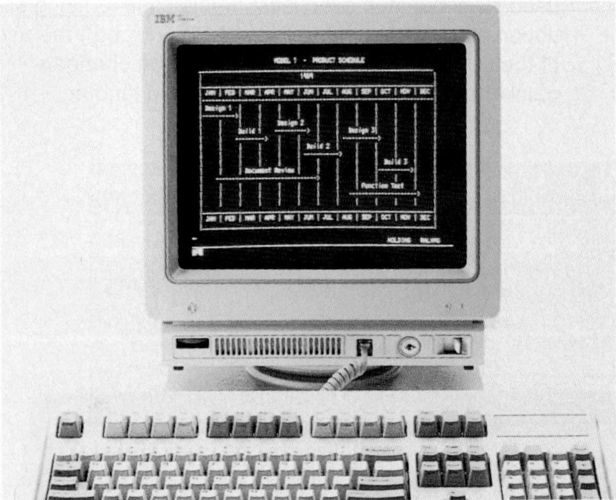

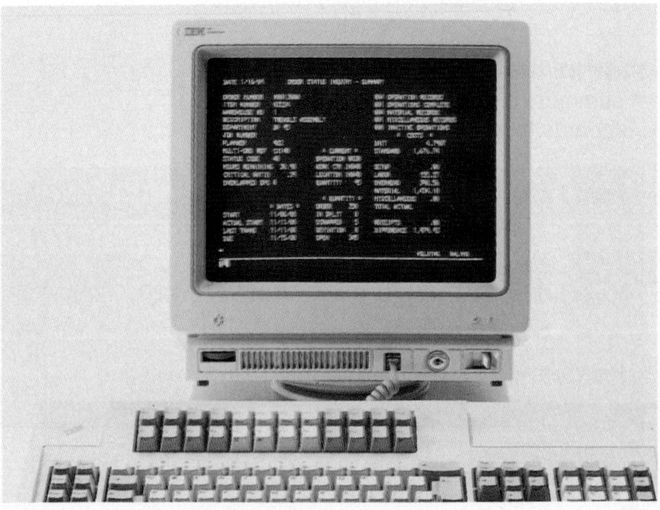

FIGURE 5-35
Many users prefer amber or green characters rather than white characters.

FIGURE 5-36
Toshiba manufactures laptop computers that use liquid crystal display (LCD) screens, such as the model T1000 on the left, and plasma technology, such as the T5200 on the right.

The use of **color screens** is increasing. Although they are more expensive than monochrome, they are desireable because much of today's software uses color. Color enables users to more easily read and understand the information on the screen. When color software is used with a monochrome monitor, the output displays as shades of a single color such as shades of grey.

With the development of truly portable computers, that could be conveniently carried by hand or in a briefcase, came a need for an output display that was equally as portable. **Liquid crystal displays (LCD)** and **plasma screens** are flat screens that are used as output displays for a number of laptop computers (Figure 5-36).

How Images Are Displayed on a CRT Screen

Most screens used with personal computers and terminals use cathode ray tube (CRT) technology. When these screens produce an image, the following four steps occur (Figure 5-37):

1. The image to be displayed on the screen is sent electronically from the CPU to the cathode ray tube.
2. An electron gun generates an electron beam of varying intensity, depending on the electronic data received from the CPU.
3. The yoke, which generates an electromagnetic field, moves the electron beam horizontally and vertically on the phosphor-coated screen.
4. The electron beam causes the desired phosphors to emit light. The higher the intensity of the beam, the brighter the phosphor glows. It is the phosphor-emitted light that produces an image on the screen.

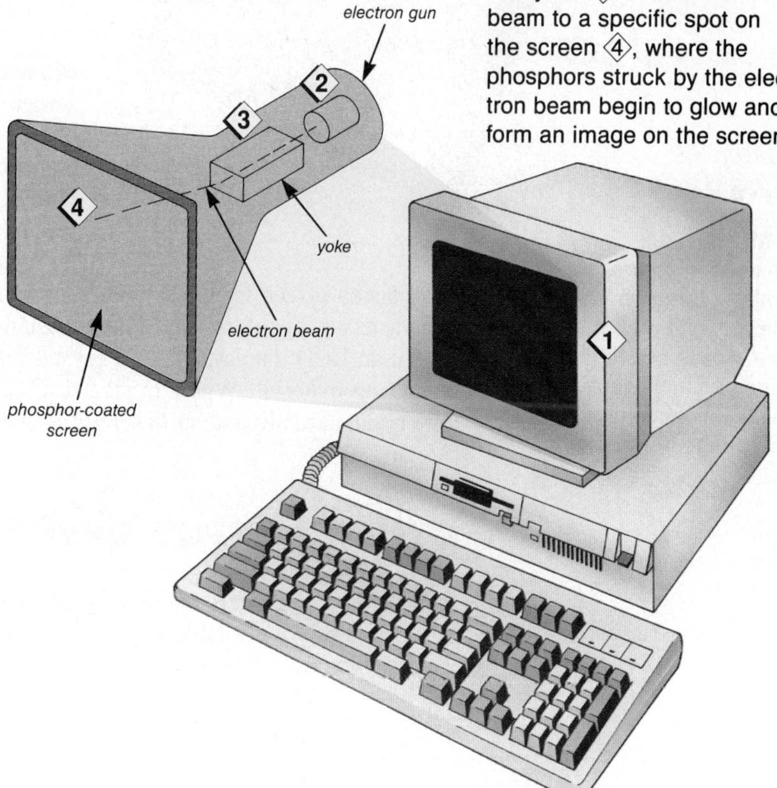

FIGURE 5-37
The process of forming an image on a screen begins when the information to be displayed is sent to the CRT ①. Then the electron gun ② generates an electron beam. The yoke ③ directs the beam to a specific spot on the screen ④, where the phosphors struck by the electron beam begin to glow and form an image on the screen.

On most screens, the phosphors that emit the light causing the image on the screen do not stay lit very long. They must be refreshed by having the electron beam light them again. If the screen is not scanned enough times per second, the phosphors will begin to lose their light. When this occurs, it appears that the image on the screen is flickering. To eliminate flicker, the entire screen is refreshed 30 times per second.

The brightness of the image on the screen depends on the intensity of the electron beam striking the phosphor, which in turn depends on the voltage applied to the beam. As the beam scans each phosphor dot, the intensity is varied precisely to turn each dot on or off.

How Color Is Produced Color is produced on a screen in several ways. Remember that on a monochrome screen, a single electron beam strikes the phosphor-coated screen, causing the chosen phosphor dot to light. If the characters are green on a black background, the phosphors emit a green light when they are activated. Similarly, if the characters are amber on black, the phosphors emit an amber light.

To show color on a screen, each pixel must have three phosphor dots. These dots are red, blue, and green (Figure 5-38). The electron beam must turn on the desired color phosphors within the pixel to generate an image. In the simplest configuration, eight colors can be generated—no color (black), red only, blue only, green only, red and blue (magenta), red and green (yellow), blue and green (blue-green), and red, blue, and green together (white). By varying the intensity of the electron beam striking the phosphors, many more colors can be generated.

Two types of color screens are composite video monitors and RGB monitors. Both monitors produce color images, and both monitors can be used for color graphics. A **composite video monitor** uses a single electron signal to turn on the color phosphors within the pixel. An **RGB monitor** uses three signals, one for each color, red, green, and blue, to turn on the required phosphors. The difference is that the RGB monitor produces a much clearer display with much better color and character resolution.

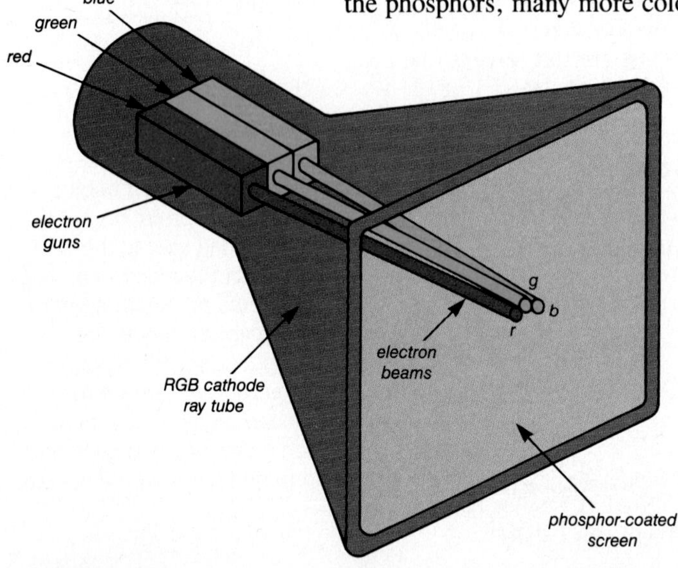

FIGURE 5-38
On color monitors, each pixel contains three phosphor dots: one red, one green, and one blue. These dots can be turned on individually or in combinations to display a wide range of colors.

How Flat Panel Displays Work A plasma screen is one type of flat panel display. It consists of a grid of conductors sealed between two flat plates of glass. The space between the glass is filled with neon/argon gas. When the gas at an intersection in the grid is electronically activated, it creates an image. Each intersection of the grid of wires in a plasma screen is addressable. Therefore, this type of screen can display characters in a variety of typefaces and graphics such as line drawings, charts, or even pictures.

In an LCD display, a liquid crystal material is deposited between two sheets of polarizing material. When an electrical current passes between crossing wires, the liquid crystals are aligned so that light cannot shine through, producing an image on the screen.

OTHER OUTPUT DEVICES

Although printers and display devices provide the majority of computer output, other devices are available for particular uses and applications. These include data projectors, plotters, computer output microfilm devices, and voice output devices.

Data Projectors

A variety of devices are available to take the image that appears on a computer screen and project it so that it can be clearly seen by a room full of people. Smaller, lower cost units, called **projection panels**, use liquid crystal display (LCD) technology and are designed to be placed on top of an overhead projector (Figure 5-39).

Larger, more expensive units use technology similar to large screen projection TV sets; separate red, green and blue beams of light are focused onto the screen (Figure 5-40). The projection panels are easily portable and depending on the overhead projector with which they are used, can be located at different distances from the projection screen. The three-beam projectors must be focused and aligned for a specific distance and thus once installed, are usually not moved.

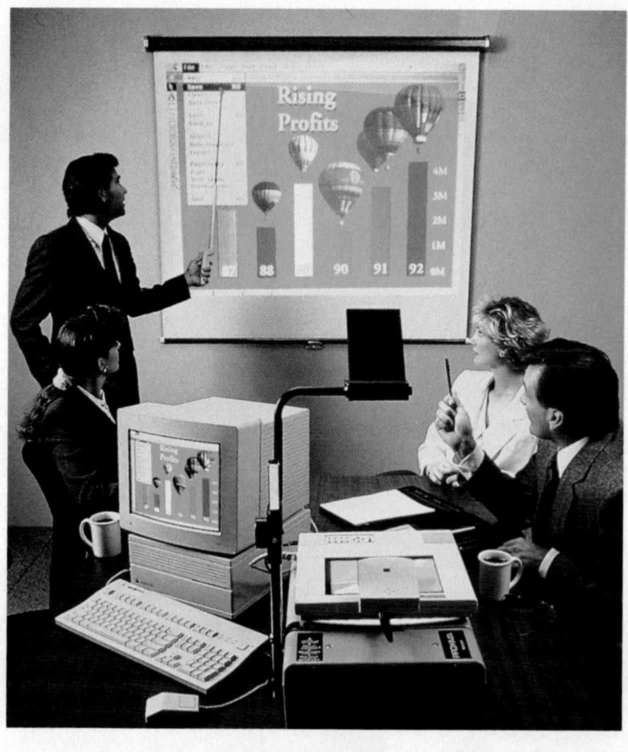

FIGURE 5-39
Projection panels are used together with overhead projectors to display computer screen images to a room full of people.

Plotters

A **plotter** is an output device used to produce high-quality line drawings such as building plans, charts, or circuit diagrams. These drawings can be quite large; some plotters are designed to handle paper up to 40 inches by 48 inches, much larger than would fit in a standard printer. Plotters can be classified by the way they create the drawing. The two types are pen plotters and electrostatic plotters.

As the name implies, **pen plotters** create images on a sheet of paper by moving one or more pens over the surface of the paper or by moving the paper under the tip of the pens.

Two different kinds of pen plotters are flatbed plotters and drum plotters. When a **flatbed plotter** is used to plot, or draw, the pen or pens are instructed by the software to move to the down position so the pen contacts the flat surface of the paper. Further instructions then direct the movement of the pens to create the image. Most flatbed plotters have one or more pens of varying colors or widths. The plotter shown in Figure 5-41 is a flatbed plotter that can create color drawings. Another kind of flatbed plotter holds the pen stationary and moves the paper under the pen.

FIGURE 5-40
This data projector uses three separate red, green, and blue beams to project data onto a screen.

FIGURE 5-41
A color flatbed plotter.

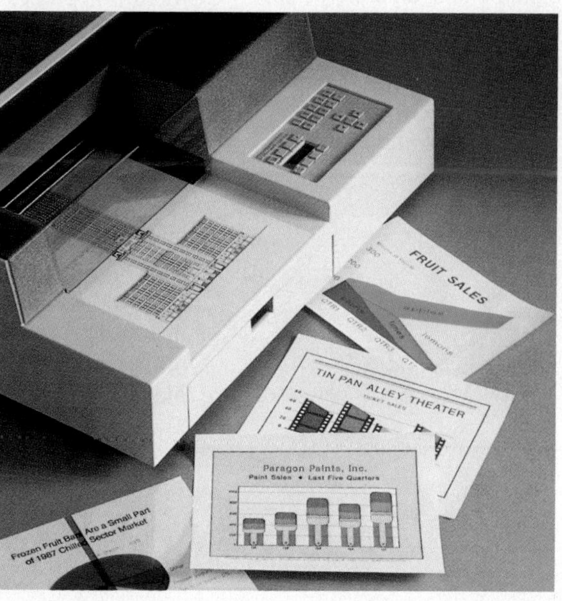

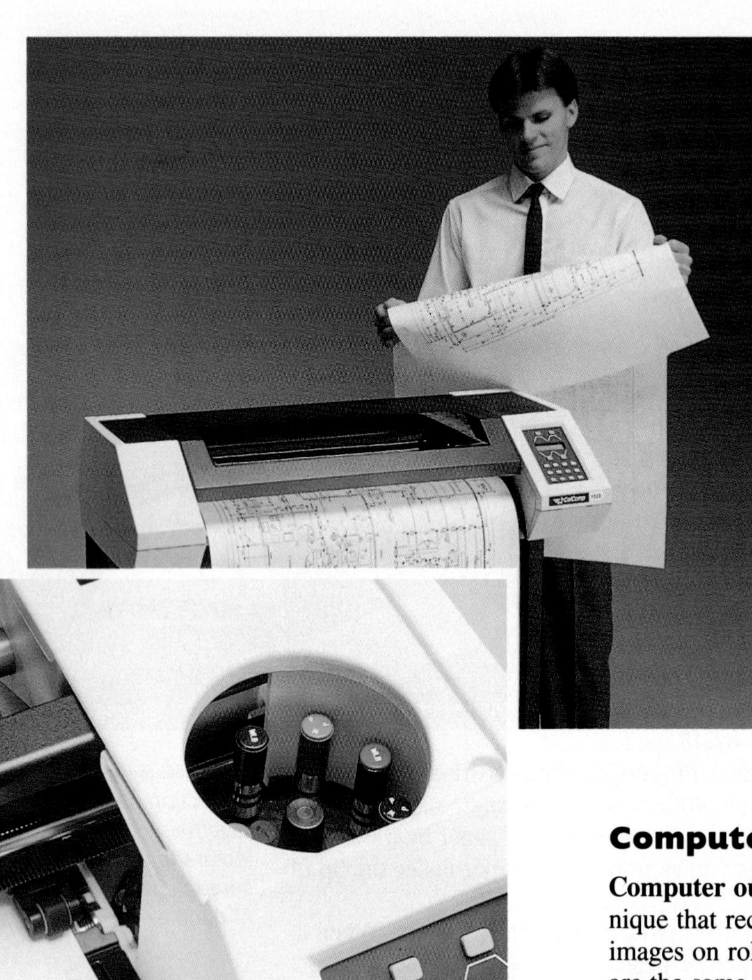

FIGURE 5-42
This drum plotter utilizes eight pens of different colors to create diagrams. As the paper moves forward and back, the pens move left and right and, under software control, draw where instructed.

A **drum plotter** uses a rotating drum, or cylinder, over which drawing pens are mounted. The pens can move to the left and right as the drum rotates, creating an image (Figure 5-42). An advantage of the drum plotter is that the length of the plot is virtually unlimited, since roll paper can be used. The width of the plot is limited by the width of the drum.

With an **electrostatic plotter**, the paper moves under a row of wires (called styli) that can be turned on to create an electrostatic charge on the paper. The paper then passes through a developer and the drawing emerges where the charged wires touched the paper. The electrostatic printer image is composed of a series of very small dots, resulting in relatively high-quality output. In addition, the speed of electrostatic plotting is faster than with pen plotters.

Computer Output Microfilm

Computer output microfilm (COM) is an output technique that records output from a computer as microscopic images on roll or sheet film. The images stored on COM are the same as the images that would be printed on paper. The COM recording process reduces characters 24, 42, or 48 times smaller than would be produced on a printer. The information is then recorded on sheet film called **microfiche** or on 16mm, 35mm, or 105mm roll film.

The data to be recorded by the device can come directly from the computer (online) or from a magnetic tape that was previously produced by the computer (offline) (Figure 5-43). After the COM film is processed, the user can view it.

Microfilm has several advantages over printed reports or other storage media for certain applications. Some of these advantages are:

1. Data can be recorded on the film up to 30,000 lines per minute—faster than all but very high-speed printers.
2. Costs for recording the data are lower. The cost of printing a three-part, 1,000-page report is approximately $28, whereas the cost of producing the same report on microfilm is approximately $3.
3. Less space is required to store microfilm than printed materials. Microfilm that weighs one ounce can store the equivalent of 10 pounds of paper.
4. Microfilm provides a less expensive way to store data. For example, the cost per million characters (megabyte) on a disk is approximately $10, whereas the cost per megabyte on microfilm is approximately 65 cents.

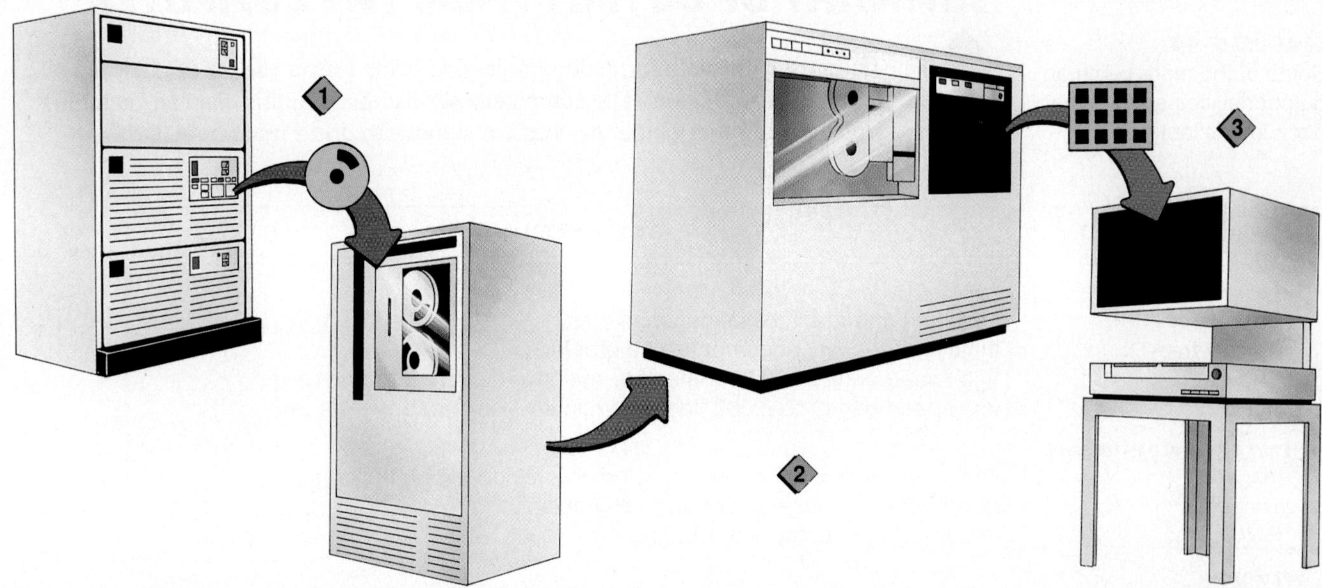

To access data stored on microfilm, a variety of readers are available. They utilize indexing techniques to provide a quick reference to the data. Some microfilm readers can perform automatic data lookup, called **computer-assisted retrieval (CAR)**, under the control of an attached computer. With the powerful indexing software and hardware now available for microfilm, a user can usually locate any piece of data in a 200 million character database in less than 10 seconds, at a far lower cost per inquiry than using an online inquiry system consisting of a computer system that stores the data on a hard disk.

FIGURE 5-43
The computer output microfilm (COM) process is illustrated here. The computer generates printed images on an output tape that is transferred to the tape drive attached to the COM machine ①. The COM machine reads the tape and produces reduced images of the printed output on the film ②—in this example, microfiche sheet film. Then the film can be viewed using special microfilm reader devices ③.

Voice Output

Another important means of generating output from a computer is voice output. **Voice output** consists of spoken words that are conveyed to the user from the computer. Thus, instead of reading words on a printed report or monitor, the user hears the words over earphones, the telephone, or other devices from which sound can be generated.

The data that produces voice output is usually created in one of two ways. First, a person can talk into a device that will encode the words in a digital pattern. For example, the words *The number is* can be spoken into a microphone, and the computer software can assign a digital pattern to the words. The digital data is then stored on a disk. At a later time, the data can be retrieved from the disk and translated back from digital data into voice, so that the person listening will actually hear the words.

A second type of voice generation that holds great promise is called a **voice synthesizer**. It can transform words stored in main memory into speech. The words are analyzed by a program that examines the letters stored in memory and generates sounds for the letter combinations. The software can apply rules of intonation and stress to make it sound as though a person were speaking. The speech is then projected over speakers attached to the computer.

You may have heard voice output used by the telephone company for giving number information. Automobile and vending machine manufacturers are also incorporating voice output into their products. The potential for this type of output is great and it will undoubtedly be used in many products and services in the future.

SUMMARY OF OUTPUT FROM THE COMPUTER

FIGURE 5-44
Some of the more common output devices are summarized in this table.

The output step of the information processing cycle uses a variety of devices to provide users with information. The equipment we discussed in this chapter, including printers, screens, and other output devices are summarized in Figure 5-44.

OUTPUT DEVICE	DESCRIPTION
Printers—Impact	
Dot matrix	Prints text and graphics using small dots.
Daisy wheel	Prints letter-quality documents—no graphics.
Chain	High-speed printer to 3,000 lines per minute—designed to print text.
Band	High-speed printer to 2,000 lines per minute—designed to print text.
Printers—Nonimpact	
Ink jet	Sprays ink onto page to form text and graphic output—prints quietly.
Thermal	Uses heat to produce fully formed characters.
Page	Produces high-quality text and graphics.
Screens	
Monochrome	Displays white, green, or amber images on a black background.
Color	Uses multiple colors to enhance displayed information.
Plasma	A flat screen that produces bright, clear images with no flicker.
LCD	A flat screen used on many laptop computers.
Data Projector	Projects computer screen images to a room full of people.
Plotters	Produces hard-copy graphic output.
COM	Records reduced-size information on sheet film called microfiche or on roll film.
Voice	Conveys information to the user from the computer in the form of speech.

CHAPTER SUMMARY

1. **Output** is data that has been processed into a useful form called information that can be used by a person or a machine.
2. Output that is printed is called **hard copy** and output that is displayed on a screen is called **soft copy**.
3. A **report** is information presented in an organized form.
4. An **internal report** is used within an organization by people performing their jobs.
5. An **external report** is used outside the organization.
6. The major consideration for internal reports is that they are clear and easy to use. For external reports, the quality of the printed output may be important.
7. **Narrative reports** may contain some graphic or numeric information, but are primarily text-based reports.
8. In a **detail report**, each line on the report usually corresponds to one input record.
9. A **summary report** contains summarized data, consisting of totals from detailed input data.
10. An **exception report** contains information that will help users to focus on situations that may require immediate decisions or specific actions.
11. **Periodic reports**, also called **scheduled reports**, are produced on a regular basis such as daily, weekly, or monthly.
12. **On-demand reports** are created for information that is not required on a scheduled basis, but only when it is requested.
13. **Computer graphics** are used to present information so it can be quickly and easily understood.
14. **Multimedia** combines text, graphics, video, and audio output on a screen.

15. The key to use of full-motion video in multimedia is **video compression**, making large amounts of data take up less storage space. **Digital video interactive (DVI)** is one compression technique currently being developed.
16. Computer printer features include speed, paper types and sizes, print quality, typefaces, color capability, size, and interface.
17. The printing rate for low-speed printers is rated in **characters per second (cps)**. The printing rate for medium- and high-speed printers is rated in either **lines per minute (lpm)** or **pages per minute (ppm)**.
18. The pages of **continuous-form paper** are connected for continuous flow through the printer.
19. Print quality is rated as **letter quality (LQ)**, **near letter quality (NLQ)**, or **draft quality**.
20. A **typeface** is a set of letters, numbers, and special characters that have a similar design.
21. Character sizes are measured in points. A **point** is 1/72 of an inch.
22. A complete set of characters in the same typeface, style, and size is called a **font**.
23. Computer printers fall into two broad categories: impact printers and nonimpact printers.
24. **Impact printing** devices transfer the image onto paper by some type of printing mechanism striking the paper, ribbon, and character together.
25. A **nonimpact printer** creates an image without having characters strike against a sheet of paper.
26. Although impact printing is noisy, multiple copies can be made at the same time.
27. Nonimpact printers are quiet and produce high-quality output.
28. **Dot matrix printers** can print text and graphics and are used with more personal computers than any other type of printer.
29. Dot matrix printers have small pins that are contained in a print head. The pins strike the paper and ribbon to print a character.
30. The quality of a dot matrix printer is partly dependent on the number of pins used to form the character.
31. Most dot matrix printers can print condensed print, standard print, and enlarged print.
32. Most dot matrix printers print **bidirectionally**, meaning the print head can print while moving in either direction.
33. **Tractor feed mechanisms** transport continuous-form paper by using sprockets inserted into holes on the sides of the paper.
34. **Friction feed mechanisms** move paper through a printer by pressure between the paper and the carriage.
35. Some dot matrix printers can print in color.
36. **Daisy wheel printers** can print high-quality text, but they cannot print graphics.
37. **Chain printers** use a rotating chain to print up to 3,000 lines per minute.
38. **Band printers** can use interchangeable bands with different fonts.
39. An **ink jet printer** uses a nozzle to spray liquid ink drops onto the page. Some ink jet printers print in color.
40. **Thermal printers** use heat to produce fully formed characters, usually on chemically treated paper.
41. **Page printers** use a process similar to a copying machine to produce high-quality text and graphic output.
42. **High-speed page printers** use a dedicated computer and tape drive and can print several hundred pages per minute.
43. **Screens**, also referred to as **monitors**, **CRTs**, or **VDTs** are used to display data.
44. Most screens are 12 to 16 inches and display 80 characters per line with 25 lines on the screen at one time.
45. The **resolution**, or clarity, of a screen is determined by the number of **pixels** that can be illuminated.
46. The **cursor** is a symbol such as an underline character or an arrow that indicates where you are working on the screen.
47. **Scrolling** refers to the movement of screen data up or down one line or one screen at a time.
48. **Reverse video**, also called **inverse video**, **underlining**, **bold**, and **blinking** are screen features that can be used to emphasize displayed characters.
49. Types of screens include **monochrome screens**, **color screens**, **plasma screens**, and **LCD screens**.
50. **Monochrome screens** usually display green, white, or amber images on a black background or black images on a white background.
51. **Color screens** are being used more because color enables the user to more easily read and understand the information displayed on the screen.
52. **Plasma screens** and **liquid crystal display (LCD) screens** are flat screens often used with portable computers.
53. Most screens utilize cathode ray tube (CRT) technology.
54. To display color on a color monitor, three separate dots (red, blue, and green) are turned on by an electron beam.
55. Two types of color monitors are: **composite video monitors** and **RGB monitors**.
56. **Data projectors** can be used to project a screen image so that it can be seen by a room full of people.
57. A **plotter** is an output device that can create line drawings, diagrams, and similar types of output.

58. **Computer output microfilm (COM)** is an output technique that records output from a computer as microscopic images on roll or sheet film.
59. COM offers the advantages of faster recording speed, lower costs of recording the data, less space required for storing the data, and lower costs for storing the data.
60. Some microfilm readers can perform automatic data lookup, called **computer-assisted retrieval (CAR)**.
61. **Voice output** consists of spoken words that are conveyed to the computer user from the computer.
62. A **voice synthesizer** can transform words stored in main memory into human speech.

KEY TERMS

Band printer *5.12*
Bidirectional *5.10*
Bit-mapped display *5.16*
Blinking *5.18*
Bold *5.18*
Chain printer *5.12*
Characters per second (cps) *5.6*
Color screen *5.19*
Composite video monitor *5.20*
Computer-assisted retrieval (CAR) *5.23*
Computer graphics *5.4*
Computer output microfilm (COM) *5.22*
Continuous-form paper *5.6*
CRT (cathode ray tube) *5.16*
Cursor *5.18*
Daisy wheel printer *5.11*
Detail report *5.3*
Digital video interactive (DVI) *5.5*
Dot-addressable display *5.16*
Dot matrix printer *5.8*
Draft quality *5.6*
Drum plotter *5.22*
Electrostatic plotter *5.22*
Exception report *5.3*
External report *5.2*
Flatbed plotter *5.21*
Flat panel display screen *5.18*
Font *5.6*
Friction feed mechanism *5.10*
Hard copy *5.2*
High-speed page printer *5.15*
Impact printer *5.7*
Ink jet printer *5.13*
Internal report *5.2*
Inverse video *5.18*
Laser printer *5.14*
Letter quality (LQ) *5.6*
Line printer *5.6*
Lines per minute (lpm) *5.6*
Liquid crystal display (LCD) *5.19*
Microfiche *5.22*
Monitor *5.16*
Monochrome screen *5.18*
Multimedia *5.4*
Narrative report *5.2*
Near letter quality (NLQ) *5.6*
Nonimpact printing *5.7*
On-demand report *5.4*
Output *5.2*
Page printer *5.14*
Pages per minute (ppm) *5.6*
Parallel interface *5.7*
Pen plotter *5.21*
Periodic report *5.4*
Picture element *5.16*
Pixel *5.16*
Plasma screen *5.19*
Plotter *5.21*
Projection panel *5.21*
Report *5.2*
Resolution *5.16*
Reverse video *5.18*
RGB monitor *5.20*
Scheduled report *5.4*
Screen *5.16*
Scrolling *5.18*
Serial interface *5.7*
Soft copy *5.2*
Summary report *5.3*
Thermal printer *5.14*
Thermal transfer printer *5.14*
Tractor feed mechanism *5.10*
Typeface *5.6*
Underlining *5.18*
VDT (video display terminal) *5.16*
Video compression *5.5*
Voice output *5.23*
Voice synthesizer *5.23*

REVIEW QUESTIONS

1. Name and describe four types of commonly used reports.
2. What is multimedia? Give an example of multimedia.
3. Define the terms typeface, point, and font.
4. Identify the two major classifications of printers and discuss the advantages and disadvantages of each.
5. How does a dot matrix printer produce an image? What techniques are used on dot matrix printers to improve the print quality?
6. What are the two types of impact printers often used to print large volumes of data?
7. How does an ink jet printer produce images?
8. Explain how a page printer works.
9. List four graphics standards that have been developed for screens.
10. List the steps involved in displaying an image on a CRT screen.
11. Identify two types of flat panel display screens that are commonly used with portable computers.
12. What is a projection panel and how is it used?
13. List several advantages of microfilm over printed reports.
14. Describe the two ways of creating voice output.

CONTROVERSIAL ISSUES

1. When computers were first used in business, some people predicted the paperless office; a place where most documents would only exist electronically in the computer database. While some people think this will still happen, others believe that the widespread use of computers, word processing and spreadsheet software, and low-cost printers has actually resulted in an increase in the amount of paperwork. Do you think computers increase or decrease the amount of paper required?
2. Some people believe that multimedia will revolutionize the way information is presented and the way people learn. Others believe multimedia will have only a limited number of successful applications. For which new applications do you think multimedia can be used?

RESEARCH PROJECTS

1. Make a list of the places where you have heard synthesized voice output. Discuss these with others in your class.
2. Visit a computer store and obtain information on the lowest and highest priced printers. Make a presentation explaining the differences between the two printers.

Auxiliary Storage

OBJECTIVES

- Define auxiliary storage
- Identify the primary devices used for auxiliary storage
- Explain how data is stored on diskettes and hard disks
- Describe how data stored on magnetic disks can be protected
- Explain how magnetic tape storage is used with computers
- Describe three other forms of auxiliary storage: optical disks, solid-state devices, and mass storage devices
- Describe how special-purpose storage devices such as smart cards are used

Storage is the fourth and final operation in the information processing cycle. In this chapter we explain storage operations and the various types of auxiliary storage devices that are used with computers. Combining what you learn about storage with your knowledge of input, processing, and output will allow you to complete your understanding of the information processing cycle.

WHAT IS AUXILIARY STORAGE?

It is important to understand the difference between how a computer uses main memory and how it uses auxiliary storage. As you have seen, main memory temporarily stores programs and data that are being processed. **Auxiliary storage**, also called **secondary storage**, stores programs and data when they are not being processed, just as a filing cabinet is used in an office to store records. Records that are not being used are kept in the filing cabinet until they are needed. In the same way, data and programs that are not being used on a computer are kept in auxiliary storage until they are needed. Auxiliary storage devices that are used with computers include devices such as disk and tape drives (Figure 6-1).

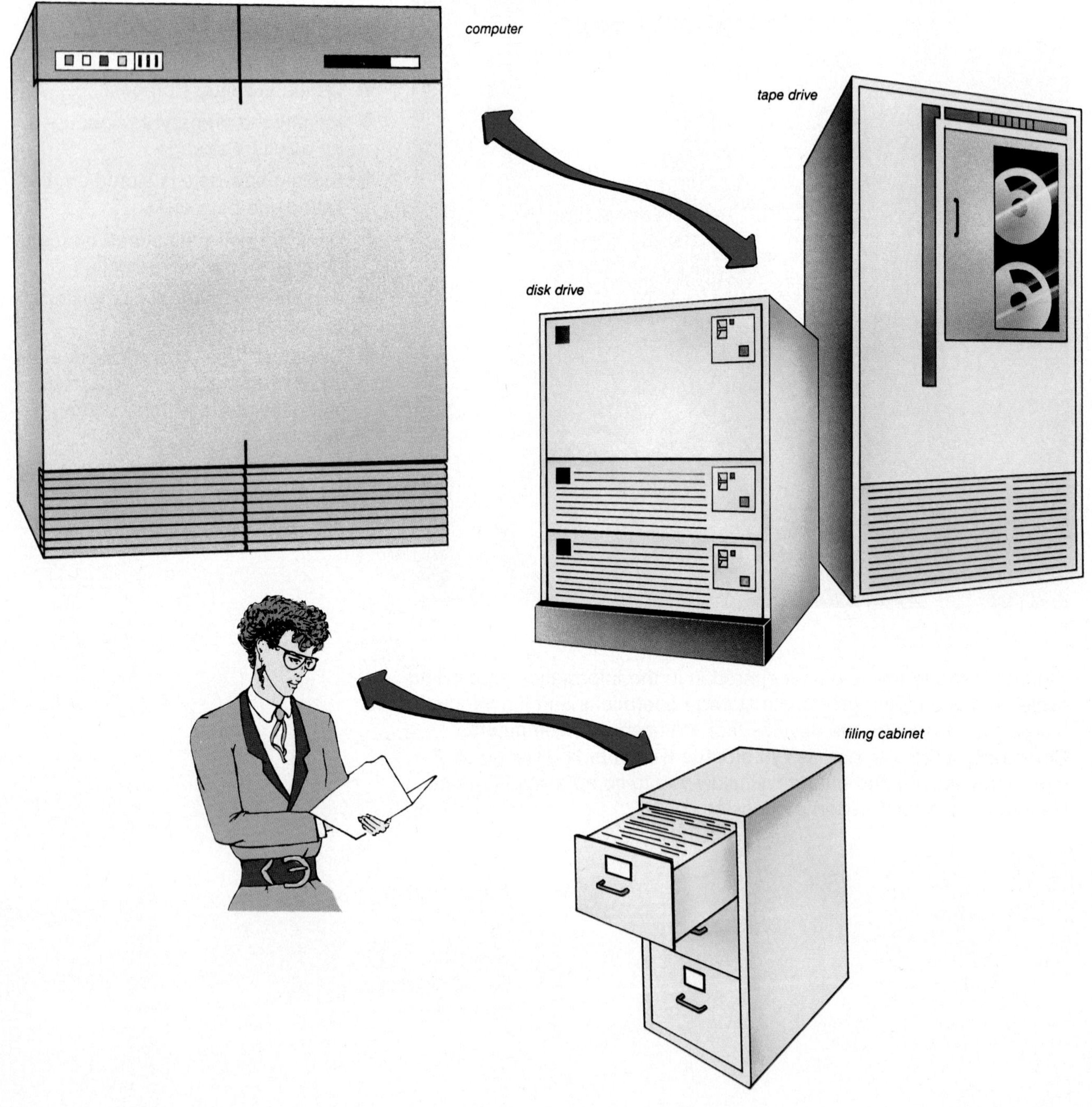

FIGURE 6-1
Auxiliary storage is like a filing cabinet in which data is stored until you need it.

Most auxiliary storage devices provide a more permanent form of storage than main memory because they are **nonvolatile**, that is, data and programs stored on auxiliary storage devices are retained when the power is turned off. Main memory is volatile, which means that when power is turned off, whatever is stored in main memory is erased.

Auxiliary storage devices can be used as both input and output devices. When they are used to receive data that has been processed by the computer, they are functioning as output devices. When some of their stored data is transferred to the computer for processing, they are functioning as input devices.

User auxiliary storage needs can vary greatly. Personal computer users might find the amount of data to be stored to be relatively small. For example, the names, addresses, and telephone numbers of several hundred friends or customers of a small business might require only 20,000 bytes of auxiliary storage (200 records × 100 characters per record). Users of large computers, such as banks or insurance companies, however, might need auxiliary storage devices that can store billions of characters. To meet the different needs of users, a variety of storage devices are available. We discuss magnetic disk, magnetic tape, and other auxiliary storage devices in this chapter.

FIGURE 6-2
Here, a user is inserting a diskette into the disk drive of an IBM personal computer.

MAGNETIC DISK STORAGE

Magnetic disk is the most widely used storage medium for all types of computers. **Magnetic disk** offers high storage capacity, reliability, and the capability to directly access stored data. There are several types of magnetic disk including diskettes, hard disks, and removable disk cartridges.

Diskettes

In the early 1970s, IBM introduced the diskette as a new type of auxiliary storage. These diskettes were eight inches in diameter and were thin and flexible, hence the name **floppy disks**, or *floppies*. Today, **diskettes** are used as a principal auxiliary storage medium for personal computers (Figure 6-2). This type of storage is convenient, reliable, and inexpensive.

Diskettes are available in a number of different sizes. The most common sizes today are 5 1/4" and 3 1/2" diameters (Figure 6-3).

A diskette consists of a circular piece of thin mylar plastic (the actual disk), which is coated with an oxide material similar to that used on recording tape. On a 5 1/4" disk, the circular piece of plastic is enclosed in a flexible square protective jacket. The jacket has an opening so that a portion of the disk's surface is exposed for reading and writing (recording) as shown on the next page in Figure 6-4.

FIGURE 6-3
The most commonly used diskette for personal computers are 5 1/4" and 3 1/2".

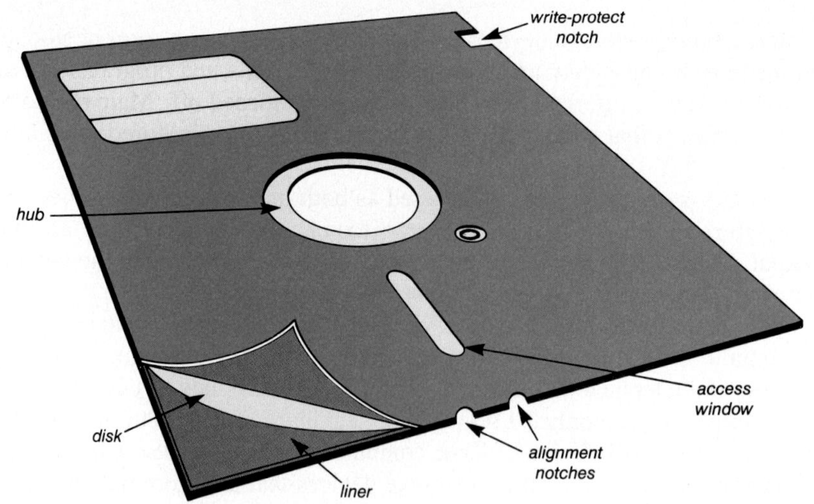

FIGURE 6-4
A 5 1/4" diskette consists of the disk itself enclosed within a protective jacket, usually made of vinyl material. The liner of the diskette is essentially friction-free so that the disk can turn freely, but the liner does contact the disk and keep it clean. The magnetic surface of the diskette, which is exposed through the window in the jacket, allows data to be read and stored. The large hole (hub) in the diskette is used to mount the diskette in the disk drive. The small hole is used by some disk drives as an indicator for where to store data.

On a 3 1/2" disk, the circular piece of plastic is enclosed in a rigid plastic cover and a piece of metal called the shutter covers the reading and writing area. When the 3 1/2" diskette is inserted into a disk drive, the drive slides the shutter to the side to expose the diskette surface (Figure 6-5).

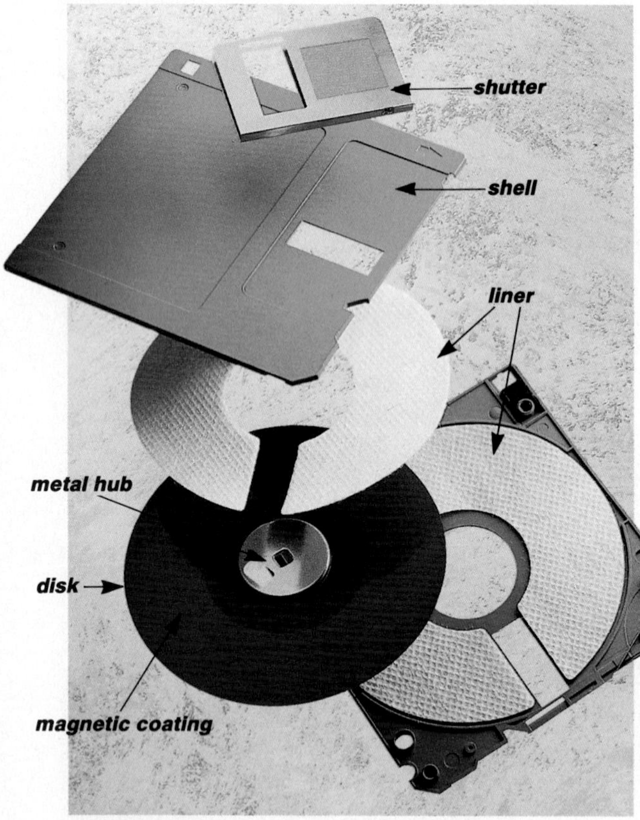

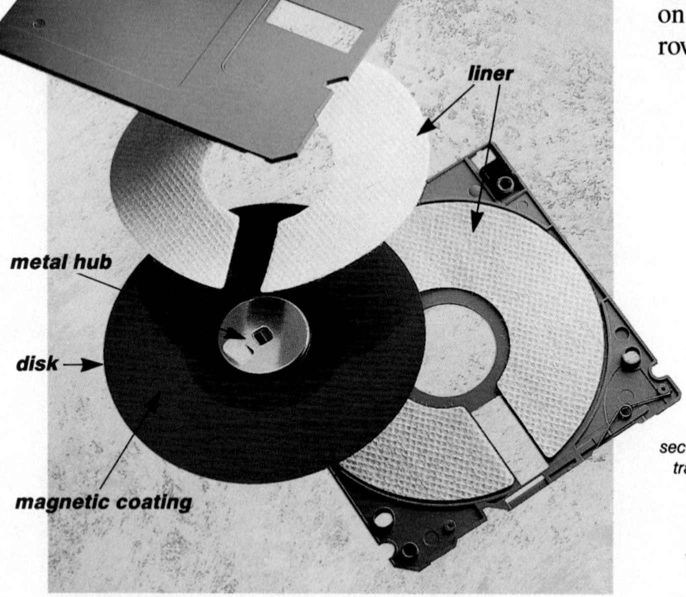

FIGURE 6-5
In a 3 1/2" diskette, the flexible plastic disk is enclosed between two liners that clean the disk surface of any microscopic debris and help to disperse static electricity. The outside cover is made of a rigid plastic material, and the recording window is covered by a metal shutter that slides to the side when the disk is inserted into the disk drive.

How Is a Diskette Formatted? Before a diskette can be used for auxiliary storage, it must be formatted. The **formatting** process prepares the diskette so that it can store data and includes defining the tracks, cylinders, and sectors on the surfaces of a diskette (Figure 6-6). A **track** is a narrow recording band forming a full circle around the diskette.

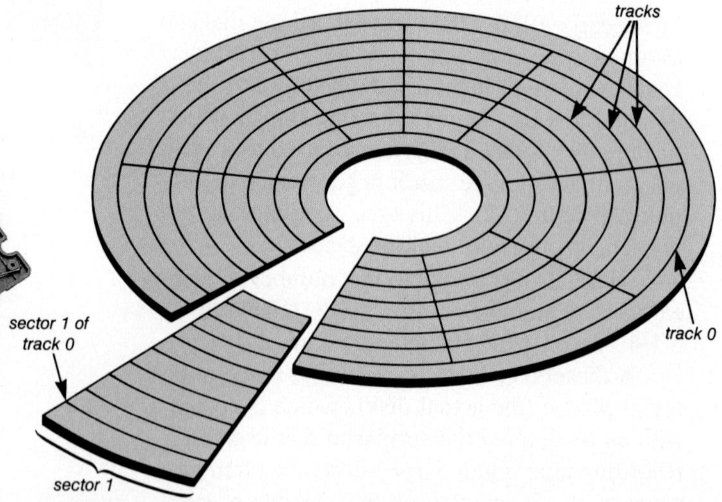

FIGURE 6-6
Each track on a diskette is a narrow, circular band. On a diskette containing 40 tracks, the outside track is called track 0 and the inside track is called track 39. The distance between track 0 and track 39 on a 5 1/4" diskette is less that one inch. The disk surface is divided into sectors. This example shows a diskette with nine sectors.

A **cylinder** is defined as all tracks of the same number. For example, track 0 on side 1 of the diskette and track 0 on side 2 of the diskette would be called cylinder 0. The term **sector** is used to refer to a pie-shaped section of the disk. It is also used to refer to a section of a track. When data is read from a diskette, a minimum of one full sector of a track is read. When data is stored on a diskette, at least one full sector of a track is written. The number of tracks and sectors created on a diskette when it is formatted varies based on the capacity of the diskette, the capabilities of the diskette drive being used, and the specifications in the software that does the formatting. Many 5 1/4" diskettes are formatted with 40 tracks and 9 sectors on the surface of the diskette. The 3 1/2" diskettes are usually formatted with 80 tracks and 9 sectors on each side. Even though it is smaller in size, a 3 1/2" diskette has a larger storage capacity than a 5 1/4" diskette.

Formatting is not usually done by the disk manufacturer because different operating systems define the surface of the diskette differently. In addition to defining the disk surface, the formatting process erases any data that is on the disk, analyzes the disk surface for any defective spots, and establishes a directory that will be used to record information about files stored on the diskette.

What Is the Storage Capacity of a Diskette? Knowing the storage capacity of a diskette gives you an idea of how much data or how many programs you can store on the diskette. The amount of data you can store depends on three factors: (1) the number of sides of the diskette used; (2) the recording density of the bits on a track; and (3) the number of tracks on the diskette.

Early diskettes and drives were designed so that data could be recorded on only one side of the diskette. These drives are called **single-sided drives**. Similarly, diskettes on which data can be recorded on one side only are called **single-sided diskettes**. Today, disk drives are designed to record and read data on both sides of the diskette. Drives that can read and write data on both sides of the diskette are called **double-sided drives** and the diskettes are called **double-sided diskettes**. The use of double-sided drives and diskettes *doubles* the amount of data that can be stored on the diskette.

Another factor in determining the storage capacity of a diskette is the recording density provided by the drive. The **recording density** is the number of bits that can be recorded on one inch of the innermost track on the diskette. This measurement is referred to as **bits per inch (bpi)**. The higher the recording density, the higher the storage capacity of the diskette.

The third factor that influences the amount of data that can be stored on a diskette is the number of tracks onto which data can be recorded. This measurement is referred to as **tracks per inch (tpi)**. As we saw earlier in this chapter, the number of tracks depends on the size of the diskette, the drive being used, and how the diskette was formatted.

The capacity of diskettes varies and increases every two or three years as manufacturers develop new ways of recording data more densely. Commonly used diskettes are referred to as either low density or high density. **Low-density diskettes** can store 360K for a 5 1/4" diskette and 720K for a 3 1/2" diskette. Personal computers using **high-density diskettes** (sometimes abbreviated as HD) can store 1.2 megabytes (million characters) on a 5 1/4" diskette and 1.44 megabytes on a 3 1/2" diskette.

How Is Data Stored on a Diskette? Regardless of the type of diskette or how it is formatted, the method of storing data on a diskette is essentially the same. When a 5 1/4" diskette is inserted in a disk drive, the center hole fits over a hub mechanism that positions the diskette in the unit (Figure 6-7). The circular plastic diskette rotates within its cover at approximately 300 revolutions per minute. Data is stored on tracks of the disk, using the same code, such as ASCII, that is used to store the data in main memory. To do this, a recording mechanism in the drive called the **read/write head** rests on the surface of the rotating diskette, generating electronic impulses (Figure 6-8). The electronic impulses change the magnetic polarity, or alignment, of magnetic spots along a track on the disk. The plus or minus polarity represents the 1 or 0 bits being recorded. To access different tracks on the diskette, the drive moves the read/write head from track to track. When reading data from the disk, the read/write head senses the magnetic spots that are recorded on the disk along the various tracks and transfers the data to main memory. When writing, the read/write head transfers data from main memory and stores it as magnetic spots on the tracks on the recording surface.

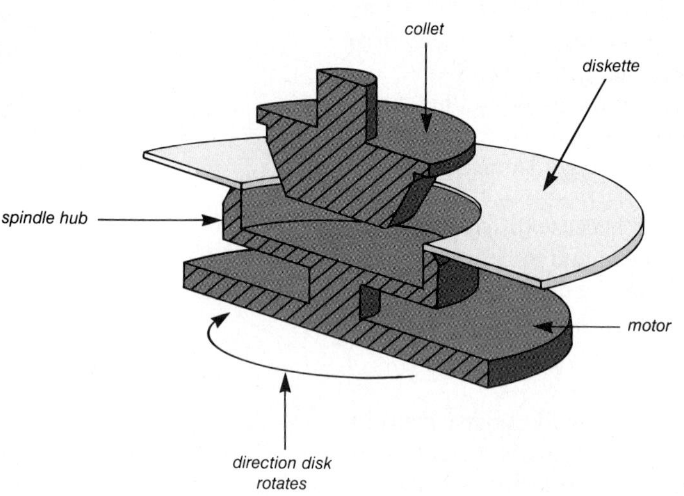

FIGURE 6-7
A cutaway drawing of a 5 1/4" disk drive. When you insert a diskette in a drive, the center hole is positioned between the collet and the hub. After you close the door to the disk drive, the disk is engaged and begins rotating within the protective jacket at approximately 300 RPM.

What Is Access Time? Data stored in sectors on a diskette must be retrieved and placed in main memory to be processed. The time required to access and retrieve the data is called the **access time**.

The access time for a diskette drive depends on four factors:

1. **Seek time**, the time it takes to position the read/write head over the proper track.
2. **Rotational delay** (also called **latency**), the time it takes for the sector containing the data to rotate under the read/write head.
3. **Settling time**, the time required for the read/write head to be placed in contact with the disk.
4. **Data transfer rate**, the time required to transfer the data from the disk to main memory.

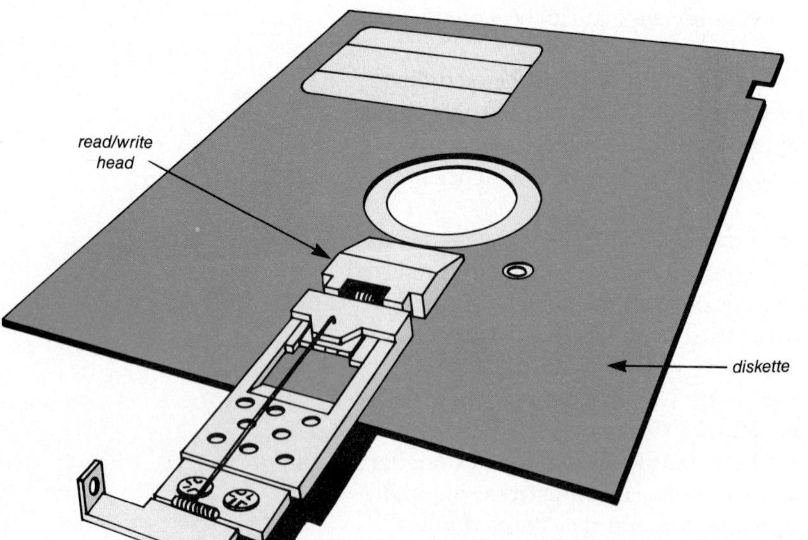

FIGURE 6-8
The read/write heads move back and forth over the openings on both sides of the protective jacket to read or write data on the disk.

The access time for diskettes varies from about 175 milliseconds (one millisecond equals 1/1000 of one second) to approximately 300 milliseconds. What this means to the user is that, on the average, data stored in a single sector on a diskette can be retrieved in approximately 1/5 to 1/3 of one second.

The Care of Diskettes With reasonable care, diskettes provide an inexpensive and reliable form of storage. In handling diskettes, you should take care to avoid exposing them to heat, magnetic fields, and contaminated environments such as dust, smoke, or salt air. One advantage of the 3 1/2" diskette is that its rigid plastic cover provides more protection for the data stored on the plastic disk inside than the flexible cover on a 5 1/4" diskette. Figure 6-9 shows you ways to properly care for your diskettes. Because the read/write head actually comes in contact with the diskette surface, wear takes place and the diskette will eventually become unreadable. To protect against loss, you should backup or copy data onto other diskettes.

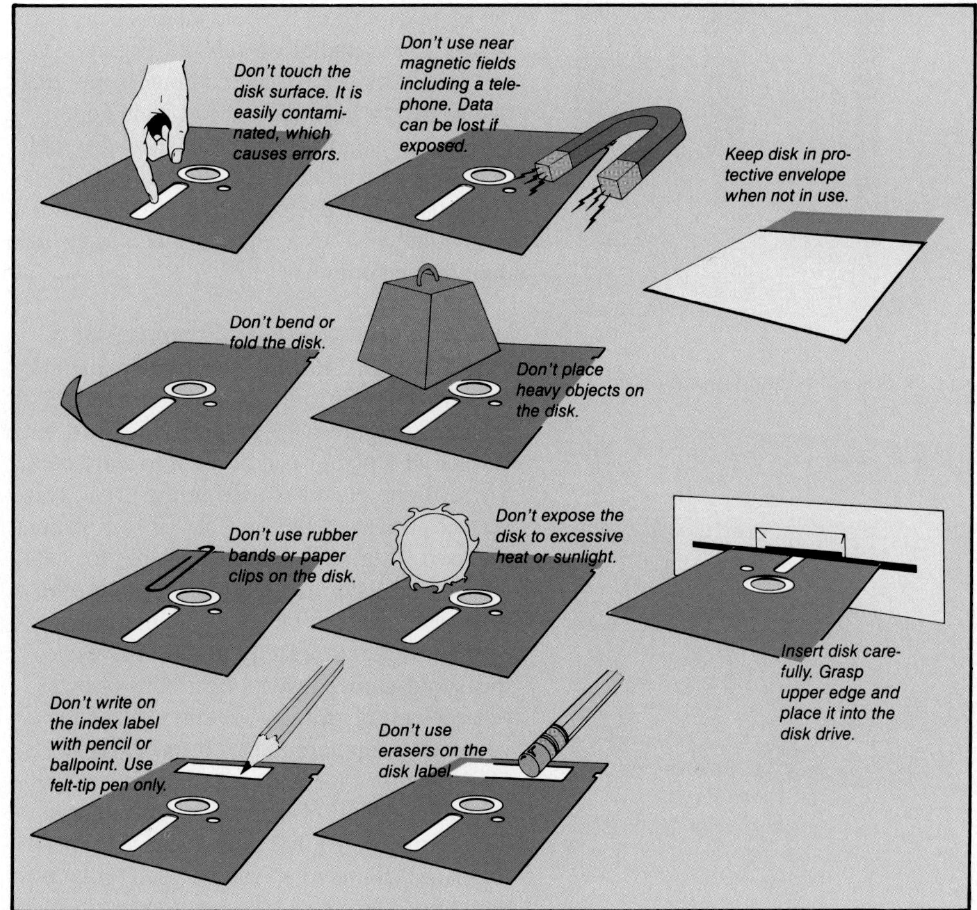
Don't touch the disk surface. It is easily contaminated, which causes errors.
Don't use near magnetic fields including a telephone. Data can be lost if exposed.
Keep disk in protective envelope when not in use.
Don't bend or fold the disk.
Don't place heavy objects on the disk.
Don't use rubber bands or paper clips on the disk.
Don't expose the disk to excessive heat or sunlight.
Insert disk carefully. Grasp upper edge and place it into the disk drive.
Don't write on the index label with pencil or ballpoint. Use felt-tip pen only.
Don't use erasers on the disk label.

FIGURE 6-9
Guidelines for the proper care of 5 1/4" diskettes. Most of the guidelines also apply to 3 1/2" diskettes.

Hard Disks

Hard disks provide larger and faster auxiliary storage capabilities than diskettes. **Hard disks** consist of one or more rigid metal platters coated with an oxide material that allows data to be magnetically recorded on the surface of the platters (Figure 6-10). These disks are permanently mounted inside the computer and are not removable like diskettes. On hard disks, the metal platters, the read/write heads, and the mechanism for moving the heads across the surface of the disk are enclosed in an airtight, sealed case. This helps to ensure a clean environment for the disk.

FIGURE 6-10
A hard disk consists of one or more disk platters. Each side of the platter is coated with an oxide substance that allows data to be magnetically stored.

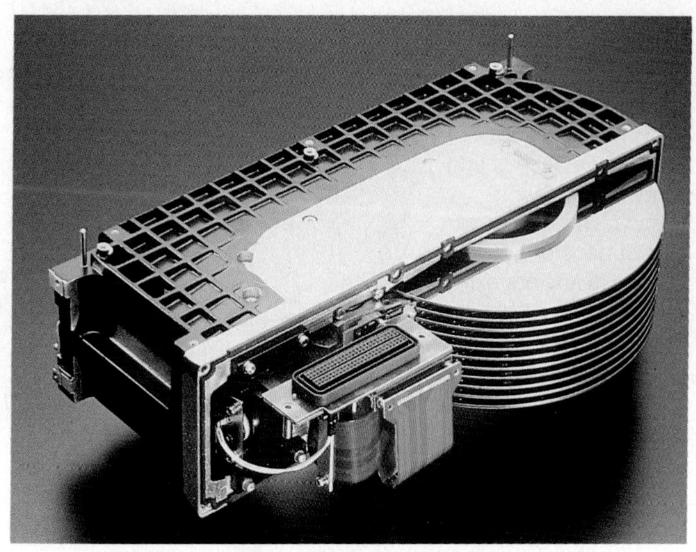

FIGURE 6-11
A high-speed, high-capacity fixed disk drive in a stand-alone cabinet.

FIGURE 6-12
A mainframe computer can have dozens of fixed disk storage devices attached to it.

FIGURE 6-13
This hard disk drive shows the access arm and the read/write heads, which are over the surface of the disks. These heads are extremely stable. They can read and write tracks very close together on the surface of the disk.

On minicomputers and mainframes, hard disks are sometimes called **fixed disks** because they cannot be removed like diskettes. They are also referred to as **direct-access storage devices (DASD)**. These hard disks are larger versions of the hard disks used on personal computers and can be either mounted in the same cabinet as the computer or enclosed in their own stand-alone cabinet (Figure 6-11).

While most personal computers are limited to two to four disks drives, minicomputers can support 8 to 16 disk devices, and mainframe computers can support over 100 high-speed disk devices. Figure 6-12 shows a large number of disk units attached to a single mainframe computer.

What Is the Storage Capacity of a Hard Disk? Hard drives contain a spindle on which one or more disk platters are mounted (Figure 6-13). On many drives, each surface of a platter can be used to store data. Thus, if one platter is used in the drive, two surfaces are available for data. If two platters are used, four surfaces are available for data, and so on. Naturally, the more platters, the more data that can be stored on the drive.

The storage capacity of hard drives is measured in megabytes or millions of bytes (characters) of storage. Common sizes for personal computers range from 20MB to 100MB of storage and even larger sizes are available; 20MB of storage is equivalent to approximately 10,000 double-spaced typewritten pages. Some disk devices used on large computers can store billions of bytes of information (Figure 6-14). A billion bytes of information is called a **gigabyte**.

FIGURE 6-14
The IBM 3390 disk drive, shown here being assembled, can store 22.7 billion bytes of data.

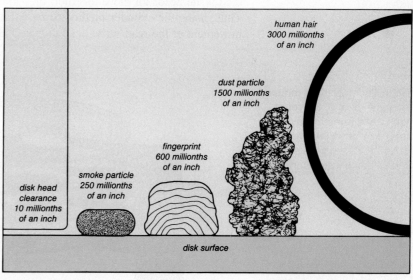

How Is Data Stored on a Hard Disk? Storing data on hard disks is similar to storing data on diskettes. In order to read or write data on the surface of the spinning disk platter, the disk drives are designed with access arms, or actuators. The **access arms**, or **actuators**, contain one or more read/write heads per disk surface. As the disk rotates at a high rate of speed, usually 3600 revolution per minute, the read/write heads move across its surface. These read/write heads *float* on a cushion of air and do not actually touch the surface of the disk. The distance between the head and the surface varies from approximately ten to twenty millionths of an inch. As shown in Figure 6-15, the close tolerance leaves no room for any type of contamination. If some form of contamination is introduced or if the alignment of the read/write heads is altered by something accidentally jarring the computer, the disk head can collide with and damage the disk surface, causing a loss of data. This event is known as a **head crash**. Because of the time needed to repair the disk and to reconstruct the data that was lost, head crashes can be extremely costly to users in terms of both time and money.

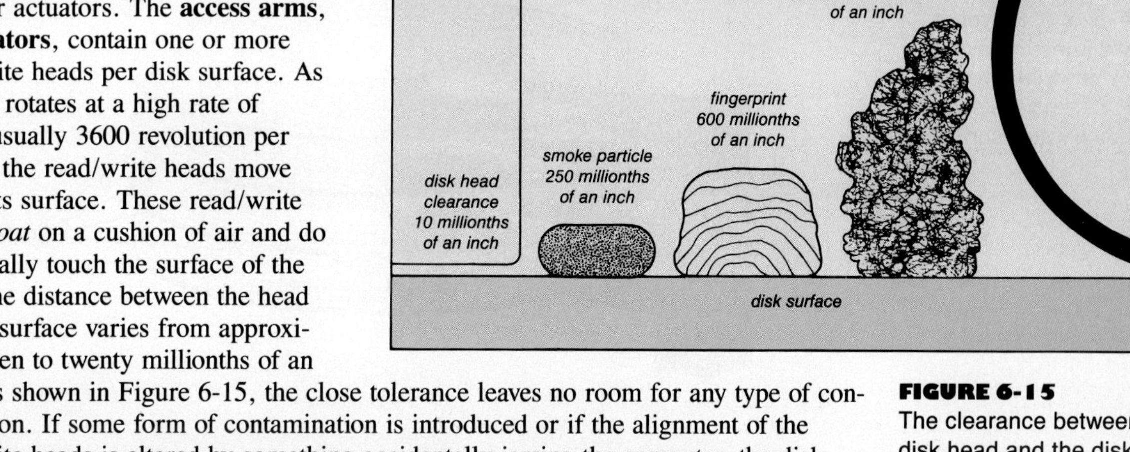

FIGURE 6-15
The clearance between a disk head and the disk surface is about 10 millionths of an inch. With this small difference, contamination such as a smoke particle, fingerprint, dust particle, or human hair could render the drive unusable. Sealed disk drives are designed to minimize contamination.

How Is Data Physically Organized on a Hard Disk? Depending on the type of disk drive, data is physically organized in one of two ways. One way is the sector method and the other is the cylinder method.

The **sector method** for physically organizing data on disks divides each track on the disk surface into individual storage areas called sectors (Figure 6-16). Each sector can contain a specified number of bytes. Data is referenced by indicating the surface, track, and sector where the data is stored.

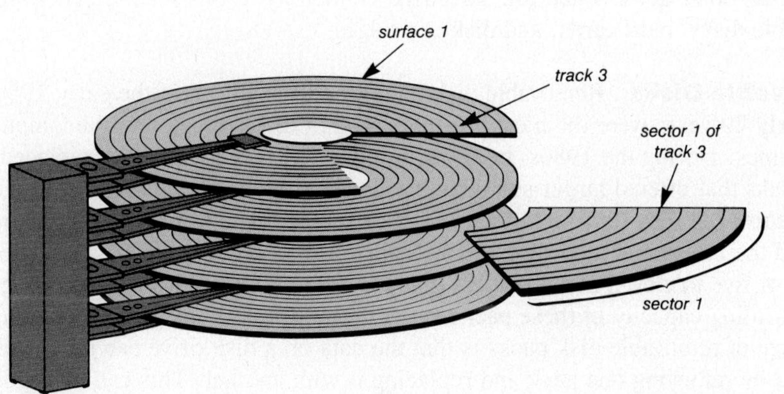

FIGURE 6-16
The sector method of disk addressing divides each track into a number of sectors. To locate data, the surface, track, and sector where the data is stored are specified.

With the **cylinder method**, all tracks of the same number on each recording surface are considered part of the same cylinder (shown on the next page in Figure 6-17). For example, the fifth track on all surfaces would be considered part of cylinder five. All twentieth tracks would be part of cylinder twenty, and so on. When the computer requests data from a disk using the cylinder method, it must specify the cylinder, recording surface, and record number. Because the access arms containing the read/write heads all move together, they are always over the same track on all surfaces. Thus, using the cylinder method to record data *down* the disk surfaces reduces the movement of the read/write head during both reading and writing of data.

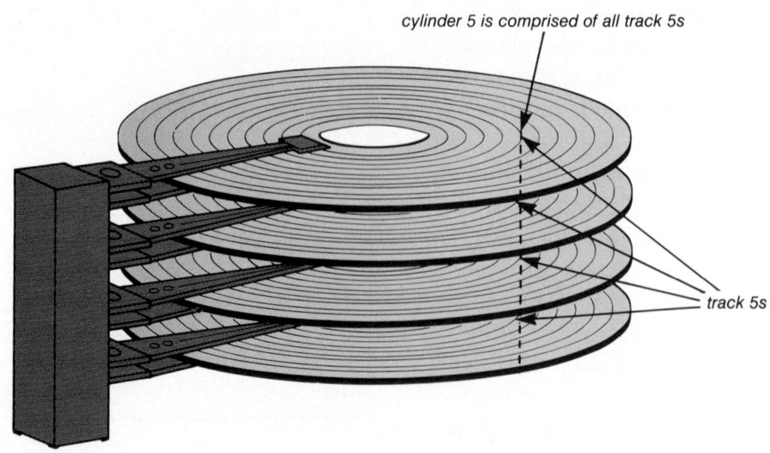
cylinder 5 is comprised of all track 5s
track 5s

FIGURE 6-17
The cylinder method reduces the movement of the read/write head (thereby saving time) by writing information *down* the disk on the same track of successive surfaces.

Advantages of Using a Hard Disk on a Personal Computer

A hard disk drive on a personal computer provides many advantages for users. Because of its large storage capacity, a hard disk can store many software application programs and data files. When a user wants to run a particular application or access a particular data file on a hard disk, it is always available. The user does not have to find the appropriate diskette and insert it into the drive. In addition, the faster access time of a hard disk reduces the time needed to load programs and access data. The typical access time of a hard disk for a personal computer is between 15 and 80 milliseconds.

Other Types of Hard Disks

We discuss other devices that use hard disk technology in this section. These include removable disks, hard cards, and disk cartridges.

Removable Disks Removable disk units were introduced in the early 1960s and for nearly 20 years were the most prevalent type of disk storage on minicomputers and mainframes. During the 1980s, however, removable disks began to be replaced by hard fixed disks that offered larger storage capacities and higher reliability.

Removable disk devices consist of the drive unit, which is usually in its own cabinet, and the removable recording media, called a **disk pack**. Removable disk packs consist of five to eleven metal platters that are used on both sides for recording data. The recording capacity of these packs varies from 10 to 300 megabytes of data. One advantage of removable disk packs is that the data on a disk drive can be quickly changed by removing one pack and replacing it with another. This can be accomplished in minutes. When removable disk packs are not mounted in a disk drive they are stored in a protective plastic case. When the packs are being used, the plastic case is usually placed on top of the drive unit. Figure 6-18 shows a large installation of removable disk devices with the empty protective disk pack cases on top of the drives.

FIGURE 6-18
A large installation of removable disk drives showing the protective disk pack cases on top of the drive units.

Hard Cards One option for installing a hard disk in a personal computer is a hard card. The **hard card** is a circuit board that has a hard disk built onto it. Hard cards provide an easy way to expand the storage capacity of a personal computer because the board can be installed into an expansion slot of the computer (Figure 6-19).

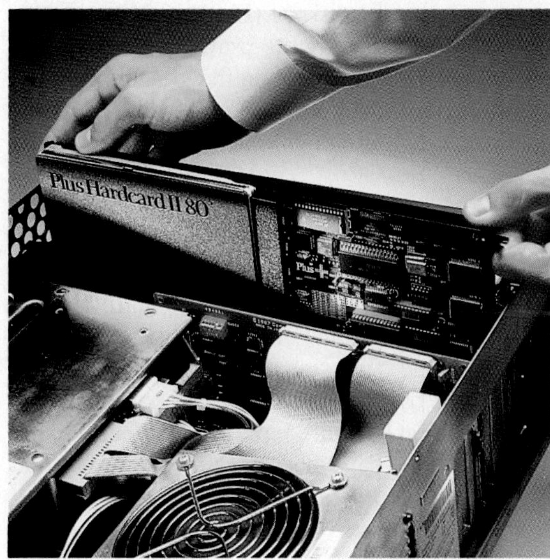

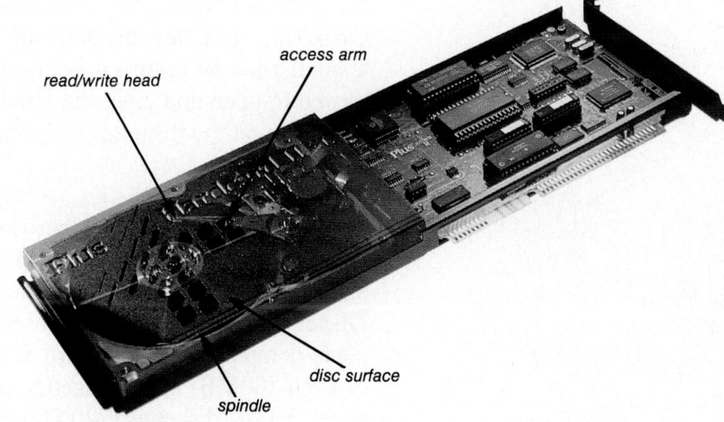

FIGURE 6-19
A hard card is a hard disk on a circuit board that can be mounted in a computer's expansion slot. Notice that a transparent cover (above) allows you to see the disk platter and access arm.

FIGURE 6-20
A removable hard disk cartridge allows a user to remove and transport the entire hard disk from computer to computer or to lock it up in a safe.

Disk Cartridges Another variation of disk storage available for use with personal computers is the removable disk cartridge. **Disk cartridges**, which can be inserted and removed from a computer (Figure 6-20), offer the storage and fast access features of hard disks and the portability of diskettes. Disk cartridges are often used when data security is an issue. At the end of a work session, the disk cartridge can be removed and locked up, leaving no data on the computer.

Protecting Data Stored on a Disk

Regardless of whether you are using diskettes or hard disks, you must protect the data you store on the disk from being lost. Disk storage is reusable, and data that is stored on a disk may be overwritten and replaced with new data. This is a desirable feature allowing users to remove or replace unwanted files. However, it also raises the possibility of accidentally removing or replacing a file that you wanted to keep. To protect programs and data stored on disks, there are several things you can do.

How Is a Diskette Write-Protected? One way to protect the data and programs stored on a 5 1/4" diskette is to use the write-protect notch. This notch is located on the side of the diskette. To prevent writing to a diskette, you cover this notch with a small piece of removable tape. Before writing data onto a diskette, the disk drive checks the notch. If the notch is open, the drive will proceed to write on the diskette. If the notch is covered, the disk drive will not write on the diskette (Figure 6-21).

On 3 1/2" diskettes, the situation is reversed. Instead of a write-protect notch, there is a small window in the corner of the diskette. A piece of plastic in the window can be moved to open and close the window. If the write-protect window is closed, the drive can write on the diskette. If the window is open, the drive will not write on the diskette.

Backup Storage Another way to protect programs and data stored on disks is by creating backup storage. Backup storage means creating a copy of important programs and data. To backup diskettes, simply copy the data on one diskette to another diskette. Diskettes are also commonly used to backup the data stored on a hard disk of a personal computer. Because hard disks can store large quantities of data (20MB, 40MB, or even 100MB) many diskettes are required for backup. For example, approximately thirty 3 1/2" diskettes (720,000 characters each) are required to back up a hard disk containing 20 million characters. Data stored on the hard disks of minicomputers and mainframes must also be backed up. Magnetic tape, another form of auxiliary storage, is commonly used to backup data stored on large-capacity hard disks.

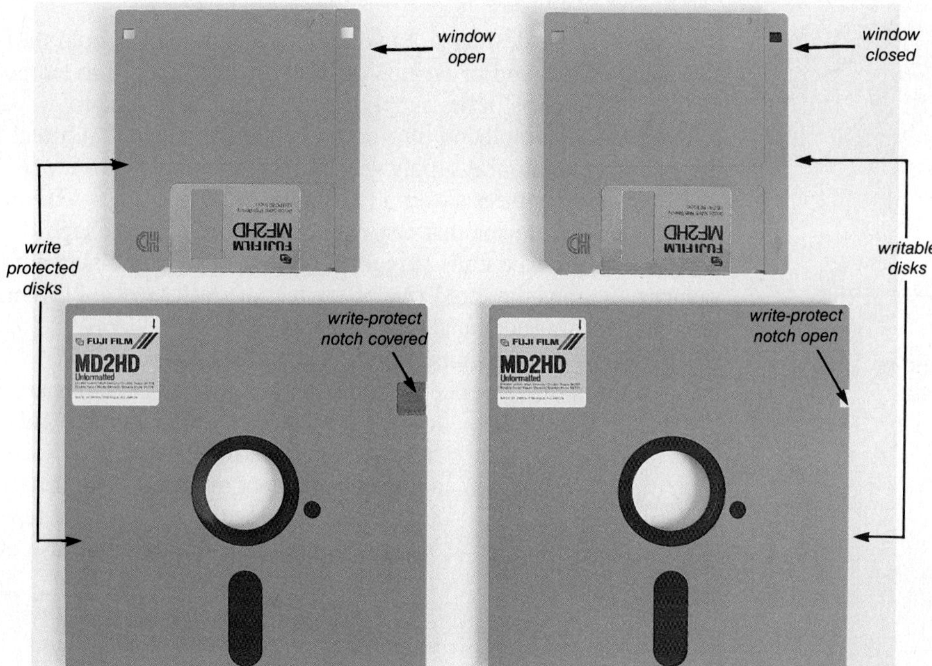

FIGURE 6-21
Data cannot be written on the 3½-inch diskette on the upper left because the window in the corner of the diskette is open. A small piece of plastic covers the window of the 3½-inch diskette on the upper right, so data can be written on this diskette. The reverse situation is true for the 5¼-inch diskettes. The write-protect notch of the 5¼-inch diskette on the lower left is covered and, therefore, data cannot be written to the diskette. The notch of the 5¼-inch diskette on the lower right, however, is open. Data can be written to this diskette.

MAGNETIC TAPE

During the 1950s and early 1960s, prior to the introduction of removable disk pack drives, magnetic tape was the primary method of storing large amounts of data. Today, even though tape is no longer used as the primary method of auxiliary storage, it still functions as a cost-effective way to store data that does not have to be accessed immediately. In addition, tape serves as the primary means of backup for most medium and large systems and is often used when data is transferred from one system to another.

Magnetic tape consists of a thin ribbon of plastic. The tape is coated on one side with a material that can be magnetized to record the bit patterns that represent data. The most common types of magnetic tape devices are reel-to-reel and cartridge. Reel-to-reel tape is usually 1/2-inch wide and cartridge tape is 1/4-inch wide (Figure 6-22).

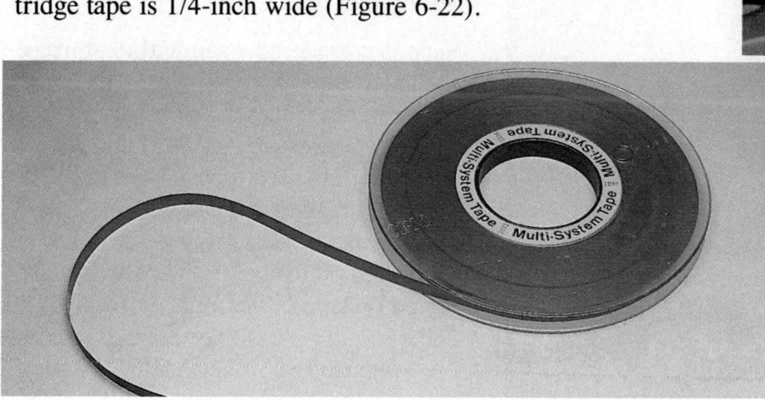

FIGURE 6-22
A computer operator is positioning a reel of magnetic tape on a tape device (top). A standard 10 1/2-inch reel of magnetic tape (left).

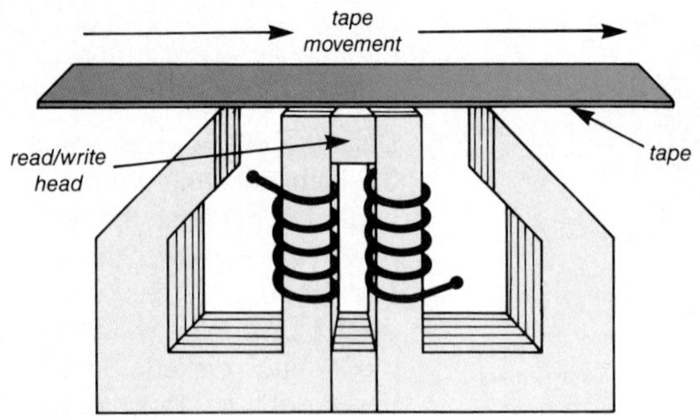

FIGURE 6-23
The tape read/write head senses and records the electronic bits that represent data.

Reel-to-Reel Tape Devices

Reel-to-reel tape devices use two reels: a supply reel to hold the tape that will be read or written on, and the take-up reel to temporarily hold portions of the supply reel tape as it is being processed. At the completion of processing, tape on the take-up reel is wound back onto the supply reel. As the tape moves from one reel to another, it passes over a read/write head (Figure 6-23), an electromagnetic device that can read or write data on the tape.

Older style tape units (Figure 6-24) are vertical cabinets with vacuum columns that hold five or six feet of slack tape to prevent breaking during sudden start or stop operations.

Newer style tape units (Figure 6-25) allow a tape to be inserted through a slot opening similar to the way videotapes are loaded in a videocassette recorder. This front-loading tape drive takes less space and can be cabinet mounted. The drive automatically threads the end of the tape onto an internal take-up reel. Because of their size and cost, reel-to-reel tape drives are used almost exclusively on minicomputer and mainframe systems.

Reels of tape usually come in lengths of 300, 1,200, 2,400 and 3,600 feet and can store up to 200 megabytes of data.

FIGURE 6-24
Older style reel-to-reel magnetic tape storage devices are shown behind newer style tape units.

Cartridge Tape Devices

Cartridge tape is frequently used for backup on personal computers. Faster and higher storage capacity cartridge tapes are also increasingly replacing reel-to-reel tape devices on minicomputers and mainframes. Cartridge tape units are designed to be internally mounted or in a separate external cabinet (Figure 6-26).

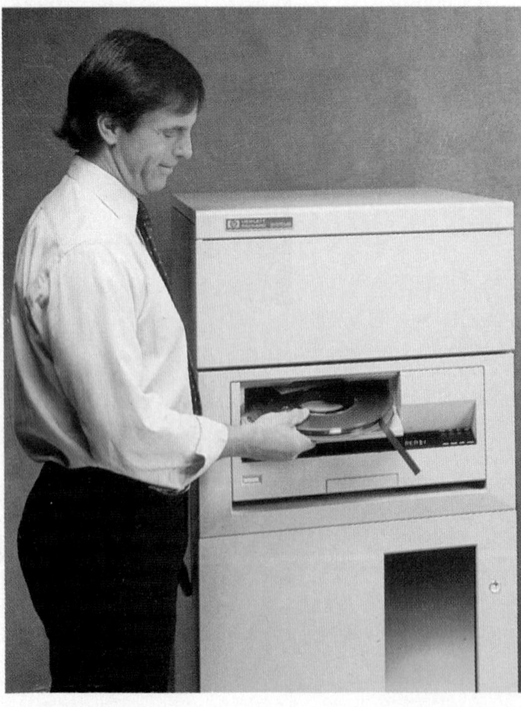

FIGURE 6-25
Newer style tape drives allow the user to slide the tape into a slot at the front of the unit. The drive automatically threads the tape onto an internal take-up reel.

How Is Data Stored on Magnetic Tape?

Tape is considered a **sequential storage** media because the computer must record and read tape records one after another. Binary codes, such as ASCII and EBCDIC, are used to represent data stored on magnetic tape. Within a code, each character is represented by a unique combination of bits. The bits are stored on tape in the form of magnetic spots (Figure 6-27). The magnetic spots are organized into rows, called channels, that run the length of the tape. A combination of bits in a vertical column (one from each channel) is used to represent a character. An additional bit is used as a parity bit for error checking.

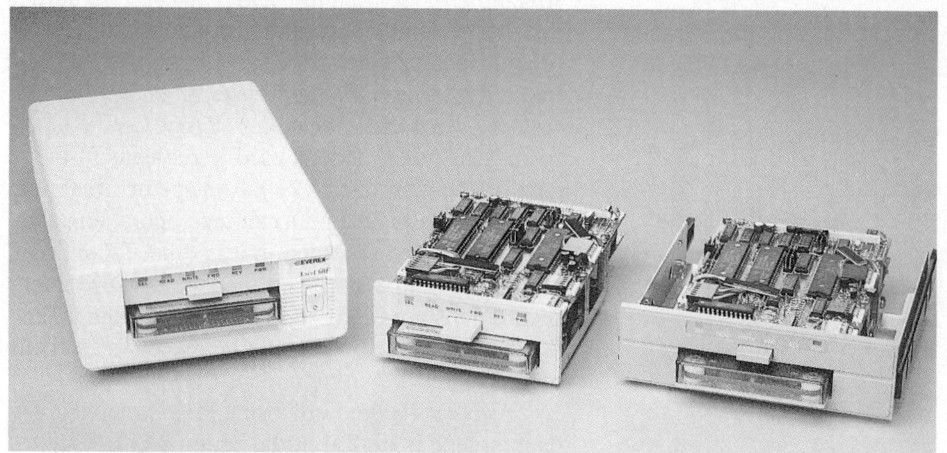

FIGURE 6-26
Cartridge tape drives are an effective way to back up and store data that would otherwise require numerous diskettes.

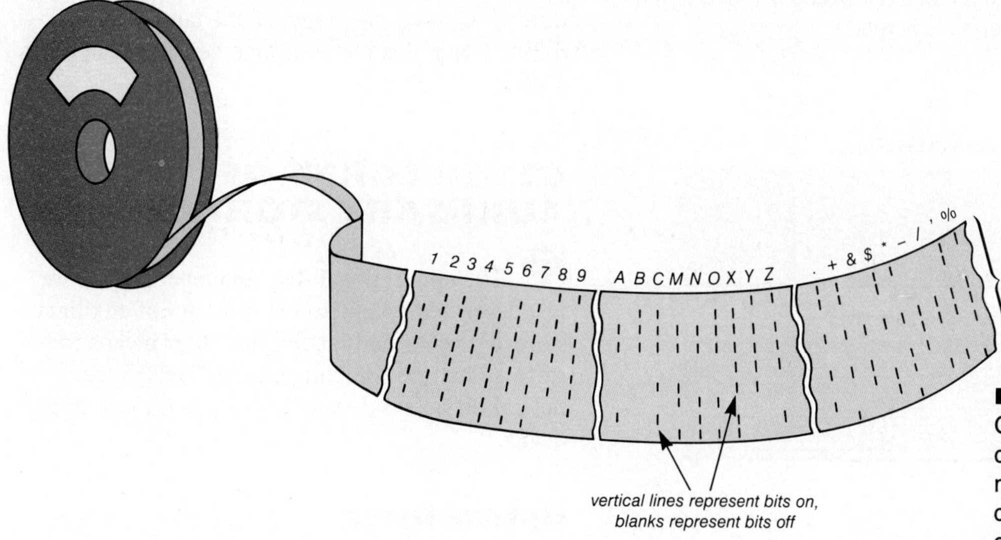

FIGURE 6-27
One of the most common coding structures found on magnetic tape is the EBCDIC code, which is stored in nine channels on the tape. Eight channels are used to store the bits representing a character. The ninth channel is for the error-checking parity bit.

Tape density is the number of bits that can be stored on an inch of tape. As on disk drives, tape density is expressed in bits per inch, or bpi. Commonly used tape densities are 800, 1,600, 3,200 and 6,250 bpi. Some of the newer cartridge tape devices can record at densities of over 60,000 bpi. The higher the density, the more data that can be stored on a tape.

Data is recorded on tape in **blocks** which usually consist of two or more records. The individual records are referred to as **logical records**. The group of records making up the block is referred to as a **physical record**. For example, there could be three employee payroll records (three logical records) contained within one block (one physical record) on tape. Each time a tape read or write operation takes place, one physical record is processed. In between each block is a gap of approximately .6 inches called and **interblock gap (IBG)**, or an **interrecord gap (IRG)**. This gap provides room for the tape to slow down and stop after each block has been read. Blocking logical records together has two advantages. First, the space on the tape is used more efficiently than if logical records were written one at a time. Second, because an entire physical record is read into memory each time data is read from tape, reading data takes place faster. A diagram of a section of tape is shown at Figure 6-28.

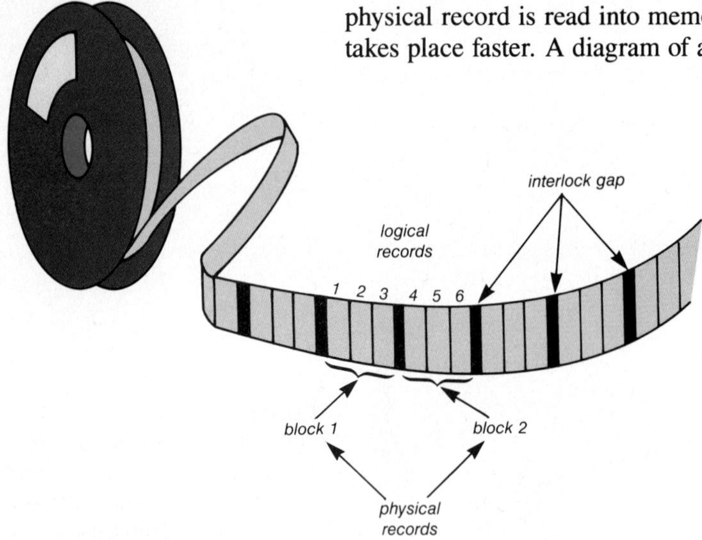

FIGURE 6-28
Three logical records are stored in each block, or physical record, in this diagram. An entire block of records is brought into main memory each time the tape file is read.

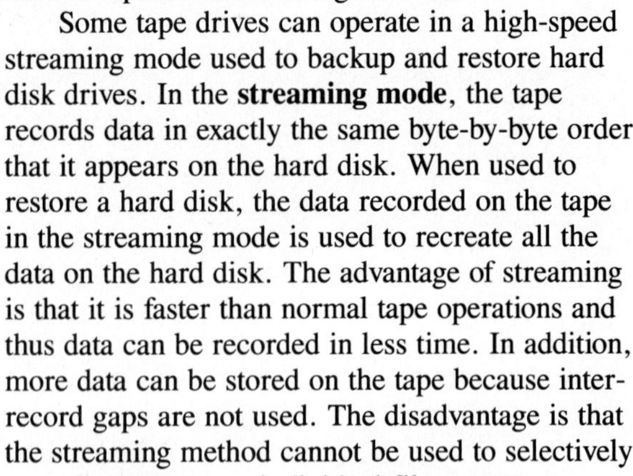

Some tape drives can operate in a high-speed streaming mode used to backup and restore hard disk drives. In the **streaming mode**, the tape records data in exactly the same byte-by-byte order that it appears on the hard disk. When used to restore a hard disk, the data recorded on the tape in the streaming mode is used to recreate all the data on the hard disk. The advantage of streaming is that it is faster than normal tape operations and thus data can be recorded in less time. In addition, more data can be stored on the tape because inter-record gaps are not used. The disadvantage is that the streaming method cannot be used to selectively record or restore an individual file.

Another method of storing large amounts of data on tape is **digital audio tape (DAT)**. DAT uses **helical scan technology** to write data at much higher densities across the tape at an angle instead of down the length of the tape (Figure 6-29). Using this method, tape densities can be as high as 61,000 bpi.

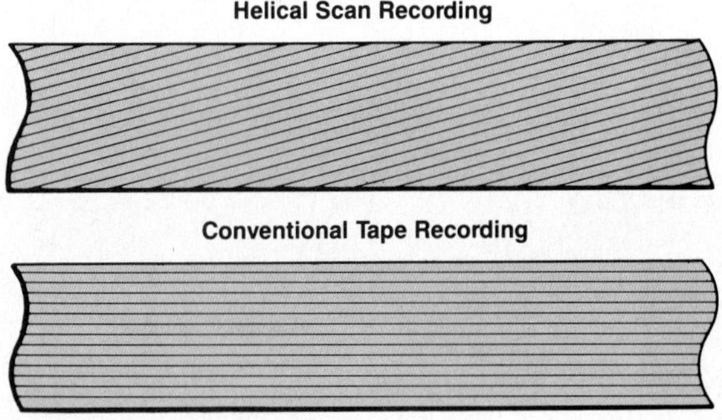

FIGURE 6-29
Using helical scan technology, data is recorded at a higher density across the tape at an angle. Conventional tape drives record data in channels running the length of the tape.

OTHER FORMS OF AUXILIARY STORAGE

The conventional disk and tape devices we just described comprise the majority of auxiliary storage devices and media, but other means for storing data are sometimes used. These include optical disks, solid-state devices, and mass storage devices.

Optical Disks

Enormous quantities of information are stored on **optical disks** by using a laser to burn microscopic holes on the surface of a hard plastic disk (Figure 6-30).

FIGURE 6-30
To record data on an optical disk (left), a laser burns microscopic holes on the surface (right).

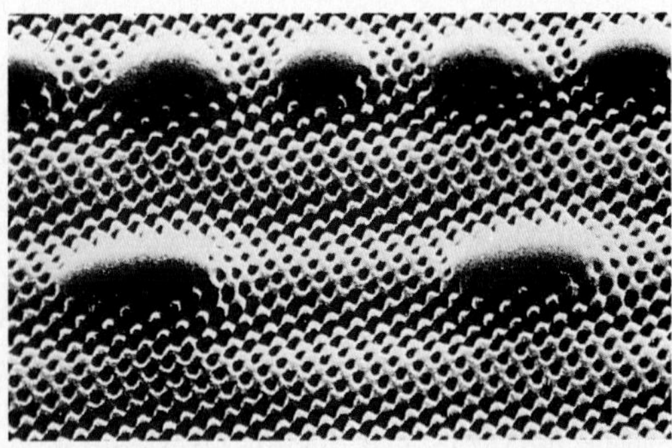

A lower power laser reads the disk by reflecting light off the disk surface. The reflected light is converted into a series of bits that the computer can process (Figure 6-31).

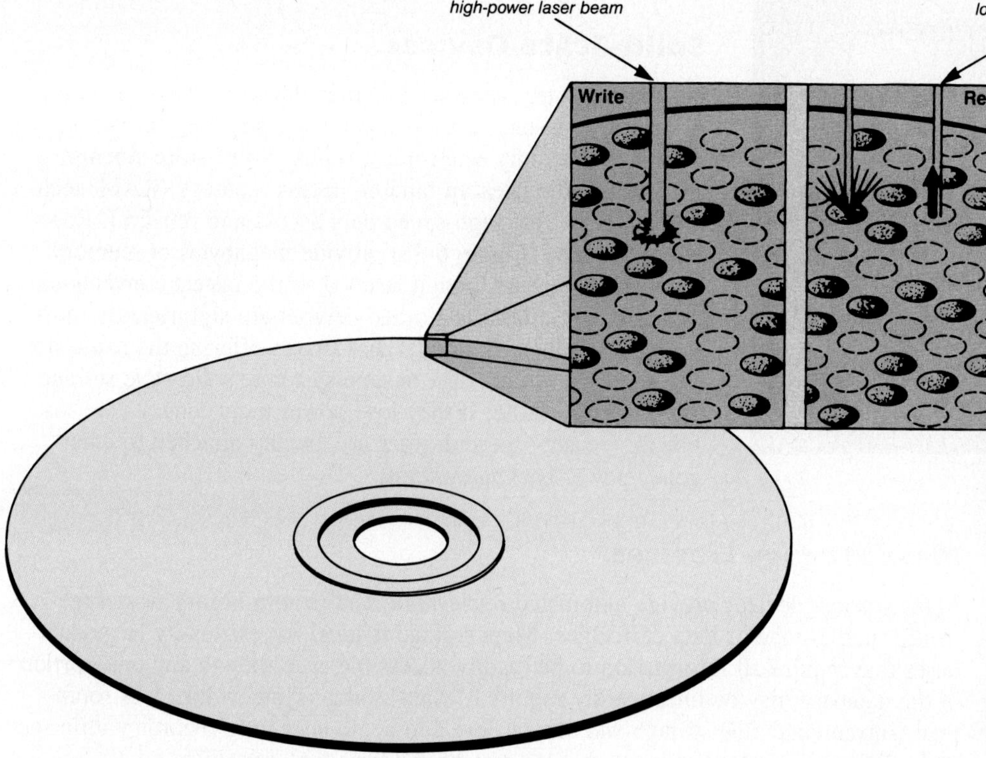

FIGURE 6-31
To record data on an optical disk, a high-power laser heats the surface and makes a microscopic pit. To read data, a low-power laser light is reflected from the smooth unpitted areas and is interpreted as a 1 bit. The pitted areas do not reflect the laser beam and are interpreted as 0 bits.

A full-size, 14-inch optical disk can store 6.8 billion bytes of information. Up to 150 of these disks can be installed in automated disk library systems that provide over one trillion bytes (called a **terabyte**) of online storage. The smaller disks, just under five inches in diameter, can store over 800 million characters, or approximately 1100 times the data that can be stored on a standard density 3 1/2" diskette. That's enough space to store approximately 400,000 pages of typed data. The smaller optical disks are called **CDROM**, an acronym for compact disk read-only memory (Figure 6-32). They use the same laser technology that is used for the CDROM disks that have become popular for recorded music.

FIGURE 6-32
An optical compact disk can store hundreds of times the data as on a diskette of similar dimensions.

Most optical disks are prerecorded and cannot be modified by the user. These disks are used for applications such as an auto parts catalog where the information is changed only occasionally, such as once a year, and a new updated optical disk is created. Optical disk devices that provide for one-time recording are called **WORM** devices, an acronym for write once, read many. Erasable optical disk drives are just starting to be used. The most common erasable optical drives use **magneto-optical technology**, in which a magnetic field changes the polarity of a spot on the disk that has been heated by a laser.

FIGURE 6-33
Solid-state storage devices use rows of RAM chips to emulate a conventional rotating disk drive. This solid-state device, with a RAM memory board shown in front, can transfer data 15 to 20 times faster than a rotating disk system.

Because of their tremendous storage capacities, entire catalogs or reference materials can be stored on a single optical disk. Some people predict that optical disks will someday replace data now stored on film such as microfiche.

Solid-State Devices

To the computer, solid-state storage devices act just like disk drives, only faster. As their name suggests, they contain no moving parts, only electronic circuits. **Solid-state storage** devices use the latest in random access memory (RAM) technology to provide high-speed data access and retrieval. Rows of RAM chips (Figure 6-33) provide megabytes of memory that can be accessed much faster than the fastest conventional disk drives. Solid-state storage devices are significantly more expensive than conventional disk drives offering the same storage capacity. Unlike disk or tape systems, solid-state storage devices are volatile; if they lose power their contents are lost. For this reason, these devices are usually attached to emergency power backup systems.

Mass Storage Devices

Mass storage devices provide automated retrieval of data from a library of storage media such as tape or data cartridges. Mass storage is ideal for extremely large databases that require all information to be readily accessible even though any one portion of the database may be infrequently required. Mass storage systems take less room than conventional tape storage and can retrieve and begin accessing records within seconds. Figure 6-34 shows a mass storage system that uses tape cartridges.

FIGURE 6-34
This is the inside of an automated mass storage system that uses tape cartridges. A robot arm with a camera mounted on top can access and load any one of thousands of tape cartridges in an average of 11 seconds. Each cartridge is a 4 × 4-inch square and about one-inch thick and can hold up to 200 megabytes of data. The tapes are stored in a circular cabinet referred to as a silo.

Special-Purpose Storage Devices

Several devices have been developed for special-purpose storage applications. Two of these are smart cards and optical cards.

Smart cards are the same size and thickness of a credit card and contain a thin microprocessor capable of storing recorded information (Figure 6-35). When it is inserted into compatible equipment, the information on the smart card can be read and if necessary, updated. A current user of smart cards is the U.S. Marine Corps, who issues the cards to recruits instead of cash. Each time a recruit uses the card, the transaction amount is subtracted from the previous balance. Other uses of the card include employee time and attendance tracking (instead of time cards) and security applications where detailed information about the card holder is stored in the card.

Optical cards can store up to 800 pages of text or images on a device the size of a credit card (Figure 6-36). Applications include automobile records and the recording of personal and health-care data.

FIGURE 6-35
Smart cards are credit card-sized devices that contain a microprocessor in the left center of the card. The microprocessor can store up to 64,000 bits of information.

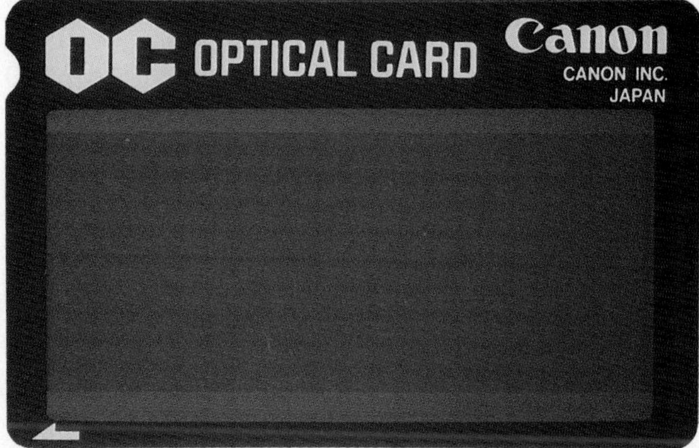

FIGURE 6-36
This optical card can store up to 800 pages of information and images. It is about the size of a credit card.

SUMMARY OF AUXILIARY STORAGE

Auxiliary storage is used to store programs and data that are not currently being processed by the computer. In this chapter, we discussed the various types of auxiliary storage used with computers. The chart on the next page in Figure 6-37 provides a summary of the auxiliary storage devices we covered. What you have learned about these devices and storage operations in general can now be added to what you have learned about the input, processing, and output operations to complete your understanding of the information processing cycle.

FIGURE 6-37
A summary of the various auxiliary storage devices.

DEVICE	DESCRIPTION
Magnetic Disk	
Diskette	Plastic storage media that is reliable and low in cost.
Hard disk	Fixed metal platter storage media that provides large storage capacity and fast access.
Removable disk	Large disk drives with removable disk packs.
Hard card	Hard disk that is built on a circuit board and installed in an expansion slot of a personal computer.
Disk cartridge	Combines storage and access features of hard disks and portability of diskettes.
Magnetic Tape	
Reel tape	Magnetic tape device using the reel-to-reel method of moving tape.
Tape cartridge	Magnetic tape device using the cartridge method of holding tape.
Other Storage Devices	
Optical storage	Uses lasers to record and read data on a hard plastic disk. Provides high quality and large storage capacity.
Solid-state	Uses RAM chips to provide high-speed data access and retrieval.
Mass storage	Automated retrieval of storage media such as tape or data cartridges.
Special-Purpose Storage Devices	
Smart card	Contains a thin microprocessor capable of storing recorded information.
Optical card	Credit card-sized device that stores text and images.

CHAPTER SUMMARY

1. **Auxiliary storage** is used to store data that is not being processed on the computer.
2. **Magnetic disk** is the most widely used storage medium for all types of computers and offers high storage capacity, reliability, and the capability to directly access stored data.
3. The most common diskette sizes are 5 1/4" and 3 1/2" in diameter.
4. A diskette consists of a plastic disk enclosed within a square protective jacket. A portion of the surface of the disk is exposed so data can be stored on it.
5. The **formatting** process prepares the diskette so that it can store data and includes defining the tracks, cylinders, and sectors on the surfaces of a diskette.
6. Data is stored along the tracks of a diskette. A **track** is a narrow recording band forming a full circle around the diskette.
7. A **cylinder** is defined as all tracks of the same number.
8. The term **sector** is used to refer to a pie-shaped section of the disk. It is also used to refer to a section of a track.
9. When data is read from a diskette, a minimum of one full sector of a track is read. When data is stored on a diskette, at least one full sector of a track is written.
10. The factors affecting disk storage capacity are the number of sides of the disk used; the recording density; and the number of tracks on the disk.
11. The **recording density** is stated as the number of bits that can be recorded on one inch of the innermost track on a disk. The measurement is referred to as **bits per inch (bpi)**.
12. To read or write data on a diskette, it is placed in the disk drive. Within its protective covering the diskette rotates at about 300 revolutions per minute. The **read/write head** rests on the diskette and senses the magnetic spots or generates electronic impulses that represent the bits.

13. The time required to access and retrieve data stored on a diskette is called the **access time**.
14. Access time depends on four factors: (1) **seek time**, the time it takes to position the read/write head on the correct track; (2) **rotational delay time**, or **latency**, the time it takes for the data to rotate under the read/write head; (3) **settling time**, the time required for the head to be placed in contact with the disk; and (4) **data transfer rate**, the amount of data that can be transferred from the disk to main memory.
15. Diskettes should not be exposed to heat or magnetic fields. With proper care, diskettes provide an inexpensive and reliable form of storage.
16. A **hard disk** consists of one or more rigid metal platters coated with an oxide material.
17. On hard disks, the metal platters, read/write heads, and access arm are enclosed in an airtight, sealed case.
18. To read and write data on a hard disk, an **access arm** moves read/write heads in and out. The heads float very close to the surface of the disk, generating or sensing the magnetic spots that represent bits.
19. The **sector method** (identifying the surface, track, and sector number) or the **cylinder method** (identifying the cylinder, recording surface, and record number) can be used to physically organize and address data stored on disk.
20. **Removable disk** devices consist of the drive unit, which is usually in its own cabinet, and the removable recording media, called a **disk pack**.
21. A **hard card** consists of a circuit board that has a hard disk built onto it. The board can be installed into an expansion slot of a personal computer.
22. **Disk cartridges**, which can be inserted and removed from a computer, offer the storage and fast access features of hard disks and the portability of diskettes.
23. The write-protect notch on 5 1/4" diskettes and the window on 3 1/2" diskettes can be used to protect the data stored on a disk from being overwritten.
24. To backup storage means to create a copy of important programs and data on a separate disk or tape.
25. The normal method for diskette backup is to copy the data onto another diskette. For large-capacity hard disks, the data is often copied to magnetic tape.
26. **Magnetic tape** consists of a thin ribbon of plastic. The tape is coated on one side with a material that can be magnetized to record the bit patterns that represent data.
27. The most common types of magnetic tape devices are reel-to-reel and cartridge.
28. Data is recorded on magnetic tape as a series of magnetic spots along a horizontal channel. Each spot represents a bit in a coding scheme.
29. **Tape density** is the number of bits that can be stored on one inch of tape. Common densities are 800, 1,600, 3,200, and 6,520 bytes per inch.
30. Data is recorded on tape in **blocks** which usually consist of two or more records. The individual records are referred to as **logical records**. The group of records making up the block is referred to as a **physical record**.
31. An **interblock gap (IBG)**, also called an **interrecord gap (IRG)**, separates the blocks stored on tape.
32. In the **streaming mode**, a tape records data in exactly the same byte-by-byte order as it appears on the disk.
33. **Digital audio tape (DAT)** uses **helical scan technology** to write data at much higher densities across the tape at an angle instead of down the length of the tape.
34. **Optical disks** use a laser to burn microscopic holes on the surface of a hard plastic disk. Optical disks can store enormous quantities of data.
35. **CDROM** is an acronym for compact disk read-only memory.
36. Optical disks that provide for one-time recording are called **WORM** devices.
37. Most erasable optical disk drives use **magneto-optical technology** that uses a magnetic field to change the polarity of a spot on the disk that has been heated by a laser.
38. RAM chips are used in **solid-state storage** devices to provide fast data access and retrieval. These devices are volatile.
39. Automated retrieval of storage media is provided by **mass storage** devices.
40. **Smart cards** are the same size and thickness of a credit card and contain a thin microprocessor capable of storing recorded information.
41. **Optical cards** can store up to 800 pages of text or images on a device the size of a credit card.

KEY TERMS

Access arm *6.9*
Access time *6.6*
Actuator *6.9*
Auxiliary storage *6.2*
Bits per inch (bpi) *6.5*
Block *6.15*
Cartridge tape *6.14*
CDROM *6.17*
Cylinder *6.5*
Cylinder method *6.9*
Data transfer rate *6.6*
Digital audio tape (DAT) *6.16*
Direct-access storage device (DASD) *6.8*
Disk cartridge *6.12*
Diskette *6.3*
Disk pack *6.10*
Double-sided diskette *6.5*
Double-sided drive *6.5*
Fixed disk *6.8*
Floppy disk *6.3*
Formatting *6.4*
Gigabyte *6.8*
Hard card *6.11*
Hard disk *6.7*
Head crash *6.9*
Helical scan technology *6.16*
High-density diskette *6.5*
Interblock gap (IBG) *6.15*
Interrecord gap (IRG) *6.15*
Latency *6.6*
Logical record *6.15*
Low-density diskette *6.5*
Magnetic disk *6.3*
Magnetic tape *6.13*
Magneto-optical technology *6.17*
Mass storage *6.18*
Nonvolatile *6.3*
Optical card *6.19*
Optical disk *6.16*
Physical record *6.15*
Read/write head *6.6*
Recording density *6.5*
Reel-to-reel *6.14*
Removable disk *6.10*
Rotational delay *6.6*
Secondary storage *6.2*
Sector *6.5*
Sector method *6.9*
Seek time *6.6*
Sequential storage *6.14*
Settling time *6.6*
Single-sided diskette *6.5*
Single-sided drive *6.5*
Smart card *6.19*
Solid-state storage *6.18*
Streaming mode *6.16*
Tape density *6.15*
Terabyte *6.17*
Track *6.4*
Tracks per inch (tpi) *6.5*
WORM *6.17*

REVIEW QUESTIONS

1. Write a definition for auxiliary storage. Explain how auxiliary storage differs from main memory.
2. Draw a diagram of a diskette and label the main parts.
3. Explain the terms track, cylinder, and sector.
4. What are the three factors influencing the storage capacity of a diskette? Briefly describe each of them.
5. What is the difference in storage capacity between low-density and high-density diskettes? Give values for both 5 1/4" and 3 1/2" diskettes.
6. What is access time? List the four factors that influence the access time of a disk drive.
7. Describe how data is stored on a hard disk.
8. What are the advantages of using a hard disk drive on a personal computer?
9. Explain how 5 1/4" and 3 1/2" diskettes may be write-protected.
10. Write a definition for magnetic tape. What are the two most common types of magnetic tape devices?
11. What is the streaming mode of tape operation and how is it used?
12. What is a WORM device? How do they differ from magneto-optical technology?

CONTROVERSIAL ISSUES

1. Some people believe that the increasing capacities and decreasing costs of storage devices such as CDROM will eventually result in the replacement of most books, magazines, and other printed matter. What do you think?
2. Many personal computer users and some businesses do not regularly backup the data on their computer systems. Rather than spending time each day to perform backup, they are willing to take the risk that they may have to spend a considerable amount of time recreating their database if their system should experience a disk failure. Discuss the pros and cons of such a policy.

RESEARCH PROJECTS

1. Visit a computer store and obtain information on the different types of hard disk drives that are available for personal computers. Summarize your findings and include data on price, storage capacity, and access speed. Calculate the cost per megabyte of storage for each drive.
2. Pick several different types of businesses. Write a paper on how their information storage requirements differ. Comment on what types of data should be online and available for immediate access.
3. Write a paper on the possible applications of smart card technology.

File and Database Management

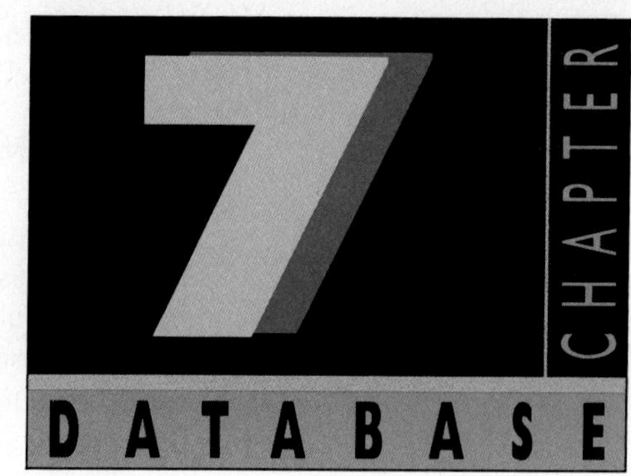

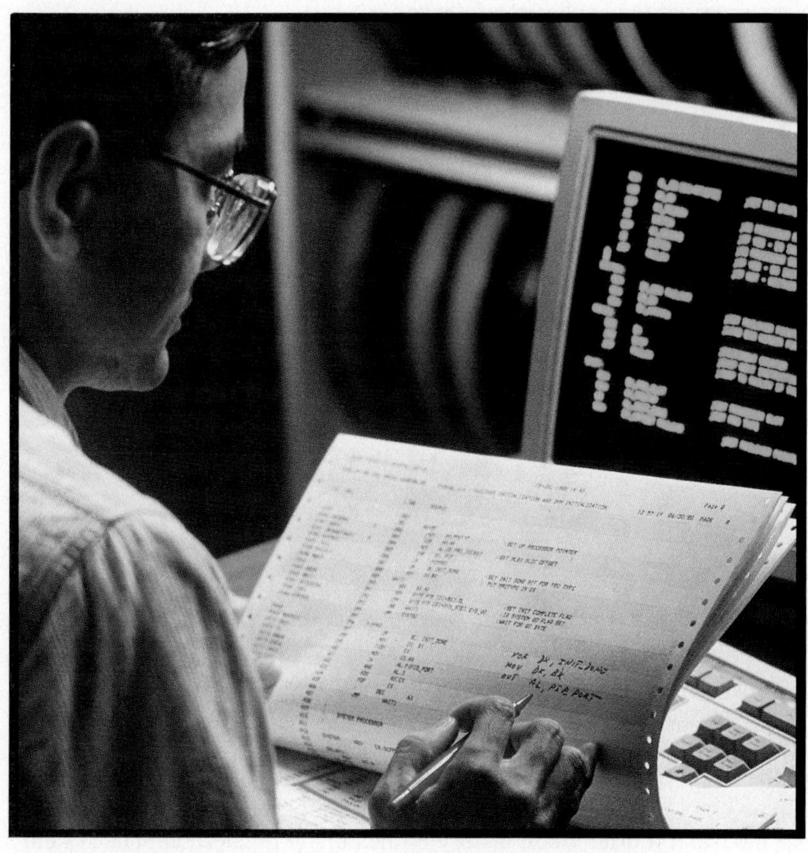

OBJECTIVES

- Discuss data management and explain why it is needed
- Describe sequential files, indexed files, and direct (or relative) files
- Explain the difference between sequential retrieval and random retrieval of records from a file
- Describe the data maintenance procedures for updating data including adding, changing, and deleting
- Discuss the advantages of a database management system (DBMS)
- Describe hierarchical, network, and relational database systems
- Explain the use of a query language
- Describe the responsibilities of a database administrator
- Discuss personal computer database systems

In order to provide maximum benefit to a company, data must be carefully managed, organized, and used. The purpose of this chapter is to explain the need for data management, how files on auxiliary storage are organized and maintained (kept current), and the advantages, organization, and use of databases. Learning this information will help you to better understand how data and information is stored and managed on a computer.

DATA MANAGEMENT

For data to be useful, it must be accurate and timely. **Data management** refers to procedures that are used to keep data accurate and timely and provide for the security and maintenance of data. The purpose of data management is to ensure that data required for an application will be available in the correct form and at the proper time for processing. Both data processing professionals and users share the responsibility for data management.

To illustrate the need for data management, we use an example of a credit bureau (Figure 7-1). A summary of the application follows.

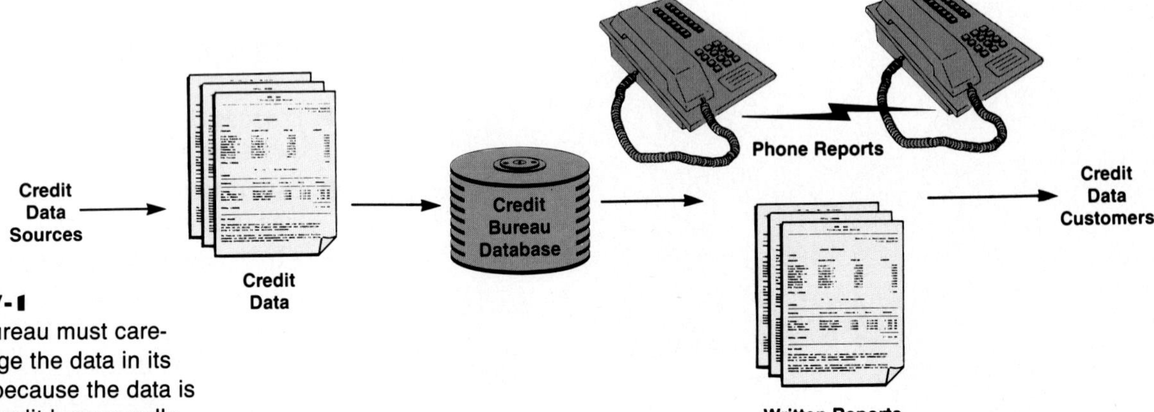

FIGURE 7-1
A credit bureau must carefully manage the data in its database because the data is what the credit bureau sells to its customers. Data management procedures must be in place to make sure the data is accurate and timely and to provide for the proper security and maintenance of the data.

- Data entered into the database of the credit bureau is acquired from numerous sources such as banks and stores. The data includes facts such as income, history of paying debts, bankruptcies, and certain personal information.
- When the data is entered into the computer, it becomes a part of the database. The database is stored on an auxiliary storage device such as a hard disk.
- Customers of the credit bureau can call and request information about an individual. The credit bureau employee uses a terminal to retrieve information from the database and gives the caller a brief credit history of the person in question. The system also generates a record that causes a complete credit history to be printed that night. The credit report will be mailed to the credit bureau customer the following day.

Data Accuracy

For a user, such as a credit bureau customer, to have confidence in the information provided by a computer system, he or she first must be confident that the data used to create the information is accurate. **Data accuracy**, sometimes called **data integrity**, means that the source of the data is reliable and the data is correctly reported and entered. For example, if someone incorrectly reports to the credit bureau that an individual did not pay a bill and this information becomes part of the database, a customer could be denied credit unjustly. Users must be confident that the people and organizations providing data to the credit bureau provide accurate data. In addition, the data they obtain must be entered into the computer correctly. This is called reliable data entry. In the credit bureau example, if a bank reports that the balance on a credit card account is $200.00, but the balance is incorrectly entered as $2,000.00, the information generated would be invalid.

Accurate data must also be timely. Timely data has not lost its usefulness because time has passed. For example, assume that two years ago a salary of $15,000.00 was entered for an individual. Today, that data is not timely because two years have passed and the person may be earning either less or more.

Data Security

Data management also includes managing data security. **Data security** refers to protecting data to keep it from being misused or lost. This is important because misuse or loss of data can have serious consequences. In the credit bureau example, a person's credit rating and history of financial transactions are confidential. People do not want their credit information made available to unauthorized persons. Therefore, the credit bureau must develop systems and procedures that allow only authorized personnel to access the data stored in the database. In addition, if the data in the database should be lost or destroyed, the credit bureau must have a way to recover the correct data. Therefore, data in an information system is periodically copied, or backed up. **Backup** refers to making copies of data files so that if data is lost or destroyed, a timely recovery can be made and processing can continue. Backup copies are normally kept in fireproof safes or in a separate building so that a single disaster, such as a fire, will not destroy both the primary and the backup copy of the data.

Data Maintenance

Data maintenance, another aspect of data management, refers to the procedures used to keep data current. When data is maintained it is called **updating** and includes procedures for **adding** new data, such as creating a record for a new person to include in the credit bureau database; **changing** existing information, such as posting a change of address to an existing record; and **deleting** obsolete information, such as removing inactive records.

Summary of Data Management

Data management includes managing data accuracy, data security, and data maintenance (Figure 7-2). If your attention to data management is inadequate, the information processing system will not perform as intended and the output will have little value.

ACCURACY	SECURITY	MAINTENANCE
Reliable Source Data Reliable Data Entry Timeliness	Authorized Access Backup	Updating: Adding Changing Deleting

FIGURE 7-2
Data management is concerned with data accuracy, data security, and data maintenance.

The data accumulated by companies is stored in files and databases. In the next section we discuss files and how they are organized and maintained. Then we continue with a discussion of databases.

WHAT IS A FILE?

A *file* is a collection of related records that is usually stored on an auxiliary storage device. A *record* is a collection of related fields and a *field*, also called a *data item* or *data element*, is a fact. Figure 7-3 shows a portion of a payroll file that is stored on a diskette. The file contains a separate record for each employee. Each record contains a social security field, a name field and a paycheck amount field. Files contain data that relates to one topic. For example, a business can have separate files that contain data related to payroll, personnel, inventory, customers, vendors, and so forth. Most companies have hundreds, sometimes thousands of files that store the data pertaining to their business. Files that are stored on auxiliary storage devices can be organized in several different ways, and there are advantages and disadvantages to each of these types of file organization.

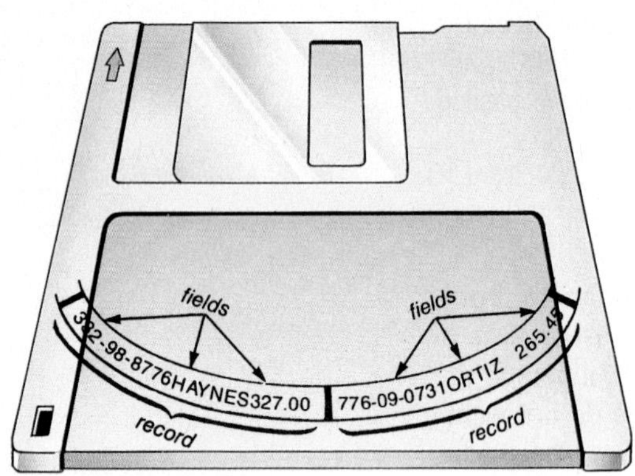

FIGURE 7-3
This payroll file stored on a diskette contains payroll records. Each payroll record contains a social security field, a name field, and a paycheck amount field.

TYPES OF FILE ORGANIZATION

Three types of file organization are used on auxiliary storage devices. These are sequential, indexed, and direct or relative, file organization.

Sequential File Organization

Sequential file organization means that records are stored one after the other, normally in ascending or descending order, based on a value in each record called the key. The **key** is a field that contains unique data, such as a Social Security number, part number, or customer number that is used to identify the records in a file (Figure 7-4). Files stored on tape are processed as sequential files. Files on disk may be sequential, indexed, or direct.

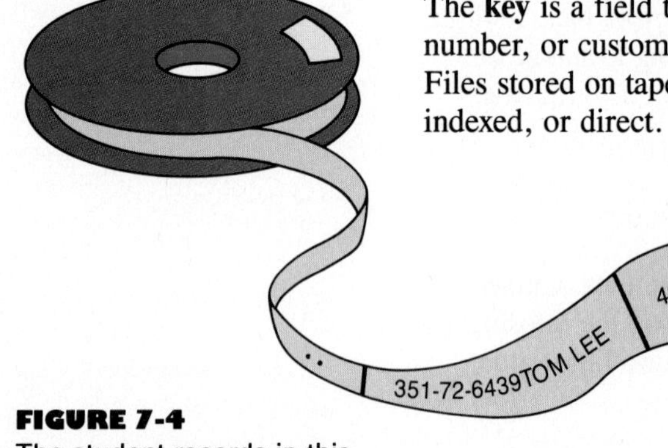
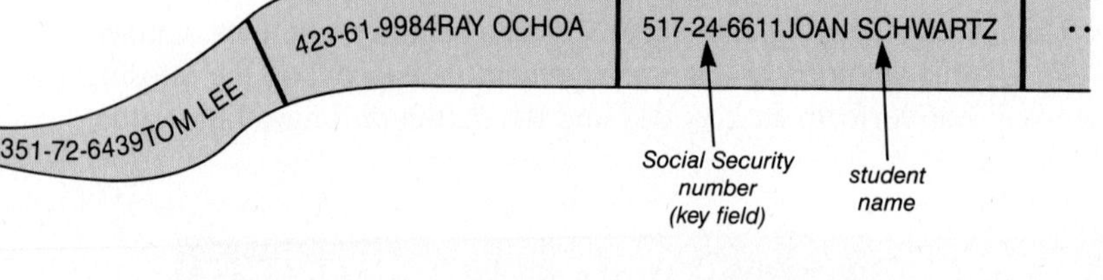

FIGURE 7-4
The student records in this file are stored sequentially in ascending order using the Social Security number as the key field. The records in this file will be retrieved sequentially.

Records stored using sequential file organization are also retrieved sequentially. **Sequential retrieval**, also called **sequential access**, means that the records in a file are retrieved one record after another in the same order that the records are stored. For example, in Figure 7-4, the file contains student records stored in sequence by Social Security number. The data in the file is retrieved one record after another in the same sequence that it is stored in the file.

Sequential retrieval has a major disadvantage — since records must be retrieved one after another in the same sequence as they are stored, the only way to retrieve a record is to read all preceding records first. Therefore, in Figure 7-4, if the record for Joan Schwartz must be retrieved, the records for Tom Lee and Ray Ochoa must be read before retrieving the Joan Schwartz record. Because of this, sequential retrieval is not used when fast access to a particular record is required. However, sequential retrieval is appropriate when records are processed one after another. An example is a weekly payroll application where employee records are processed sequentially.

A common use of sequential files in a computer center is as backup files, where data from a disk is copied onto a tape or another disk so that if the original data becomes unusable, the original file can be restored from the backup file. Sequential files can also be used for batch processing where records are all processed at one time.

Indexed File Organization

A second type of file organization is called **indexed file organization**. Just as in a sequential file, records are stored in an indexed file in an ascending or descending sequence based on the value in the key field of the record.

An indexed file, however, also has an index which itself is a file. An **index** consists of a list containing the values of a key field and the corresponding disk address for each record in a file (Figure 7-5). In the same way that an index for a book points to the page where a particular topic is covered, the index for a file points to the place on a disk where a particular record is located. The index is updated each time a record is added to or deleted from the file. The index is retrieved from the disk and placed in main memory when the file is to be processed.

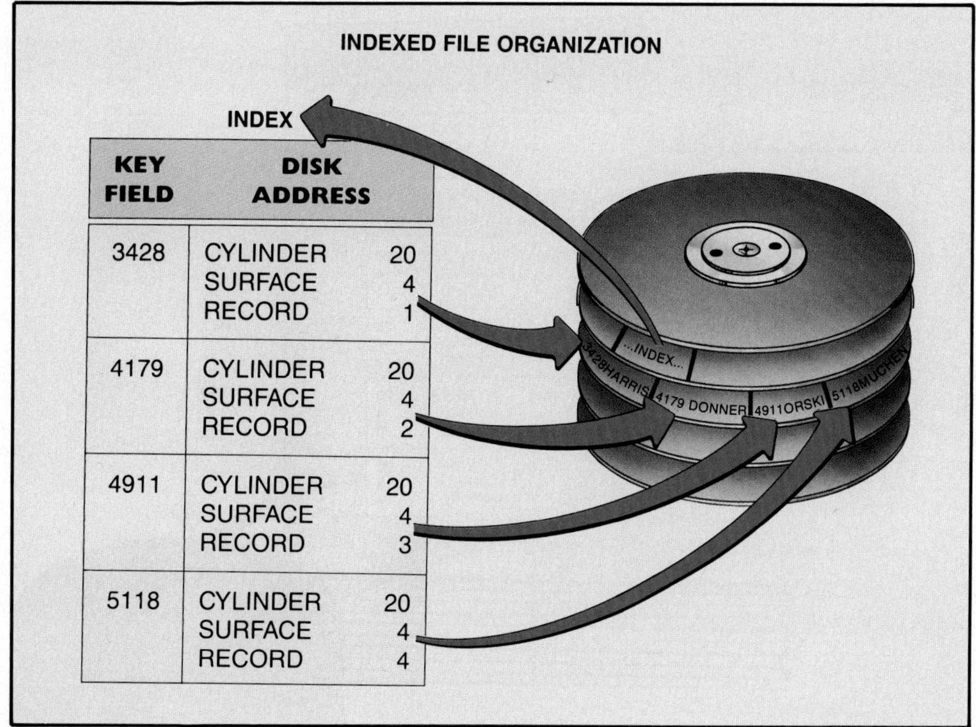

FIGURE 7-5
The index in an indexed file contains the record key and the corresponding disk address for each record in the file. Here, the index contains the employee number, which is the key for the employee file and the disk address for the corresponding employee record.

Records can be accessed in an indexed file both sequentially and randomly. As we previously discussed, sequential retrieval means that the records in a file are retrieved one record after another in the same order that the records are stored. **Random retrieval**, also called **random access** or **direct access**, means the system can go directly to a record without having to read the preceding records. For example, with sequential retrieval, to read the fiftieth record in a file, records 1 through 49 would be read first. With random retrieval, the system can go directly to the fiftieth record. To directly access a record in an indexed file, the index is searched until the key of the record to be retrieved is found. The address of the record (also stored in the index) is then used to retrieve the record directly from the file without reading any other records. For example, if the personnel office asked for the name of employee number 5118, the index could be searched until key 5118 was found (Figure 7-6). The corresponding disk address (cylinder 20, surface 4, record 4) would then be used to read the record directly from the disk into main memory. An advantage of indexed files is that usually more than one index can be maintained. Each index can be used to access or report records in a particular order. For example, an employee file might have three separate indexes; one for employee number, a second for employee name, and a third for Social Security number. A disadvantage of indexed files is that searching an index for a record in a large file can take a long time. In addition, maintaining one or more indexes adds to the processing time whenever a record is added or deleted.

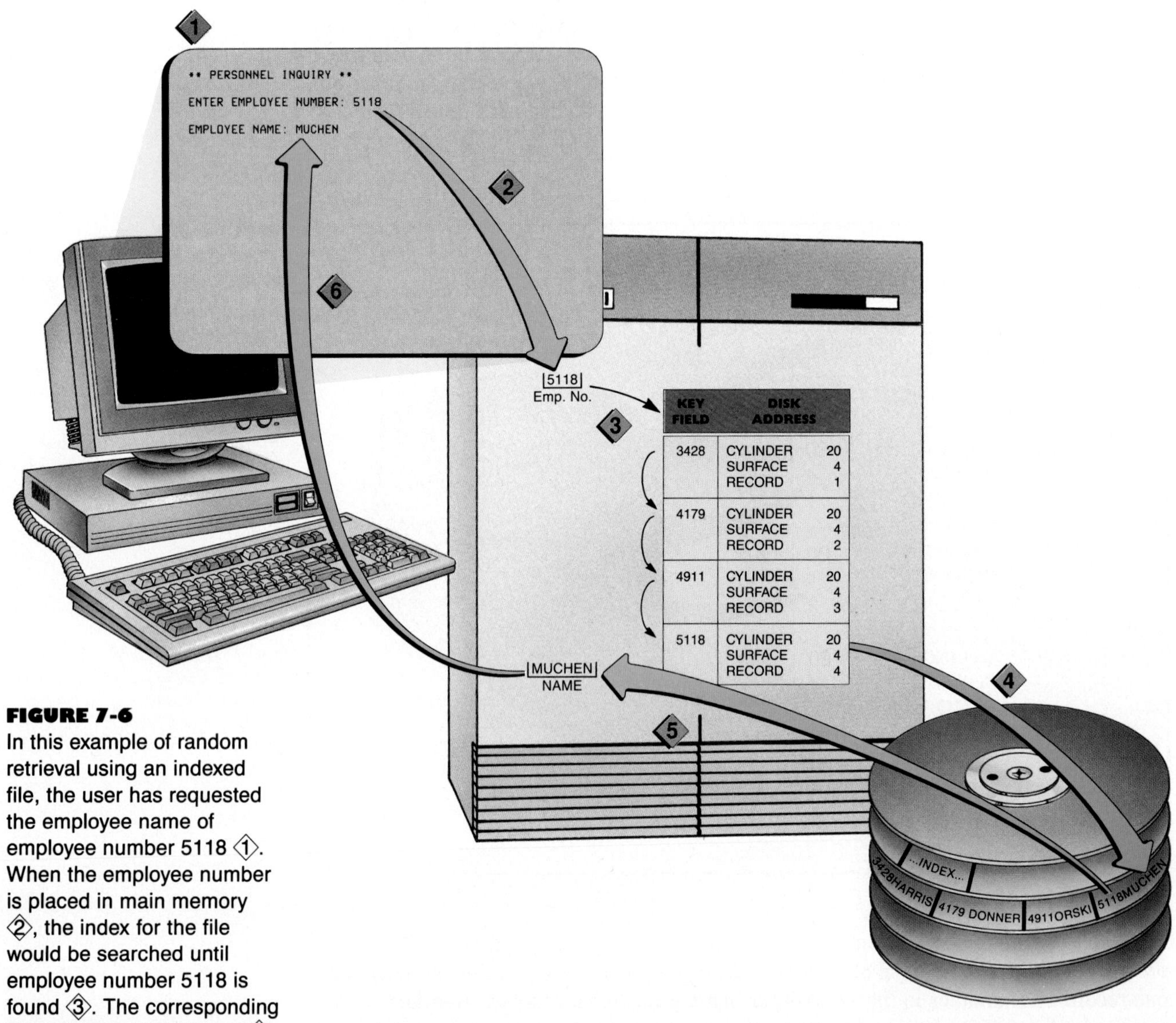

FIGURE 7-6
In this example of random retrieval using an indexed file, the user has requested the employee name of employee number 5118 ①. When the employee number is placed in main memory ②, the index for the file would be searched until employee number 5118 is found ③. The corresponding disk address in the index ④ is then used to access the record stored at that address. Here, the record containing the employee name Muchen is retrieved and placed in main memory ⑤. This name is then sent back to the terminal to answer the user's request ⑥.

Direct or Relative File Organization

A **direct file** or **relative file** (sometimes called a random file) uses the key value of a record to determine the location on the disk where the record is or will be stored. For example, a program could establish a file that has nine locations where records can be stored. These locations are sometimes called **buckets**. A bucket can contain multiple records. If the key in the record is a one-digit value (1–9), then the value in the key would specify the relative location within the file where the record was stored. For example, the record with key 3 would be placed in relative location, or bucket, 3, the record with key 6 would be placed in relative location 6, and so on.

Usually, the storage of records in a file is not so simple. For instance, what if the maximum number of records to be stored in a direct file is 100 and the key for the record is a four-digit number? In this case, the key of the record could not be used to specify the relative or actual location of the record because the four-digit key could result in up to 9,999 records. In cases such as these, an arithmetic formula is used to calculate the relative or actual location in the file where the record is stored. The process of using a formula and performing the calculation to determine the location of a record is called **hashing**.

One hashing method is the division/remainder method. With this method, the computer uses a prime number close to but not greater than the number of records to be stored in the file. A **prime number** is a number divisible by only itself and 1. For example, suppose you have 100 records. The number 97 is the closest prime number to 100 without being greater than 100. The key of the record is then divided by 97 and the remainder from the division operation is the relative location where the record is stored. For example, if the record key is 3428, the relative location where the record will be stored in the file is location 33 (Figure 7-7).

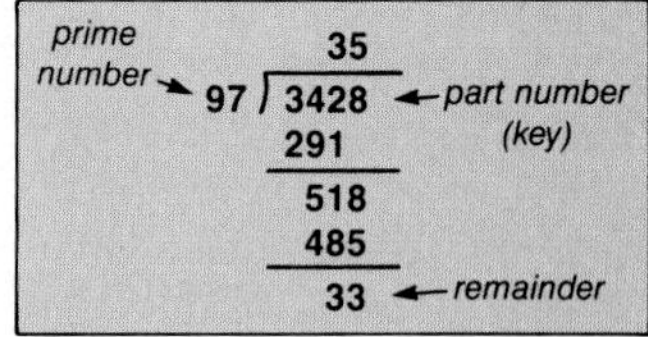

FIGURE 7-7
When the value 3428 is divided by the prime number 97, the remainder is 33. This remainder is used as the bucket where the record with key 3428 is stored in the direct file.

Direct files present one problem you do not encounter with sequential or indexed files. In all three file organization methods, the key in the record must be unique so that it can uniquely identify the record. For example, the employee number, when acting as the key in an employee file, must be unique. No two employees can have the same number. When a hashing technique is used to calculate a disk address, however, it is possible that two different keys could identify the same location on disk. For example, employee number 3331 generates the same relative location (33) as employee number 3428. When the locations generated from the different keys are the same, they are called **synonyms**. The occurrence of this event is called a **collision**. A method that is often used to resolve collisions is to place the record that caused the collision in the next available storage location. This location may be in the same bucket (if multiple records are stored in a bucket) or in the next bucket (Figure 7-8).

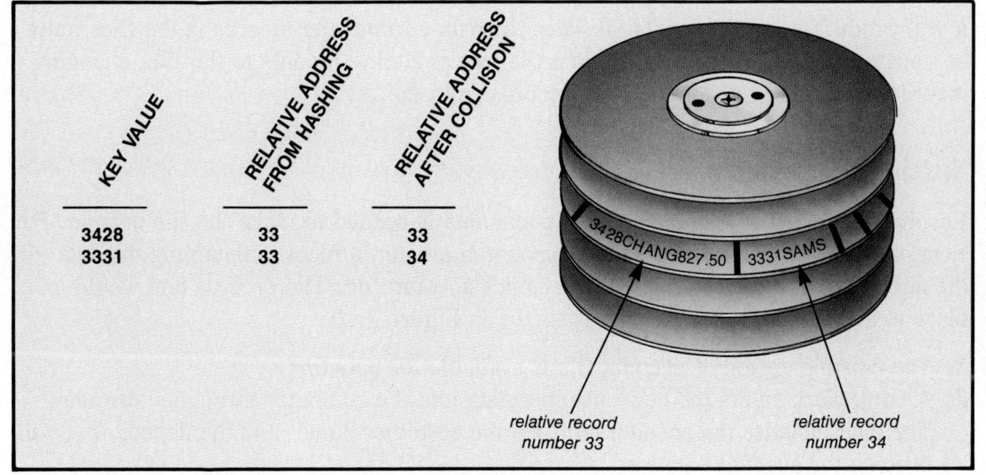

FIGURE 7-8
Sometimes the hashing computation produces synonyms, or records that have the same relative address. In this example, both records have a relative address of 33. When the computer tries to store the second record and finds that location 33 is already full, it stores the second record at the next available location. Here, record 3331 would be stored in location 34.

Once a record is stored in its relative location within a direct file, it can be retrieved either randomly or sequentially. The method normally used with direct files is random retrieval. A record is retrieved from a direct file by performing three steps.

1. The program obtains the key of the record to be retrieved. The valuc of the key, such as a part number, is entered by the user or is read from another file record such as a sales invoice.

2. The program determines the location of the record to be retrieved by performing the same hashing process as when the record was initially stored. Thus, to retrieve the record with key 3428, the key value would be divided by the prime number 97. The remainder, 33, specifies the location of the bucket where the record is stored.
3. The software directs the computer to bucket 33 to retrieve the record.

Sequential retrieval from a direct file can be accomplished by indicating that the record from the first relative location is to be retrieved, followed by the record from the second relative location, and so on. All the records in the file are retrieved based on their relative location in the file.

Summary of File Organization Concepts

Files are organized as either sequential, indexed, or direct files. Sequential file organization can be used on tape or disk and requires that the records in the file be retrieved sequentially. Indexed files must be stored on disk and the records can be accessed either sequentially or randomly. Direct files are stored on disk and are usually accessed randomly (Figure 7-9).

FIGURE 7-9
The types of storage and the access methods that can be used with each of the three file types.

FILE TYPE	TYPE OF STORAGE	ACCESS METHOD
Sequential	Tape or Disk	Sequential
Indexed	Disk	Random* or Sequential
Direct (Relative)	Disk	Random* or Sequential

* *Primarily accessed as random files*

HOW IS DATA IN FILES MAINTAINED?

Data stored on auxiliary storage must be kept current so that when it is processed it will produce accurate results. To keep the data current, the records in the files must be updated. Updating records within a file means adding records to the file, changing records within the file, and deleting records from the file.

Adding Records

Records are added to a file when additional data is needed to make the file current. For example, if a customer opens a new account at a bank, a record containing the data for the new account must be added to the bank's account file. The process that would take place to add this record to the file is shown in Figure 7-10.

1. The existing customer account file is available for updating.
2. A bank clerk enters the new customer data into the computer through a terminal. The data includes the account number, the customer name, and the deposit that will become the account balance.
3. The update program moves the data entered by the user into the new record area in main memory.
4. The update program writes the new record to the file. The location on the disk where the record is written will be determined by the program that manages the disk. In some cases, a new record will be written between other records in the file. In other cases, such as illustrated in Figure 7-10, the new record will be added to the end of the file.

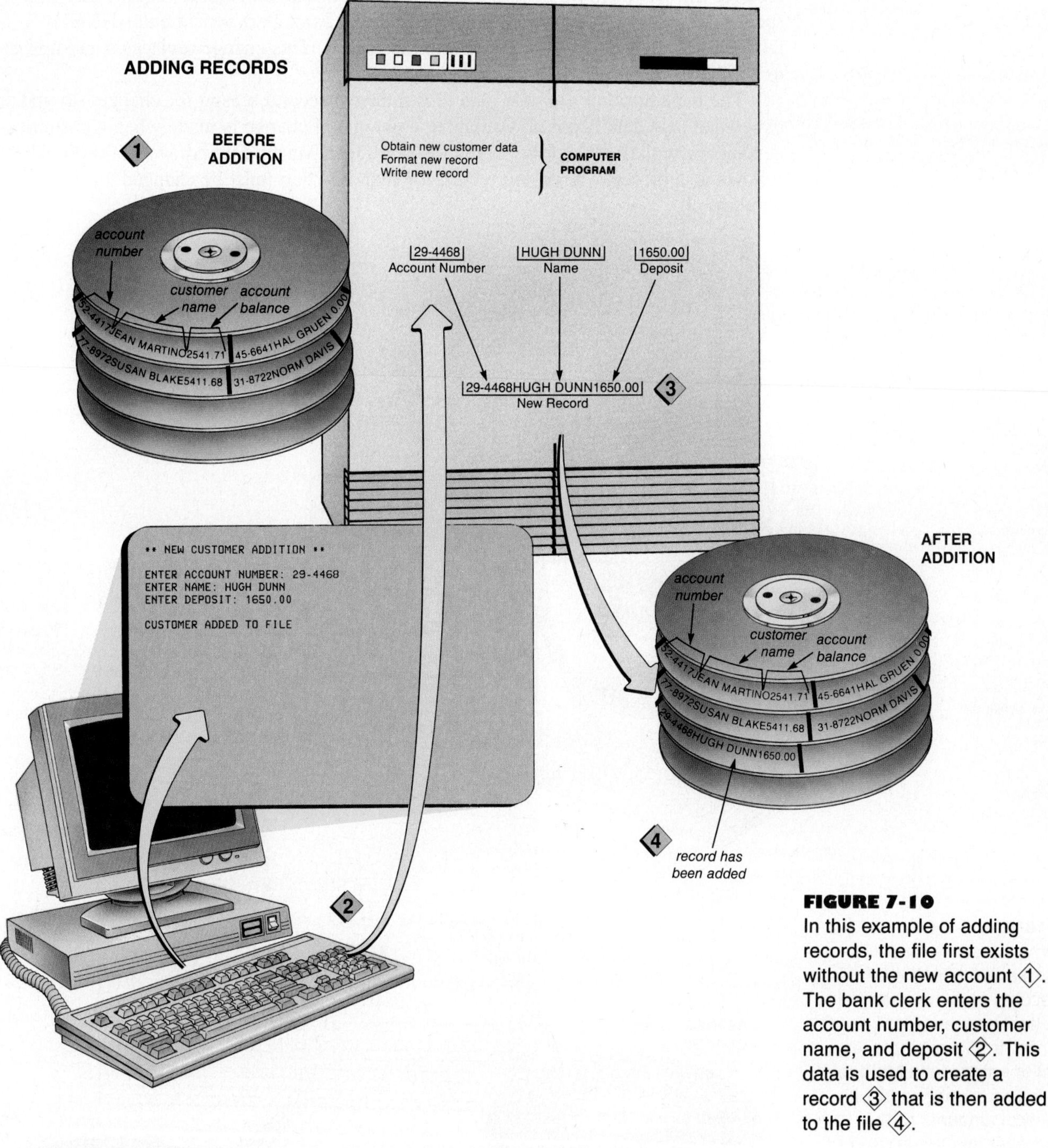

FIGURE 7-10
In this example of adding records, the file first exists without the new account ①. The bank clerk enters the account number, customer name, and deposit ②. This data is used to create a record ③ that is then added to the file ④.

Whenever data is stored on auxiliary storage for subsequent use, the capability to add records must be present in order to keep the data current.

Changing Records

Changing data takes place for two primary reasons: (1) to correct data that is known to be incorrect, and (2) to update data when new data becomes available.

As an example of the first type of change, assume in Figure 7-10 that instead of entering HUGH DUNN as the name for the customer, the bank clerk enters HUGH DONE. The error is not noticed and the customer leaves the bank. When the customer receives his statement he notices the error and contacts the bank to request that the spelling of his name be corrected. To do this, the bank clerk would enter HUGH DUNN as a change to the name field in the record. This change replaces data known to be incorrect with data known to be correct.

The bank account example also illustrates the second reason for change—to update data when new data becomes available. This type of change is made when a customer deposits or withdraws money. In Figure 7-11, Jean Martino withdraws $500.00. The following steps occur when the record for Jean Martino must be changed to reflect her withdrawal.

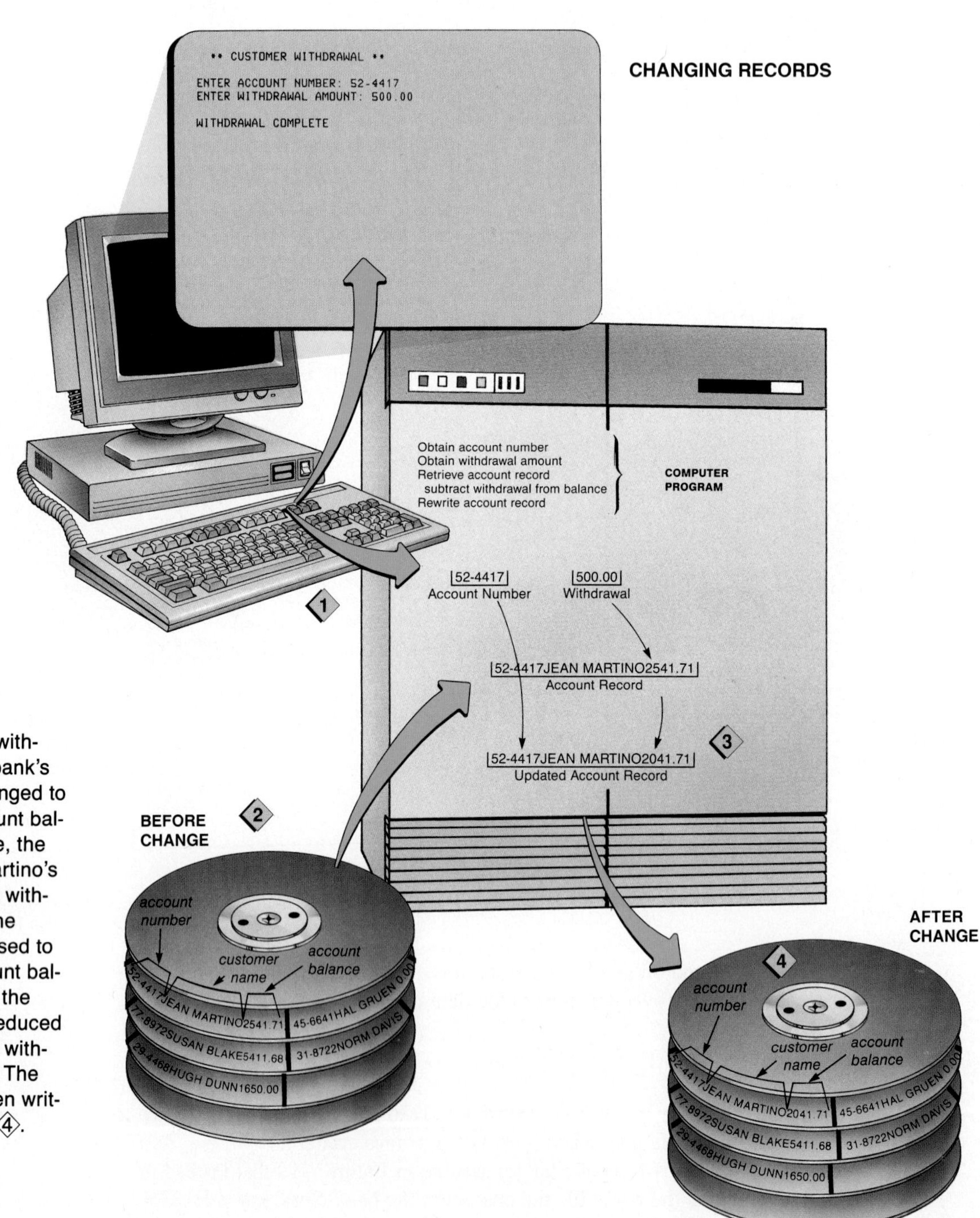

FIGURE 7-11
When Jean Martino withdraws $500.00, the bank's records must be changed to reflect her new account balance. In this example, the teller enters Jean Martino's account number and withdrawal amount ⟨1⟩, the account number is used to retrieve Jean's account balance record ⟨2⟩; and the account balance is reduced by the amount of the withdrawal ($500.00) ⟨3⟩. The updated record is then written back to the disk ⟨4⟩.

1. The bank clerk enters Jean Martino's account number 52-4417 and the amount 500.00.
2. The update program retrieves the record for account number 52-4417 and stores the record in main memory.
3. The program subtracts the withdrawal amount from the account balance in the record. This changes the account balance to reflect the correct balance in the account.
4. After the balance has been changed in memory, the updated record is written back onto the disk. After the change, the account balance has been updated, and the record stored on auxiliary storage contains the new correct account balance.

Changing data stored on auxiliary storage to reflect the correct and current data is an important part of the updating process that is required for data.

Deleting Records

Records are deleted when they are no longer needed as data. Figure 7-12 shows the updating procedures to delete a record for Hal Gruen who has closed his account. The following steps occur to delete the record.

FIGURE 7-12
Here, the account number entered by the teller ① is used to retrieve Hal Gruen's account record ②. The account record is identified as deleted by placing an asterisk in the first position of the record ③. The record is then written back to the file ④. The application software is designed to not process records that begin with an asterisk.

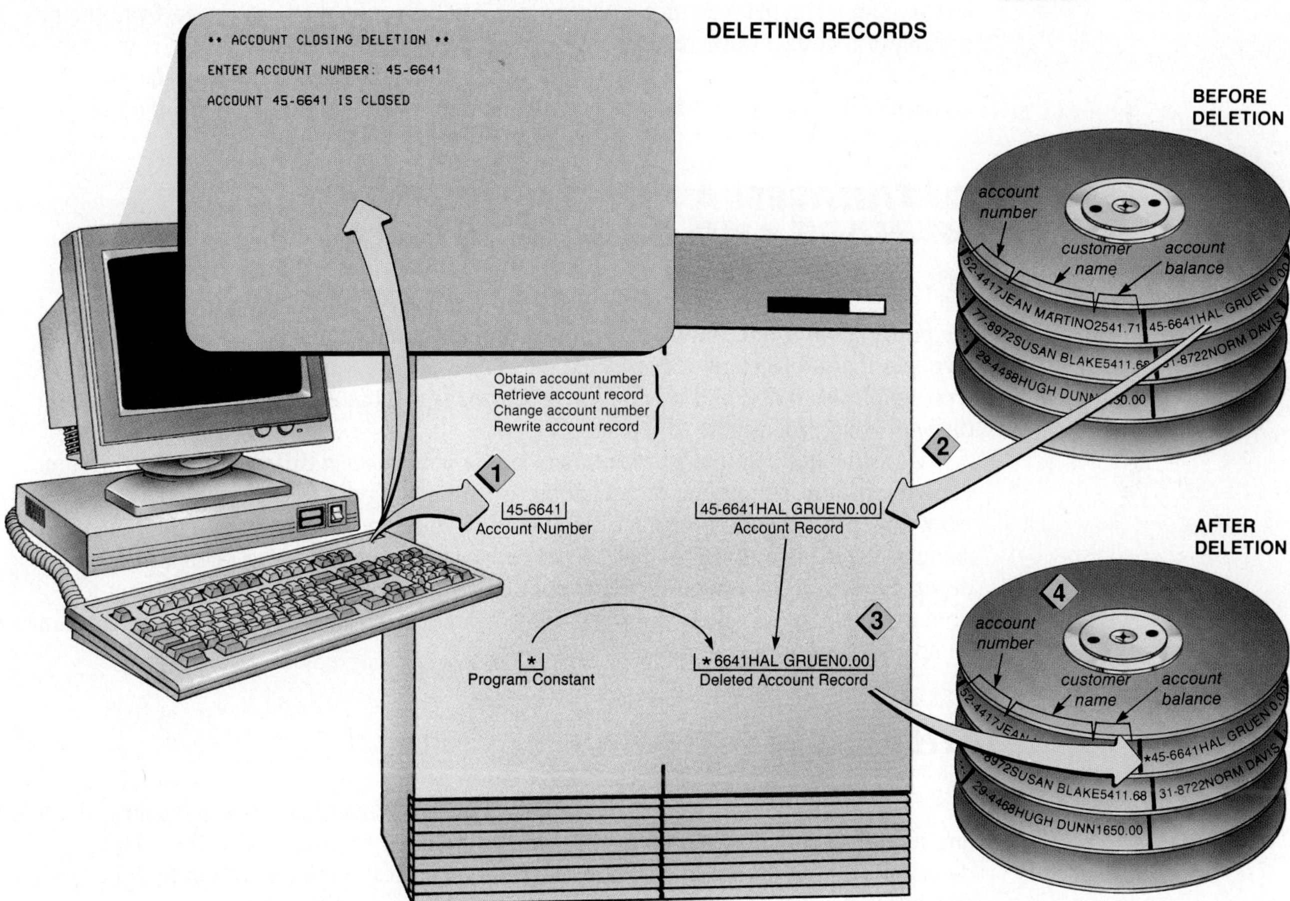

1. The teller enters Hal Gruen's account number (45-6641).
2. The update program retrieves the record from the disk using the account number as the key. The record is placed in main memory.

3. The actual processing that occurs to delete a record from a file depends on the type of file organization being used and the processing requirements of the application. Sometimes the record is removed from the file. Other times, as in this example, the record is not removed from the file. Instead, the record is *flagged*, or marked in some manner, so that it will not be processed again. In this example, an asterisk (*) is added at the beginning of the record.
4. After the asterisk is added, the record is written back to the file. The application program is designed to not process records that begin with an asterisk. Even though the record is still physically stored on the disk, it is effectively deleted because it will not he retrieved for processing.

Flagged records are used in applications where data should no longer be processed but must be maintained for some period of time, such as until the end of the year. Periodically, the user can run a utility program that reorganizes the current records and removes the flagged records. Deleting records from auxiliary storage removes records that are no longer needed and makes additional disk space available.

Summary of How Data Is Maintained

Data maintenance is updating or adding, changing, and deleting data stored on auxiliary storage. The maintenance of data is essential for information derived from the processing of that data to be reliable. When updating data, it does not matter if the data is stored as a single file or if it is part of a series of files organized into a database. The concept of adding, changing, and deleting data to keep it current remains the same.

DATABASES: A BETTER WAY TO MANAGE AND ORGANIZE DATA

Most business people realize that next to the skills of their employees, data (and the information it represents) is one of a company's most valuable assets. They recognize that the information accumulated on sales trends, competitors' products and services, employee skills, and production processes is a valuable resource that would be difficult if not impossible to replace.

Unfortunately, in many cases this resource is located in different files in different departments throughout the organization, often known only to the individuals who work with their specific portion of the total information. In these cases, the potential value of the information goes unrealized because it is not known to people in other departments who may need it or it cannot be accessed efficiently. In an attempt to organize their information resources and provide for timely and efficient access, many companies have implemented databases.

WHAT IS A DATABASE?

Previously in this chapter, we've discussed how data elements (characters, fields, and records) can be organized in files. In file-oriented systems, each file is independent and contains all the information necessary to process the records in that file. In a **database**, the data is organized in multiple related files. Because these files are related, users can access data in multiple files at one time. A **database management system (DBMS)** is the software that allows the user to create, maintain, and report the data and file relationships. By contrast, a **file management system** is software that allows the user to create, maintain, and access one file at a time.

WHY USE A DATABASE?

The following example (Figure 7-13) illustrates some of the advantages of a database system as compared to a file-oriented system. Assume that a business periodically mails catalogs to its customers. If the business is using a file-oriented system, it would probably have a file used for the catalog mailing application that contains information about the catalog plus customer information such as customer account number, name, and address. Files that are used in a file-oriented system are independent of one another. Therefore, other applications such as the sales application, that also need to have customer information would each have files that contain the same customer information stored in the catalog mailing file. Thus, in a file-oriented system, the customer data would be duplicated several times in different files. This duplication of data wastes auxiliary storage space. In addition, it makes maintaining the data difficult because when a customer record must be updated, all files containing that data must be individually updated.

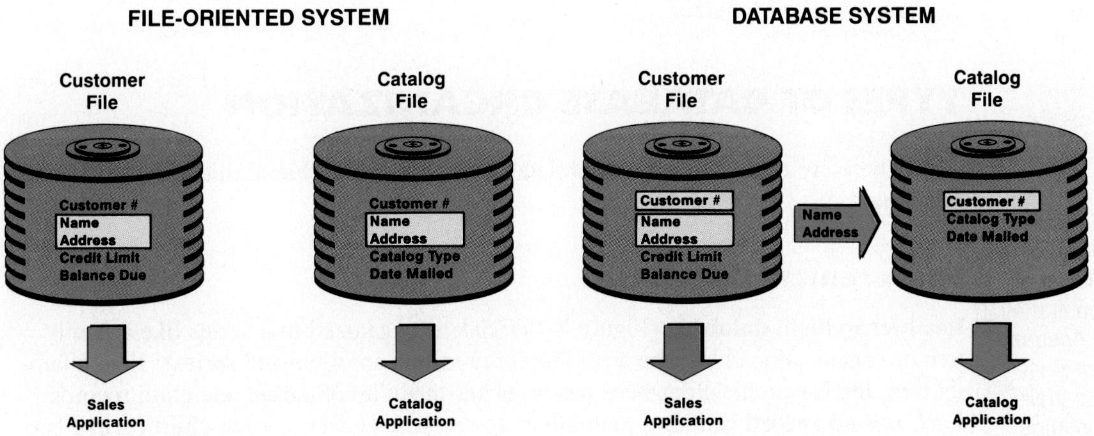

FILE-ORIENTED SYSTEM

DATABASE SYSTEM

Customer File: Customer #, Name, Address, Credit Limit, Balance Due → Sales Application

Catalog File: Customer #, Name, Address, Catalog Type, Date Mailed → Catalog Application

Customer File: Customer #, Name, Address, Credit Limit, Balance Due → Sales Application

Name, Address →

Catalog File: Customer #, Catalog Type, Date Mailed → Catalog Application

FIGURE 7-13
In a file-oriented system, each file contains the customer name and address. In the database system, only the customer file contains the name and address. Other files, such as the catalog file, use the customer number to retrieve the customer name and address when it is needed for processing.

In a database system, however, only one of the applications would have a file containing the customer name and address data. That is because in a database system, files are integrated; that is, related files are linked together by the database software either through predefined relationships or through common data fields. In this example, the link could be the customer account number. If the sales file contained the customer account number, name, and address, the catalog mailing file would only need to contain the customer's account number plus the other catalog information. When the catalog application software is executed, the customer's name and address would be obtained from the sales file. The advantage of the database is that because the files are integrated, the customer name and address would only be stored once. This saves auxiliary storage space. It also allows data to be maintained more easily because update information need only be entered once.

As the previous example illustrates, a database system offers a number of advantages over a file-oriented system. These advantages and several others are summarized as follows:

- **Reduced data redundancy**. Redundant, or duplicate, data is greatly reduced in a database system. Frequently used data elements such as names, addresses, and descriptions are stored in one location. Having such items in one instead of many locations lowers the cost of maintaining the data.
- **Improved data integrity**. Closely related to reduced data redundancy is the database advantage of improved data integrity. Because data is only stored in one place, it is more likely to be accurate. When it is updated, all applications that use the data will be using the most current version.

- **Integrated files**. As we demonstrated by the catalog mailing example in Figure 7-13, a key advantage of a database management system is its capability to *integrate*, or join together, data from more than one file for inquiry or reporting purposes.
- **Improved data security**. Most database management systems allow the user to establish different levels of security over information in the database. For example, a department manager may have *read only* privileges on certain payroll data: the manager could inquire about the data but not change it. The payroll supervisor would have *full update* privileges: the supervisor could not only inquire about the data but could also make changes. A nonmanagement employee would probably have no access privileges to the payroll data and could neither inquire about nor change the data.
- **Reduced development time**. Because data is better organized in a database, development of programs that use this data is more efficient and takes less time. The need to create new files is reduced. Instead, new attributes are added to existing files.

Now that we've discussed some of their advantages, let's discuss the ways that databases can be organized.

TYPES OF DATABASE ORGANIZATION

◆ There are three major types of database organization: hierarchical, network, and relational.

Hierarchical Database

In a **hierarchical database** (Figure 7-14), data is organized in a series like a family tree or organization chart (the term hierarchy means an organized series). Like a family tree, the hierarchical database has branches made up of parent and child records. Each **parent record** can have multiple child records. However, each **child record** can have only one parent. The parent record at the top of the database is referred to as the **root record**.

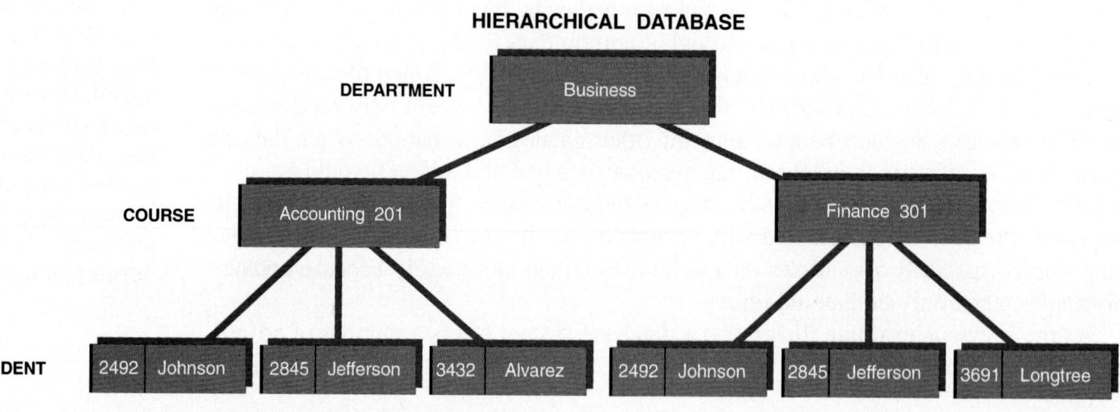

FIGURE 7-14
In this hierarchical database, Johnson, Jefferson, and Longtree are the children of Finance, and Finance is their parent. Finance and Accounting are the children of Business, and Business is their parent. These relationships must be established before the database can be used.

Hierarchical databases are the oldest form of database organization and reflect the fact that they were developed when the disk and memory capacity of computers was limited and most processing was done in batch mode. Data access is sequential in the sense that an inquiry begins at the root record and proceeds down the branch until the requested data is found. All parent-child relationships are established when the database is created in a separate process that is sometimes called *generating the database.*

After the database is created, access must be made through the established relationships. This points out two disadvantages of hierarchical databases. First, records located in separate branches of the database cannot be accessed easily at the same time. Second, adding new fields to database records or modifying existing fields, such as adding the four-digit ZIP code extension, requires the redefinition of the entire database. Depending on the size of the database, this redefinition process can take a considerable amount of time. The advantage of a hierarchical database is that because the data relationships are predefined, access to and updating of data is very fast.

Network Database

A **network database** (Figure 7-15) is similar to a hierarchical database except that each child record can have more than one parent. In network database terminology, a child record is referred to as a **member** and a parent record is referred to as an **owner**. Unlike the hierarchical database, the network database is able to establish relationships between different branches of the data and thus offers increased access capability for the user. However, like the hierarchical database, these data relationships must be established prior to the use of the database and must be redefined if fields are added or modified.

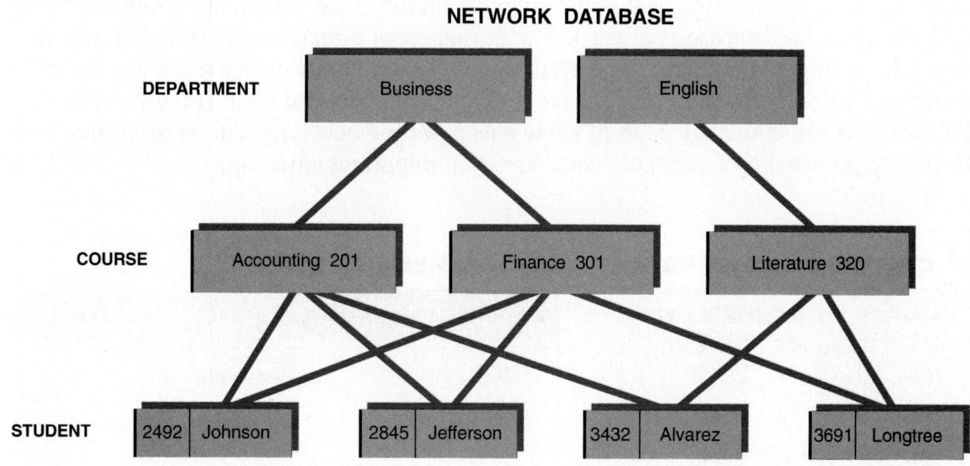

FIGURE 7-15
In a network database, lower level (member) records can be related to more than one higher level (owner) record. For example, Longtree's owners are Finance and Literature. Accounting has three members, Johnson, Jefferson, and Alvarez. As in a hierarchical database, these relationships must be established before the database can be used.

Relational Database

The relational database structure is the most recently developed of the three methods and takes advantage of large-capacity, direct-access storage devices that were not available when the hierarchical and network methods were developed. In a **relational database**, data is organized in tables that in database terminology are called **relations**. The tables are further divided into rows (called **tuples**) and fields (called **attributes**). The tables can be thought of as files and the rows as records. The range of values that an attribute can have is called a **domain**. These terms with a Student Master Table are illustrated on the next page in Figure 7-16.

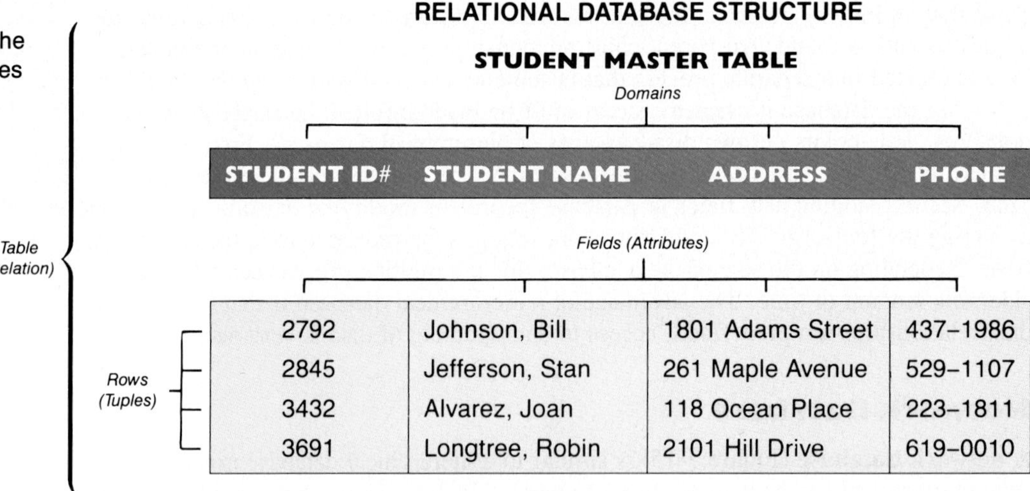

STUDENT ID#	STUDENT NAME	ADDRESS	PHONE
2792	Johnson, Bill	1801 Adams Street	437–1986
2845	Jefferson, Stan	261 Maple Avenue	529–1107
3432	Alvarez, Joan	118 Ocean Place	223–1811
3691	Longtree, Robin	2101 Hill Drive	619–0010

FIGURE 7-16
In a relational database, the terms used to describe files are called tables.

Recall that a key advantage of a database is its capablity to link multiple files together. A relational database accomplishes this by using a common field that exists in each file. For example, in a database for a college, the link between files containing student information could be the student identification number. Hierarchical and network databases can also extract data from multiple files, but in these database structures, the data relationships that will enable the multiple file combination must be defined when the database is created. The advantage of a relational database is that the data relationships do not have to be predefined. The relational database needs only a common field in both data files to make a relationship between them (Figure 7-17). Because it is sometimes difficult to know ahead of time how data will be used, the flexibility provided by a relational database is an important advantage.

FIGURE 7-17
In a relational database, files (called tables) do not require predefined relationships as they do with hierarchal or network databases. Instead, common fields are used to link one table to another. For example, Student ID# could be used to link the Student Master Table in Figure 7-16 above with the Course-Student Table ⓐ. Department ID could be used to link the Department Table ⓑ with the Course-Master Table ⓒ.

ⓐ **COURSE–STUDENT TABLE**

COURSE #	STUDENT ID#
ACC201	2942
ACC201	2845
ACC201	3432
FIN301	2492
FIN301	2845
FIN301	3691
LIT320	3691

ⓑ **DEPARTMENT TABLE**

DEPARTMENT ID	DEPARTMENT NAME
BUS	Business
ENG	English

ⓒ **COURSE–MASTER TABLE**

COURSE #	COURSE NAME	DEPARTMENT ID	UNITS	MAX ENROLLMENT
ACC201	Advanced Accounting	BUS	4	50
FIN301	Investments	BUS	2	30
LIT320	Modern Literature	ENG	3	20

Another advantage of a relational database is its capability to add new fields. All that need be done is to define the fields in the appropriate table. With hierarchical and network database systems, the entire database has to be *redefined*: existing relationships have to be reestablished to include the new fields. A disadvantage of a relational database is that its more complex software requires more powerful computers to provide acceptable performance.

DATABASE MANAGEMENT SYSTEMS

A number of common database management system features are available, including the following described in Figure 7-18.

FEATURE	DESCRIPTION
Data Dictionary	Defines data files and fields.
Utility Program	Creates files and dictionaries, monitors performance, copies data, and deletes unwanted records.
Security	Controls different levels of access to a database.
Query Language	Allows user to specify report content and format.

FIGURE 7-18
A summary of common database management system features.

- **Data dictionary**. The data dictionary defines each data field that will be contained in the database files. The dictionary is used to record the field name, size, description, type of data (e.g., text, numeric, or date), and relationship to other data elements.
- **Utilities**. Database management system utility programs provide for a number of maintenance tasks including creating files and dictionaries, monitoring performance, copying data, and deleting unwanted records.
- **Security**. Most database management systems allow the user to specify different levels of user access privileges. The privileges can be established for each user for each type of access (retrieve, update, and delete) to each data field. Be aware that without some type of access security, the data in a database is more subject to unauthorized access than in a decentralized system of individual files.
- **Query language**. The query language is one of the most valuable features of a database management system. It allows the user to retrieve information from the database based on the criteria and in the format specified by him or her.

QUERY LANGUAGES: ACCESS TO THE DATABASE

A **query language** is a simple English-like language that allows users to specify what data they want to see on a report or screen display. Although each query language has its own grammar, syntax, and vocabulary, these languages can generally be learned in a short time by persons without a programming background.

A Query Example

Figure 7-19 shows how a user might query a relational database. In this example, we illustrate the relational operations that might be performed when a relational database inquiry is made. These three **relational operations** are select, project, and join. They allow the user to manipulate the data from one or more files to create a unique **view**, or subset, of the total data.

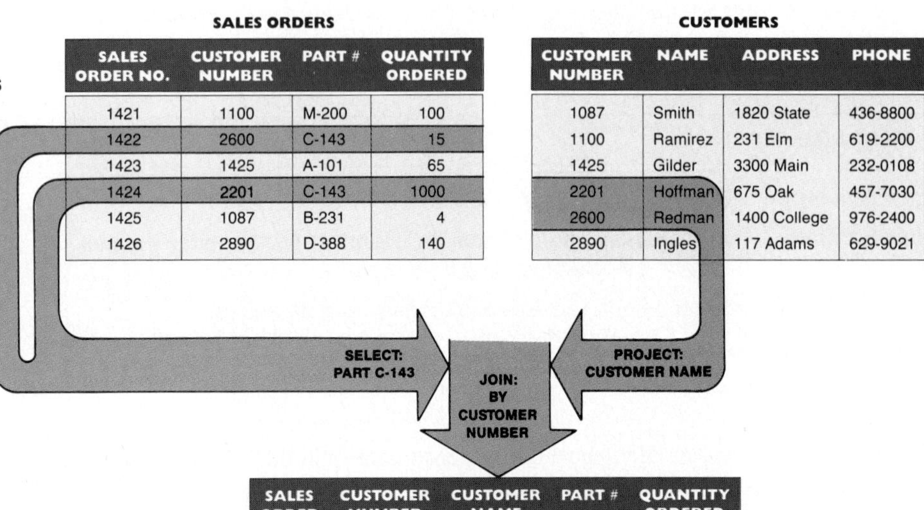

SALES ORDERS

SALES ORDER NO.	CUSTOMER NUMBER	PART #	QUANTITY ORDERED
1421	1100	M-200	100
1422	2600	C-143	15
1423	1425	A-101	65
1424	2201	C-143	1000
1425	1087	B-231	4
1426	2890	D-388	140

CUSTOMERS

CUSTOMER NUMBER	NAME	ADDRESS	PHONE
1087	Smith	1820 State	436-8800
1100	Ramirez	231 Elm	619-2200
1425	Gilder	3300 Main	232-0108
2201	Hoffman	675 Oak	457-7030
2600	Redman	1400 College	976-2400
2890	Ingles	117 Adams	629-9021

Response to Query (view)

SALES ORDER	CUSTOMER NUMBER	CUSTOMER NAME	PART #	QUANTITY ORDERED
1422	2600	Redman	C-143	15
1424	2201	Hoffman	C-143	1000

FIGURE 7-19
The three relational operations (select, project, and join) that would be used to produce a response to the query. The query response is referred to as a view.

The **select relational operation** selects certain records (rows or tuples) based on user-supplied criteria. In the example, the user queries the database to select records from the sales order file that contain part number C-143. Selection criteria can be applied to more than one field and can include tests to determine if a field is greater than, less than, equal to, or not equal to a value specified by the user. Connectors such as AND and OR can also be used.

The **project relational operation** specifies the fields (attributes) that appear on the query output. In the example, the user wants to see the names of the customers who placed orders for part number C-143.

The **join relational operation** is used to combine two files (relations or tables). In the example, the customer number, a field contained in each file, is used to join the two files. After the query is executed, most query languages allow the user to give the query a unique name and save it for future use.

Structured Query Language

One of the most widely used query languages is **Structured Query Language**, often referred to as **SQL** or *sequel*. Originally developed during the 1970s by IBM, SQL has been incorporated into a number of relational database software packages including ORACLE by Oracle Corporation and INGRES by Relational Technology. IBM actively supports SQL and incorporates it into their two major relational database system products, SQL/DS and DB2. SQL received increased support as the emerging relational database management system query language when, in 1985, the American National

Standards Institute formed a committee to develop industry standards for SQL. The standards were issued in 1987. Today, most database software vendors have incorporated SQL into their products. The standardization of SQL will further accelerate its implementation on a wide range of computer systems from micros to supercomputers. This fact, coupled with the increasing dominance of relational databases, will mean that SQL will be available to many computer users. Figure 7-20 shows an example of the SQL statements that would be used to create the response (view) shown in Figure 7-19.

```
SELECT ORDNO, CUSTNO, CUSTNAME, PARTNO, QTYORD
FROM SALESORDERS, CUSTOMERS
WHERE SALESORDERS.CUSTNO = CUSTOMERS.CUSTNO
ORDER BY ORDNO
```

FIGURE 7-20
These Structured Query Language (SQL) statements will generate the response (view) shown in Figure 7-19. The statements specify that the sales order number (ORDNO), customer number (CUSTNO), part number (PARTNO), and quantity ordered (QTYORD) appear on the report. This information will be taken from the SALESORDERS and CUSTOMERS files. The report information will be taken from records where the customer number (CUSTNO) in the SALESORDERS file matches the customer number in the CUSTOMERS file. Information on the report will be listed in sales order (ORDNO) sequence.

DATABASE ADMINISTRATION

◆ The centralization of an organization's data into a database requires a great deal of cooperation and coordination on the part of the database users. In file-oriented systems, if a user wanted to keep track of some data, he or she would just create another file, often duplicating some data that was already being tracked by someone else. In a database system, the user must first check to see if some or all of the data is already on file and if not, how it can be added to the system. The role of coordinating the use of the database belongs to the database administrator.

The Database Administrator

The **database administrator**, or **DBA**, is the person responsible for managing all database activities (Figure 7-21). In small organizations, this person usually has other responsibilities such as the overall management of the computer resources. In medium and large organizations, the role of the DBA is a full-time job for one or more people. The job of the DBA usually includes the following responsibilities:

- **Database design**. The DBA determines the design of the database and specifies where to add additional data files and records when they are needed.
- **User coordination**. The DBA is responsible for letting users know what data is available in the database and how the users can retrieve it. The DBA also reviews user requests for additions to the database and helps establish priorities for their implementation.
- **Backup and recovery**. The centralization of data in a database makes an organization particularly vulnerable to a computer system failure. The DBA is often responsible for minimizing this risk, making sure that all data is regularly backed up and preparing (and periodically testing) contingency plans for a prolonged equipment or software malfunction.
- **System security**. The DBA is responsible for establishing and monitoring system access privileges to prevent the unauthorized use of an organization's data.

FIGURE 7-21
The database administrator plays a key role in the managing of a company's data. The DBA should possess good technical and management skills.

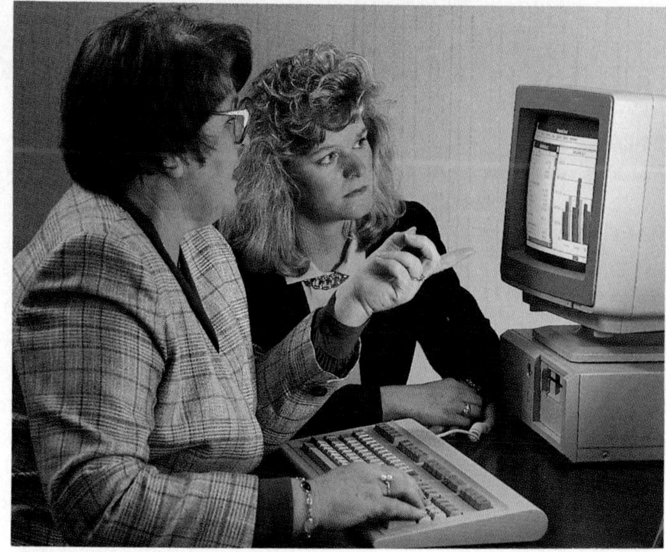

- **Performance monitoring**. The performance of the database, usually measured in terms of response time to a user request, can be affected by a number of factors such as file sizes and the types and frequency of inquiries during the day. Most database management systems have utility programs that enable the DBA to monitor these factors and make adjustments to provide for more efficient database use.

In addition to the DBA, the user also has a role in a database management system.

The Responsibility of the User in a Database Management System

One of the user's first responsibilities is to become familiar with the data in the existing database. First-time database users are often amazed at the wealth of information available to help them perform their jobs more effectively.

Another responsibility of the user, in organizations of any size, is to play an active part in the specification of additions to the database. The maintenance of an organization's database is an ongoing task that must be constantly measured against the overall goals of the organization. Therefore, users must participate in designing the database that will be used to help them achieve those goals and measure their progress.

PERSONAL COMPUTER DATABASE SYSTEMS

A variety of software packages are available for personal computers, ranging from simple file management programs to full relational database management systems. Some of the popular database packages designed for personal computer include dBASE III PLUS, dBASE IV, Paradox, Rbase and Foxpro (Figure 7-22).

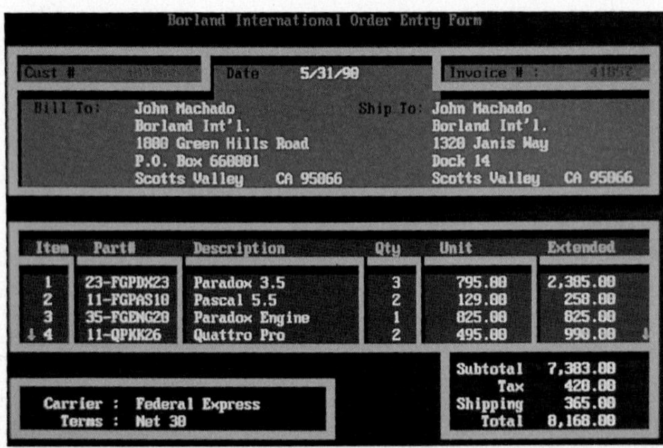

FIGURE 7-22
Paradox and dBASE IV are two of the more popular database software packages. The screen on the left shows an order entry form that was designed with Paradox. The screen on the right shows a name and address file developed using dBASE IV.

As with large system packages, many personal computer software vendors have developed or modified existing packages to support Structured Query Language (SQL). The advantage of SQL packages for personal computers is that they can directly query mainframe databases that support SQL.

The increased computing power of the newest personal computers now allows modified versions of database management packages originally written for mainframe computers to be run on the personal computers. ORACLE (Oracle Corporation) and INFORMIX-SQL (Informix Software) are two SQL-based packages that have been adapted to personal computers.

With so many software packages available (a recent survey included 43), it's difficult to decide which one to choose. If you have simple needs, a file management package is probably all that you need. If you need the capability of a database, one of the more popular database management systems will offer you increased capability and growth potential. For your complex database requirements, the packages originally developed on mainframes should provide all the database resources you require. If you need to select a database software package for your personal computer, you may want to refer to the sections in Chapter 2 that discuss personal computer databases and how to choose software packages for a personal computer.

SUMMARY OF FILE AND DATABASE MANAGEMENT

◆ Understanding the data management, file, and database concepts that we have presented in this chapter gives you a knowledge of how data is stored and managed on a computer. This information will be useful to you, whether you are a home computer user who wants to store personal data on diskettes or a hard drive, or a computer user accessing the database of the company where you are employed.

CHAPTER SUMMARY

1. **Data management** refers to procedures that are used to keep data accurate and timely and provide for the security and maintenance of data.
2. **Data accuracy**, sometimes called **data integrity**, means that the source of the data is reliable and the data is correctly reported and entered.
3. Accurate data must also be timely meaning that it has not lost its usefulness because time has passed.
4. **Data security** refers to protecting data to keep it from being misused or lost.
5. **Backup** procedures provide for maintaining copies of data so that in the event the data is lost or destroyed it can be recovered.
6. Data maintenance refers to **updating** data. This includes **adding**, **changing**, or **deleting** data in order to keep it current.
7. A **file** is a collection of related records that is usually stored on an auxiliary storage device.
8. The three types of file organization are sequential, indexed, and direct or relative.
9. When **sequential file organization** is used, records are stored one after the other, normally in ascending or descending order, based on a value in each record called the key.
10. The **key** is a field that contains unique data, such as a Social Security number, that is used to identify the records in a file.
11. **Sequential retrieval** means that the records on a tape or disk file are retrieved (accessed) one after another in the same order that the records are stored on the tape or disk.
12. With **indexed file organization**, the records are stored on the disk in an indexed file in ascending or descending sequence based on a key field. An index is used to retrieve records.
13. An **index** is a file that consists of a list containing the key field and the corresponding disk address for each record in a file.
14. **Random retrieval**, or **random access**, means the system can go directly to a record without having to read the preceding records.
15. An advantage of indexed files is that usually more than one index can be maintained. Each index can be used to access the records in a file in a particular order.
16. A **direct file**, or **relative file**, uses the key value of a record to determine the location on the disk where the record is or will be stored.
17. The locations on a disk where records in a direct file can be stored are called **buckets**.
18. **Hashing** means the program managing the disk uses a formula or performs a calculation to determine the location (position) where a record will be placed on a disk.
19. A **collision** occurs when the hashing operation generates the same disk location (called **synonyms**) for records with different key values.

20. In a **database**, the data is organized in multiple related files.
21. A **database management system (DBMS)** is the software that allows the user to create, maintain, and report the data and file relationships.
22. By contrast, a **file management system** allows a user to access only one file at a time.
23. The major advantages of using a database include: **reduced data redundancy** (data is not duplicated in several different files); **improved data integrity** (data accuracy); **integrated files** (joining data from more than one file); **improved data security** (ensuring that the data is accessible only to those with the proper authorization); and **reduced development time** (for program development and data preparation).
24. A **hierarchical database** is organized in a top to bottom series of parent-child relationships. Each **parent record** can have multiple child records. However, each **child record** can have only one parent. The parent record at the top of the hierarchy is called the **root record**.
25. A **network database** is organized similar to a hierarchical database except each child record (called a **member**) may have more than one parent record (called an **owner**).
26. Data relationships in both the hierarchical database and the network database must be established prior to the use of the database.
27. A **relational database** is organized into tables called **relations**. The relations are divided into **tuples** (rows) and **attributes** (fields). Each attribute is given a unique name, called the **domain**.
28. In a relational database, a common field is used to connect multiple files.
29. The advantage of a relational database is that the data relationships do not need to be predefined.
30. The database management system (DBMS) consists of a **data dictionary** that defines each data field to be used in the database; **utilities**, or programs, that provide a number of special functions (such as copying data, creating files, and deleting records); **security levels** that control access to the data; and a **query language** that allows users to specify what data they wish to view.
31. When a user queries a relational database, the three **relational operations** are the select, project, and join.
32. The **select relational operation** selects certain records (rows or tuples) based on user-supplied criteria.
33. The **project relational operation** specifies the fields (attributes) that appear on the query output.
34. The **join relational operation** is used to combine two files.
35. A widely used query language is **Structured Query Language (SQL)**.
36. The **database administrator (DBA)** is the person who coordinates all database activities.
37. The database administrator is responsible for database design, user coordination, backup and recovery, database security, and database performance monitoring.
38. Users should become familiar with the data in their organization's database and should actively participate in the specification of additions to the database that will affect their jobs.
39. A variety of data management systems are available for personal computers, ranging from file management programs to full relational database management systems.

KEY TERMS

Adding *7.3*
Attribute *7.15*
Backup *7.3*
Bucket *7.6*
Changing *7.3*
Child record *7.14*
Collision *7.7*
Data accuracy *7.2*
Data dictionary *7.17*
Data integrity *7.2*
Data maintenance *7.3*
Data management *7.2*
Data security *7.3*
Database *7.12*
Database administrator (DBA) *7.19*
Database management system (DBMS) *7.12*
Deleting *7.3*
Direct access *7.5*
Direct file *7.6*
Domain *7.15*
File management system *7.12*
Hashing *7.7*
Hierarchical database *7.14*
Index *7.5*
Indexed file organization *7.5*
Join relational operation *7.18*
Key *7.4*
Member *7.15*
Network database *7.15*
Owner *7.15*
Parent record *7.14*
Prime number *7.7*
Project relational operation *7.18*
Query language *7.17*
Random access *7.5*
Random retrieval *7.5*
Relational database *7.15*
Relational operation *7.18*
Relation *7.15*
Relative file *7.6*
Root record *7.14*

Security *7.17*
Select relational operation *7.18*
Sequential access *7.4*
Sequential file organization *7.4*
Sequential retrieval *7.4*
Structured Query Language (SQL) *7.18*
Synonym *7.7*
Tuple *7.15*
Updating *7.3*
Utilities *7.17*
View *7.18*

REVIEW QUESTIONS

1. List and describe the three areas of data management.
2. Describe sequential file organization. What is a key?
3. What is an indexed file? Describe how the index is used to retrieve records from an indexed file.
4. Write a definition for a direct file.
5. What is hashing? What are buckets?
6. Write a definition for the term database.
7. Describe what a database management system allows a user to do.
8. What are the advantages of a database management system over a file-oriented system?
9. Draw an example of a hierarchical and network database.
10. Describe how data is organized in a relational database.
11. Discuss two advantages and one disadvantage of a relational database.
12. What are the common features of database management systems?
13. How is a database query used?
14. What are the responsibilities of a database administrator?
15. What are the responsibilities of the user in a database management system?

CONTROVERSIAL ISSUES

1. Database management systems allow the user to establish different levels of security that can be used to restrict access and update privileges. Using a student record file as an example, discuss the different access and update privileges that students, teachers, administrators, and outside organizations should have concerning student file records.
2. Commercial attempts to market databases consisting of personal information on citizens have met strong opposition from critics that contend that the dissemination of such information is an invasion of privacy. Discuss how such a database could be used and misused. What limits, if any, should be placed on the creation of databases that contain information on private citizens?

RESEARCH PROJECTS

1. Visit a local computer store and obtain information on a file management system and a database management system. What features does the database management system have that the file management system does not have?
2. Prepare a report on a database management system that supports Structured Query Language (SQL).

Communications

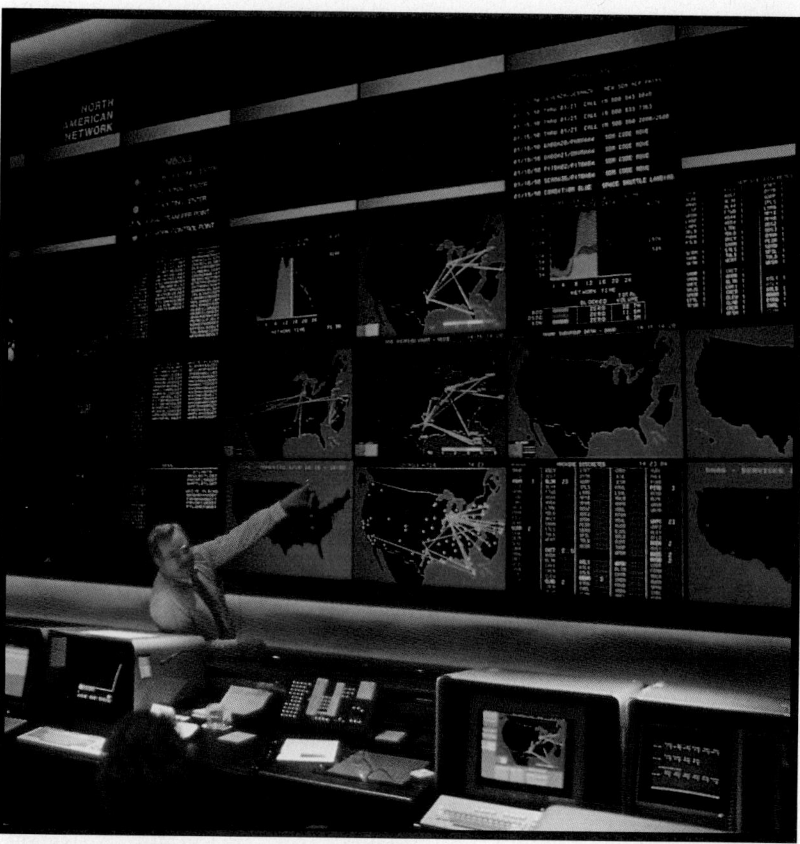

OBJECTIVES

- Define the term communications
- Describe the basic components of a communications system
- Describe the various transmission media used for communications channels
- Describe the different types of line configurations
- Describe how data is transmitted
- Identify and explain the communications equipment used in a communications system
- Describe the functions performed by communications software
- Explain the two major categories of networks and describe three common network configurations
- Describe how bridges and gateways are used to connect networks

Computers are well recognized as important computing devices. They should also be recognized as important communications devices. It is now possible for a computer to communicate with other computers anywhere in the world. This capability, sometimes referred to as *connectivity*, allows users to quickly and directly access data and information that otherwise would have been unavailable or that probably would have taken considerable time to acquire. Banks, retail stores, airlines, hotels, and many other businesses use computers for communications purposes. Personal computer users communicate with other personal computer users. They can also access special databases available on larger machines to quickly and conveniently obtain information such as weather reports, stock market data, airline schedules, news stories, or even theater and movie reviews.

In this chapter we provide an overview of communications with an emphasis on the communication of data and information. We explain some of the terminology, equipment, procedures, and applications that relate to computers and their use as communications devices. Chapter 14 explains more about some of the specialized communications devices that have been developed for transmitting text, graphics, voice, and video over communications channels.

WHAT IS COMMUNICATIONS?

Communications, sometimes called **data communications**, refers to the transmission of data and information over a communications channel such as a standard telephone line, between one computer or terminal and another computer. Other terms such as telecommunications and teleprocessing are also used to describe communications. **Telecommunications** describes any type of long-distance communications including television signals. **Teleprocessing** refers to the use of telephone lines to transmit data. As communications technology continues to advance, the distinction between these terms is blurred. Therefore, most people refer to the process of transmitting data or information of any type as data communications, or simply communications.

A COMMUNICATIONS SYSTEM MODEL

Figure 8-1 shows the basic model for a communications system. This model consists of the following equipment:

- A computer or a terminal
- Communications equipment that sends (and can usually receive) data
- The communications channel over which the data is sent
- Communications equipment that receives (and can usually send) data
- Another computer

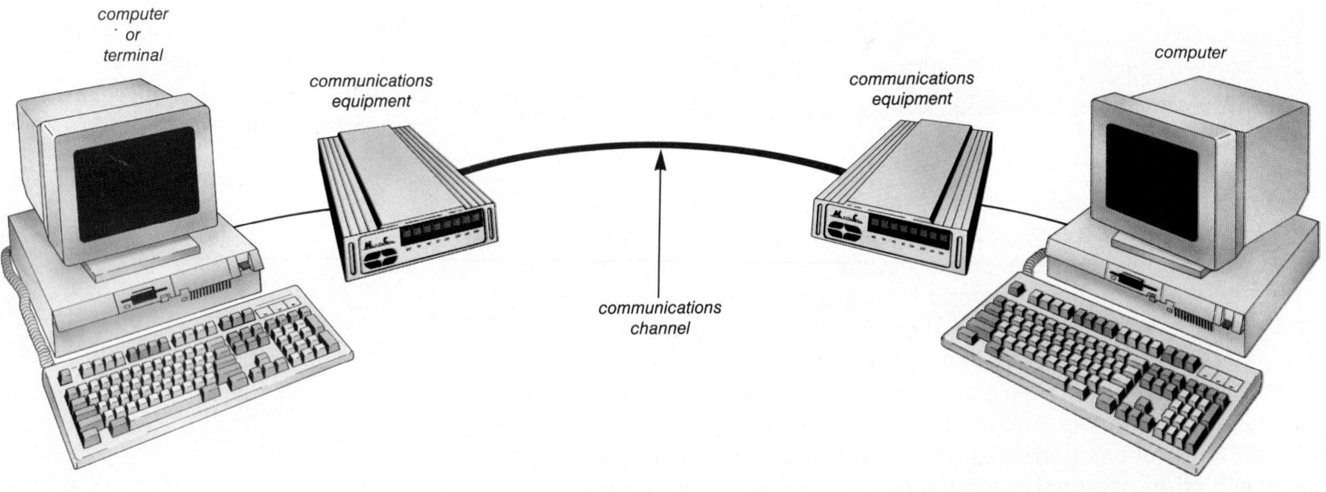

FIGURE 8-1
The basic model of a communications system. In addition to the equipment, communications software is also required.

The basic model also includes communications software. If two computers are communicating with each other, compatible communications software is required on each system. If a computer is communicating with a terminal, communications are directed by either a separate program running on the computer or the computer operating system.

COMMUNICATIONS CHANNELS

A **communications channel**, also called a **communications line** or **communications link**, is the path that the data follows as it is transmitted from the sending equipment to the receiving equipment in a communications system. These channels are made up of one or more **transmission media**, including twisted pair wire, coaxial cable, fiber optics, microwave transmission, satellite transmission, and wireless transmission.

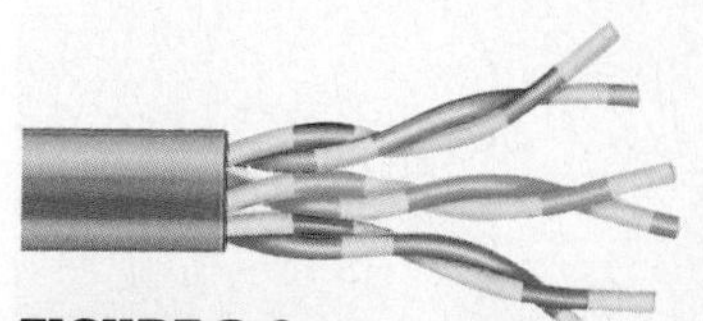

FIGURE 8-2 ▲
Twisted pair wire is most commonly used as telephone wire. It is inexpensive but can be affected by electrical interference that can cause errors in data transmission.

Twisted Pair Wire

Twisted pair wire (Figure 8-2) consists of pairs of copper wires that are twisted together. To insulate and identify the wires, each wire is covered with a thin layer of colored plastic. Twisted pair wire is commonly used for telephone lines. It is an inexpensive transmission medium, and it can be easily strung from one location to another. The disadvantage of twisted pair wire is that it can be affected by outside electrical interference generated by machines such as fans or air conditioners. While this interference might be acceptable on a voice call, it can garble the data as it is sent over the line, causing transmission errors to occur.

FIGURE 8-3 ▼
On coaxial cable, data travels through the copper wire conductor. The outer conductor is made of woven metal mesh that acts as an electrical ground. Coaxial cable can carry up to 100 times as many communication signals as twisted pair wire.

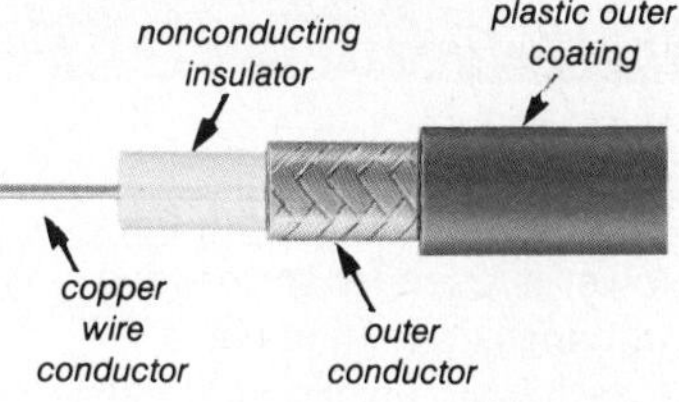

Coaxial Cable

A **coaxial cable** is a high-quality communications line that is used in offices and laid under the ground and under the ocean. Coaxial cable consists of a copper wire conductor surrounded by a nonconducting insulator that is in turn surrounded by a woven metal outer conductor, and finally a plastic outer coating (Figure 8-3). Because of its more heavily insulated construction, coaxial cable is not susceptible to electrical interference and can transmit data at higher data rates over longer distances than twisted pair telephone wire.

There are two types of coaxial cable, named for the transmission techniques they support: baseband and broadband. **Baseband** coaxial cable carries one signal at a time. The signal, however, can travel very fast — in the area of ten million bits per second for the first 1,000 feet. The speed drops significantly as the length of the cable increases, and special equipment is needed to amplify (boost) the signal if it is transmitted more than approximately one mile.

Broadband coaxial cable can carry multiple signals at one time. It is similar to cable TV where a single cable offers a number of channels to the user. A particular advantage of broadband channels is that data, audio, and video transmission can occur over the same line.

FIGURE 8-4 ▼
The two-strand, fiber-optic cable (bottom) can transmit as much information as the 1,500-pair copper cable (top).

Fiber Optics

Fiber optics is a technology that may eventually replace conventional wire and cable in communications systems. This technology is based on the capability of smooth, hair-thin strands of glass to conduct light with high efficiency (Figure 8-4). The major advantages of fiber optics over wire cables include substantial weight and size savings and increased speed of transmission. Another advantage is that fiber-optic cable is not affected by electrical and magnetic fields. A single fiber-optic cable can carry several hundred thousand voice communications simultaneously. The disadvantages of fiber-optic cable are that it is more expensive than twisted pair or coaxial cable and it is more difficult to install and modify than metal wiring. Fiber optics is frequently being used in new voice and data installations.

Microwave Transmission

Microwaves are radio waves that can be used to provide high-speed transmission of both voice and data. Data is transmitted through the air from one microwave station to another in a manner similar to the way radio signals are transmitted (Figure 8-5). A disadvantage of microwaves is that they are limited to line-of-sight transmission. This means that microwaves must be transmitted in a straight line and that there can be no obstructions, such as buildings or mountains, between microwave stations. For this reason, microwave stations are characterized by antennas positioned on tops of buildings, towers, or mountains.

Satellite Transmission

Communications satellites receive signals from earth, amplify the signals, and retransmit the signals back to the earth. **Earth stations** (Figure 8-6) are communications facilities that use large, dish-shaped antennas to transmit and receive data from satellites. The transmission *to* the satellite is called an **uplink** and the transmission *from* the satellite to a receiving earth station is called a **downlink**.

Communications satellites are usually placed about 22,300 miles above the earth in a **geosynchronous orbit** (Figure 8-7). This means that the satellite is placed in an orbit where it rotates with the earth, so that the same dish antennas on earth that are used to send and receive signals can remain fixed on the satellite at all times.

FIGURE 8-5 ▲
The round antenna on this tower is used for microwave transmission. Microwave transmission is limited to line-of-sight. Antennas are usually placed 25 to 75 miles apart.

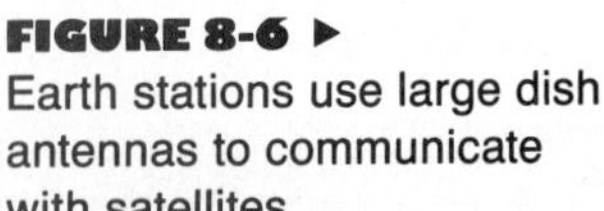

FIGURE 8-6 ▶
Earth stations use large dish antennas to communicate with satellites.

◀ FIGURE 8-7
Communications satellites are placed in geosynchronous orbits approximately 22,300 miles above the earth.

Wireless Transmission

Wireless transmission uses one of three techniques to transmit data: light beams, radio waves, or carrier-connect radio, which uses the existing electrical wiring of a building. These methods are sometimes used by companies to connect devices that are in the same general area such as an office or business park. For example, the unit shown in Figure 8-8 uses light beams to transmit or receive data over a distance up to 70 feet. Local wireless systems offer design flexibility and portability, but provide slower transmission speed than wired connections.

For longer distances, radio-wave wireless systems are becoming more widely used. IBM and Motorola combined their private nationwide radio networks and are selling its use to other companies. The combined network contains over 1,100 radio base stations that can serve over 8,000 cities in 50 states. Potential users include companies with large numbers of service personnel who need access to their company's computer data when they are at a customer site. For example, a repair technician may need to know the nearest location of a particular part. Using a portable radio data terminal (Figure 8-9) the technician could access the company's inventory database and obtain information about the availability of the required part.

A wireless device available to the general public that offers many of the same advantages as private radio networks is a cellular telephone. A **cellular telephone** uses radio waves to communicate with a local antenna assigned to a specific geographic area called a cell. Each cell is shaped like a hexagon (Figure 8-10) so that it will precisely fit with adjacent cells. Cellular phones are often used in automobiles. As a cellular telephone user travels from one cell to another, a computer that monitors the activity in each cell switches the conversation from one radio channel to another. By switching channels in this manner, the same channel can be used by another caller in a nonadjacent cell. Individual cells range from one to ten miles in width and use between 50 and 75 radio channels.

FIGURE 8-8
Wireless communications devices are well suited for open office environments where they can be mounted on office partitions. The units work by bouncing light beams off reflective surfaces such as a ceiling or a wall. Multiple terminals or computers can be connected to each device.

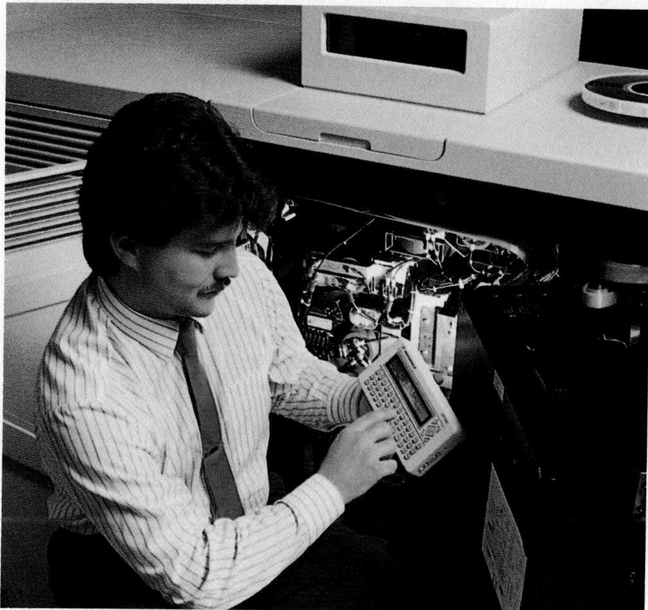

◀ **FIGURE 8-9**
This portable terminal uses radio waves to communicate with a base radio station that is connected to a host computer. Using such a terminal, service technicians can instantly inquire as to the availability of repair parts.

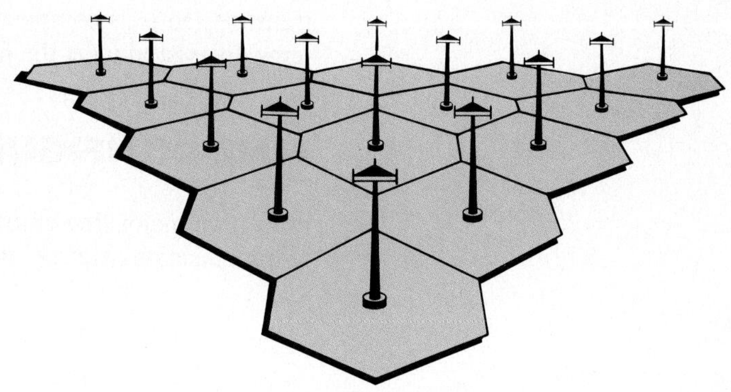

FIGURE 8-10 ▶
Each cell in a cellular phone system is shaped like a hexagon so that it precisely fits with adjacent cells. If a cellular phone user is traveling between cells, such as in a car, a central computer automatically transfers the communication signal from one antenna to another.

An Example of a Communications Channel

When data is transmitted over long distances, several different transmission media are generally used to make a complete communications channel. Figure 8-11 illustrates how some of the various transmission media could be used to transmit data from a personal computer on the west coast of the United States to a large computer on the east coast. An example of the steps that could occur are as follows.

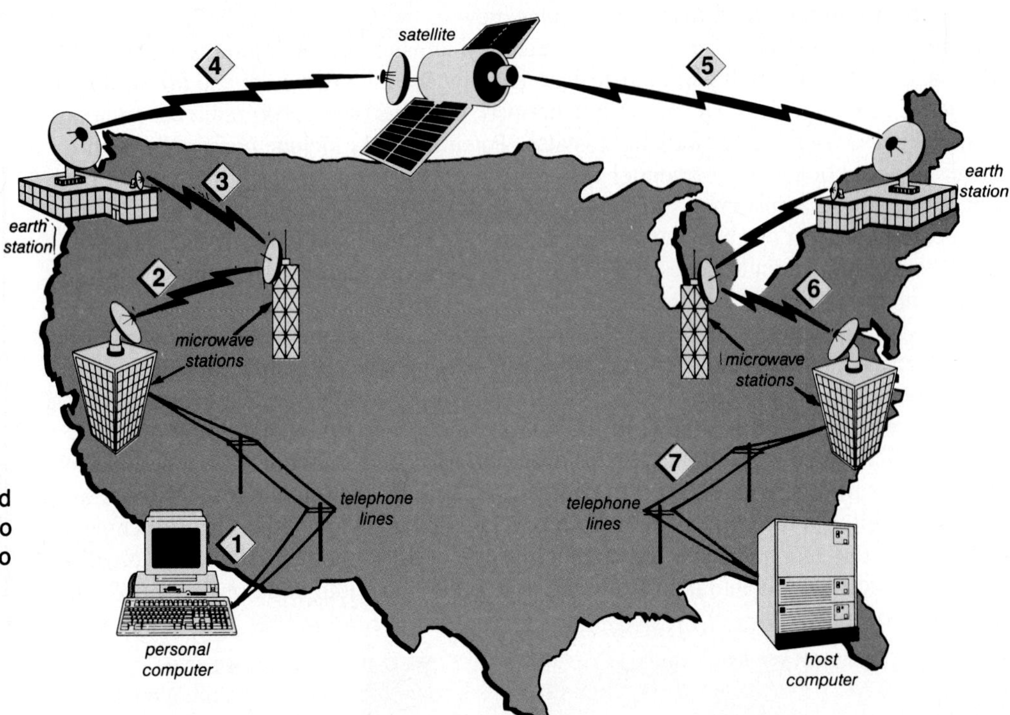

FIGURE 8-11
The use of telephone wires, microwave transmission, and a communications satellite to allow a personal computer to communicate with a large host computer.

1. An entry is made on the personal computer. The data is sent over telephone lines from the computer to a microwave station.
2. The data is then transmitted from one microwave station to another.
3. The data is transmitted from the last microwave station to an earth station.
4. The earth station transmits the data to the communications satellite.
5. The satellite relays the data to another earth station on the other side of the country.
6. The data received at the earth station is transmitted to microwave stations.
7. The data is sent by the telephone lines to the large computer.

This entire transmission process would take less than one second. Not all data transmission is as complex as this example, but such sophisticated communications systems do exist to meet the needs of some users.

LINE CONFIGURATIONS

Two major **line configurations** (types of line connections) commonly used in communications are: point-to-point lines and multidrop, or multipoint, lines.

Point-to-Point Lines

A **point-to-point line** is a direct line between a sending and a receiving device. It may be one of two types: a switched line or a dedicated line (Figure 8-12).

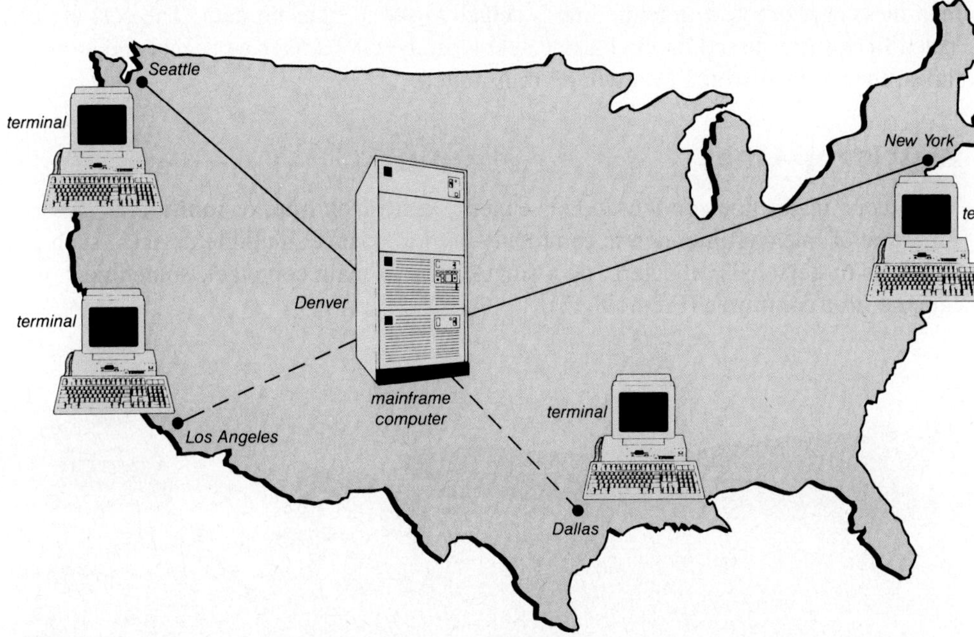

FIGURE 8-12
A point-to-point line configuration using both switched telephone (dial up) lines (----) and dedicated lines (_____) are connected to a main computer in Denver. The dedicated lines are always connected, whereas the switched lines have to be connected each time they are used.

Switched Line A **switched line** uses a regular telephone line to establish a communications connection. Each time a connection is made, the line to be used for the call is selected by the telephone company switching stations (hence the name switched line). Using a switched line for communicating data is the same process as one person using a telephone to call another person. The communications equipment at the sending end dials the telephone number of the communications equipment at the receiving end. When the communications equipment at the receiving end answers the call, a connection is established and data can be transmitted. The process of establishing the communication connection is sometimes referred to as the **handshake**. When the transmission of data is complete, the communications equipment at either end terminates the call by hanging up and the line is disconnected.

An advantage of using switched lines is that a connection can be made between any two locations that have telephone service and communications equipment. For example, a personal computer could dial one computer to get information about the weather and then hang up and place a second call to another computer to get information about the stock market. A disadvantage of a switched line is that the quality of the line cannot be controlled because the line is chosen at random by the telephone company switching equipment. The cost of a switched line is the same for data communications as for a regular telephone call.

Dedicated Line A **dedicated line** is a line connection that is always established (unlike the switched line where the line connection is reestablished each time it is used). The communications device at one end is always connected to the device at the other end. A user can create his or her own dedicated line connection by running a wire or cable between two points, such as between two offices or buildings, or the dedicated line can be provided by an outside organization such as a telephone company or some other communications service company. If the dedicated line is provided by an outside organization, it is sometimes called a **leased line**, or a **private line**. The quality and consistency of the connection is better than on a switched line because a dedicated line is always established. Use of dedicated lines provided by outside organizations are usually charged on a flat-fee basis, a fixed amount each month regardless of how much time the line is actually used to transmit data. The cost of dedicated lines varies based on the distance between the two connected points and, sometimes, the speed at which data will be transmitted.

Multidrop Lines

The second major line configuration is called a **multidrop line**, or **multipoint line**. This type of line configuration is commonly used to connect multiple devices, such as terminals or personal computers, on a single line to a main computer, sometimes called a **host computer** (Figure 8-13).

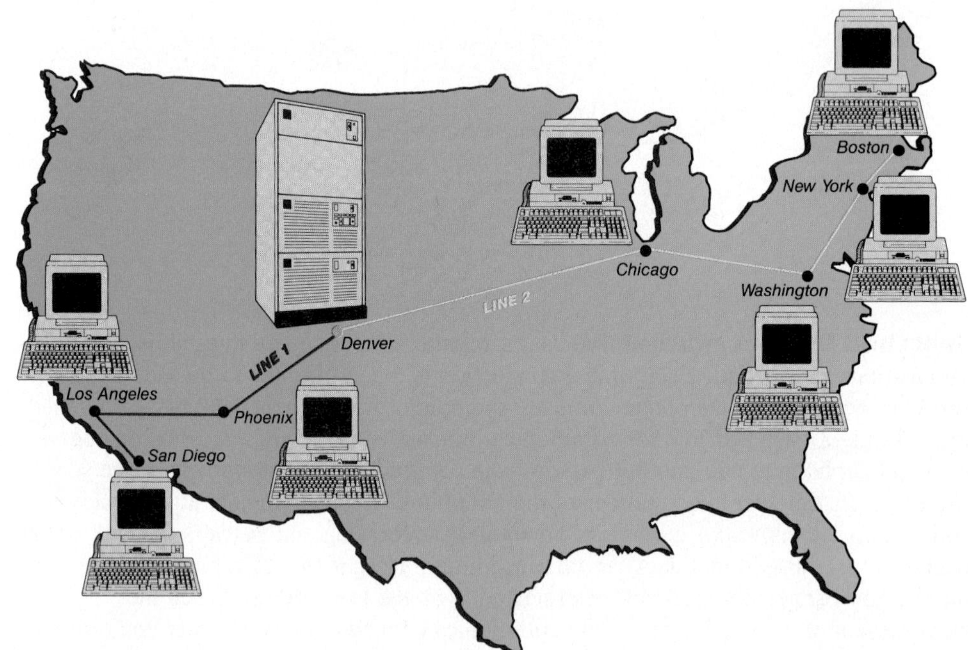

FIGURE 8-13
Two multidrop lines connect several cities with a computer in Denver. Each line is shared by terminals at several locations. Multidrop line configurations are less expensive than individual lines to each remote location.

For example, a ticket agent could use a terminal to enter an inquiry requesting flight information from a database stored on a main computer (Figure 8-14). While the request is being transmitted to the main computer, other terminals on the line are not able to transmit data. The time required for the data to be transmitted to the main computer, however, is short—most likely less than one second. As soon as the inquiry is received by the computer, a second terminal can send an inquiry. With such short delays, it appears to the users that no other terminals are using the line, even though multiple terminals may be sharing the same line.

The number of terminals to be placed on one line is a decision made by the designer of the system based on the anticipated amount of traffic on the line. For example, 100 or more terminals could be contained on a single line, provided each one would send only short messages, such as inquiries, and each terminal would use the communications line only a few hours per day. But if longer messages, such as reports, were required and if the terminals were to be used almost continuously, the number of terminals on one line would have to be smaller.

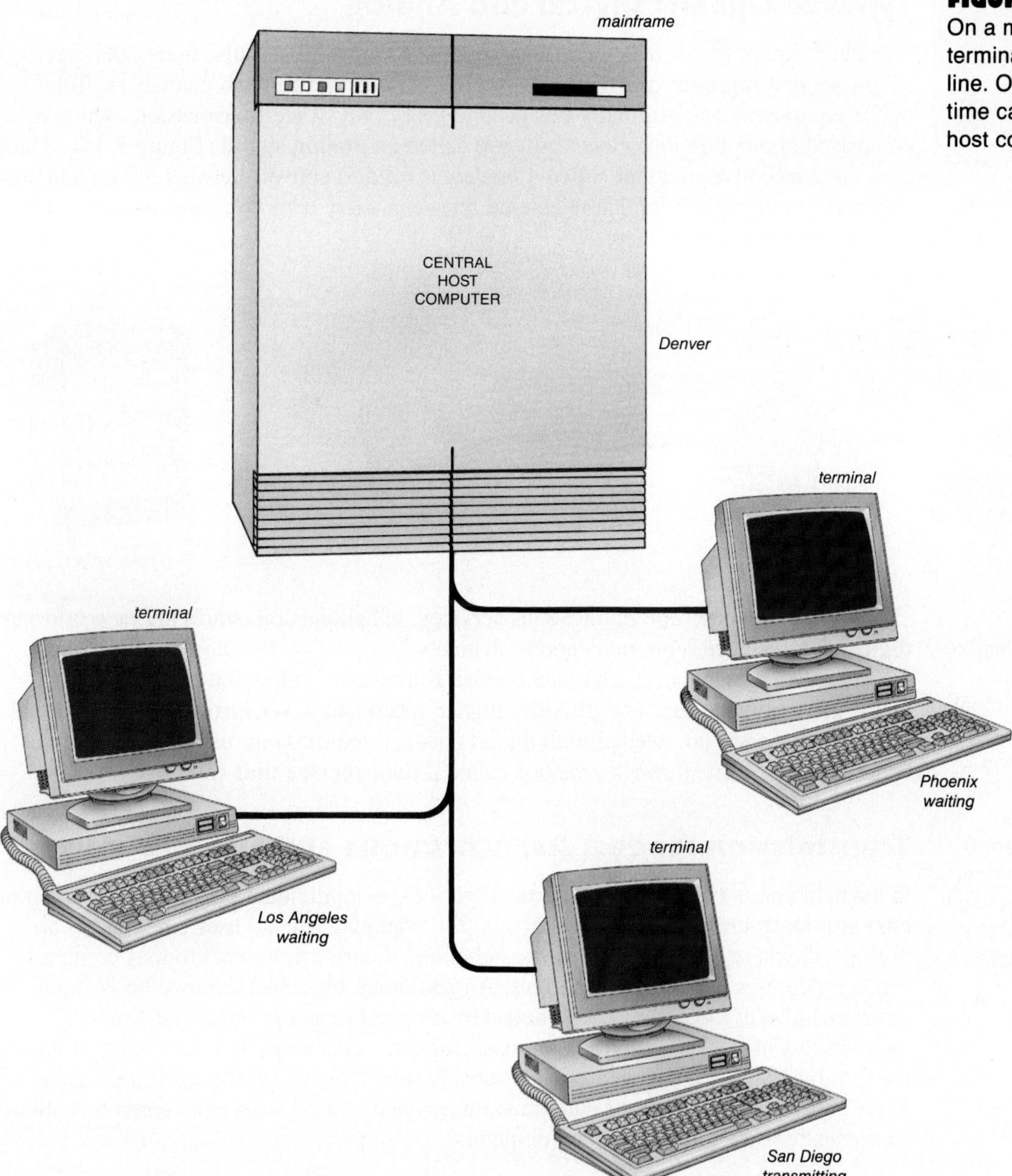

FIGURE 8-14
On a multidrop line, several terminals share the same line. Only one terminal at a time can transmit data to the host computer.

A leased line is almost always used for multidrop line configurations. The use of multidrop lines can decrease line costs considerably because one line is used by many terminals.

CHARACTERISTICS OF COMMUNICATIONS CHANNELS

The communications channels we have just discussed can be categorized by a number of characteristics including the type of signal, transmission mode, transmission direction, and transmission rate.

Types of Signals: Digital and Analog

Computer equipment is designed to process data as **digital signals**, individual electrical pulses that represent the bits that are grouped together to form characters. Telephone equipment was originally designed to carry only voice transmission, which is comprised of a continuous electrical wave called an **analog signal** (Figure 8-15). Thus, a special piece of equipment called a *modem* is used to convert between the digital signals and analog signals so that telephone lines can carry data. We discuss modems in more detail later in this chapter.

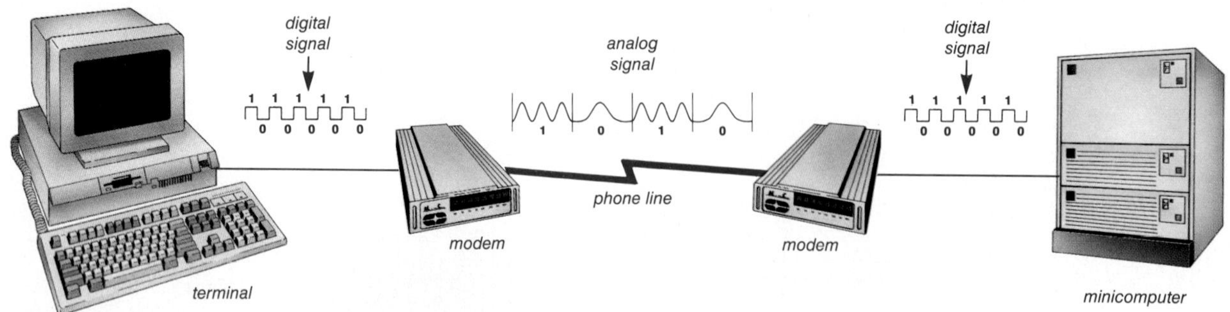

FIGURE 8-15
Individual electrical pulses of the digital signal are converted into analog (electrical wave) signals for transmission over voice telephone lines. The 1s represent ON bits and the 0s represent OFF bits. At the main computer receiving end, another modem converts the analog signals back into digital signals that can be processed by the computer.

To provide better communications services, telephone companies are now offering **digital data service**, communications channels specifically designed to carry digital instead of voice signals. Digital data service is available within and between most major metropolitan areas and provides higher speed and lower error rates than voice lines. Modems are not needed with digital data service; instead, users connect to the communications line through a device called a **data service unit (DSU)**.

Transmission Modes: Asynchronous and Synchronous

In **asynchronous transmission mode** (Figure 8-16), individual characters (made up of bits) are transmitted at irregular intervals, for example, when a user enters data. To distinguish where one character stops and another starts, the asynchronous communication mode uses a start and a stop bit. An additional bit called a *parity bit* is sometimes included at the end of each character. As you learned in our discussion of memory in Chapter 4, parity bits are used for error checking, and they detect if one of the data bits has been changed during transmission. The asynchronous transmission mode is used for lower speed data transmission and is used with most communications equipment designed for personal computers.

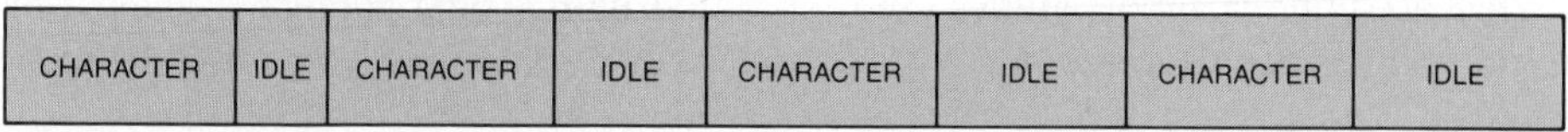

FIGURE 8-16
In asynchronous transmission mode, individual characters are transmitted. Each character has start, stop, and error-checking bits. In synchronous transmission mode, multiple characters are sent in a block with start bytes at the beginning of the block and error-checking bits and stop bytes at the end of the block. Synchronous transmission is faster and more accurate.

In the **synchronous transmission mode** (Figure 8-16), large blocks of data are transmitted at regular intervals. Timing signals synchronize the communications equipment at both the sending and receiving ends and eliminate the need for start and stop bits for each character. Error-checking bits and start and end indicators called sync bytes are also transmitted. Synchronous transmission requires more sophisticated and expensive equipment, but it does give much higher speeds and accuracy than asynchronous transmission.

Direction of Transmission: Simplex, Half-Duplex, and Full-Duplex

The direction of data transmission is classified as either simplex, half-duplex, or full-duplex (Figure 8-17). In **simplex transmission**, data flows in one direction only. Simplex is used only when the sending device, such as a temperature sensor, never requires a response from the computer. For example, if a computer is used to control the temperature of a building, numerous sensors are placed throughout it. Each sensor is connected to the computer with a simplex transmission line because the computer only needs to receive data from the temperature sensors and does not need to send data back to the sensors.

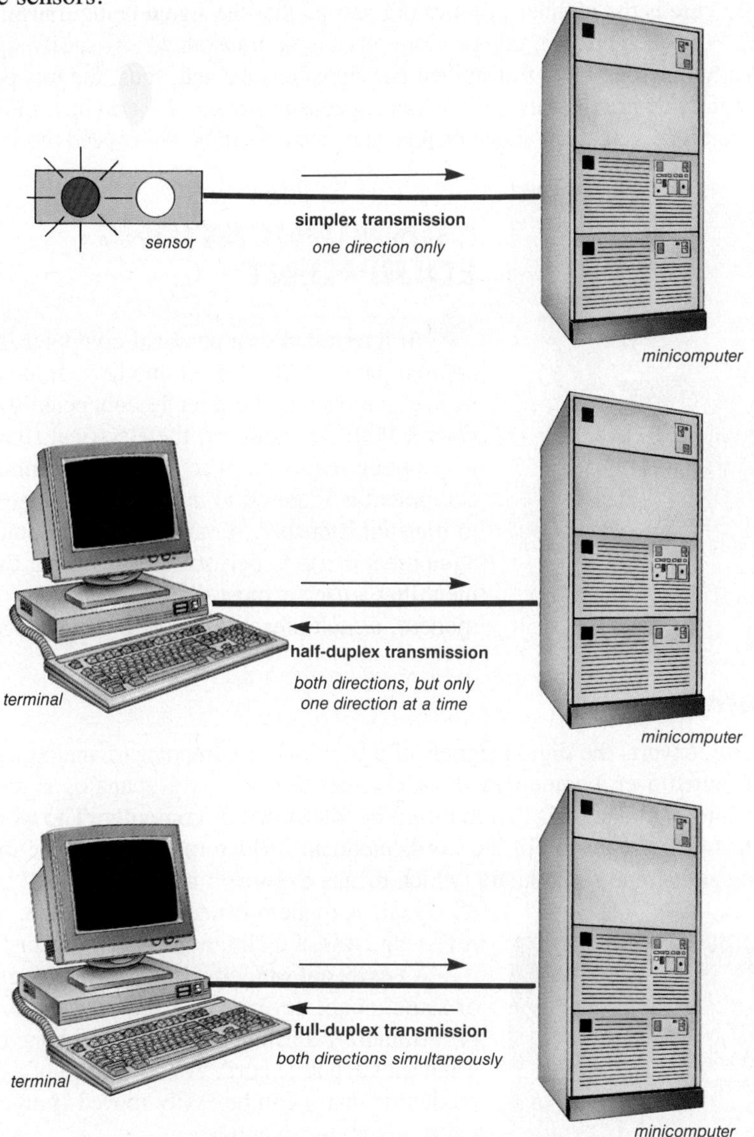

FIGURE 8-17
Simplex transmission allows data to flow in one direction only. Half-duplex transmission allows data to flow in both directions but not at the same time. Full-duplex transmission allows data to flow in both directions simultaneously.

In **half-duplex transmission**, data can flow in both directions but in only one direction at a time. An example is a citizens band radio. The user can talk or listen but not do both at the same time. Half-duplex is often used between terminals and a central computer.

In **full-duplex transmission**, data can be sent in both directions at the same time. A normal telephone line is an example of full-duplex transmission. Both parties can talk at the same time. Full-duplex transmission is used for most interactive computer applications and for computer-to-computer data transmission.

Transmission Rate

The transmission rate of a communications channel is determined by its bandwidth and its speed. The **bandwidth** is the range of frequencies that a channel can carry. Since transmitted data can be assigned to different frequencies, the wider the bandwidth, the more frequencies, and the more data that can be transmitted at the same time.

The speed at which data is transmitted is usually expressed as bits per second or as a baud rate. **Bits per second (bps)** is the number of bits that can be transmitted in one second. Using a 10-bit byte to represent a character (7 data bits, 1 start, 1 stop, and 1 parity bit), a 2,400 bps transmission would transmit 240 characters per second. At this rate, a 20-page, single-spaced report would be transmitted in approximately five minutes. The **baud rate** is the number of times per second that the signal being transmitted changes. With each change, one or more bits can be transmitted. At speeds up to 2,400 bps, usually only one bit is transmitted per signal change and, thus, the bits per second and the baud rate are the same. To achieve speeds in excess of 2,400 bps, more than one bit is transmitted with each signal change and, thus, the bps will exceed the baud rate.

FIGURE 8-18
An external modem is connected to a terminal or computer and to a telephone outlet.

COMMUNICATIONS EQUIPMENT

If a terminal or a personal computer is within approximately 1,000 feet of another computer, the two devices can usually be directly connected by a cable. Over 1,000 feet, however, the electrical signal weakens to the point that some type of special communications equipment is required to increase or change the signal to transmit it farther. A variety of communications equipment exists to perform this task, but the equipment that a user is most likely to encounter is a modem, a multiplexor, and a front-end processor.

Modems

A **modem** converts the digital signals of a terminal or computer to analog signals that are transmitted over a communications channel. It also converts analog signals it receives into digital signals that are used by a terminal or computer. The word modem comes from a combination of the words *mo*dulate, which means to change into a sound or analog signal,and *dem*odulate, which means to convert an analog signal into a digital signal. A modem is needed at both the sending and receiving ends of a communications channel.

FIGURE 8-19
An internal modem is mounted inside a personal computer.

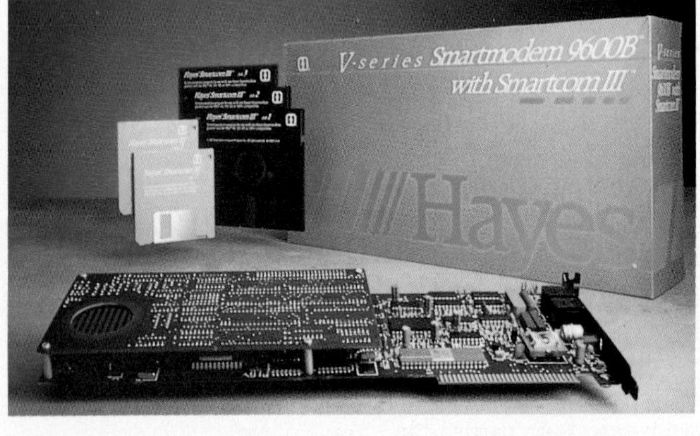

An **external modem** (Figure 8-18) is a separate, or stand-alone, device that is attached to the computer or terminal by a cable and to the telephone outlet by a standard telephone cord. An advantage of an external modem is that it can be easily moved from one terminal or computer to another.

An **internal modem** (Figure 8-19) is a circuit board that is installed inside a computer or terminal. Internal modems are generally less expensive than comparable external modems but once installed, they are not as easy to move.

An **acoustic modem**, also called an **acoustic coupler**, is designed to be used with a telephone handset (Figure 8-20). The acoustic coupler converts the digital signals generated by the terminal or personal computer into a series of audible tones, which are picked up by the mouthpiece in the headset in the same manner that a telephone picks up a person's voice. The analog signals are then transmitted over the communications channel. An acoustic coupler provides portability, but is generally less reliable than an internal or external modem because small outside sounds can be picked up by the acoustic coupler and cause transmission errors. Acoustic couplers are no longer common and are primarily used for special applications, such as with portable computers.

FIGURE 8-20
The acoustic coupler (lower left) allows a portable computer user to communicate with another computer over telephone lines. The telephone handset is placed in the molded rubber cups on the acoustic coupler.

Modems can transmit data at rates from 300 to 38,400 bits per second (bps). Most personal computers would use either a 1,200 or 2,400 bps modem. Business or heavier volume users would use faster and more expensive modems.

Multiplexors

A **multiplexor**, sometimes referred to as a MUX, combines more than one input signal into a single stream of data that can be transmitted over a communications channel (Figure 8-21). The multiplexor at the sending end codes each character it receives with an identifier that is used by the multiplexor at the receiving end to separate the combined data stream into its original parts. A multiplexor may be connected to a separate modem or may have a modem built in. By combining the individual data streams into one, a multiplexor increases the efficiency of communications and saves the cost of individual communications channels.

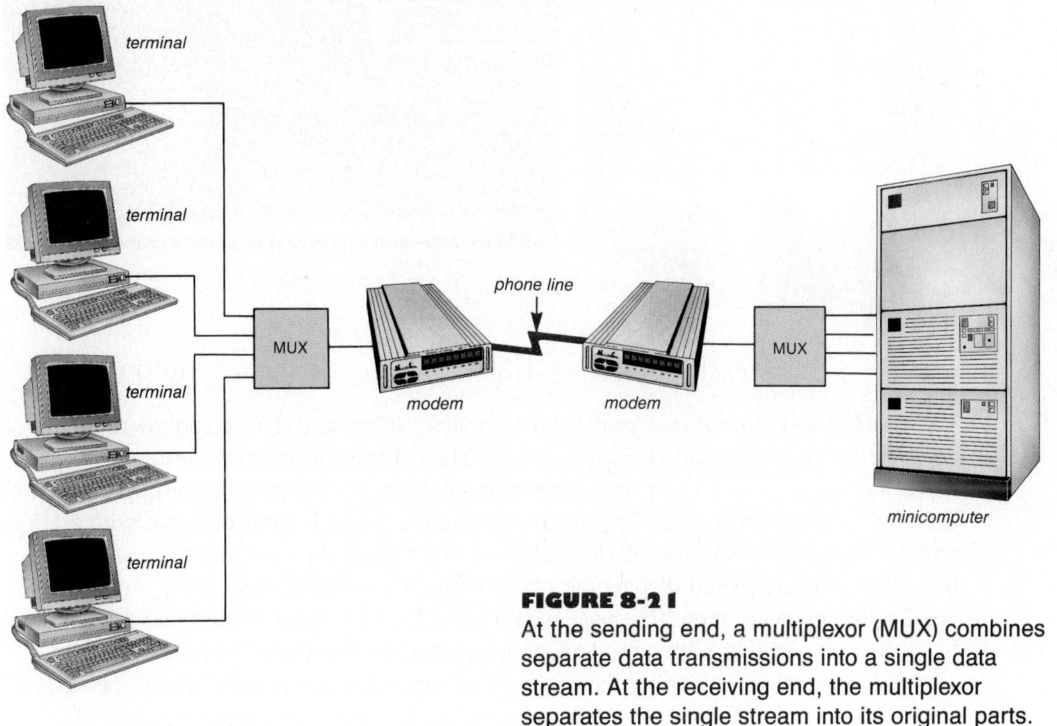

FIGURE 8-21
At the sending end, a multiplexor (MUX) combines separate data transmissions into a single data stream. At the receiving end, the multiplexor separates the single stream into its original parts.

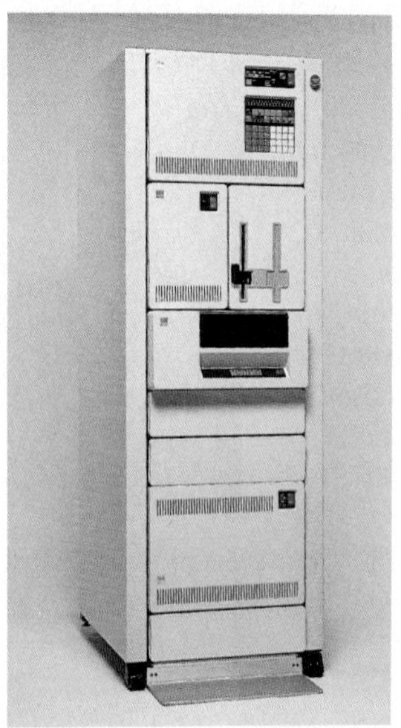

FIGURE 8-22
This IBM Series 1 minicomputer is often used as a front-end processor to relieve the main computer of communications tasks.

Front-End Processors

A **front-end processor** (Figure 8-22) is a computer that is dedicated to handling the communications requirements of a larger computer. Relieved of these tasks, the large computer is then dedicated to processing data, while the front-end processor communicates the data. Tasks that the front-end processor would handle include **polling** (checking the connected terminals or computers to see if they have data to send), error checking and correction, and access security to make sure that a connected device or the user of the connected device is authorized to access the computer.

COMMUNICATIONS SOFTWARE

Sometimes communications equipment is preprogrammed to accomplish its designed communications tasks. Other times, the user must load a program before transmitting data. These programs, referred to as **communications software**, can perform a number of tasks including dialing (if a switched telephone line is used), file transfer, terminal emulation, and data encryption (Figure 8-23).

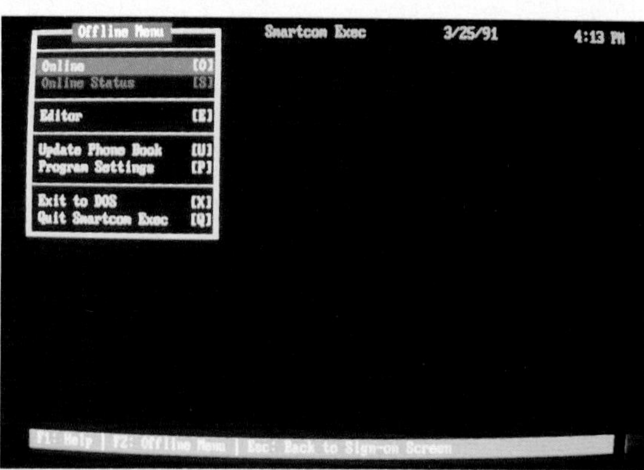

FIGURE 8-23
Communications software performs a variety of tasks that assist the user in operating communications equipment.

Dialing software allows you to store, review, select and dial telephone numbers of computers that can be called (Figure 8-24). The software provides a variety of meaningful messages to assist you in establishing a connection before transmitting data. For example, a person who uses a personal computer at home to communicate with a computer at the office could use dialing software to establish the communications connection. The software would display the office computer's telephone number on the user's personal computer screen. The user would enter the appropriate command for the dialing software, working with a modem, to begin dialing the office computer and to establish a connection. During the 10 or 15 seconds that this process takes, the software would display messages to indicate specifically what was happening, such as "DIALING," "CARRIER DETECT" (which means that the office computer has answered), and "CONNECTED" (to indicate that the communications connection has been established and data transmission can begin).

File transfer software allows you to move one or more files from one system to another. Generally, you have to load the file transfer software on both the sending and receiving computers.

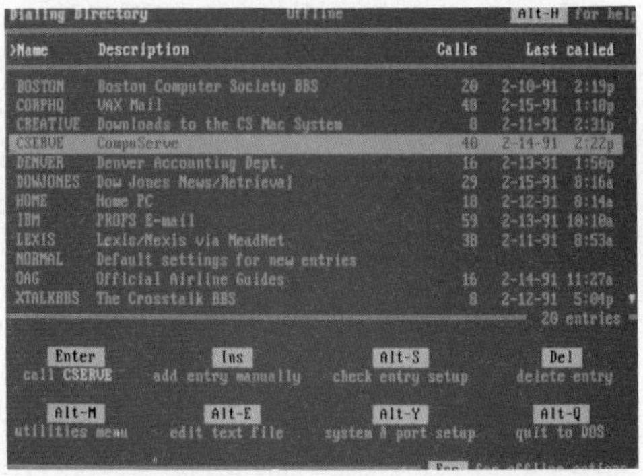

Terminal emulation software allows a personal computer to imitate or appear to be a specific type of terminal, so that the personal computer can connect to another usually larger computer. Most minicomputers and mainframes are designed to work with terminals that have specific characteristics such as speed and parity. Terminal emulation software performs the necessary speed and parity conversion.

FIGURE 8-24
This screen from *Crosstalk Communicator* is a popular communications software package for personal computers. The screen shows the information that is displayed when the software is being used to dial the CompuServe Information Service.

Data encryption protects confidential data during transmission. **Data encryption** is the conversion of data at the sending end into an unrecognizable string of characters or bits and the reconversion of the data at the receiving end. Without knowing how the data was encrypted, someone who intercepted the transmitted data would have a difficult time determining what the data meant.

COMMUNICATIONS PROTOCOLS

Communications software is written to work with one or more protocols. A **protocol** is a set of rules and procedures for exchanging information between computers. Protocols define how the communications link is established, how information is transmitted, and how errors are detected and corrected. Using the same protocol, different types and makes of computers can communicate with each other. Over the years, numerous protocols have been developed. Today, however, there are strong efforts to establish standards that all computer and communications equipment manufacturers will follow. The International Standards Organization (ISO) based in Geneva, Switzerland has defined a set of communications protocols called the **Open Systems Interconnection (OSI) model**. The OSI model has been endorsed by the United Nations.

COMMUNICATIONS NETWORKS

A communications **network** is a collection of terminals, computers, and other equipment that uses communications channels to share data, information, hardware, and software. Networks can be classified as either local area networks or wide area networks.

Local Area Networks (LANs)

A **local area network**, or **LAN**, is a communications network that is privately owned and that covers a limited geographic area such as an office, a building, or a group of buildings.

The LAN consists of a communications channel that connects either a series of computer terminals together with a minicomputer or, more commonly, a group of personal computers to one another. Very sophisticated LANs can connect a variety of office devices such as word processing equipment, computer terminals, video equipment, and personal computers.

Two common applications of local area networks are hardware resource sharing and information resource sharing. **Hardware resource sharing** allows each personal computer in the network to access and use devices that would be too expensive to provide for each user or would not be justified for each user because of only occasional use. For example, when a number of personal computers are used on the network, each may need to use a laser printer. Using a LAN, a laser printer could be purchased and made a part of the network. Whenever a user of a personal computer on the network needed the laser printer, it could be accessed over the network. Figure 8-25 depicts a simple local area network consisting of four personal computers linked together by a cable. Three of the personal computers (computer 1 in the sales and marketing department, computer 2 in the accounting department, and computer 3 in the personnel department) are available for use at all times. Computer 4 is used as a **server**, sometimes called a **network control unit**, which is dedicated to handling the communications needs of the other computers in the network. The users of this LAN have connected the laser printer to the server. Using the LAN, all computers and the server can use the printer.

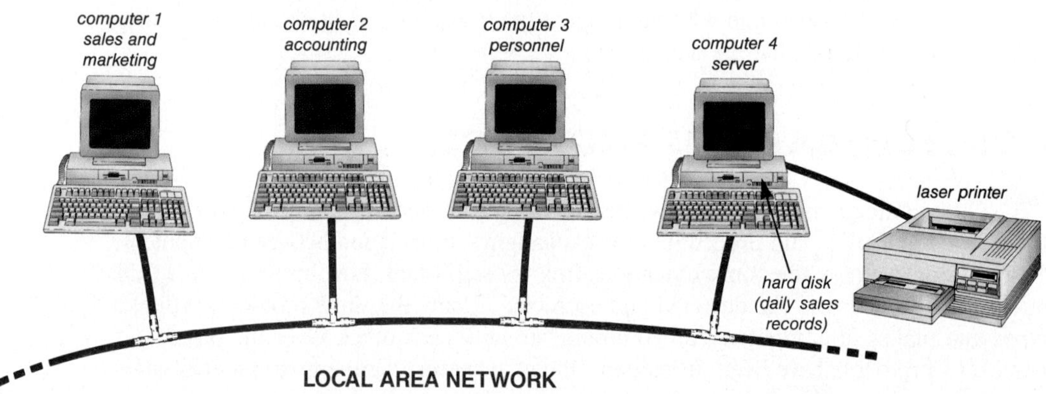

FIGURE 8-25
A local area network (LAN) consists of multiple personal computers or terminals connected to one another. The LAN allows users to share hardware and information.

Information resource sharing allows anyone using a personal computer on the local area network to access data stored on any other computer in the network. In actual practice, hardware resource sharing and information resource sharing are often combined. For example, in Figure 8-25, the daily sales records could be stored on the hard disk associated with the server unit personal computer. Anyone needing access to the sales records could use this information resource. The capability to access and store data on common auxiliary storage is an important feature of many local area networks.

Information resource sharing is usually provided by using either the file-server or client-server method. Using the **file-server** method, the server sends an entire file at a time. The requesting computer then performs the processing. With the **client-server** method, as much processing as possible is done on the server system before data is transmitted. Figure 8-26 illustrates how the two methods would process a request for information stored on the server system for customers with balances over $1,000. With the file-server method, the user transmits a request for the customer file to the server unit ⟨1⟩. The server unit locates the customer file ⟨2⟩ and transmits the entire file to the requesting computer ⟨3⟩. The requesting computer selects customers with balances over $1,000 and prepares the report ⟨4⟩. With the client-server method, the user transmits a request for customers with a balance over $1,000 to the server unit ⟨1⟩. The server unit selects the customer records that meet the criteria ⟨2⟩ and transmits the selected records to the requesting computer ⟨3⟩. The requesting computer prepares the report ⟨4⟩. The client-server method greatly reduces the amount of data sent over a network but requires a more powerful server system.

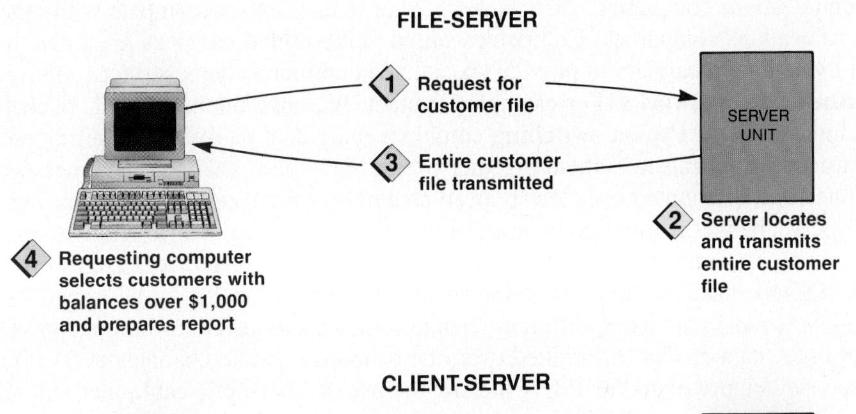
FILE-SERVER
1 Request for customer file
3 Entire customer file transmitted
SERVER UNIT
2 Server locates and transmits entire customer file
4 Requesting computer selects customers with balances over $1,000 and prepares report

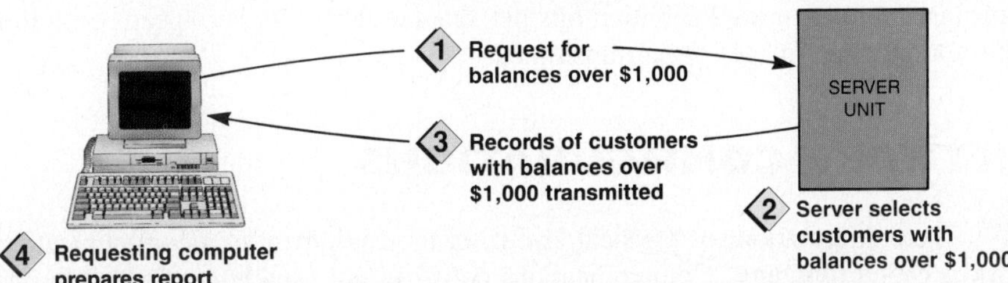
CLIENT-SERVER
1 Request for balances over $1,000
3 Records of customers with balances over $1,000 transmitted
SERVER UNIT
2 Server selects customers with balances over $1,000
4 Requesting computer prepares report

FIGURE 8-26
A request for information about customers with balances over $1,000 would be processed differently by file-server and client-server networks.

Frequently used software is another type of resource that is often shared on a local area network. For example, if all users need access to word processing software, the software can be stored on the hard disk of the server and accessed by all users as needed. This is much more convenient and faster than having the software stored on a diskette and available at each computer. Sharing software is a common practice for both in-house and commercial software. Many software vendors now sell a network version of their software. When a commercial software package is accessed by many users, it is sometimes necessary to obtain a special agreement from the software vendor, called a **site license**. The site license fee is usually based on the number of computers on the network and is less than if individual copies of the software package were purchased for each computer.

Wide Area Networks (WANs)

A **wide area network**, or **WAN**, is geographic in scope (as opposed to local) and uses telephone lines, microwaves, satellites, or a combination of communications channels. Public wide area network companies include so-called **common carriers** such as the telephone companies. Telephone company deregulation has encouraged a number of companies to build their own wide area networks. For example, EDS has built one of the largest private communications network (Figure 8-27) to handle the needs of their computer services business and the needs of their parent company, General Motors.

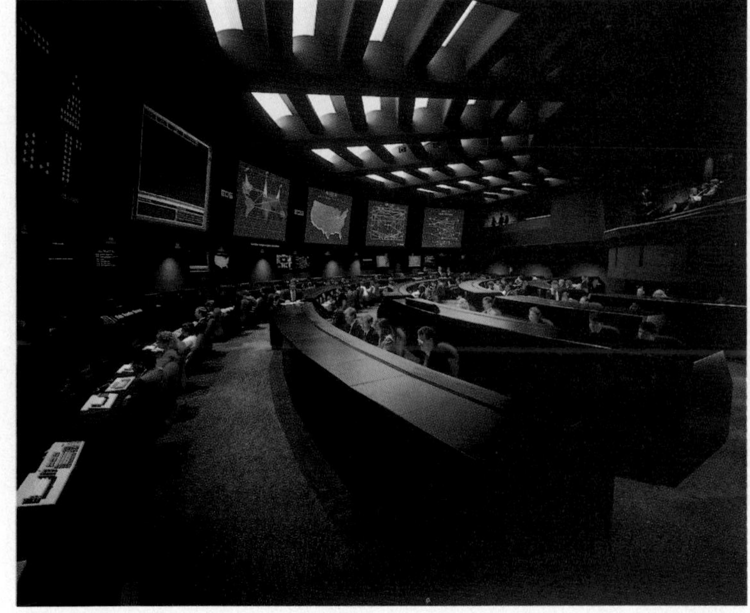

FIGURE 8-27
The control room for EDSNET, the private communications network of Electronic Data Systems Corporation (EDS). The network was built by EDS over a three-year period and a cost of more than $1 billion. The network provides communications for EDS, its computer services customers, and its parent company, General Motors.

Communications companies, such as MCI, have built WANs to compete with other communications companies. Companies called **value-added carriers** lease channels from the common carriers to provide specialized communications services referred to as **value-added networks**. For example, Tymnet, Inc. and Telenet provide packet-switching services. **Packet-switching** combines individual packets of information from various users and transmits them together over a high-speed channel. The messages are separated and distributed over lower speed channels at the receiving end. Sharing the high-speed channel is more economical than each user having their own high-speed channel. Most common carriers are now offering **Integrated Services Digital Network (ISDN)** services. ISDN is an international standard for the digital transmission of both voice and data using different channels and communications companies. Using ISDN lines, data can be transmitted over one or more separate channels at 64,000 bits per second. Future plans for ISDN include the use of fiber-optic cable that will allow transmission rates up to 2.2 billion bits per second. These higher speeds will allow full-motion video images to be transmitted.

NETWORK CONFIGURATIONS

The configuration, or physical layout, of the equipment in a communications network is called **topology**. Communications networks are usually configured in one or a combination of three patterns. These configurations are star, bus, and ring networks. Although these configurations can be used with wide area networks, we illustrate them with local area networks. Devices connected to a network, such as terminals, printers, or other computers, are referred to as **nodes**.

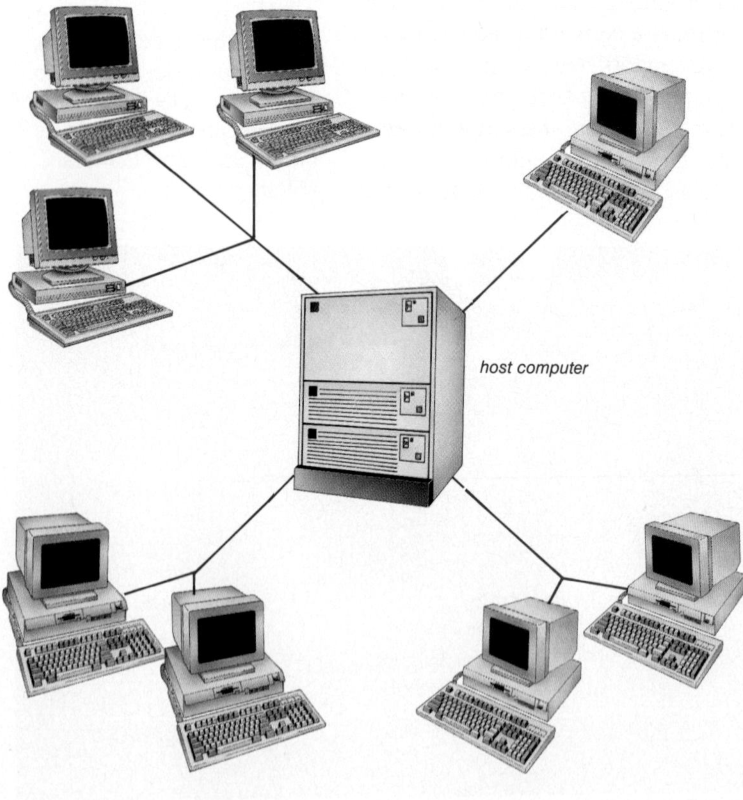

FIGURE 8-28
A star network contains a single, centralized host computer with which all the terminals or personal computers in the network communicate. Both point-to-point and multidrop lines can be used in a star network.

Star Network

A **star network** (Figure 8-28) contains a central computer and one or more terminals or personal computers connected to it, forming a star. A pure star network consists of only point-to-point lines between the terminals and the computer, but most star networks, such as the one shown in Figure 8-28, include both point-to-point lines and multidrop lines. A star network configuration is often used when the central computer contains all the data required to process the input from the terminals, such as an airline reservation system. For example, if inquiries are being processed in the star network, all the data to answer the inquiry would be contained in the database stored on the central computer.

A star network can be relatively efficient, and close control can be kept over the data processed on the network. Its major disadvantage is that the entire network is dependent on the central computer and the associated hardware and software. If any of these elements fail, the entire network is disabled. Therefore, in most large star networks, backup computer systems are available in case the primary system fails.

Bus Network

When a **bus network** is used, all the devices in the network are connected to and share a single cable. Information is transmitted in either direction from any one personal computer to another. Any message can be directed to a specific device. An advantage of the bus network is that devices can be attached or detached from the network at any point without disturbing the rest of the network. In addition, if one computer on the network fails, this does not affect the other users of the network. Figure 8-25 illustrates a simple bus network.

Ring Network

A **ring network** does not use a centralized host computer. Rather, a circle of computers communicate with one another (Figure 8-29). A ring network can be useful when the processing is not done at a central site, but at local sites. For example, computers could be located in three departments: accounting, personnel, and shipping and receiving. The computers in each of these departments could perform the processing required for each of the departments. On occasion, however, the computer in the shipping and receiving department could communicate with the computer in the accounting department to update certain data stored on the accounting department computer. Data travels around a ring network in one direction only and passes through each node. Thus, one disadvantage of a ring network is that if one node fails, the entire network fails because the data does not get past the failed node. An advantage of a ring network is that less cable is usually needed and therefore network cabling costs are lower.

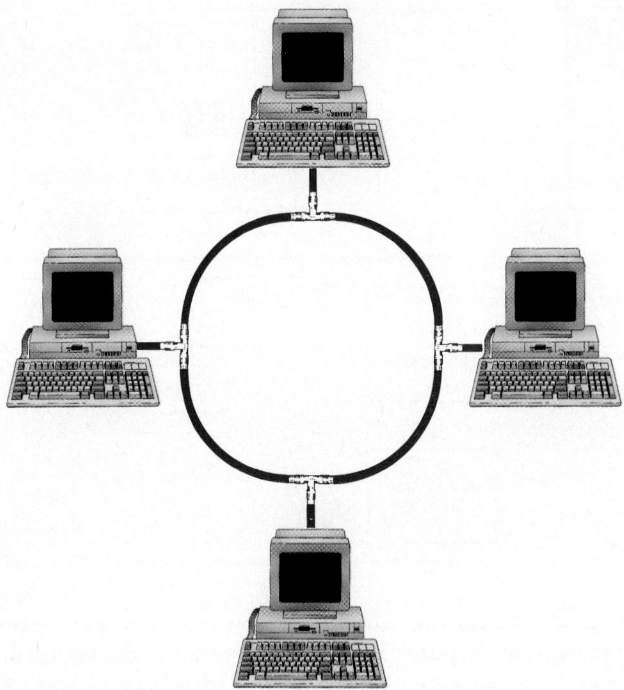

FIGURE 8-29
In a ring network, all computers are connected in a continuous loop. Data flows around the ring in one direction only.

CONNECTING NETWORKS

◆ Sometimes you might want to connect separate networks. You do this by using gateways and bridges. A **gateway** is a combination of hardware and software that allows users on one network to access the resources on a *different* type of network. For example, a gateway could be used to connect a local area network of personal computers to a mainframe computer network. A **bridge** is a combination of hardware and software that is used to connect *similar* networks. For example, if a company had similar but separate local area networks of personal computers in their accounting and marketing departments, the networks could be connected with a bridge. In this example, using a bridge makes more sense than joining all the personal computers together in one large network because the individual departments only occasionally need to access information on the other network.

AN EXAMPLE OF A COMMUNICATIONS NETWORK

The diagram in Figure 8-30 illustrates how two personal computer networks and a mainframe computer can be connected to share information with each other and with outside sources.

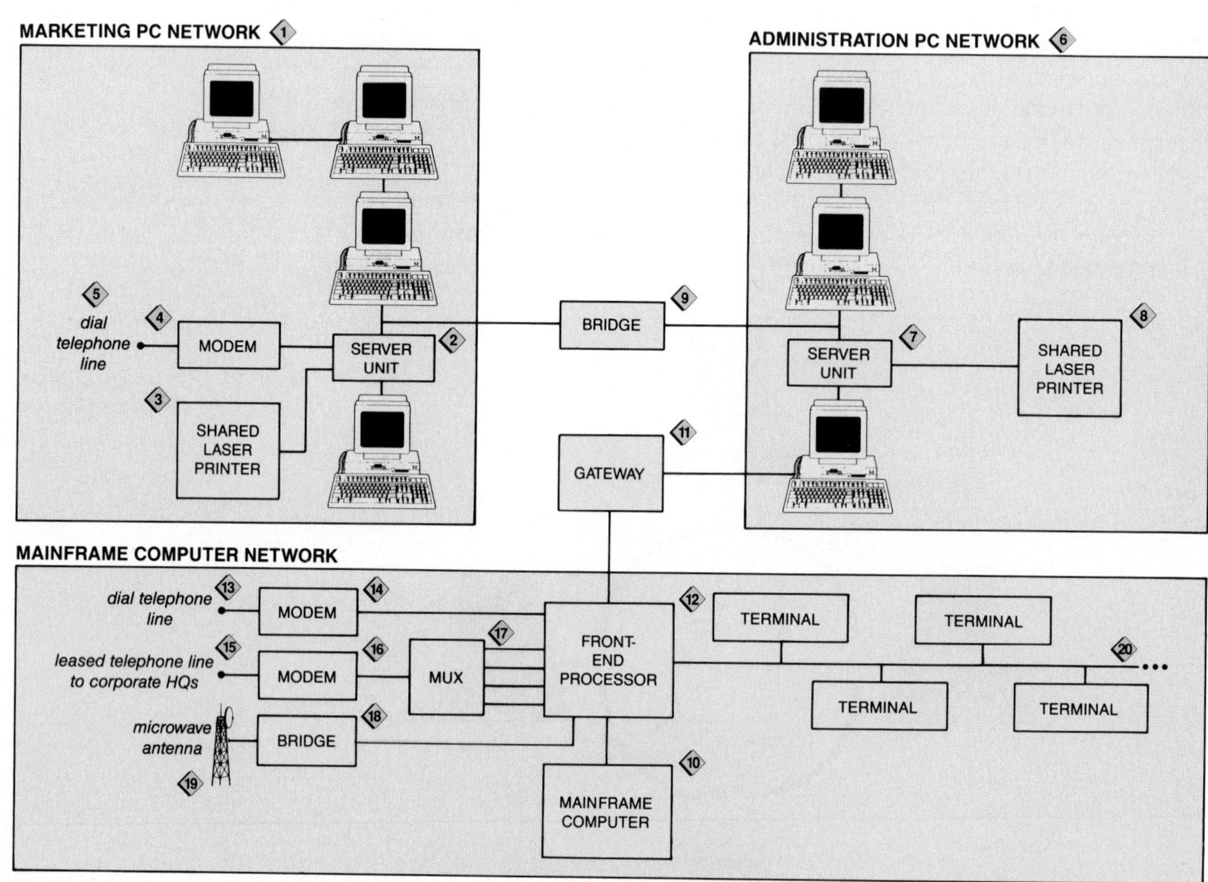

FIGURE 8-30
These two personal computer networks are connected to a mainframe computer system with a bridge. A gateway is used to connect the personal computer network with the mainframe. All communications with the mainframe are controlled by a separate computer called a front-end processor. Modems are used to connect the networks to leased and dial telephone lines.

The marketing department operates a bus network of four personal computers ①. Frequently used marketing data and programs are stored in the server unit ②. The personal computers in the marketing department share a laser printer ③. A modem ④ is attached to the marketing server unit so that outside sales representatives can use a dial telephone line ⑤ to call the marketing system and obtain product price information.

The administration department operates a bus network of three personal computers ⑥. As with the marketing network, common data and programs are stored on a server unit ⑦ and the administration personal computers share a laser printer ⑧. Because the administration department sometimes needs information from the marketing system, the two similar networks are connected with a LAN bridge ⑨. The bridge allows users on either network to access data or programs on the other network.

Administration department users sometimes need information from the company's mainframe computer system ⟨10⟩. They can access the mainframe through the use of a gateway ⟨11⟩ that allows different types of network systems to be connected. All communications with the mainframe computer are controlled by a front-end processor ⟨12⟩. A dial telephone line ⟨13⟩ connected to a modem ⟨14⟩ allows remote users to call the mainframe and allows mainframe users to call other computers. A leased telephone line ⟨15⟩ and a modem ⟨16⟩ are used for a permanent connection to the computer at the corporate headquarters, several hundred miles away. The leased line can carry the signals of up to four different users. The signals are separated by the use of a multiplexor (MUX) ⟨17⟩. A bridge ⟨18⟩ connects the front-end processor and mainframe system to a microwave antenna ⟨19⟩ on the roof of the building. The microwave antenna sends and receives data from a computer at the manufacturing plant located two miles away. The front-end processor also controls mainframe computer terminals located throughout the company ⟨20⟩.

SUMMARY OF COMMUNICATIONS

Communications will continue to affect how people work and how they use computers. Individuals and organizations are no longer limited to local data resources but instead, with communications capabilities, they can obtain information from anywhere in the world at electronic speed. With communications technology rapidly changing, today's businesses are challenged to find ways to adapt the technology to provide better products and services for their customers and make their operations more efficient. For individuals, the new technology offers increased access to worldwide information and services, and provides new opportunities in business and education.

CHAPTER SUMMARY

1. **Communications**, sometimes called **data communications** refers to the transmission of data or information over a communications channel between one computer or a terminal and another computer.
2. **Telecommunications** describes any type of long-distance communications including television signals.
3. **Teleprocessing** refers to the use of telephone lines to transmit data.
4. The basic components of a communications system are: a personal computer or terminal; communications equipment that sends (and can usually receive) data; the communications channel over which data is sent; communications equipment that receives (and can usually send) data; and a computer. Communications software is also required.
5. A **communications channel**, also called a **communications line** or **communications link** is the link, or path, that the data follows as it is transmitted from the sending equipment to the receiving equipment in a communications system.
6. A communications channel can consist of various **transmission media** including twisted pair wire, coaxial cable, fiber optics, microwave transmission, satellite transmission, and wireless transmission.
7. **Twisted pair wire** is the color-coded copper wires that are twisted together and commonly used as telephone wire.
8. **Coaxial cable** is a high-quality communications line that is used in offices and laid underground and under the ocean. Coaxial cable consists of a copper wire conductor surrounded by a nonconducting insulator that is in turn surrounded by a woven metal mesh outer conductor, and finally a plastic outer coating.
9. Coaxial cable can be either **baseband**, carrying one signal at a time at very high rates of speed, or **broadband**, carrying multiple signals at a time.
10. **Fiber optics** uses technology based on the capability of smooth, hair-thin strands of glass that conduct light waves to rapidly and efficiently transmit data.

11. **Microwaves** are radio waves that can be used to provide high-speed transmissions of voice and data that are sent through the air between microwave stations.
12. **Communications satellites** are man-made space devices that receive, amplify, and retransmit signals from earth.
13. **Earth stations** are communications facilities that contain large, dish-shaped antennas used to transmit data to and receive data from communications satellites.
14. The transmission *to* the satellite is called an **uplink** and the transmission *from* the satellite to a receiving earth station is called a **downlink.**
15. Communications satellites are normally placed about 22,300 miles above the earth in a **geosynchronous orbit.**
16. **Wireless systems** use one of three transmission techniques: light beams, radio waves, or carrier-connect radio.
17. A **cellular telephone** uses radio waves to communicate with a local antenna assigned to a specific geographic area called a cell.
18. **Line configurations** can be either point-to-point lines or multidrop lines.
19. A **point-to-point line** is a direct line between a sending and receiving device. It may be either a **switched line** (a connection established through regular telephone lines) or a **dedicated line** (a line whose connection between devices is always established).
20. If the dedicated line is provided by an outside organization, it is sometimes called a **leased line**, or a **private line**.
21. The process of establishing the communications connection is sometimes referred to as the **handshake.**
22. A **multidrop line**, also known as a **multipoint line**, uses a single line to connect multiple devices to a main computer.
23. A multidrop line, or multipoint line, configuration is commonly used to connect multiple devices, such as terminals or personal computers, on a single line to a main computer sometimes called a **host computer**.
24. Computer equipment processes data as **digital signals**, which are individual electrical pulses representing the bits that are grouped together to form characters.
25. **Analog signals** are continuous electrical waves that are used to transmit data over standard telephone lines.
26. Companies offering **digital data service** provide communications channels specifically designed to carry digital instead of voice signals.
27. Modems are not needed with digital data service; instead, users connect to the communications line through a device called a **data service unit (DSU)**.
28. There are two modes of transmitting data: **asynchronous transmission mode**, which transmits one character at a time at irregular intervals using start and stop bits, and **synchronous transmission mode**, which transmits blocks of data at regular intervals using timing signals to synchronize the sending and receiving equipment.
29. Transmissions may be classified according to the direction in which the data can flow on a line: sending only (**simplex transmission**); sending or receiving but in only one direction at a time (**half-duplex transmission**); and sending and receiving at the same time (**full-duplex transmission**).
30. The transmission rate of a communications channel depends on the **bandwidth** and its speed. The wider the bandwidth, the greater the number of signals that can be carried on the channel at one time and the more data that can be transmitted.
31. **Bits per second (bps)** is the number of bits that can be transmitted in one second.
32. The **baud rate** is the number of times per second that the signal being transmitted changes. With each change, one or more bits can be transmitted.
33. A **modem** converts the digital signals of a terminal or computer to analog signals that are transmitted over a communications channel.
34. There are three basic types of modems: an **external modem**, which is a separate, stand-alone device attached to the computer or terminal by a cable and to the telephone outlet by a standard telephone cable; an **internal modem**, which is a circuit board installed inside a computer or terminal; and an **acoustic modem**, or **acoustic coupler**, which is a device used with a telephone handset.
35. A **multiplexor**, or MUX, combines more than one input signal into a single stream of data that can be transmitted over a communications channel.
36. A **front-end processor** is a computer dedicated to handling the communications requirements of a larger computer.
37. A front-end processor would use **polling** to check the connected terminals or computers to see if they have data to send.
38. **Communications software** consists of programs that perform tasks such as **dialing** (software that stores, selects, and dials telephone numbers); **file transfer**; (moving files from one system to another); **terminal emulation**

(software that allows the personal computer to imitate or appear to be a specific type of terminal, so that the personal computer can connect to specific types of computers); and **data encryption** (software that can code and decode transmitted data for security purposes).

39. A **protocol** is a set of rules and procedures for exchanging information between computers.
40. A **network** is a collection of terminals, computers, and other equipment that use communications channels to share data, information, hardware, and software.
41. A **local area network (LAN)** is a communications network that covers a limited geographic area and is privately owned.
42. Two common uses of local area networks are **hardware resource sharing**, which allows all network users to access a single piece of equipment rather than each user having to be connected to his or her own device, and **information resource sharing**, which allows the network users to access data stored on other computers in the network.
43. A **server**, sometimes called a **network control unit**, is a computer that is dedicated to handling the communications needs of the other computers in a network.
44. Information sharing is usually provided by using either the **file-server** or **client-server** method.
45. When a commercial software package is accessed by many users within the same organization, a special agreement called a **site license** can usually be obtained from the software vendor.
46. A **wide area network (WAN)** is a network that covers a large geographical area.
47. Public wide area network companies include so-called **common carriers** such as the telephone companies.
48. Companies called **value-added carriers** lease channels from the common carriers to provide specialized communications services referred to as **value added networks**.
49. **Packet-switching** combines individual packets of information from various users and transmits them together over a high-speed channel.
50. **Integrated Services Digital Network (ISDN)** services is an international standard for the digital transmission of both voice and data using different channels and communications companies.
51. Network **topology** describes the configuration, or physical layout, of the equipment in a communications network.
52. Devices connected to a network, such as terminals, printers, or other computers, are referred to as **nodes**.
53. A **star network** contains a central computer and one or more terminals or computers connected to it, forming a star.
54. In a **bus network**, all the devices in the network are connected to and share a single cable.
55. A **ring network** has a series of computers connected to each other in a ring.
56. A **gateway** is a combination of hardware and software that allows users on one network to access the resources on a *different* type of network.
57. A **bridge** is a combination of hardware and software that is used to connect *similar* networks.

KEY TERMS

Acoustic coupler *8.13*
Acoustic modem *8.13*
Analog signal *8.10*
Asynchronous transmission mode *8.10*
Bandwidth *8.12*
Baseband *8.3*
Baud rate *8.12*
Bits per second (bps) *8.12*
Bridge *8.19*
Broadband *8.3*
Bus network *8.19*
Cellular telephone *8.5*
Client-server *8.16*
Coaxial cable *8.3*
Common carrier *8.17*
Communications channel *8.3*
Communications line *8.3*
Communications link *8.3*
Communications satellite *8.4*
Communications *8.2*
Communications software *8.14*
Data communications *8.2*
Data encryption *8.15*
Data service unit (DSU) *8.10*
Dedicated line *8.7*
Dialing software *8.14*
Digital data service *8.10*
Digital signal *8.10*
Downlink *8.4*
Earth station *8.4*
External modem *8.12*
Fiber optics *8.3*
File transfer software *8.15*
File-server *8.16*
Front-end processor *8.14*
Full-duplex transmission *8.11*
Gateway *8.19*
Geosynchronous orbit *8.4*
Half-duplex transmission *8.11*
Handshake *8.7*
Hardware resource sharing *8.16*
Host computer *8.8*

REVIEW QUESTIONS

1. Draw and label the basic components of a communications system.
2. List six kinds of transmission media used for communications channels.
3. Describe the two major types of line configurations. What are the advantages and disadvantages of each?
4. List and describe the three types of data transmission (direction) that are used.
5. Why is a modem used? Describe three types of modems that are available.
6. List and explain four tasks that communications software can perform.
7. What is a communications protocol?
8. Discuss the reasons for using a local area network.
9. Name three topologies, or configurations, that are used with networks. Draw a diagram of each.
10. Explain bridges and gateways and how they are used.

CONTROVERSIAL ISSUES

1. Some people believe that better control is maintained if data is stored and processed on a central minicomputer or mainframe. Others believe that personal computer networks that provide decentralized storage and processing are best. Discuss the advantages and disadvantages of both types of systems.
2. Some personal computer users have used communications equipment and software to illegally gain access to private databases. These individuals, known as *hackers*, often claim that their illegal access was only a harmless prank. Do you think this type of computer usage is harmless? Explain your position.

RESEARCH PROJECTS

1. Call or visit a communications company and obtain information relating to the types of services they provide for customers who transmit computer data. Prepare a report on this information for your class.
2. Obtain information about modems for personal computers. Prepare a report for your class that discusses the features and cost of both internal and external models.

Operating Systems and Systems Software

OBJECTIVES

- Describe the three major categories of systems software
- Define the term operating system
- Describe the various types of operating systems and explain the differences in their capabilities
- Describe the functions of an operating system, including allocating system resources, monitoring system activities, and disk and file management
- Explain the difference between proprietary and portable operating systems
- Name and briefly describe the major operating systems that are being used today
- Discuss utilities and language translators

When most people think of software they think of applications software such as word processing, spreadsheet, and database software. For applications software to run on a computer, however, another type of software is needed to interface between the user, the applications software, and the equipment. This software consists of programs that are referred to as the operating system. The operating system is part of what is called systems software.

In this chapter, we discuss operating system features of both large and small computer systems. It is important to understand the features of large computer operating systems because these features are steadily being implemented on small systems such as personal computers.

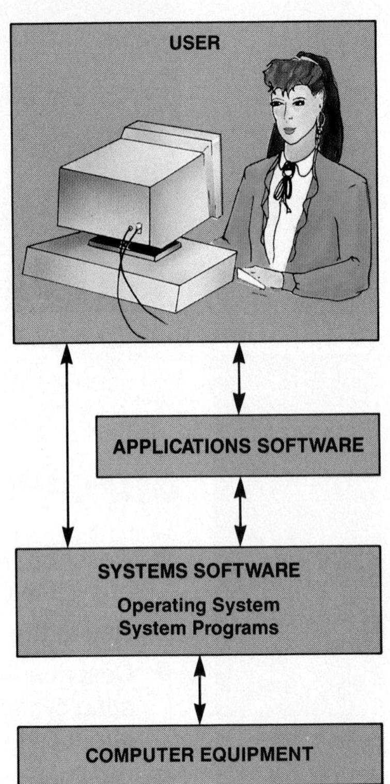

FIGURE 9-1
The operating system and other systems software programs act as an interface between the user, the applications software, and the computer equipment.

WHAT IS SYSTEMS SOFTWARE?

Systems software consists of all the programs including the operating system that are related to controlling the operations of the computer equipment. Some of the functions that systems software perform include: starting up the computer; loading, executing, and storing applications programs; storing and retrieving files; and performing a variety of functions such as formatting disks, sorting data files, and translating program instructions into machine language. Systems software can be classified into three major categories; operating systems, utilities, and language translators.

WHAT IS AN OPERATING SYSTEM?

An **operating system (OS)** consists of one or more programs that manage the operations of a computer. These programs function as an interface between the user, the applications programs, and the computer equipment (Figure 9-1).

The operating system is usually stored on a disk. For a computer to operate, the essential and most frequently used instructions in the operating system must be copied from the disk and stored in the main memory of the computer. This *resident* portion of the operating system is called by many different names: the **supervisor**, **monitor**, **executive**, **master program**, **control program**, or **kernel**. The *nonresident* portion of the operating system, which consists of the less frequently used instructions, remains stored on a disk and is available to be loaded into main memory whenever it is needed.

LOADING AN OPERATING SYSTEM

The process of loading an operating system into main memory is called **booting** the system. Figure 9-2 shows the steps that occur when an operating system is loaded on a personal computer. This process is not identical to that used on large computers, but it is similar.

1. A diskette that contains the operating system is placed in the disk drive. If the operating system is already stored on a hard disk, the diskette would not be necessary.
2. When the computer is turned on, a series of instructions stored in ROM called the boot routine issue the commands to load the operating system into main memory. To do this, a copy of the operating system is transferred from the diskette or hard disk into main memory.

3. The instructions that loaded the operating system transfer control of the computer to the operating system. In many cases, the operating system displays a message requesting that the user enter the correct date and time, after which the **operating system prompt** appears. This prompt indicates to the user that the operating system has been loaded and is ready to accept a command such as to begin an application program.

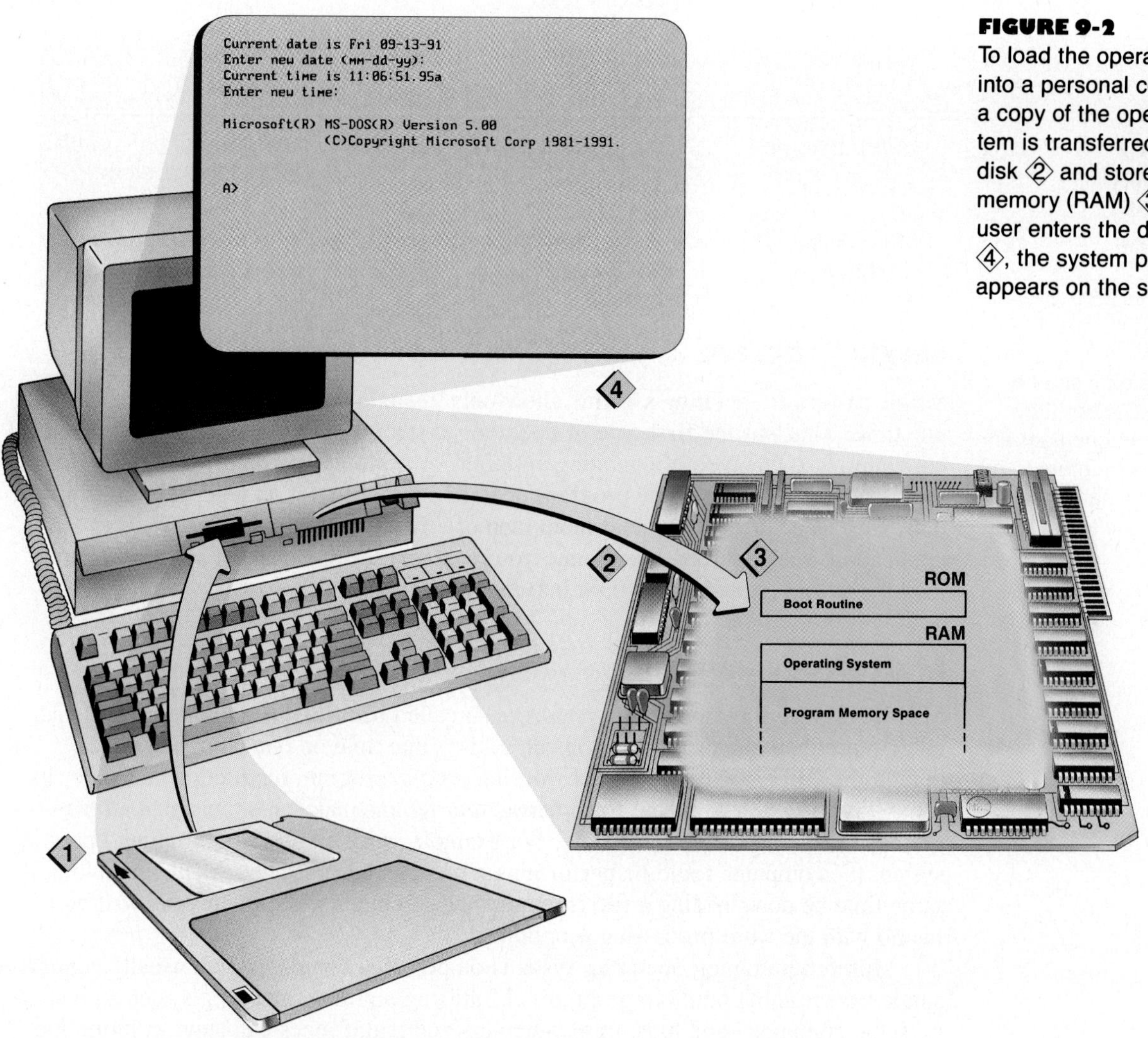

FIGURE 9-2
To load the operating system into a personal computer ⟨1⟩, a copy of the operating system is transferred from the disk ⟨2⟩ and stored in main memory (RAM) ⟨3⟩. After the user enters the date and time ⟨4⟩, the system prompt A> appears on the screen.

Once the operating system is loaded into main memory, it usually remains in memory until the computer is turned off. The operating system controls the loading and manages the execution of each application program that is requested by the user. When an application program completes its task or a user finishes using the application program, the operating system displays the system prompt again.

TYPES OF OPERATING SYSTEMS

The types of operating systems include single program, multiprogramming, multiprocessing, and virtual machine operating systems. These operating systems can be classified by two criteria: (1) whether they allow more than one user to use the computer at the same time and (2) whether they allow more than one program to run at the same time (Figure 9-3).

	SINGLE PROGRAM	MULTIPROGRAMMING	MULTIPROCESSING	VIRTUAL MACHINE
NUMBER OF PROGRAMS RUNNING	One	More than one	More than one on each CPU	More than one on each operating system
NUMBER OF USERS	One	One or more than one (Multiuser)	More than one on each CPU	More than one on each operating system

FIGURE 9-3
Operating systems can be classified by whether they allow more than one user and more than one program to be operating at the same time.

Single Program

Single program operating systems allow only a single user to run a single program at one time. This was the first type of operating system developed. Today, many personal computers use this type of operating system. For example, if you are working on a personal computer with a single program operating system you can load only one application, such as a spreadsheet, into main memory. If you want to work on another application, such as word processing, you must exit the spreadsheet application and load the word processing program into memory.

Multiprogramming

Multiprogramming operating systems, also called **multitasking** operating systems, allow more than one program to be run at the same time on one computer. Even though the CPU is only capable of working on one program instruction at a time, its capability to switch back and forth between programs makes it appear that all programs are running at the same time. For example, with a multiprogramming operating system the computer could be performing a complex spreadsheet calculation and at the same time be downloading a file from another computer while the user is writing a memo with the word processing program.

Multiprogramming operating systems on personal computers can usually support a single user running multiple programs. Multiprogramming operating systems on some personal computers and most minicomputers and mainframes can support more than one user running more than one program. This version of a multiprogramming operating system is sometimes called a **multiuser-multiprogramming** operating system. Most of these operating systems also allow more than one user to be running the same program. For example, a wholesale distributor may have dozens of terminal operators entering sales orders using the same order entry program on the same computer.

Multiprocessing

Computers that have more than one CPU are called **multiprocessors**. A **multiprocessing** operating system coordinates the operations of computers with more than one CPU. Because each CPU in a multiprocessor computer can be executing one program instruction, more than one instruction can be executed simultaneously. Besides providing an increase in performance, most multiprocessors offer another advantage. If one CPU fails, work can be shifted to the remaining CPUs. In addition to an extra CPU, some systems, called **fault-tolerant computers**, are built with redundant components such as memory, input and output controllers, and disk drives. If any one of the components fail, the system can continue to operate with the duplicate component. Fault-tolerant systems are used for airline reservation systems, communications networks, bank teller machines, and other applications where it is important to keep the computer operating at all times.

Virtual Machine

A **virtual machine (VM)** operating system allows a single computer to run two or more different operating systems. The VM operating system allocates system resources such as memory and processing time to each operating system. To users it appears that they are working on separate systems, hence the term virtual machine. The advantage of this approach is that an organization can run different operating systems (at the same time) that are best suited to different tasks. For example, some operating systems are best for interactive processing and others are best for batch processing. With a VM operating system both types of operating systems can be run concurrently.

FUNCTIONS OF OPERATING SYSTEMS

◆ The operating system performs a number of functions that allow the user and the applications software to interact with the computer. These functions apply to all operating systems but become more complex for operating systems that allow more than one program to run at a time. The functions can be grouped into three types: allocating system resources, monitoring system activities, and disk and file management (Figure 9-4).

ALLOCATING RESOURCES	MONITORING ACTIVITIES	DISK AND FILE MANAGEMENT
CPU management	System performance	Formatting
Memory management	System security	Copying
Input/output management		Deleting

FIGURE 9-4
Operating system functions.

Allocating System Resources

The primary function of the operating system is to allocate, or assign, the resources of the computer system. That is, like a police officer directing traffic, the operating system decides what resource will currently be used and for how long. These resources include the CPU, main memory, and the input and output devices such as disk and tape drives and printers.

CPU Management Because a CPU can only work on one program instruction at a time, a multiprogramming operating system must keep switching the CPU among the different instructions of the programs that are waiting to be performed. A common way of allocating CPU processing is time slicing. A **time slice** is a fixed amount of CPU processing time, usually measured in milliseconds (thousandths of a second). With this technique, each user in turn receives a time slice. Since some instructions take longer to execute than others, some users may have more instructions completed in their time slice than other users. When a user's time slice has expired, the operating system directs the CPU to work on another user's program instructions, and the most recent user moves to the end of the line to await the next time slice (Figure 9-5). Unless the system has a heavy work load, however, users may not even be aware that their program has been temporarily set aside. Before they notice a delay, the operating system has allocated them another time slice and their processing continues.

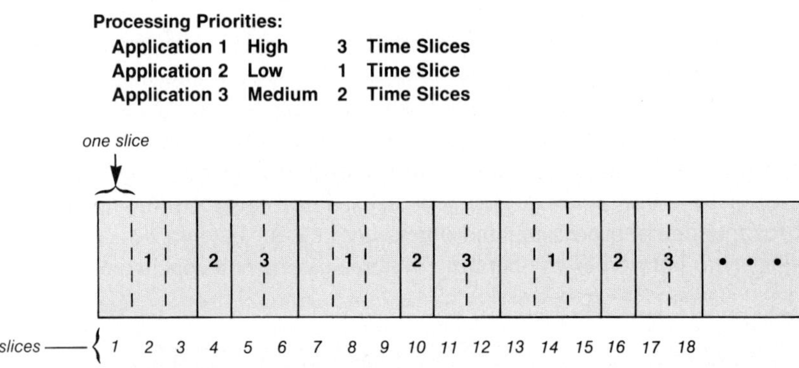

FIGURE 9-5
With the time slice method of CPU management, each application is allocated one or more fixed amounts of time called slices. Higher priority (more important) applications receive more consecutive slices than lower priority applications. When its processing time has expired, an application goes to the end of the line until all other applications have received at least one time slice. Here, application 2 is the lowest priority and so receives only one time slice. Application 1 is the highest priority and receives three time slices.

Because some work has a higher priority or is more important than other work, most operating systems have ways to adjust the amount of time slices a user receives, either automatically or based on user-specified criteria. One technique for modifying the number of time slices is to have different priorities assigned to each user. For each time slice received by the lowest priority, the highest priority would receive several consecutive time slices. For example, it would be logical to assign a higher priority to a program that processes orders and records sales than to an accounting program that could be run at a later time. Another way to allocate time slices is based on the type of work being performed. For example, some operating systems automatically allocate more time slices to interactive processes such as keyboard entry than they do to CPU-only processes such as calculations or batch processing. This gives a higher priority to users entering data than to a report being output to a printer.

Another way of assigning processing priorities is to designate each job as either foreground or background. **Foreground** jobs receive a higher processing priority and therefore more CPU time. Data entry would be an example of a job that would be classified as a foreground job. **Background** jobs receive a lower processing priority and less CPU time. Printing a report or calculating payroll are examples of jobs that could be classified as background jobs. Background jobs usually involve batch processing or require little or no computer operator intervention.

Memory Management During processing, main memory stores such items as the operating system, application program instructions for one or more programs, data waiting to be processed, and work space used for calculations, sorting, and other temporary tasks. It is the operating system's job to allocate, or assign, each of these items to areas of main memory. Data that has just been read into main memory from an input device or is waiting to be sent to an output device is stored in areas of main memory called **buffers**. The operating system assigns the location of the buffers in main memory and manages the data that is stored in them.

Operating systems allocate at least some portion of memory into fixed areas called partitions (Figure 9-6). Some operating systems allocate all memory on this basis while others use partitions only for the operating system instructions and buffers.

Another way of allocating memory is called virtual memory management, or virtual storage. **Virtual memory management** increases the effective (or *virtual*) limits of memory by expanding the amount of main memory to include disk space. Without virtual memory management, an entire program must be loaded into main memory during execution. With virtual memory management, only the portion of the program that is currently being used is required to be in main memory. Virtual memory management is used with multiprogramming operating systems to maximize the number of programs using memory at the same time. The operating system performs virtual memory management by transferring data and instructions to and from memory and the disk by using one or both of the two methods, segmentation and paging.

In **segmentation**, programs are divided into logical portions called **segments**. For example, one segment of a program might edit data and another segment might perform a calculation. Because the segments are based on logical portions of a program, some segments are larger than others. When a particular program instruction is required, the segment containing that instruction is transferred from the disk into main memory.

In **paging**, a fixed number of bytes is transferred from the disk each time data or program instructions are required. This fixed amount of data is called a **page**, or a **frame**. The size of a page, generally from 512 to 4,000 bytes, is determined by the operating system. Because a page is a fixed number of bytes, it may not correspond to a logical division of a program like a segment.

In both segmentation and paging, a time comes when memory is full but another page or segment needs to be read into memory. When this occurs, the operating system makes room for the new data or instructions by writing back to disk one or more of the pages or segments currently in memory. This process is referred to as **swapping** (Figure 9-7). The operating system usually chooses the least recently used page or segment to transfer back to disk.

MAIN MEMORY
OPERATING SYSTEM
PARTITION 1 Program A – Spreadsheet
PARTITION 2 Program B – Word Processing
PARTITION 3 Program C – Payroll Data
PARTITION 4 (Available)

FIGURE 9-6
Some computer systems allocate memory into fixed blocks called partitions. The CPU then keeps track of programs and data by assigning them to a specific partition.

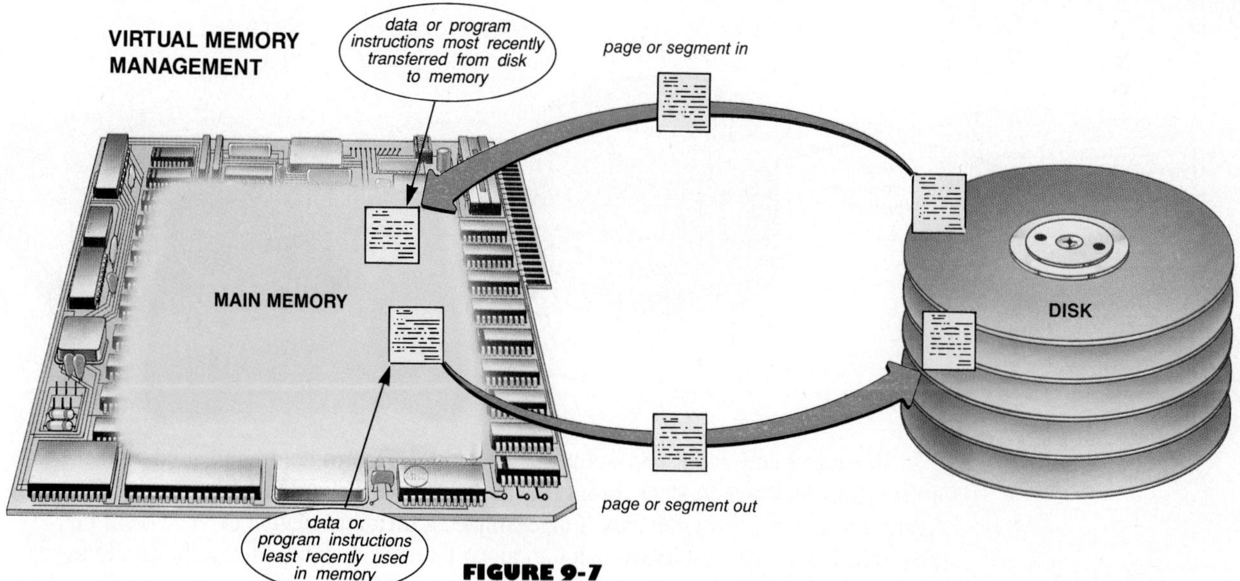

FIGURE 9-7
With virtual memory management, the operating system expands the amount of main memory to include available disk space. Data and program instructions are transferred to and from memory and disk as required. The segmentation technique transfers logical portions of programs that might be different sizes. The paging technique transfers pages of the same size. To make room for the new page or segment, the least recently used page or segment is *swapped*, or written back to the disk.

Input and Output Management At any given time, more than one input device can be sending data to the computer. At the same time, the CPU could be ready to send data to an output device such as a terminal or printer or a storage device such as a disk. The operating system is responsible for managing these input and output processes.

Some devices, such as a tape drive, are usually allocated to a specific user or application program. This is because tape is a sequential storage medium, and generally it would not make sense to have more than one application writing records to a single tape. Disk drives are usually allocated to all users because the programs and data files that users need are stored on these devices. The operating system keeps track of disk read and write requests, stores these requests in buffers along with the associated data for write requests, and usually processes them sequentially. A printer could be allocated to all users or restricted to a specific user. For example, a printer would be restricted to a specific user if the printer was going to be used with preprinted forms such as payroll checks.

Because the printer is a relatively slow device compared to other computer system devices, the technique of spooling is used to increase printer efficiency and reduce the number of printers required. With **spooling** (Figure 9-8), a report is first written (saved) to the disk before it is printed. Writing to the disk is much faster than writing to the printer. For example, a report that may take one-half hour to print (depending on the speed of the printer) may take only one minute to write to the disk. After the report is written to the disk, the CPU is available to process other programs. The report saved on the disk can be printed at a later time or, on a multiprogramming operating system, a print program can be run (at the same time other programs are running) to process the **print spool** (the reports on the disk waiting to be printed).

FIGURE 9-8
Spooling increases both CPU and printer efficiency by writing reports to the disk before they are printed. After the reports are written to disk, the CPU can begin processing other programs. Writing to the disk is much faster than writing directly to the printer.

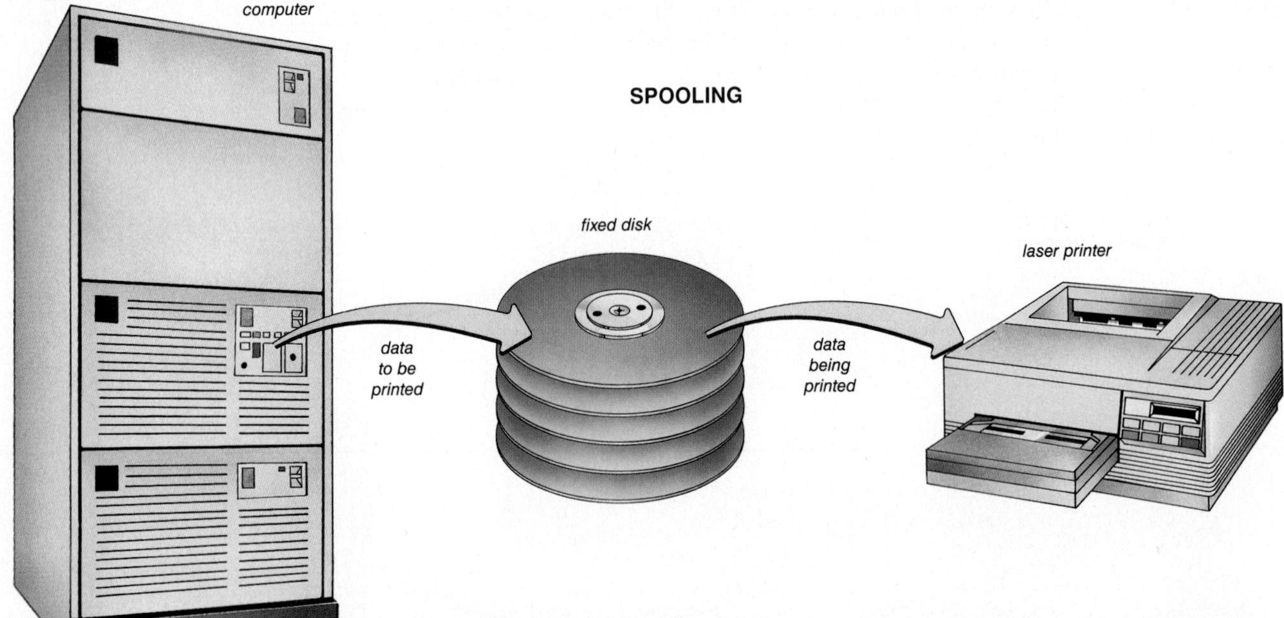

Because many input and output devices use different commands and control codes to transmit and receive data, programs called **device drivers** are used by the operating system to control these devices. For example, a different device driver would be required for a high-resolution color monitor than for a standard-resolution monochrome monitor. Output device drivers for monitors and printers are usually supplied by applications software developers along with their specific application such as word processing or spreadsheet. Input device drivers for equipment such as a mouse or scanner are usually supplied by the equipment manufacturer.

Monitoring System Activities

Another function of the operating system is monitoring the system activity. This includes monitoring system performance and system security.

System Performance System performance can be measured in a number of ways but is usually gauged by the user in terms of response time. **Response time** is the amount of time from the moment a user enters data until the computer responds. Response time can vary based on what the user has entered. If the user is simply entering data into a file, the response time is usually within a second or two. However, if the user has just completed a request for a display of sorted data from several files, the response time could be minutes.

A more precise way of measuring performance is to run a program that is designed to record and report system activity. Among other information, these programs usually report **CPU utilization**, the amount of time that the CPU is working and not idle, waiting for data to process. Figure 9-9 shows a CPU performance measurement report.

CONNECT SEC : CPU SEC

HOUR	CONNECT	CPU SEC
12-1A	1925.	1742.
1-2	802.	2057.
2-3	5788.	5164.
3-4	7200.	4368.
4-5	14692.	3791.
5-6	73585.	3172.
6-7	154932.	2490.
7-8	343274.	3909.
8-9	778287.	4828.
9-10	896538.	4405.
10-11	970041.	4736.
11-12	950215.	4620.
12-1P	769632.	3297.
1-2	868651.	4875.
2-3	890501.	4321.
3-4	799440.	4264.
4-5	651196.	3135.
5-6	221613.	3053.

TO CONTINUE SCROLL PRESS RETURN

FIGURE 9-9
System performance measurement programs report the amount of time the CPU is actually working and not waiting to process data.

Another measure of performance is to compare the CPU utilization with the disk input and output rate, referred to as disk I/0. We previously discussed how a virtual memory management operating system swaps pages or segments from disk to memory as they are needed. Systems with heavy work loads and insufficient memory or CPU power can get into a situation called **thrashing**, where the system is spending more time moving pages to and from the disk than processing the data. System performance reporting can alert the computer operations manager to this problem.

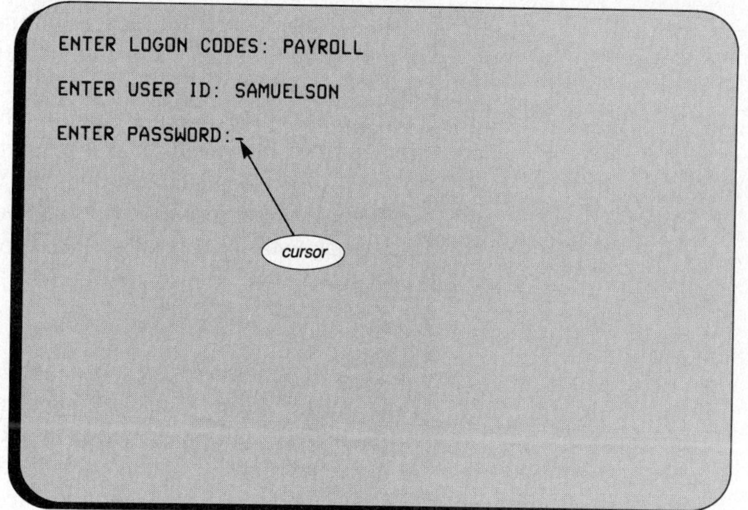

FIGURE 9-10
The logon code, user ID, and password must all be entered correctly before the user is allowed to use the computer. Because the password is confidential, it is usually not displayed on the screen when the user enters it.

System Security Most multiuser operating systems provide for a logon code, a user ID, and a password that must all be entered correctly before a user is allowed to use an application program (Figure 9-10). Each is a word or series of characters. A **logon code** usually identifies the application that will be used, such as accounting, sales, or manufacturing. A **user ID** identifies the user, such as Jeffrey Ryan or Mary Gonzales. The **password** is usually confidential; often it is known only to the user and the computer system administrator. The logon code, user ID, and password must match entries in an authorization file. If they don't match, the user is denied access to the system. Both successful and unsuccessful logon attempts are often recorded in a file so that management can review who is using or attempting to use the system. These logs can also be used to allocate data processing expenses based on the percentage of system use by an organization's various departments.

Disk and File Management

In addition to allocating system resources and monitoring system activities, most operating systems contain programs that can perform functions related to disk and file management. Some of these functions include formatting disks and diskettes, deleting files from a disk, copying files from one auxiliary storage device to another, and renaming stored files.

POPULAR OPERATING SYSTEMS

The first operating systems were developed by manufacturers for the computers in their product line. When the manufacturers came out with another computer or model, they often produced an improved and different operating system. Since programs are designed to be used with a particular operating system, this meant that users who wanted to switch computers, either from one vendor to another or to a different model from the same vendor, would have to convert their existing programs to run under the new operating system. Today, however, the trend is away from operating systems limited to a specific model and toward operating systems that will run on any model by a particular manufacturer. For example, part of Digital Equipment Corporation's success has been attributed to the fact that their VMS operating system is used on all their computer systems.

Going even further, many computer users are supporting the move away from **proprietary operating systems** (meaning privately owned) and toward **portable operating systems** that will run on many manufacturers' computers. The advantage of portable operating systems is that the user is not tied to a particular manufacturer. Using a portable operating system, a user could change computer systems, yet retain existing software and data files, which usually represent a sizable investment in time and money. For example, say a small business purchased a computer system to handle their immediate needs and to provide for several years of anticipated growth. Five years later, the business has reached the capacity of the computer; no more memory or terminals can be added. In addition, the manufacturer of the five-year-old computer does not make a larger or more powerful model. But because they originally chose a computer that used a portable operating system, the business can purchase a more powerful computer from another manufacturer that offers the same portable operating system and continue to use their existing software and data files.

One of the most popular portable operating systems is UNIX, which we will discuss along with the several personal computer operating systems.

UNIX

The **UNIX** operating system was developed in the early 1970s by scientists at Bell Laboratories. It was specifically designed to provide a way to manage a variety of scientific and specialized computer applications. Because of federal regulations, Bell Labs (a subsidiary of AT&T) was prohibited from actively promoting UNIX in the commercial marketplace. Instead, for a low fee Bell Labs licensed UNIX to numerous colleges and universities where it obtained a wide following. With the deregulation of the telephone companies in the 1980s, AT&T was allowed to enter the computer system marketplace. With AT&T's increased promotion and the trend toward portable operating systems, UNIX has aroused tremendous interest. One of the advantages of UNIX is its extensive library of over 400 instruction modules that can be linked together to perform almost any programming task. Today, most major computer manufacturers offer a multiuser version of the UNIX operating system to run on their computers.

With all its strengths, however, UNIX has not yet obtained success in the commercial business systems marketplace. Some people attribute this to the fact that UNIX has never been considered user friendly. For example, most of the UNIX program modules are identified by obscure names such as MAUS, SHMOP, and BRK. Other critics contend that UNIX lacks the file management capabilities to support the online interactive databases that more and more businesses are implementing. With the support of most major computer manufacturers, however, these problems are being worked on and UNIX has a good chance of becoming one of the major operating systems of the coming years.

MS-DOS

The Microsoft Disk Operating System, or **MS-DOS**, was released by Microsoft Corporation in 1981. MS-DOS was originally developed for IBM for their first personal computer system. IBM calls their equivalent version of the operating system **PC-DOS**. Because so many personal computer manufacturers followed IBM's lead and chose MS-DOS for their computers, MS-DOS quickly became an industry standard. Other personal computer operating systems exist, but by far the majority of personal computer software is written for MS-DOS. This single-user operating system is so widely used that it is often referred to simply as DOS.

Macintosh

The Apple **Macintosh** multiprogramming operating system provides a graphic interface that uses icons (figures) and windows (Figure 9-11). Macintosh users interface with the operating system through the use of features called Finder and Multifinder. Finder allows the user to run single programs and perform utility functions such as organizing and finding files.

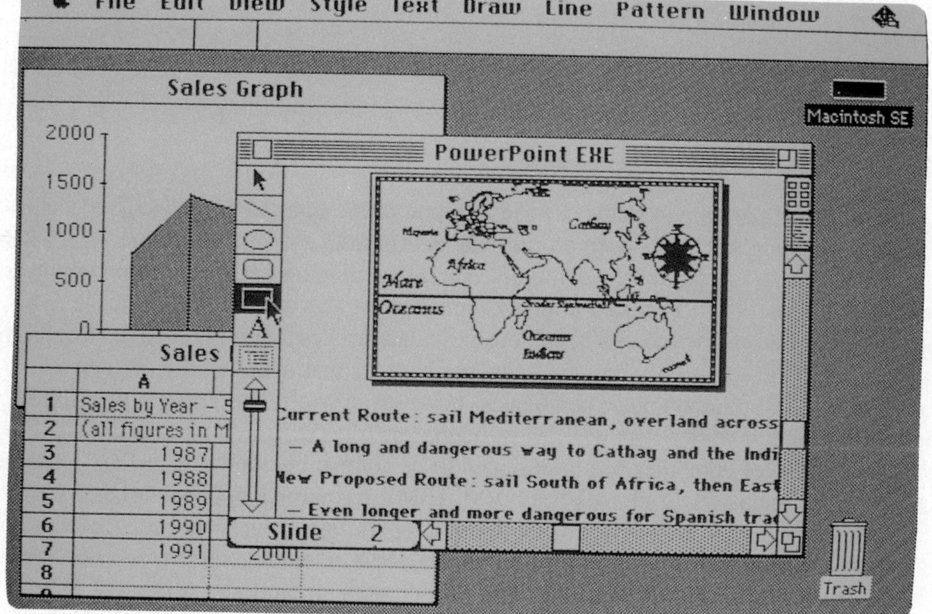

"Reprinted by permission from 'IBM Operating Systems/2 Standard Edition' Getting Started; Version 1.2, page 15 © by International Business Machines Corporation"

FIGURE 9-11
The Macintosh operating system offers a graphic user interface and the capability to display information in separate windows.

Multifinder allows the user to have certain processes, such as printing a document, run in the background while other processes, such as working on a spreadsheet, are currently being accessed. The Macintosh operating system has set the standard for operating system ease of use and has been the model for most of the new graphic user interfaces developed for non-Macintosh systems.

OS/2

In 1988, IBM released the **OS/2** operating system for its new family of PS/2 personal computers (Figure 9-12). Microsoft Corporation, which developed OS/2 for IBM, also released their equivalent version, called MS-OS/2. OS/2 is designed to take advantage of the increased computing power of the Intel 80286, 80386, and 80486 microprocessors and will run only on systems that use these chips. OS/2 also requires more computing power to operate. For example, OS/2 requires 5MB of hard disk and a minimum of 2MB of main memory just to run the operating system. Additional features offered by OS/2 include the capability to run larger and more complex programs and the capability to do multiprogramming (OS/2 can have up to 12 programs running at the same time).

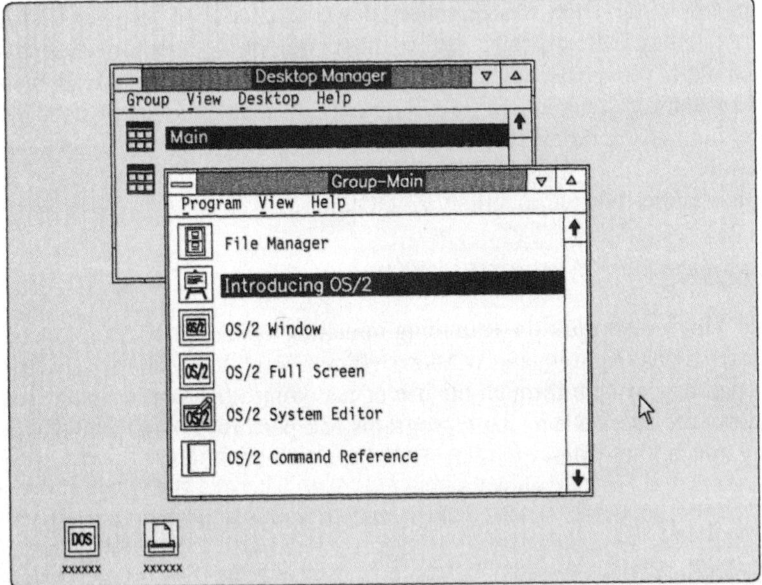

FIGURE 9-12
IBM's OS/2 operating system takes advantage of the increased processing power of the latest personal computer systems.

Other Operating Systems

Other popular operating systems exist in addition to the ones we just discussed. The ProDos operating system is used on millions of Apple II computer systems. The PICK operating system is a portable operating system that runs on personal, minicomputers, and mainframes. The PICK operating system incorporates a relational database manager and has had much success in the business data processing marketplace. Minicomputer manufacturers usually provide operating systems that operate only on their equipment. Most minicomputer companies, however, now offer versions of the UNIX and Pick operating systems as well. Most mainframe operating systems are unique to a particular make of computer or are designed to be compatible with one of IBM's operating systems such as DOS/VS, MVS, or VM, IBM's virtual machine operating system.

Although not yet widely used, the MACH operating system has been called a possible replacement for the increasingly popular UNIX operating system and possibly the standard operating system of the future. Considered a streamlined version of UNIX, MACH has the support of several large governmental and educational organizations. Currently being developed by Carnegie Mellon University, MACH has also been chosen by the Open Software Foundation (OSF), a 170 member organization that is trying to establish an industrywide operating system standard.

OPERATING ENVIRONMENTS

Because of the success of the Macintosh operating system, systems software developers have looked for ways to make other operating systems easier to use. One way has been to create an operating environment. An **operating environment**, sometimes called a **windowing environment**, is a graphic interface between the user and the operating system such as DOS, OS/2, or UNIX. Some operating environments, such as Microsoft's Windows (Figure 9-13), are separate software programs that can be added to existing DOS-based systems. Other operating environments, such as IBM's Presentation Manager for OS/2, are included with the operating system. Common features and advantages of an operating environment include use of a mouse, pull-down menus, the capability to have several applications open at the same time, and the capability to easily move data from one application such as a spreadsheet to another application such as a word processing document.

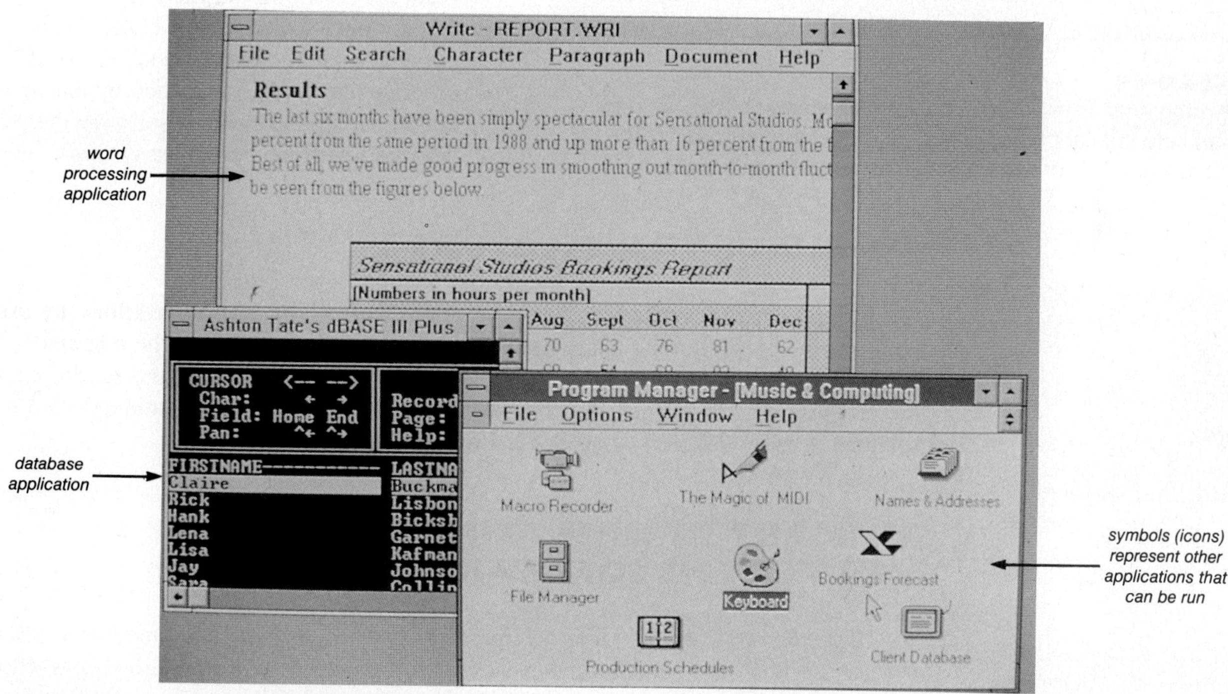

FIGURE 9-13
Microsoft's Windows operating environment provides a graphic user interface for computers that use the DOS operating system. Windows provides the capability to have different applications running in separate windows. The window on the left shows a dBASE III PLUS database application. The window at the top shows a word processing document. The window at the lower right is used to start other application programs represented by the symbols (called icons) shown in the window.

Closely related to operating environments are operating system shell programs. Like an operating environment, a **shell** program acts as an interface between the user and the operating system. Shell programs, however, usually offer a limited number of utility functions such as file maintenance and do not offer applications windowing or graphics.

UTILITIES

In addition to the programs in the operating system, systems software also contains programs called utilities. **Utilities** are programs that provide commonly needed tasks such as file backups, sorting, and editing. Sort utilities place the data stored in files into ascending or descending order based on a value stored in one or more specified fields of each record in a file. For example, a sort utility program could be used

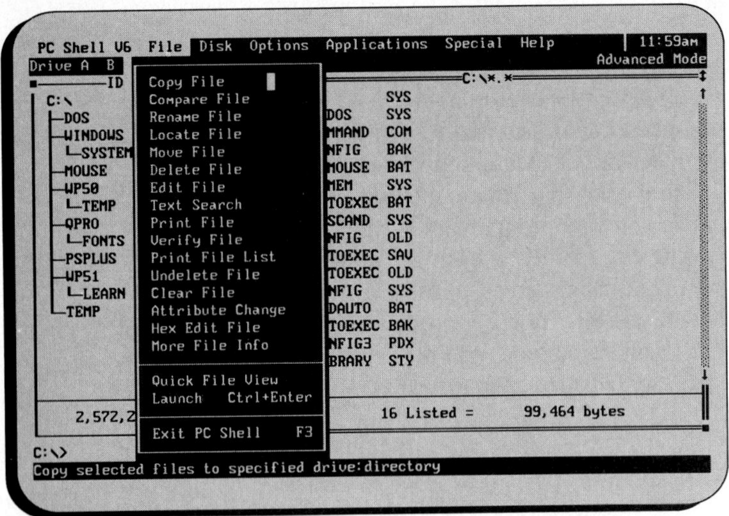

FIGURE 9-14
Utility programs such as PC Tools Deluxe offer a number of functions to help the user perform routine tasks more efficiently. The functions available for maintaining files appear on the screen.

to sort the records in a personnel file in alphabetical order by the employees' last names. An **editor** is a utility program that allows users to make direct changes to programs and data. A programmer can use an editor to change a program instruction that was incorrect or needs to be modified.

Microcomputer operating systems usually contain programs that provide some utility functions such as copying files. In addition, software packages can be purchased to enhance a user's library of systems software. Three popular packages are The Mace Utilities, PC Tools Deluxe, and The Norton Utilities, Advanced Edition. Figure 9-14 shows the file utility functions that are part of PC Tools Deluxe. With larger computer systems, a set of utility programs are usually supplied by the vendor as part of the systems software that is delivered with the computer system.

LANGUAGE TRANSLATORS

Special-purpose systems software programs called **language translators** are used to convert the programming instructions written by programmers into the machine instructions that a computer can understand. Language translators are written for specific programming languages and computer systems. Language translators are explained in more detail in Chapter 12, Program Development.

SUMMARY OF OPERATING SYSTEMS AND SYSTEMS SOFTWARE

Systems software, including the operating system, utilities, and language translators, are essential parts of a computer system and should be understood by users who want to obtain the maximum benefits from their computer. This is especially true for the latest personal computer operating systems that include features such as virtual memory management and multiprogramming. Understanding and being able to use these and other features will give users more control over their computer resources.

CHAPTER SUMMARY

1. **Systems software** consists of all the programs including the operating system that are related to controlling the operations of the computer.
2. An **operating system (OS)** consists of one or more programs that manage the operations of a computer.
3. Operating systems function as an interface between the user, the application programs, and the computer equipment.
4. The essential and most frequently used instructions in an operating system must be stored in main memory for the computer to operate.

5. The *resident* portion of the operating system is called by many different names: the **supervisor**, **monitor**, **executive**, **master program**, **control program**, or **kernel**.
6. The *nonresident* portion of the operating system, which consists of the less frequently used instructions, remains stored on a disk and is available to be loaded into main memory whenever it is needed.
7. **Booting** the system is the process of loading the operating system into the main memory of a computer.
8. The **operating system prompt** indicates that the operating system has been loaded and is ready to accept a command.
9. **Single program** operating systems allow a single user to run a single program at one time.
10. **Multiprogramming** operating systems, also called **multitasking** operating systems, allow more than one program to be run at the same time.
11. A multiprogramming operating system that allows multiple users is called a **multiuser-multiprogramming** operating system.
12. A **multiprocessor** computer has more than one CPU. **Multiprocessing** operating systems coordinate the operations of these computers.
13. **Fault-tolerant computers** are built with redundant components to allow processing to continue if any single component fails.
14. A **virtual machine (VM)** operating system allows a single computer to run two or more different operating systems.
15. The functions of an operating system include allocating system resources, monitoring system activities, and disk and file management.
16. The system resources that the operating system allocates include the CPU, main memory, and the input/output devices.
17. A **time slice** is a common way for an operating system to allocate CPU processing time.
18. **Foreground** jobs have a higher priority than **background** jobs and thus receive more CPU time.
19. **Buffers** are areas of main memory used to store data that has just been read or is being sent to an output device.
20. **Virtual memory management** increases the effective (or *virtual*) limits of memory by expanding the amount of main memory to include disk space. With virtual memory management, the operating system transfers data and programs between main memory and the disks by segmentation and paging.
21. In **segmentation**, programs are divided into logical portions called **segments**.
22. In **paging**, a fixed number of bytes called a **page**, or **frame**, is transferred from the disk each time data or program instructions are required.
23. The operating system is responsible for managing the input and output processes of the computer.
24. **Spooling** increases printer and computer system efficiency by writing a report to disk before it is printed.
25. The **print spool** refers to reports that have been stored on the disk and are waiting to be printed.
26. **Device drivers** are programs used by the operating system to control different input and output equipment.
27. **Response time** is the amount of time from the moment a user enters data until the computer responds.
28. System performance can be measured by the response time and by comparing the **CPU utilization** with the disk I/O to determine if the system is **thrashing**.
29. Most multiuser operating systems provide for a **logon code**, a **user ID**, and a **password** which all must be entered correctly before a user is allowed to use an application program.
30. Most operating systems contain programs that perform functions that are related to disk and file management.
31. Many computer users are supporting the move away from **proprietary operating systems** and toward **portable operating systems**.
32. Some of the popular operating systems being used today include **UNIX**, **MS-DOS**, **PC-DOS**, **Macintosh**, and **OS/2**.
33. An **operating environment**, sometimes called a **windowing environment**, is a graphic interface between the user and the operating system.
34. A **shell** program acts as an interface between the user and the operating system.
35. **Utilities** are programs that provide commonly needed tasks such as file backups, sorting, and editing.
36. An **editor** is a utility program that allows users to make direct changes to programs and data.
37. **Language translators** are used to convert the programming instructions written by programmers into the machine instructions that a computer can understand.

KEY TERMS

Background *9.6*
Booting *9.2*
Buffer *9.6*
Control program *9.2*
CPU utilization *9.9*
Device driver *9.8*
Editor *9.14*
Executive *9.2*
Fault-tolerant computer *9.5*
Foreground *9.6*
Frame *9.7*
Kernel *9.2*
Language translators *9.14*
Logon code *9.9*
Macintosh *9.11*
Master program *9.2*
Monitor *9.2*
MS-DOS *9.11*
Multiprocessing *9.4*
Multiprocessor *9.4*
Multiprogramming *9.4*
Multitasking *9.4*
Multiuser-multiprogramming *9.4*
Operating environment *9.13*
Operating system (OS) *9.2*
Operating system prompt *9.3*
OS/2 *9.12*
Page *9.7*
Paging *9.7*
Password *9.9*
PC-DOS *9.11*
Portable operating system *9.10*
Print spool *9.8*
Proprietary operating system *9.10*
Response time *9.9*
Segment *9.7*
Segmentation *9.7*
Shell *9.13*
Single program *9.4*
Spooling *9.8*
Supervisor *9.2*
Swapping *9.7*
Systems software *9.2*
Time slice *9.5*
Thrashing *9.9*
UNIX *9.10*
User ID *9.9*
Utilities *9.13*
Virtual machine (VM) *9.5*
Virtual memory management *9.7*
Windowing environment *9.13*

REVIEW QUESTIONS

1. How does systems software differ from applications software?
2. Describe how to boot an operating system on a personal computer.
3. What are the different types of operating systems? How are they different?
4. The functions of an operating system can be grouped into which three types?
5. How does an operating system use time slices to assign different processing priorities to jobs?
6. Describe how an operating system uses the disk drive to perform virtual memory management.
7. How does spooling increase printer and computer system efficiency?
8. Discuss several techniques used to measure computer system performance.
9. Describe three types of authorization that an operating system can use to provide system access security.
10. What are the advantages of a portable operating system.
11. List several tasks that the utility programs can perform.

CONTROVERSIAL ISSUE

1. Many people believe that a graphics user interface will eventually be part of all operating systems. Others prefer a nongraphic, command-line operating system. Discuss the advantages and disadvantages of both.

RESEARCH PROJECTS

1. Prepare a paper comparing the MS-DOS and Unix operating systems.

Management Information Systems

OBJECTIVES

- Define the term management information systems
- Describe why information is important to an organization
- Discuss the different levels in an organization and how the information requirements differ for each level
- Explain the qualities that all information should have
- Define the term information system and identify the six elements of an information system
- Describe the different types of information systems and the trend toward integration
- Explain how personal computers are used in management information systems

Management information systems, often abbreviated MIS, is a frequently used computer industry term. It is often used, however, to mean different things. It can describe the total system from which information flows to employees of an organization. This could include manual and automated methods as well as computerized systems. The term MIS can also be used to refer to only those portions of a system that provide information to management. Finally, MIS can refer to the department that manages the computer resources of an organization. For the purposes of this chapter, we use a broad definition of **management information systems (MIS)** to mean any computer-based system that provides timely and accurate information for managing an organization. To better understand how a MIS system provides this information, we first need to discuss why information is important to an organization.

WHY IS INFORMATION IMPORTANT TO AN ORGANIZATION?

More and more organizations are realizing that the information in their databases is an important asset that must be protected. Like more tangible assets such as buildings and equipment, an organization's information assets have both a present and future value and have costs associated with their acquisition, maintenance, and storage. Information is no longer thought of as a by-product of doing business, but rather as a key ingredient in both short- and long-range decision making.

Several factors have contributed to the increased need for timely and accurate information. Among these factors are expanded markets, increased competition, shorter product life cycles, and government regulation.

Expanded markets means that to be successful today, many businesses must sell their products in as many markets as possible. Often this means national as well as international distribution of a product. Companies that produce a product for local or regional use are at a disadvantage against companies that produce larger volumes of products for a wider distribution. When companies expand their markets they must have more information about a larger number of potential selling areas (markets) and the different ways of getting their products to those markets. Automobiles are an example of this trend. The number of automobile producers has decreased, and the surviving companies are moving toward worldwide distribution of their products.

Increased competition means that competing companies are financially stronger and better organized. It is, therefore, more important for organizations to have current information on how competitors are selling their products. Many companies now maintain large databases that include information on competitive product features, prices, and methods of distribution. For consumer product companies, this information often includes sales and percent of the total market. This information is important in measuring the impact of advertising campaigns. For example, many companies will measure the impact of a new advertising campaign in a limited geographic area such as a large metropolitan city, before they use the advertising nationwide.

Shorter product life cycles means that companies have less time to perfect a product. More often than not, the product has to be successful when it is first introduced because companies will have less time to make corrections after a product is introduced. This means that before they introduce products, they must have accurate information about what potential customers want. This has led to the increased use of test marketing. Company managers then use the results of tests to decide on advertising, packaging, and product features. Shorter product life cycles also require companies to begin work earlier on the next generation of products. To do this, managers must have information about existing product features that customers want changed and new features they want added.

Government regulation has also contributed to the need for more information. One good example of this is in human resource management. To comply with equal employment opportunity (EEO) guidelines and laws, organizations must keep detailed records on testing, hiring, and promotion practices. The employee database, once used almost exclusively for payroll purposes, has now been expanded to include valuable information on employee skill and education levels as well as the results of performance reviews. With this information companies can document their compliance with government regulations and guidelines.

HOW DO MANAGERS USE INFORMATION?

All employees in an organization need information to effectively perform their jobs; but the primary users of information are managers. **Managers** of an organization are the men and women responsible for directing the use of resources such as people, money, materials, and information so the organization can operate efficiently and prosper. Managers work toward this goal by performing the four management tasks of planning, organizing, directing, and controlling.

1. *Planning* involves establishing goals and objectives. Upper levels of management also plan by establishing the strategies of the organization that will help meet these goals and objectives. For example, upper management often prepares a three- to five-year plan that includes strategies on how to enter new markets or increase existing market share. Lower levels of management plan by establishing specific policies and procedures to implement the strategies. A lower level management plan might include a specific inventory quantity to be maintained for a part.
2. *Organizing* includes identifying and bringing together the resources necessary to achieve the plans of an organization. Resources include people, money, materials (facilities, equipment, raw materials), and information. Organizing also involves establishing the management structure of an organization such as the departments and reporting relationships. For example, to introduce a new product, a company can assign responsibility to an existing department or form a new group whose sole responsibility is the new product.
3. *Directing* involves instructing and authorizing others to perform the necessary work. To direct effectively, managers must be able to communicate what needs to be done and motivate people to do the work. Directing often takes place at daily or weekly meetings where managers meet with their employees to discuss job priorities.
4. *Controlling* involves measuring performance and, if necessary, taking corrective action. Daily production reports are a control device that give managers the information they need to make any necessary adjustments in production rate or product mix.

Figure 10-1 shows how the four management tasks are usually performed in a sequence that becomes a recurring cycle. Actual performance is measured against a previously established plan as part of the control task; this often results in a revised plan. The revised plan may result in additional organizational and directional activities, and so the cycle repeats itself. The four tasks are related and a change in one task usually affects one or more of the other tasks.

All managers perform these management tasks but their area of focus, such as finance or production, and the information they need to perform the tasks is influenced by their level in the organization.

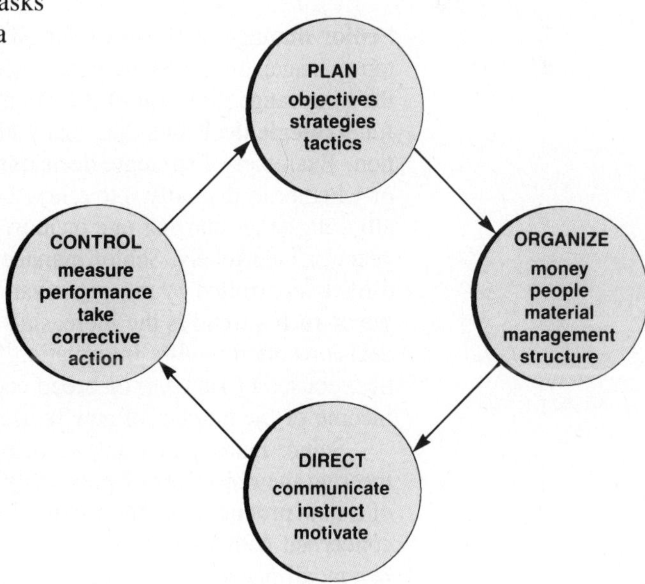

FIGURE 10-1
The four management tasks performed by management are to plan, organize, direct, and control. These tasks are part of a recurring cycle; actions connected with any one task usually affect one or more of the other tasks.

MANAGEMENT LEVELS IN AN ORGANIZATION

Management is usually classified into three levels. The names for these three levels can vary; we call them senior management, middle management and operational management. As shown in Figure 10-2, these three levels of management are above a fourth level of the organization consisting of the production, clerical, and nonmanagement staff. Together, these four levels make up the entire organization. The following sections discuss these levels and their different information requirements.

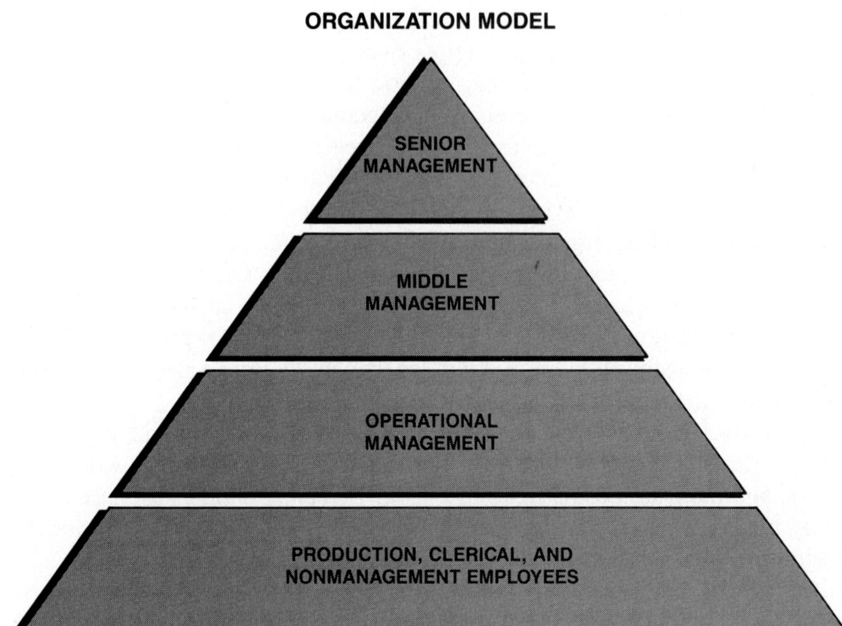

FIGURE 10-2
The model of an organization's management includes three levels with a fourth level made up of the production, clerical, and other non-management employees. Each level makes different types of decisions and requires different types and amounts of information.

Senior Management — Strategic Decisions

Senior management, also referred to as executive or top management, includes the top management positions in an organization. Senior management is concerned with the long-range direction of the organization. Senior managers are primarily responsible for **strategic decisions** that deal with the overall goals and objectives of an organization. Examples of strategic decisions are whether to add or discontinue a product line or whether to diversify into a new business. The time frame for such decisions is usually long-range starting one or more years in the future and continuing for several years or indefinitely. Senior management decisions often involve factors that cannot be directly controlled by the organization such as the changing trends of society. An example of such a trend is the increasing average age of the population. Senior management decisions often require information from outside the company such as industry statistics, consumer surveys, or broad economic indicators such as the change in personal income or the number of new houses being built.

Senior management is also responsible for monitoring how current operations are meeting the objectives of previously made strategic decisions. For example, are sales of a new product meeting previously forecasted levels? Because senior management is concerned with all areas of an organization, it must rely on summarized information to review all operations in a timely manner. Often information on current operations is presented only if it is significantly above or below what was planned. This helps senior management to focus on only the variations that require its involvement.

Another senior management responsibility is to supervise middle management personnel.

Middle Management — Tactical Decisions

Middle management is responsible for implementing the strategic decisions of senior management. To do this, middle managers make **tactical decisions** that implement specific programs and plans necessary to accomplish the stated objectives. Tactical decisions could include how to best advertise and promote a company's products. Such decisions usually involve a shorter time frame than strategic decisions but often cover an entire year. Although they are interested in external events that may influence their work, middle managers are more concerned with the internal operations of the organization and, therefore, rely on information generated by the organization. Middle management also uses summarized and exception-oriented reports although not to the extent of senior management. Middle management sometimes must review detailed information in order to understand performance variances.

Middle management is also responsible for supervising operational management.

Operational Management — Operational Decisions

Operational management supervises the production, clerical, and nonmanagement staff of an organization. In performing their duties, operational managers make **operational decisions** that usually involve an immediate action such as accepting or rejecting an inventory delivery or approving a purchase order. The decision time frame of operational managers tasks is usually very short, such as a day, a week, or a month. Operational managers directly supervise the production and support of an organization's product or service; thus they need detailed information telling them what was produced. Summary and exception reporting, long an important tool for senior and middle level managers, is increasingly being used by operational managers. There are two reasons for this change. First, upper levels of management are allowing lower levels of management to make more decisions. Second, because of computerized systems, the information necessary to make decisions at lower levels is more easily available.

Nonmanagement Employees — On-the-Job Decisions

Nonmanagement employees, which include production, clerical, and staff personnel, also need frequent information to perform their jobs. The trend toward flexible manufacturing systems has increased the need for information to be available to the production worker. Instead of working at the same task all the time, production workers often work as a group on related tasks. Some manufacturing plants allow a group of workers to move with the product from the beginning of production to the end. Such changes require production workers to understand more about the production process than ever before. Often, this information is made available to the workers through the use of production-floor terminals that can be used to inquire on the next production process or tool required. Some systems tell the workers what job they should work on next.

Today, clerical and nonproduction workers also have more information available to them than in the past. For example, more documentation of administrative systems is being placed on-line for immediate access. As we previously mentioned, this is part of a trend toward giving lower level, nonmanagement employees the information they need to make decisions made formerly by managers.

Although we have classified the organization and its corresponding information requirements into four levels as is usually done, in the real world there is often a crossover from one level to another. For example, management and nonmanagement employees frequently join together in committees where all participants have an equal voice. Organizations have realized that formal or informal distinctions between managers and employees hinder communication and can restrict the flow of useful ideas and information. As we will discuss later in this chapter, recent technology, especially the personal computer, has significantly contributed to the flow of timely information to all levels within an organization.

Now that we have discussed why information is important to an organization and how it is used by the various levels, we explain the characteristics, or qualities, that all information should have.

QUALITIES OF INFORMATION

As we have discussed, the purpose of processing data is to create information. Just as data should have certain characteristics, so too should information. These characteristics are often called the qualities of information (Figure 10-3). Terms used to describe these qualities include: accurate, verifiable, timely, organized, meaningful, useful, and cost effective.

QUALITIES OF INFORMATION

- Accurate
- Verifiable
- Timely
- Organized
- Meaningful
- Useful
- Cost Effective

FIGURE 10-3
The qualities of information are characteristics that all information should have, whether or not it is produced by a computer.

Although it may seem obvious, the first quality of information is that it should be *accurate*. Inaccurate information is often worse than no information at all. Accuracy is also a characteristic of data. Although accurate data does not guarantee accurate information, it is impossible to produce accurate information from erroneous data. The computer jargon term **GIGO** states this point very well; it stands for *Garbage In, Garbage Out*.

Closely related to accuracy is that information be *verifiable*. This means that if necessary, the user can confirm the information. For example, before relying on the amounts in a summary report, an accountant would want to know that the totals could be supported by details of the transactions. The accountant could verify the accuracy of the report totals by testing some or all of the totals by adding up the supporting detail records and comparing the results to the report.

Another quality of information is that it must be *timely*. Although most information loses its value with time, some information, such as trends, becomes more valuable as time passes and more information is obtained. The point to remember is that the timeliness must be appropriate for any decisions that will be made based on the information. Up-to-the-minute information may be required for some decisions such as the inventory level of a key part, while older information may be satisfactory or more appropriate for other decisions such as the number or employees planning vacations next month.

To be most valuable, information should be *organized* to suit users' requirements. For example, a sales manager that assigns territories on a geographic basis would need prospect lists sorted by ZIP code and not by prospect name.

Meaningful information indicates that the information is relevant to the person who receives it. Certain information is only meaningful to specific individuals or groups within an organization. Management should eliminate extraneous and unnecessary information and always consider the audience when it is accumulating or reporting information.

To be *useful*, information should result in an action being taken or specifically being not taken, depending on the situation. Often, this quality can be improved through exception reporting, which focuses only on the information that exceeds certain limits. An example of exception reporting is an inventory report showing items whose balance on hand is less than a predetermined minimum quantity. Rather than looking through an entire inventory report to find such items, the exception report would quickly bring these items to the attention of the managers responsible for maintaining the inventory.

Last, but not least, information must be *cost effective*. That is, the cost to produce the information must be less than the value of the information. This can sometimes be hard to determine. If the value of the information cannot be determined, perhaps the information should be produced only as managers require it, instead of on a regular basis. Many organizations periodically review the information they produce in reports to determine if the reports maintain the qualities of information we just described. The cost of producing these reports can therefore still be justified or possibly reduced.

Although we have discused the qualities of information in conjunction with computer systems, these qualities apply to all information regardless of how it is produced. Knowing these qualities will help you evaluate the information you receive and you provide every day, whether or not it is generated by a computer.

The elements of an information system and the general categories of information systems are discussed in the next section.

WHAT IS AN INFORMATION SYSTEM?

◆ An **information system** is a collection of elements that provides accurate, timely, and useful information. As we discussed in Chapter 1, all information systems that are implemented on a computer are comprised of the six elements: equipment, software, accurate data, trained information systems personnel, knowledgeable users, and documented procedures. Each element contributes to a successful information system and conversely, a weakness in any of these elements can cause an information system to fail. People who create, use, or change any type of information system should consider all six elements to ensure success.

Information systems that are implemented on a computer are generally classified into four categories: (1) operational systems; (2) management information systems; (3) decision support systems; and (4) expert systems.

Operational Systems

Operational systems process data generated by the day-to-day transactions of an organization (Figure 10-4). Some examples of operational systems are billing systems, inventory control systems, and order entry systems.

When computers were first used for processing business applications, the information systems developed were primarily operational systems. Usually, the purpose was to computerize an existing manual system. This approach often resulted in faster processing, reduced clerical costs, and improved customer service. Although these operational systems were originally designed to process daily transactions, they were modified over time to provide summaries, trends, and exception data useful to management. Today, operational systems are often a part of management information systems, which we discuss in the next section.

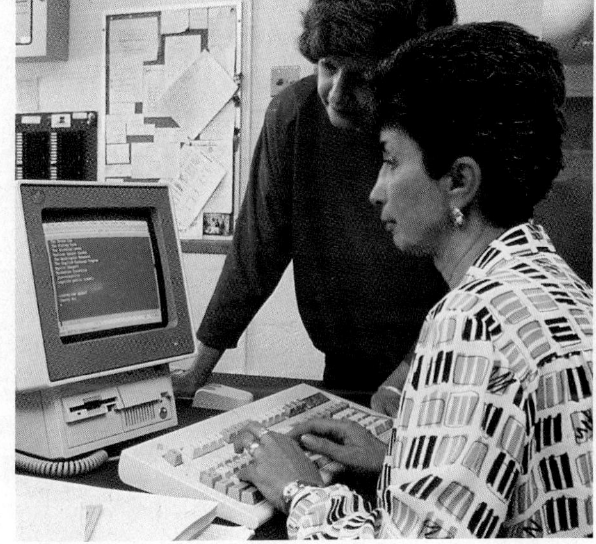

FIGURE 10-4
Operational systems process the day-to-day transactions of an organization.

Management Information Systems

In this section we discuss management information systems defined as systems that provide information to management. The concept of management information systems evolved as managers realized that computer processing could be used for more than just day-to-day transaction processing and that the computer's capability to perform rapid calculations and compare data could be used to produce meaningful information

FIGURE 10-5
Management information systems focus on the summary information and exceptions that managers use to perform their jobs.

for management. As we stated at the beginning of the chapter, a management information system (MIS) refers to a computer-based system that generates timely and accurate information for managing an organization. Frequently a management information system is integrated with an operational system. For example, to process a sales order, the operational system would record the sale, update the customer's accounts receivable balance, and make a deduction from the inventory. In the related management information system, reports would be produced that show slow or fast moving items, customers with past due accounts receivable balances, and inventory items that need reordering. In the management information system, the focus is on the information that management needs to do its job (Figure 10-5).

A special type of management information system is the executive information system. **Executive information systems (EIS)** are management information systems that have been designed for the information needs of senior management. Company-wide management information systems usually address the information needs of all levels of management. Because senior managers may not be familiar (or comfortable) working with computer systems, EIS have features that make them easier for executives to use. The EIS user interface often uses a mouse or a touch screen to help executives that are not familiar with using a keyboard. One leading system uses a remote control device similar to those used to control a television set. Another aspect of the EIS user interface is the graphic presentation of information. EIS rely heavily on graphic presentation of both the processing options (Figure 10-6) and data. Again, this is designed to make the system easier to use.

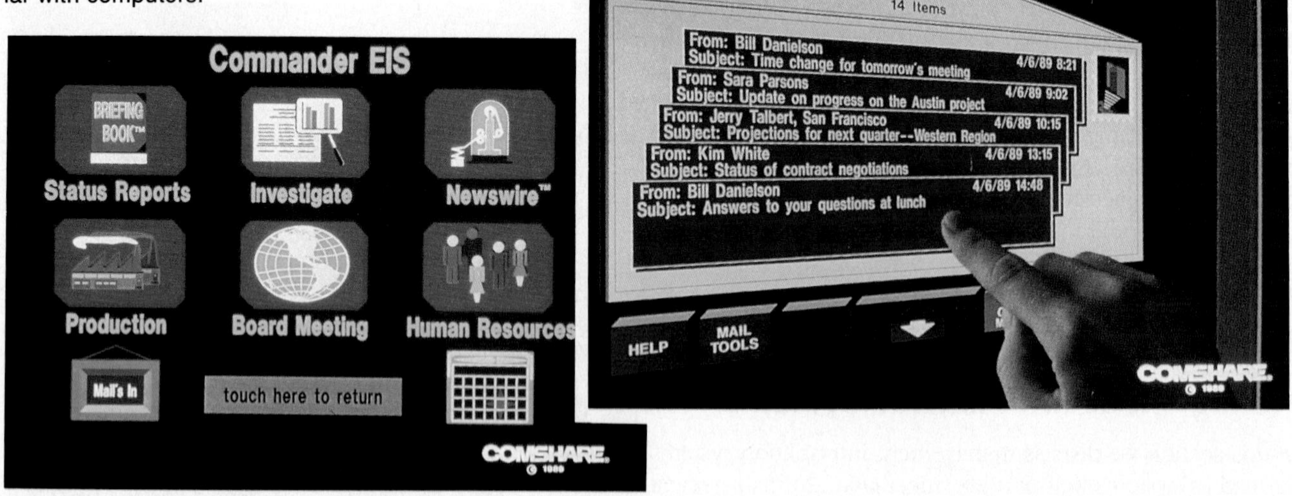

FIGURE 10-6
Executive information systems (EIS) often use graphics and touch screens to make the systems easier to use by executives who are not familiar with computers.

Because executives focus on strategic issues, EIS often have access to external databases such as the Dow Jones News/Retrieval service. Such external sources of information can provide current information on interest rates, commodity prices, and other leading economic indicators.

Although they offer great promise, many EIS have not been successfully implemented and many executives have stopped using them. A common reason cited in several failed attempts is the mistake of not modifying the system to the specific needs of the individual executives who will use the system. For example, many executives prefer to have information presented in a particular sequence with the option of seeing different levels of supporting detail information such as cost data on a spreadsheet. The desired sequence and level of detail varies for each executive. It appears that EIS must be tailored to the executives' requirements or the executives will continue to manage with information they have obtained through previously established methods.

Decision Support Systems

Frequently, management needs information that is not routinely provided by operational and management information systems. For example, a vice president of finance may want to know the net effect on company profits if interest rates on borrowed money increase and raw material prices decrease. Operational or management information systems do not usually provide this type of information. Decision support systems have been developed to provide this information.

A **decision support system (DSS)** is a system designed to help someone reach a decision by summarizing or comparing data from either or both internal and external sources. Internal sources include data from an organization's database such as sales, manufacturing, or financial data. Data from external sources could include information on interest rates, population trends, new housing construction, or raw material pricing. Frito Lay, for example, collects and reports sales data on its own and competitors products every day (Figure 10-7). The information is part of a DSS that allows Frito Lay to analyze important trends in days or weeks instead of the months that it used to take.

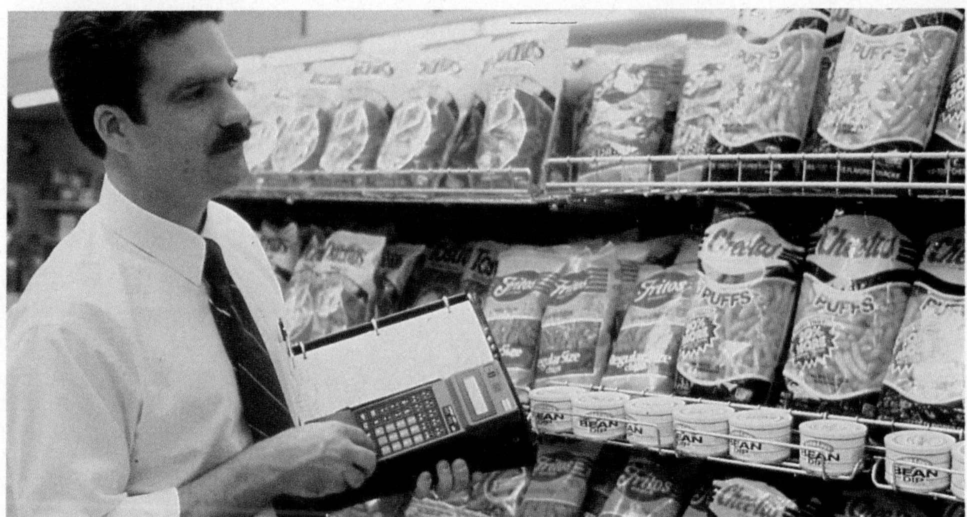

FIGURE 10-7
Frito Lay, a major producer of snack foods, has developed a decision support system that uses sales information collected daily on hand-held terminals by over 10,000 salespeople. The system helps Frito Lay spot sales trends in days or weeks instead of the months it used to take.

Decision support systems often include query languages, statistical analysis capabilities, spreadsheets, and graphics to help the user evaluate the decision data. More advanced decision support systems also include capabilities that allow users to create a model of the variables affecting a decision. With a **model**, users can ask *what-if* questions by changing one or more of the variables and seeing what the projected results would be. A simple model for determining the best product price would include factors for the expected sales volume at each price level. Many people use electronic spreadsheets for simple modeling tasks. DSS are sometimes combined with executive information systems (EIS). Generally speaking, DSS are more analytical and are designed

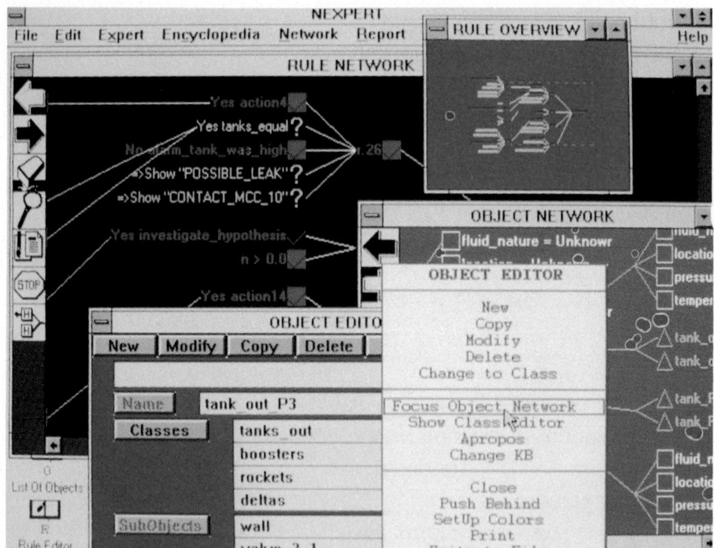

FIGURE 10-8
Nexpert Object is a powerful expert system that provides a highly visual presentation of its data, rules, and conclusions.

to work on unstructured problems that do not have a predefined number of variables. For example, a problem involving how to finance a company's growth would involve estimates of sales, income, depreciation, interest rates, and other variables that would best be handled by a DSS. EIS are primarily oriented toward collecting and presenting meaningful information from a variety of sources.

Expert Systems

Expert systems combine the knowledge on a given subject of one or more human experts into a computerized system that simulates the human experts' reasoning and decision making processes (Figure 10-8). Thus, the computer also becomes an *expert* on the subject. Expert systems are made up of the combined subject knowledge of the human experts, called the **knowledge base** and the **inference rules** that determine how the knowledge is used to reach decisions. Although they may appear to *think*, the current expert systems actually operate within narrow preprogrammed limits and cannot make decisions based on common sense or on information outside of their knowledge base. An example of how a simple expert system uses rules to identify an animal is shown in Figure 10-9.

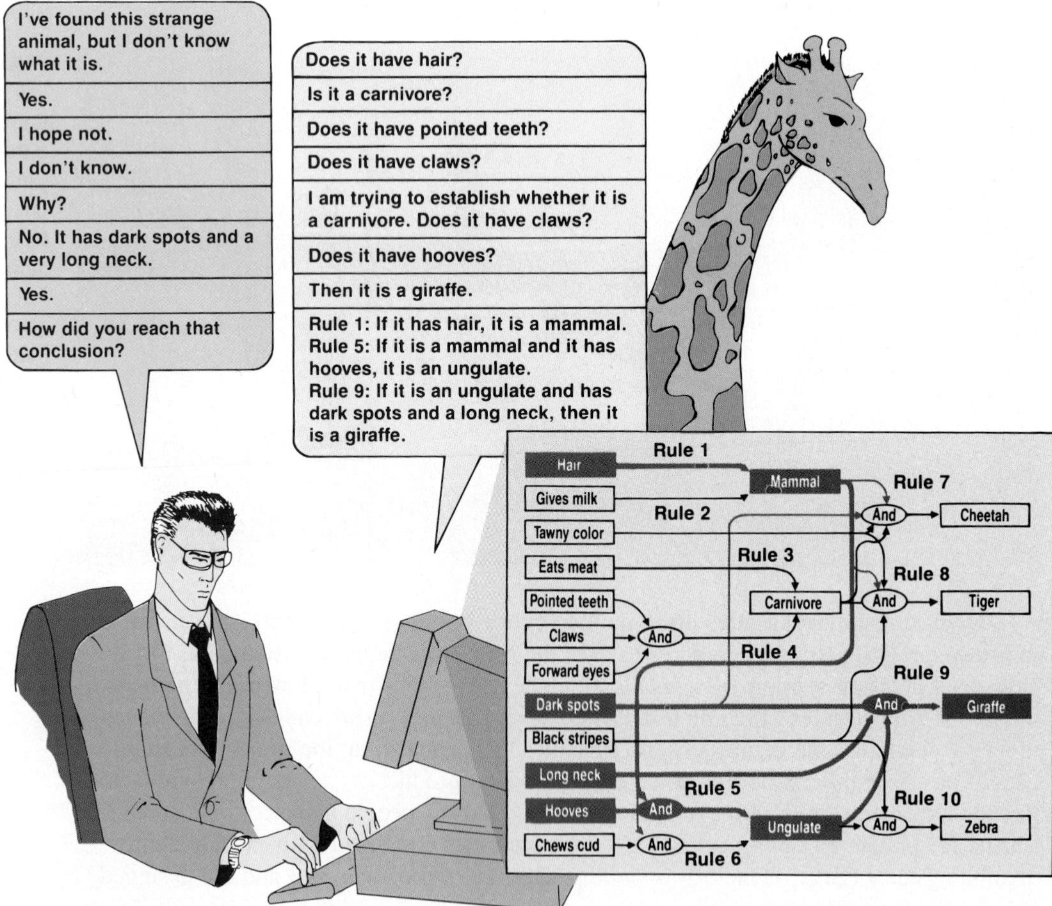

FIGURE 10-9
A simulated dialogue between a user and a simple expert system is designed to identify an animal based on observations about the animal provided by the user. Notice how answers to certain questions result in other questions that narrow the possible conclusions. Once a conclusion is reached, the expert system can display or print the rules upon which the conclusion was based.

A more practical application of an expert system has been implemented by Ford Motor Company to help their dealers diagnose engine repair problems. Previously, when they encountered an engine problem that they could not solve, dealers would call Dearborn, Michigan to talk with Ford engine expert Gordy Kujawski. Now dealers can access a nationwide computer system that Ford has developed to duplicate the reasoning that Kujawski uses when troubleshooting a problem (Figure 10-10).

Although expert systems can be used at any level in an organization, to date they have been primarily used by nonmanagement employees for job-related decisions. Expert systems have also been successfully applied to problems as diverse as diagnosing illnesses, searching for oil, and making soup. These systems are part of an exciting branch of computer science called **artificial intelligence**, the application of human intelligence to computer systems.

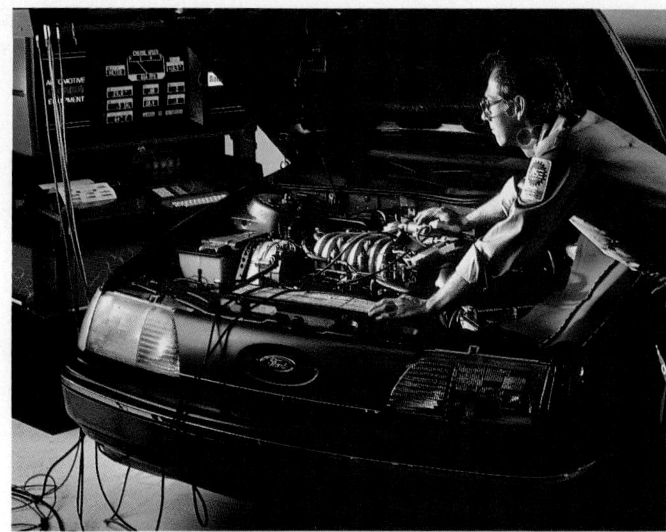

FIGURE 10-10
Ford Motor Company has developed an expert system that incorporates the knowledge of engine repair expert Gordy Kujawski. Instead of calling Kujawski, Ford dealers can now access the expert system when they are trying to diagnose engine problems.

INTEGRATED INFORMATION SYSTEMS

With today's sophisticated software, it can be difficult to classify a system as belonging uniquely to one of the four types of information systems we have discussed. For example, much of today's application software provides both operational and MIS information and some of the more advanced software even includes some decision support capabilities. Although expert systems still operate primarily as separate systems, the trend is clear: combine all of an organization's information needs into a single, integrated information system.

THE ROLE OF PERSONAL COMPUTERS IN MANAGEMENT INFORMATION SYSTEMS

The personal computer is playing an increasingly significant role in modern management information systems. Some professionals have said that the personal computer is the right tool at the right time. As organizations have moved toward decentralizing decision making, personal computers have given managers access to the information they need to make their decisions. Nonmanagement employees also benefit from having information available through networked personal computers on their desk or in the production area. For many MIS applications, personal computers are more cost effective than larger systems. One study estimated that the cost to process a million transactions on a mainframe is fifty times more expensive than on a personal computer. Flexibility is another advantage of personal computers. Individual or networks of personal computers can often be added more quickly than the corresponding amount of equipment that would be needed with minicomputer or mainframe systems. Many professionals believe that the ideal MIS decision involves a network of personal computers attached to a central mainframe, minicomputer, or file server that stores the common information that many users access. This centralized data and decentralized computing arrangement allow users and organizations the most flexibility over controlling their information resources.

SUMMARY OF MANAGEMENT INFORMATION SYSTEMS

Numerous factors have combined to make information an increasingly important asset for most organizations. Organizations manage this asset through the use of management information systems, computer-based systems that provide the information necessary to manage the activities of the organization. Management information systems provide different types of information based on the users' needs, which is often related to the users' levels in the organization.

The trend of management information systems is to combine and integrate operational, MIS, decision support, and expert systems that previously operated independently.

CHAPTER SUMMARY

1. **Management information system (MIS)** refers to any computer-based system that provides timely and accurate information for managing an organization.
2. Information that is stored in a database is no longer thought of as a by-product of doing business, but rather as a key ingredient in both short- and long-range decision making.
3. Factors that have contributed to the increased need for information include: expanded markets; increased competition; shorter product life cycles; and government regulation.
4. **Managers** of an organization are responsible for performing four different types of tasks: planning, organizing, directing, and controlling.
5. Management is usually divided into three levels: senior management, middle management, and operational management. A fourth level of an organization consists of the production, clerical, and nonmanagement staff.
6. **Senior management** makes strategic decisions and is concerned with the long-range direction of the company.
7. **Strategic decisions** deal with the overall goals and objectives of an organization.
8. **Middle management** makes tactical decisions and is responsible for implementing the strategic decisions of senior management.
9. **Tactical decisions** involve specific programs and plans necessary to accomplish the strategic objectives of an organization.
10. **Operational management** makes operational decisions and provides direct supervision over the production, clerical, and nonmanagement staff of an organization.
11. **Operational decisions** usually involve an immediate action such as accepting or rejecting an inventory delivery or approving a purchase order.
12. The terms used to describe the qualities of information include accurate, verifiable, timely, organized, meaningful, useful, and cost effective.
13. **GIGO** is an acronym that stands for *Garbage In, Garbage Out*.
14. An **information system** is a collection of elements that provide accurate, timely, and useful information. These elements include: equipment, software, accurate data, trained information systems personnel, knowledgeable users, and documented procedures.
15. The types of computer information systems include: (1) operational systems; (2) management information systems; (3) decision support systems; and (4) expert systems.
16. **Operational systems** process data generated by the day-to-day transactions of an organization.
17. **Executive information systems (EIS)** are management information systems that have been designed for the information needs of senior management.
18. A **decision support system (DSS)** is a system designed to help someone reach a decision by summarizing or comparing data from either or both internal and external sources.
19. Some decision support systems allow users to create a **model** where they can ask *what-if* questions by changing one or more of the variables and see what the projected results will be.

20. **Expert systems** combine the knowledge on a given subject of one or more human experts into a computerized system that simulates the human experts' reasoning and decision-making processes.
21. Expert systems are made up of the combined subject knowledge of the human experts, called the **knowledge base** and the **inference rules** that determine how the knowledge is used to reach decisions.
22. An exciting branch of computer science is **artificial intelligence**, the application of human intelligence to computer systems.
23. The trend is to combine all of an organization's information needs into a single, integrated information system.
24. The personal computer is playing an increasingly significant role in modern management information systems.

KEY TERMS

Artificial intelligence *10.11*
Decision support system (DSS) *10.9*
Executive information system (EIS) *10.8*
Expert system *10.10*
GIGO *10.6*
Inference rules *10.10*
Information system *10.7*
Knowledge base *10.10*
Manager *10.2*
Management information system (MIS) *10.1*
Middle management *10.5*
Model *10.9*
Operational decision *10.5*
Operational management *10.5*
Operational system *10.7*
Senior management *10.4*
Strategic decision *10.4*
Tactical decision *10.5*

REVIEW QUESTIONS

1. Define the term management information systems. Discuss three ways that the term is used.
2. List five factors that have contributed to the increased need for organizations to have information.
3. Describe the four different types of tasks that managers perform.
4. Identify the three levels of management in an organization, and describe the types of decisions that are made at each level.
5. What are the six qualities that information should have?
6. List the four general types of information systems.
7. What is an EIS? What are some of the user interfaces frequently used with an EIS?
8. Discuss how the personal computer is being used in management information systems.

CONTROVERSIAL ISSUE

1. Some people are concerned that the increased application of expert systems will lead to real life situations of robots gone wild or uncontrollable computers as they are sometimes portrayed in science fiction. Discuss what limits you think should be placed on computerized decision making.

RESEARCH PROJECTS

1. Think of an application for an expert system. Make a list of the inference rules that would be used.
2. Interview a manager at a local company or your school. Ask him or her what information he or she uses to make decisions. Identify the information that is not provided by the computer system being used at the local company or the school. Could it be provided by the system?

The Information System Life Cycle

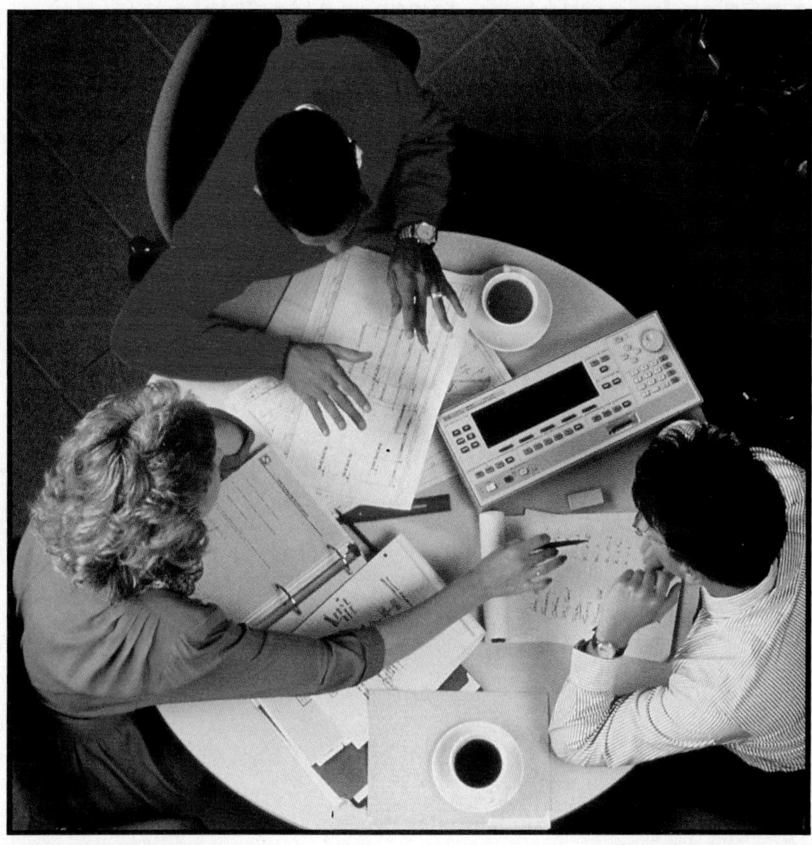

Every day, competition, government regulations, and other such influences cause people to face new challenges as they try to obtain the information they need to perform their jobs. A new product, a new sales commission plan, or a change in tax rates are just three examples of why an organization must change the way it processes information. Sometimes, these challenges can be met by existing methods but other times, meeting the challenge requires an entirely new way of processing data. In these cases, a new or modified information system is needed. As a computer user, either as an individual or within your organization, it is very likely that someday you will participate in acquiring, developing, or modifying a system. Creating an information system can be described by phases known as the information system life cycle. In this chapter, we illustrate each phase of the system life cycle by using a case study about the wholesale auto parts division of the Sutherland Company.

OBJECTIVES

- Explain the phases and paths of the information system life cycle
- Explain the importance of project management and documentation
- Define commercial applications software and describe the difference between horizontal and vertical applications
- Discuss each of the steps of acquiring commercial applications software
- Discuss the reasons for developing custom software
- Describe how various analysis and design tools, such as data flow diagrams, are used
- Explain how program development is part of the information system life cycle
- Explain several methods that can be used for a conversion to a new system
- Discuss the installation and maintenance of an information system

WHAT IS THE INFORMATION SYSTEM LIFE CYCLE?

The **information system life cycle (ISLC)** is an organized approach to obtaining an information system. Regardless of the type or complexity of an information system, the structured process of the information system life cycle should be followed whenever an information system is acquired or developed. The activities of the information system life cycle can be grouped into distinct phases.

The Phases of the Information System Life Cycle

As shown in Figure 11-1, the phases of the information system life cycle are:

- Analysis
- Acquisition or Design
- Customizing or Development
- Implementation
- Maintenance

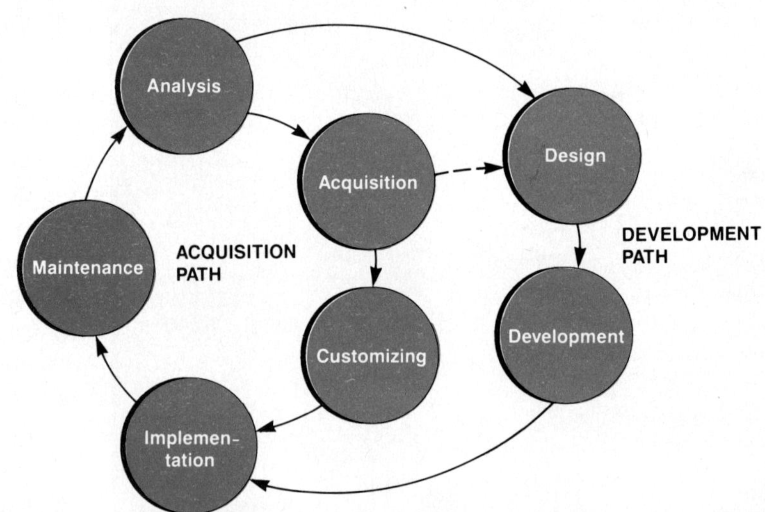

FIGURE 11-1
The information system life cycle consists of several phases. The phases of the acquistion path are analysis, acquisition, customizing, implementation, and maintenance. The phases of the development path include analysis, design, development, implementation, and maintenance.

Each of the phases includes important activities that relate to the acquisition or development of an information system.

As Figure 11-1 also shows, there is an acquisition path and a development path in the information system life cycle. After the analysis phase, an organization can either choose to acquire a system by purchasing software or develop one by writing their own software. If an organization does not find a suitable system during the acquisition phase, it will move to the design phase of the development path. All systems have analysis, implementation, and maintenance phases.

Before explaining each of the phases, we will discuss project management and documentation because these two activities are ongoing processes that are performed throughout the cycle. First, we will identify the information system specialists and users who participate in the various phases of the ISLC.

Project Management

Project management involves planning, scheduling, reporting, and controlling the individual activities that make up the information system development life cycle. These activities are usually recorded in a **project plan** on a week-by-week basis that includes an estimate of the time to complete the activity and the start and finish dates. As you might expect, the start of many activities depends on the successful completion of other activities. For example, implementation activities cannot begin until you have completed at least some, if not all, of the development activities. An effective way of showing the relationship of project activities is with a Gantt chart (Figure 11-2). A Gantt chart usually shows time across the top of the chart and a list of activities to be completed down the left side. Marks on the chart indicate when an activity begins and is completed. Lines or bars between the marks indicate progress toward completing the task.

The importance of maintaining a realistic schedule for project management cannot be overstated. Without a realistic schedule, the success of a development project is in jeopardy from the start. If project members do not believe the schedule is realistic, they may not participate to the full extent of their abilities. Project management is a place for realistic, not wishful, thinking.

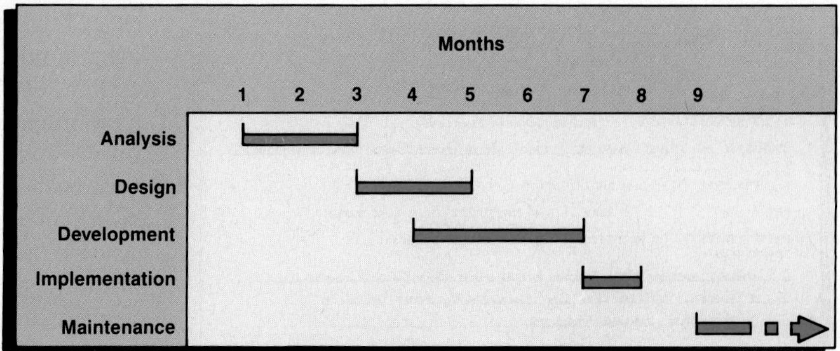

FIGURE 11-2
A Gantt chart is often used in project management to show the time relationships of the project activities.

Project management should be practiced throughout the development process. In most projects, activities need frequent rescheduling. Some activities will take less time than originally planned and others will take longer. To measure the impact of the actual results and revised estimates, they should be recorded regularly and a revised project plan issued. Project management software provides an efficient method of recording results and revising project plans.

Documentation

Documentation refers to written materials that are produced as part of the information system development life cycle such as a report describing the overall purpose of the system or layout forms that are used to design reports and screens. Documentation should be identified and agreed on prior to beginning the project. Well-written, thorough documentation makes it easier for users and others to understand why particular decisions are made. Too often, documentation is put off until the completion of a project and is never adequately finished. Documentation should be an ongoing part of the entire development process and should not be thought of as a separate phase. Well-written, thorough documentation can also extend the useful life of a system. Unfortunately, systems are sometimes replaced simply because no one understands how they work.

Who Participates in the Information System Development Life Cycle?

Every person who will be affected by the new system should have the opportunity to participate in its development. The participants fall into two categories: users and information system personnel such as systems analysts and computer programmers. The systems analyst works closely with both the users and the programmers to define the system. The systems analyst's job is challenging, requiring good communication, analytical, and diplomatic skills to keep the development process on track and on schedule. Good communication skills are especially important during analysis, the first phase of the information system life cycle.

ANALYSIS PHASE

Analysis is the separation of a system into its parts to determine how the system works. In addition, the analysis phase of a project also includes the identification of a proposed solution to the problems identified in the current system. A system project can originate in several ways, but a common way is for the manager of a user department, such as accounting or personnel, to contact the information systems department with a request for assistance. The initial request may be oral, but it is eventually written on a standard form that becomes the first item of documentation (Figure 11-3). In most organizations, requests for new system projects exceed the capacity of the information systems department to implement them. Therefore, the manager of the systems department must review each request and make a preliminary determination as to the potential benefit for the company. Requests for large development projects, such as an entirely new system, are often reviewed by committees made up of both user and information systems personnel and representatives of top management. When the managers of both the user and information systems departments determine that a request warrants further review, one or more systems analysts will be assigned to begin a preliminary investigation, the first step in the analysis phase.

REQUEST FOR SYSTEM SERVICES

ISD CONTROL #: 2143

I. To Be Completed By Person Requesting Services

SUBMITTED BY: MIKE CHARLES DEPT: AUTO PARTS SALES DATE: 1/22/92

REQUEST TYPE: ☐ MODIFICATION ✓ NEW SYSTEM

NEED: ☐ ASAP ✓ IMMEDIATE ☐ LONG RANGE

BRIEF STATEMENT OF REQUEST (attach additional material, if necessary)

NEED AUTOMATED ORDER ENTRY AND INVOICING CAPABILITY. MANUAL PROCEDURES CAN NO LONGER KEEP UP WITH INCREASED SALES VOLUME.

☐ ADDITIONAL MATERIAL ATTACHED

II. To Be Completed By Information Systems Department

REQUEST INVESTIGATED BY: FRANK PEACOCK DATE: 2/4/92

COMMENTS: MANUAL INVOICING RUNNING 3 DAYS BEHIND SHIPMENTS. RECOMMEND DETAILED SYSTEM ANALYSIS FOR DEVELOPMENT OF COMPUTERIZED SYSTEM.

III. Disposition

✓ REQUEST APPROVED FOR IMMEDIATE IMPLEMENTATION

☐ ANALYST ASSIGNED: MARY RUIZ

☐ REQUEST APPROVED FOR IMPLEMENTATION AS SOON AS POSSIBLE

☐ REQUEST REJECTED

COMMENTS:

SIGNED: George Lucey DATE: 2/15/92

FIGURE 11-3
The system development project usually starts with a request from a user. The request should be documented on a form such as this one to provide a record of the action taken.

The Preliminary Investigation

The purpose of the **preliminary investigation** is to determine if a request justifies further detailed investigation and analysis. The most important aspect of the preliminary investigation is **problem definition**, the identification of the true nature of the problem. Often the stated problem and the real problem are not the same. For example, suppose the manager of the accounting department requests a new accounts receivable report that shows recent customer payments. An investigation might reveal that the existing accounts receivable reports would be acceptable if the customer payments were recorded daily instead of once a week. The real problem is that customer payments are being recorded too late to be included in the existing reports. Thus, the preliminary investigation determines the real source of the problem.

The preliminary investigation begins with an interview of the manager who submitted the request. Depending on the request, other users can be interviewed as well. For example, a request might involve data or a process that affects more than one department or clerical workers may have to be interviewed to obtain detail information.

The preliminary investigation is usually quite short when compared to the remainder of the project. At the end of the investigation, the systems analyst presents the findings to both user and information system management and recommends the next action. Sometimes the results of a preliminary investigation indicate an obvious solution that can be implemented at minimal cost. Other times, however, the only thing the preliminary investigation does is confirm that there is a problem that needs further study. In these cases, detailed system analysis is recommended. The user, the information systems management, and the systems analyst work together to decide how to proceed.

Detailed System Analysis

Detailed system analysis involves both a thorough study of the current system and at least one proposed solution to the problems found.

The study of the current system is important for two reasons. First, it helps increase the systems analyst's understanding of the activities that a new system might perform. Second, and perhaps most important, studying the current system builds a relationship between the systems analyst and the user. The systems analyst will have much more credibility with users if he or she understands how the users currently do their job. This may seem an obvious point, but surprisingly, many systems are created or modified without studying the current system or without adequately involving the users.

The basic fact-gathering techniques used during the detailed system analysis are: (1) interviews, (2) questionnaires, (3) reviewing current system documentation, and (4) observing current procedures. During this phase of the system study, the systems analyst must develop a critical, questioning approach to each procedure within the current system to determine what is actually taking place. Often systems analysts find that operations are being performed not because they are efficient or effective, but because they have always been done this way.

Information gathered during this phase includes: (1) the output of the current system, (2) the input to the current system, and (3) the procedures used to produce the output.

An increasingly popular method for documenting this information is called structured analysis. **Structured analysis** is the use of analysis and design tools such as data flow diagrams, data dictionaries, process specifications, structured English, decision tables, and decision trees to document the specifications of an information system.

Data Flow Diagrams One of the difficulties in analyzing any system is how to document the findings in a way that can be understood by users, programmers, and other systems analysts. Structured analysis addresses this problem by using graphics to represent the flow of data. These graphics are called data flow diagrams.

A **data flow diagram (DFD)** graphically shows the flow of data through a system. The key elements of a DFD (Figure 11-4) are arrows, or vectors, called data flows that represent data; circles (also called bubbles) that represent processes such as verifying an order or creating an invoice; parallel lines that represent data files; and squares, called sources, or sinks, that represent either or both an originator or a receiver of data such as a customer.

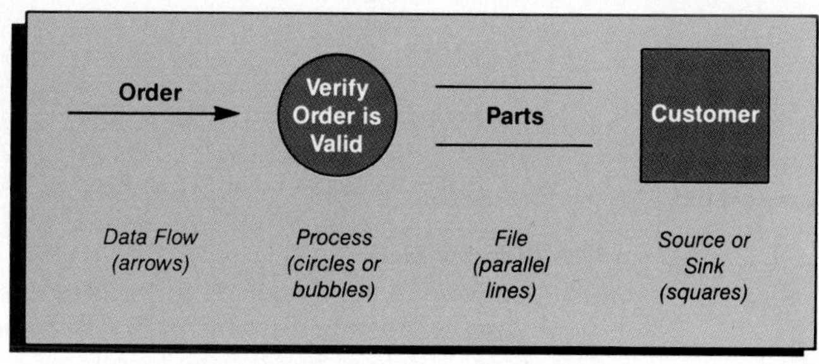

FIGURE 11-4
The symbols used to create data flow diagrams.

Because they are visual, DFDs are particularly useful for reviewing the existing or proposed system with the user (Figure 11-5). One of the features of DFDs is that they are done on a level-by-level basis. The top level would only identify major processes and flows. Lower levels further define the higher levels. For example, in Figure 11-5 the Apply Invoice Payment process in the lower left corner could have its own separate DFD to define subprocesses that take place.

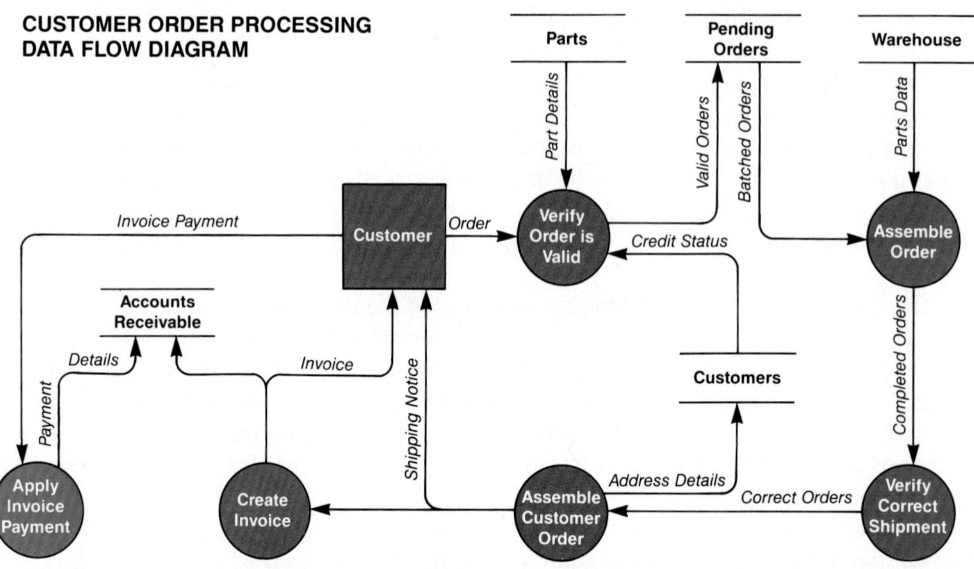

FIGURE 11-5
Data flow diagrams (DFDs) are used to graphically illustrate the flow of information through a system. The customer (box) both originates and receives data (arrows). The circles indicate where actions take place on the data. Files are shown as parallel lines.

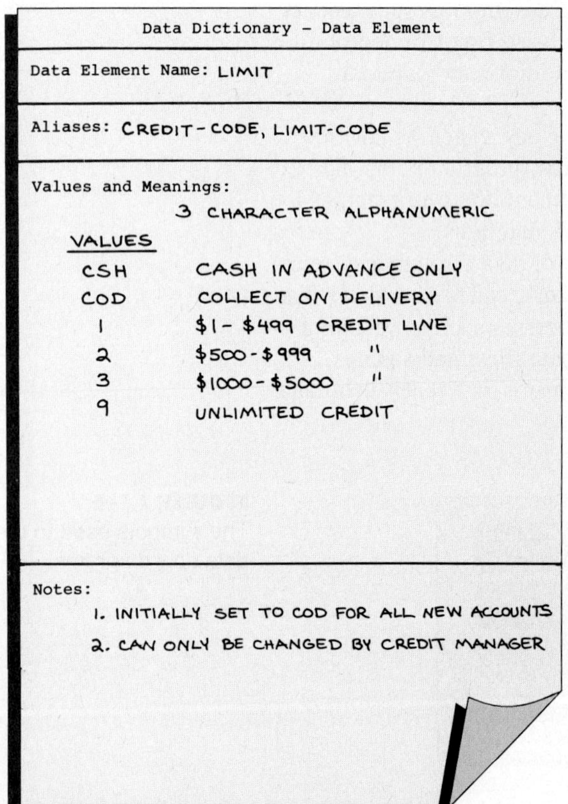

Data Dictionary - Data Element

Data Element Name: LIMIT

Aliases: CREDIT-CODE, LIMIT-CODE

Values and Meanings:
3 CHARACTER ALPHANUMERIC

VALUES	
CSH	CASH IN ADVANCE ONLY
COD	COLLECT ON DELIVERY
1	$1 - $499 CREDIT LINE
2	$500 - $999 "
3	$1000 - $5000 "
9	UNLIMITED CREDIT

Notes:
1. INITIALLY SET TO COD FOR ALL NEW ACCOUNTS
2. CAN ONLY BE CHANGED BY CREDIT MANAGER

Data Dictionaries The **data dictionary** describes the elements that make up the data flow. Each element can be thought of as equivalent to a field in a record. The data dictionary also includes information about the attributes of each element such as length, where the element is used (which files and data flows include the element), and any values or ranges the element might have, such as a value of 2 in Figure 11-6 for a credit limit code to indicate a purchase limit of $1,000.00. The data dictionary is created by the systems analyst in the analysis phase and is used in all subsequent phases of the information system life cycle. Although data dictionaries are often first prepared manually, they are usually entered and maintained on a computer system.

FIGURE 11-6
A data dictionary form such as this one is used to document each of the data elements that are included in the data flows. The form records the length, type of data, and possible values for each data element.

Structured English **Process specifications** describe and document what happens to a data flow when it reaches a process circle. For example in Figure 11-5, process specifications describe what goes on in each of the circles. One way of writing process specifications is to use **structured English**, a style of writing and presentation that highlights the alternatives and actions that are part of the process. Figure 11-7 shows an example of a structured English process specification describing a policy for order processing.

```
If the order amount exceeds $1,000,
    If customer has any unpaid invoices over 90 days old,
        Do not issue order confirmation,
        Write message on order reject report.
    Otherwise (account is in good standing),
        Issue order confirmation.
Otherwise (order is $1,000 or less),
    If customer has any unpaid invoices over 90 days old,
        Issue order confirmation,
        Write message on credit follow-up report.
    Otherwise (account is in good standing),
        Issue order confirmation.
```

FIGURE 11-7
Structured English is an organized way of describing what actions are taken on data. This structured English example describes an order processing policy.

Decision Tables and Decision Trees Another way of documenting the system during the analysis phase is with a decision table or decision tree. A **decision table** or a **decision tree** identifies the actions that should be taken under different conditions. Figures 11-8 and 11-9 show a decision table and decision tree for the order processing policy described with structured English in Figure 11-7. Decision tables and trees are an excellent way of showing the desired action when the action depends on multiple conditions.

	Rules			
	1	2	3	4
Conditions				
1. Order > $1,000	Y	Y	N	N
2. Unpaid invoices over 90 days old	Y	N	Y	N
Actions				
1. Issue confirmation	N	Y	Y	Y
2. Reject order	Y	N	N	N
3. Credit follow-up	N	N	Y	N

FIGURE 11-8
Decision tables help a user quickly determine the course of action based on two or more conditions. This decision table is based on the order processing policy described in Figure 11-7. For example, if an order is $1,000 or less and the customer has an unpaid invoice over 90 days old, the policy (Rule 3) is to issue an order confirmation and perform a credit follow-up on the past due invoice.

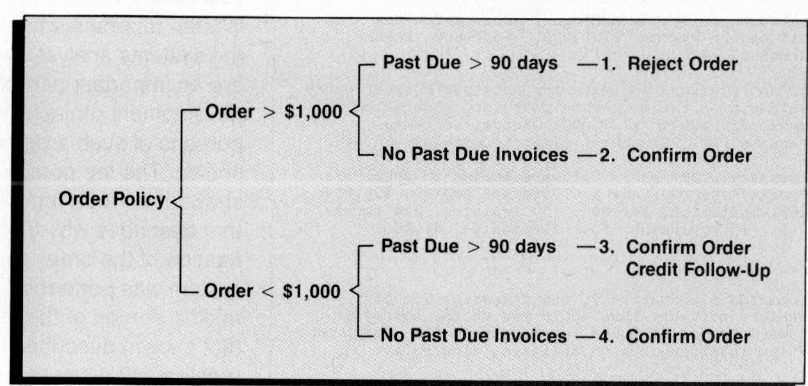

FIGURE 11-9
Like a decision table, a decision tree illustrates the action to be taken based on the given conditions, but presents it graphically. This decision tree is based on the order processing policy described in Figure 11-7.

Making the Decision on How to Proceed

Just as at the completion of the preliminary investigation, at the completion of the analysis phase, the user, systems analyst, and management face another decision on how to proceed. At this point the systems analyst should have completed a study of the current system and, using the same tools and methods, developed one or more proposed solutions to the current system's identified problems. Sometimes, the systems analyst is asked to prepare a feasibility study and a cost/benefit analysis. These two reports are often used together. The **feasibility study** discusses whether the proposed solution is practical and capable of being accomplished. The **cost/benefit analysis** identifies the estimated costs of the proposed solution and the benefits (including potential cost savings) that are expected. If there are strong indications at the beginning of the project that some type of new system will likely be developed, the feasibility study and cost/benefit analysis are sometimes performed as part of the preliminary investigation.

The systems analyst presents the results of his or her work in a written report (Figure 11-10) to both user and information systems management who consider the alternatives and the resources, such as time, people, and money of the organization. The end of the analysis phase is usually when organizations decide either to acquire a commercial software package from an outside source or to develop the software. If a decision is made to proceed, the project enters the acquisition phase if a software package is going to be obtained or the design phase if software is going to be developed. If a suitable software package cannot be found, an organization will start the design phase of the development path.

DATE: April 1, 1992
TO: Management Review Committee
FROM: George Lacey, Corporate Systems Manager
SUBJECT: Detailed Investigation and Analysis of Order Entry System

Introduction

A detailed system investigation and analysis of the order entry system was conducted as a result of approval given by the Management Review Committee on March 1. The findings of the investigation are presented below.

Objectives of Detailed Investigation and Analysis

The study investigated reported problems of the wholesale auto parts order entry system. We have received complaints that orders were not being shipped promptly and that customers were not notified about out-of-stock parts when they placed their orders. In addition, invoices are not sent to customers until twelve to sixteen days after orders are shipped. The objective of this study was to determine where the problems existed and to develop alternative solutions.

Findings of the Detailed Investigation and Analysis

The following problems appear to exist within the order entry system:

Possible Solutions:

1. Acquire a separate minicomputer system and order entry software. Estimated costs: Minicomputer system, $150,000. Software license, $50,000. Annual maintenance, $20,000.

2. Investigate commercial applications software for auto parts order entry and invoicing that would run on the corporate computer. Estimated costs: Software license, $50,000 to $100,000. Annual software maintenance, 10% of license fee. Equipment (four terminals), $6,000.

3. Internally develop necessary order entry software to run on corporate computer. Estimated costs: (1) Systems analysis and design, $26,000; (2) Programming and implementation, $40,000; (3) Training, new forms, and maintenance, $7,000; (4) Equipment (four terminals), $6,000.

Recommended Action

The systems department recommends alternative 2, the investigation of existing commercial applications software that could run on the corporate computer. If suitable software cannot be found, we recommend the design of a computerized order entry and invoicing system utilizing alternative 3.

George Lacey

FIGURE 11-10
Written reports summarizing the systems analyst's work are an important part of the development project. Two portions of such a report are shown. The top portion shows the report introduction that describes why the investigation of the order entry system was performed. The middle portion of the report (not shown) describes the problems that were found during the investigation. The bottom portion shows three possible solutions and the action recommended by the corporate systems manager.

ANALYSIS AT SUTHERLAND

The Sutherland Company is a large corporation with three separate divisions that sell tools, electric motors, and auto parts. Although the tool and electric motor divisions have been computerized for some time, the auto parts division, started just two years ago, has been small enough that it has relied on manual procedures. In the last six months, however, auto parts sales doubled and the manual order entry and invoicing systems are incapable of keeping up with the increased work load.

Mike Charles, the auto parts sales manager, decides to submit a request for system services to the information systems department that provides computer services for all three Sutherland divisions. George Lacey, the head of the Information Systems department assigns Frank Peacock, a senior systems analyst, to investigate Mike's request.

As part of the preliminary investigation, Frank interviews Mike to try to determine the problem. During his interview with Mike and a subsequent tour of the auto parts sales department, Frank discovers that invoices are not being sent to customers until twelve to sixteen days after their parts orders have shipped. In addition, Frank discovers that customers complain about shipments being late and about not being notified when parts they ordered are not available. To quantify the expected increases in sales volume, Frank has Mike prepare the transaction volume summary shown in Figure 11-11. As a result of his preliminary investigation, Frank recommends a detailed system analysis. George Lacey, the corporate systems manager, agrees with Frank's recommendation and assigns systems analyst Mary Ruiz to perform a detailed analysis.

Transaction Volume Summary

	LAST YEAR	CURRENT	1 YEAR	3 YEARS
Number of Customers	175	300	400	600
Orders per Month	525	950	1250	1900
Invoices per Month	600	1100	1375	2100

FIGURE 11-11
A transaction volume summary should be prepared to estimate the projected growth of an application. Systems should be designed to handle the projected volume of transactions, not just the current volume.

Mary reviews Frank's notes and begins to perform a detailed analysis of the auto parts order entry and invoicing systems. As part of her study, Mary interviews several people in the auto parts division and prepares several documents including a data flow diagram (Figure 11-5), a data dictionary definition for the different credit limits assigned to customers (Figure 11-6), and a structured English statement of the order processing policy (Figure 11-7).

After studying the manual procedures for a week, Mary discusses her findings with her supervisor, George Lacey. Based on Mary's work, George writes a report to the management review committee recommending that the order entry and invoicing systems be computerized (Figure 11-10). The report contains three possible solutions; one, obtain a separate minicomputer system; two, obtain a commercial applications software package to run on the corporate computer; and three, internally develop the necessary software for the corporate computer. Before proceeding to develop the necessary software internally, George recommends that Sutherland try to find a suitable commercial software package that would run on Sutherland's central computer. The management review committee meets every month to review requests for additional computer equipment and software. The committee is made up of top management representatives from each division, the finance department, and the information systems department. Based on George's report, the management review committee authorizes the corporate systems department to try and find a commercial package to satisfy the auto parts division's order entry and invoicing requirements.

ACQUISITION PHASE

Once the analysis phase has been completed, the **acquisition** phase begins; it has four steps: (1) summarizing the application requirements, (2) identifying potential software vendors, (3) evaluating software alternatives, and (4) making the purchase. Before we describe these steps, let's discuss commercial applications software.

What is Commercial Applications Software?

Commercial applications software is software that has already been developed and is available for purchase. Prewritten software is available for computers of all sizes. Most users know about the numerous application packages available for microcomputers. In addition, users should be aware that numerous packages are available for larger machines. This section discusses the categories of commercial applications software that are available, how to determine software requirements, and how to acquire the software. This information is important to know because it is very likely that some day you will either acquire applications software for yourself or participate in software selection for your organization.

It's probably safe to say that at least some part of every type of business, government branch, or recreational pastime has been computerized. Figure 11-12 is an excerpt from a category listing from an applications software catalog. Within each category, numerous programs are available to perform different types of tasks. This catalog contains listings for over 20,000 individual software packages. Notice that this list is divided into two parts: nonindustry specific and industry specific. The more commonly used terms are horizontal and vertical applications.

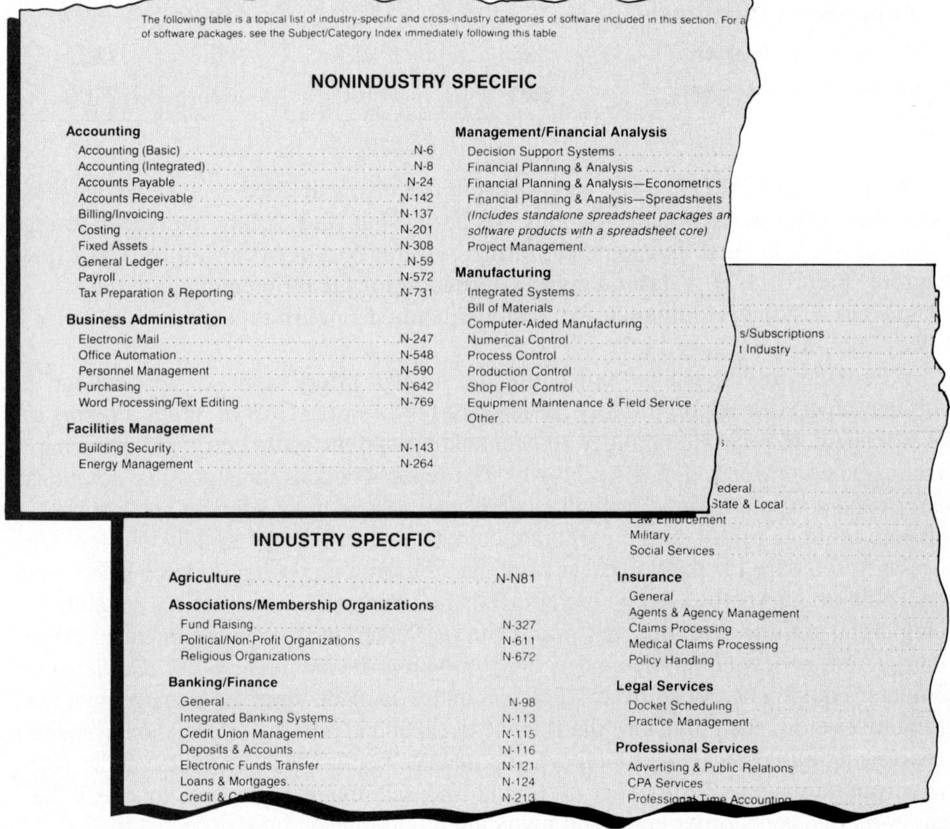

The following table is a topical list of industry-specific and cross-industry categories of software included in this section. For a of software packages, see the Subject/Category Index immediately following this table

NONINDUSTRY SPECIFIC

Accounting
Accounting (Basic) N-6
Accounting (Integrated) N-8
Accounts Payable N-24
Accounts Receivable N-142
Billing/Invoicing N-137
Costing N-201
Fixed Assets N-308
General Ledger N-59
Payroll N-572
Tax Preparation & Reporting N-731

Business Administration
Electronic Mail N-247
Office Automation N-548
Personnel Management N-590
Purchasing N-642
Word Processing/Text Editing N-769

Facilities Management
Building Security N-143
Energy Management N-264

Management/Financial Analysis
Decision Support Systems
Financial Planning & Analysis
Financial Planning & Analysis—Econometrics
Financial Planning & Analysis—Spreadsheets
(Includes standalone spreadsheet packages an software products with a spreadsheet core)
Project Management

Manufacturing
Integrated Systems
Bill of Materials
Computer-Aided Manufacturing
Numerical Control
Process Control
Production Control
Shop Floor Control
Equipment Maintenance & Field Service
Other

s/Subscriptions
t Industry

ederal
State & Local
Law Enforcement
Military
Social Services

INDUSTRY SPECIFIC

Agriculture N-N81

Associations/Membership Organizations
Fund Raising N-327
Political/Non-Profit Organizations N-611
Religious Organizations N-672

Banking/Finance
General N-98
Integrated Banking Systems N-113
Credit Union Management N-115
Deposits & Accounts N-116
Electronic Funds Transfer N-121
Loans & Mortgages N-124
Credit & C N-213

Insurance
General
Agents & Agency Management
Claims Processing
Medical Claims Processing
Policy Handling

Legal Services
Docket Scheduling
Practice Management

Professional Services
Advertising & Public Relations
CPA Services
Professional Time Accounting

FIGURE 11-12
An excerpt from a category listing in an applications software catalog that contains information on over 20,000 individual software packages.

Horizontal application software is software that can be used by many different types of organizations. Accounting packages are a good example of horizontal applications because they apply to most organizations. If, however, an organization has a unique way of doing business, then it requires a package that has been developed specifically for that job. Software developed for a unique way of doing business, usually within a specific industry, is called **vertical application software**. Examples of specific industries that use vertical software include food service, construction, and real estate. Each of these industries has unique information processing requirements.

The difference between horizontal and vertical application software is important to understand. If you become involved in selecting software, one of the first things you will have to decide is how unique is the task for which you are trying to obtain software. If the task is not unique to your business, you will probably be able to use a horizontal application package. Horizontal application packages tend to be widely available (because they can be used by a greater number of organizations) and less expensive. If your task is unique to your type of organization, you will probably have to search for a vertical software solution. Often an organization's total software requirements are made up of a combination of unique and common requirements.

Now that we understand what commercial applications software is, let's discuss the steps used to acquire it.

FIGURE 11-13
A request for proposal (RFP) documents the key features that a user wants in a software package.

REQUEST FOR PROPOSAL
ACCOUNTS PAYABLE

Features	Standard Feature	Comments
1. Interface to general ledger	✓	
2. Matching to receiving documents	✓	
3. Matching to purchasing documents	✓	
4. Automatic check printing	✓	
5. Recurring payments		PLANNING FOR NEXT RELEASE
6. Flexible payment selection	✓	
7. Checking statement reconciliation		WILL DO ON CUSTOM BASIS
8. Consolidated check preparation	✓	
9. Duplicate invoice check		NO PLANS FOR THIS FEATURE
10. Manual check processing	✓	
Reports		
1. Vendor listing	✓	BY NAME, BUYER
2. Invoice register	✓	
3. Check register	✓	
4. Cash requirements	✓	WEEKLY & MONTHLY
5. Detail aging	✓	30, 60, 90, 120+ DAYS
6. Form 1099 reports		PLANNED FOR NEXT RELEASE
7. Account distribution	✓	
8. Bank statement reconciliation		WILL DO ON CUSTOM BASIS

Summarizing the Application Requirements

One way organizations summarize their software requirements is in a request for proposal. A **request for proposal**, or **RFP**, is a written list of an organization's software requirements. This list is given to prospective software vendors to help the vendors determine if they have a product that is a possible software solution. Just as the depth of application evaluations varies, so do RFPs. RFPs for simple applications might be only a single page consisting of the key features and a transaction volume summary. Other RFPs for large systems might consist of over a hundred pages that identify both key and secondary desired features. An example of a page from an RFP is shown in Figure 11-13.

Identifying Potential Software Vendors

After you have an idea of the software features you want, your next step is to locate potential vendors that sell the type of software you are interested in buying. If the software will be implemented on a personal computer, a good place to start looking for software is a local computer store. Most computer stores have a wide selection of applications software and can suggest several packages for you to consider. If you have prepared an RFP, even a simple one, it will help the store representative to narrow the choices. If you require software for a minicomputer or mainframe, you won't find it at the local personal computer store. For this type of software, which can cost tens to hundreds of thousands of dollars, the best place to start is the computer manufacturer.

In addition to having some software themselves, most manufacturers have a list of software companies with which they work—companies that specialize in developing software for the manufacturer's equipment. **Software houses** are businesses that specialize in developing software for sale. **System houses** not only sell software but also sell the equipment. System houses usually take full responsibility for equipment, software, installation, and training. Sometimes, they even provide equipment maintenance, although this is usually left to the equipment manufacturer. The advantage of dealing with a system house is that the user has to deal with only a single company for the entire system.

Another place to find software suppliers, especially for vertical applications, is to look in trade publications, magazines written for specific businesses or industries. Companies and individuals who have written software for these industries often advertise in the trade publications. Some industry trade groups also maintain lists of companies that provide specific software solutions.

For horizontal applications, many computer magazines publish regular reviews of individual packages and often have annual reviews of several packages of the same type. Figure 11-14 shows a software review of an accounting package.

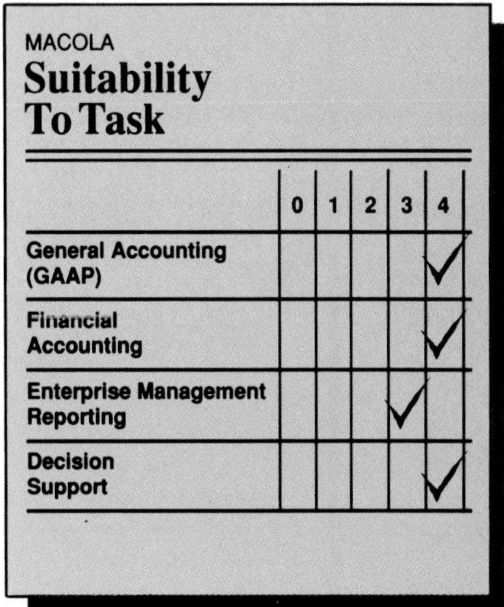

MACOLA
Suitability To Task

	0	1	2	3	4
General Accounting (GAAP)					✓
Financial Accounting					✓
Enterprise Management Reporting				✓	
Decision Support					✓

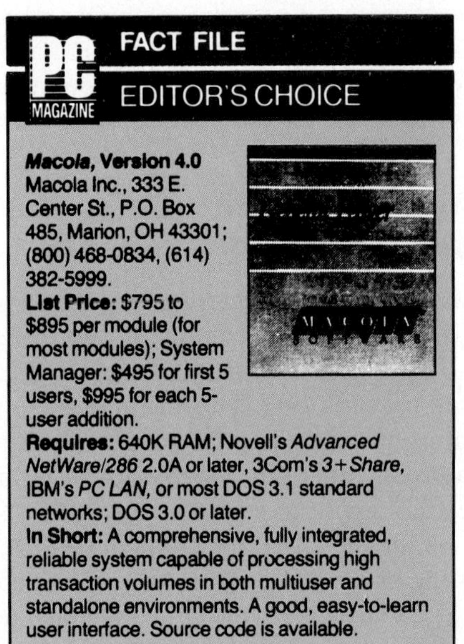

PC MAGAZINE FACT FILE
EDITOR'S CHOICE

Macola, Version 4.0
Macola Inc., 333 E. Center St., P.O. Box 485, Marion, OH 43301; (800) 468-0834, (614) 382-5999.
List Price: $795 to $895 per module (for most modules); System Manager: $495 for first 5 users, $995 for each 5-user addition.
Requires: 640K RAM; Novell's *Advanced NetWare/286* 2.0A or later, 3Com's *3+Share*, IBM's *PC LAN*, or most DOS 3.1 standard networks; DOS 3.0 or later.
In Short: A comprehensive, fully integrated, reliable system capable of processing high transaction volumes in both multiuser and standalone environments. A good, easy-to-learn user interface. Source code is available.

FIGURE 11-14
Many publications regularly evaluate applications software. This review includes a narrative discussion of the package.

Another way to identify software suppliers is to hire a knowledgeable consultant. Although the fee paid to a consultant increases your software costs, it may be worth it, considering the real cost of making a bad decision. Many consultants specialize in assisting organizations of all sizes to identify and implement software packages. A good place to start looking for a consultant would be to contact professional organizations in your industry. Your accountant may also be able to recommend a possible software solution or a consultant.

Evaluating Software Alternatives

After you have identified several possible software solutions, you have to evaluate them and choose one. First, match each choice against your original requirements list. Be as objective as possible—try not to be influenced by the salesperson or representative demonstrating the software or the appeal of the marketing literature. Match each package against your list or RFP and give each package a score. If some key features are more important than others, take that into consideration. Try to complete this rating either during or immediately after a demonstration of the package while the features are still fresh in your mind (Figure 11-15).

The next step is to talk to existing users of the software. For minicomputer and mainframe software packages, software vendors routinely provide user references. User references are important because if a software package does (or doesn't) work for an organization like yours, it probably will (or won't) work for you. For personal computer packages, if the computer store can't provide references, call the software manufacturer directly.

Finally, try the software yourself. For a small application, this may be as simple as entering a few simple transactions using a demonstration copy of the software at the computer store. For large applications, it may require one or more days of testing at the vendor's office or on your existing computer to be sure that the software meets your needs.

If you are concerned about whether the software can handle a certain transaction volume efficiently, you may want to perform a benchmark test. A **benchmark test** measures the time it takes to process a set number of transactions. For example, a benchmark test might consist of measuring the time it takes a particular software package to produce a sales summary report using 1,000 sales transactions. Comparing the time it takes different packages to perform the same task using the same data and the same equipment is one way of measuring the packages' relative performance.

FIGURE 11-15
You should ask to see a demonstration of any program you are considering purchasing. During or after the demonstration, you should rate how well the package meets your requirements.

Making the Purchase

When you purchase software you usually don't own it. What you are actually purchasing is a **software license** (Figure 11-16), the right to use the software under certain terms and conditions. One of the usual terms and conditions of a software license is that you can use the software on a single computer only. In fact, some software is licensed to a specific computer and the serial number of the system is recorded in the license agreement. Other license restrictions include prohibitions against making the software available to others (for example, renting it or leasing it) and modifying or translating the software into another language. These restrictions are designed to protect the rights of the software developer, who doesn't want someone else to benefit unfairly from the developer's work. For personal computer users, software license terms and conditions usually cannot be modified. But for minicomputer and mainframe users, terms of the license agreements can be modified and, therefore, should be carefully reviewed and considered a part of the overall software selection process. Modifications to the software license are generally easier to obtain before the sale is made than after.

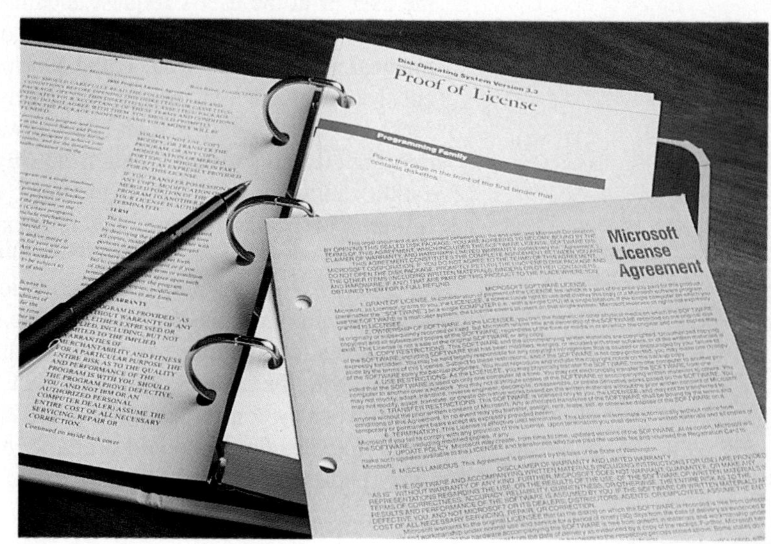

FIGURE 11-16
A software license grants the purchaser the right to use the software but does not include ownership rights.

ACQUISITION AT SUTHERLAND

Based on the directions of the management review committee, a software selection committee is formed with Mike Charles as the chairperson. Mary Ruiz and Frank Peacock from the MIS department are also members as are the order entry and billing supervisors from the auto parts division. Also asked to participate is Bill Comer, computer systems specialist with Sutherland's CPA firm. Mary and Frank take the information developed during the analysis phase and summarize it into a request for proposal (RFP). The RFP is sent to ten software vendors which Bill Comer has identified. Eight of the ten vendors send a response to the RFP within the one month deadline set by Sutherland. Most of the vendors had contacted and visited the auto parts operation to gather information necessary for their responses. Of the eight replies, Sutherland chooses three vendors for further discussions. The committee eliminates five of the vendors because they believe that these systems do not meet the requirements of an auto parts distributor. The software selection committee visits the offices of all three remaining software vendors for a thorough demonstration of their respective packages. In addition, the committee visits a customer of each of the three vendors. The vendor and customer site visits are conducted over a one-month period.

At this point, Sutherland faces a difficult choice. None of the commercial software packages is significantly better than the other and all three have areas that have to be substantially modified to meet Sutherland's way of doing business. The software selection committee summarizes their findings in a report to the management review committee. After discussing the report, the management review committee authorizes the MIS department to begin development of an order entry and invoicing system to run on Sutherland's existing computer system.

COMMERCIAL APPLICATIONS VERSUS CUSTOM SOFTWARE

Each year, the number of applications software packages increases. With all that software available, why would an organization choose to develop its own applications? There could be several reasons. The most common reason is that the organization's software requirements are so unique that it is unable to find a package that will meet its needs. In such a case, the organization would choose to develop the software itself or have it developed specifically for them. Applications software that is developed by the user or at the user's request is called **custom software**. An example of a requirement for custom software might be a government agency that is implementing a new medical assistance service. If the service has new forms and procedures and is different from previous services, it is unlikely that any appropriate software exists. Another reason to develop rather than buy software is that the new software must work with existing custom software. This is an important point to keep in mind; once an organization chooses to use custom software, it will usually choose custom software for future applications as well. This is because it is often difficult to make custom software work with purchased software. The following example illustrates this point.

Let's say a company that has previously developed a custom inventory control software system now wants to computerize their order entry function. Order entry software packages allow the user to sell merchandise from stock and, therefore, must work closely with the inventory files. In fact, many order entry systems are sold together with inventory control systems. If the company wants to retain its existing inventory control application, it would probably have a hard time finding a commercial order entry package that would be able to work with its custom inventory files. This is because the software and the file structures used in the commercial package will not be the same as the existing software. For this reason, the company would probably decide to develop a custom order entry application.

Both custom and commercial software have their advantages and disadvantages. The advantage of custom software is that if it is correctly done, it will match an organization's exact requirements. The disadvantages of custom software are that it is one of a kind, difficult to change, often poorly documented, and usually more expensive than commercial software. In addition, custom software projects are often difficult to manage and complete on time.

The advantage of commercial software is that it's ready to install immediately. After sufficient training, usually provided by the vendor who developed or sold the software, people can begin using the software for productive work. The disadvantage of commercial software is that an organization will probably have to change some of its methods and procedures to adapt to the way the commercial software functions.

A good guideline for evaluating your need for custom or commercial software is to look for a package with an 80% or better fit with your requirements. If there is less than an 80% fit, an organization should either consider custom software or reevaluate its requirements. Figure 11-17 shows the most likely software solutions for different application requirements.

FIGURE 11-17
Software guidelines for different types of applications.

APPLICATION CHARACTERISTICS	APPLICATION EXAMPLE	MOST LIKELY SOFTWARE SOLUTION
Applicable to many different types or organizations	Accounts receivable	Horizontal application package
Specific to a particular type of business or organization	Hotel room reservations	Vertical application package
Unique to a specific organization or business	Space shuttle launch program	Custom software

CUSTOMIZING PHASE

Ideally, acquired commercial applications software will meet 80% or more of an organization's requirements. But what about the other 20% or so? For these requirements, the organization has two choices: change their way of doing business to match the way the software works or modify the way the software works to match their organization. Usually, they will choose a combination of the two alternatives.

Modifying a commercial application package is usually referred to as **customizing**, or **tailoring**. The process of customizing a commercial package involves the following four steps:

1. Identifying potential modifications.
2. Determining the impact of changing current operations to match the software and thus avoiding making a modification.
3. Specifying the amount of work required to make the modifications and the corresponding cost.
4. Choosing which modifications will be made. If possible, the modifications should be made prior to the system being implemented. This avoids users having to relearn how the system works.

Some software vendors do not recommend or support modifications to their packages. Other vendors facilitate modifications by providing copies of the programs or by doing the modifications themselves, usually for a fee. Generally speaking, the larger and more expensive the application package, the more likely that modifications will be required and will be permitted.

CUSTOMIZING AT SUTHERLAND

Because the software selection committee does not choose a commercial applications software package, the customizing phase does not take place at Sutherland.

DESIGN PHASE

The proposed solution developed as part of the analysis phase usually consists of what is called a **logical design**, which means that the design was deliberately developed without regard to a specific computer or programming language and that no attempt was made to identify which procedures should be automated and which procedures should be manual. This approach avoids early assumptions that might limit the possible solutions.

During the **design** phase the logical design will be transformed into a **physical design** that will identify the procedures to be automated, choose the programming language, and specify the equipment needed for the system.

Structured Design Methods

The system design usually follows one of two methods, top-down design or bottom-up design.

Top-Down Design **Top-down design**, also called **structured design**, focuses on the major functions of the system, such as recording a sale or generating an invoice, and keeps breaking those functions down into smaller and smaller activities, sometimes called modules, that can eventually be programmed. Top-down design is an increasingly popular method because it focuses on the total requirements and helps users and systems analysts reach an early agreement on what the major functions of the new system are.

Bottom-Up Design **Bottom-up design** focuses on the data, particularly the output of the system. The approach used determines what output is needed and moves *up* to the processes needed to produce the output.

In practice, most systems analysts use a combination of the top-down and bottom-up designs. Some information requirements such as payroll checks, for example, have required data elements that lend themselves to bottom-up design. Other requirements, such as management-oriented exception reports that are based on the needs of a particular user, are better suited to a top-down design. Regardless of the structured design method he or she uses, the systems analyst will eventually need to complete the design activities.

Design Activities

Design activities include individual tasks that a systems analyst performs to design an information system. These include designs for the output, input, database, processes, system controls, and testing.

Output Design The design of the output is critical to the successful implementation of the system. Output provides information to the users, and information is the basis for the justification of most computerized systems. For example, most users don't know (or necessarily care) how the data will be processed, but they usually do have clear ideas on how they want the information output to look. Often, requests for new or modified systems begin with a user-prepared draft of a report that the current system doesn't produce. During **output design**, the systems analyst and the user document specific screen and report layouts for output to display or report information from the new system. The example in Figure 11-18 illustrates a report layout form.

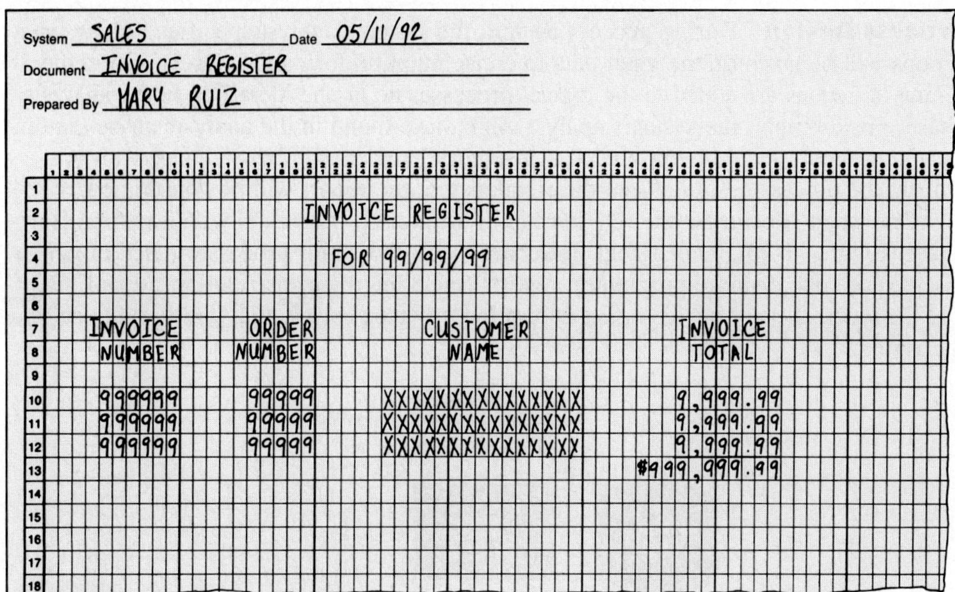

System SALES Date 05/11/92
Document INVOICE REGISTER
Prepared By MARY RUIZ

INVOICE REGISTER
FOR 99/99/99

INVOICE NUMBER	ORDER NUMBER	CUSTOMER NAME	INVOICE TOTAL
999999	99999	XXXXXXXXXXXXXXXXX	9,999.99
999999	99999	XXXXXXXXXXXXXXXXX	9,999.99
999999	99999	XXXXXXXXXXXXXXXXX	9,999.99
			$999,999.99

FIGURE 11-18
The report layout form is used to design printed output. Column titles, data width, and report totals are shown on the layout form.

Input Design During **input design** the systems analyst and the user identify what information needs to be entered into the system to produce the desired output, and where and how the data will be entered. With interactive systems, the systems analyst and the user must determine the sequence of inputs and computer responses, called a **dialogue**, that the user will encounter when he or she enters data. Figure 11-19 shows a display screen layout form commonly used to document the format of a screen display.

COLUMN

ROW	
01	99/99 ** ENTER ORDERS **
02	- SCREEN 1 -
03	
04	CUSTOMER NUMBER: 9999999
05	ORDER NUMBER: 99999
06	
07	BILL TO: XXXXXXXXXXXXXXXXXXXX SHIP TO: XXXXXXXXXXXXXXXXXXXX
08	XXXXXXXXXXXXXXXXXXXX XXXXXXXXXXXXXXXXXXXX
09	XXXXXXXXXXXXXXXXXXXX XXXXXXXXXXXXXXXXXXXX
10	
11	ORDER DATE: 99/99
12	TERMS: XXXXXXXXXXX
13	SALESPERSON: XXXXX
14	DISCOUNT %: 999

FIGURE 11-19
The display screen layout sheet is similar to the report layout form but is used only for information that will be displayed on a screen. Each row and column corresponds to a row and column on the screen.

Database Design During **database design** the systems analyst uses the data dictionary information developed during the analysis phase and merges it into new or existing system files. During this phase of the design, the systems analyst works closely with the database administrator to identify existing database elements that can be used to satisfy design requirements.

Efficient file design can be a challenging task, especially with relational database systems that stress minimum data redundancy (duplicate data). The systems analyst must also consider the volume of database activity. For example, large files that will be frequently accessed may need a separate index file to allow inquiries to be processed in an amount of time acceptable to the user.

Process Design During **process design**, the systems analyst specifies exactly what actions will be taken on the input data to create output information. Decisions on the timing of actions are added to the logical processes he or she identified in the analysis phase. For example, the systems analyst might have found in the analysis phase that an exception report should be produced if inventory balances fall below a certain level. During the process design phase, the frequency of the report will be determined.

One way to document the relationship of different processes is with a **system flowchart** (Figure 11-20). The system flowchart shows the major processes (each of which may require one or more programs), reports (including their distribution), data files, and the types of input devices such as terminals or tape drives, that will provide data to the system.

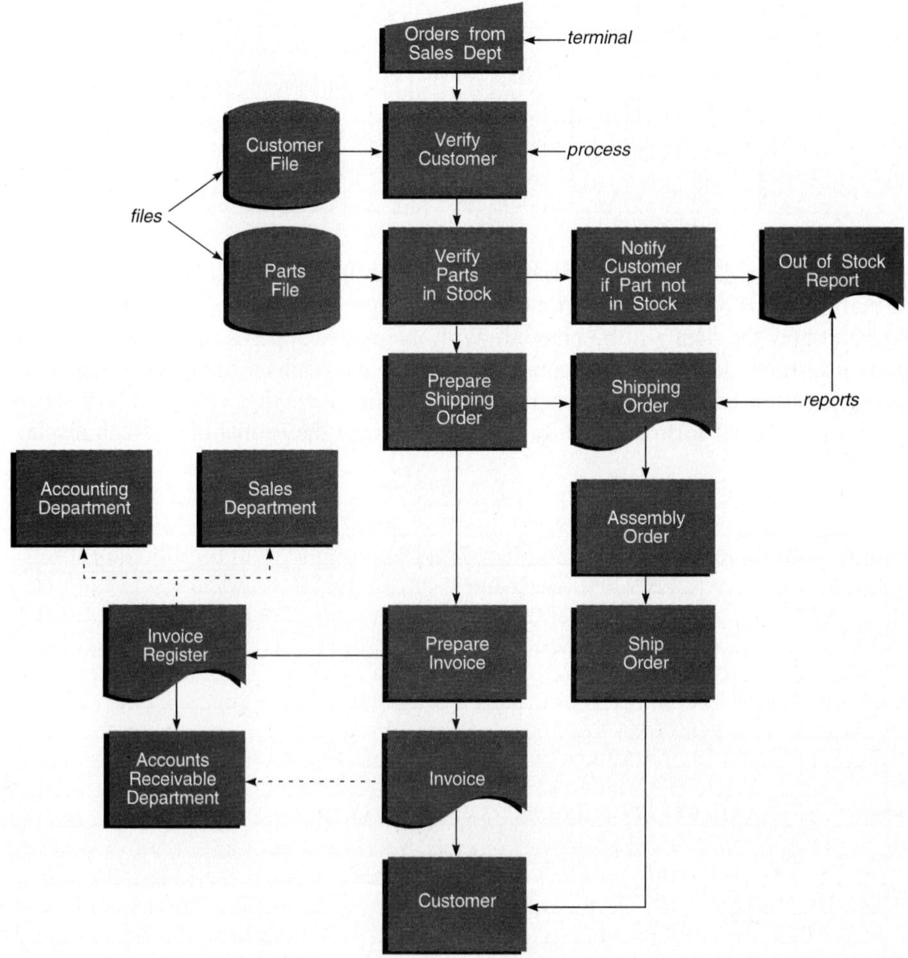

FIGURE 11-20
The system flowchart documents the equipment used to enter data, such as the terminals for the salespeople and the order department, the processes that will take place, such as the Verify Customer process, the files that will be used, such as the Parts and Customer files, and the reports that will be produced, such as the Shipping Order. Dotted lines indicate additional copies of reports, such as the copy of the Invoice that is sent to the accounts receivable department.

The special symbols used in a system flowchart are shown in Figure 11-21.

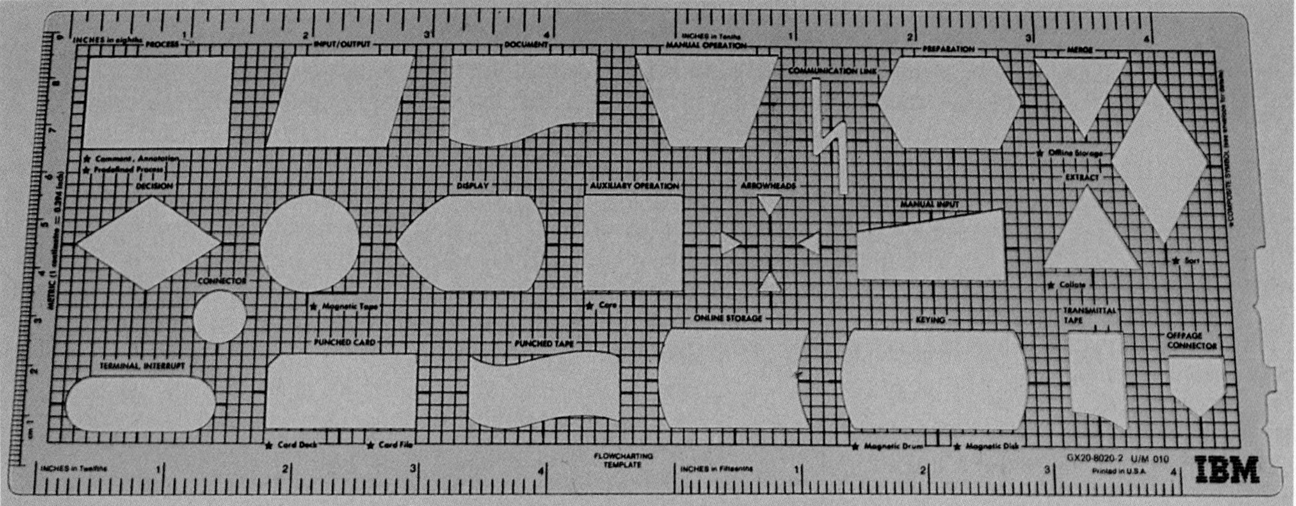

FIGURE 11-21
Symbols used for preparing a system flowchart.

During process design the systems analyst, the user, and the other members of the development project sometimes meet to conduct a **structured walk-through**, a step-by-step review of the process design. The purpose of these sessions is to identify any design logic errors and to continue the communication between the systems analyst and the user.

System Controls An important aspect of the design phase is the establishment of a comprehensive set of system controls. **System controls** ensure that only valid data is accepted and processed. Adequate controls must be established for two reasons: (1) to ensure the accuracy of the processing and the information generated from the system, and (2) to prevent computer-related fraud.

There are four types of controls that must be considered by the systems analyst. These controls are: (1) source document controls, (2) input controls, (3) processing controls, and (4) accounting controls.

1. **Source document controls** include serial numbering of input documents such as invoices and paychecks, document registers in which each input document is recorded and time-stamped as it is received, and batch totaling and balancing to predetermined totals to assure the accuracy of processing.

2. **Input controls** are established to assure the complete and accurate conversion of data from the source documents or other sources to a machine-processable form. Editing data as it enters the system is the most important form of input controls.

3. **Processing controls** refer to procedures that are established to determine the accuracy of information after it has been input to the system. For example, the accuracy of the total accounts receivable could be verified by taking the prior day's total, adding the current day's sales invoices, and subtracting the current day's payments.

4. **Accounting controls** provide assurance that the dollar amounts recorded in the accounting records are correct. One type of accounting control is making sure that detail reports are created to support the summary reports used to make entries in an organization's financial system. For example, many companies record sales by product line based on a summary report showing product line totals. In addition to this summary report, a detail report showing individual product sales should also be prepared and agreed to the summary report.

Testing Design During the design phase, test specifications are developed. The exact tests to be performed should be specified by someone other than the user or the systems analyst, although both should be consulted. Users and systems analysts have a tendency to test only what has been designed. An impartial third party, who has not been actively involved in the design, is more likely to design a test for, and therefore discover, a procedure or type of data that may have been overlooked in the design. Sometimes organizations avoid test design and test their systems with actual transactions. While such *live* testing is valuable, it might not test all conditions that the system is designed to process. This is especially true of error or exception conditions that do not occur regularly. For example, payroll systems are usually designed to reject input for hours worked over some limit, say 60 hours in a week. If only actual data are used to test the system, this limit may not be tested. Thus, it is important to design testing specifications that will test each system control that is part of the system by using both valid and invalid data.

Design Review

At the end of the design phase, management performs a **design review** and evaluates the work completed so far to determine whether to proceed (Figure 11-22). This is a critical point in any development project and all parties must take equal responsibility for the decision.

FIGURE 11-22
The design review is a critical point in the development process. Representatives from the user and information systems departments and top management meet to determine if the system should be developed as designed or if additional design work is necessary.

Usually, the design review will result only in requests for clarification of a few items. But sometimes an entire project will be terminated. Although canceling or restarting a project from the beginning is a difficult decision, in the long run it is less costly than implementing the wrong or an inadequate solution. If management decides to proceed, the project enters the development phase.

Before discussing the development phase, we describe prototyping, a development method that can be used in several phases of a system development project, and computer-aided software engineering, an automated approach to system design.

Prototyping

Prototyping is building a working model of the new system. The advantage of prototyping is that it lets the user actually experience the system before it is completed. Some organizations use prototyping during the analysis phase, others use it during the design phase. Still other companies use prototyping to go directly from the preliminary investigation to an implemented system. These companies just keep refining the prototype until the user says that it is acceptable. A disadvantage of such an accelerated approach is that key features of a new system, especially exception conditions, may be overlooked. Another disadvantage is that documentation, an important part of any system development effort, is usually not as well or as thoroughly prepared. Used as a tool to show the user how the system will operate, prototyping can be an important system development tool.

Computer-Aided Software Engineering (CASE)

Many organizations are now using computer software specifically developed to aid the information system life cycle process. **Computer-aided software engineering (CASE)** refers to the use of automated computer-based tools to design and manage a software system (Figure 11-23). Sometimes these tools, such as a data dictionary, exist separately. Other CASE vendors have combined several tools into an integrated package referred to as a **CASE workbench**. CASE workbench tools might include:

- *Analysis and design tools* such as data dictionaries, decision tables, or data flow diagram builders
- *Prototyping tools* that can be used to create models of the proposed system
- *Code generators* that create actual computer programs
- An *information repository* that cross references and organizes all information about a system
- *Management tools* that assist in the management of a systems project

In addition to the benefits of increased productivity, CASE tools promote the completion of the design work before development begins. Starting the development work before the design is completed often results in work that has to be redone.

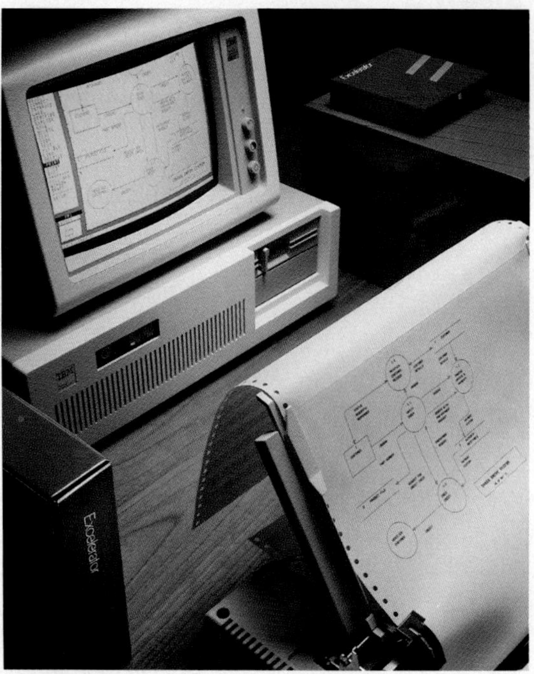

FIGURE 11-23
Computer-aided software engineering (CASE) packages help users design complex systems. Excelerator by Index Technologies allows users to create and revise data flow diagrams, data dictionary elements, screens, reports, and process specifications.

DESIGN AT SUTHERLAND

Upon approval by the management review committee, Mary Ruiz begins designing the order entry and invoicing system. After she studies existing manually prepared documents and talks to users, Mary designs printed reports and screen displays. According to Mike Charles, one of the most important reports is the daily invoice register. Using a report layout form (Figure 11-18), Mary shows Mike how the report will look after it is programmed. Using a similar form for screen displays (Figure 11-19), Mary also shows Mike what the order clerks will see when they enter auto parts orders. To graphically show how the overall system will work, Mary prepares a system flowchart (Figure 11-20). The system flowchart shows that auto parts orders will be entered on terminals in the sales department and will use data in the Parts and Customer files to verify that the orders are valid. Shipping orders and invoices are two of the reports produced. An important part of Mary's design time involves specifying the system controls used during processing. These controls include verifying the customer number before processing the order and checking to see if the ordered part is in stock. If the ordered part is not in stock, the customer is notified immediately.

After completing her design work, Mary meets with representatives from the user and information systems departments and top management to review her design. After Mary explains the design, the committee agrees to develop the system.

DEVELOPMENT PHASE

Once the system design phase has been completed, the project enters the system development phase. There are two parts to **development**: program development and equipment acquisition.

Program Development

The process of developing the software, or programs, required for a system is called **program development** and includes the following steps: (1) reviewing the program specifications, (2) designing the program, (3) coding the program, (4) testing the program; and (5) finalizing the program documentation. The primary responsibility for completing these tasks is assumed by computer programmers who work closely with the systems analyst who designed the system. Chapter 12 explains program development in depth. The important concepts to understand now are that this process is a part of the development phase of the information system life cycle and that its purpose is to develop the software required by the system.

Equipment Acquisition

During the development phase, final decisions will be made on what additional equipment, if any, will be required for the new system. A preliminary review of the equipment requirements would have been done during the analysis phase and included in the written report prepared by the systems analyst. Making the equipment acquisition prior to the development phase would be premature because any equipment selected should be based on the requirements specified in the design phase. Equipment selection is affected by factors such as the number of users who will require terminals and the disk storage that will be required for new files and data elements. In some cases, even a new or upgraded CPU is required. If an organization chose to acquire a commercial software package instead of developing software, the equipment acquisition would take place during the acquisition phase.

DEVELOPMENT AT SUTHERLAND

◆ During the development phase, Mary works closely with the two programmers who are assigned to the project. She regularly meets with the programmers to answer questions about the design and to check on the progress of their work. Prior to starting the programming, Mary arranges for the programmers to meet with the auto parts sales employees so that the programmers will have a better understanding of the purpose of the new system.

When the programming is nearly completed, Mary arranges for the terminals to be installed in the sales department.

IMPLEMENTATION PHASE

◆ **Implementation** is the phase of the system development process when people actually begin using the new system. This is a critical phase of the project that usually requires careful timing and the coordination of all the project participants. Important parts of this phase that will contribute to the success of the new system are training and education, conversion, and post-implementation evaluation.

Training and Education

Someone once said, "If you think education is expensive, you should consider the cost without it." The point is that untrained users can prevent the estimated benefits of a new system from ever being obtained or, worse, contribute to less efficiency and more costs than when the old system was operational. Training consists of showing people exactly how they will use the new system (Figure 11-24). This might include classroom-style lectures, but should definitely include hands-on sessions with the equipment they will be using, such as terminals, and realistic sample data. Education consists of learning new principles or theories that help people to understand and use the system. For example, before implementing a modern manufacturing system, many companies now require their manufacturing personnel to attend classes on material requirements planning (MRP), shop floor control, and other essential manufacturing topics.

FIGURE 11-24
All users should be trained on the system before they have to use it to process actual transactions. Training could include both classroom and hands-on sessions.

Conversion

Conversion refers to the process of changing from the old system to the new system. A number of different methods of conversion can be used including direct, parallel, phased, and pilot.

With **direct conversion**, the user stops using the old system one day and begins using the new system the next. The advantage of this approach is that it is fast and efficient. The disadvantage is that it is risky and can seriously disrupt operations if the new system does not work correctly the first time.

Parallel conversion consists of continuing to process data on the old system while some or all of the data is also processed on the new system. Results from both systems are compared, and if they agree, all data is switched to the new system (Figure 11-25).

Phased conversion is used with larger systems that can be broken down into individual modules that can be implemented separately at different times. An example would be a complete business system that could have the accounts receivable, inventory, and accounts payable modules implemented separately in phases. Phased conversions can be direct, parallel, or a combination of both.

Pilot conversion means that the new system will be used first by only a portion of the organization, often at a separate location such as a plant or office.

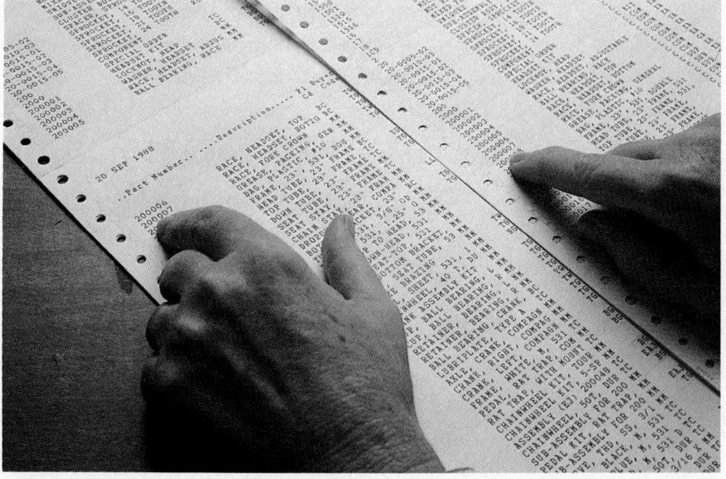

FIGURE 11-25
During parallel conversion, the user compares results from both the old and the new systems to determine if the new systems is operating properly.

Post-Implementation Evaluation

After a system is implemented, it is important to conduct a **post-implementation evaluation** to determine if the system is performing as designed, if operating costs are as anticipated, and if any modifications are necessary to make the system operate more effectively.

IMPLEMENTATION AT SUTHERLAND

Before they begin to use the new system to enter real transactions, the users participate in several training sessions about the equipment and the software. Because this is the first application in the auto parts division to be computerized, Mary begins the training sessions with an overview of how the central computer system processes data.

She conducts a basic data entry class to teach the employees how to use the terminals (Figure 11-24).

Before the system can be used, the Parts and Customer files have to be created from existing manual records. Temporary employees trained in data entry skills are hired for this task. Their work is carefully reviewed each day by Mike Charles and other permanent department employees.

Although he knows it means extra work, Mike decides that a parallel conversion is the safest way to implement the new system. Using this method, Mike verifies the results of the new system with those of the existing manual system. Actual use of the system begins on the first business day of the month so that transaction totals can be balanced to accounting reports.

Because they are thoroughly trained, the order clerks feel comfortable when they begin entering real orders. They encounter a few minor problems, such as orders for special parts not on the Parts file. These problems become less frequent and at the end of the month, after Mike compares the manual and computerized report totals, he decides to discontinue the use of the manual system.

During the post-implementation review, Mike and Mary discover that nine out of ten customer orders are now shipped the same day as the order is received. Before the new system was implemented, less than half the orders were shipped within two days of receipt. Invoices, which once lagged twelve to sixteen days behind shipments, are now mailed on the same day. Perhaps the most positive benefit of the new system is that customer complaints about order processing are practically eliminated.

MAINTENANCE PHASE

◆ **Maintenance** is the process of supporting the system after it is implemented. Maintenance consists of three activities: performance monitoring, change management, and error correction.

Performance Monitoring

Performance monitoring is the ongoing process of comparing response times, file sizes, and other system performance measures against the estimates that were prepared during the analysis, design, and implementation phases. Variances from these estimates may indicate that the system requires additional equipment resources, such as more memory or faster disk drives.

Change Management

Change is an inevitable part of any system; thus, all users of the system should be familiar with methods and procedures that provide for change. Sometimes, changes are required because existing requirements were overlooked. Other times, new information requirements caused by external sources such as government regulations will force change. A key part of change management is documentation. The same documentation standards that were followed during the analysis and design phases should also be used to record changes. In fact, in many organizations, the same document that is used to request new systems (Figure 11-3) is used to request changes to an existing system (Figure 11-26). Thus, the information system development cycle continues as the analysis phase begins on the change request.

Error Correction

Error correction deals with problems that are caused by programming and design errors that are discovered after the system is implemented. Often these errors are minor problems, such as the ZIP code not appearing on a name and address report, that can be quickly fixed by a programmer. Other times, however, the error requires more serious investigation by the systems analyst before a correction can be determined. Design errors that are not found until after a system is implemented are much more expensive to correct than had they been found earlier.

REQUEST FOR SYSTEM SERVICES

ISD CONTROL #: 4703

I. To Be Completed By Person Requesting Services

SUBMITTED BY: MIKE CHARLES DEPT: AUTO PARTS SALES DATE: 2/1/93

REQUEST TYPE: ✓ MODIFICATION □ NEW SYSTEM

NEED: ✓ ASAP □ IMMEDIATE □ LONG RANGE

BRIEF STATEMENT OF REQUEST (attach additional material, if necessary)

SALES INVOICE PROGRAM NEEDS TO PROVIDE FOR 1% COUNTY TAX THAT WILL GO INTO EFFECT JULY 1, 1993

✓ ADDITIONAL MATERIAL ATTACHED COUNTY TAX RATE SCHEDULE

II. To Be Completed By Information Systems Department

REQUEST INVESTIGATED BY: ______ DATE: ______

COMMENTS: ______

III. Disposition

□ REQUEST APPROVED FOR IMMEDIATE IMPLEMENTATION

□ ANALYST ASSIGNED: ______

□ REQUEST APPROVED FOR IMPLEMENTATION AS SOON AS POSSIBLE

□ REQUEST REJECTED

COMMENTS: ______

SIGNED: ______ DATE: ______

FIGURE 11-26
The same form used to request a new system (Figure 11-3) is also used to request a modification to an existing system.

MAINTENANCE AT SUTHERLAND

◆ During the months following the system implementation, users discover a number of minor errors in the system. The programming staff quickly corrects most of these errors, but in one case involving special credit terms for a large customer, Mary Ruiz becomes involved and prepares specifications for the necessary program changes.

Approximately one year after Mike Charles submits his original request for a computerized order entry and invoicing system, he submits another request (Figure 11-26) for a change to the system to provide for a new county sales tax. This type of request does not require a preliminary investigation and is assigned to Mary Ruiz as soon as she is available. Mike submits his request five months before the tax is scheduled to go into effect, which allows ample time for the necessary program changes to be implemented.

SUMMARY OF THE INFORMATION SYSTEM LIFE CYCLE

◆ Although the information system development process may appear to be a straightforward series of steps, in practice it is a challenging activity that calls for the skills and cooperation of all involved. New development tools have made the process more efficient but the success of any project always depends on the commitment of the project participants. The understanding you have gained from this chapter will help you participate in information system development projects and give you an appreciation for the importance of each phase.

CHAPTER SUMMARY

1. The **information system life cycle (ISLC)** is an organized approach to obtaining an information system.
2. Planning, scheduling, reporting, and controlling the individual activities that make up the information system development life cycle is called **project management**. These activities are usually recorded in a **project plan**.
3. **Documentation** refers to written materials that are produced throughout the information system development life cycle.

4. All users and information system personnel who will be affected by the new system should have the opportunity to participate in its development.
5. The **analysis** phase is the separation of a system into its parts in order to determine how the system works. This phase consists of the preliminary investigation, detailed system analysis, and making the decision to proceed.
6. The purpose of the **preliminary investigation** is to determine if a request warrants further detailed investigation. The most important aspect of this investigation is **problem definition**.
7. **Detailed system analysis** involves both a thorough study of the current system and at least one proposed solution to any problems found.
8. **Structured analysis** is the use of analysis and design tools such as **data flow diagrams (DFDs)**, **data dictionaries**, **process specifications**, **structured English**, **decision tables**, and **decision trees** to document the specifications of an information system.
9. A **feasibility study** and **cost/benefit analysis** are often prepared to show whether the proposed solution is practical and to show the estimated costs and benefits that are expected.
10. The **acquisition** phase involves four steps: (1) summarizing application requirements, (2) identifying potential software vendors, (3) evaluating software alternatives, and (4) making the purchase.
11. **Commercial applications software** is software that has already been developed and is available for purchase.
12. Software packages that can be used by many different types of organizations, such as accounting packages, are called **horizontal application software**.
13. Software developed for a unique way of doing business, usually within a specific industry, is called **vertical application software**.
14. A **request for proposal (RFP)** is a written list of an organization's software requirements that is given to prospective software vendors.
15. Identifying potential software vendors for personal computers can usually be done at a local computer store. For larger applications sources include computer manufacturers, **software houses**, **system houses**, trade publications, computer periodicals, and consultants.
16. To evaluate software alternatives, match the features of each possible solution against the original requirements list or RFP.
17. A **benchmark test** involves measuring the time it takes to process a set number of transactions.
18. A **software license** is the right to use software under certain terms and conditions.
19. Application software that is developed by a user or at the user's request is called **custom software**.
20. Modifying a commercial applications package is usually referred to as **customizing** or **tailoring**.
21. During the **design** phase the **logical design** that was created in the analysis phase is transformed into a **physical design**.
22. There are two major structured design methods: **top-down design** (or **structured design**) and **bottom-up design**.
23. **Output design**, **input design**, and **database design** all occur during the design phase.
24. A **dialogue** is the sequence of inputs and computer responses that a user will encounter when he or she enters data on an interactive system.
25. During the **process design**, the systems analyst specifies exactly what actions will be taken on the input data to create output information.
26. One method of documenting the relationship of different processes is with a **system flowchart**.
27. A **structured walk-through**, or a step-by-step review, is sometimes performed on the process design.
28. **System controls** are established to (1) ensure that only valid data is accepted and processed and (2) to prevent computer-related fraud. Types of system controls include **source document controls**, **input controls**, **processing controls**, and **accounting controls**.
29. At the end of the design phase, a **design review** is performed to evaluate the work completed so far.
30. **Prototyping** is building a working model of the new system.
31. **Computer-aided software engineering (CASE)** refers to the use of automated computer based tools to design and manage a software system.
32. A **CASE workbench** provides several CASE tools in an integrated package. These tools might include analysis and design tools, prototyping tools, code generators, information repository, and management tools.
33. The **development** phase consists of program development and equipment acquisition.
34. **Program development** includes: (1) reviewing the program specifications, (2) designing the program, (3) coding the program, (4) testing the program, and (5) finalizing the program documentation.
35. The **implementation** phase is when people actually begin using the new system. This phase includes training and education, conversion, and the **post-implementation evaluation**.

36. The process of changing from the old system to the new system is called a **conversion**. The conversion methods that may be used are **direct**, **parallel**, **phased**, and **pilot**.
37. The **maintenance** phase is the process of supporting the information system after it is implemented. It consists of three activities: **performance monitoring**, change management, and error correction.

KEY TERMS

Accounting controls *11.19*
Acquisition *11.10*
Analysis *11.4*
Benchmark test *11.13*
Bottom-up design *11.16*
CASE workbench *11.21*
Commercial applications software *11.10*
Computer-aided software engineering (CASE) *11.21*
Conversion *11.23*
Cost/benefit analysis *11.8*
Custom software *11.14*
Customizing *11.15*
Database design *11.18*
Data dictionary *11.6*
Data flow diagram (DFD) *11.5*
Decision table *11.7*
Decision tree *11.7*
Design *11.16*
Design review *11.20*
Detailed system analysis *11.5*
Development *11.21*
Dialogue *11.17*
Direct conversion *11.23*
Documentation *11.3*
Feasibility study *11.8*
Horizontal application software *11.11*
Implementation *11.22*
Information system life cycle (ISLC) *11.2*
Input controls *11.19*
Input design *11.17*
Logical design *11.16*
Maintenance *11.24*
Output design *11.17*
Parallel conversion *11.23*
Performance monitoring *11.24*
Phased conversion *11.23*
Physical design *11.16*
Pilot conversion *11.23*
Post-implementation evaluation *11.23*
Preliminary investigation *11.4*
Problem definition *11.4*
Process design *11.18*
Processing controls *11.19*
Process specification *11.7*
Program development *11.22*
Project management *11.2*
Project plan *11.2*
Prototyping *11.20*
Request for proposal (RFP) *11.11*
Software house *11.12*
Software license *11.13*
Source document controls *11.19*
Structured analysis *11.5*
Structured design *11.16*
Structured English *11.7*
Structured walk-through *11.19*
System controls *11.19*
System flowchart *11.18*
System house *11.12*
Tailoring *11.15*
Top-down design *11.16*
Vertical application software *11.11*

REVIEW QUESTIONS

1. Draw a diagram showing the phases of the information system life cycle.
2. Describe project management and when it should be performed.
3. What is the preliminary investigation? What is the most important aspect of the preliminary investigation?
4. Briefly describe detailed system analysis. What are the fact-finding techniques used during detailed system analysis?
5. What is commercial applications software? Explain the difference between horizontal and vertical applications.
6. Describe the information that an RFP should contain and how the RFP is used.
7. What is custom software and why is it appropriate for some applications?
8. Describe several things that a user can do to evaluate a software package before purchasing it. What is a benchmark test?
9. What is a software license? Describe some of the terms and conditions that are included in a software license.
10. What are the symbols used in data flow diagrams? Why are data flow diagrams useful?
11. Explain the difference between the logical and physical design of an information system.
12. What are the two methods of structured design? Briefly describe each method.
13. What is prototyping?
14. Write a description of the four types of conversion methods.
15. Describe the three major activities of system maintenance.

CONTROVERSIAL ISSUES

1. Some organizations claim that consultants have saved them considerable sums of money when acquiring applications software. Others say that they would have been better off not using a consultant. What role, if any, do you feel a consultant should play in helping an organization to select applications software?
2. "The difficulty in developing and implementing an information processing system is the user," proclaimed a systems analyst. "Users never know what they want. When they are shown what the system will do, they give their approval, but when the system is implemented they are never happy. They always want changes. It's impossible to satisfy them." How do you feel about these comments? Are the systems analyst's comments about users correct?

RESEARCH PROJECTS

1. Use the yellow pages, computer magazines or newspapers, or computer store references to locate a computer consultant. Interview the consultant over the phone or in person and ask him or her how he or she helps a user choose a computer system. Prepare a report for your class.
2. Prepare a data flow diagram of how you registered for class. Document your work by obtaining copies of any forms that you used during the registration process.

Program Development

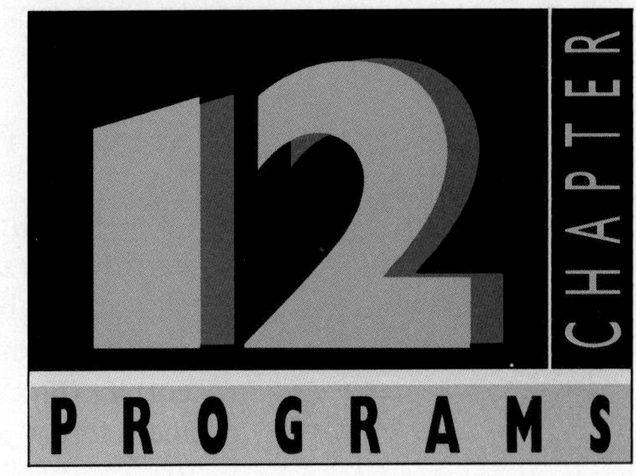

The information system life cycle covers the entire process of taking a plan for processing information through various phases until it becomes a functioning information system. During the development phase of this cycle, computer programs are written. The purpose of these programs is to process data and produce information as specified in the information system design. In this chapter we focus on the steps taken to write a program and the available tools that make the program development process more efficient. Also in this chapter we discuss the different languages used to write programs.

Although you may never write a program yourself, you might someday request information that will require a program to be written or modified; thus, you should understand how a computer program is developed.

OBJECTIVES

- Define the term computer program
- Describe the five steps in program development: review of program specifications, program design, program coding, program testing, and finalizing program documentation
- Explain the concepts of structured program design including modules, control structures, and single entry/single exit
- Explain and illustrate the sequence, selection, and iteration control structures used in structured programming
- Define the term programming language and discuss the various categories of programming languages
- Briefly discuss the programming languages that are commonly used today, including BASIC, COBOL, C, FORTRAN, Pascal, and Ada
- Explain and discuss application generators
- Explain and discuss object-oriented programming
- Explain the factors that should be considered when choosing a programming language

WHAT IS A COMPUTER PROGRAM?

A **computer program** is a detailed set of instructions that directs a computer to perform the tasks necessary to process data into information. These instructions, usually written by a computer programmer, can be coded (written) in a variety of programming languages that we discuss later in this chapter. To create programs that are correct (produce accurate information) and maintainable (easy to modify), programmers follow a process called program development.

WHAT IS PROGRAM DEVELOPMENT?

Program development is the process of producing one or more programs to perform specific tasks on a computer. The process of program development has evolved into a series of five steps that most experts agree should take place when any program is developed (Figure 12-1).

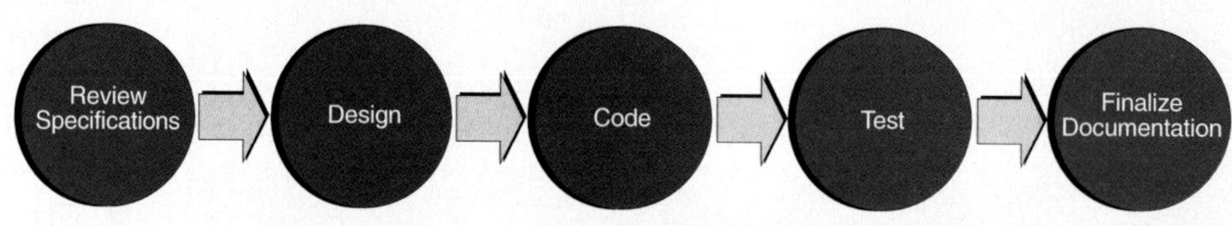

FIGURE 12-1
The five steps of program development. Although the process steps are shown sequentially, program development usually requires returning to previous steps to correct errors.

1. *Review of program specifications*. The programmer reviews the specifications created by the systems analyst during the system design phase.
2. *Program design*. The programmer determines and documents the specific actions the computer will take to accomplish the desired tasks.
3. *Coding*. The programmer writes the actual program instructions.
4. *Testing*. The written programs are tested to make sure they perform as intended.
5. *Finalizing documentation*. Throughout the program development process the programmer documents, or writes, explanatory information about the program. In this final step the documentation produced during steps 1 through 4 is brought together and organized.

Although we list these five steps sequentially, the program development process usually requires returning to previous steps to correct errors that are discovered.

FIGURE 12-2
Program development occurs during the Development phase of the information system life cycle.

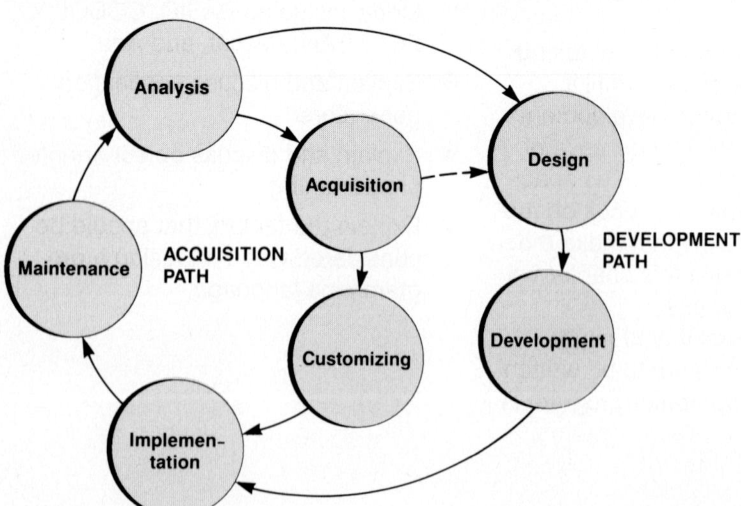

To help you to better understand how the steps in the program development process relate to the overall development of an information system, let's review the phases of the information system life cycle. As you can see in Figure 12-2, program development is a phase on the development path of the information system life cycle. If, after the analysis phase, an organization is unable to acquire commercial software that meets its needs, it moves or it proceeds to the design phase. The development phase, which refers to program development, follows the design phase and includes the five steps shown in Figure 12-1.

STEP 1—REVIEWING THE PROGRAM SPECIFICATIONS

The first step in the program development cycle is a review of the program specifications. **Program specifications** can consist of data flow diagrams, system flowcharts, process specifications that indicate the action to be taken on the data, a data dictionary identifying the data elements that will be used, screen formats, report layouts, and actual documents such as invoices or checks. These documents help the programmer understand the work that needs to be done by the program. Also, the programmer meets once or more with the user and the systems analyst who designed the system to understand the purpose of the program from the user's point of view.

If the programmer believes some aspect of the design should be changed, such as a screen layout, he or she discusses it with the systems analyst and the user. If the change is agreed on, the written design specification is changed. However, the programmer should not change the specified system without the agreement of the systems analyst and the user. If a change is authorized, it should be recorded in the system design. The systems analyst and the user, through the system design, have specified what is to be done. It is the programmer's job to determine *how* to do it.

Large programming jobs are usually assigned to more than one programmer. In these situations, a good system design is essential so that each programmer can be given a logical portion of the system to be programmed.

STEP 2—DESIGNING THE PROGRAM

After the programmer has carefully reviewed the specifications, program design begins. During **program design** a logical solution to the programming task is developed and documented. The logical solution, or **logic**, for a program is a step-by-step solution to a programming problem. Determining the logic for a computer program can be an extremely complex task. To aid in program design and development, a method called structured program design is commonly used.

Structured Program Design

Structured program design is a methodology that emphasizes three main program design concepts: modules, control structures, and single entry/single exit. Use of these concepts helps to create programs that are easy to write, read, understand, check for errors, and modify.

Modules With structured design, programming problems are *decomposed* (separated) into smaller parts called modules. Each **module**, sometimes referred to as a **subroutine** in programming, performs a given task within the program. The major benefit of this technique is that it simplifies program development because each module of a program can be developed individually. When the modules are combined, they form a complete program that accomplishes the desired result.

Structure charts, also called **hierarchy charts**, are often used to decompose and represent the modules of a program. When the program decomposition is completed, the entire structure of a program is illustrated by the hierarchy chart (on the next page in Figure 12-3), which shows the relationship of the modules within the program.

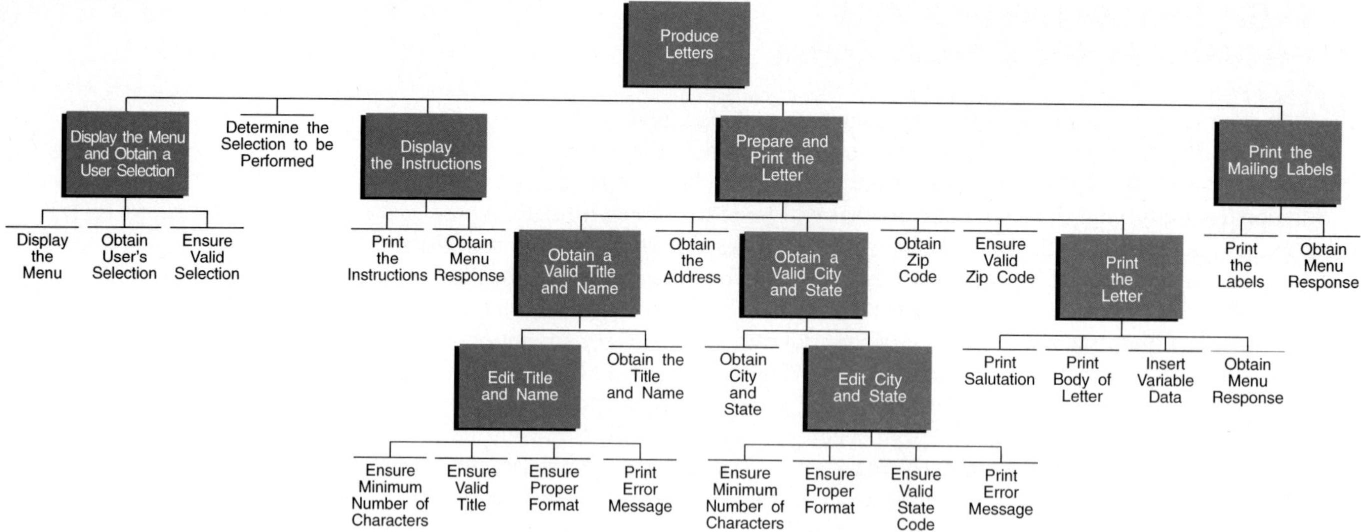

FIGURE 12-3
In this structure chart, the relationship of individual program modules are graphically shown as boxes. The text below each box indicates the processing steps that would be performed.

Control Structures In structured program design three basic **control structures** are used to form the logic of a program. All logic problems can be solved by a combination of these structures. The three basic control structures are: sequence, selection, and iteration.

1. In the **sequence structure**, one process occurs immediately after another. In Figure 12-4, each rectangular box represents a particular process that is to occur. For example, a process could be a computer instruction to move data from one location in main memory to another location. Each process occurs in the exact sequence specified, one process followed by the next.

2. The second control structure, called the **selection structure**, or **if-then-else structure**, gives programmers a way to represent conditional program logic (Figure 12-5). Conditional program logic can be expressed in the following way: *If* the condition is true, *then* perform the true condition processing, *else* perform the false condition processing. When the if-then-else structure is used, the if portion of the structure tests a given condition. The true portion of the statement is executed if the condition tested is true, and the false portion of the statement is executed if the condition is false. An if-then-else structure might be used to determine if an employee is hourly or salaried and then process the employee accordingly. To do this, an employee code might be tested to determine if an employee is hourly. If the employee is hourly, the true portion of the structure would be executed and hourly pay would be calculated. If the employee is not hourly, the false portion of the structure would be executed and salary pay would be calculated. The selection, or if-then-else, structure is used by programmers to represent conditional logic problems.

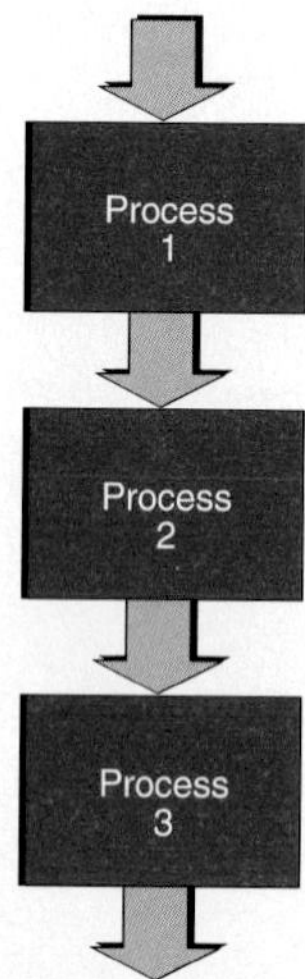

FIGURE 12-4
Each box in the sequence control structure represents a process that will occur immediately after the preceding process.

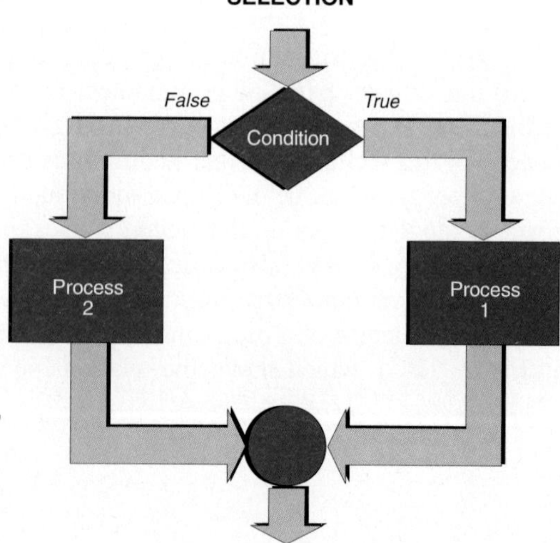

FIGURE 12-5
The selection, or if-then-else, control structure is used to direct the program to one process or another based on the test of a condition.

A variation of the selection structure is the case structure. The **case structure** is used when a condition is being tested that can lead to more than two alternatives (Figure 12-6). In a program, a menu is an example of a case structure because it provides multiple processing options.

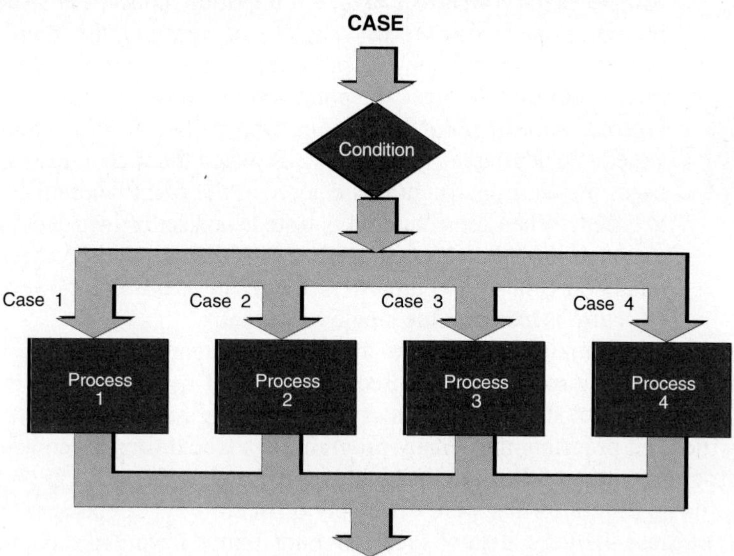

FIGURE 12-6
A case control structure with four possible processing paths is similar to the if-then-else control structure except that it provides for more than two alternatives.

3. The third control structure, called the **iteration structure**, or **looping structure**, means that one or more processes continue to occur as long as a given condition remains true. There are two forms of this control structure: the **do-while structure** and the **do-until structure** (Figure 12-7). In the do-while structure a condition is tested. If the condition is true, the process is performed. The program then *loops* back and tests the condition again. If the condition is still true, the process is performed again. This looping continues until the condition being tested is false. At that time, the program exits the loop, moves to another section of the program, and performs some other processing. An example of this type of testing would be a check to see if all records have been processed. The do-until control structure is similar to the do-while except that the condition tested is at the end instead of the beginning of the loop. Processing continues *until* the condition is met.

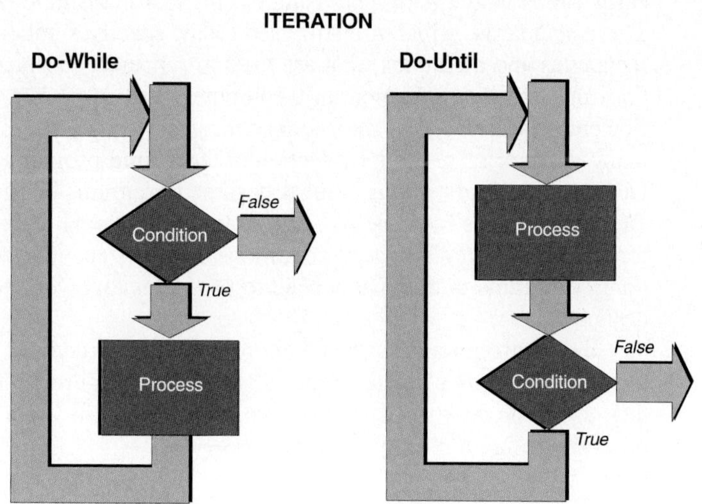

FIGURE 12-7
The iteration control structure has two forms, do-while and do-until. In the do-while structure, the condition is tested before the process. In the do-until structure, the condition is tested after the process.

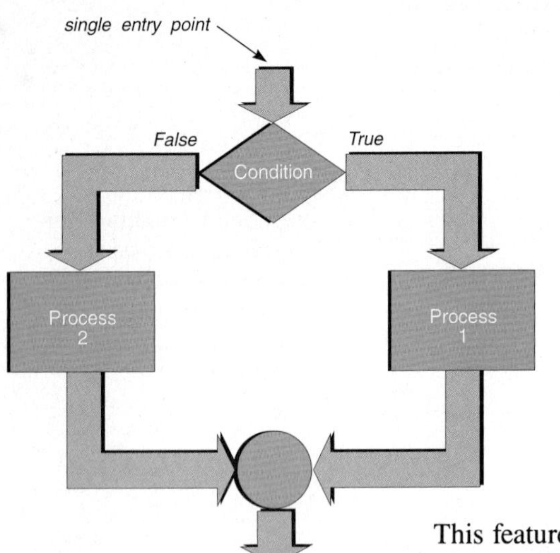

FIGURE 12-8
Structured programming concepts require that all control structures have a single entry point and a single exit point. This contributes to programs that are easier to understand and maintain.

Programmers combine these three control structures—sequence, selection, and iteration—to create program logic solutions. A structured program design rule that applies to these control structures and how they are combined is the single entry/single exit rule.

Single Entry/Single Exit An important concept in structured programming is **single entry/single exit**, meaning that there is only one entry point and one exit point for each of the three control structures. An **entry point** is the point where a control structure is entered. An **exit point** is the point where the control structure is exited. For example, in Figure 12-8, when the if-then-else structure is used, the control structure is entered at the point where the condition is tested. When the condition is tested, one set of instructions will be executed if the condition is true and another set will be executed if the condition is false. Regardless of the result of the test, however, the structure is exited at the single exit point.

This feature substantially improves the logic of a program because, when reading the program, the programmer can be assured that whatever happens within the if-then-else structure, the control structure will always be exited at a common point. Prior to the use of structured programming, many programmers would transfer control to other parts of a program without following the single entry/single exit rule. This practice led to poorly designed programs that were extremely difficult to read, check for errors, and modify. Because the logic path of such programs jumps from one section of the program to another, the programs are sometimes referred to as *spaghetti code*.

Program Design Tools

Programmers use several popular program design tools to develop and document the logical solutions to the problems they are programming. Three commonly used design tools are program flowcharts, pseudocode, and Warnier-Orr diagrams.

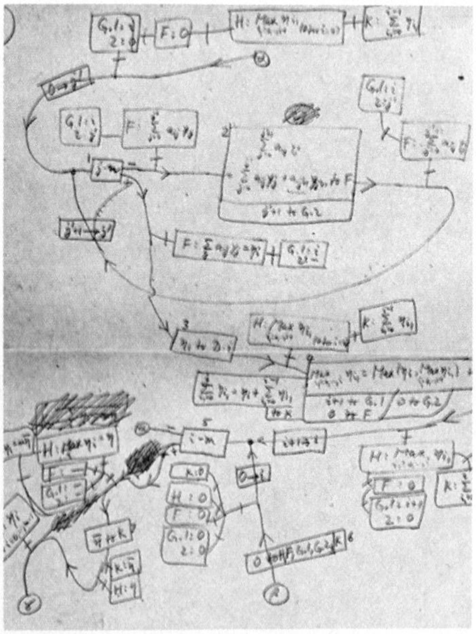

FIGURE 12-9
An example of an early flowchart developed by computer scientist Dr. John von Neumann in the 1940s to solve a problem involving game theory. This flowchart was drawn prior to the standardization of flowchart symbols and the development of structured design techniques.

Program Flowcharts Program flowcharts were one of the first program design tools. Figure 12-9 shows a flowchart drawn in the late 1940s by Dr. John von Neumann, a computer scientist and one of the first computer programmers. In a **program flowchart** all the logical steps of a program are represented by a combination of symbols and text.

A set of standards for program flowcharts was published in the early 1960s by the American National Standards Institute (ANSI). These standards, which are still used today, specify symbols, such as rectangles and diamonds, that are used to represent the various operations that can be performed on a computer (Figure 12-10). Program flowcharts were used as the primary means of program design for many years prior to the introduction of structured program design. During these years, programmers designed programs by focusing on the detailed steps required for a program and creating logical solutions for each new combination of conditions as it was encountered. Developing programs in this manner led to programs that were poorly designed.

Today, programmers are taught to apply the structured design concepts when they create program flowcharts (Figure 12-11). When they use basic control structures, program flowcharts are a valuable program design tool.

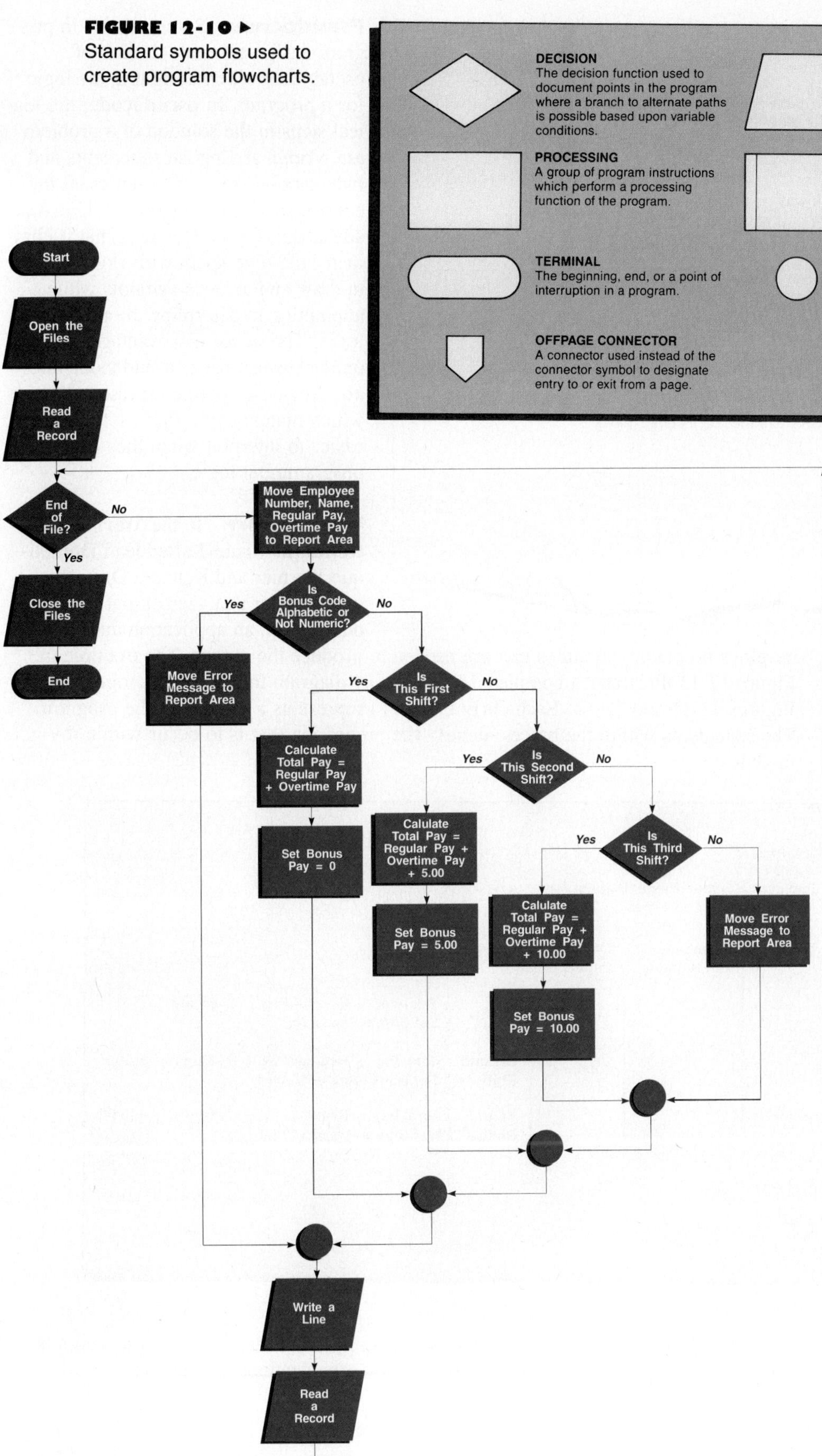
DECISION
The decision function used to document points in the program where a branch to alternate paths is possible based upon variable conditions.
INPUT/OUTPUT
Any function of an input/output device (making information available for processing, recording processing information, etc.).
PROCESSING
A group of program instructions which perform a processing function of the program.
PREDEFINED PROCESS
A group of operations not detailed in the particular set of flowcharts.
TERMINAL
The beginning, end, or a point of interruption in a program.
CONNECTOR
An entry from, or an exit to, another part of the program flowchart.
OFFPAGE CONNECTOR
A connector used instead of the connector symbol to designate entry to or exit from a page.
Start
Open the Files
Read a Record
End of File?
No
Yes
Close the Files
End
Move Employee Number, Name, Regular Pay, Overtime Pay to Report Area
Is Bonus Code Alphabetic or Not Numeric?
Yes
No
Move Error Message to Report Area
Is This First Shift?
Yes
No
Calculate Total Pay = Regular Pay + Overtime Pay
Set Bonus Pay = 0
Is This Second Shift?
Yes
No
Calulate Total Pay = Regular Pay + Overtime Pay + 5.00
Set Bonus Pay = 5.00
Is This Third Shift?
Yes
No
Calulate Total Pay = Regular Pay + Overtime Pay + 10.00
Set Bonus Pay = 10.00
Move Error Message to Report Area
Write a Line
Read a Record

FIGURE 12-10 ▸
Standard symbols used to create program flowcharts.

◂ FIGURE 12-11
This flowchart displays the logic required to solve a payroll calculation task using standard flowcharting symbols and the three control structures of structured programming.

```
Open the files
Read a record
PERFORM UNTIL end of file
   Move employee number, name, regular pay, and
      overtime pay to the report area
   IF bonus code is alphabetic or not numeric
      Move error message to report area
   ELSE
      IF first shift
         Calculate total pay = regular pay +
            overtime pay
         Set bonus pay to zero
      ELSE
         If second shift
            Calculate total pay = regular pay +
               overtime pay + 5.00
            Set bonus pay to 5.00
         ELSE
            If third shift
               Calculate total pay = regular pay +
                  overtime pay + 10.00
               Set bonus pay to 10.00
            ELSE
               Move error message to report area
            ENDIF
         ENDIF
      ENDIF
   ENDIF
   Write a line
   Read a record
ENDPERFORM
Close the files
End the program
```

FIGURE 12-12
This pseudocode is another way of documenting the logic shown in the flowchart in Figure 12-11.

Pseudocode Some experts in program design advocate the use of pseudocode when designing the logic for a program. In **pseudocode**, the logical steps in the solution of a problem are written as English statements and indentations are used to represent the control structures (Figure 12-12). An advantage of pseudocode is that it eliminates the time spent with flowcharting to draw and arrange symbols while attempting to determine the program logic. The major disadvantage is that unlike flowcharting, pseudocode does not provide a graphic representation, which many people find useful and easier to interpret when they examine programming logic.

Warnier-Orr In the **Warnier-Orr technique** (named after Jean Dominique Warnier and Kenneth Orr), the programmer analyzes output to be produced from an application and develops processing modules that are needed to produce the output. The example in Figure 12-13 illustrates a completed Warnier-Orr diagram for the same program as Figures 12-11 and 12-12. Each curly brace ({}) represents a module in the program. The statements within the braces identify the processing that is to occur within the modules.

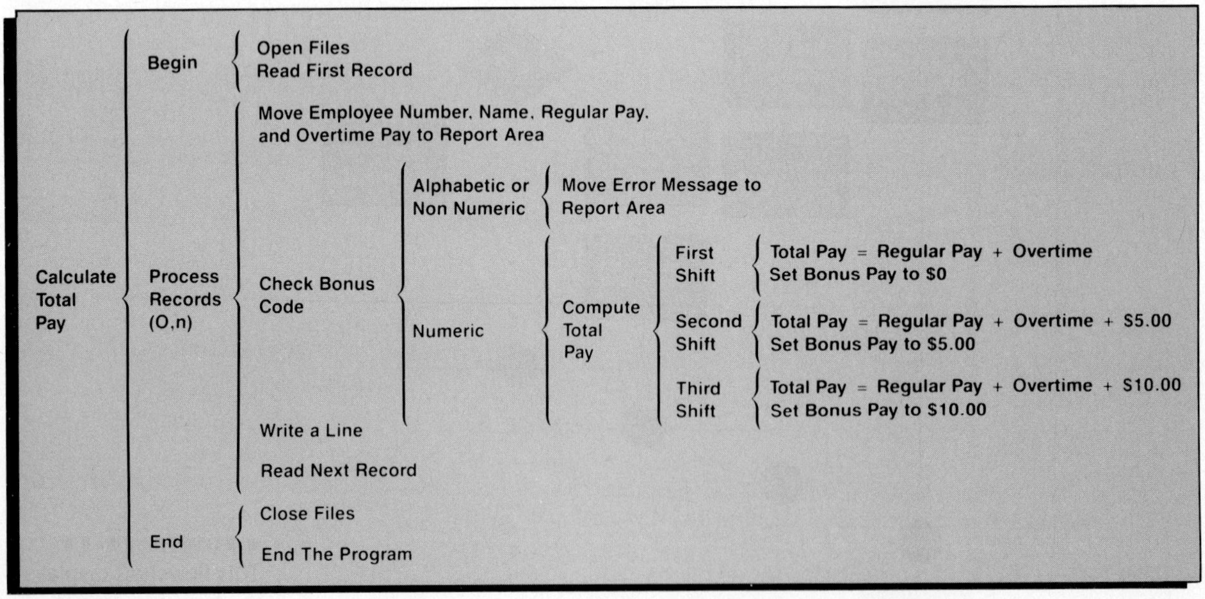

Calculate Total Pay {
- Begin { Open Files; Read First Record }
- Process Records (O,n) {
  - Move Employee Number, Name, Regular Pay, and Overtime Pay to Report Area
  - Check Bonus Code {
    - Alphabetic or Non Numeric { Move Error Message to Report Area }
    - Numeric { Compute Total Pay {
      - First Shift { Total Pay = Regular Pay + Overtime; Set Bonus Pay to $0 }
      - Second Shift { Total Pay = Regular Pay + Overtime + $5.00; Set Bonus Pay to $5.00 }
      - Third Shift { Total Pay = Regular Pay + Overtime + $10.00; Set Bonus Pay to $10.00 } } }
  - Write a Line
  - Read Next Record
- End { Close Files; End The Program }

FIGURE 12-13
This Warnier-Orr diagram also illustrates the logic for the payroll calculation problem used for Figures 12-11 and 12-12.

Regardless of the design tool you use, it is important that the program design is efficient and correct. To help ensure this, many organizations use structured walkthroughs.

Structured Walk-Through

After a program has been designed, the programmer schedules a structured walk-through of the program. The programmer, other programmers in the department, and the systems analyst attend. During the walk-through, the programmer who designs the program explains the program logic. The purpose of the design walk-through is to review the logic of the program for errors, and if possible, improve program design. Early detection of errors and approval of program design improvements reduces the overall development time and therefore the cost of the program. It is much better to find errors and make needed changes to the program during the design step than to make them later in the program development process.

Once the program design is complete, the programmer can begin to code the program.

STEP 3—CODING THE PROGRAM

Coding the program refers to the process of writing the program instructions that will process the data and produce the output specified in the program design. As we previously mentioned, programs are written in different languages, which each have particular rules on how to instruct the computer to perform specific tasks, such as read a record or multiply two numbers.

If the program design is thorough, logical, and well structured, the coding process is greatly simplified and can sometimes be a one-for-one translation of a design step into a program step. Today, program code, or instructions, are usually entered directly into the computer via a terminal and stored on a disk drive. Using this approach, the programmer can partially enter a program at one time and finish entering it at a later time. Program instructions are added, deleted, and changed until the programmer believes the program design has been fully translated into program instructions and the program is ready for testing.

STEP 4—TESTING THE PROGRAM

Before a program is used to process *real* data and produce information that people rely on, it should be thoroughly tested to make sure it is functioning correctly. A programmer can perform several different types of tests.

Desk checking is the process of reading the program and mentally reviewing its logic. This is a simple process that can be performed by the programmer who wrote the program or by another programmer. This process can be compared to proofreading a letter before you mail it. The disadvantage of this method is that it is difficult to detect other than obvious errors.

Syntax errors are violations of the grammar rules of the language in which the program was written. An example of a syntax error would be the program command READ being misspelled REED. Syntax errors missed by the programmer during desk checking are identified by the computer when it decodes the program instructions.

Logic testing is what most programmers think of when the term testing is used. During **logic testing**, the sequence of program instructions is tested to make sure it provides the correct result. Logic errors may be the result of a programming oversight, such as using the wrong data to perform a calculation, or a design error, such as forgetting to specify that some customers do not have to pay sales tax when they purchase merchandise.

Logic testing is performed with **test data**, data that simulates the type of input that the program will process when it is implemented. To obtain an independent and unbiased test of the program, test data and the review of test results should be the responsibility of someone other than the programmer who wrote the program. The test data should be developed by referring to the system design but it should also try to *break* the program by including data outside the range of data that will be input during normal operations. For example, if the specifications of a payroll program stated that the input for an employee should never exceed 60 hours of work per week, the program should be designed, coded, and tested to properly process transactions in excess of 60 hours. It would do this by displaying an error message or in some other way indicating that an invalid number of hours has been entered. Other similar tests should include alphabetic data when only numeric data is expected, and negative numbers when only positive numbers are normally input.

One of the more colorful terms of the computer industry is **debugging**, which refers to the process of locating and correcting program errors, or **bugs**, found during testing. The term was coined when the failure of one of the first computers was traced to a moth that had become lodged in the electronic components (Figure 12-14).

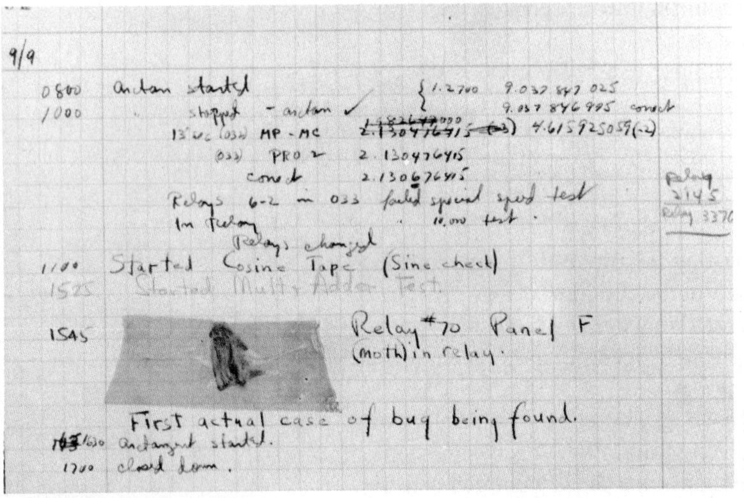

FIGURE 12-14
In 1945, the cause of the temporary failure of the world's first electromechanical computer, the Mark 1, was traced to a dead moth (shown taped to the log book) caught in the electrical components. The term *bug*, meaning a computer error, has been part of computer jargon ever since.

STEP 5—FINALIZING PROGRAM DOCUMENTATION

Documentation, or the preparation of documents, that explains the program is an essential but sometimes neglected part of the programming process. Documentation should be an ongoing part of developing a program and should only be finalized, meaning organized and brought together, after the program is successfully tested and ready for implementation. Documentation developed during the programming process should include a narrative description of the program, program design documents such as flowcharts or pseudocode, program listings, and test results. Comments in the program itself are also an important part of program documentation (Figure 12-15).

Data entry and computer operations procedures should also be documented prior to implementation. Obtaining adequate documentation may be difficult because some programmers can and do develop programs without it; when they have finished coding the program, they have little incentive to go back and complete the documentation after the fact. In addition to helping programmers develop programs, documentation is valuable because it helps the next programmer who, six months or one year later, is asked to make a change to the program. Proper documentation can substantially reduce the amount of time the new programmer will have to spend learning enough about the program to know how best to make the change.

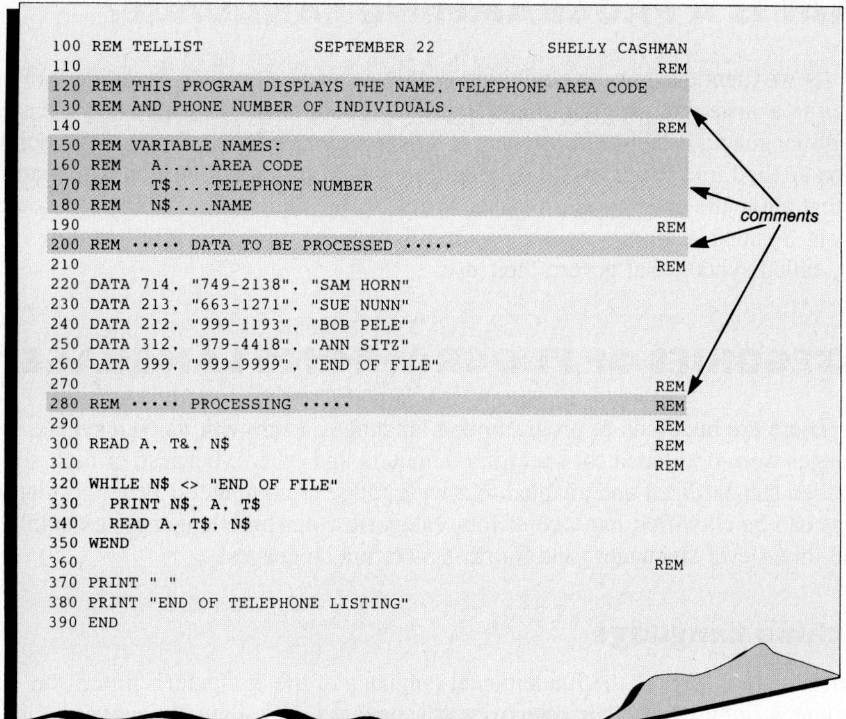

```
100 REM TELLIST              SEPTEMBER 22            SHELLY CASHMAN
110                                                             REM
120 REM THIS PROGRAM DISPLAYS THE NAME, TELEPHONE AREA CODE
130 REM AND PHONE NUMBER OF INDIVIDUALS.
140                                                             REM
150 REM VARIABLE NAMES:
160 REM   A.....AREA CODE
170 REM   T$....TELEPHONE NUMBER
180 REM   N$....NAME
190                                                             REM
200 REM ••••• DATA TO BE PROCESSED •••••
210                                                             REM
220 DATA 714, "749-2138", "SAM HORN"
230 DATA 213, "663-1271", "SUE NUNN"
240 DATA 212, "999-1193", "BOB PELE"
250 DATA 312, "979-4418", "ANN SITZ"
260 DATA 999, "999-9999", "END OF FILE"
270                                                             REM
280 REM ••••• PROCESSING •••••                                  REM
290                                                             REM
300 READ A, T&, N$                                              REM
310                                                             REM
320 WHILE N$ <> "END OF FILE"
330    PRINT N$, A, T$
340    READ A, T$, N$
350 WEND
360                                                             REM
370 PRINT " "
380 PRINT "END OF TELEPHONE LISTING"
390 END
```


FIGURE 12-15
Most programming languages allow programmers to place explanatory comments directly in the program. This is an effective way of documenting the program. In this program, comment lines are identified by the letters REM, which is an abbreviation for REMARK.

PROGRAM MAINTENANCE

Program maintenance includes all changes to a program once it is implemented and processing real transactions. Sometimes, maintenance is required to correct errors that were not found during the testing step. Other times, maintenance is required to make changes that are the result of the users' new information requirements. It may surprise you to learn that the majority of all business programming today consists of maintaining existing programs, not writing new programs.

Because so much time is spent on maintenance programming, it should be subject to the same policies and procedures, such as design, testing, and documentation, that are required for new programs. Unfortunately, this is not always the case. Because maintenance tasks are usually shorter than new programming efforts, they often aren't held to the same standards. The result is that over time, programs can become unrecognizable when compared with their original documentation. Maintaining high standards for program maintenance can not only lower overall programming costs, but also lengthen the useful life of a program.

SUMMARY OF PROGRAM DEVELOPMENT

The key to developing quality programs for an information system is to follow the steps of the program development process. Program specifications must be carefully reviewed and understood. Programmers should use structured concepts to design programs that are modular, use the three control structures, and follow the single entry/single exit rule. Programmers should carefully code and test the program and finalize documentation. If each of these steps is followed, programmers will create quality programs that are correct and that can be easily read, understood, and maintained.

WHAT IS A PROGRAMMING LANGUAGE?

As we mentioned at the beginning of this chapter, computer programs can be written in a variety of programming languages. People communicate with one another through language, established patterns of words and sounds. A similar definition can also be applied to a **programming language**, which is a set of written words and symbols that allow the programmer or user to communicate with the computer. As with English, Spanish, Chinese, or other spoken languages, programming languages have rules, called syntax, that govern their use.

CATEGORIES OF PROGRAMMING LANGUAGES

There are hundreds of programming languages, each with its own syntax. Some languages were developed for specific computers and others, because of their success, have been standardized and adapted to a wide range of computers. Programming languages can be classified into one of four categories: machine language, assembly language, high-level languages, and fourth-generation languages.

Machine Language

A **machine language** is the fundamental language of the computer's processor. Programs written in all other categories of languages are eventually converted into machine language before they are executed. Individual machine language instructions exist for each of the commands in the computer's instruction set, the operations such as add, move, or read that are specific to each computer. Because the instruction set is unique for a particular processor, machine languages are different for computers that have different processors. The advantage of writing a program in machine language is that the programmer can control the computer directly and accomplish exactly what needs to be done. Therefore, well-written machine language programs are very efficient. The disadvantages of machine language programs are that they take a long time to write and they are difficult to review if the programmer is trying to find an error. In addition, because they are written using the instruction set of a particular processor, the programs will only run on computers with the same type of processor. Because they are written for specific processors, machine languages are also called **low-level languages**. Figure 12-16(a) shows an example of machine language instructions.

FIGURE 12-16
Program instruction chart for: (a) machine language (printed in a hexadecimal form), (b) assembly language, and (c) a high-level language called C. The machine language and assembly language instructions correspond to the high-level instructions and were generated when the high-level language statements were translated into machine language. As you can see, the high-level language requires fewer program instructions and is easier to read.

(a) MACHINE LANGUAGE	(b) ASSEMBLY LANGUAGE	(c) HIGH-LEVEL LANGUAGE
9b df 46 0c 9b d9 c0 9b db 7e f2 9b d9 46 04 9b d8 c9 9b d9 5e fc	fild WORD PTR [bp+12];qty fld ST(0) fstp TBYTE PTR [bp-14] fld DWORD PTR [bp+4];price fmul ST(0),ST(1) fstp DWORD PTR [bp-4];gross	gross = qty * price;
9b d9 c0 9b dc 16 ac 00 9b dd d8 9b dd 7e f0 90 9b 8a 66 f1 9e 9b dd c0 76 19	fld ST(0) fcom QWORD PTR $T20002 fstp ST(0) fstsw WORD PTR [bp-16] fwait mov ah,BYTE PTR [bp-15] sahf ffreeST(0) jbe $I193	if (qty > ceiling)

9b d9 46 fc
9b dc 0e b4 00
9b de e9
9b d9 5e 08
90 9b
 	
eb 0d
90
	fld DWORD PTR [bp-4];gross
	fmul QWORD PTR $T20003
	fsub
	fstp DWORD PTR [bp+8];net
	fwait
	
	jmp SHORT $I194
	nop
	$I193:
		net = gross - (gross * discount_rate);
		
		else

8b 46 fc 8b 56 fe 89 46 08 89 56 0a	mov ax,WORD PTR [bp-4];gross mov dx,WORD PTR [bp-2] mov WORD PTR [bp+8],ax ;net mov WORD PTR [bp+10],dx $I194:	net = gross;

Assembly Language

To make it easier for programmers to remember the specific machine instruction codes, assembly languages were developed. An **assembly language** is similar to a machine language, but uses abbreviations called **mnemonics** or **symbolic operation code** to represent the machine operation code. Another difference is that assembly languages usually allow **symbolic addressing**, which means that a specific computer memory location can be referenced by a name or symbol, such as TOTAL, instead of by its actual address as it would have to be referenced in machine language. Assembly language programs can also include **macroinstructions** that generate more than one machine language instruction. Assembly language programs are converted into machine language instructions by a special program called an **assembler**. Even though assembly languages are easier to use than machine languages, they are still considered a low-level language because they are so closely related to the specific design of the computer. Figure 12-16⟨b⟩ shows an example of assembly language instructions.

High-Level Languages

The evolution of computer languages continued with the development of high-level languages in the late 1950s and 1960s. **High-level languages** more closely resemble what most people would think of as a language in that they contain nouns, verbs, and mathematical, relational, and logical operators that can be grouped together to form what appear to be sentences (Figure 12-16⟨c⟩). These sentences are called **program statements**. Because of these characteristics, high-level languages can be *read* by programmers and are thus easier to learn and use than machine or assembly languages. Another important advantage over low-level languages is that high-level languages are usually machine independent, which means they can run on different types of computers.

As mentioned previously, all languages must be translated into machine language before they can be executed. High-level languages are translated in one of two ways: with a compiler or an interpreter.

A **compiler** converts an entire program into machine language that is usually stored on a disk for later execution. The program to be converted is called the **source program** and the machine language produced is called the **object program** or **object code**. Compilers check the program syntax, perform limited logic checking, and make sure that data that is going to be used in comparisons or calculations, such as a discount rate, is properly defined somewhere in the program. An important feature of compilers is that they produce an error listing of all program statements that do not meet the program language rules. This listing helps the programmer make the necessary changes to debug or correct the program. Figure 12-17 illustrates the process of compiling a program.

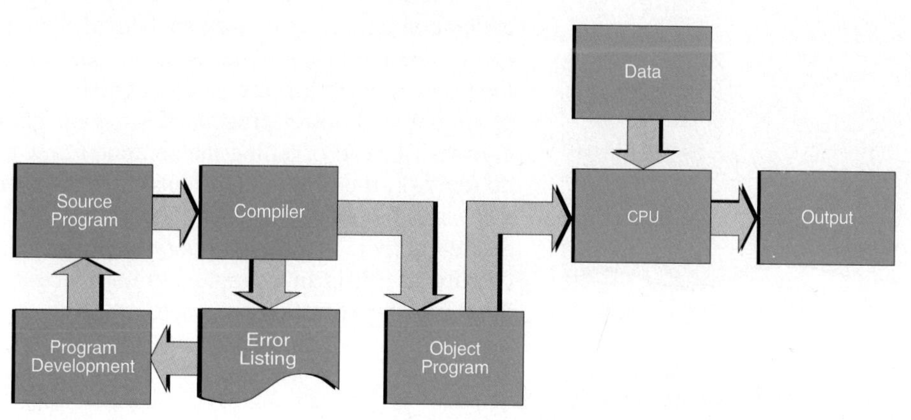

FIGURE 12-17
When a compiler is used, a source language program is compiled into a machine language object program. Usually, both the source and object programs are stored on disk. When the user wants to run the program, the object program is loaded into the main memory of the CPU and the program instructions begin executing. As instructed by the program, the CPU processes data and creates output. Errors in the source program identified during compilation are shown on an error listing that can be used to make the necessary corrections during program development.

Because machine language is unique to each processor, different computers require different compilers for the same language. For example, a mainframe, minicomputer, and personal computer would each have different compilers that would translate the same source language program into the specific machine language for each computer.

While a compiler translates an entire program, an **interpreter** translates one program statement at a time and then executes the resulting machine language before translating the next program statement. When using an interpreter, each time the program is run, the source program is interpreted into machine language and executed. No object program is produced. Figure 12-18 illustrates this process.

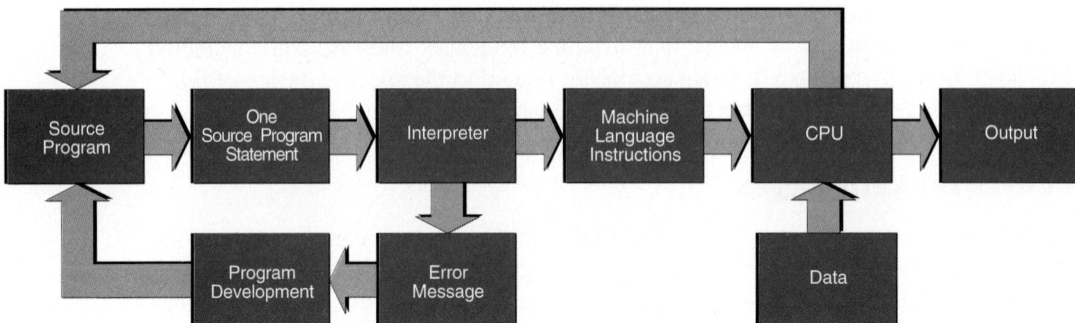

FIGURE 12-18
When an interpreter is used, one source language statement at a time is interpreted into machine language instructions that are executed immediately by the CPU. As instructed by the machine language instructions, the CPU processes data and creates output. Error messages indicating an invalid source language statement are produced as each source program statement is interpreted and are used to make the necessary corrections during program development.

Interpreters are often used with personal computers that do not have the memory or computing power required by compilers. The advantage of interpreters is that the compiling process is not necessary before program changes can be tested. The disadvantage of interpreters is that interpreted programs do not run as fast as compiled programs because the translation to machine language occurs each time the program is run. Compilers for most high-level languages are now available for the newer and more powerful personal computers.

Fourth-Generation Languages

The evolution of computer languages is sometimes described in terms of generations with machine, assembly, and high-level languages considered the first, second, and third generations, respectively. Each generation offered significant improvements in ease of use and programming flexibility over the previous generation. Although a clear definition does not yet exist, **fourth-generation languages (4GLs)**, sometimes called **very high-level languages**, continue the programming language evolution by being even easier to use than high-level languages for both the programmer and the nonprogramming user.

A term commonly used to describe fourth-generation languages is **nonprocedural**, which means that the programmer does not specify the procedures to be used to accomplish a task as is done with lower procedural language generations. Instead of telling the computer how to do the task, the programmer tells the computer *what* is to be done, usually by describing the desired output. A database query language (Figure 12-19) is an example of a nonprocedural fourth-generation language.

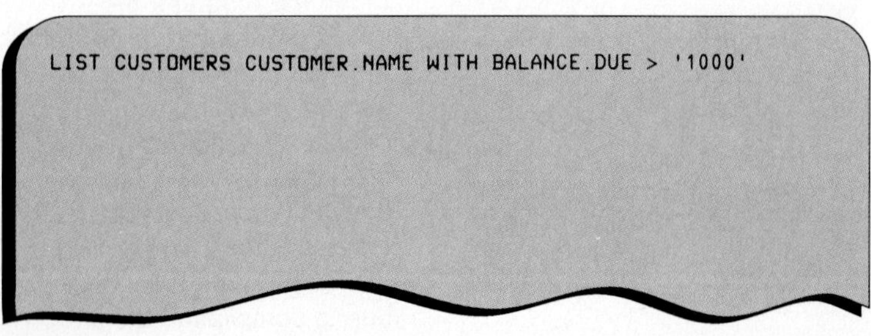

LIST CUSTOMERS CUSTOMER.NAME WITH BALANCE.DUE > '1000'

FIGURE 12-19
This database query is considered an example of a fourth-generation language because it tells the computer what the user wants, not how to perform the processing.

The advantage of fourth-generation languages is that they are *results* oriented (*what* is to be done, not *how*), and they can be used by nonprogramming personnel such as users. The disadvantage of fourth-generation languages is that they do not provide as many processing options to the programmer as other language generations and they require more computer processing power that other language generations. Most experts, however, believe that their ease of use far outweighs these disadvantages and they predict that fourth-generation languages will continue to be more widely used.

An extension of fourth-generation languages, sometimes called the fifth generation, is a natural language. A **natural language** is a type of query language that allows the user to enter a question as if he or she were speaking to another person. For example, a fourth-generation query might be stated as LIST SALESPERSON TOTAL-SALES BY REGION. A natural language version of that same query might be TELL ME THE NAME OF EACH SALESPERSON AND THE TOTAL SALES FOR EACH REGION. The natural language allows the user more flexibility in the structure of the query and can even ask the user a question if it does not understand what is meant by the initial query statement. A few natural languages are available today but they are not yet widely used.

PROGRAMMING LANGUAGES USED TODAY

Although there are hundreds of programming languages, only a few are used extensively enough to be recognized as industry standards. Most of these are high-level programming languages that can be used on a variety of computers. In this section, we discuss the popular programming languages that are commonly used, their origins, and their primary purpose.

To help you understand the differences, we show program code for each of the most popular languages. The code is from programs that solve the same problem. The problem is to compute the net price of a sale. This is done by multiplying the quantity sold times the unit price. A discount of 5% is calculated if the gross sale is over $100.00.

BASIC

BASIC, which stands for **B**eginner's **A**ll-purpose **S**ymbolic **I**nstruction **C**ode, was developed by John Kemeny and Thomas Kurtz in 1964 at Dartmouth College (Figure 12-20). They originally designed BASIC to be a simple, interactive programming language for college students to learn and use. BASIC has become one of the most popular programming languages in use on microcomputers and minicomputers today.

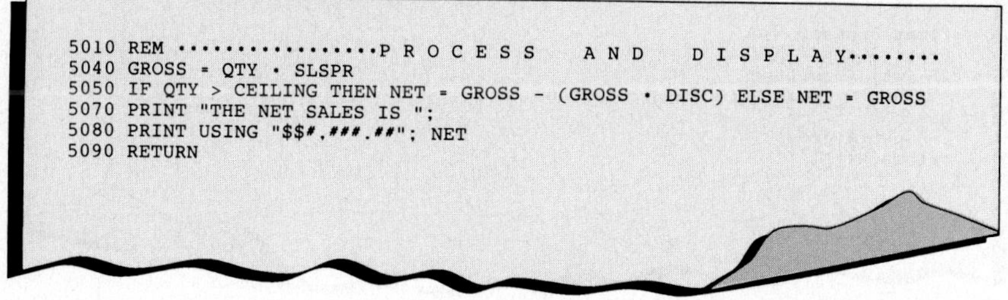

```
5010 REM ••••••••••••••••••P R O C E S S   A N D   D I S P L A Y••••••••
5040 GROSS = QTY • SLSPR
5050 IF QTY > CEILING THEN NET = GROSS - (GROSS • DISC) ELSE NET = GROSS
5070 PRINT "THE NET SALES IS ";
5080 PRINT USING "$$#,###.##"; NET
5090 RETURN
```

FIGURE 12-20
An excerpt from a BASIC program.

COBOL

COBOL (**CO**mmon **B**usiness **O**riented **L**anguage) was introduced in 1960. Backed by the U.S. Department of Defense, COBOL was developed by a committee of representatives from both government and industry. Rear Admiral Grace M. Hopper was a key person on the committee and is recognized as one of the prime developers of the COBOL language. COBOL is one of the most widely used programming languages for business applications (Figure 12-21). Using an English-like format, COBOL instructions are arranged in sentences and grouped into paragraphs. The English format makes COBOL easy to write and read, but also makes it a wordy language that produces lengthy program code. COBOL is very good for processing large files and performing relatively simple business calculations. Other languages are better suited to performing complex mathematical formulas and functions.

FIGURE 12-21
An excerpt from a COBOL program. Notice the additional words in the COBOL program compared to the BASIC program in Figure 12-20. Although the extra words increase the time it takes to write a COBOL program, they also make the program easier to read and understand.

```
016200 C010-PROCESS-AND-DISPLAY.
016400••••••••••••••••••••••••••••••••••••••••••••••••••••••••••••••
016600• FUNCTION:                          CALCULATE NET SALES AMOUNT    •
016700•                                    AND DISPLAY RESULTS           •
016800• ENTRY/EXIT:                        B000-LOOP-CONTROL             •
016900• CALLS:                             NONE                          •
017100••••••••••••••••••••••••••••••••••••••••••••••••••••••••••••••
017300   COMPUTER GROSS-SALES-WRK = QUANTITY-SOLD-WRK • SALES-PRICE-WRK.
017500   IF QUANTITY-SOLD-WRK IS GREATER THAN CEILING
017600       COMPUTE NET-SALES-WRK = GROSS-SALES-WRK -
017700            <GROSS-SALES-WRK • DISCOUNT-RATE)
017800   ELSE
017900       MOVE GROSS-SALES-WRK TO NET-SALES-WRK.
018100   MOVE NET-SALES-WRK TO NET-SALES-OUTPUT.
018300    DISPLAY CLEAR-SCREEN.
018500   WRITE PRINT-LINE FROM DETAIL-LINE
018600        AFTER ADVANCING 2.
```

C

The **C** programming language was developed at Bell Laboratories in 1972 by Dennis Ritchie (Figure 12-22). It was originally designed as a programming language for writing systems software, but it is now considered a general-purpose programming language. C is a powerful programming language that requires professional programming skills to be used effectively. The use of C to develop various types of software, including commercial applications, is increasing. C programs are often used with the Unix operating system (most of the Unix operating system is written in C).

FIGURE 12-22
An excerpt from a C program.

```
float gross;
gross = qty • price;
if (qty > ceiling)
    net = gross - (gross • discount_rate);
else
    net = gross;
return(net);
```

FORTRAN

FORTRAN (FORmula TRANslator) was developed by a team of IBM programmers led by John Backus. Released in 1957, FORTRAN was designed as a programming language to be used by scientists, engineers, and mathematicians (Figure 12-23). FORTRAN is considered the first high-level language that was developed and is noted for its capability to easily express and efficiently calculate mathematical equations.

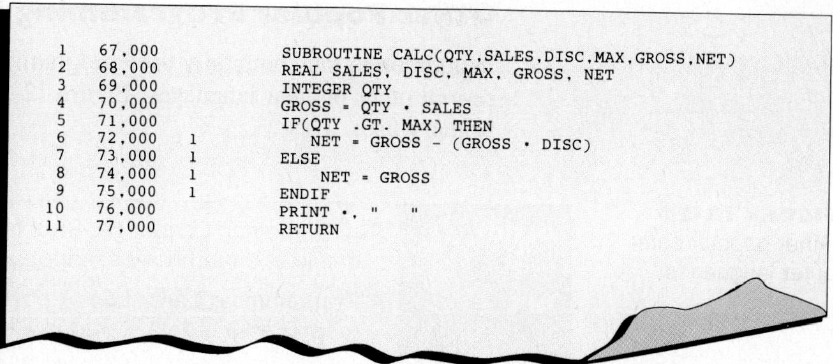

```
      SUBROUTINE CALC(QTY,SALES,DISC,MAX,GROSS,NET)
      REAL SALES, DISC, MAX, GROSS, NET
      INTEGER QTY
      GROSS = QTY * SALES
      IF(QTY .GT. MAX) THEN
         NET = GROSS - (GROSS * DISC)
      ELSE
         NET = GROSS
      ENDIF
      PRINT *, "  "
      RETURN
```

FIGURE 12-23
An excerpt from a FORTRAN program.

Pascal

The **Pascal** language was developed in 1968 by Niklaus Wirth, a computer scientist at the Institut für Informatik in Zurich, Switzerland. It was developed for teaching programming. The name Pascal is not an abbreviation or acronym, but rather the name of a mathematician, Blaise Pascal (1623–1662), who developed one of the earliest calculating machines. Pascal, available for use on both personal and large computers, was one of the first programming languages developed where the instructions in the language were designed and written so that programmers using Pascal would be encouraged to develop programs that follow structured program design (Figure 12-24).

```
BEGIN                                      (* Begin procedure *)
   GROSS := SALES * QTY;
   IF QTY > CEILING
      THEN NET := GROSS - (GROSS * DISCOUNT_RATE)
      ELSE NET := GROSS;
   WRITELN('THE NET SALES IS $',NET:6:2)
END;                                       (* End of procedure *)
```

FIGURE 12-24
An excerpt from a Pascal program.

Ada

The programming language **Ada** is named for Augusta Ada Byron, Countess of Lovelace, a mathematician in the 1800s, who is thought to have written the first program. The development of Ada was supported by the U. S. Department of Defense and its use is required on all U. S. government military projects. Ada was introduced in 1980 and designed to facilitate the writing and maintenance of large programs that would be used over a long period of time. The language encourages coding of readable programs that are also portable, allowing them to be transferred from computer to computer (Figure 12-25).

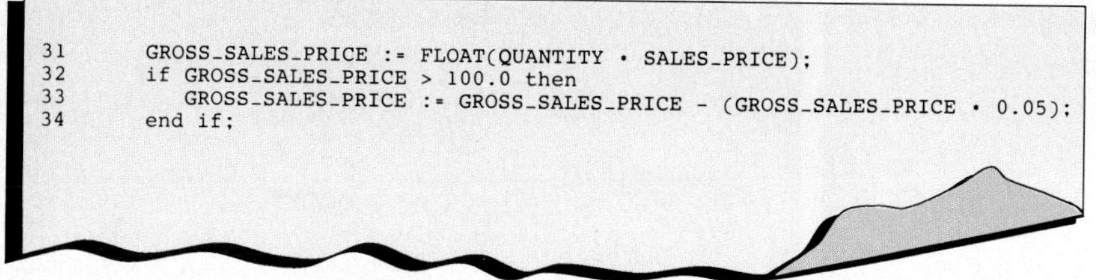

```
GROSS_SALES_PRICE := FLOAT(QUANTITY * SALES_PRICE);
if GROSS_SALES_PRICE > 100.0 then
   GROSS_SALES_PRICE := GROSS_SALES_PRICE - (GROSS_SALES_PRICE * 0.05);
end if;
```

FIGURE 12-25
An excerpt from an Ada program.

Other Popular Programming Languages

In addition to the commonly used programming languages we just discussed, there are several other popular languages. Figure 12-26 lists some of these languages and their primary uses.

FIGURE 12-26
Other popular computer languages.

ALGOL	**ALGO**rithmetic **L**anguage. Structured programming language used for scientific and mathematical applications.
APL	**A P**rogramming **L**anguage. A powerful, easy-to-learn language that is good for processing data stored in a table (matrix) format.
FORTH	Similar to C. Creates fast and efficient program code. Originally developed to control astronomical telescopes.
LISP	**LIS**t **P**rocessing. Popular artificial intelligence language.
LOGO	Primarily known as an educational tool to teach problem-solving skills.
MODULA-3	Similar to Pascal. Used primarily for developing systems software.
PILOT	**P**rogrammed **I**nquiry **L**earning **O**r **T**eaching. Used by educators to write computer-aided instruction programs.
PL/I	**P**rogramming **L**anguage/**O**ne. Business and scientific language that combines many of the features of FORTRAN and COBOL.
PROLOG	**PRO**gramming in **LOG**ic. Used for artificial intelligence.
RPG	**R**eport **P**rogram **G**enerator. Uses special forms to help user specify input, output, and calculation requirements of a program.

APPLICATION GENERATORS

Application generators, also called **program generators**, are programs that produce source-language programs, such as BASIC or COBOL, based on input, output, and processing specifications entered by the user. Application generators can greatly reduce the amount of time required to develop a program. They are predicated on the fact that most programs are comprised of standard processing modules, such as routines to read, write, or compare records, that can be combined together to create unique programs. These standard processing modules are stored in a library and are selected and grouped together based on user specifications. Application generators often use menu and screen generators to assist in developing an application.

A **menu generator** lets the user specify a menu (list) of processing options that can be selected. The resulting menu is automatically formatted with heading, footing, and prompt line text (Figure 12-27).

FIGURE 12-27
The left screen is part of a menu generator from ORACLE Corporation that can be used to quickly create professional looking menus on the right screen.

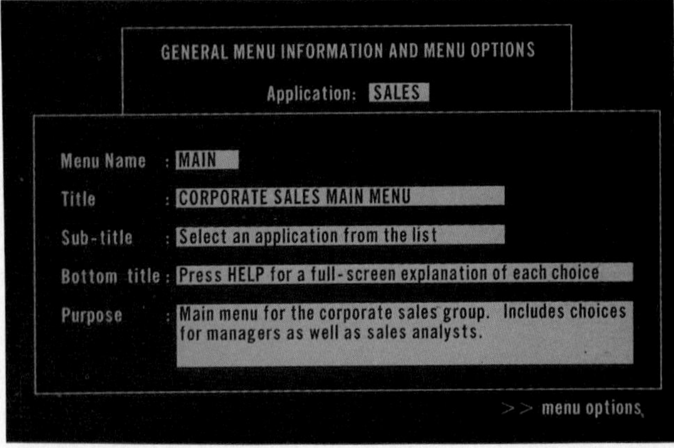

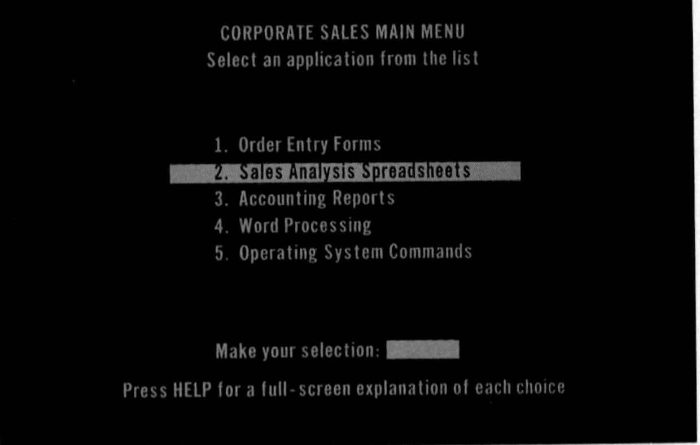

A **screen generator**, sometimes called a **screen painter**, allows the user to design an input or output screen by entering the names and descriptions of the input and output data directly on the screen. The advantage is that the user enters the data exactly as it will appear after the program is created. As each data name, such as Order No., is entered, the screen generator asks the user to specify the length and type of data that will be entered and what processing, if any, should take place before or after the data is entered. The order entry screen shown in Figure 12-28 was created in just one hour using SQL*FORMS, a screen generator product from ORACLE Corporation.

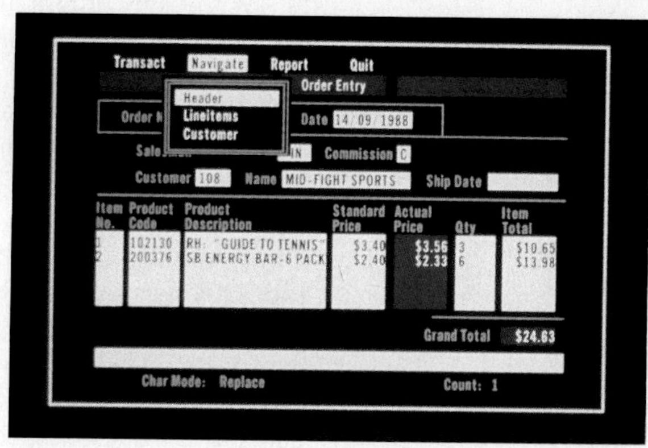

FIGURE 12-28
This order entry screen and the program to process the data were created in one hour using a screen generator from ORACLE Corporation. Using the traditional programming technique of writing individual program instructions would have taken considerably longer.

OBJECT-ORIENTED PROGRAMMING

Object-oriented programming (OOP) is a new approach to developing software that allows programmers to create **objects**, a combination of data and program instructions. Traditional programming methods keep data, such as files, independent of the programs that work with the data. Each traditional program, therefore, must define how the data will be used for that particular program. This often results in redundant programming code that must be changed every time the structure of the data is changed, such as when a new field is added to a file. With OOP, the program instructions and data are combined into objects that can be used repeatedly by programmers whenever they need them. Specific instructions, called **methods** define how the object acts when it is used by a program. The following example, illustrated in Figure 12-29, describes how OOP minimizes the number of instructions that must be defined.

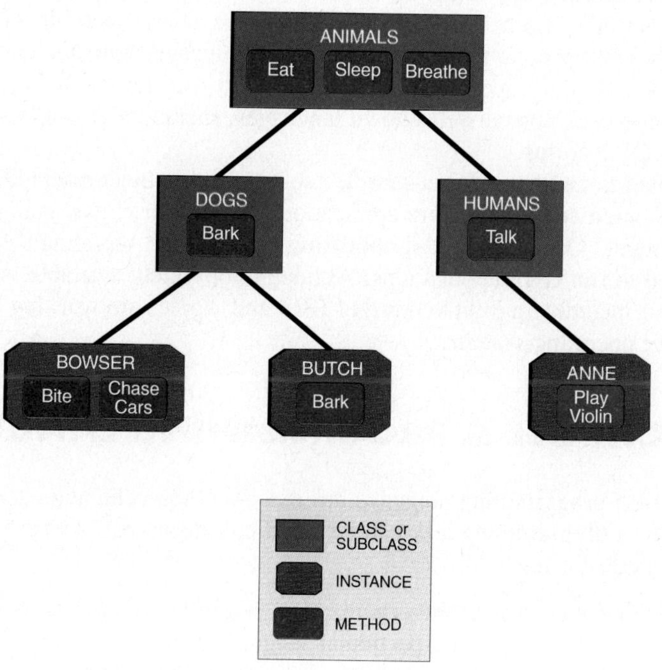

FIGURE 12-29
Object-oriented programming (OOP) allows procedures (called methods) to be combined with data to form objects. In traditional programming, procedures are defined by the program instructions that are separate from the data. In OOP, the methods define how the object will act when it is referenced and how it can be *inherited* from higher levels, called classes. For example, the method BARK can be inherited by BOWSER from the class DOGS. Objects can also have unique procedures that differ from higher levels. Thus, BUTCH can have a different BARK than BOWSER. The capability to inherit methods from higher levels makes programming more efficient because only methods unique to the specific object need to be defined. A specific occurrence of an object is called an instance.

With OOP, programmers define classes of objects. Each **class** contains the methods that are unique to that class. As shown in Figure 12-29, the class of animals could contain methods on how animals eat, sleep, and breathe. Each class can have one or more subclasses. Each subclass contains the methods of its higher level classes plus whatever methods are unique to the subclass. For example, the subclass Humans contains the method Talk. The subclass Dogs contains the method Bark. Both subclasses, Humans and Dogs, also contain the Eat, Sleep, and Breathe methods of the higher class, Animals. The OOP capability to pass methods to lower levels is called **inheritance**. A specific **instance** of an object contains all methods from its higher level classes plus any methods that are unique to the object. For example, the object Anne contains a method on how to play the violin. The object Bowser contains methods on how Bowser bites and chases cars. Although these methods may be shared by other humans and dogs, respectively, they cannot be placed at higher levels because they are not shared by all humans or dogs. When an OOP object is sent an instruction to do something, called a **message**, unlike a traditional program, the message does not have to tell the OOP object exactly what to do. *What to do* is defined by the methods that the OOP object contains or has inherited. For example, if the object Bowser was sent a message to bark, the method of barking would be defined by the bark method in the subclass Dogs. However, if the object Butch was sent the same message to bark, its actions would be defined by the bark (perhaps a growl) associated with Butch. This illustrates that higher level methods can be overridden to define actions unique to a particular object or class.

A business example of an object would include a class called Invoices. With traditional programming, each time an invoice is displayed on a screen, specific programming instructions are included in the program. With OOP, a method called Display would be part of the object Invoice. An OOP program would only have to send a message identifying the object (Invoice) and stating the desired method (Display). How to display the invoice would be defined as part of the Invoice object.

As OOP is used by an organization, the organization builds a library of OOP objects and classes that can be reused. The more extensive the library, the more powerful and efficient OOP becomes. OOP development systems, such as the Interface Builder used on NeXT computers, allow programmers to access such libraries and link objects to quickly build programs. The programming language most often associated with OOP is Smalltalk, developed by Xerox at their Palo Alto Research Center (PARC) in the 1970s. Versions of several well-known languages, including C and Pascal, also currently offer OOP features.

Closely related to OOP are object-oriented software and object-oriented operating systems. **Object-oriented software** are applications that are developed using OOP programming techniques. **Object-oriented operating systems** are operating systems specifically designed to run OOP applications. Although not widely available, several major companies, including a joint venture of IBM and Apple, are working on versions of object-oriented operating systems.

HOW TO CHOOSE A PROGRAMMING LANGUAGE

◆ Although each programming language has its own unique characteristics, selecting a language for a programming task can be a difficult decision. Factors to be considered include the following:

1. The programming standards of the organization. Many organizations have programming standards that specify that a particular language is used for all applications.
2. The need to interface with other programs. If a program is going to work with other existing or future programs, ideally it should be programmed in the same language as the other programs.

3. The suitability of a language to the application to be programmed. As we discussed, most languages are best suited to a particular type of application. For example, FORTRAN works well with applications requiring many calculations.
4. The expertise of the available programmers. Unless another language is far superior, you should choose the language used by the existing programmers.
5. The availability of the language. Not all languages are available on all machines.
6. The need for the application to be portable. If the application will have to run on different machines, you should choose a common language so the program has to be written only once.
7. The anticipated maintenance requirements. If the user anticipates that the application will have to be modified frequently, consider a language that can be maintained easily and that supports structured programming concepts.

SUMMARY OF PROGRAMMING LANGUAGES

◆ Although procedural languages such as COBOL and BASIC will continue to be used for many years, there is a clear trend toward the creation of programs using non-procedural tools, such as fourth-generation and natural languages, that allow users to specify what they want accomplished. Your knowledge of programming languages will help you to understand how the computer converts data into information and to obtain better results if you directly participate in the programming process.

CHAPTER SUMMARY

1. A **computer program** is a detailed set of instructions that directs a computer to perform the tasks necessary to process data into information.
2. **Program development** is a series of five steps that take place when a computer program is developed. These steps include: (1) review of the program specifications, (2) program design, (3) program coding, (4) program testing, and (5) finalizing the documentation.
3. In the information system life cycle, program development occurs during the development phase.
4. **Program specifications** can include many documents such as data flow diagrams, system flowcharts, process specifications, a data dictionary, screen formats, and report layouts.
5. During **program design** a logical solution, or **logic**, for a program is developed and documented.
6. **Structured program design** is methodology that emphasizes three main program design concepts: modules, control structures, and single entry/single exit.
7. **Modules**, or **subroutines**, which perform a given task within a program, can be developed individually and then combined to form a complete program.
8. **Structure charts**, or **hierarchy charts**, are used to decompose the modules of a program.
9. The three **control structures** are: the **sequence structure** , where one process occurs immediately after another; the **selection structure**, or **if-then-else structure**, which is used for conditional program logic; and the **iteration structure** or **looping structure**.
10. The **case structure**, which is a variation of the selection structure, is used when a condition is being tested that can lead to more than two alternatives.
11. The two forms of iteration are the **do-while structure** and the **do-until structure**.
12. **Single entry/single exit** means that there is only one **entry point** and one **exit point** from each of the control structures.
13. Three commonly used program design tools are **program flowcharts**, **pseudocode**, and the **Warnier-Orr technique**.
14. Structured walk-throughs are used to review the design and logic of a program.
15. **Coding** is the process of writing the program instructions.

16. Before a program is used to process *real* data it should be thoroughly tested to make sure it is functioning correctly. A simple type of testing is **desk checking**.
17. Programs can be tested for **syntax errors** (grammar). **Logic testing** checks for incorrect results using **test data**.
18. **Debugging** refers to the process of locating and correcting program errors, or **bugs**, found during testing.
19. **Program maintenance** includes all changes to a program once it is implemented and processing real transactions.
20. A **programming language** is a set of written words and symbols that allow a programmer or user to communicate with the computer.
21. Programming languages fit into one of four categories: machine language; assembly language; high-level languages; and fourth-generation languages.
22. Before they can be executed, all programs are converted into **machine language**, the fundamental language of computers, also called **low-level language**.
23. **Assembly language** is a low-level language that is closely related to machine language. It uses **mnemonics** or **symbolic operation code**.
24. Assembly languages use **symbolic addressing** and include **macroinstructions**. Assembly language programs are converted into machine language instructions by an **assembler**.
25. **High-level languages** are easier to learn and use than low-level languages. They use sentences called **program statements**.
26. **Compilers** and **interpreters** are used to translate high-level **source programs** into machine language **object code** or **object programs**.
27. **Fourth-generation languages (4GLs)**, also called **very high-level languages**, are **nonprocedural**, which means that the user tells the computer *what* is to be done, not *how* to do it.
28. A **natural language** allows the user to enter a question as if he or she were speaking to another person.
29. Commonly used programming languages include **BASIC**, **COBOL**, **C**, **FORTRAN**, **Pascal**, and **Ada**.
30. **BASIC** is one of the most commonly used programming languages on microcomputers and minicomputers.
31. **COBOL** is the most widely used programming language for business applications.
32. **C** is an increasingly popular programming language that requires professional programming skills to be used effectively.
33. **FORTRAN** is noted for its capability to easily express and efficiently calculate mathematical equations.
34. **Pascal** contains programming statements that encourage the use of structured program design.
35. **Ada**, developed and supported by the U.S. Department of Defense, was designed to facilitate the writing and maintenance of large programs that would be used over a long period of time.
36. **Application generators**, or **program generators**, produce source-language programs based on input, output, and processing specifications entered by the user.
37. A **menu generator** lets the user specify a menu of options.
38. A **screen generator**, or **screen painter**, allows the user to design an input or output screen.
39. **Object-oriented programming (OOP)** is a new approach to developing software that allows programmers to create objects.
40. **Objects** are a combination of data and program instructions.
41. **Methods** define how the object acts when it is used by a program.
42. With OOP, each **class** contains the methods that are unique to that class.
43. **Inheritance** is the OOP capability to pass methods to lower levels of classes or objects.
44. A specific **instance** of an object contains all methods inherited from its higher level classes plus and methods that are unique to it.
45. A **message** is an instruction to do something that is sent to an OOP object.
46. **Object-oriented software** are applications that are developed using OOP programming techniques.
47. **Object-oriented operating systems** are operating systems specifically designed to run OOP applications.
48. Some of the factors that you should consider when you choose a programming language are: the programming standards of the organization; the need to interface with other programs; the suitability of a language to the application to be programmed; the expertise of the available programmers; the availability of the language; the need for the application to be portable; and the anticipated maintenance requirements.

KEY TERMS

Ada *12.17*
Application generator *12.18*
Assembler *12.13*
Assembly language *12.13*
BASIC *12.15*
Bugs *12.10*
C *12.16*
Case structure *12.5*
Class *12.20*
COBOL *12.16*
Coding *12.9*
Compiler *12.13*
Computer program *12.2*
Control structure *12.4*
Debugging *12.10*
Desk checking *12.9*
Do-until structure *12.5*
Do-while structure *12.5*
Entry point *12.6*
Exit point *12.6*
FORTRAN *12.17*
Fourth-generation language (4GL) *12.14*
Hierarchy chart *12.3*
High-level language *12.13*
If-then-else structure *12.4*
Inheritance *12.20*
Instance *12.20*
Interpreter *12.14*
Iteration structure *12.5*
Logic *12.3*
Logic testing *12.9*
Looping structure *12.5*
Low-level language *12.12*
Machine language *12.12*
Macroinstruction *12.13*
Menu generator *12.18*
Message *12.20*
Methods *12.19*
Mnemonics *12.13*
Module *12.3*
Natural language *12.15*
Nonprocedural *12.14*
Object *12.19*
Object code *12.13*
Object-oriented operating system *12.20*
Object-oriented programming (OOP) *12.19*
Object-oriented software *12.20*
Object program *12.13*
Pascal *12.17*
Program design *12.3*
Program development *12.2*
Program flowchart *12.6*
Program generator *12.18*
Program maintenance *12.11*
Programming language *12.12*
Program specifications *12.3*
Program statement *12.13*
Pseudocode *12.8*
Screen generator *12.19*
Screen painter *12.19*
Selection structure *12.4*
Sequence structure *12.4*
Single entry/single exit *12.6*
Source program *12.13*
Structure chart *12.3*
Structured program design *12.3*
Subroutine *12.3*
Symbolic addressing *12.13*
Symbolic operation code *12.13*
Syntax error *12.9*
Test data *12.10*
Very high-level language *12.14*
Warnier-Orr technique *12.8*

REVIEW QUESTIONS

1. What is a computer program?
2. List the five steps in program development and give a brief description of each step. Explain how the program development steps relate to the information system life cycle.
3. List at least four types of documents that might be included in the program specifications. Explain the procedures that should be followed if a programmer believes that some aspect of the design should be changed.
4. Draw the three control structures and the two variations that are used in structured program design.
5. Explain the structured programming concept of single entry/single exit. Why is it important?
6. Briefly describe three types of program design tools that are used by programmers.
7. What is desk checking?
8. List at least five types of program documentation. When should documentation be performed?
9. Describe the four categories of programming languages.
10. Explain the advantage of fourth-generation languages.
11. List six commonly used programming languages and explain their primary uses.
12. How do application generators reduce the amount of time required to program?
13. What is object-oriented programming? Explain its advantages over traditional programming methods.
14. List seven factors that you should consider when you choose a programming language.

CONTROVERSIAL ISSUES

1. Although there is a trend toward standardized operating systems, different versions of programming languages are frequently made available. Discuss the advantages and disadvantages of using a single programming language for all applications.
2. Some people believe that programming languages as we know them today will eventually be eliminated. Instead of writing program instructions in a specific computer language, programmers will be able to use a fifth-generation natural language to instruct the computer what to do. Do you think this will happen? If so, when?

RESEARCH PROJECTS

1. Choose a major application at your school or place of work such as registration, payroll, or accounting. Find out what language was used to write the application and why it was chosen. Report to your class.
2. Review the employment advertisements in your local newspaper for computer programming positions. Prepare a report discussing which programming languages are in demand.

Career Opportunities in Information Processing

OBJECTIVES

- Discuss the three areas that provide the majority of computer-related jobs
- Describe the career positions available in an information systems department
- Describe information processing career opportunities in sales, service and repair, consulting, and education and training
- Discuss the compensation and growth trends for information processing careers
- Discuss the three fields in the information processing industry
- Discuss career development, including professional organizations, certification, and professional growth and continuing education

As society becomes more information oriented, computers are becoming an integral part of most jobs. For this reason, the knowledge you have gained from this text will apply in some way to *any* career you choose. You might, however, want to consider a career in the information processing industry itself.

The purpose of this chapter is to show you the opportunities that exist in the industry, present computer industry career trends, and discuss how to prepare for a career in information systems. Even if you don't choose a computer industry career, you will profit in whatever career you choose if you understand the jobs that computer professionals perform, because any job you choose will likely involve you with one or more of these computer professionals.

THE INFORMATION PROCESSING INDUSTRY

The information processing industry is one of the largest industries in the world with annual sales of well over $100 billion. Job opportunities in the industry come primarily from three areas: the companies that provide the computer equipment; the companies that develop computer software; and the companies that hire information processing professionals to work with these products. As in any major industry, there are also many service companies that support each of these three areas. An example would be a company that sells computer supplies such as printer paper and diskettes.

FIGURE 13-1
Personal-computer keyboards are being assembled and packaged.

The Computer Equipment Industry

The computer equipment, or hardware, industry includes all manufacturers and distributors of computers and computer-related equipment such as disk and tape drives, terminals, printers, and communications equipment (Figure 13-1).

The five largest minicomputer and mainframe manufacturers in the United States—IBM, Digital Equipment Corporation, UNISYS, Hewlett-Packard, and NCR— are huge organizations with tens of thousands of employees worldwide. Major microcomputer manufacturers include IBM, Apple, Compaq, and Tandy. The largest company, IBM, has had annual sales of over $70 billion. In addition to the major companies, the computer equipment industry is also known for the many new start-up companies that appear each year. These new companies take advantage of rapid changes in equipment technology, such as laser printers, video disks, and fiber optics, to create new products and new job opportunities. Besides the companies that make end user equipment, thousands of companies make components that most users never see. These companies manufacture chips (processor, memory), power supplies, wiring, and the hundreds of other parts that go into computer equipment.

The Computer Software Industry

The computer software industry includes all the developers and distributors of applications and system software. Thousands of companies provide a wide range of software from operating systems to complete business systems. The personal computer boom in the early 1980s provided numerous opportunities in the software industry. Thousands of individuals went into business for themselves by creating useful programs for the new microcomputers. Many of these people started by working out of their homes, developing their first software products on their own time while holding other jobs.

Today, software alone is a huge industry that includes leading companies such as MSA, ASK, Microsoft, Lotus, and Borland, with annual sales in the hundreds of millions of dollars. Most of these companies specialize in one particular type of software product such as business application software or productivity tools such as word processing or spreadsheets.

Information Processing Professionals

Information processing professionals are the people who put the equipment and software to work to produce information for the end user (Figure 13-2). This includes people such as programmers and systems analysts who are hired by companies to work in an information systems department. We discuss these and other positions available in the information processing industry in the next section.

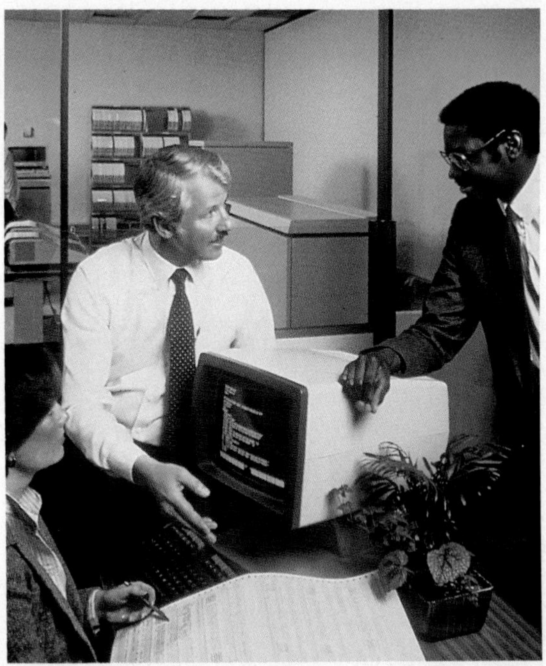

FIGURE 13-2
Computer professionals must be able to understand the end user's point of view and often meet with the user to review his or her information processing requirements.

WHAT ARE THE CAREER OPPORTUNITIES IN INFORMATION PROCESSING?

The use of computers in so many aspects of life has created thousands of new jobs. Some of these occupations, such as personal computer network sales representative, didn't even exist ten years ago. We describe some of the current career opportunities, and encourage you to consider them as you prepare for your future profession.

Working in an Information Systems Department

In Chapter 1 we discussed the various jobs within an information systems department. These positions include: data entry personnel, computer operators, computer programmers, systems analysts, database administrator, manager of information systems, and vice president of information systems.

The people in these positions work together as a team to meet the information demands of their organizations. Throughout this book we have discussed the responsibilities associated with many of these positions, including the role of the systems analysts in the information system life cycle (Chapter 11) and the steps programmers perform in program development (Chapter 12). Another way to visualize the positions and their relationships is to look at an organization chart such as the one shown in Figure 13-3. In addition to management, the jobs in an information systems department can be classified into five categories:

1. Operations
2. Data administration
3. Systems analysis and design
4. Programming
5. Information center

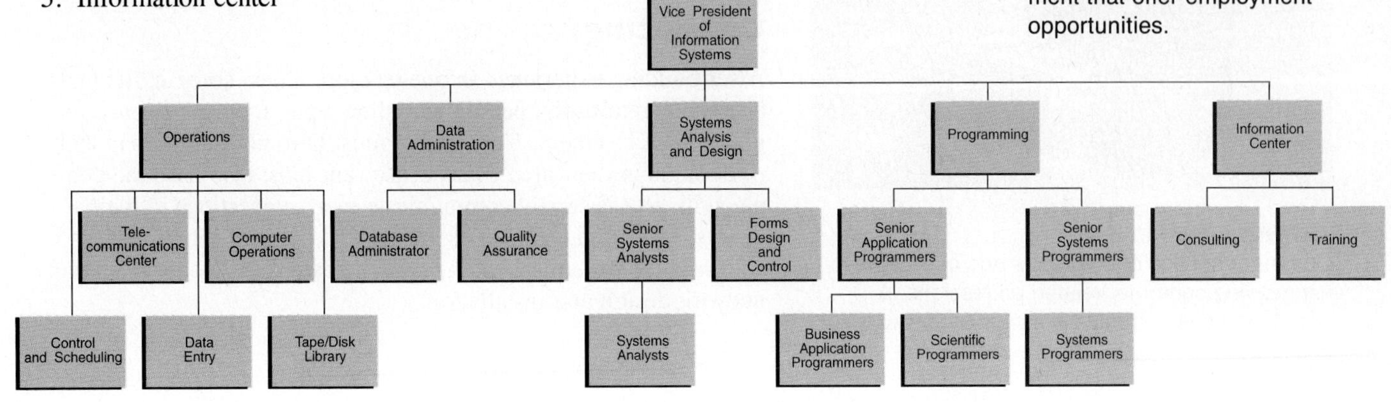

FIGURE 13-3
The organization chart shows the many areas within an information systems department that offer employment opportunities.

Operations personnel are responsible for carrying out tasks such as operating the computer equipment that is located in the computer center. The primary responsibility of data administration is to maintain and control the organization's database. In systems analysis and design, the various information systems needed by an organization are created and maintained. Programming develops the programs needed for the information systems, and the information center provides teaching and consulting services within an organization to help users meet their departmental and individual information processing needs. As you can see, an information systems department provides career opportunities for people with a variety of skills and talents.

FIGURE 13-4
Computer retailers, such as Computerland, need salespeople who understand personal computers and have good people skills.

Sales

Sales representatives must have a general understanding of computers and a specific knowledge of the product they are selling. Strong interpersonal, or people, skills are important, including listening ability and strong oral and written communication skills. Sales representatives are usually paid based on the amount of product they sell, and top sales representatives are often the most highly compensated employees in a computer company.

Some sales representatives work directly for equipment and software manufacturers and others work for resellers. Most personal computer products are sold through dealers such as Computerland (Figure 13-4). Some dealers, such as Egghead Discount Software, specialize in selling the most popular software products.

Service and Repair

Being a **service and repair technician** is a challenging job for individuals who like to troubleshoot and solve problems and who have a strong background in electronics (Figure 13-5). In the early days of computers, repairs were often made at the site of the computer equipment. Today, however, malfunctioning components, such as circuit boards, are usually replaced and taken back to the service technician's office or sent to a special facility for repair. Many equipment manufacturers are now including special diagnostic software with their computer equipment that helps the service technician identify the problem. Using a modem, some computer systems can automatically telephone another computer at the service technician's office and leave a message that a malfunction has been detected.

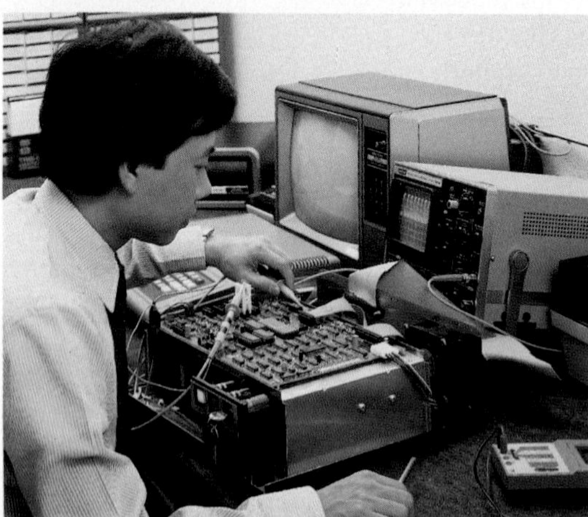

FIGURE 13-5
Computer service and repair is one of the fastest growing computer-related professions. A knowledge of electronics is essential for this occupation.

Consulting

After building experience in one or more areas, some individuals become **consultants**, people who draw upon their experience to give advice to others. Consultants must have not only strong technical skills in their area of expertise, but must also have the people skills to effectively communicate their suggestions to their clients. Qualified consultants are in high demand for such tasks as computer system selection, system design, and communications network design and installation.

Education and Training

The increased sophistication and complexity of today's computer products has opened wide opportunities in computer education and training (Figure 13-6). Qualified instructors are needed in schools, colleges, and universities and in private industry as well. In fact, the high demand for teachers has created a shortage at the university level, where many instructors have been lured into private industry because of higher pay. This shortage probably will not be filled in the near future; the supply of Ph.D.s, usually required at the university level, is not keeping up with the demand.

FIGURE 13-6
There is a high demand in schools and industry for qualified instructors who can teach information processing subjects.

COMPENSATION AND GROWTH TRENDS FOR INFORMATION PROCESSING CAREERS

◆ Compensation is a function of experience and demand for a particular skill. Demand is influenced by geographic location, with metropolitan areas usually having higher pay than rural areas. Figure 13-7 shows the result of a salary survey of over 80,000 computer professionals across the United States and Canada.

	YEARS EXP.	MEDIAN SALARY ($1,000)
PROGRAMMING:		
Commercial	<2 2–3 4–6 >6	27 33 35 40
Engineering/Scientific	<2 2–3 4–6 >6	31 35 38 43
Microcomputer/ Minicomputer	<2 2–3 4–6 >6	27 32 34 40
Software Engineer	<2 2–3 4–6 >6	30 36 41 46
Systems Software	<2 2–3 4–6 >6	32 38 40 49
MANAGEMENT:		
Data Center Operations		45
Programming Development		61
Systems Development		58
Technical Services		59
MIS Director/VP		67
BUSINESS SYSTEMS:		
Consultant		45
Project Leader/Sys. Analyst		43

	YEARS EXP.	MEDIAN SALARY ($1,000)
SPECIALISTS:		
Data Base Management Analyst	<4 4–6 >6	39 41 49
Information Center Analyst	<4 4–6 >6	30 33 43
Office Automation Analyst	<4 4–6 >6	30 34 40
Edp Auditor	<4 4–6 >6	35 38 44
Technical Writer	<4 4–6 >6	30 32 37
Telecommunications (Planning)	<4 >4	35 45
SALES:		
Hardware		55
Software		57
Services		56
Technical Support	<2 2–3 4–6 >6	32 35 38 45
Management		68
DATA CENTER:		
Computer Operator	<2 2–3 4–6 >6	20 23 25 29
Technical Data Center Analyst	<4 4–6 >6	37 44 46
Operations Support Technician	<4 >4	24 30
Communications/ Network Analyst	<4 >4	26 34

FIGURE 13-7
Salary levels (in thousands of dollars) for various computer industry positions are based on the number of years of experience. (Source: Source EDP, 1991 Professional Compensation Data, National Statistics).

As shown in Figure 13-8, some industries pay higher than others for the same job. According to the survey, the communications, utility, and aerospace industries pay the highest salaries. These industries have many challenging applications and pay the highest rate to obtain the best qualified employees.

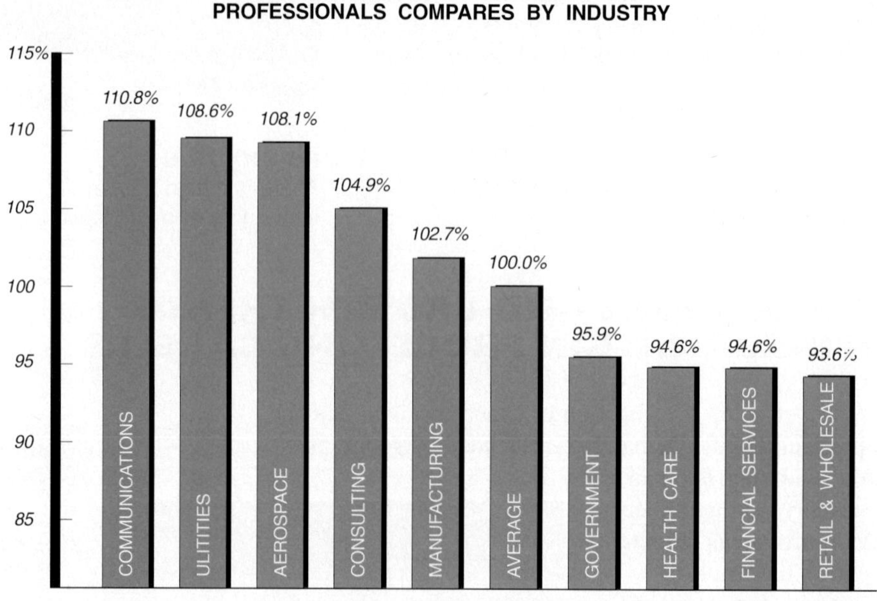

FIGURE 13-8
Some industries pay more for the same job position.

According to the U.S. Bureau of Labor Statistics, the fastest growing computer career positions through 1995 will be systems analyst, applications programmer, machine operator, and computer repair technician (Figure 13-9).

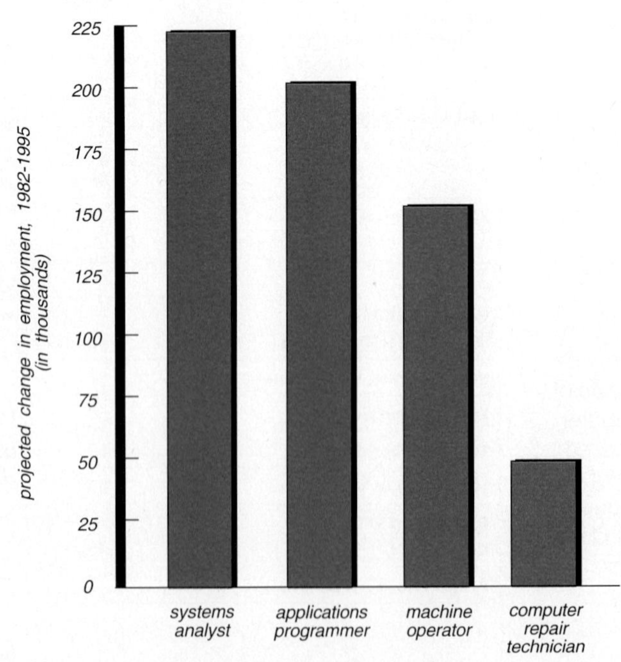

FIGURE 13-9
Computer careers with the highest projected growth, as compiled by the U.S. Bureau of Labor Statistics.

PREPARING FOR A CAREER IN INFORMATION PROCESSING

To prepare for a career in the information processing industry, individuals must decide what computer field they are interested in and obtain education in the field they chose. In this section we discuss the three major computer fields and some of the opportunities for obtaining education in those fields.

What Are the Fields in the Information Processing Industry?

While this book has primarily focused on the use of computers in business, there are actually three broad fields in the information processing industry (Figure 13-10): computer information systems; computer science; and computer engineering. **Computer information systems (CIS)** refers to the use of computers to provide the information needed to operate businesses and other organizations. The field of **computer science** includes the technical aspects of computers such as hardware operation and systems software. **Computer engineering** deals with the design and manufacturing of electronic computer components and computer hardware. Each field provides unique career opportunities and has specialized requirements.

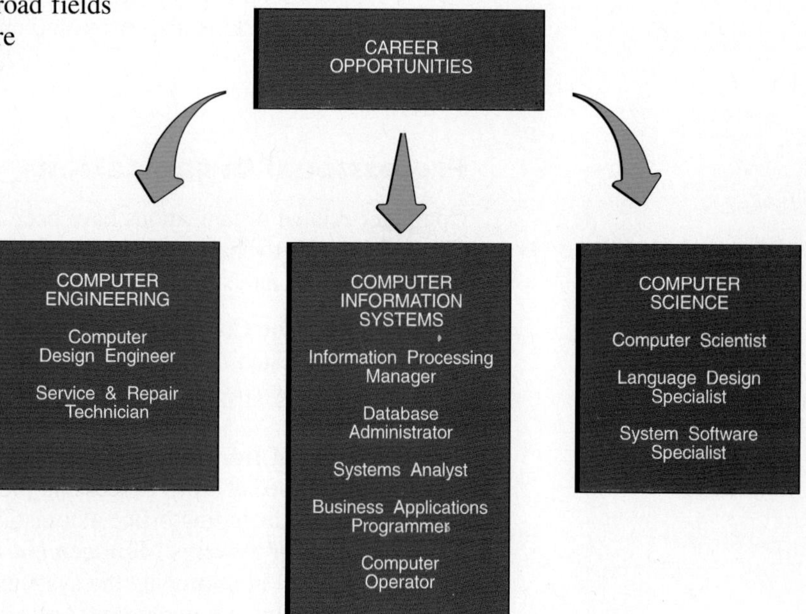

FIGURE 13-10
There are three broad fields of study in the information processing industry; each with specialized study requirements.

Obtaining Education for Information Processing Careers

The expanded use of computers in today's world has increased the demand for properly trained computer professionals. Educational institutions have responded to this demand by providing a variety of options for students to study information systems. Trade schools, technical schools, community colleges, colleges, and universities offer formal education and certification or degree programs in computer-related fields. If you are evaluating a program offered by one of these institutions, remember the three areas of information processing: computer information systems, computer science, and computer engineering. Frequently, schools will have separate programs for each area.

Understanding the differences among the three fields will help you to find the courses you want. For example, in a university, courses relating to computer information systems may be listed with the business courses, computer science courses may be with math, and computer engineering may be with electronic technology or electrical engineering. Because schools list and organize their computer courses in different ways, you should carefully read individual course descriptions whenever you are selecting computer education classes.

With the wide variety of career opportunities that exist in information processing, it is difficult to make anything other than broad general statements when it comes to discussing degree requirements for employment in the industry. As in most other industries, the more advanced degree an individual has in a chosen field, the better that individual's chances are for success. While not having a degree may limit a person's opportunities for securing a top position, it will neither prevent entry nor preclude success in information processing.

CAREER DEVELOPMENT IN THE INFORMATION PROCESSING INDUSTRY

◆ There are several ways for persons employed in the information processing industry to develop their skills and increase their recognition among their peers. These include professional organizations, certification, and professional growth and continuing education activities.

Professional Organizations

Computer-related organizations have been formed by people who have common interests and a desire to share their knowledge. Some of the organizations that have been influential in the industry include:

1. **Association for Computing Machinery (ACM)**. This association is composed of persons interested in computer science and computer science education. The association has many special interest groups such as computer graphics, database, and business.
2. **Association of Information Systems Professionals (AISP)**. This association was originally aimed at word processing professionals, but now includes a much broader membership, including office automation professionals.
3. **Association of Systems Management (ASM)**. This group is composed of individuals interested in improving the systems analysis and design field.
4. **Data Processing Management Association (DPMA)**. This is a professional association of programmers, systems analysts, and information processing managers.
5. **Institute of Electrical and Electronic Engineers (IEEE) and IEEE Computer Society (IEEE/CS)**. These organizations are primarily composed of computer scientists and engineers.

Each of these organizations has chapters throughout the United States (several have chapters throughout the world), offers monthly meetings, and sponsors periodic workshops, seminars, and conventions. Some organizations have student chapters or offer reduced membership fees for students. Attending professional meetings provides an excellent opportunity for students to learn about the information processing industry and to meet and talk with professionals in the field.

In addition to these and other professional organizations, user groups exist for most makes of computers. A **user group** is a group of people with common computer equipment or software interests that meet regularly to share information. Most metropolitan areas have one or more local computer societies that meet monthly to discuss topics of common interest about personal computers. For anyone employed or simply interested in the computer industry, these groups can be an effective and rewarding way to learn and continue career development.

Certification

Many professions offer certification programs as a way of encouraging and recognizing the efforts of their members to attain a level of knowledge about their profession. The best known certification programs in the information processing industry are administered by the **Institute for the Certification of Computer Professionals (ICCP)**. The ICCP offers four certification designations: Certified Computer Programmer (CCP); Certified Data Processor (CDP); Certified Systems Professional (CSP); and Associate Computer Professional (ACP). The CCP, CDP, and CSP designations are earned by passing three examinations. The ACP designation is obtained by passing a general computer knowledge test and any one of seven programming language tests. A summary of the test requirements for all of the designations is shown in Figure 13-11. To be eligible to take the CCP, CDP, and CSP examinations, a person must have a minimum of five years of experience in the information processing industry. The ACP examination, which is designed for entry level personnel, requires no previous industry experience.

```
                    ICCP CERTIFICATION EXAMINATIONS

A.  Examination Requirements for Certified Computer Programmer
    (CCP), Certified Data Processor (CDP), and Certified Systems
    Professional (CSP)

    1.  Core Examination (required for all designations)
        a.  Human and Organization Framework
        b.  Systems Concepts
        c.  Data and Information
        d.  Systems Development
        e.  Technology
        f.  Associated Disciplines
    2.  Professional Designation Examinations
        a.  Certified Computer Programmer (CCP)
            1)  Data and File Organization
            2)  Program Design
            3)  Procedural Program Structure
            4)  Procedural Programming Considerations
            5)  Integration with Hardware and Software
        b.  Certified Data Processor (CDP)
            1)  General Management and Organization Concepts
            2)  Project Management
            3)  Information Systems Management
        c.  Certified Systems Professional (CSP)
            1)  Systems Analysis
            2)  Systems Design and Implementation
            3)  The Systems Analyst as a Professional
    3.  Specialty Examinations (one required)
        a.  Business Information Systems
        b.  Communications
        c.  Office Information Systems
        d.  Scientific Programming
        e.  Software Engineering
        f.  Systems Programming

B.  Associate Computer Professional (ACP) Examination

    1.  Core Examination (same as for CCP, CDP, and CSP)
    2.  Programming Language Examinations (one required)
        a.  FORTRAN
        b.  Pascal
        c.  BASIC
        d.  RPG
        e.  COBOL
        f.  C
        g.  ADA
```

FIGURE 13-11
The subject areas for each of the four certification examinations offered by the Institute for the Certification of Computer Professionals (ICCP). Three of the designations (CCP, CDP, and CSP) are designed for experienced professionals with five or more years of industry experience. The fourth designation (ACP) does not require previous industry experience.

Professional Growth and Continuing Education

Because of rapid changes in technology, staying aware of new products and services in the information processing industry can be a challenging task. One way of keeping up is by participating in professional growth and continuing education activities. This broad category includes events such as workshops, seminars, conferences, conventions, and trade shows that provide both general and specific information on equipment, software, services, and issues affecting the industry, such as computer security. Workshops and seminars usually last a day or two, while conferences, conventions, and trade shows often last a week. The largest trade show in the United States, **COMDEX**, brings together nearly 2,000 vendors to display their newest products and services to over 125,000 attendees (Figure 13-12).

FIGURE 13-12
COMDEX is one of the largest computer product trade shows in the world. Nearly 2,000 vendors come together to demonstrate their new equipment, software, and services to over 125,000 prospective customers.

Another way of keeping informed about what is going on in the computer industry is to regularly read one or more computer industry publications (Figure 13-13). There are hundreds of publications to choose from. Some publications, such as *Computerworld* and *InfoWorld*, are like newspapers and cover a wide range of issues. Other publications are oriented toward a particular topic area such as communications, personal computers, or a specific equipment manufacturer. Many of the more popular publications can be found in public or school libraries.

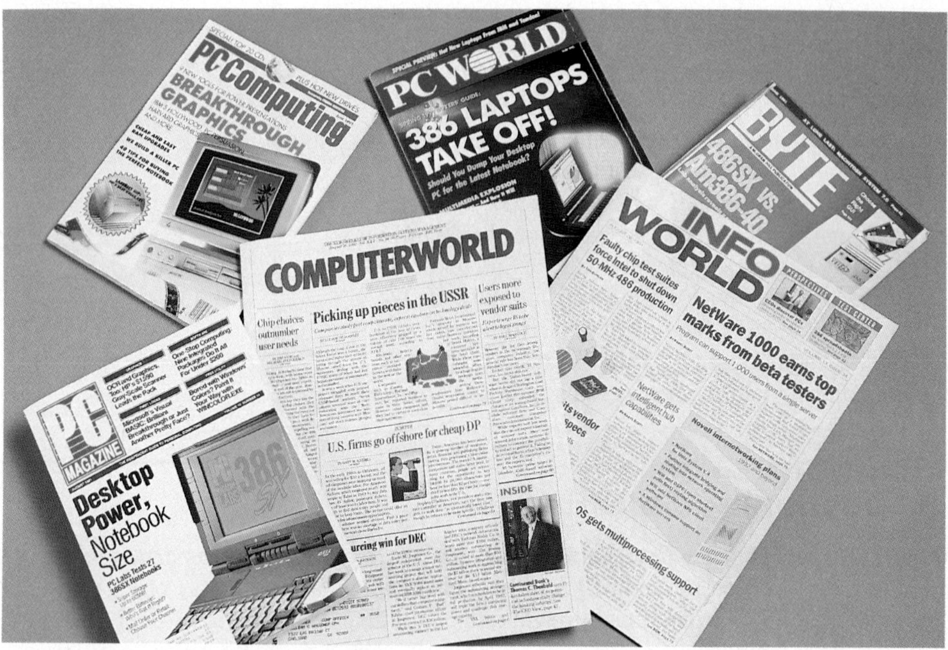

FIGURE 13-13
Computer industry publications number in the hundreds, with general- and specific-interest topics available to keep you informed.

SUMMARY OF COMPUTER CAREER OPPORTUNITIES

With the increased use of computers, the prospects for computer-related career opportunities are excellent. Not only are the numbers of traditional information processing jobs, such as programmer and systems analyst, expected to increase, but the application of the computer to existing occupations will create additional job opportunities. Regardless of an individual's career choice, a basic understanding of computers should be an essential part of any employee's job skills.

CHAPTER SUMMARY

1. As society becomes more information oriented, computers are becoming an integral part of most jobs.
2. Job opportunities in the information processing industry come from three areas: computer equipment companies, computer software companies, and companies that hire information processing professionals.
3. The computer equipment industry includes all manufacturers and distributors of computers and computer-related equipment.
4. The computer software industry includes all developers and distributors of application and system software.

5. Information processing professionals are the people that put the equipment and software to work to produce information for the end user.
6. Career opportunities in information processing include: working in an information systems department, sales, service and repair, consulting, and education and training.
7. The jobs in an information systems department can be classified into five categories: (1) operations, (2) data administration, (3) systems analysis and design, (4) programming, and (5) information center.
8. **Sales representatives** are often the most highly compensated employees in a computer company.
9. Being a **service and repair technician** is a challenging job for individuals who like to solve problems and who have a strong background in electronics.
10. **Consultants**, people who draw upon their experience to give advice to others, are in high demand for such tasks as computer system selection, system design, and communications network design and installation.
11. According to the U.S. Bureau of Labor Statistics, the fastest growing computer career positions through 1995 will be systems analyst, applications programmer, machine operator, and computer repair technician.
12. The three fields in information processing are computer information systems; computer science; and computer engineering.
13. **Computer information systems (CIS)** refers to the use of computers to provide the information needed to operate businesses and other organizations.
14. **Computer science** includes the technical aspects of computers such as hardware operation and systems software.
15. **Computer engineering** deals with the design and manufacturing of electronic computer components and computer hardware.
16. Trade schools, technical schools, community colleges, colleges, and universities offer formal education and certification or degree programs in computer-related fields.
17. Computer professionals may continue to develop their skills and increase their recognition among their peers through professional organizations, certification, and professional growth and continuing education activities.
18. Professional organizations include the **Association for Computing Machinery (ACM)**, the **Association of Information Systems Professionals (AISP)**, the **Association of Systems Management (ASM)**, the **Data Processing Management Association (DPMA)**, and the **Institute of Electrical and Electronic Engineers (IEEE) and IEEE Computer Society (IEEE/CS)**.
19. A **user group** is a group of people with common computer equipment or software interests that meet regularly to share information.
20. The **Institute for Certification of Computer Professionals (ICCP)** offers four certification programs.
21. Computer professionals stay current by participating in professional growth and continuing education activities such as conferences, workshops, conventions, and trade shows.

KEY TERMS

Association for Computing Machinery (ACM) *13.8*
Association of Information Systems Professionals (AISP) *13.8*
Association of Systems Management (ASM) *13.8*
COMDEX *13.9*
Computer engineering *13.7*
Computer information systems (CIS) *13.7*
Computer science *13.7*
Consultant *13.4*
Data Processing Management Association (DPMA) *13.8*
IEEE Computer Society (IEEE/CS) *13.8*
Institute for the Certification of Computer Professionals (ICCP) *13.9*
Institute of Electrical and Electronic Engineers (IEEE) *13.8*
Sales representative *13.4*
Service and repair technician *13.4*
User group *13.8*

REVIEW QUESTIONS

1. List the three areas that provide the majority of computer related jobs.
2. Identify seven jobs within an information systems department. The jobs in an information systems department can be classified into what five categories?
3. Describe the people skills that are important for a sales representative.
4. What does a consultant do? List three areas of knowledge where consultants are in high demand.
5. What are the four fastest growing computer career positions?
6. Describe the three fields in information processing and list at least two types of jobs in each field.
7. List and describe the purpose of five computer-related professional organizations.
8. What are the four certifications administered by the Institute for the Certification of Computer Professionals (ICCP)?
9. Name two computer industry publications that are like newspapers.

CONTROVERSIAL ISSUES

1. Because the industry is changing so rapidly, computer professionals often disagree as to what should be taught in an introductory computer course. What topics do you think should be included or excluded?
2. Some people believe that computer professions such as programming should be subject to mandatory certification or licensing, like certified public accountants. Others believe that because the industry is changing so rapidly, certification programs should be encouraged but remain voluntary. Discuss the advantages and disadvantages of mandatory programs.

RESEARCH PROJECTS

1. Contact a graduate of your school who is currently working in the computer industry. Write a report on his or her current job responsibilities. Ask the graduate to comment on how his or her education prepared him or her for this current job.
2. Contact a local computer employment specialist. Ask him or her for information on entry level computer positions in your community. Report to your class.

Trends and Issues in the Information Age

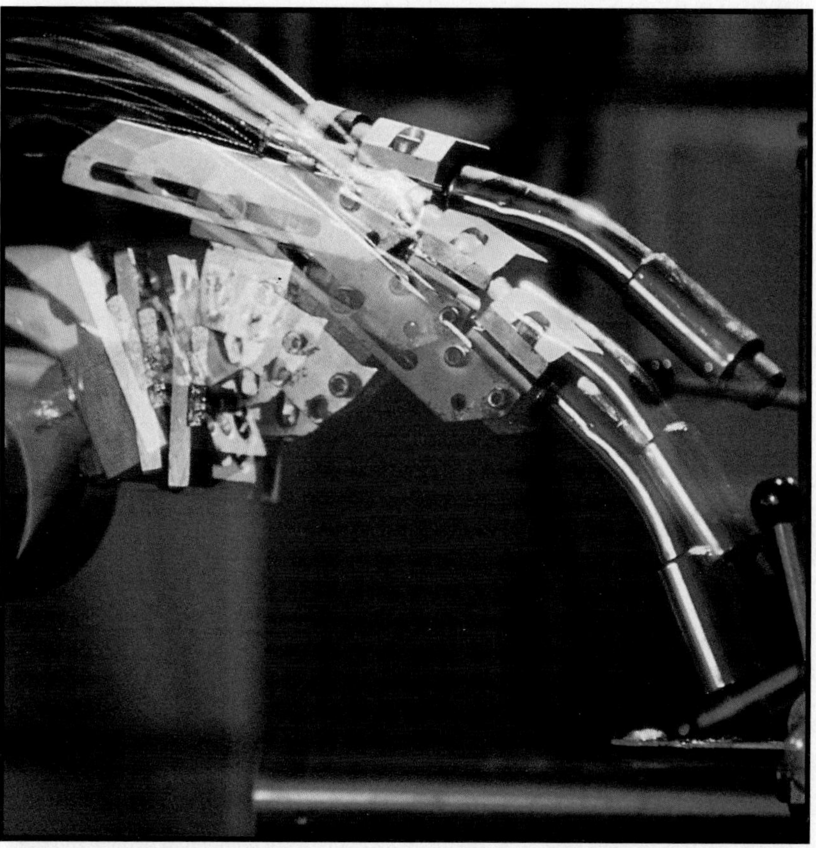

OBJECTIVES

- Discuss the electronic devices and applications that are part of the automated office
- Describe the technologies that are developing for the automated factory, including CAD, CAE, CAM, and CIM
- Discuss the trend toward the computer-integrated enterprise
- Discuss the use of personal computers in the home
- Describe the methods used in computer-aided instruction (CAI)
- Explain guidelines for purchasing personal computers
- Discuss social issues related to computers, such as computer crime and privacy

After reading the preceding chapters, you know what a computer is, what a computer does, how it does it, and why a computer is so powerful. You have learned about computer equipment and software and how the system development process is used to combine these elements with data, personnel, users, and procedures to create a working information system. The purpose of this chapter is to talk about current and future trends, including changes taking place in information systems in the workplace. We also discuss the use of personal computers in the home and some of the social issues related to computers such as security and computer crime, privacy, and ethics.

INFORMATION SYSTEMS IN BUSINESS

The largest use of computers is in business. Millions of systems ranging from mainframes to microcomputers are installed and used for applications such as inventory control, billing, and accounting. This section discusses how these traditional applications will be affected by changes in technology and methods. It also covers the automated office, the automated factory, and the computer-integrated enterprise. Although the term automated can be applied to any process or machine that can operate without human intervention, the term is commonly used to describe computer-controlled functions.

How Will Existing Information Systems Change?

Existing business information systems will continue to undergo profound changes as new technology, software, and methods are applied to the huge installed base of traditional business system users. Important overall trends include more online, interactive systems and less batch processing. In addition, the expansion of communications networks and the increased use of relational database systems means that users will have a wider variety of data and information available for decision making, and more flexibility presenting information on reports and displays. The increased number of people using computers will make the computer-user interface even more important. Graphical user interfaces will continue to replace command- and menu-driven interfaces. These and other trends that will affect the information systems of tomorrow are shown in Figure 14-1.

FIGURE 14-1
Trends affecting information systems of tomorrow.

◄ EQUIPMENT

- Increased use of personal computers networked to other personal computers and to central minicomputers or mainframes
- Mainframes and minicomputers used as central storehouses of data with processing done on a decentralized basis by powerful personal computers
- Increased disk storage capacity using new technologies such as laser disks
- High-resolution color graphics screens that can display photo-quality pictures
- Increased use of page printers that can print high-quality graphics and text
- Reduced instruction set computers (RISC) and parallel processing greatly increasing the number of instructions that can be processed at one time
- Increased use of portable computing equipment such as notebook computers
- Handwriting recognition systems allowing users to interact with a computer using a pen-shaped stylus

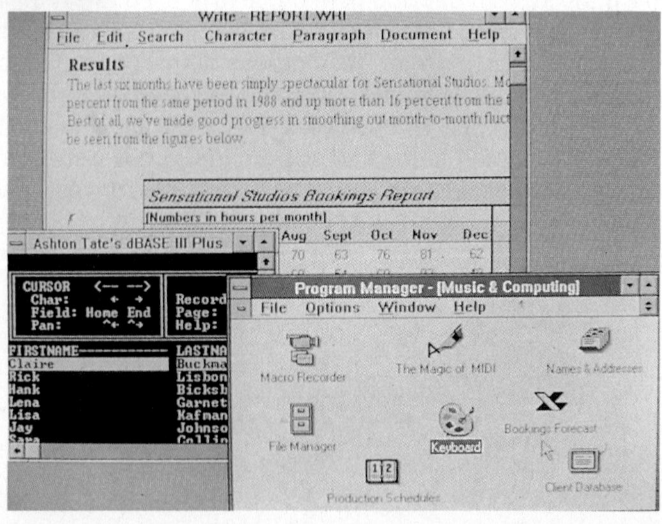

SOFTWARE ►

- Fourth-generation and natural languages enabling the user to communicate with the computer in a more conversational manner
- Object orientation combining processes and methods with data
- Computer-aided software engineering (CASE) shortening the system development time frame
- Increased use of decision support and artificial intelligence systems to help users make decisions
- Widespread implementation of graphic user interfaces using icons and symbols to represent information and processes
- Integrated applications to eliminate the need for separate programs for word processing, spreadsheets, graphics, telecommunications, and other applications

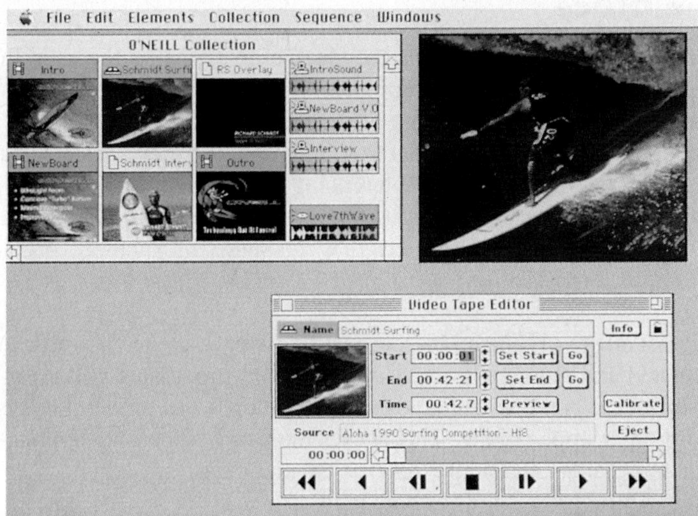

◀ DATA

- Automatic input of data at the source where it is created
- Compound documents that combine text, numbers, and nontext data such as voice, image, and full-motion video

USERS ▶

- Most people being computer literate, with a basic understanding of how computers work and how to use them in their jobs
- Increased responsibility for design, operation, and maintenance of information processing systems
- Users increasingly relying on computers to manage the continuing proliferation of information (the worldwide volume of printed information doubles every eight years)

◀ INFORMATION SYSTEMS PERSONNEL

- Increased interface with users
- Shift from machine and software orientation to user application orientation
- Emphasis from how to capture and process data to how to more effectively use the data available and create information
- Reduced staff levels handling increased processing work loads
- Some processing operations being outsourced to independent contractors
- Continuous need for retraining and education to keep up with new technology

The Automated Office

The **automated office**, sometimes referred to as the **electronic office**, is the term that describes the use of electronic devices such as computers, facsimile machines, and computerized telephone systems to make office work more productive. Automated office applications, such as word processing, electronic mail, voice mail, desktop publishing, facsimile, image processing, and teleconferencing, started out as separate, stand-alone applications. In recent years, however, the trend has been to integrate these applications into a network of devices and services that can share information. A brief review of each of these applications follows.

Word Processing For many organizations, word processing was the first office application to be automated and among all organizations, word processing still ranks as the most widely used office automation technology. Today, most word processing systems are integrated with other applications. This allows the word processing applications to extract data such as names and addresses or financial data from other application files.

Electronic Mail **Electronic mail** is the capability to use computers to transmit messages to and receive messages from other computer users. The other users may be on the same computer network or on a separate computer system reached through the use of a modem or some other communications device. Electronic mail eliminates the need to hand deliver messages or use a delivery service such as the post office or Federal Express. Electronic mail usage will grow as previously separate personal computers are attached to local area networks.

Voice Mail **Voice mail** can be considered verbal electronic mail. Made possible by the latest computerized telephone systems, voice mail reduces the problem of telephone tag, where two people trying to reach each other wind up leaving a series of messages to please call back. With voice mail, the caller can leave a message, similar to leaving a message on an answering machine. The difference is that with a voice mail system, the caller's message is digitized (converted into binary ones and zeros) so that it can be stored on a disk like other computer data. This allows the party who was called to hear the message later (by reconverting it to an audio form) and also, if desired, add a reply or additional comments and forward the message to someone else who has access to the system. Some software applications are now incorporating voice messages as part of stored documents. For example, a budget worksheet could be created with verbal instructions on how it should be completed.

Desktop Publishing Desktop publishing allows the user to control the process of creating high-quality newsletters, brochures, and other documents that previously would had to have been developed by professional artists. Trends in desktop publishing include more sophisticated high-resolution graphics and the increased use of color. More powerful computer systems and the availability of desktop publishing systems for different levels of user sophistication will increase their use in small as well as large organizations.

Facsimile **Facsimile**, or **FAX**, machines are used to transmit a reproduced image of a document over standard phone lines (Figure 14-2). The document can contain text or graphics, can be hand-written, or be a photograph. FAX machines optically scan the document and convert the image into digitized data that can be transmitted, using a modem, over the phone. A FAX machine at the receiving end converts the digitized data back into its original image. Besides the separate FAX machines, plug-in circuit boards are also available for personal computers. Using either a separate or a built-in modem, these fax boards can directly transmit computer-prepared documents or documents that have been digitized with the use of a scanner. FAX machines are having an increasing impact on the way businesses transmit documents. Many documents that were previously sent through the mail are now sent by FAX. With the speed and convenience of a phone call, a document sent by FAX can be transmitted anywhere in the world.

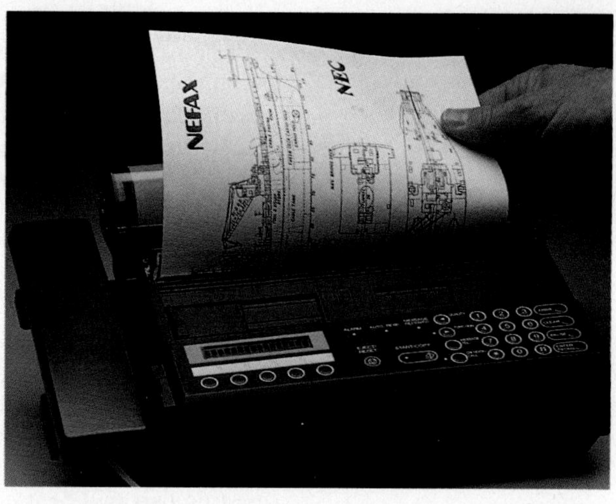

FIGURE 14-2
A facsimile (FAX) machine can send and receive copies of documents to and from any location where there is phone service and another FAX machine.

Image Processing Image processing is the capability to store and retrieve a reproduced image of a document. Image processing is often used when an original document, such as an insurance claim, must be seen to verify data. Image processing and traditional applications will continue to be combined in many areas. For example, in 1988 American Express began sending cardholders copies of the individual charge slips that were related to the charges on their statement. These charge slips were recorded by an image processing system and then merged with the customer statement program.

Teleconferencing **Teleconferencing** once meant three or more people sharing a phone conversation. Today, however, teleconferencing usually means **video conferencing**, the use of computers and television cameras to transmit video images and the sound of the conference participants to other participants with similar equipment at a remote location (Figure 14-3). Special software and equipment is used to digitize the video image so that it can be transmitted along with the audio over standard communications channels. Although the video image is not as clear for moving objects as is commercial television, it does contribute to the conference discussion and is adequate for nonmoving objects such as charts and graphs.

FIGURE 14-3
Video conferencing is used to transmit and receive video and audio signals over standard communications channels. This meeting is being transmitted to a video conference center at another location. The people at the other location are also being recorded and transmitted and can be seen on the TV monitor.

Summary of the Automated Office The trend toward integrated automated office capabilities will continue. Currently incompatible devices such as stand-alone FAX machines, copiers, and telephone switches will be standardized or will be provided with software that will enable them to communicate and transfer data with other devices. The higher productivity provided by automated office devices will encourage more organizations to adopt them.

The Automated Factory

As in the automated office, the goal of the **automated factory** is to increase productivity through the use of automated, and often computer-controlled, equipment. Technologies used in the automated factory include computer-aided design, computer-aided engineering, computer-aided manufacturing, and computer-integrated manufacturing.

Computer-Aided Design (CAD) **Computer-aided design (CAD)** uses a computer and special graphics software to aid in product design (Figure 14-4). The CAD software eliminates the laborious drafting that used to be required and allows the designer to dynamically change the size of some or all of the product and view the design from different angles. The capability to store the design electronically offers several advantages over traditional manual methods. One advantage is that the designs can be changed more easily than before. Another is that the design database can be reviewed more easily by other design engineers. This increases the likelihood that an existing part will be used in a product rather than a new part designed. For example, if a support bracket was required for a new product, the design engineer could review the design database to see if any existing products used a support bracket that would be appropriate for the new product. This not only decreases the overall design time but increases the reliability of the new product by using proven parts.

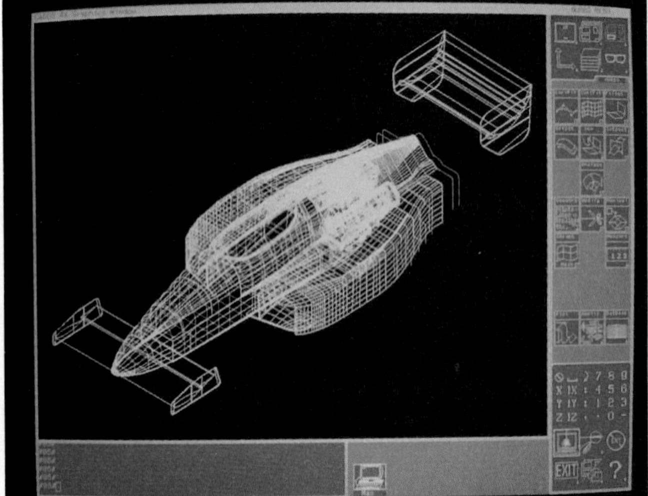

FIGURE 14-4
Computer-aided design (CAD) is an efficient way to develop plans for new products.

Computer-Aided Engineering (CAE) **Computer-aided engineering (CAE)** is the use of computers to test product designs. Using CAE, engineers can test the design of an airplane or a bridge before it is built (Figure 14-5). Sophisticated programs simulate the effects of wind, temperature, weight, and stress on product shapes and materials. Before the use of CAE, prototypes of products had to be built and subjected to testing that often destroyed the prototype. CAE allows engineers to create a computer prototype that can be tested under a variety of conditions. CAE allows products to be tested in some conditions, such as earthquakes, that could not previously be simulated.

FIGURE 14-5
Computer-aided engineering (CAE) allows the user to test product designs before they are built and without damaging the product.

Computer-Aided Manufacturing (CAM) **Computer-aided manufacturing (CAM)** is the use of computers to control production equipment. CAM production equipment includes software-controlled drilling, lathe, and milling machines as well as robots (Figure 14-6). The use of robots has aroused much interest, partially because of preconceived ideas of robots as intelligent, humanlike machines. In practice, most industrial robots rarely look like a human and can perform only preprogrammed tasks. Robots are often used for repetitive tasks in hazardous or disagreeable environments such as welding or painting areas, or when chemicals that are hazardous to humans are used.

FIGURE 14-6
Computer-aided manufacturing (CAM) is used to control production equipment such as these welding robots on an automobile assembly line.

Computer-Integrated Manufacturing (CIM) **Computer-integrated manufacturing (CIM)** is the total integration of the manufacturing process using computers (Figure 14-7). Using CIM concepts, individual production processes are linked so that the production flow is balanced and optimized and products flow at an even rate through the factory. In a CIM factory, automated design processes are linked to automated machining processes that are linked to automated assembly processes that are linked to automated testing and packaging. Under ideal CIM conditions, a product will move through the entire production process under computer control. Many companies may never fully implement CIM because it is so complex. But CIM's related concepts of minimum inventory and efficient demand-driven production are valid and will be incorporated into many manufacturers' business plans.

The Computer-Integrated Enterprise

Although in the previous sections we discuss the automated office and automated factory separately, the long-range trend is the **computer-integrated enterprise**—an organization in which all information storage and processing is performed by a network of computers and intelligent devices. In a computer-integrated enterprise, all office, factory, warehouse, and communications systems are linked using a common interface allowing authorized users in any functional area of the organization to access and use data stored anywhere in the organization. Rather than being machine or software oriented as today's systems, future systems will be document or information oriented. The user won't need to separately start a word processing, spreadsheet, or communications program. Instead, users will be able to create and distribute compound documents that contain text, graphics, numbers, and full-motion video. They will be able to record, in their own voice, comments or questions about the document before it is stored or routed to someone else in the organization. For example, a new product marketing plan could contain a text description of the product, a spreadsheet showing projected sales, and a narrated video showing the product in use. If the president of a company had questions about the plan, he or she could add questions to the plan in his or her own voice, and route the plan to the appropriate person for a response.

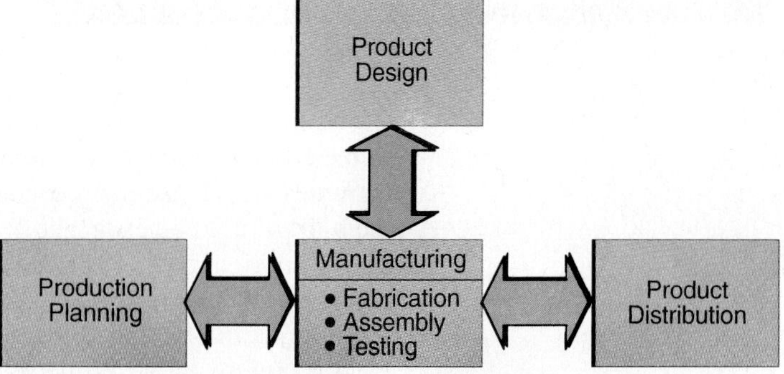

FIGURE 14-7
The concept of computer-integrated manufacturing (CIM) is to use computers to integrate all phases of the manufacturing process from planning and design to manufacturing and distribution.

BRINGING THE INFORMATION AGE HOME

Millions of personal computers have been purchased for home use, and the use of personal computers in the home is expected to increase. Just as the use of computers in the workplace has changed how we work, the use of computers in our homes is changing our personal lives. In the next two sections we discuss how people use personal computers in homes today, how they might use them in the future, and things you should consider when purchasing a personal computer system.

The Use of Personal Computers in the Home

People use personal computers in their homes in a variety of ways. These ways usually fall into five general categories: (1) personal services, (2) control of home systems, (3) telecommuting, (4) education, and (5) entertainment.

FIGURE 14-8
The Prodigy online information service offers the latest news, weather, sports, and financial information along with shopping, entertainment, and electronic mail.

Personal Services In many ways running a home is similar to running a small business. The productivity tools you use in the office, such as word processing, spreadsheet, and database, can also be used in the home to help you with creating documents, with financial planning and analysis, and filing and organizing data. Personal computer software is also available to assist you with home accounting applications such as balancing checkbooks, making household budgets, and preparing tax returns. In addition, using a personal computer to transmit and receive data over telephone lines allows home users to access a wealth of information and services. For example, teleshopping, electronic banking, and airline reservations are services that are becoming more popular, and information such as stock prices, weather reports, and headline news is available to home users who subscribe to online information services such as Prodigy (Figure 14-8), Genie, and CompuServe. The personal services provided by home computer use allows people to perform personal and business-related tasks quickly and conveniently in the comfort of their own homes. Without a personal computer, completing similar activities would take them considerably more time because it would frequently require them to travel to other locations to conduct this business and acquire information.

A different type of service available to users who have personal computers with communications capabilities is the access and use of electronic **bulletin board systems**, called **BBSs**, that allow users to communicate with one another and share information (Figure 14-9). While some bulletin boards provide specific services such as buying and selling used computer equipment, many bulletin boards function as electronic clubs for special-interest groups and are used to share information about hobbies as diverse as stamp collecting, music, genealogy, and astronomy. Some BBSs are strictly social; users meet new friends and conduct conversations by entering messages through their keyboards.

Control of Home Systems Another use of computers in the home is to control home systems such as security, environment, lighting, and landscape sprinkler systems. Personal computers used in this manner are usually linked to special devices such as alarms for security; thermostats for temperature control; and timing devices for lighting and sprinkler systems. For example, if the personal computer system has communications capabilities, a homeowner who is away can use a telephone or another computer to call home and change the operation of one of the control systems. Suppose a homeowner is on vacation in Texas and learns that heavy rains have been falling at home in Pennsylvania. He or she could call the computer and use the keys of a touch-tone telephone to instruct the computer to turn off the garden sprinkler system.

Most existing home control systems were installed after the home was built and often consist of separate systems to control each set of devices. This will change in the future, however. In 1990, the Electronic Industries Association released a new wiring standard called the Consumer Electronics Bus (CEBus). The CEBus sets standards for sending information throughout a home using existing electrical wiring, phone lines, TV cable, and nonwired techniques such as radio waves. In a related effort, Echelon Corporation is designing chips to be used in consumer electronics and building products. The chips will allow appliances, lighting systems, and other home products to be networked together and controlled by a single system using a consistent set of commands. Although they are not yet widely implemented, these changes will result in what many refer to as the intelligent home or smart house.

San Diego Electronic Bulletin Boards

1 OMNIBUS BBS	464-6271 ¥
also	280-2696
A&B Express	447-1009 ¥Z
ABC	436-3525 ¥
Adventure Board	224-2636 §
Adventure Games of America	695-3011 •
Adventures In Palancia	222-1785 ¥
Alabaster's cave	528- 9218 §
Alcatraz	723- 0537 ¥
Amber Knights	460-9762 §
Aquarium BBS	462-1732 ß
ARC Modem	589-0339 ¥
Artworld BBS	462- 6887 ¥
Ashley's BBS	565-2029 ¥
Astralite	276-7623 ¥
The Asylum	293-0158 ¥
Atari/Amiga	691-7862 ¥
Awesome's Place	482-3025 ¥
The Ballyhoo BBS	447-1008 ¥
The BBS Summit	576-0077 ¥
The Black Box	747-2304 ¥
Bootcamp I	941-0996 ß
Border Town BBS	466-3173 ¥
The Bosn's Locker	442-9252 ¥
Brian Smith's BBS	582-0875 ¥
The Bicycle Bulletin Board	720-1830 ¥
Bullit Proof Software	284-6729 Ω
Bytes 'R Us	428-9773 ß
California Sands GS	541-7048 ß
California Computer Connection	944-1804 ß
Camelot 3000	462-0542 ¥
Casa de Cricket	823-1583 ¥
The Chief's Mess	469-1354 ß
Christ Line	268-3568 ¥
Classified Connection	566-1745 ¥
The Closet BBS	480-9686 §
also	726-4419
CMS:Lakeside	390-2689 §
CMUG	433-3162 §
Coconet Demo BBS	456-0815 ¥
COM2 (node #1): Remote BBS	471-8730 ß
COM2 (node #2): Remote BBS	471-8839 ¥
Commodore Connection	429-6227 ¥
Commodore Edition	575-8364 §
The Commodore Shop	423-7901 §
Commadore User's Network	267-8056 §
Communication link	726-7834 §
Communicore	484-5811 ¥
Computer Buyer's Guide	689-0500 ¥
Computer Outlet, North County	740-0113 ¥Z
The Computer Room	287-6006 ¥
ComputorEdge On-Line	573-1675 ¥
Cornucopia	748-8096 ¥
Cougar Country	480-3056 §Z
Covey's Concepts	439-5131 ¥
Cygnus X-1 BBS	457-2665 ¥
The Crypt BBS	457-1836 ¥
Cuyamaca College	660-2010 §
Data Trax, USRobotics HST	433-8564 ß
The Dark Alley	728-5497 ¥
DataWorks BBS	423-9352 Ω
Dave's Place	562-3248 ß
Deadwood BBS	598-4088 ¥
dBored	748-3644 ß
The Dead Zone BBS/PDSE	755-3350 ¥
also	942-0848
Demon's Den	284-3439 ¥
Digex:SDCS DIGSIG	454-8078 §
DJM BBS	588-6941 ß
Dollars and Bytes	483-5477 ¥Z
Don's House	440-6038 ¥
DOOGER'S PLACE	588-8931 ß
Dragon's Nest BBS	449-7052 ¥
Dragon's Domain BBS	565-4424 ¥
The Dream Clinic	670-9522 ¥
Eight-Bit Tandy	571-6366 ¥
The Edge Elite	695-6949 ¥
Electro-shok Therapy	723-3065 ¥
Elephant's Graveyard (node #9):	270-3148 ¥
Enigma	453-1819 ¥
Especially Yours	226-3042 ¥
The Evergreen Forest	426-2057 §
Falcon's BBS	726-8001 ¥
Family Historians	297-5746 ¥
Far Star Prev. ST Sig atar	225-1775 ¥
Fax Satellite System	224-3853 ¥
The File Bank	728-4318 ß
The File Cabinet	427-5459 Ω
The Final Experience	670-4445 ß
The Final Frontier	966-0114 ß
Fightertown BBS	537-4217 ¥
The Flare Path	561-2999 Ω
The Forgotten Realm BBS	578-4093 ¥
Foundations Edge	287-2996 ¥
Foy's Trading Post	562-3646 ¥
FSMAO-2	725-6322 ¥
Fuel Dump	390-7896 ¥
The Fun House	697-8714 ¥
The Funny Farm	746-6564 Ω
The Game Board BBS	281-0675§
Gandalf's	466-9505 ¥
The General	281-4185 ¥
The General	281-5538 Ω
The Ginko BBS	566-4165 ¥
The G.T. Connection	263-0347 ¥
The Hero Network	222-5961 ¥
High Country East	789-4391
Hillcrest Host & BBS	291-0544 ¥
Hog Heaven	561-0058 ¥
The Family Historian	279-5746 ¥
IEEE (San Diego)	452-3131 ¥
I.D.I.C.	461-0982 ¥
Imperial Beach BBS	575-1562 ¥
The Internal Stack II	741-2686 ¥
Inve$tment Club BB$	476-0692 ¥
Jim's BBS of San Diego	492-9714 ¥
Katatania Tales	420-4120 ¥
Key Point BBS	479-8032 Ω
Kit's Hideout	741-0692 §
Knight Shadows' Grotto	792-0455 ¥
Knowledge Works BBS	528-1058 ¥
Lake Murray's Support BBS	460-2292 ¥
Lakeside Wildcat!	390-7328 Ω
The Landing Strip	672-0846 Ω
Launching Acadamy	562-6337 ¥
La Verne & PC Street Again	222-9483 ¥
The Lemonade Stand	941-6158 §
The Lemon Grove BBS	463-9037 ¥
Lips BBS	693-0735 ¥
Light Impressions	538-9131 §
L.O.L.A.	582-6969 §
Longshot	465-9764¥√
also	465-0327
The Looney Bin	390-9470 ¥
LoticTek BBS	280-6725 ¥
L.V. Wanderer	560-8203 §
Mac Underground Safehouse	272-2059 ¥
Magic 102 BBS	560-1534 §
Mainstreet Data	439-6624 ¥
Marzland	578-9086 §
MBC Broadcast	422-0239 ¥
MediaLine BBS	298-4027 ß
MicroMiga	670-1095 ¥
Milliway's	268-9614 ¥
Mister Rick's Neighborhood	695-1163 ß
Molakai Express	462-6319 §
Morning Star	575-3310 Ω
Mount Olympous	465-8236 §
Mousetrap	464-2134 Ω
Multitech PC	578-9221
Mushin BBS	535-9580 ß
also	222-3097 ß
My House	447-1422 ¥
Mystic Lounge	679-7691 §
Nassau Xpress	433-9777 ¥
The Nesting Ground	484-7283 ¥
New-Ware	455-5226 ¥
NEXUS Z (node #63)	486-0735 ¥
Night Owl, Ham Radio	279-3921 ß
Nola's Nemesis	461-1336 ¥
North Clairemont BBS	272-3087Ω
North San Diego Apple Club	571-9010 ¥
Ocean Beach BBS	224-4878 §
Ocean Sports	558-2691 ¥
Oh No Not Just Another BBS	298-7475 ¥
Orcus's Den BBS	268-4498 ¥
Osborne-CPM User Group	299-1604 §
OtherWorlds	630-1147 §
Outer Limits	596-0667 ¥
PC•LawCom BBS	272-6615 ¥
also	483-1324 •
P-Net (pnet03)	569-9195 ¥
P-Net (pnet01)	444-7006 ¥
Paulette's Playhouse	484-2690 ¥
PD-SIG	749-2741 ¥ß$
also	749-2589¥$, 749-3432¥$,
also	749-6222¥ß$, 749-6384¥$
People-Net (pnet12)	259-3704 Σ
The Place BBS	479-5244 ¥
Pro-BEAGLE	558-6151 ¥
Pro-Grouch	260-0492 ß
ProLine [avalon]	632-7161 ß
ProLine [mercury]	697-0261 ¥
ProLine [simasd]	238-2333 ß
ProLine [sol]	670-5379 ß
The Rabbit Hole	941-3505 §
Radio-Active	268-9625 ¥
The Rasta Think Tank	282-1211 Σ
The Rat's Nest	275-6129 ß
The Real Estate BBS	464-4540 ¥
R-n-S Info Foneline	268-0964 ¥
Rogues' Roost C-64	262-6106 §
Rom-Burner	424-7213 ¥
The RPC Library	461-6642 ¥
Rosie's Lair	589-4599 ¥
Rudy's Place BBS	670-3040 ¥
Sabaline	692-1961 ß
S.D. Fantasy	476-7733 ¥
San Diego PC Board (node #1)	584-4172 ¥
San Diego PC Board (node #2)	584-1715 ¥
Santee Experiment	562-8758 ¥
Sawyer College of Business BBS	286-8614 ¥Z
Scanline	298-2023 ß
SCCG:TIBBS	278-8155 §
SCH Editor's BBS	563-1598 ¥
Scripps Ranch	586-0703 ¥
SDC BBS	754-5425 ¥
S.D. CLIP*BOARD	279-4662 ¥
S.D. Computer Society	549-3788 ¥
The Seaside Connection	481-6479 ¥
Serenity	259-3704 ß
Serenity	259-7757 Σ
Serial Port	755-3123 ¥
The Service Center	275-1448 ¥
Sharky's MAChine	747-8719 ¥
S.I.G.H. Amiga	788-0449 ¥
Silver's Cave	561-7206 ¥
Skanked BBS!	480-2441 ¥
SKYNET II	754-1659 ¥
So Cal Graphics BBS	292-0186 ¥
Software Revenge	431-4444 ß
The Software Corner	588-6238 ¥
The Software Market Place	669-1581 ¥
SomeWares Bet. Heaven	436-9861 ¥
Sound of Money	461-2521 ¥
ST-NET BBS	268-3996 Ω
ST-SDACE	689-8157 §
also	689-8397
ST SIG Atari ST & Others	726-4419 §
also	726-4419
Star Base 23	560-2996 ¥
Starhelm Graystaff	479-3006 ß
Suburbia?	447-5489 Ω
The Surf Shack	967-6017 §
SW/SE Connection	479-0411 ß
also	479-3006
Sys-Jam Productions	432-9057 ¥
Tech Pro BBS	755-7357 §
TeleMac	576-1820 √$
The 64 & More Store	258-0951 ¥
Tinker Toys BBS	738-0471 ¥
Trader's World	284-8729 ß
The Treehouse	424-6375 ¥
Tunnels of Versarius NODE I	453-1781 √
The Underground Cavern	748-8157 §
The Underground Press	444-4163 §
The VOID! BBS	455-5957 ¥
UN*x Lips Service BBS	693-0735 Ω
USA BBS	443-5968 ¥
USRobotics	286-0841 √
USS Perpetrators	561-4681 ¥
Viking BBS	756-9567 ¥
Waduki's Graphics Pad	425-5831 ¥
The Warezhouse	575-7914 §
The White House	432-0787 §
Willy-NET	535-0816 ¥$
Wisdom BBS	270-3083 ¥
The Wizard's Domain	426-5028 ¥
Xanadu (new users)	287-2044 ¥
Xanadu (validated users)	287-2140 ¥
Zeke	755-5675 ¥

Legend

§ 300/1200 baud, ¥ 300-2400 baud, ß 9600 baud HSTs, Ω 14,400 baud HSTs, √ Dual Standard (14,400 HST and 9600 V.32), Σ V.32 19,200 Telebit Trailblazer, Z After hours or weekends, $ Requires a donation for access.

ComputorEdge acknowledges this is not a complete list of all the BBSs in the San Diego area and reserves the right to reject or cancel, for any reason, any BBS submission for inclusion on this list.

62 October 19, 1990 — ComputorEdge

FIGURE 14-9
Some of the bulletin boards available in the San Diego, California area. Bulletin board systems are an excellent source for answers to questions about personal computer equipment and software.

Telecommuting **Telecommuting** refers to the capability of individuals to work at home and communicate with their offices by using personal computers and communications lines. With a personal computer, an employee can access the main computer at the office. He or she can read and answer electronic mail. An employee can access databases, and can transmit completed projects. Some predictions claim that by the end of the 1990s, ten percent of the work force will be telecommuters. Most of these people will probably arrange their business schedules so they can telecommute two or three days a week. Telecommuting provides flexibility, allowing companies and employees to increase productivity and, at the same time, meet the needs of individual employees. Some of the advantages possible with telecommuting include reducing the time needed to commute to the office each week; eliminating the need to travel during poor weather conditions; providing a convenient and comfortable work environment for disabled employees or workers recovering from injuries or illnesses; and allowing employees to combine work with personal responsibilities such as child care.

Education The use of personal computers for education, called **computer-aided instruction (CAI)**, is another rapidly growing area. Whereas CAI is frequently used to describe software that is developed and used in schools, much of the same software is available for home users. CAI software can be classified into three types: drill and practice, tutorials, and simulations.

Drill and practice software uses a flash-card approach to teaching by allowing users to practice skills in subjects such as math and language. A problem or word appears on the computer screen and the user enters the answer. The computer accepts the answer and responds by telling the student whether the answer is correct or incorrect. Sometimes the user gets second and third chances to select the correct answer before the computer software reveals the correct answer.

With **tutorial software**, the computer software uses text, graphics, and sometimes sound to teach a user concepts about subjects such as chemistry, music theory, or computer literacy. Following the instruction, tutorial software might present true/false or multiple-choice questions to help the user ensure that he or she understands the concepts. The increased use of optical disk storage provides high-quality graphics and direct access capability; it promises to greatly enhance this type of CAI.

The third type of CAI, **simulation software**, is designed to teach a user by creating a model of a real-life situation. For example, many simulation packages are available to teach business concepts. One program designed for children simulates running a lemonade stand and another program for adults simulates the stock market. In the lemonade simulation, the user makes decisions about *How many quarts of lemonade to make* and *What price to charge customers for a glass of lemonade*. The computer software accepts the user's decisions, performs computations using the software model, and then responds to the user with the amount of profit or loss for the day. Good CAI software is designed to be user friendly and motivate the user to succeed (Figure 14-10).

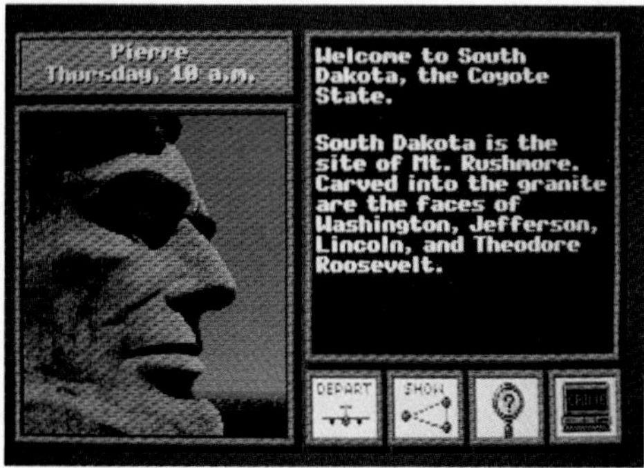

FIGURE 14-10
Computer-aided instruction (CAI) software provides a structured yet motivating way to learn. This CAI software helps the user to develop deductive reasoning, reference, and research skills while learning geography, history, economics, government, and culture.

In addition to CAI software, some trade schools, colleges and universities are now offering students with personal computers a chance to take electronic correspondence courses from their homes. Lessons and assignments for classes are transmitted between the student and the school over communications lines.

Education in the home through CAI or electronic correspondence courses allows home users to learn at their own pace, in the convenience of their home, and at a time that fits into their personal schedule. Well-written educational software can be so entertaining that it is sometimes difficult to distinguish between it and entertainment software.

FIGURE 14-11
Flight simulators can be both fun and educational. Some simulators offer realistic instrument consoles and flight patterns that help teach the user about flying.

Entertainment Entertainment software, or game playing, on home computers has always had a large following among the younger members of the family. However, many adults are surprised to find that entertainment software can also provide them with hours of enjoyment. Popular types of entertainment software include arcade games, board games, simulations, and interactive graphics programs. Most people are familiar with the arcade-type games (similar to video games) that are available for computers. A popular board game is computer chess. Simulations include games such as baseball and football and a variety of flight simulators that allow users to pretend they are controlling and navigating different types of aircraft (Figure 14-11).

Also available are a wide variety of interactive graphic adventure games that range from rescuing a princess from a castle's dungeon to solving a murder mystery. People can play many of these games alone or in small groups. The software usually allows players to adjust the level of play to match their abilities, that is, beginner through advanced. With entertainment software, the computer becomes a fun, skillful, and challenging game partner.

In addition to playing games, some personal computer users use their home computer as a tool for personal hobbies. Computers are used by hobbyists to design quilt and stained glass patterns, run model trains, organize stamp, doll, and photography collections, and write, transpose, play, and print musical scores.

Summary of the Use of Personal Computers in the Home As you can see, personal computers are used in homes in a variety of ways. Whether or not you now use a personal computer in your home, it is very probable that you will at some time in the near future. In fact, it is very possible that within the next decade you will have multiple computers in your home. Because computers can be used in so many different ways and also because computer technology is changing so rapidly, you should carefully choose any computer system you purchase. We discuss some general guidelines for purchasing personal computers in the next section.

Guidelines for Buying a Personal Computer

When you purchase a personal computer, you should make every effort to select a computer system that matches your individual needs as closely as possible. The six steps for purchasing a personal computer system recommend that you:

1. **Become computer literate**. This is truly the first and most important step in making a wise purchase. You might be surprised that many people buy computer equipment without understanding the capability of a personal computer or the tasks it can and cannot perform. Many times these people buy a computer like the one their neighbor or friend purchased, and expect it to meet their needs. Sometimes it does, but frequently they are disappointed. Hopefully, this will not happen to you. You already have an advantage because by reading this book, you now know a great deal about computers and have developed a foundation of knowledge on which you can base your software and equipment decisions. In short, you already are computer literate. But computer technology is changing rapidly, to stay computer literate you will need to stay current with the changes in the field. You can do this by reading periodicals or attending seminars on state-of-the-art computer technology.
2. **Define and prioritize the type of tasks you want to perform on your computer**. This step will help you to see more clearly exactly what you want to do with your computer and will help you select software and equipment that will match these needs. Define your needs in writing. Create a numbered list with the most important application at the top and the least important application at the bottom. General applications such as word processing, spreadsheets, database, and communications are easy to include on the list. You may, however, have a special application in mind such as controlling a household security system. Being computer literate will help you know if a special application is feasible. It will also help you to discuss any special needs you might have with computer professionals who can help you. Once your list is completed you can begin to evaluate the available software.
3. **Select the software packages that best meet your needs**. Publications, computer stores, and user groups are all good resources when it comes to evaluating the available software. For more on evaluating software, review the section in Chapter 2, Guidelines for Purchasing Microcomputer Applications Software.

In addition to purchasing commercial software, you can also consider selecting shareware and public domain software. **Shareware** is software that users may try out on their own systems before paying a fee. If a user decides to keep and use the software, he or she sends a registration fee to the software publisher (Figure 14-12).

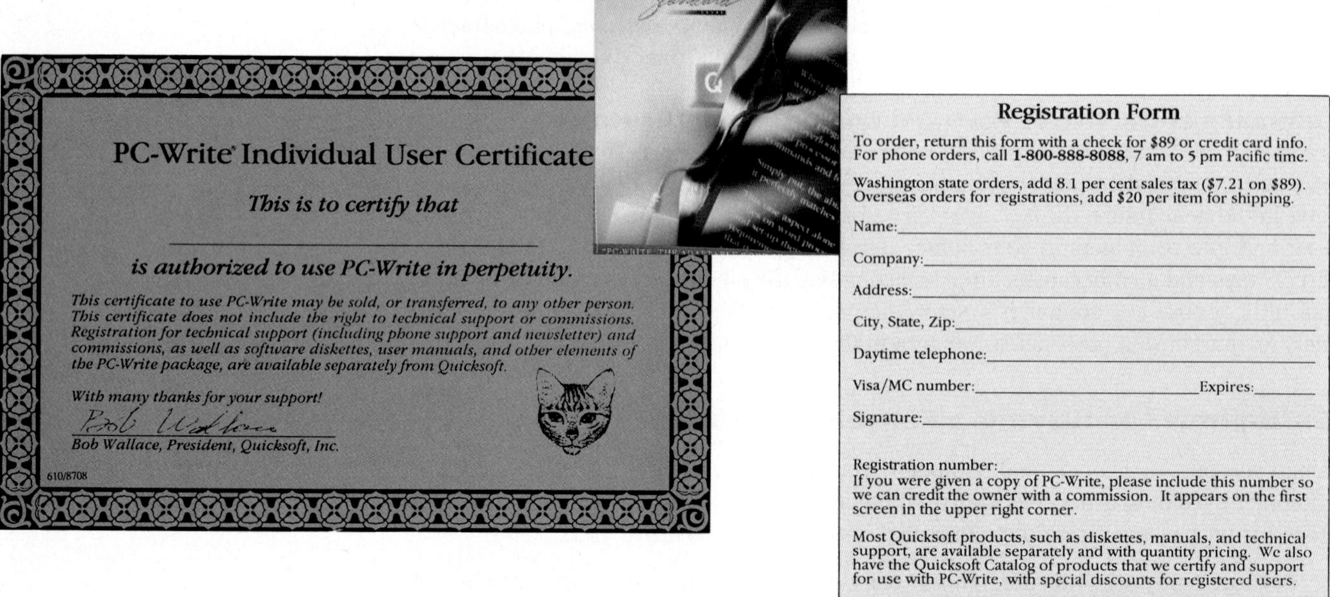

PC-Write® Individual User Certificate

This is to certify that

is authorized to use PC-Write in perpetuity.

This certificate to use PC-Write may be sold, or transferred, to any other person. This certificate does not include the right to technical support or commissions. Registration for technical support (including phone support and newsletter) and commissions, as well as software diskettes, user manuals, and other elements of the PC-Write package, are available separately from Quicksoft.

With many thanks for your support!

Bob Wallace, President, Quicksoft, Inc.

610/8708

Registration Form

To order, return this form with a check for $89 or credit card info. For phone orders, call **1-800-888-8088**, 7 am to 5 pm Pacific time.

Washington state orders, add 8.1 per cent sales tax ($7.21 on $89). Overseas orders for registrations, add $20 per item for shipping.

Name:

Company:

Address:

City, State, Zip:

Daytime telephone:

Visa/MC number: Expires:

Signature:

Registration number:
If you were given a copy of PC-Write, please include this number so we can credit the owner with a commission. It appears on the first screen in the upper right corner.

Most Quicksoft products, such as diskettes, manuals, and technical support, are available separately and with quantity pricing. We also have the Quicksoft Catalog of products that we certify and support for use with PC-Write, with special discounts for registered users.

Quicksoft, 219 First Ave N #224, Seattle, WA 98109. 206/282-0452.

FIGURE 14-12
After trying the PC-Write software, users fill out a registration form and mail it with a fee to Quicksoft, the publisher of PC-Write. A user certificate is then sent to the user.

Public domain software is free software that is not copyrighted and can therefore be distributed among users. While the quality of shareware and public domain software varies greatly, some of the software is quite good. You can obtain this type of software from BBSs and also from public domain software libraries.

4. **Select equipment that will run the software you have selected**. The capabilities of the different types of personal computers vary greatly. For example, some personal computers can perform extensive graphics while others cannot. Selecting the software that meets your needs before selecting your equipment guides you in selecting appropriate equipment. Some software only runs on certain types of personal computers. Also, knowing the software you want to run prevents overbuying (purchasing a machine that is more powerful than you need) or underbuying (purchasing a machine that is not powerful enough). Capabilities to consider when you evaluate equipment include: processing speed of the microprocessor, memory size, system expandability, compatibility of the system with other personal computers, monochrome or color display, graphics capability, amount and type of auxiliary storage, printer type and speed, and communications capabilities. If you can't decide between two configurations, choose the system with more storage and/or processing power. Today's latest software applications require more disk space and CPU speed than applications released in prior years. This trend is expected to continue. Although you don't want to overbuy, you do want to buy a system that will meet your immediate needs and provide room for storage growth and additional applications.
5. **Select the suppliers for the software and equipment**. Your options include used equipment and software, mail order, and computer stores. Price, warranties, training, service, and repair are all details to consider when you select a supplier.

Obtaining the best overall value may not mean paying the lowest price. A store that is willing to provide you with assistance in assembling your system or furnish some training may be well worth a slightly higher price. Student purchasers should always check to see if systems and software are available through their school or if an educational discount is offered.

6. **Purchase the software and equipment**. If you have followed these guidelines you will probably feel both excited and confident with the decisions you have made. Your efforts to define your computing needs and to select software, equipment, and a supplier that will meet those needs should help you to select a personal computer system that is appropriate for you and with which you will be satisfied.

Summary of Bringing the Information Age Home

Personal computers are used in homes to aid in a variety of tasks such as personal services, control of home systems, telecommuting, education, and entertainment. When users purchase a personal computer system for the home, they should first become computer literate and evaluate their computer processing needs, then purchase software and equipment that meets those needs. The trend is clear. Personal computers will continue to bring the information age into our homes.

The changes that accompany the information age raise several issues that are related to society as a whole. We discuss some of these issues in the next section.

SOCIAL ISSUES

◆ Significant inventions such as the automobile and television have always challenged existing values and caused society to think about the right and wrong ways to use the new invention. The computer is no exception; including the social issues related to security and computer crime, privacy, and ethics.

Computer Security and Crime

Computer security and computer crime are closely related topics. **Computer security** refers to the safeguards established to prevent and detect unauthorized use and deliberate or accidental damage to computer systems and data. **Computer crime** is the use of a computer to commit an illegal act. Here we discuss three types of crimes that can be committed and the security measures that can be taken to prevent and detect them.

Software Theft Software theft, often called **software piracy**, became a major problem with the increased use of personal computers. Some people have difficulty understanding why they should pay hundreds, perhaps thousands, of dollars for what appears to be an inexpensive diskette or tape, and instead of paying for an authorized copy of the software they make an illegal copy. Estimates are that for every authorized copy of a commercial program, there is at least one illegal copy. However, it should be stated that software theft is a violation of copyright law and is a crime. Software companies take illegal copying seriously and in some cases offenders who have been caught have been vigorously prosecuted. For large users, the financial incentives for stealing software have been lowered by site licensing and multiple-copy discounts. Site licensing allows organizations to pay a single fee for multiple copies of a program used at a single location. Multiple-copy discounts reduce the fee of each additional copy of a program license.

Unauthorized Access and Use **Unauthorized access** can be defined as computer trespassing, in other words, being logged on a system without permission. Many so-called computer hackers boast of the number of systems that they have been able to access by using a modem. These hackers usually don't do any damage and merely wander around the accessed system before logging off.

Unauthorized use is the use of a computer system or computer data for unapproved and possibly illegal activities. Unauthorized use may range from an employee using the company computer for keeping his or her child's soccer league scores to someone gaining access to a bank funds system and creating an unauthorized transfer. Unauthorized use could also include the theft of computerized information such as customer lists or product plans. Courts have been taking a harsher view of both unauthorized access and use, and more frequently sentence violators to jail terms and substantial fines.

The key to preventing both unauthorized access and unauthorized use is computer security that controls and monitors an appropriate level of authorization for each user. Authorization techniques range from simple passwords to advanced biometric devices that can identify individuals by their fingerprint, voice, or eye pattern (Figure 14-13). The authorization technique should match the degree of risk associated with unauthorized access. An organization should regularly review the levels of authorization for users to determine if the levels are still appropriate.

FIGURE 14-13
Biometric security devices use biological characteristics to allow or deny access to would-be computer users. A retinal scanner reads a small area of a person's eye (left). An individual's retina pattern is as unique as a fingerprint, which can also be tested by a fingerprint recognition device (right). Other equipment exists to identify people by their voices or by their signatures.

Malicious Damage Malicious or deliberate damage to the data in a computer system is often difficult to detect because the damaged data may not be used or carefully reviewed on a regular basis. A disgruntled employee or an outsider might gain access to the system and delete or alter individual records or an entire file. One of the most potentially dangerous types of malicious damage is done by a **virus**, a computer program designed to copy itself into other software and spread through multiple computer systems. Figure 14-14 shows how a virus can spread from one system to another. Although they have existed for a some time, viruses have become a serious problem only recently.

Organizations have developed specific programs called **vaccines** to locate and remove viruses; in addition organizations are becoming more aggressive in prosecuting persons suspected of planting viruses. In what was described as the first computer virus trial, in 1988 a former programmer was convicted in Texas of planting a program in his employer's computer system that deleted 168,000 sales commission records.

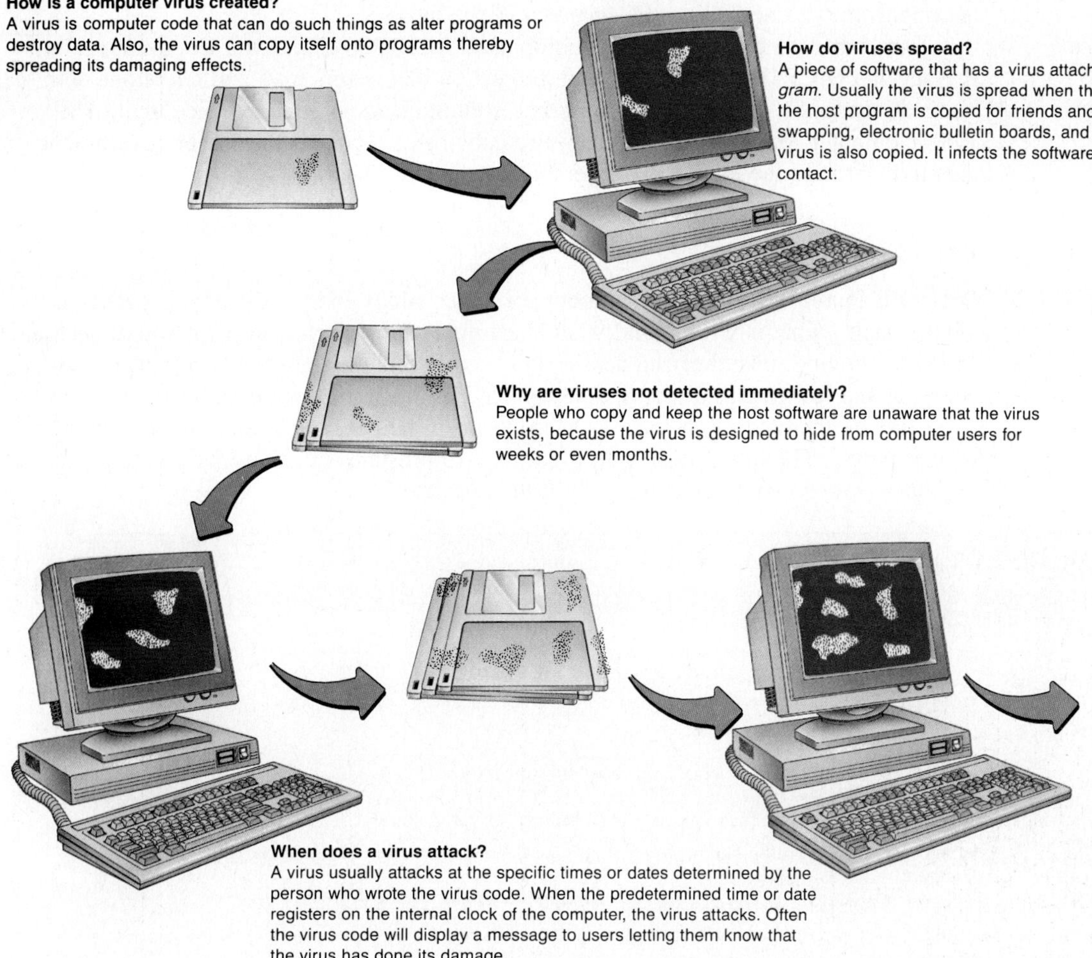

A COMPUTER VIRUS: WHAT IT IS AND HOW IT SPREADS
How is a computer virus created?
A virus is computer code that can do such things as alter programs or destroy data. Also, the virus can copy itself onto programs thereby spreading its damaging effects.
How do viruses spread?
A piece of software that has a virus attached to it is called the host program. Usually the virus is spread when the host program is shared. As the host program is copied for friends and business associates through swapping, electronic bulletin boards, and other usual channels, the virus is also copied. It infects the software with which it comes into contact.
Why are viruses not detected immediately?
People who copy and keep the host software are unaware that the virus exists, because the virus is designed to hide from computer users for weeks or even months.
When does a virus attack?
A virus usually attacks at the specific times or dates determined by the person who wrote the virus code. When the predetermined time or date registers on the internal clock of the computer, the virus attacks. Often the virus code will display a message to users letting them know that the virus has done its damage.

FIGURE 14-14
How a virus program can be transmitted from one computer system to another.

Single acts of malicious damage, especially when performed by employees with authorized access to the computer system, are very difficult to prevent. The best protection against this type of act remains adequate backup files that enable organizations to restore damaged or lost data.

Privacy

In the past, one way to maintain privacy was to keep information in separate locations—individual stores had their own credit files, government agencies had separate records, doctors had separate files, and so on. However, it is now technically and economically feasible to store large amounts of related data about individuals in one database. Some people believe that this increases the possibility for unauthorized use.

The concern about information privacy has led to federal and state laws regarding the storage and disclosure of personal data. Common points in these laws include: (1) information collected and stored about individuals should be limited to what is necessary to carry out the function of the business or government agency collecting the data. (2) Once collected, provisions should be made to restrict access to the data to those employees within the organization who need access to it to perform their job duties. (3) Personal information should be released outside the organization collecting the data only when the person has agreed to its disclosure. (4) When information is collected about an individual, the individual should know that data is being collected and have the opportunity to determine the accuracy of the data.

Two laws deal specifically with computers. The 1986 Electronic Communications Privacy Act (ECPA) provides the same protection that covers mail and telephone communications to the new forms of electronic communications such as voice mail. The 1988 Computer Matching and Privacy Protection Act regulates the use of government data to determine the eligibility of persons for federal benefits.

Ethics

Society is increasingly concerned about computer ethics and the difference between what is right, what is wrong, and what is criminal. Issues relate to many topics such as software copying, unauthorized access and use of computer systems, and privacy. By studying and learning the information provided in this book, you have become a computer literate member of society. As such, you will be better able to evaluate computer-related issues. The questionnaire in Figure 14-15 presents situations for you to evaluate. How do you feel about each of the questions?

FIGURE 14-15
Ethics questionnaire.

ETHICS OF INFORMATION PROCESSING

1. A computer operator runs a program at work for a friend and uses ten minutes of computer time. The program was run when the computer was idle and not being used for company business.
   Ethical ________ **Unethical** ________ **Computer Crime** ________
2. A student gives a password to another student not enrolled in a computer class for which a laboratory fee is charged. The password allows access to the school computer. The student not enrolled uses three hours of computer time in a time-sharing environment.
   Student enrolled in class:
   Ethical ________ **Unethical** ________ **Computer Crime** ________
   Student not enrolled in class:
   Ethical ________ **Unethical** ________ **Computer Crime** ________
3. A company hires a consultant to develop a payroll program. After completing the project, the consultant gives a copy of the program (without data) to a friend at another company.
   Ethical ________ **Unethical** ________ **Computer Crime** ________
4. Using a terminal, an individual breaks a security code and reviews confidential salaries of corporate executives. No use is made of the information. "I was just curious" is the individual's response when caught.
   Ethical ________ **Unethical** ________ **Computer Crime** ________
5. A bank employee electronically transfers money from a relatively inactive customer account to his own personal account and then transfers the money to a credit card account to pay current credit card charges. After money is deposited into his personal account on pay day, he electronically transfers the money back to the customer's account. No money physically changes hands, and no interest is lost to the customer's account.
   Ethical ________ **Unethical** ________ **Computer Crime** ________
6. While reviewing a list of available programs on a bulletin board, a user notices a title of a program that is the same as a popular spreadsheet package. After downloading the program onto his system, the user discovers that the program appears to be an exact copy of the spreadsheet program that is sold in computer stores for $300.00. The user keeps and uses the program.
   Ethical ________ **Unethical** ________ **Computer Crime** ________
7. A programmer is asked to write a program that she knows will generate inaccurate information for stockholders of the company. When she questions her manager about the program, she is told she must write it or lose her job. She writes the program.
   Manager: **Ethical** ________ **Unethical** ________ **Computer Crime** ________
   Programmer: **Ethical** ________ **Unethical** ________ **Computer Crime** ________
8. As a practical joke, a student enters a virus program onto the hard disk of a microcomputer in the school's computer lab. Each time another student uses that machine, the virus program is copied onto that student's diskette. The program is designed so that the first time the disk is used after the first of January a "Happy New Year" message will be displayed on the screen.
   Ethical ________ **Unethical** ________ **Computer Crime** ________
9. A photojournalist uses a computer graphics program to retouch the background of a photo that is used on the front page of the newspaper.
   Ethical ________ **Unethical** ________ **Computer Crime** ________
10. A company uses software to monitor the productivity of the clerical staff. Supervisors are notified of staff members who fall below what management considers to be the minimum productivity standards.
   Ethical ________ **Unethical** ________ **Computer Crime** ________

SUMMARY OF TRENDS AND ISSUES IN THE INFORMATION AGE

Based on current and planned developments, the impact of computers and the information age will be even greater in the future than it has been to date. However, as a society and as individuals, we have an obligation to use the computer responsibly and not abuse the power it provides. This presents constant challenges that sometimes weigh the rights of the individual against increased efficiency and productivity. The computer must be thought of as a tool whose effectiveness is determined by the skill and experience of the user. With the computer knowledge that you have acquired you will be better able to participate in decisions on how to best use computerized information systems.

CHAPTER SUMMARY

1. Existing business information systems will continue to undergo profound changes as new technology, software, and methods become available.
2. Trends will include; more online, interactive systems; less batch processing; expanded communications networks and increased use of relational database systems; and replacing command- and menu-driven interfaces with graphical-user interfaces.
3. The **automated office**, sometimes referred to as the **electronic office**, is the term that describes the use of electronic devices such as computers, facsimile machines, and computerized telephone systems to make office work more productive.
4. Word processing ranks as the most widely used office automation technology.
5. **Electronic mail** is the capability to transmit messages to and receive messages from other computer users.
6. **Voice mail** can be considered verbal electronic mail.
7. Desktop publishing involves the use of computers to produce printed documents that can combine different sizes and styles of text and graphics.
8. **Facsimile**, or **FAX**, machines are used to transmit a reproduced image of a document over standard phone lines.
9. Image processing is the capability to store and retrieve a reproduced image of a document.
10. **Teleconferencing** usually means **video conferencing**, the use of computers and television cameras to transmit video images and the sound of the conference participants to other participants with similar equipment at a remote location.
11. The goal of the **automated factory** is to increase productivity through the use of automated, and often computer-controlled, equipment.
12. **Computer-aided design (CAD)** uses a computer and special graphics software to aid in product design.
13. **Computer-aided engineering (CAE)** is the use of computers to test product designs.
14. **Computer-aided manufacturing (CAM)** is the use of computers to control production equipment.
15. **Computer-integrated manufacturing (CIM)** is the total integration of the manufacturing process using computers.
16. The long-range trend is the **computer-integrated enterprise**; an organization where all information storage and processing is performed by a network of computers and intelligent devices.
17. Personal computers are used in the home in many different ways, including: (1) personal services, (2) control of home systems, (3) telecommuting, (4) education, and (5) entertainment.
18. The personal services provided by home computer use allow people to perform personal and business-related tasks quickly and conveniently in the comfort of their own homes.
19. Electronic **bulletin board systems**, called **BBSs**, allow users to communicate with one another and share information.
20. Another use of computers in the home is to control home systems such as security, environment, lighting, and landscape sprinkler systems.

21. **Telecommuting** refers to the capability of individuals to work at home and communicate with their offices by using personal computers and communication lines.
22. The use of personal computers for education, called **computer-aided instruction (CAI)**, is a rapidly growing area.
23. **Drill and practice software** uses a flash-card approach to teaching by allowing users to practice skills in subjects such as math and language.
24. **Tutorial software** uses text, graphics, and sometimes sound to teach a user concepts about a subject and follows the instruction with questions to help the user ensure that he or she understands the concepts.
25. **Simulation software** is designed to teach a user by creating a model of a real-life situation.
26. Popular types of entertainment software include arcade games, board games, simulations, and interactive graphics programs.
27. The guidelines for purchasing a personal computer recommend that you: (1) become computer literate; (2) define and prioritize the type of tasks you want to perform on your computer; (3) select the software packages that best meet your needs; (4) select equipment that will run the software you have selected; (5) select the suppliers for the software and equipment; and (6) purchase the software and equipment.
28. **Shareware** is software that users may try out on their own systems before paying a fee.
29. **Public domain software** is not copyrighted and can therefore be distributed among users.
30. **Computer security** refers to the safeguards established to prevent and detect unauthorized use and deliberate or accidental damage to computer systems and data.
31. **Computer crime** is the use of a computer to commit an illegal act.
32. Software theft, often called **software piracy**, refers to illegal copying of software.
33. **Unauthorized access** can be defined as computer trespassing, in other words, being logged on a system without permission.
34. **Unauthorized use** is the use of a computer system or computer data for unapproved and possibly illegal activities.
35. The key to preventing both unauthorized access and unauthorized use is computer security that controls and monitors an appropriate level of authorization for each user.
36. One of the most potentially dangerous types of malicious damage is done by a **virus**, a computer program designed to copy itself into other software and spread through multiple computer systems.
37. **Vaccines** are programs that locate and remove viruses.
38. The concern about information privacy has led to federal and state laws regarding the storage and disclosure of personal data.

KEY TERMS

INTRODUCTION TO

PROJECT 1

Working with Files on Disks

PROJECT 2

Managing and Organizing Files on Disks

Working With Files on Disks

OBJECTIVES

You will have mastered the material in this project when you can:

- Identify the purpose of DOS
- Boot your computer
- Establish the default disk drive
- Enter and correct DOS commands
- Clear the screen
- Format a disk
- View filenames on a disk
- Copy a file
- Rename a file
- Delete a file
- Recover a file
- Obtain help for DOS commands

INTRODUCTION

Without an operating system, a computer is a useless piece of equipment. An **operating system** is a collection of programs that enables the user to communicate with the computer; it is the interface between you and the hardware (Figure 1-1). You make requests of the operating system, and the operating system, in turn, controls and manages the hardware. Thus, you issue instructions, and the operating system interprets and executes these instructions. For example, the instruction `cls` tells the operating system to clear the computer's screen.

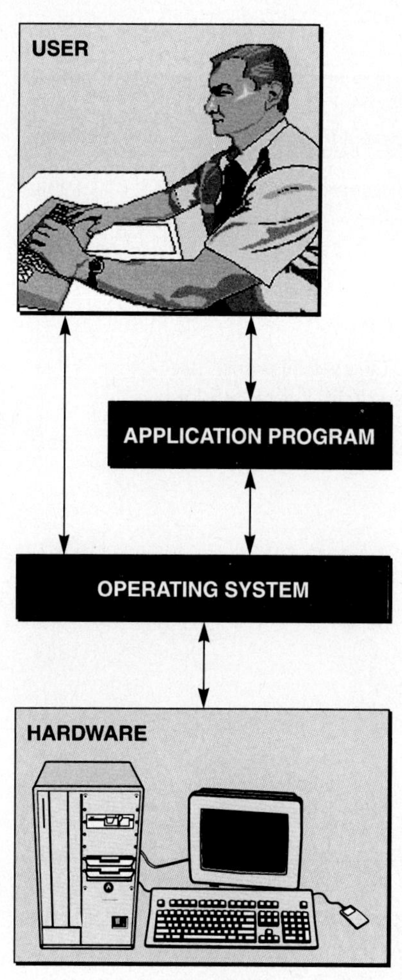

FIGURE 1-1

When you use an application program, such as a word processor, electronic spreadsheet, or database management system, the application program interacts with the operating system. To use a computer to print a memo, for example, you first use the operating system to start the computer. You next instruct the operating system to begin the word processing program. At this point, you are interacting with the word processing program, which is interacting with the operating system, which is interacting with the hardware. When you instruct the word processing program to display the memo on the screen, or *open* the file, the word processing program requests that the operating system find the memo file on disk, retrieve the file from the disk, and display its contents on the screen. The operating system provides essential services that the application software uses to perform its functions for you.

To use your computer effectively, you need to know when and how to interact with the operating system. IBM and IBM-compatible personal computers use the disk operating system called DOS. In Project 1, you will learn how to use DOS to work with your disk files.

PC Versus MS-DOS

Microsoft Corporation developed the operating system called **DOS** (pronounced doss), an acronym for **Disk Operating System**. DOS has been used since 1981 on IBM and IBM-compatible personal computers. Depending on the type of personal computer you are using, your operating system is called either PC-DOS or MS-DOS. **PC-DOS** is distributed by IBM for its Personal Computer (PC) and Personal System/2 lines of personal computers. All IBM-compatible personal computers use **MS-DOS**, distributed by Microsoft Corporation. PC-DOS and MS-DOS are essentially the same product. For purposes in this book, the term DOS is used to refer to both the PC-DOS and MS-DOS products.

DOS Versions

The numbers following a software product name, like DOS, indicate the specific version number and release number of the product. The version number is the number in front of the decimal point; the release number is the number following the decimal point. All software products have version and release numbers. Changes in a version number indicate a major improvement to the product, whereas changes in the release number indicate corrections or minor changes to a version of the product. Often, new releases of a version are prompted by a user(s) notifying the software manufacturer of a problem with the current release. For example DOS 1.1 corrected some minor problems with DOS 1.0; but DOS 2.0 made significant changes over DOS 1.1. New releases are also issued to accommodate minor hardware changes and upgrades. Table 1-1 lists the hardware changes and new features added with each new release, or version, of DOS.

TABLE 1-1

DOS Version & Release	*Major Features Supported*	*Year*
6.2	New Data-Protection Technology, Disk Uncompression, Copy Overwrite Protection, Removal of DOS Shell—except for Step-Up program	1993
6.0	Disk Compression and Defragmenter, Memory Optimization, Improved Backup Utility, Anti-Virus Program	1993
5.0	Improved Memory Management, Recover Deleted Files and Formatted Disks, Online Help, Full-Screen Editor, 2.88 MB Disks	1992
4.0	Hard Disks Larger than 32MB, File Manager Shell (DOS Shell), Memory Supported Beyond 640KB	1988
3.3	IBM PS/2	1987
3.2	Token-Ring Networks, 3 1/2" Disks	1986
3.1	Networking	1985
3.0	IBM PC/AT, High Density 5 1/4" Disks	1984
2.1	PC Jr and Portables	1983
2.0	IBM PC/XT, Hard Disks	1983
1.1	Double-Sided Disks	1982
1.0	IBM PC, Single-Sided Disks	1981

Software developers try to maintain **upward compatibility** in their products. That is, all of the features in an earlier version and release remain supported by a later one. A word processing package that works when you use DOS 3.2, for example, should also work when you use DOS 6.2. Downward compatibility, however, is not common. Programs or equipment that require the features of DOS 6.2 will not function with DOS 5.0 or earlier versions.

Disk Configurations

You will probably use a computer with one of two common disk configurations. The first configuration has a hard drive and one or two diskette drives and operates as a stand-alone unit (Figures 1-2 and 1-3). Each drive has a **drive name**, which is a unique letter name preassigned to the drive. The hard drive name is C, and the diskette drive name is A.

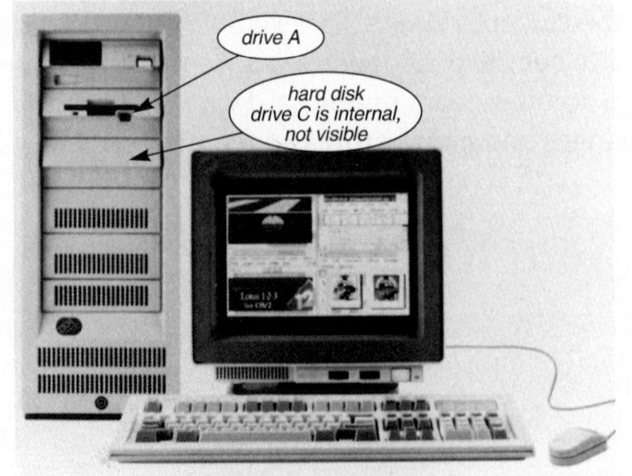

(a) Tower unit

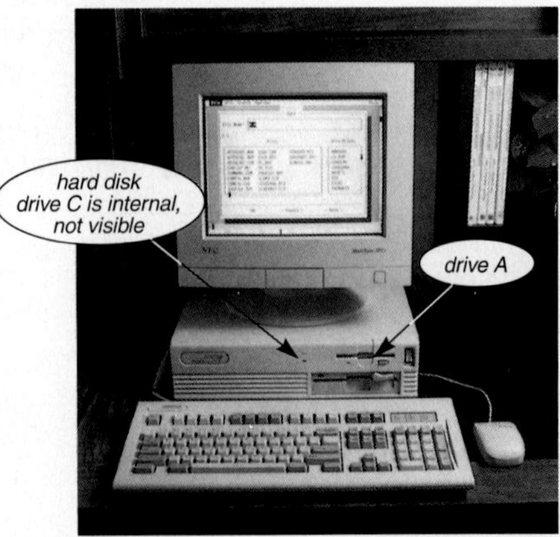

(b) Desktop unit

FIGURE 1-2
(a) Courtesy IBM Corporation
(b) Courtesy Compaq Computer

(a) **Notebook unit**

(b) **Desktop unit with a CD ROM drive**

FIGURE 1-3
(a) Courtesy Texas Instruments
(b) Courtesy IBM Corporation

The second configuration connects your computer through a local area network with other computers (Figure 1-4). A **local area network**, or **LAN**, is a collection of connected computers that share data. One special computer on the LAN, called the **server**, has a high-capacity hard drive containing files that you can access from any connected computer. The server hard drive name is usually F. Each computer connected to the LAN may have either two diskette drives; one hard drive and one diskette drive; or one hard drive and two diskette drives. In a two diskette drive environment, the top or left drive name is A, and the bottom or right drive name is B.

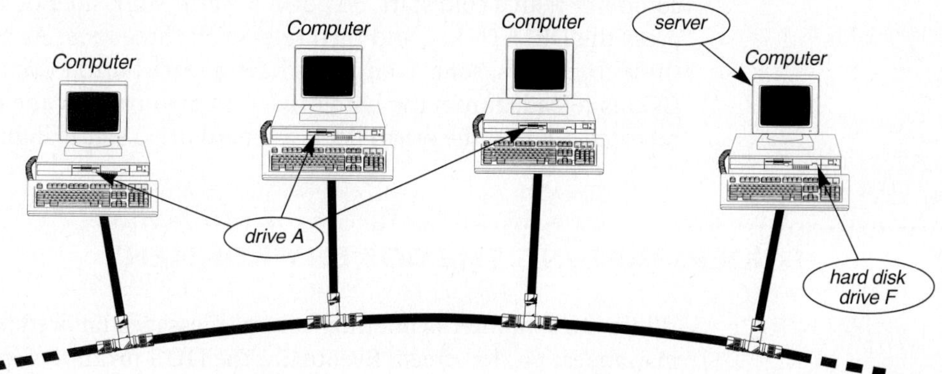

FIGURE 1-4

These DOS projects assume you have one hard drive and one diskette drive, unless otherwise stated. If you are using a computer with a different configuration, your instructor will inform you of the changes you need to make in the DOS projects.

▼ STARTING THE COMPUTER

DOS programs are originally purchased on diskettes, and then usually **installed**, or unpacked and copied, from the diskettes to a hard drive. To begin using DOS, it must be loaded from the hard drive into the memory of the computer, which is a process known as **booting** the computer. How you begin using the computer depends on your disk configuration and whether the computer has already been turned on.

LAN Environment

If you are using a computer on a LAN, the laboratory attendant will have already booted your computer. You do not need to perform any startup activities, unless your instructor gives you special instructions.

Stand-alone Mode

If your computer is not connected to a LAN, you are using it in **stand-alone mode.** You can boot stand-alone computers with a cold or warm boot. When cold or warm starting a computer, many computers require that the diskette drives be empty. If you boot many computers with a disk in the diskette drive, the message, Non-System disk or disk error Replace and press any key when ready, displays on the screen and the system halts. In this case, simply remove the disk from the drive and press any key to continue the boot process.

Cold Boot Starting a computer by turning on the power switch is called a **cold start,** or **cold boot.** In a cold boot, the computer first runs some diagnostic tests on the circuitry and then loads DOS from the hard drive into memory. While DOS is booting, the hard drive status light flashes for a few seconds.

Because turning a computer off and then immediately on again can adversely affect its internal components, you should use a warm boot to restart a running computer.

Warm Boot If the computer is already turned on, you can restart the computer without turning the power switch off and on. Restarting the computer in this way is called a **warm start, warm boot,** or **reset.** A warm start is much less stressful on a computer than a cold start. To begin a warm start, hold down the CTRL and ALT keys, press the DELETE key, and then release all three keys. As an alternative to pressing these three keys, some computers have a reset button you may press. In a warm boot, DOS is reloaded from the hard drive into memory, but the circuitry tests are not repeated. During the warm boot, the hard drive status light flashes for a few seconds.

▼ UNDERSTANDING THE DOS ENVIRONMENT

While the computer is booting, several messages tailored for your specific computer may appear on the screen. Eventually, the **DOS prompt** displays on the screen (Figures 1-5 and 1-6), indicating DOS is ready to receive your commands. (If your DOS prompt differs from the one in Figure 1-5 or 1-6, your instructor will explain the difference(s) to you.) The initial letter that appears in the DOS prompt indicates the drive that DOS was on when the computer was booted. Thus, the letter will vary depending on the disk configuration you are using. If DOS was loaded from the hard drive, the letter is a C (Figure 1-5); if DOS was loaded from a network server, the letter is usually an F (Figure 1-6).

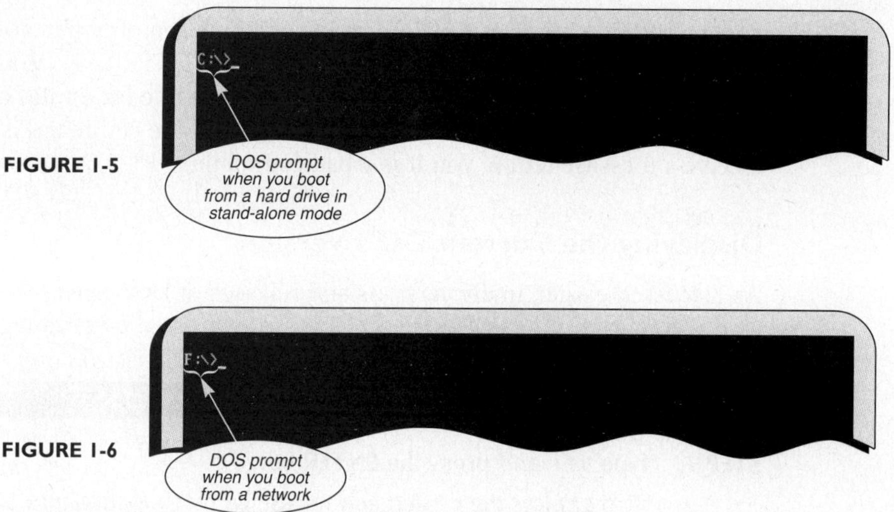
C:\>_
DOS prompt when you boot from a hard drive in stand-alone mode
F:\>_
DOS prompt when you boot from a network

FIGURE 1-5

FIGURE 1-6

The Default Drive

The drive letter in the DOS prompt is also called the default drive. The **default drive** is the drive that DOS assumes contains programs and data to be used. Another term for the default drive is the **current drive**, because it is the drive in which DOS *currently* looks for files. At times you will need to change the default drive assignment. If you change the default drive assignment to a diskette drive, you must first place a disk in the drive. Follow these steps to change the default drive assignment from C to A.

TO CHANGE THE DEFAULT DRIVE ASSIGNMENT

STEP 1: Insert the Student Diskette that accompanies this book into drive A.

A disk must be inserted into drive A before you change the default drive assignment.

STEP 2: Type a: **and press the ENTER key.**

The default drive in the DOS prompt is now drive A (Figure 1-7). You could have entered the a in the a: in either uppercase or lowercase.

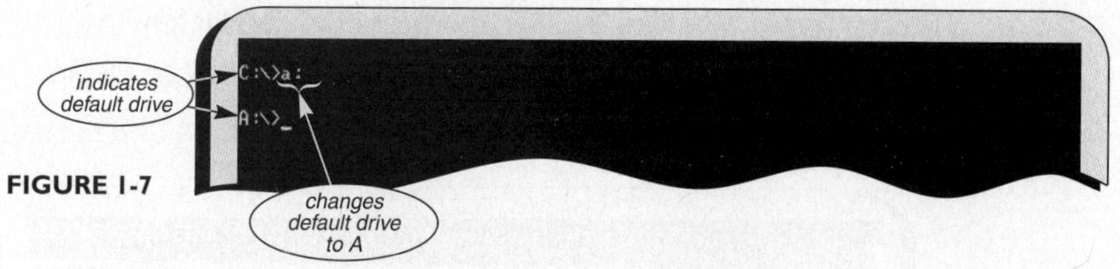
indicates default drive
C:\>a:
A:\>_
changes default drive to A

FIGURE 1-7

ENTERING DOS COMMANDS

Now that you have booted the computer, you can enter DOS commands. **Commands** are instructions you type to tell DOS what you want to do. DOS includes a variety of commands to assist you in using the computer. Some commands might be status, or informative, commands because they instruct DOS to give you information. Other commands direct DOS to perform actions for you. You can enter commands, drive names, and other entries to DOS, in any combination of uppercase and lowercase letters. Following DOS commands, you press the ENTER key. When you press the ENTER key, DOS scans the most recently entered line for a valid command and then executes the command if it is found to be valid. If the command is not valid, you will receive a message telling you it is a bad command.

Displaying the Current DOS Version

As discussed earlier, many versions and releases of DOS exist today. To verify the version and release number loaded on your system, use the **ver command.**

TO DISPLAY THE LOADED DOS VERSION

STEP 1: Type `ver` **and press the ENTER key.**

DOS displays the version and release currently loaded into memory (Figure 1-8).

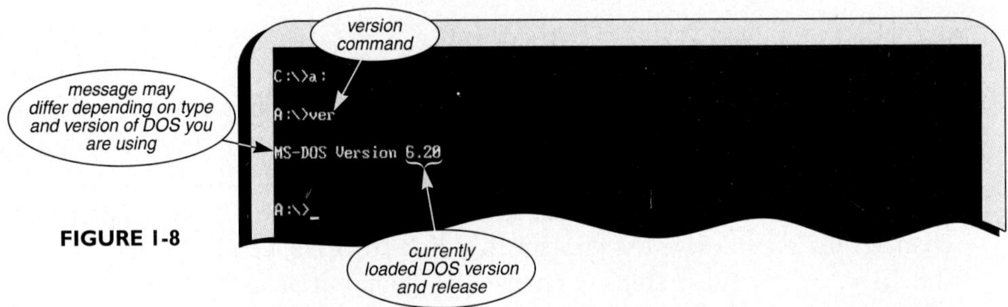

FIGURE 1-8

Clearing the Screen

Frequently, as you issue several commands or perform lengthy processes, the screen becomes cluttered. To clear the screen and place the DOS prompt on the first line of the screen, you use the **cls command.**

TO CLEAR THE SCREEN

STEP 1: Type `cls` **(Figure 1-9a) and press the ENTER key.**

The screen clears and the DOS prompt displays on the first line of the screen (Figure 1-9b).

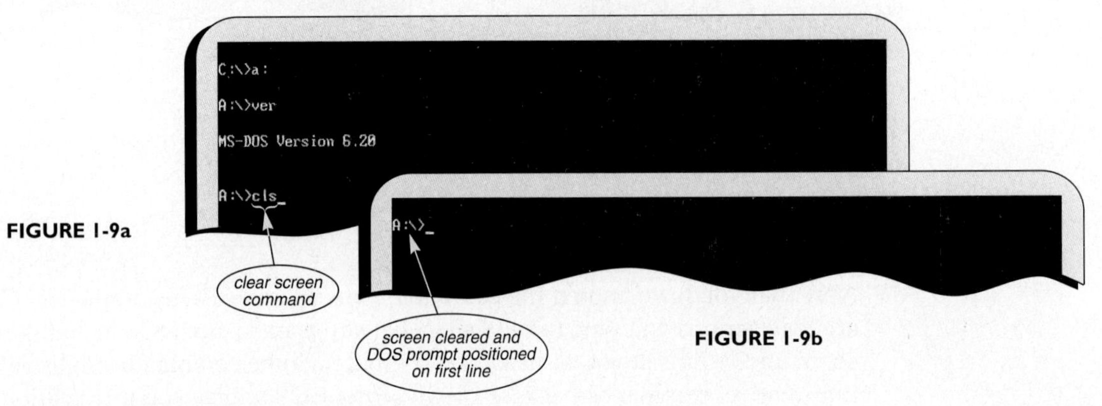

FIGURE 1-9a

FIGURE 1-9b

Whenever your screen becomes cluttered, you can enter the CLS command. As you proceed through this and the next project, you will notice we clear the screen frequently between DOS commands. Because the CLS command is used only to enhance readability, these two projects do not explicitly tell you to clear the screen.

Correcting DOS Commands

Even if you are an expert typist, you will sometimes make mistakes when you enter DOS commands. For this reason, DOS provides several keys that allow you to correct mistakes.

If you realize you have made a mistake and have *not yet* pressed the ENTER key, you can press the **BACKSPACE** key to erase the character(s) to the left of the cursor. For example, if you type vet to display the DOS version, you can press the BACKSPACE key once and then type the letter r to complete the ver command. Then, press the ENTER key to display the DOS version.

If you type xls to clear the screen and have *not* yet pressed the ENTER key, you could press the BACKSPACE key three times to erase the three letters or you can press the ESC key and retype the entire command. When you press the **ESC key**, a backslash character (\) displays at the end of the typed line, and the cursor advances to the next line. You are now at the beginning of the next line and can begin over again (Figure 1-10). (If the backslash character does not display on your screen, your instructor will explain that the difference(s) is due to a program called doskey.)

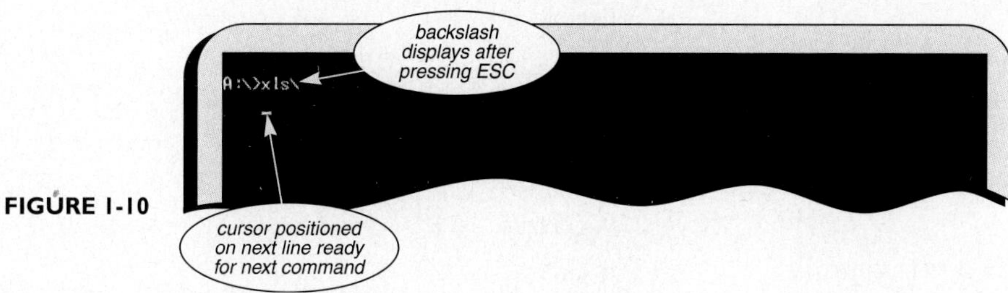

FIGURE 1-10

If you have already pressed the ENTER key after typing an erroneous command, DOS displays the error message, Bad command or file name, on the screen with a new DOS prompt below the error message. When this occurs, you either retype the entire command correctly and press the ENTER key, or press the **F3** function key to redisplay the command you just entered and modify it. The F3 key works well if the error you made occurred at the end of the command. For example, if you entered vet, you can press F3 to redisplay the entry vet (Figure 1-11), press the BACKSPACE key once to erase the letter t, type the letter r to correctly conclude the ver command, and press the ENTER key to display the DOS version.

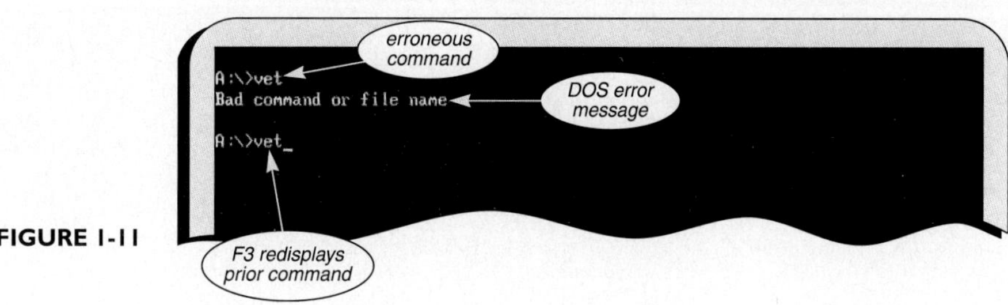

FIGURE 1-11

FORMATTING A DISKETTE

Most diskettes you buy can be used immediately; that is, they have already been formatted. Because you can also buy *unformatted* diskettes, you need to know how to format a disk. **Formatting** is the process of preparing a disk so it can store data. DOS formats a disk by dividing it into **cylinders**, which are narrow recording bands forming a full circle around the disk, and **sectors**, which are sections of a cylinder.

Be careful with the disks you format because *formatting erases any existing files on the disk*. This is true for hard disks as well as diskettes. You must be extremely careful, therefore, with the disk drives you choose when you use the format command.

Diskettes are available in three sizes: 2 inch, 3 1/2 inch, and 5 1/4 inch. Diskettes are classified as double density, high density, and very high density. Very high density diskettes store more data than high-density diskettes; high-density diskettes store more data than double-density diskettes. Table 1-2 shows a comparison of these disks. To store data on a very high density diskette, you need a very high density drive on your PC. Likewise, you need a high density drive to store data on a high-density diskette.

TABLE 1-2

Disk Size	*Density*	*Capacity in Bytes*	*Number of Double-Spaced Typewritten 8 1/2 by 11 Inch Pages*
5 1/4″	Double	360K	125
5 1/4″	High	1.2M	375
3 1/2″	Double	720K	250
3 1/2″	High	1.44M	500
3 1/2″	Very High	2.88M	1000
2″	Double	360K	125

The read/write head in the disk unit comes into magnetic contact with the recording surface of all three disk sizes. With the 5 1/4-inch diskette, the read/write heads make contact through the slot hole in the diskette's protective jacket (Figure 1-12a). The 2- and 3 1/2-inch diskettes each have a shutter that automatically opens and exposes the recording surface when the diskette is placed in the disk drive (Figure 1-12b). Once inside the disk drive, the diskette spins inside its protective jacket.

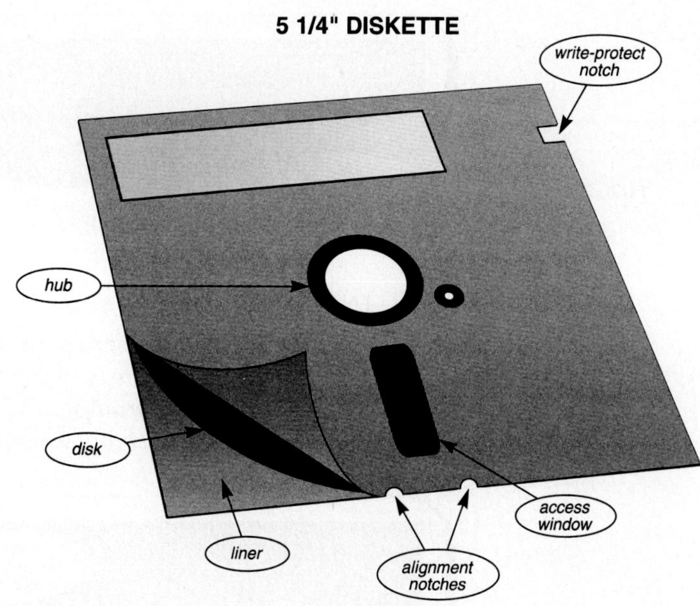

FIGURE 1-12a

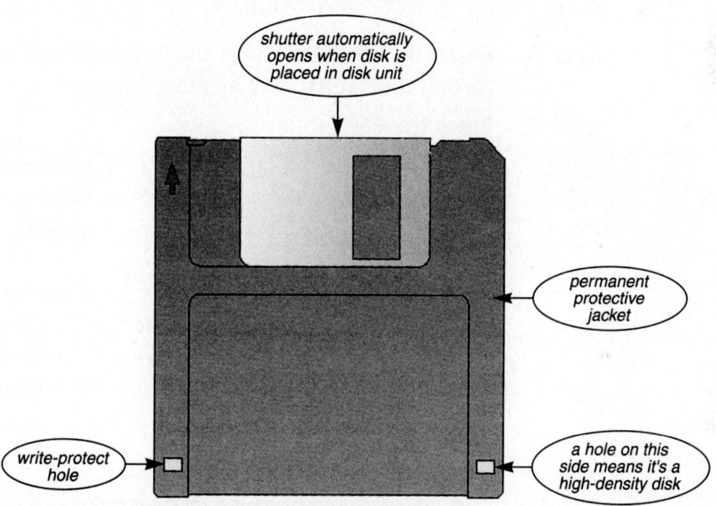

FIGURE 1-12b

Because disks vary by size and recording density, your **format command** may differ slightly from this book's description (see Table 1-3 on page DOS14). If it does, your instructor will inform you of necessary changes. Follow these steps to format a disk that is the same density as the drive in which you place it.

TO FORMAT A DISKETTE

STEP 1: Remove the Student Diskette from drive A.

STEP 2: Type `format a:`

DOS displays the format command followed by the drive to be formatted (Figure 1-13 on the next page). The disk you place in the A drive, indicated by the a:, will be formatted. To format a disk in a different drive, simply change the drive name before the colon.

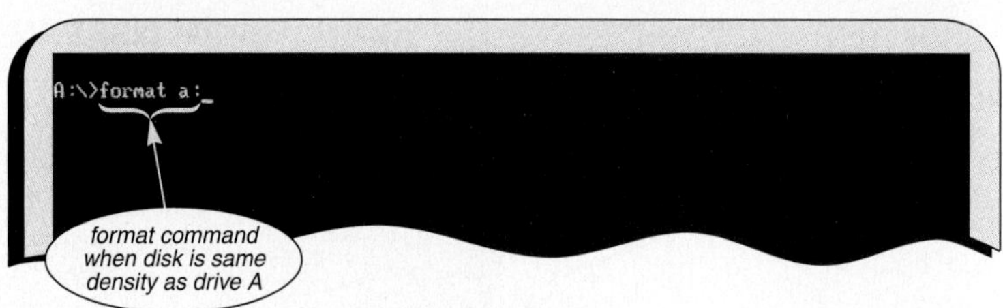

FIGURE 1-13

STEP 3: Press the ENTER key.

DOS loads the format program to memory, begins to execute the format program, and displays the prompt, Insert new diskette for drive A: and press ENTER when ready... *(Figure 1-14). A **prompt** is a message providing you with information or instructions regarding an entry you must make or an action you must take.*

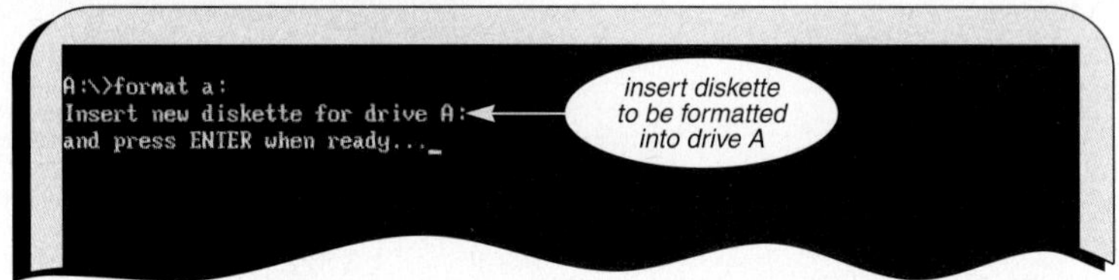

FIGURE 1-14

STEP 4: Insert the diskette you want to format into drive A. (Remember, when you format a diskette, any existing files are erased!)

STEP 5: Press the ENTER key.

*DOS displays the disk capacity on the screen and the progress of the format process in terms of the percentage completed. When formatting is 100 percent complete (Figure 1-15), DOS asks you to enter a volume label with the prompt, Volume label (11 characters, ENTER for none)? You respond to this prompt by typing a volume label and pressing ENTER, or omitting the volume label by simply pressing ENTER. A **volume label** is an optional identifying name you give to a disk to help you distinguish one disk from another. A volume label consists of one to eleven characters. Although you can choose to not enter a volume label, it is recommended you use your last name as the volume label to identify your disk.*

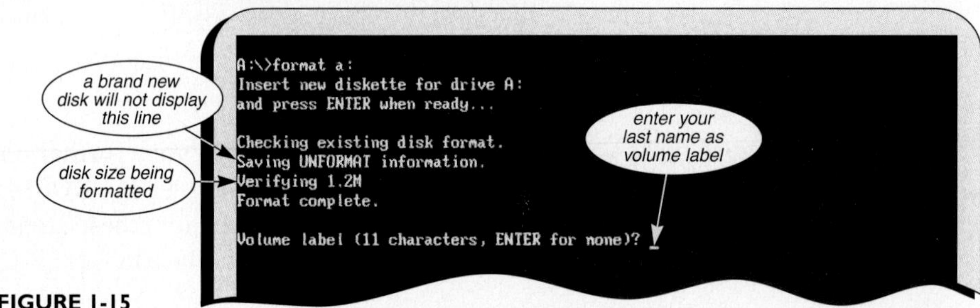

FIGURE 1-15

STEP 6: (You should enter your last name as the volume label). Type the volume label (vermaat in the example), and press the ENTER key.

DOS reports the total disk storage space; the number of bytes available for storage, which is the number of characters that may be saved; the size of each allocation unit, which equals one sector on a disk; the number of allocation units; and the assigned volume serial number (Figure 1-16). Beneath these informative messages, DOS asks you if you want to format another disk. You respond to this prompt by typing the letter Y for Yes or N for No.

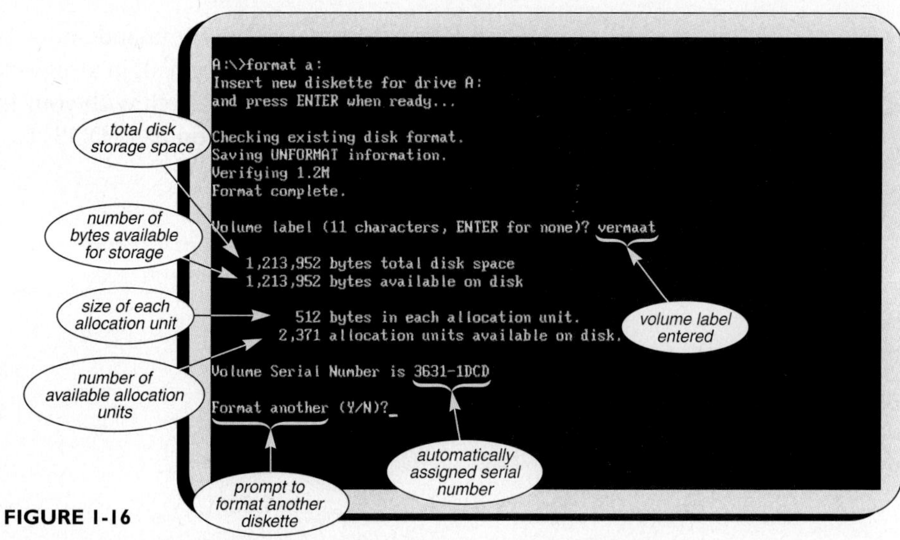
A:\>format a:
Insert new diskette for drive A:
and press ENTER when ready...
Checking existing disk format.
Saving UNFORMAT information.
Verifying 1.2M
Format complete.
Volume label (11 characters, ENTER for none)? vermaat
1,213,952 bytes total disk space
1,213,952 bytes available on disk
512 bytes in each allocation unit.
2,371 allocation units available on disk.
Volume Serial Number is 3631-1DCD
Format another (Y/N)?_
total disk storage space
number of bytes available for storage
size of each allocation unit
number of available allocation units
volume label entered
automatically assigned serial number
prompt to format another diskette

FIGURE 1-16

STEP 7: Type the letter n **for No and press the ENTER key.**

STEP 8: Remove the disk from drive A. With a felt-tipped pen, write your first and last names and the words, Data Disk, on the external disk label supplied with the disk. Then, apply the disk label firmly on the disk. Reinsert the data disk into drive A.

The external label is used to identify one disk from another (Figure 1-17). The volume label you entered in Step 6 is an internal label and does not replace the need for an external label.

5 1/4" DISK
external label
Misty Vermaat
Data Disk
3 1/2" DISK
external label
Misty Vermaat
Data Disk

FIGURE 1-17

The format command shown in Step 2 on page DOS11 assumes the diskette and the drive are the same recording density. If you want to format a double-density diskette in a high-density drive, your method of formatting will differ slightly from this description. That is, you need to modify the parameters of the format command as shown in Table 1-3 on the next page. A **parameter** is the character or set of characters that follow the basic command. That is, format is the command and a: is the parameter. If, for example, you have a 5 1/4 inch double-density disk in a high-density drive, you need to enter format a: /f:360 as the command. Check with your instructor to see what, if any changes you need to make to Step 2 on page DOS11.

TABLE 1-3

Disk Size	*Density*	*Capacity in Bytes*	*Format Command*
5 1/4"	Double	360K	format a: /f:360
5 1/4"	High	1.2M	format a: /f:1.2
3 1/2"	Double	720K	format a: /f:720
3 1/2"	High	1.44M	format a: /f:1.44
3 1/2"	Very High	2.88M	format a: /f:2.88
2"	Double	360K	format a: /f:360

▼ SETTING UP YOUR DATA DISK

The Student Diskette that accompanies this book has several files you need for the remaining examples in this and the next project. A program has been written to copy the necessary files from the Student Diskette to your data disk. The program is on the Student Diskette that accompanies this book. Follow these steps to set up your data disk.

TO SET UP YOUR DATA DISK

STEP 1: Remove your data disk from drive A. Insert the Student Diskette that accompanies this book into drive A. (Your system configuration may require you to insert the Student Diskette into drive B.)

STEP 2: Type `copydata` **and press the ENTER key.**

STEP 3: Follow the instructions given by the copydata program.

STEP 4: If it is not already in drive A, insert your data disk into drive A.

▼ DISPLAYING FILENAMES ON A DISK

A disk is essentially an electronic filing cabinet. Just like you manage file folders in a filing cabinet, one of the functions of DOS is to store files containing programs and data on disks. To manage that file storage, DOS maintains a **directory**, or listing, of all of the files stored on a disk. To display the directory of a disk, you use the **dir command**.

TO DISPLAY FILENAMES ON A DISK

STEP 1: Type `dir` **and press the ENTER key.**

The directory, or listing, of files on the data disk in drive A displays on the screen (Figure 1-18). The directory listing itself consists of the filenames and extensions of the files on the disk, the number of bytes consumed by each file on the disk, the date and time the file was created or most recently modified. The message at the end of the directory listing indicates the number of files on the disk (in Figure 1-18 there are 11 files on the disk) and the remaining space available on the disk (1,173,504 unused bytes remain on the disk in Figure 1-18, but your number may differ if your data disk is a different size or has a different recording density). At the end of the directory listing, the DOS prompt redisplays on the screen, indicating that DOS is ready for your next command.

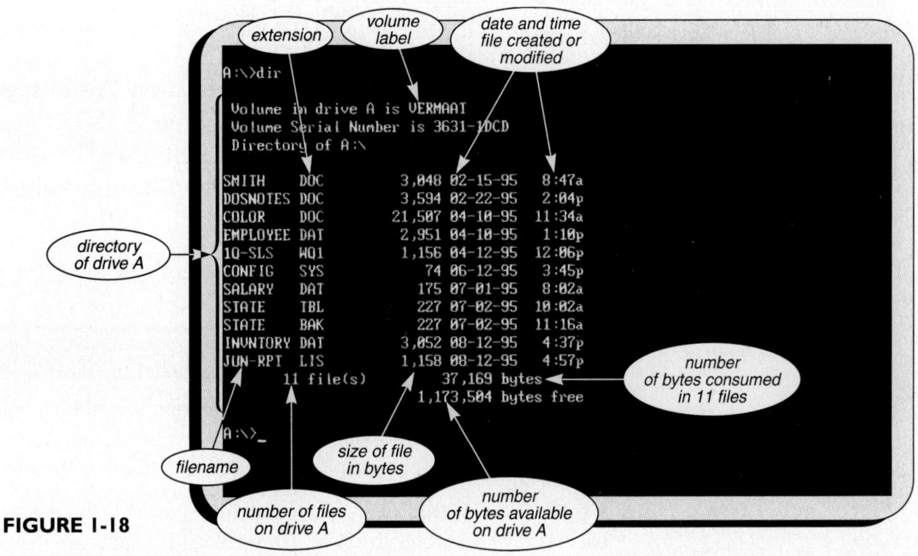

FIGURE 1-18

Filenames

In a filing cabinet, you place labels on the file folders to identify the contents of the folder. On a disk, a **filename** is a name that identifies the contents of the electronic file. Two basic types of files can appear on a disk: data files and program files. A **data file** is a collection of data created by an application program and used by the program. For example, the data can be numbers used to show sales revenue in a spreadsheet; names and addresses in a database file; or a word processing memo announcing the arrival of a new employee. A **program file** contains instructions that the computer follows to perform tasks. For example, a word processing software package contains a program(s) that enables you to create, modify, and print documents.

A filename consists of one to eight characters, which may include letters (A-Z), digits (0-9), or these special characters: underscore (_), caret (^), dollar sign ($), tilde (~), exclamation point (!), number sign (#), percent sign (%), ampersand (&), hyphen (-), braces ({}), parentheses ( ), at sign (@), apostrophe ('), or the grave accent (').

Because you only have eight characters to represent the name of a file, you should create filenames that help to remind you what data is stored in the file. If your file contains employee data, for example, the filename EMPLOYEE is more meaningful than the filename FILE1, even though DOS will accept either filename.

Extensions

A filename can also have an optional extension, which identifies a file more specifically or describes its purpose. An **extension** consists of one to three characters and is separated from the filename by a period. The same characters permitted for a filename are permitted for an extension. Many application programs automatically assign special extensions to the files they create. For example, one version of Lotus automatically adds the extension WQ3. In this way, whenever you see the filename WQ3, you can identify the file as a Lotus file. If your application does not add an extension to a file, you may add an extension. If you create a word processing document file containing a letter to John Smith, for example, you could use the filename SMITH and the extension DOC to identify the file as a document file. The entire filename would be SMITH.DOC.

File Specifications

DOS identifies a file on a disk through a file specification. A **file specification** informs DOS where the file is located and gives its exact name. A DOS file specification can have up to four components: a drive, a path, a filename, and an extension. You cannot have any spaces in a file specification. Table 1-4 describes the contents of each of the four components in a DOS file specification.

TABLE 1-4

Name	*Description*
Drive	A drive consists of the one-letter drive name followed by a colon. The drive name specifies the drive containing the file you are requesting. For example, A: represents disk drive A. If you omit the drive, DOS assumes the default, or current, drive.
Path	A path is an optional reference to a subdirectory of files on the specified disk. A backslash (\) separates the drive from the path. (Paths are discussed in Project 2.)
Filename	A filename consists of one to eight characters.
Extension	An extension, if present, consists of one to three characters. A period separates a filename from an extension.

If you have a filename SMITH with an extension of DOC on the disk in drive A, the complete file specification would be A:SMITH.DOC. To see if this file exists on a disk, you would use the dir command as shown in the following steps. Remember, you do not put any spaces in the file specification.

TO USE A FILE SPECIFICATION IN THE DIR COMMAND

STEP 1: Type `dir a:smith.doc` **and press the ENTER key.**

The directory entry for the file SMITH.DOC displays on the screen (Figure 1-19).

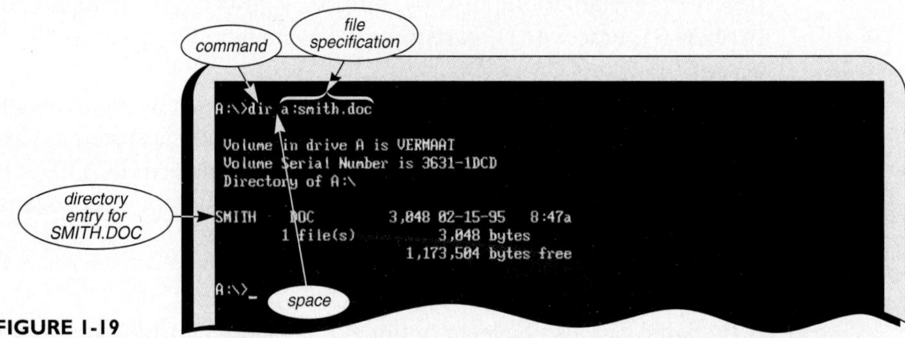

FIGURE 1-19

Internal Versus External Commands

When you boot a computer, several commands are placed into memory with DOS. These commands, called **internal commands**, may be entered at the DOS prompt at any time. Examples of internal commands used in this project are ver, cls, dir, copy, del, and rename.

An **external command** is one stored on the DOS disk as a program file. External commands must be read from the DOS disk into memory before they can be executed. For a hard disk or LAN configuration, the default drive contains these external commands, so no special steps are needed to use an external command. The format command is an example of an external command.

All DOS external commands have the special extensions COM, EXE, or BAT. To use external commands, simply type the filename (the extension is not required) with its required parameters and press the ENTER key.

▼ COPYING A FILE

Once you have formatted a disk, you can use it to store data or program files. When you store files on a disk, you may want to make duplicates of them. Using the **copy command**, you can copy a file to the same disk or to a different disk. It is *always* a good idea to copy the original files supplied with software you purchase to another disk, called a **working disk**, or **working copy**. Then, use the working copy for everyday work to protect the original disk from possible damage. A similar use of the copy command is to make a **backup copy** of a disk to guard against accidental loss of data. One frequently used technique is to make a backup copy of a file whenever you revise an existing file. For example, you might want to keep a disk backup copy of your personal financial statement in your safe-deposit box. Some application programs create a backup file automatically, using the extension BAK to indicate a backup file.

Copying a File from One Disk to Another Using the Same Name

Copying a file can be accomplished from any drive and to any drive. Follow these steps to copy the file DOSNOTES.DOC from drive A to drive C.

TO COPY A FILE FROM ONE DISK TO ANOTHER USING THE SAME NAME

STEP 1: **Type** `copy dosnotes.doc c:` **and press the ENTER key. (If DOS asks Overwrite C:DOSNOTES.DOC (Yes/No/All)?, type the letter** `y` **and press the ENTER key.)**

DOS displays the message, ***1 file(s) copied****, indicating it made a duplicate of DOSNOTES.DOC on drive C (Figure 1-20 on the next page). Notice that after typing the command* `copy`*, you leave a space, then state the file specification of the file to be copied. In DOS terminology, this file is called the* ***source file****. Because you omitted the drive name from the source file, DOS looks on drive A, the default drive, for a source file with a filename of DOSNOTES and an extension of DOC. Following the source file, you leave a space and then type the* ***target file****, which is the file specification of the file once it is copied. The drive specifier c: in the target specification indicates that the file is to be copied to the hard drive. Because you omitted the filename and extension from the target specification, the target file will have the same filename and extension as the source file.*

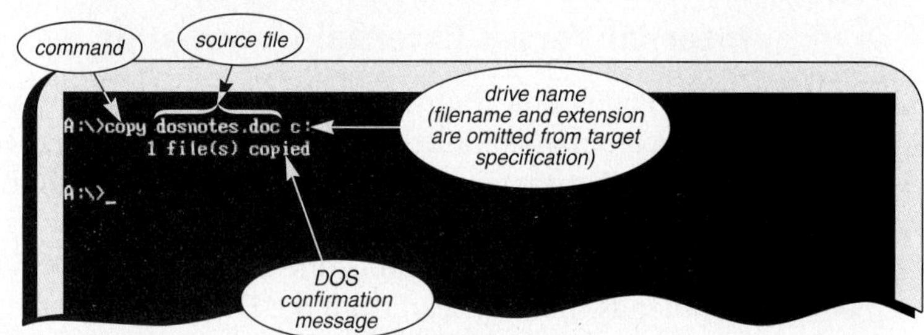

FIGURE 1-20

DOSNOTES.DOC is now on the disk in drive A and on drive C. To verify that DOSNOTES.DOC is on drive C, follow these steps.

TO VERIFY A FILE IS ON A DISK

STEP 1: Type `dir c:dosnotes.doc` **and press the ENTER key.**

The directory entry for the file DOSNOTES.DOC displays on the screen (Figure 1-21).

```
A:\>copy dosnotes.doc c:
        1 file(s) copied

A:\>dir c:dosnotes.doc

 Volume in drive C has no label
 Volume Serial Number is 1E79-4A83
 Directory of C:\

DOSNOTES DOC        3,594 02-22-95   2:04p
        1 file(s)          3,594 bytes
                      71,196,672 bytes free

A:\>_
```

file specification

displayed file is on drive C

your bytes free will differ depending on your hard disk

directory entry of DOSNOTES.DOC

FIGURE 1-21

Copying a File from One Disk to Another Using a Different Name

When you copy a file from one disk to another, you can assign the target file a different name than the source file. For example, you might want to make a backup copy of the file DOSNOTES.DOC and then make draft changes to the original file. Follow these steps to copy the file DOSNOTES.DOC from drive C to drive A with the name DOSNOTES.BAK.

TO COPY A FILE FROM ONE DISK TO ANOTHER USING A DIFFERENT NAME AND VERIFY THE RESULTS

STEP 1: Type `copy c:dosnotes.doc a:dosnotes.bak` **and press the ENTER key.**

DOS copies the file DOSNOTES.DOC from drive C to drive A, giving it the name DOSNOTES.BAK on drive A. Notice the target filename and extension must be supplied when you want the target file to have a different name than the source.

STEP 2: Type `dir dosnotes.bak` **and press the ENTER key.**

The directory entry for the file DOSNOTES.BAK displays on the screen (Figure 1-22). Because you omitted the drive name from the file specification, DOS scans drive A, the default drive, for DOSNOTES.BAK.

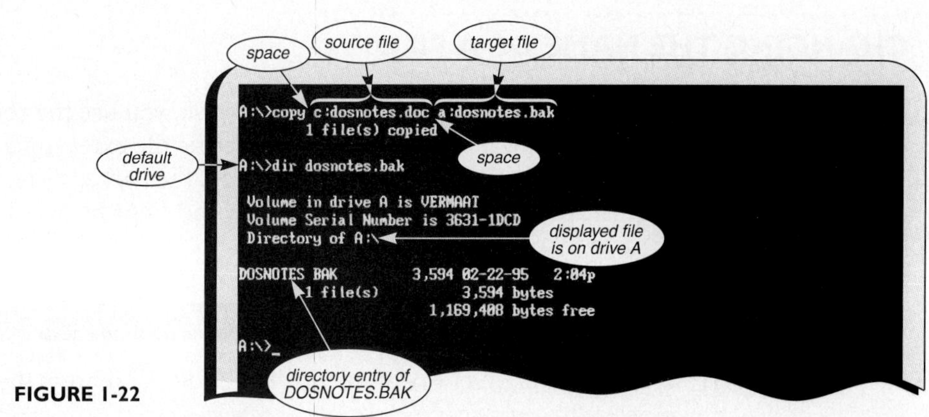

FIGURE 1-22

You have now verified that DOSNOTES.BAK is on drive A. It is an exact copy of DOSNOTES.DOC.

Copying a File to the Same Disk

In order to make a backup copy of a file on the same disk as the original file, the backup copy *must* have a different name than the source file. That is, you could not have a source file DOSNOTES.DOC and a target file DOSNOTES.DOC both on drive A. You could, however, have a source file DOSNOTES.DOC and a target file DOSFILE.TXT as illustrated in the following steps.

TO COPY A FILE TO THE SAME DISK AND VERIFY THE RESULTS

STEP 1: Type `copy dosnotes.doc dosfile.txt` **and press the ENTER key.**

DOS makes a duplicate of the file DOSNOTES.DOC on drive A, with the name DOSFILE.TXT. Recall that when you omit a drive from the file specification, DOS assumes the default drive. Thus, DOSFILE.TXT is being copied to drive A, the same drive as DOSNOTES.DOC.

STEP 2: Type `dir dosfile.txt` **and press the ENTER key.**

DOS displays the target file's directory entry (Figure 1-23).

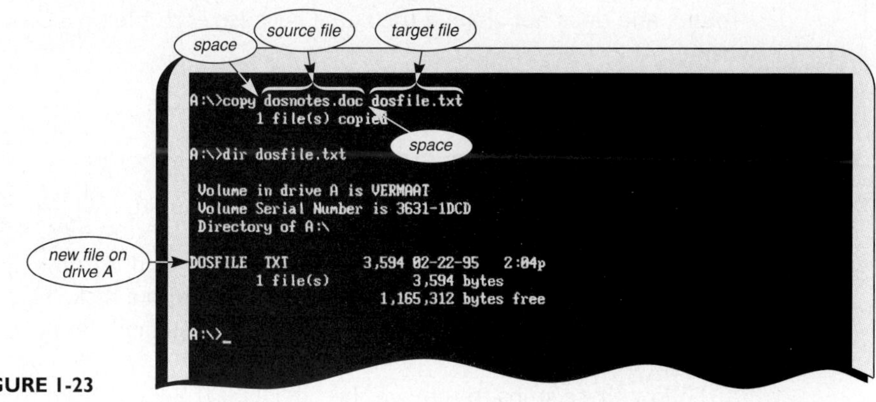

FIGURE 1-23

The file DOSNOTES.DOC now exists twice on the disk in drive A, once with the filename DOSNOTES.DOC and again under the name DOSFILE.TXT.

CHANGING THE NAME OF A FILE

When you want to change the name of a file on a disk, you use the **rename command**. For example, some software packages require specific file extensions, and you might need to change one of your file's extensions to meet the package's requirements before you can use it with that software package. Follow the steps below to change the name DOSFILE.TXT to DOSFILE.DOC on drive A.

TO RENAME A FILE AND VERIFY THE RESULTS

STEP 1: Type `rename dosfile.txt dosfile.doc` **and press the ENTER key.**

DOS renames the file DOSFILE.TXT as DOSFILE.DOC. Notice DOS does not display a message confirming a successful renaming of the file. When using the rename command, you may abbreviate it with the characters ren.

STEP 2: Type `dir dosfile.doc` **and press the ENTER key.**

DOS displays the renamed file's directory entry (Figure 1-24).

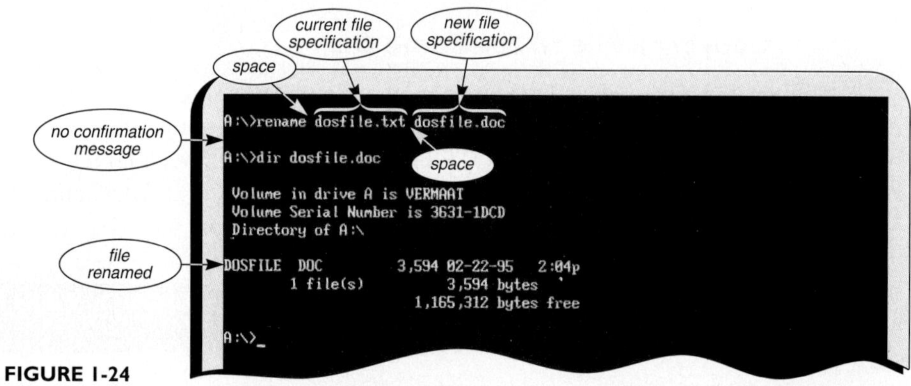

FIGURE 1-24

You must be careful not to place a drive name on the file specification for the file's new name. Thus, you cannot rename a file and place the renamed file on a different drive. If you put a drive name on the new name, DOS displays the error message, `Invalid parameter`. If you attempt to change a file's name to a name already used by a file on the disk, DOS displays the error message, Duplicate file name or file not found, and does not change the name because each file on a disk must have a unique name.

REMOVING A FILE FROM A DISK

Because a disk has a limited amount of space for storing files, you should periodically remove unneeded files from your disks to make room for new files. You use the **del command** or **erase command** to remove a file from a disk. Take care when using these commands because you do not want to mistakenly remove a file you mean to keep.

Follow these steps to remove the file DOSFILE.DOC from the disk in drive A.

TO DELETE A FILE AND VERIFY THE RESULTS

STEP 1: Type `dir` **and press the ENTER key.**

DOS displays the list of files on the default drive (Figure 1-25).

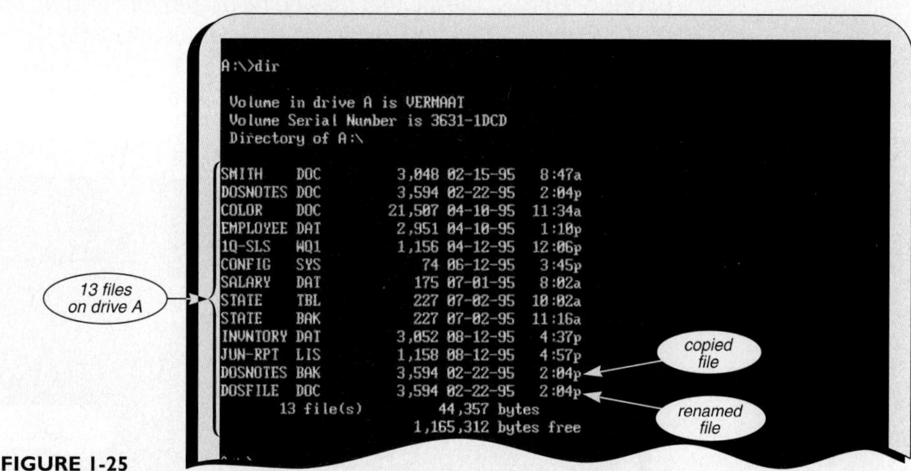

FIGURE 1-25

STEP 2: Type `del dosfile.doc` **and press the ENTER key.**

DOS deletes the file DOSFILE.DOC from the disk in drive A. Notice DOS does not display a message confirming a successful deletion of the file.

STEP 3: Type `dir` **and press the ENTER key.**

DOS displays the list of files on the default drive (Figure 1-26). Notice DOSFILE.DOC has been removed from the directory.

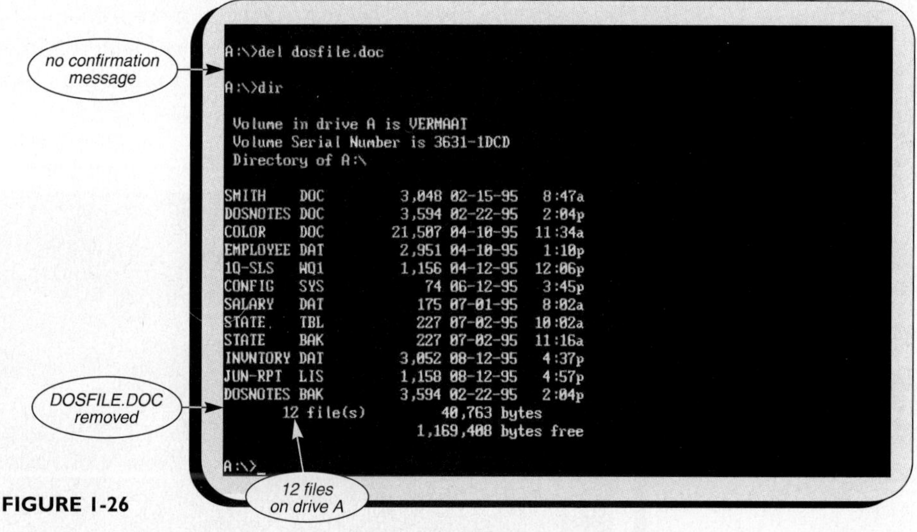

FIGURE 1-26

The file DOSFILE.DOC has been deleted. When you use the del command, DOS does not actually erase the file from the disk. Rather, it *flags* the file as deleted, which allows DOS to reuse the area of the disk occupied by the deleted file. Thus, you can recover, or *bring back*, a deleted file as long as DOS has not reused its space. To successfully recover a deleted file, you should use the **undelete command** as soon as you discover the file has been accidentally deleted. Follow the steps on the next page to recover the file DOSFILE.DOC from the disk in drive A.

TO RECOVER A DELETED FILE AND VERIFY THE RESULTS

STEP 1: Type `undelete` **and press the ENTER key.**

DOS scans the default disk drive for files that may be recovered and displays the directory entry of the file that may be recovered followed by the prompt, Undelete (Y/N)? (Figure 1-27). Notice the first letter of the filename has been replaced with a question mark (?). (Depending on the type of DOS you have, your screen may display slightly different messages for the undelete command.)

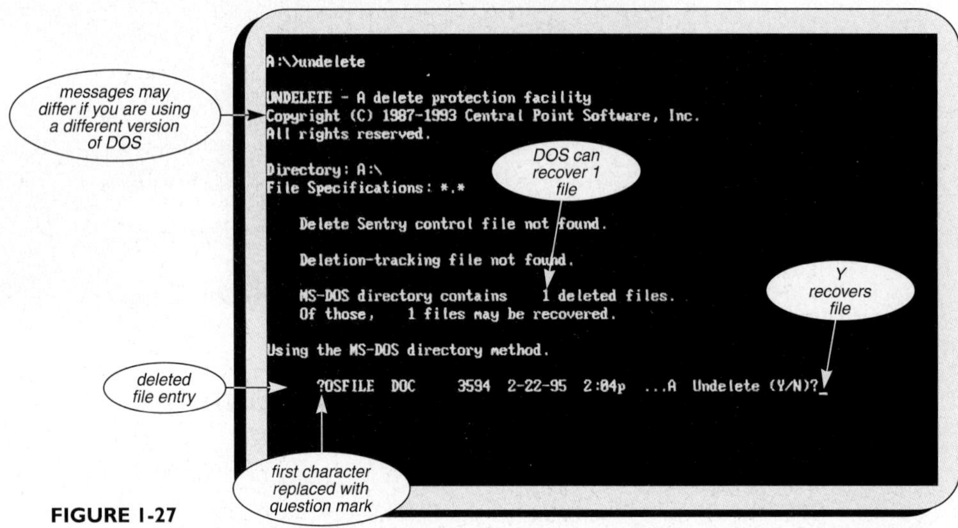

FIGURE 1-27

STEP 2: Type the letter `y`.

DOS requests you to type the first character of the filename (Figure 1-28). Because the first character of the filename is replaced with a question mark when you use the delete command to erase a file, you need to supply a character for DOS to fill in as the first character of the filename.

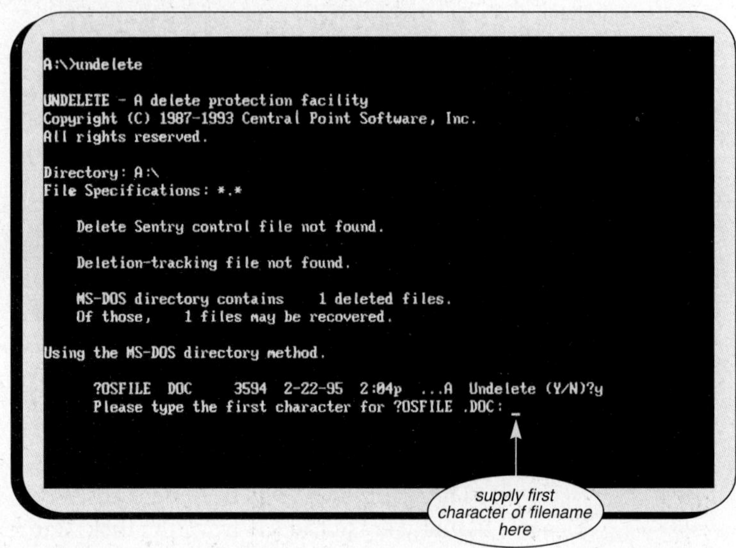

FIGURE 1-28

STEP 3: Type the letter `d`.

DOS recovers the file DOSFILE.DOC and displays the message, File successfully undeleted.

STEP 4: Type `dir` **and press the ENTER key.**

DOS displays the list of files on the default drive (Figure 1-29). Notice DOSFILE.DOC has been recovered.

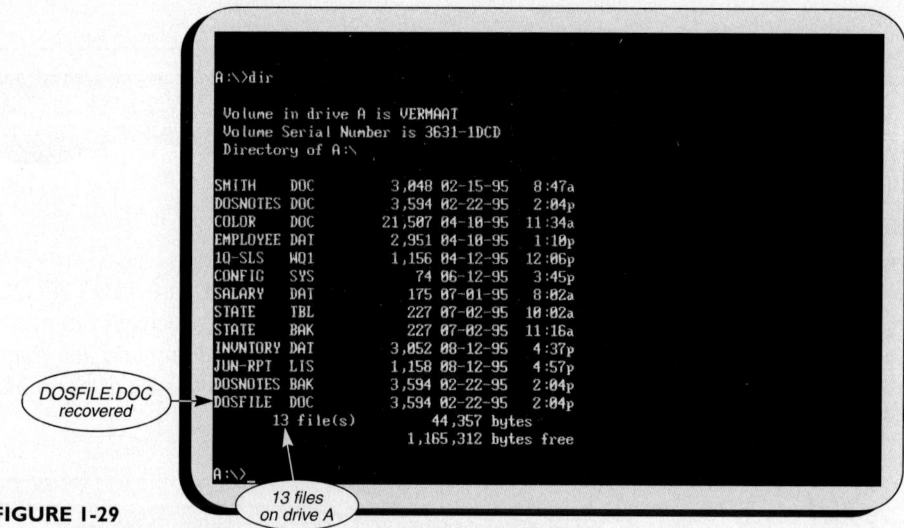

FIGURE 1-29

▼ OBTAINING HELP FOR DOS COMMANDS

Often, you are unsure of the purpose of a DOS command or how to correctly enter it. To assist you, DOS provides **online help** for all DOS commands. You can obtain help on a specific command from the DOS prompt. Follow these steps to obtain online help for the rename command.

TO OBTAIN HELP FOR THE RENAME COMMAND

STEP 1: Type `ren` **and press the SPACEBAR once. Type** `/?` **and press the ENTER key.**

DOS displays online help for the rename command (Figure 1-30).

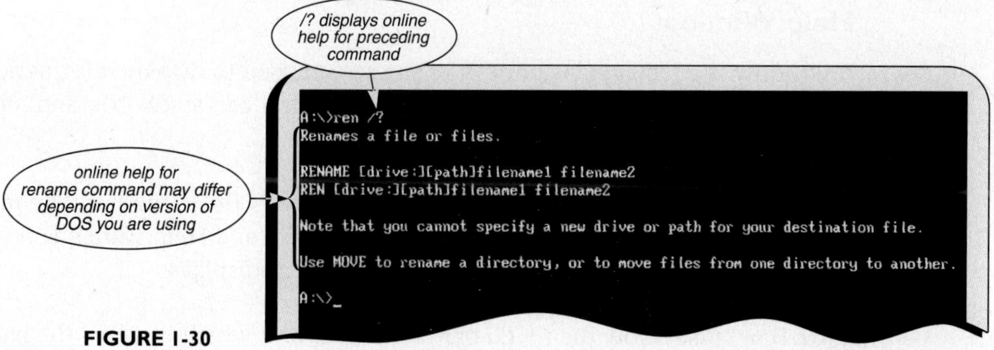

FIGURE 1-30

If you are unsure of which DOS command to use, you need to see a list of available commands by invoking the **Help window**, which displays all valid DOS commands.

TO INVOKE THE HELP WINDOW

STEP 1: Type `help` **(Figure 1-31).**

FIGURE 1-31

STEP 2: Press the ENTER key.

The Help window displays on the screen (Figure 1-32). All DOS commands display in the Help window. To obtain help on a particular command, use the arrow keys and/or TAB key to move the cursor to the command and then press the ENTER key. (Earlier versions of DOS have a different help system or no help at all.)

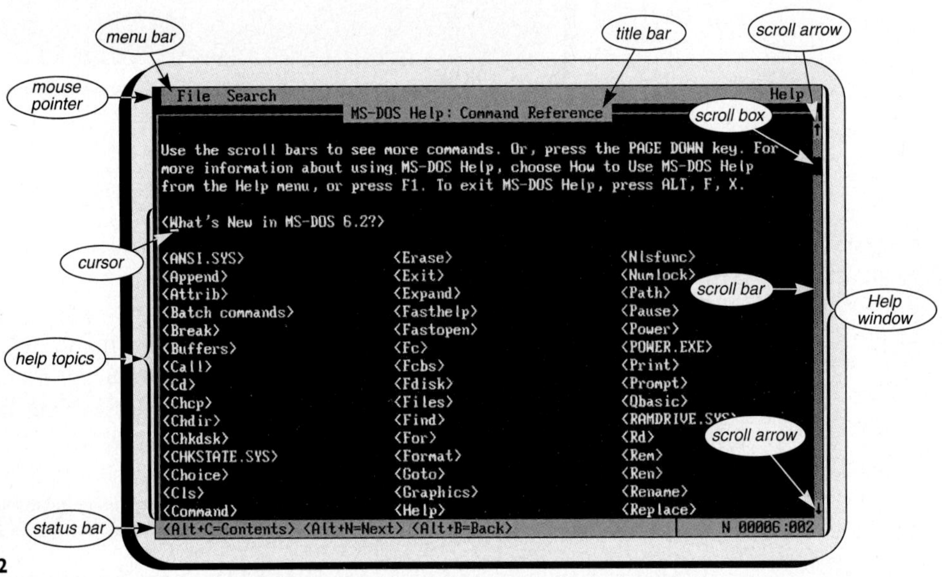

FIGURE 1-32

Help Window

A **window** is a rectangular portion of the screen used to display information. The Help window consists of a menu bar, title bar, scroll bar, status bar, and mouse pointer.

Menu Bar The first line at the top of the window is the menu bar. The **menu bar** lists the names of the available menus: File, Search, and Help. When you select a menu name from the menu bar, a list of commands displays.

Title Bar Just below the menu bar is the **title bar**, which displays the name of the current window. Initially, the title bar displays MS-DOS Help: Command Reference. (Your title bar may differ depending on the type of DOS you are using.)

Scroll Bar Located along the right edge of the Help window, you use the **scroll bar** with a mouse to bring a portion of a document into view when the complete help discussion will not fit in the window. **Scroll arrows**, represented by upward and downward pointing arrows, are located at the top and bottom of the scroll bar. The **scroll box** is a solid, nonblinking box on the scroll bar, which moves as you move the cursor.

Status Bar The line at the very bottom of the window is the **status bar**, which displays the special key combinations you use to move around the Help window and other informative messages.

Mouse Pointer The **mouse pointer** is a character-sized, nonblinking rectangle that appears *only* if you have a mouse installed on your system.

Moving Around the Help Window

When you first start online help, the cursor is blinking below the first jump. A **jump** is a topic surrounded by angle brackets (< >). To display help information on a topic, you choose a jump. You can choose a jump with either the keyboard or the mouse.

Using the Keyboard One method of moving the cursor from topic to topic is to use the following keys: TAB, HOME, END, PAGE UP, PAGE DOWN, and the four directional arrow keys. Table 1-5 illustrates how each of these keys moves the cursor in the Help window.

TABLE 1-5

Key	*Action*
TAB	Moves the cursor right to the next jump
SHIFT+TAB	Moves the cursor left to the previous jump
DOWN ARROW	Moves the cursor down one jump
UP ARROW	Moves the cursor up one jump
letter	Moves the cursor to the next jump beginning with the entered letter
SHIFT+letter	Moves the cursor to the previous jump beginning with the entered letter
PAGE DOWN	Moves the cursor down one screen
PAGE UP	Moves the cursor up one screen
HOME	Moves the cursor to the beginning of a line
END	Moves the cursor to the end of a line

Practice moving the cursor with the keyboard. Press the TAB key twice to move the cursor to the Erase topic. Next, type the letter u to move the cursor to the Undelete topic. Press the HOME key to move the cursor to the Dosshell topic, the first topic in the same line. Then, type the letter a to return the cursor to the DBLSPACE.SYS topic. Now, press the PAGE DOWN key to move the cursor down one screenful to the topic, and then press the PAGE UP key to return the cursor to the ANSI.SYS topic.

To display help on a topic, you first move the cursor to the topic and then press the ENTER key as shown in the steps on the next page.

TO DISPLAY HELP ON A TOPIC WITH THE KEYBOARD

STEP 1: Press the TAB key twice.

DOS positions the cursor in the Erase topic (Figure 1-33).

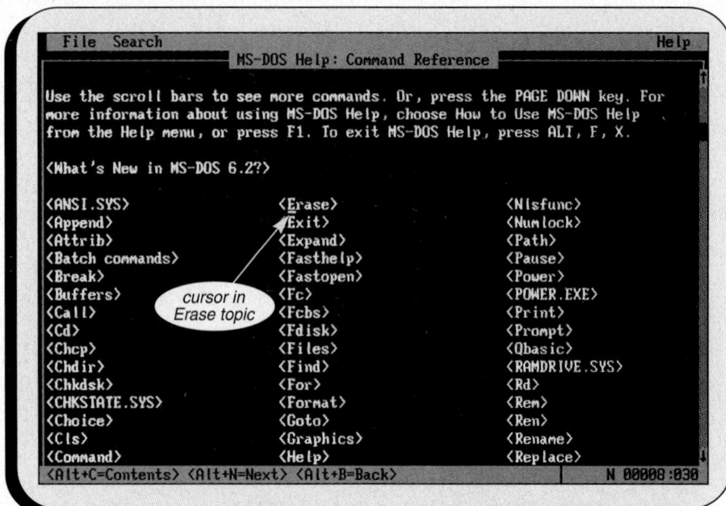

FIGURE 1-33

STEP 2: Press the ENTER key.

DOS displays help on the Erase command (Figure 1-34).

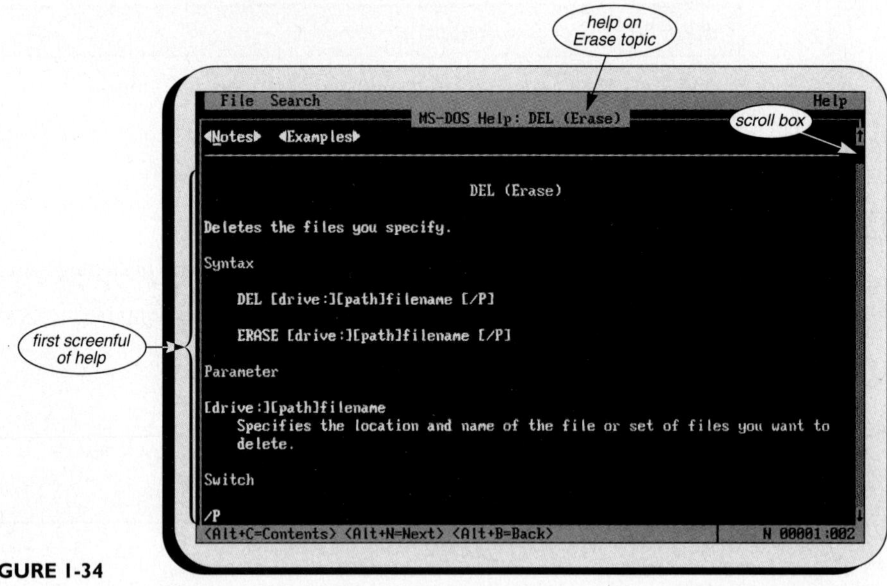

FIGURE 1-34

STEP 3: Press the PAGE DOWN key.

DOS displays the second screen of help on the Erase command (Figure 1-35).

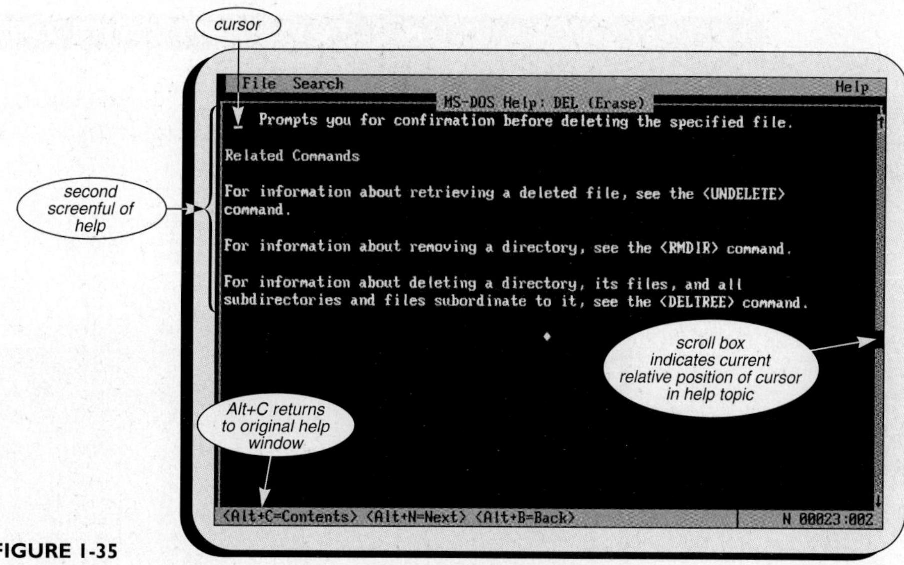

FIGURE 1-35

STEP 4: Press ALT+C; that is, while holding down the ALT key, press the letter C.

DOS returns you to the Command Reference Help window (see Figure 1-33 on the previous page).

Using a Mouse If you do not have a mouse installed on your computer, you can move the cursor only by using the keyboard. When you have a mouse connected to your computer and the mouse driver software is loaded, you can use either the keyboard or the mouse to position the cursor on a help topic.

The mouse pointer is usually displayed on the screen as a highlighted rectangle. As you move the mouse on a flat surface, the mouse pointer moves on the screen. You can perform four basic operations with a mouse: point, click, double-click, and drag. Table 1-6 discusses each of these operations.

TABLE 1-6

Mouse Term	*Action*
Point	Move the mouse until the mouse pointer is in the desired location
Click	Press the left mouse button once and release it
Double-click	Press and release the left mouse button twice in rapid succession
Drag	Hold down the left mouse button; move the mouse pointer to the desired location; release the left mouse button

As described in Table 1-6, *point and click* means move the mouse pointer to a specified location and press the left mouse button.

TO DISPLAY HELP ON A TOPIC WITH THE MOUSE

STEP 1: Point to the Erase topic.

The mouse pointer is positioned in the Erase topic (Figure 1-36).

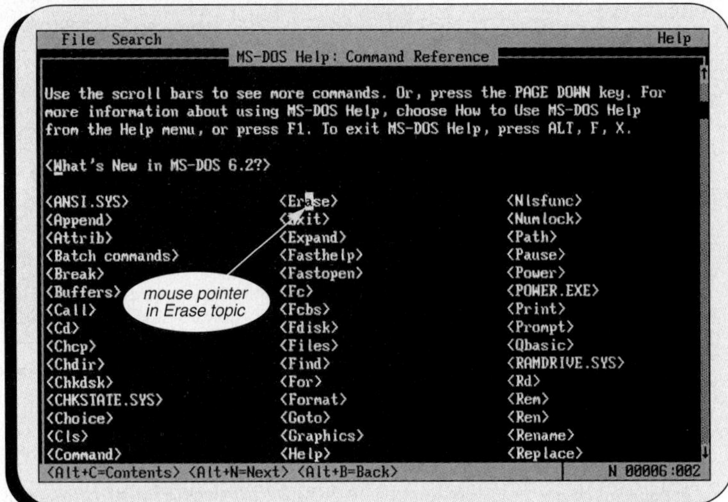

FIGURE 1-36

STEP 2: Click the left mouse button; that is, press the left mouse button once and release it.

DOS displays help on the Erase command.

STEP 3: Point to the scroll bar beneath the scroll box (Figure 1-37).

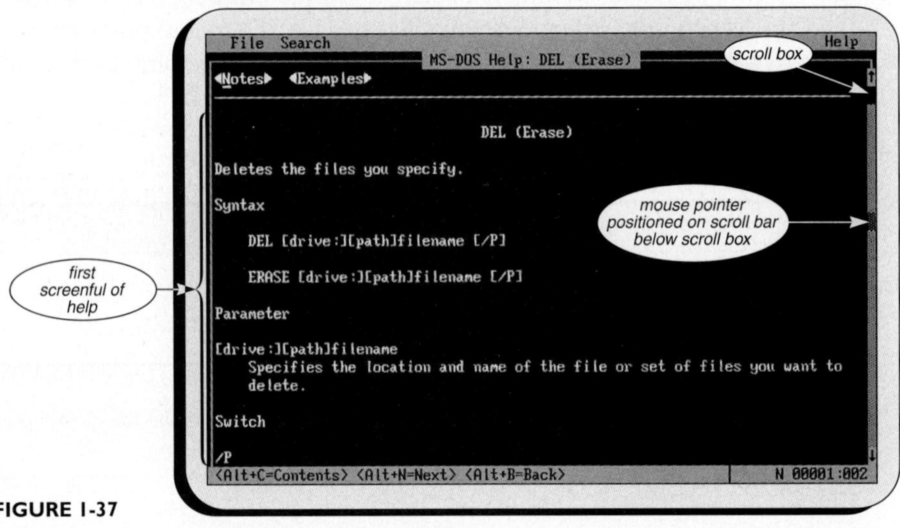

FIGURE 1-37

STEP 4: Click the left mouse button.

DOS displays the second screenful of help on the Erase command (Figure 1-38). The scroll box moves downward on the scroll bar to indicate the current relative location of the cursor in the help topic.

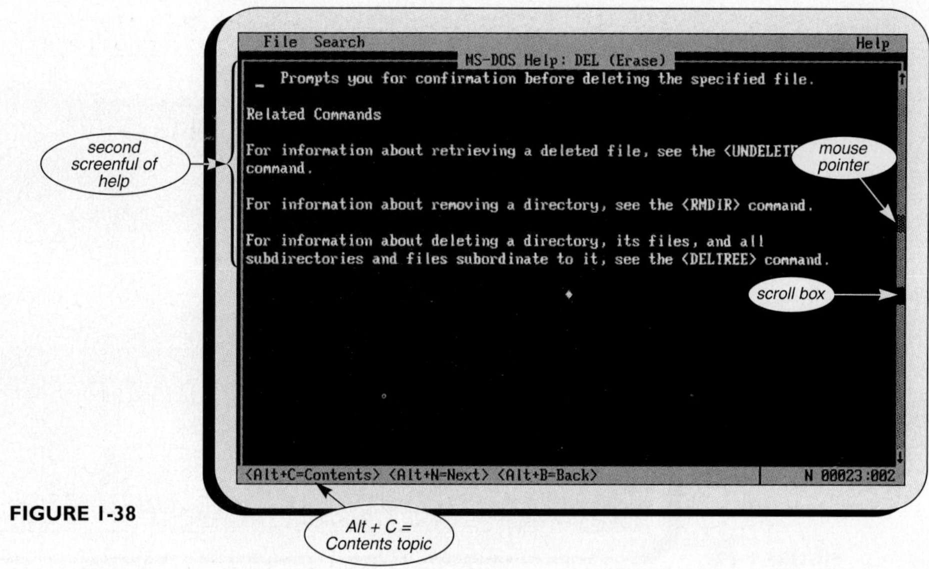

FIGURE 1-38

STEP 5: **Click the** `Alt+C=Contents` **topic on the status bar; that is, point to the Alt+C and click the left mouse button.**

DOS returns you to the Command Reference Help window (see Figure 1-36 on the previous page).

The word click is often used when referring to the point and click operation. That is, point to the Erase topic and click is often stated simply as click the Erase topic.

The scroll bar is used with the mouse to scroll through a series of screens. You can drag the scroll box upward or downward to scroll up or down through the screens. To move up or down one screenful at a time, you can click anywhere above or below the scroll box on the scroll bar. To move the screen up or down one line at a time in the window, you can click the scroll arrow at the top or bottom of the scroll bar.

TO PRINT INFORMATION ON A HELP TOPIC

STEP 1: **Press the TAB key twice and then press the ENTER key.**

DOS displays help on the Erase command.

STEP 2: **Press the ALT key.**

The word File is highlighted on the menu bar, which indicates the menu bar is activated (Figure 1-39 on the next page). The menu bar has three menu names: File, Search, and Help. To ***pull-down*** *the commands in these menus, you type the highlighted letter in the menu name. That is, to pull-down the File menu, you type the letter f.*

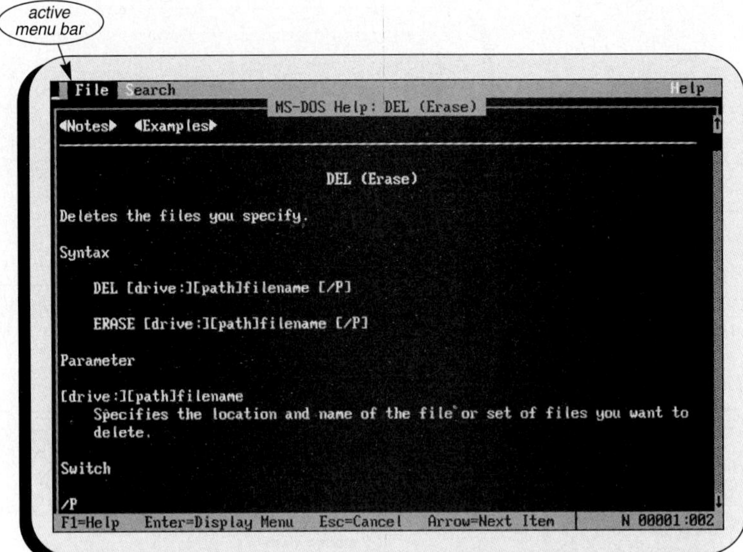

FIGURE 1-39

STEP 3: Type the letter f.

The commands in the File menu display (Figure 1-40). Two commands are available in the File menu: Print and Exit. To execute a command, you type the highlighted letter in the command. That is, to print information displayed in the Help window, you type the letter p; to exit from the Help window, you type the letter x.

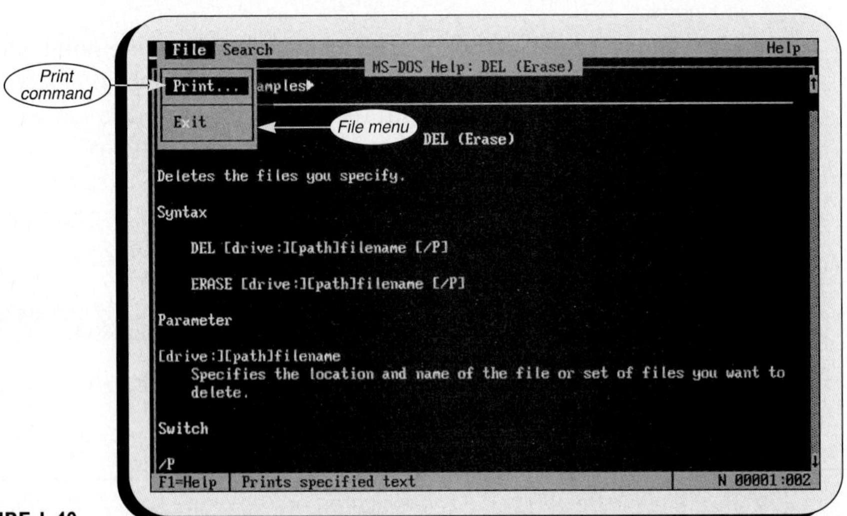

FIGURE 1-40

STEP 4: Type the letter p.

DOS displays the Print dialog box (Figure 1-41). A ***dialog box*** *is a window requesting additional information from you. DOS asks if you want to send the help information to the printer or to a file. In the Print dialog box, the dot in parentheses (•) to the left of Printer on LPT1 is called a* ***bullet****. The bullet indicates the printer is selected. Thus, you press the ENTER key to send the help information to the printer.*

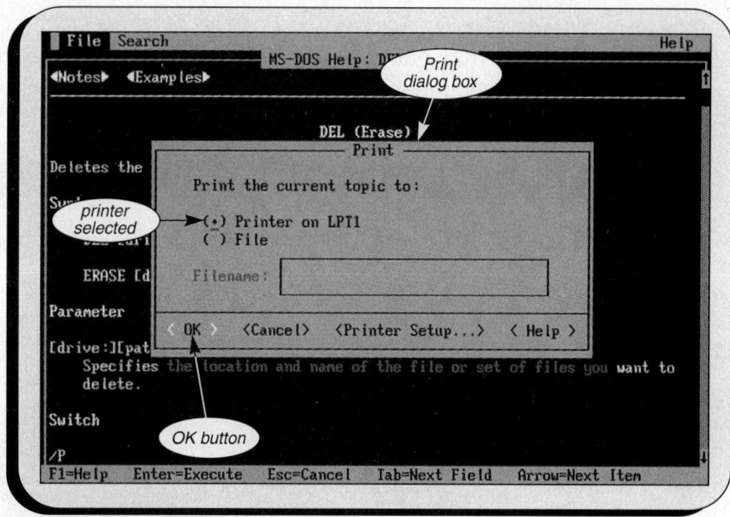

FIGURE 1-41

STEP 5: Press the ENTER key. Remove the printout from the printer.

DOS prints the help information for the Erase command (Figure 1-42).

```
Notes►  Examples►
------------------------------------------------------------------
                          DEL (Erase)

Deletes the files you specify.

Syntax

    DEL [drive:][path]filename [/P]

    ERASE [drive:][path]filename [/P]

Parameter

[drive:][path]filename
    Specifies the location and name of the file or set of files you want to
    delete.

Switch

/P
    Prompts you for confirmation before deleting the specified file.

Related Commands

For information about retrieving a deleted file, see the <UNDELETE>
command.

For information about removing a directory, see the <RMDIR> command.

For information about deleting a directory, its files, and all
subdirectories and files subordinate to it, see the <DELTREE> command.
```

FIGURE 1-42

STEP 6: Press ALT+C.

DOS returns you to the Command Reference Help window (see Figure 1-36 on page DOS28).

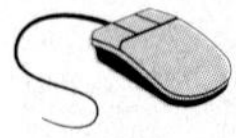

Mouse Users: *Choose the Erase topic by clicking it. Click the File menu and choose the Print command by clicking it. Click the OK button in the Print dialog box. Click Alt+C=Contents on the status bar to return to the Command Reference Help window.*

TO EXIT THE HELP WINDOW

STEP 1: Press the ALT key to activate the menu bar. Type the letter `f`**.**

DOS pulls down the File menu (Figure 1-43).

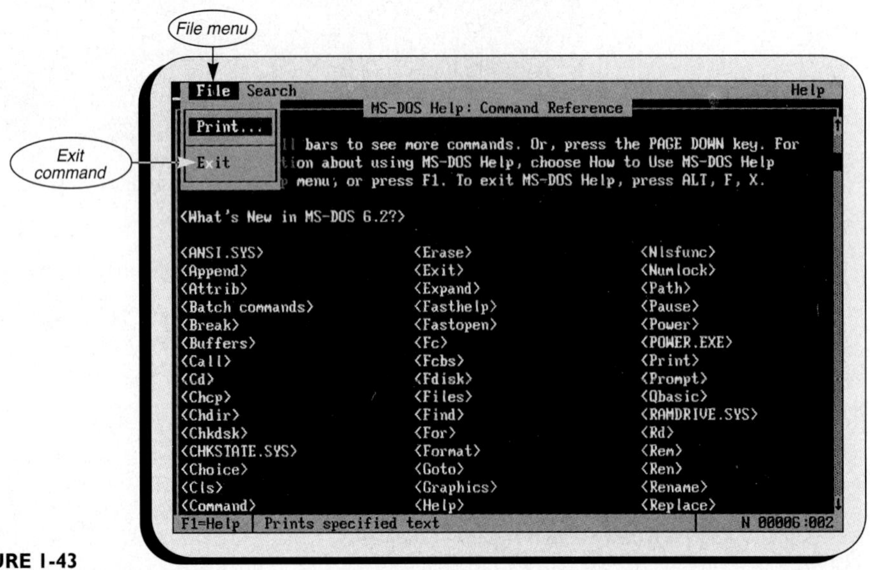

FIGURE 1-43

STEP 2: Type the letter `x`**.**

The Help window disappears from the screen and the DOS prompt displays.

Mouse Users: *Click the File menu and choose the Exit command by clicking it.*

▼ PROJECT SUMMARY

Project 1 illustrates how to boot DOS, format diskettes, name and display files, and access online help for DOS commands. In Project 1, you learned how to use these DOS commands to work with your files: ver, cls, copy, rename, delete, and undelete. All the activities you learned in this project are summarized in the Quick Reference.

KEY TERMS

BACKSPACE *(DOS9)*
backup copy *(DOS17)*
booting *(DOS6)*
bullet *(DOS30)*
cls command *(DOS8)*
cold boot *(DOS6)*
cold start *(DOS6)*
commands *(DOS7)*
copy command *(DOS17)*
current drive *(DOS7)*
cylinders *(DOS10)*
data file *(DOS15)*
default drive *(DOS7)*
del command *(DOS20)*
dialog box *(DOS30)*
dir command *(DOS14)*
directory *(DOS14)*
Disk Operating System *(DOS3)*
DOS *(DOS3)*
DOS prompt *(DOS6)*
drive name *(DOS4)*
erase command *(DOS20)*
ESC key *(DOS9)*
extension *(DOS15)*
external command *(DOS17)*
F3 *(DOS9)*
file specification *(DOS16)*
filename *(DOS15)*
format command *(DOS11)*
formatting *(DOS10)*
help *(DOS23)*
Help window *(DOS23)*
installed *(DOS6)*
internal command *(DOS17)*
jump *(DOS25)*
LAN *(DOS5)*
local area network *(DOS5)*
menu bar *(DOS24)*
mouse pointer *(DOS25)*
MS-DOS *(DOS3)*
online help *(DOS23)*
operating system *(DOS2)*
parameter *(DOS13)*
PC-DOS *(DOS3)*
program file *(DOS15)*
prompt *(DOS12)*
pull-down menu *(DOS29)*
release number *(DOS3)*
rename command *(DOS20)*
reset *(DOS6)*
scroll arrows *(DOS25)*
scroll bar *(DOS25)*
scroll box *(DOS25)*
sector *(DOS10)*
server *(DOS5)*
source file *(DOS17)*
stand-alone mode *(DOS6)*
status bar *(DOS25)*
target file *(DOS17)*
title bar *(DOS24)*
undelete command *(DOS21)*
upward compatibility *(DOS4)*
ver command *(DOS8)*
version number *(DOS3)*
volume label *(DOS12)*
warm boot *(DOS6)*
warm start *(DOS6)*
window *(DOS24)*
working copy *(DOS17)*
working disk *(DOS17)*

QUICK REFERENCE

The following table provides a quick reference to each task presented in the project.

Task	Command Syntax	Description
Change Default	drive name:	Changes the default or current drive
Clear Screen	cls	Clears the screen
Copy File	copy source target	Duplicates the source file specification to the target file specification
Directory	dir file-specification	Displays filenames on a disk
Erase File	del file-specification	Removes a file from a disk
Format Disk	format drive-name:	Prepares a new disk for use
Help	help	Invokes help window
Recover Deleted	undelete drive-name:	Attempts to bring back a deleted file
Rename File	ren currentname	Changes the name of the file
Version	ver	Displays DOS version loaded in memory

SHORT ANSWER ASSIGNMENTS

SHORT ANSWER ASSIGNMENT I

True/False

Instructions: Circle T if the statement is true or F if the statement is false.

T F 1. DOS is an example of application software.

T F 2. Microsoft developed DOS for use on IBM PCs.

T F 3. The DOS version number identifies minor changes or corrections to a release.

T F 4. The server hard disk on a LAN is usually drive C.

T F 5. During a cold start, the computer first runs tests to diagnose its own circuitry.

T F 6. To begin a warm boot, hold down the CTRL and ALT keys, press the ENTER key, and then release all three keys.

T F 7. The dir command displays the contents of the files on a disk.

T F 8. The format command is an example of a DOS prompt.

T F 9. To change the default disk drive assignment to drive B, type `b:` and press the ENTER key.

T F 10. You must enter all DOS commands in uppercase characters.

T F 11. To access online help for DOS commands, type `doshelp` and press the ENTER key.

T F 12. A:\> is an example of an extension.

T F 13. A DOS file specification can contain a filename of one to eight characters and an extension of one to three characters.

T F 14. A colon (:) separates a filename from an extension.

T F 15. The format command is an external command.

T F 16. You can format more than one diskette with one format command.

T F 17. To make a duplicate of a file, use the copy command.

T F 18. You can use the delete command to remove a file from a disk.

T F 19. To bring back a deleted file, use the recover command.

T F 20. To exit from online help, type `Exit`.

SHORT ANSWER ASSIGNMENT 2

Multiple Choice

Instructions: Circle the correct response.

1. DOS was developed by ________.
   a. Disk Operating Systems
   b. IBM
   c. LAN
   d. Microsoft
2. The 3 in DOS 3.2 refers to the ________.
   a. default
   b. release number
   c. version number
   d. prompt
3. The symbols C:\> ________.
   a. are collectively called the DOS prompt
   b. indicate the name of a program
   c. indicate the default disk drive
   d. both a and c
4. A file specification consists of all of the following except the ________.
   a. extension
   b. drive
   c. prompt
   d. filename
5. The ________ command divides a diskette into cylinders and sectors to prepare it to store data.
   a. delete
   b. rename
   c. copy
   d. format
6. To change the name of a file, use the ________ command.
   a. alter
   b. change
   c. rename
   d. assign
7. To remove a file from a disk, use the ________ command
   a. remove
   b. delete
   c. zap
   d. none of these
8. Listing the files on a disk is accomplished by typing ________ at the DOS prompt and pressing the ENTER key.
   a. list
   b. dir
   c. display
   d. files
9. To activate the menu bar in DOS online help, press the ________ key.
   a. F1
   b. ENTER
   c. CTRL
   d. ALT
10. To print a help topic in DOS online help, choose the ________ command from the ________ menu.
    a. Print, Print
    b. Print, Help
    c. Print, File
    d. File, Print

SHORT ANSWER ASSIGNMENT 3

Fill in the Blanks

1. ________ is a collection of programs that controls and manages the operation of the computer.
2. Microsoft Corporation developed the operating system known as ________.
3. ________ is a unique one-letter name preassigned to a disk drive.
4. The ________ on a LAN has a high-capacity hard disk containing files you can access from your computer.
5. To change the default drive, you type the letter of the new drive to be used, followed by a(n) ________.
6. In a file specification, C: is an example of a(n) ________.

7. In a file specification, the ________ is optional and consists of one to three characters.
8. The ________ command established cylinders and sectors on a disk in preparation for storing data.
9. Use the ________ command to change the name of a file on a disk.
10. Use the ________ command to recover a deleted file.
11. In DOS online help, the ALT key activates the ________ bar.

SHORT ANSWER ASSIGNMENT 4

Using DOS Commands

Instructions: Explain how to accomplish each of the following tasks using DOS.

Problem 1: Prepare a diskette using the format command and determine the amount of free space remaining on the disk.

Explanation: ____

____

____

Problem 2: List the files stored on the disk in drive A and determine the name of the most recently created or modified file.

Explanation: ____

____

____

Problem 3: Create a backup copy on drive A of the file DOSNOTES.DOC, using an extension of BAC and the same filename.

Explanation: ____

____

____

Problem 4: Change the name of the file DOSNOTES.BAC on drive A to THATFILE.DOC.

Explanation: ____

____

____

Problem 5: Remove the file THATFILE.DOC from the disk in drive A.

Explanation: ____

____

____

Problem 6: Recover the file THATFILE.DOC deleted from the disk in drive A.

Explanation: ____

____

____

SHORT ANSWER ASSIGNMENT 5

Understanding DOS Options

Instructions: Explain what happens after you perform each of the following DOS commands.

Problem 1: Type `format a:` at the C:\> prompt and press the ENTER key.

Explanation: ______________________________

____

____

Problem 2: Type `dir b:` at the A:\> prompt and press the ENTER key.

Explanation: ______________________________

____

____

Problem 3: Type `rename oldfile.abc newfile.abc` at the A:\> prompt and press the ENTER key.

Explanation: ______________________________

____

____

Problem 4: Press the ALT key in the Help window.

Explanation: ______________________________

____

____

Problem 5: Point and click a help topic in the Help window.

Explanation: ______________________________

____

____

SHORT ANSWER ASSIGNMENT 6

Recovering from Problems

Instructions: In each of the following situations, a problem occurred. Explain the cause of the problem and how it can be corrected.

Problem 1: You attempt to boot the computer and the message, Non-System disk or disk error Replace and press any key when ready, displays on the screen.

Cause of Problem: ______________________________

____

Method of Correction: ______________________________

____

Problem 2: You are at the DOS prompt, and the default drive is A. You type `C` and press the ENTER key to change the default drive. DOS responds with the message, Bad command or file name.

Cause of Problem: ____________________

____

Method of Correction: ____________________

____

Problem 3: You are at the DOS prompt and the default drive is A. You type `dir` to display a list of files, but nothing happens.

Cause of Problem: ____________________

____

Method of Correction: ____________________

____

Problem 4: You type `rename oldfile.bak b:newfile.new` at the A:\> prompt and press the ENTER key. DOS responds with the message, `Invalid parameter`.

Cause of Problem: ____________________

____

Method of Correction: ____________________

____

SHORT ANSWER ASSIGNMENT 7

Understanding the Help Window

Instructions: In Figure SA1-7, arrows point to major components of the Help window. Identify the various parts of the screen in the space provided.

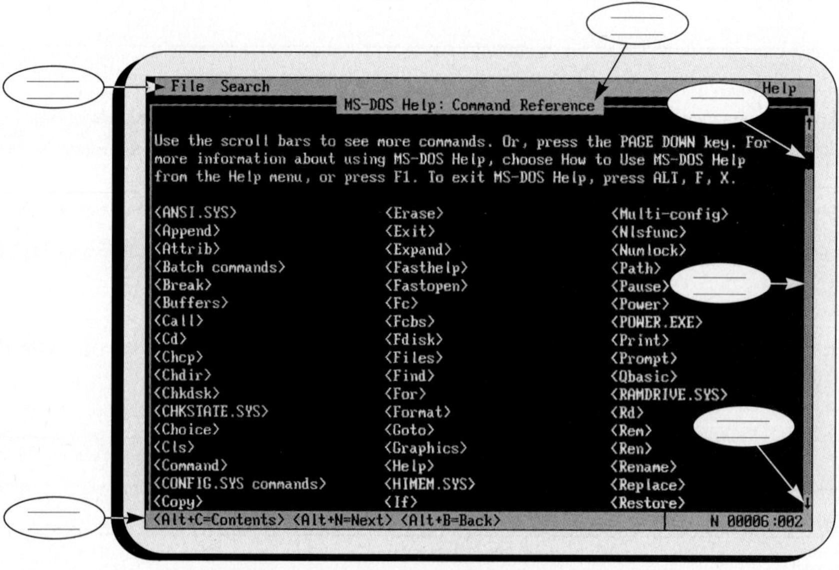

FIGURE SA1-7

HANDS-ON EXERCISES

HANDS-ON EXERCISE 1

Booting DOS and Formatting a Disk

Instructions: At the DOS prompt, perform the following tasks to boot your computer and format a new disk.

1. If the computer is not on a LAN:
   a. perform a cold boot.
   b. perform a warm boot.
2. If the computer is on a LAN:
   a. find out from your instructor if you are allowed to perform a cold boot. If so, perform a cold boot.
   b. find out from your instructor if you are allowed to perform a warm boot. If so, perform a warm boot.
3. Format a new disk using a volume label of seconddisk.
4. Do a directory of the newly formatted disk.
5. Print the directory by pressing the PRINT SCREEN key.

HANDS-ON EXERCISE 2

Working with DOS Commands

Instructions: At the DOS prompt, perform the following tasks to work with the files on your data disk. Each printout should be on a separate sheet of paper and labeled with the task number.

1. Insert your data disk that was originally created on page DOS14 and modified in the project, into drive A.
2. List all of the files on the disk with the dir command.
3. Print the directory listing by pressing the PRINT SCREEN key.
4. Clear the screen.
5. List just the file called SMITH.DOC with the dir command.
6. Print the directory listing by pressing the PRINT SCREEN key.
7. Clear the screen.
8. Display the version of DOS you are using.
9. Print the version by pressing the PRINT SCREEN key.
10. Clear the screen.
11. Copy the file SMITH.DOC to a file called SMITH.TXT on the same disk in drive A.
12. Print the copy command by pressing the PRINT SCREEN key.
13. Rename the file SMITH.TXT to JONES.TXT.
14. Print the rename command by pressing the PRINT SCREEN key.

15. Delete the file JONES.TXT.
16. Print the delete command by pressing the PRINT SCREEN key.
17. Display all of the files on your data disk.
18. Print the directory listing by pressing the PRINT SCREEN key.

HANDS-ON EXERCISE 3

Working with DOS Help

Instructions: Invoke the Help window by typing `help` at the DOS prompt. Print Help on the following DOS commands. If Examples and/or Notes exist for any of the commands, print those as well. Each printout should be on a separate sheet of paper and properly labeled. Help on the cls command is shown in HOE1-3.

1. cls
2. ver
3. dir
4. format
5. copy
6. rename
7. del
8. undelete

```
                          CLS

Clears the screen.

The cleared screen shows only the command prompt and cursor.

Syntax

    CLS
```

FIGURE HOE1-3

Managing and Organizing Files on Disks

OBJECTIVES

You will have mastered the material in this project when you can:

- Create subdirectories
- List a subdirectory's files
- Change the current subdirectory
- Specify a path
- Use wildcard characters with DOS commands
- Copy groups of files from one disk or subdirectory to another
- Move files from one subdirectory to another
- Display and print large directory listings
- Remove subdirectories
- Check the status of a disk
- Copy an entire disk

INTRODUCTION

Just as you organize the drawers in a filing cabinet, you must organize files on a disk. Disk files are usually organized by application. That is, word processing files are placed in a location separate from spreadsheet files. Because these locations often contain large numbers of files, you may copy, move, or delete a group of files, rather than just one file. In Project 2, you will learn how to organize and manage files on a disk.

Changing the Default Drive

Again in this project, it is assumed you are using a hard disk and one diskette drive with the drive names C and A, respectively. If you are using a different disk configuration, check with your instructor for the changes you should make in Project 2.

Continue to use the same data disk in this project that you used to complete Project 1. Follow these steps to change the default drive to A and to display the files on your data disk.

TO CHANGE THE DEFAULT DRIVE AND LIST A DIRECTORY

STEP 1: Insert your data disk from your completed Project 1 into drive A.

STEP 2: Type `a:` **and press the ENTER key.**

STEP 3: Type `dir` **and press the ENTER key.**

The default drive is changed to A (Figure 2-1). The list of files on the default drive, which is drive A in this case, displays on the screen. (Depending on your data disk's size and density, the bytes free at the bottom of your directory listing may differ from Figure 2-1.)

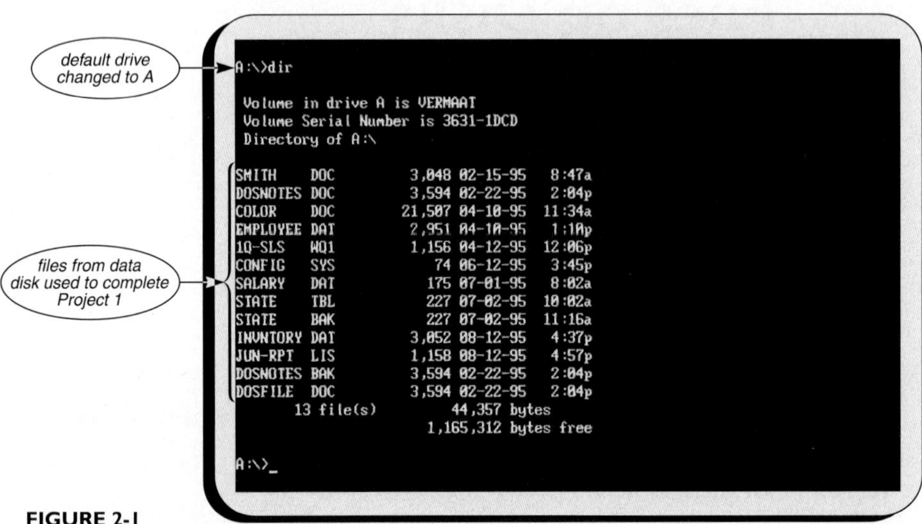

FIGURE 2-1

THE ROOT DIRECTORY AND SUBDIRECTORIES

As you learned in Project 1, a disk is essentially an electronic filing cabinet. You organize the folders in a filing cabinet by placing them in appropriate drawers. On a disk, you organize the files by placing them into appropriate directories. Recall from Project 1 that a directory is a listing of files. Two types of directories exist on a disk: the root directory and subdirectories.

The Root Directory

Every disk has at least one directory, called the **root directory**. The root directory is automatically created when you format a disk. You have thirteen files in the root directory on your data disk in drive A (see Figure 2-1 above).

The root directory on a disk is limited in size. For example, a hard disk allows up to 512 entries, while a double-density diskette has room for 112 entries and a high density diskette holds 224 entries. If you reach the maximum number of entries, you cannot place another file on the disk even if you have space left on the disk.

If you had a few hundred file entries in the root directory, you would have difficulty managing these disk files. Imagine scanning through a list of several hundred files to find the names of files you created months ago. For this reason, you divide your files into smaller logical groups. For example, all word processing files can be placed in one location and spreadsheet files in a separate location.

Subdirectories

Subdirectories are logical divisions of a disk that *you* create. Because the number of entries in the root directory is limited, you can create subdirectories to place more files on a disk. Unlike the root directory, the number of files in a subdirectory is limited only by the amount of storage available on the disk. The main reason, though, to create subdirectories is for disk and file organization. The way you use a filing cabinet is similar to the way you use subdirectories; the filing cabinet (similar to a disk) is divided into separate drawers (similar to subdirectories) to store the file folders (similar to the disk files) in an organized and manageable way.

Subdirectories are often called directories. Technically speaking, though, all directories other than the root are subdirectories. Each subdirectory itself can contain one or more subdirectories. In these cases, the directory containing the subdirectory is called the **parent directory**, and the subdirectory in the parent directory is called the **child directory**.

You may, for example, create one subdirectory called WP to hold all your word processing files and another called SS for your spreadsheet files (Figure 2-2). The root directory then would contain fifteen entries: the thirteen files in the root directory and the WP and SS subdirectories.

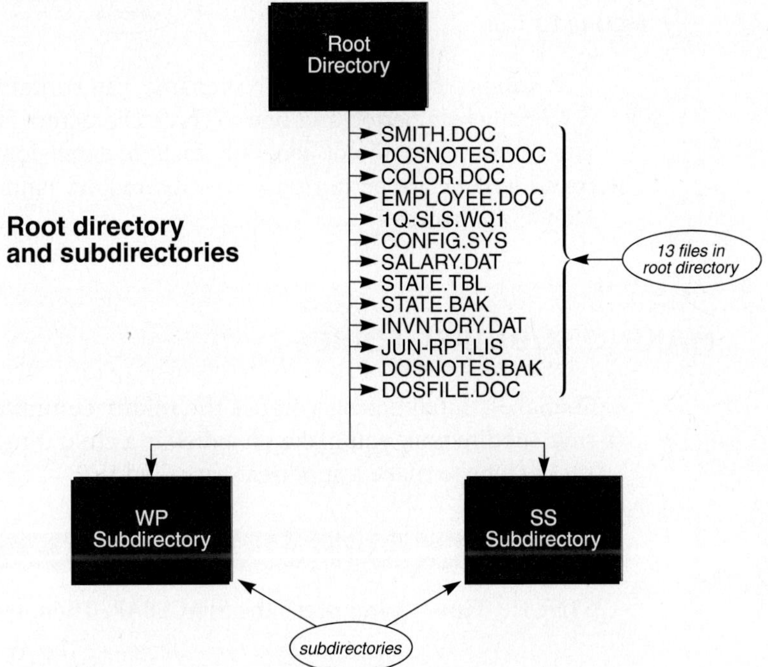

FIGURE 2-2

You may want to further divide your WP subdirectory files into two groups, placing word processing program files in the WP subdirectory and word processing document files in a new subdirectory called WPDOCS. Because you can create a subdirectory under an existing subdirectory, you can create the WPDOCS subdirectory under the

WP subdirectory (Figure 2-3). In this case, WP would be the parent directory, and WPDOCS would be the child directory.

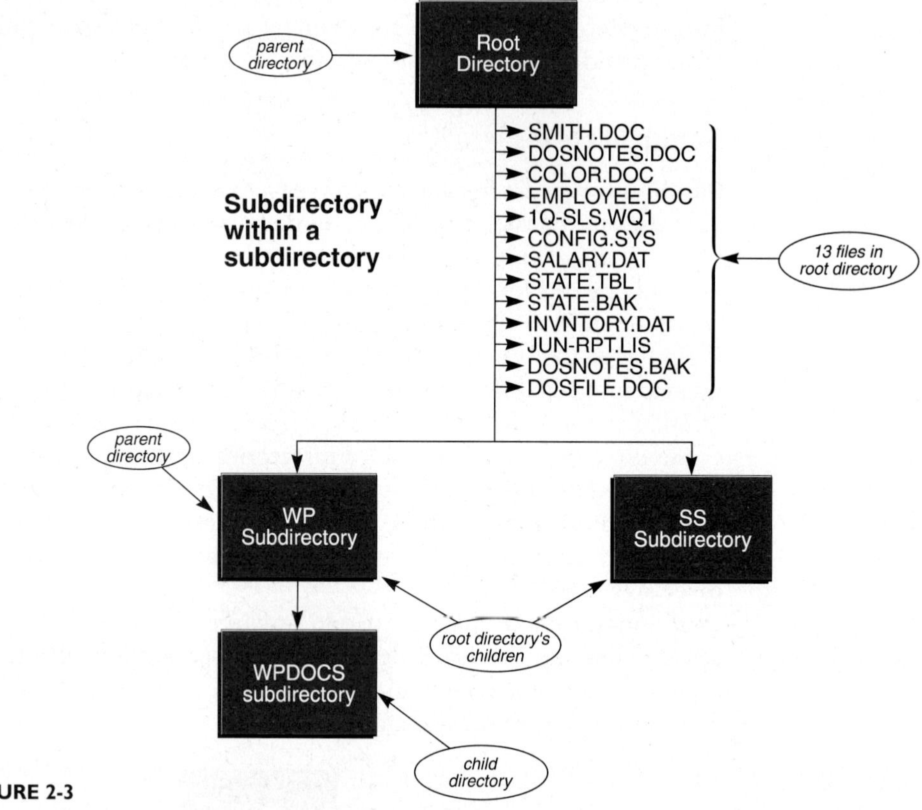

FIGURE 2-3

A subdirectory name, like a filename, can contain one to eight characters, followed optionally by a period and one to three characters for an extension. Subdirectory names, however, do not generally include extensions. The same characters permitted for a filename are permitted for a subdirectory name, which were discussed on page DOS15 in Project 1.

▼ MAKING SUBDIRECTORIES

To make a subdirectory, you use the **mkdir command**, usually abbreviated **md**. The first subdirectory you make on a disk is a child directory to the root directory. Follow these steps to make a subdirectory called WP.

TO MAKE A SUBDIRECTORY AND VERIFY THE RESULTS

STEP 1: Type `md` **and press the SPACEBAR. Then, type** `\wp` **and press the ENTER key.**

DOS makes a subdirectory called WP. The root, indicated by the backslash character, is the parent directory, and WP is the child directory.

STEP 2: Type `dir` **and press the ENTER key.**

DOS displays the files on drive A (Figure 2-4). The backslash following the A: in the Directory of A:\ message designates the root directory. Thus, A:\ indicates the files in the root directory on drive A are displayed. Notice the root directory now contains fourteen files. The new fourteenth file is actually the WP subdirectory entry and is identified as such by the <DIR> label in the directory listing.

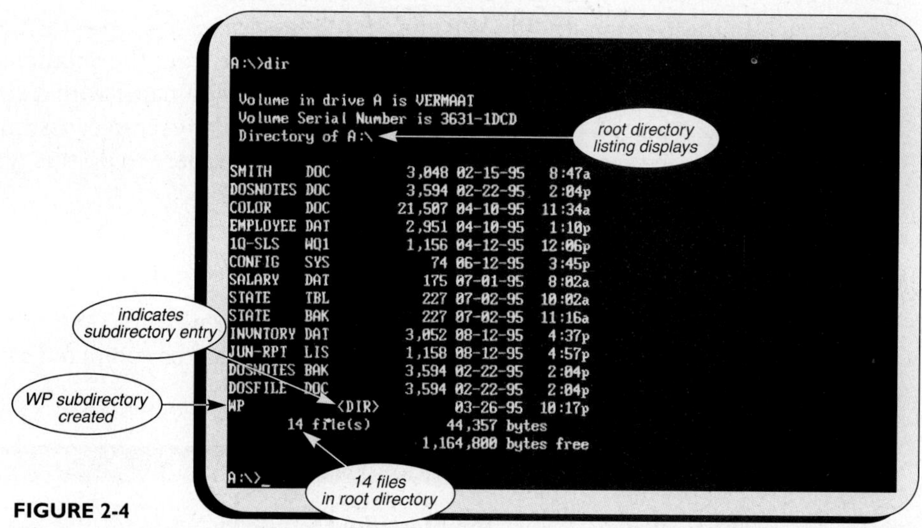

FIGURE 2-4

Follow these steps to make another subdirectory called SS.

TO MAKE ANOTHER SUBDIRECTORY AND VERIFY THE RESULTS

STEP 1: Type `md \ss` **and press the ENTER key.**

DOS makes a subdirectory called SS. The root is the parent directory, and SS is the child directory.

STEP 2: Type `dir` **and press the ENTER key.**

DOS displays the files on drive A (Figure 2-5). The root directory now contains fifteen files. The new fifteenth file is actually the `SS` *subdirectory entry and is identified as such by the* `<DIR>` *label in the directory listing.*

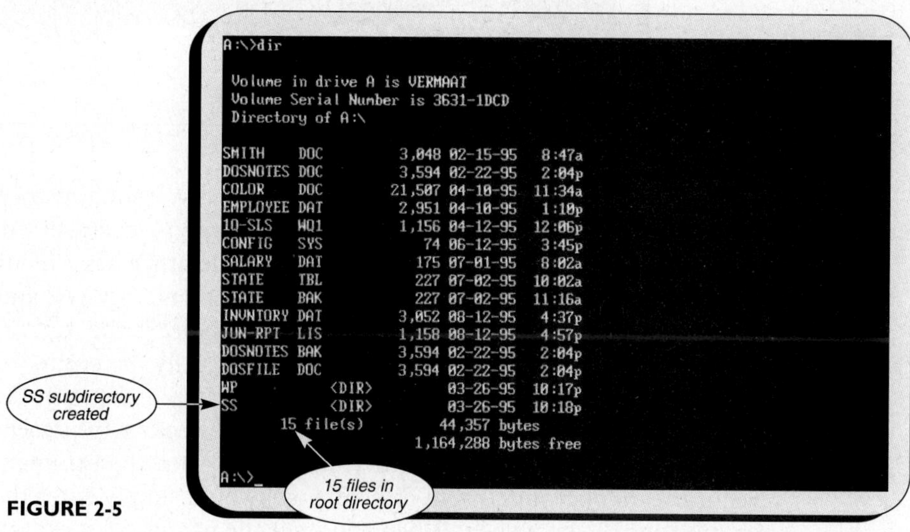

FIGURE 2-5

In these examples, the WP and SS subdirectories reside on the default drive (which is A) because you omitted the drive name from the subdirectory name when you created the subdirectories. If you specify a drive name with a subdirectory name, you must place a colon (:) after the drive name. For example, assume you wanted to make a subdirectory on drive C for your database files. To do this, you would enter `md c:\db` at the A prompt (A:\>).

Viewing the Contents of a Subdirectory

If you want to see the directory listing of the newly created WP or SS subdirectories, you need to specify the subdirectory's name in the dir command as shown in the following step.

TO DISPLAY A DIRECTORY LISTING OF A CHILD DIRECTORY

STEP 1: Type `dir \wp` and press the ENTER key.

DOS displays the message Directory of A:\WP, followed by the listing of files in the subdirectory (Figure 2-6). The \WP notation is called a ***path*** *because its sequence indicates the path from the root to the list of files. The backslash character precedes the subdirectory name in the path, indicating the root directory is the parent and WP is the child directory.*

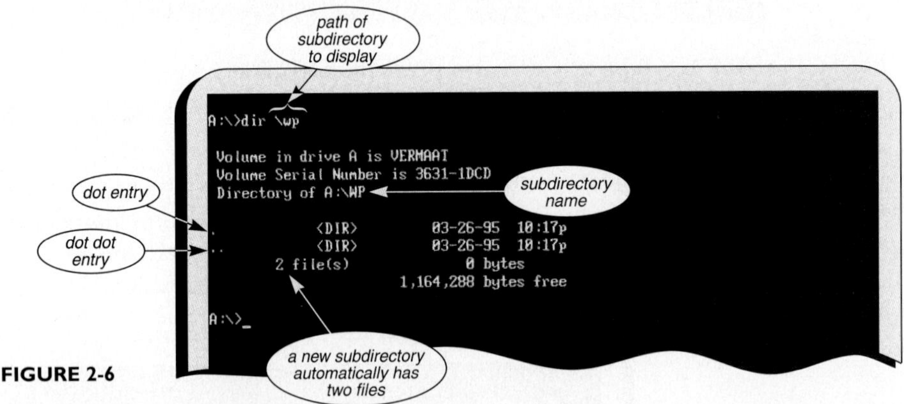

FIGURE 2-6

Because you have not yet placed any files in the WP subdirectory, you expect it to be empty; yet, its directory listing indicates 2 file(s), each with the <DIR> label. One has a filename of . (pronounced dot), and the other has a filename of .. (pronounced dot dot). The **dot entry** refers to the subdirectory WP, and the **dot dot entry** refers to the parent directory of WP, which in this case is the root directory on drive A.

When working with subdirectories, you can specify the entire path or, in some cases, just a partial path in the command. For example, the path \WP indicates the WP subdirectory is immediately below the root directory (represented by the backslash). To make the WP subdirectory, you just entered the command md \wp. However, if the root is your current directory, you could simply enter the command md wp, omitting the backslash. When you omit the parent directory(s) from a path, DOS assumes the subdirectory named in the command is a child to the current directory. For example, the command dir wp yields the same result shown in Figure 2-6 above because the root is the current directory and WP is a child to the root.

▼ MAKING SUBDIRECTORIES WITHIN SUBDIRECTORIES

As discussed earlier, you can make subdirectories within an existing subdirectory. You can, for example, make a subdirectory called WPDOCS beneath the WP subdirectory. You perform the same steps to make a subdirectory within a subdirectory as you did to make a subdirectory in the root directory. Follow these steps to create a subdirectory called WPDOCS under the WP subdirectory.

TO MAKE A SUBDIRECTORY WITHIN A SUBDIRECTORY AND VERIFY THE RESULTS

STEP 1: Type `md \wp\wpdocs` **and press the ENTER key.**

DOS makes a subdirectory called WPDOCS under the WP subdirectory. WPDOCS is the child directory, and WP is the parent. The first backslash represents the root directory; the second backslash separates the parent directory from the child directory. Recall the series of characters \wp\wpdocs is referred to as a path.

STEP 2: Type `dir` **and press the ENTER key.**

DOS displays the files on drive A (Figure 2-7). Notice the root directory still contains fifteen files, but the number of bytes free has changed from 1,164,288 (Figure 2-6 on the previous page) to 1,163,776 because you made a new subdirectory. Thus, this new empty subdirectory consumes 488 bytes of disk space (1,164,288 - 1,163,776).

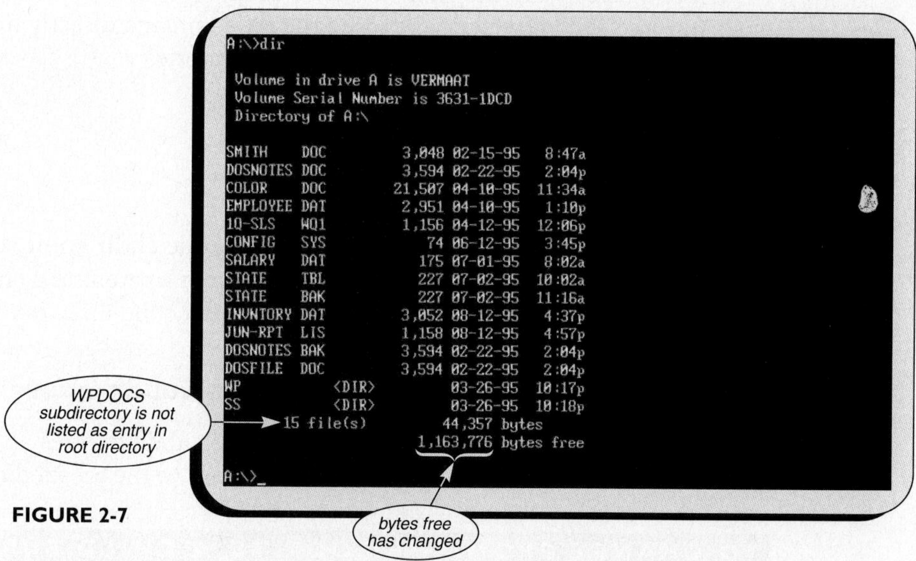

FIGURE 2-7

The child directory, WPDOCS, is not in the root directory listing because it is a subdirectory to WP. To see the directory entry for WPDOCS, you must display the directory listing for the WP subdirectory.

TO DISPLAY A DIRECTORY LISTING OF A CHILD DIRECTORY

STEP 1: Type `dir wp` **and press the ENTER key.**

DOS displays the directory for the WP subdirectory (Figure 2-8). Notice the subdirectory now contains three files: the dot entry, the dot dot entry, and the WPDOCS subdirectory entry. Because the root is the current directory and WP is a child to the root, the backslash is omitted from the path in this command.

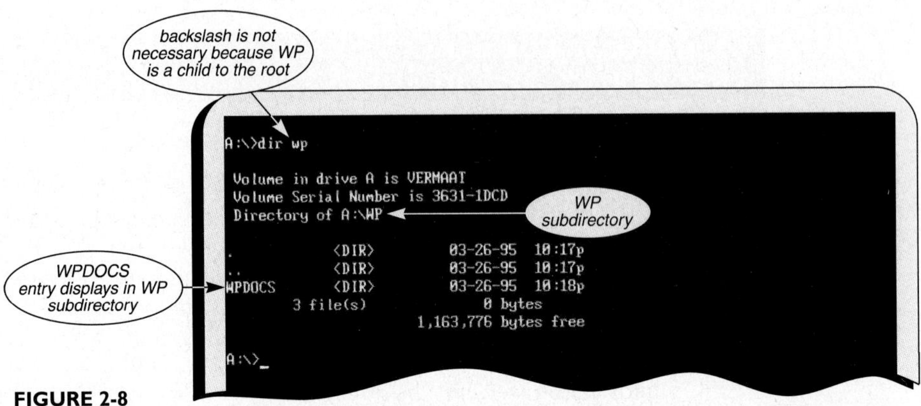

FIGURE 2-8

Instead of specifying the path to a child directory in the dir command, you can move into the child directory and issue the dir command directly from within the child directory. To do this, you must change directories.

CHANGING DIRECTORIES

To change from one directory to another, you use the **chdir command**, usually abbreviated **cd**. With this command, you can change from a parent to a child directory, from one subdirectory to another subdirectory, or from a child directory to its parent.

Changing from the Root Directory to a Subdirectory

The root directory on the disk in drive A has two subdirectories as its children: WP and SS. Follow these steps to change from the root to the SS subdirectory.

TO CHANGE FROM THE ROOT TO A CHILD SUBDIRECTORY AND VIEW IT

STEP 1: Type `cd ss` **and press the ENTER key.**

The DOS prompt changes to reflect the current subdirectory name (Figure 2-9). This way, you always can tell what directory you are currently in simply by looking at the DOS prompt. Because the SS subdirectory is a child to the root, the backslash may be omitted from the path. (If your prompt does not change, consult your instructor regarding the prompt command.)

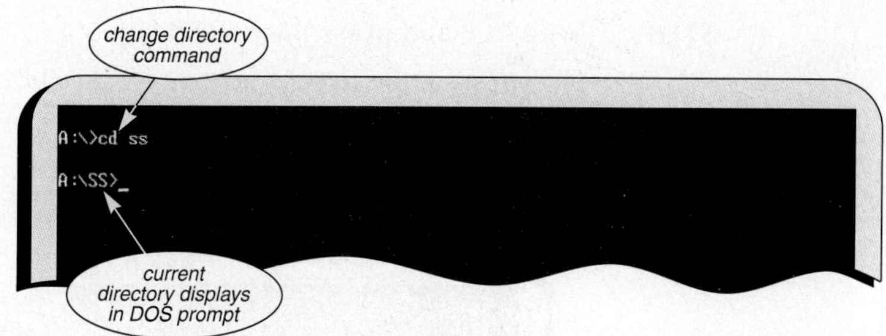

FIGURE 2-9

STEP 2: Type `dir` **and press the ENTER key.**

DOS displays the directory listing for the current directory, which is SS in this case (Figure 2-10).

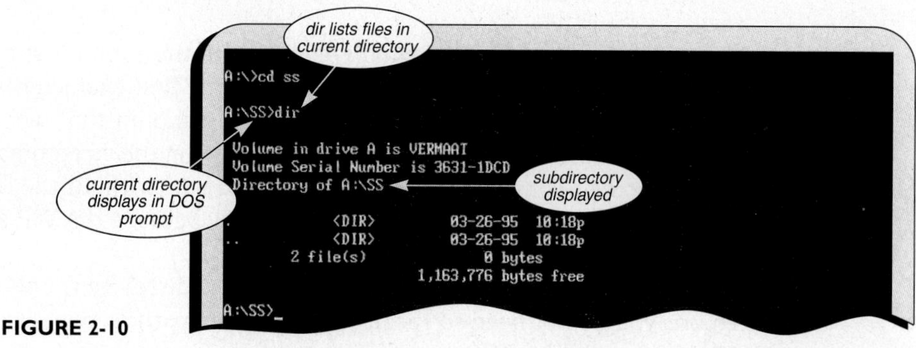

FIGURE 2-10

The Current Directory

Just as a default, or current, drive exists, each drive has a current directory. The **current directory** for a drive is the directory on which you are currently working; that is, DOS looks by default for files in the current directory of a drive. When you first access a disk, the root directory is the current directory. You can identify the current directory by looking at the DOS prompt or by entering the dir command as shown in Figure 2-10 above. You use the cd command to direct DOS to a subdirectory, which then becomes the current directory for that disk.

Changing from One Subdirectory to Another

On your data disk, WP and SS are two subdirectories, both children to the root. WPDOCS is a child to the WP subdirectory. Follow these steps to move from the SS subdirectory to the WP subdirectory.

TO CHANGE FROM ONE SUBDIRECTORY TO ANOTHER AND VIEW IT

STEP 1: Type `cd \wp` **and press the ENTER key.**

The DOS prompt changes to reflect the current subdirectory name. That is, the prompt is now A:\WP>, signifying you are in the WP subdirectory on drive A (see Figure 2-11 on the next page). Because WP is not a child to the SS directory, the complete path to the WP subdirectory is required in the cd command. That is, the backslash character is required.

STEP 2: Type `dir` and press the ENTER key.

DOS displays the directory listing for the current directory, which is the WP subdirectory (Figure 2-11).

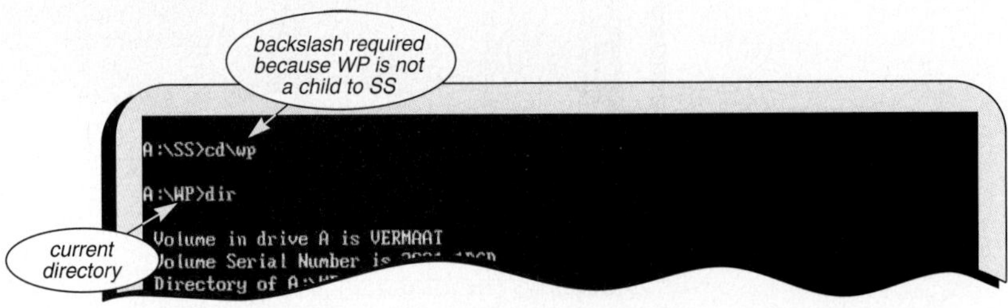

FIGURE 2-11

When you change from one subdirectory to another, you must specify the complete path to the subdirectory from the root. That is, the first character in the path is the backslash followed by the subdirectory name. If you omit the leading backslash for the root, DOS assumes the directory name following the cd command is a child to the current directory. For example, if you entered cd wp (without the leading backslash), DOS displays the error message Invalid directory because the WP subdirectory is not a child to the SS subdirectory.

However, if you want to move from the WP subdirectory to the WPDOCS subdirectory, you do not need to specify the complete path of \wp\wpdocs because WPDOCS is a child to WP as shown in the following steps.

TO CHANGE FROM A PARENT TO A CHILD DIRECTORY AND VIEW IT

STEP 1: Type `cd wpdocs` and press the ENTER key.

The DOS prompt changes to reflect the current subdirectory name (Figure 2-12 below). That is, the prompt is now A:\WP\WPDOCS>, signifying you are in the WPDOCS subdirectory, which is a child to the WP subdirectory on drive A.

STEP 2: Type `dir` and press the ENTER key.

DOS displays the directory listing for the current directory, which is the WPDOCS subdirectory (Figure 2-12).

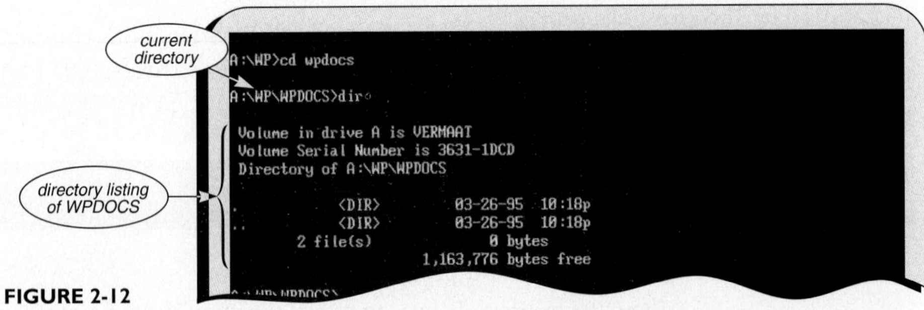

FIGURE 2-12

If you want to change from a child directory to its parent, you do not need to specify the path to the parent. Instead, you can specify the dot dot entry. Follow these steps to move from the WPDOCS subdirectory to the WP subdirectory.

TO CHANGE FROM A CHILD TO ITS PARENT AND VIEW IT

STEP 1: Type `cd ..` **and press the ENTER key.**

The DOS prompt changes to reflect the parent directory name. That is, the prompt is now A:\WP>, indicating you are in the WP subdirectory on drive A.

STEP 2: Type `dir` **and press the ENTER key.**

DOS displays the directory listing for the current directory, which is the WP subdirectory (Figure 2-13).

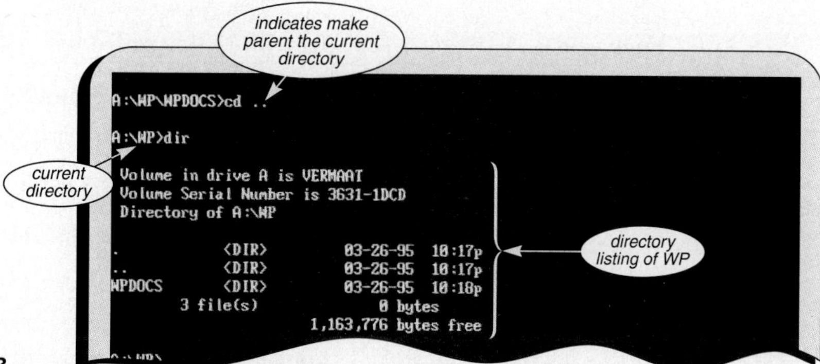

FIGURE 2-13

Changing Back to the Root Directory

The root directory is identified by a backslash. Thus, to change to the root directory, you enter a single backslash after the cd command as shown below.

TO CHANGE BACK TO THE ROOT DIRECTORY AND VIEW IT

STEP 1: Type `cd\` **and press the ENTER key.**

The DOS prompt changes to reflect the current directory name. That is, the prompt A:\> signifies you are in the root directory of drive A.

STEP 2: Type `dir` **and press the ENTER key.**

DOS displays the directory listing for the root directory, which is the current directory (Figure 2-14).

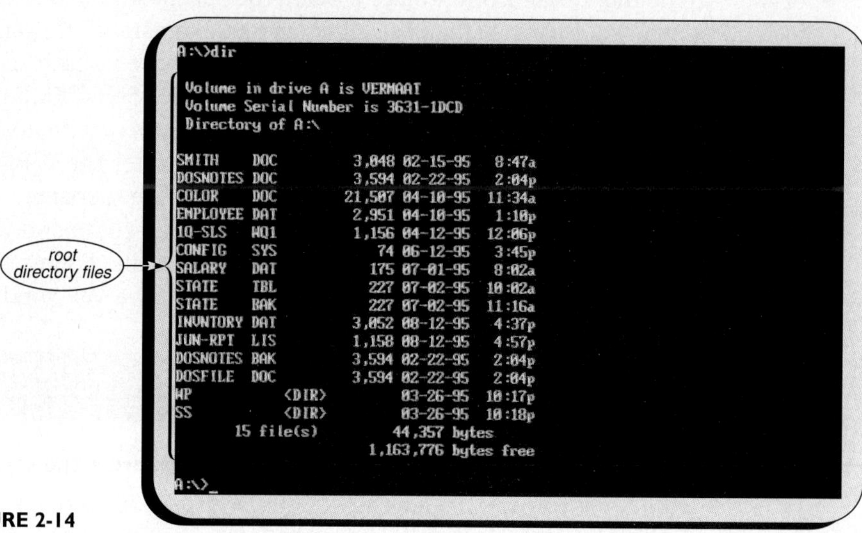

FIGURE 2-14

Summarizing Valid and Invalid Change Directory Command Entries

Because of the variety of ways you can change directories, Table 2-1 lists a variety of cd commands entered at the A:\> prompt. Some are valid; others are invalid. If valid, the table lists the result of the cd command; if invalid, the table lists the reason it is invalid.

TABLE 2-1

Assume you are at the A:\> prompt when you first enter the command.			
Command	**Valid/Invalid**	**Result/Reason**	**Display After Command Entered**
cd \wp\wpdocs	Valid	Makes WPDOCS the current directory	A:\WP\WPDOCS>
cd ..	Valid	Makes WP the current directory	A:\WP>
cd ss	Invalid	SS is not a child to the WP subdirectory	Invalid directory
cd \ss	Valid	Makes SS the current directory	A:\SS>
cd \	Valid	Makes the root directory the current directory	A:\>
cd ..	Invalid	Root does not have a parent directory	Invalid directory
cd wpdocs	Invalid	WPDOCS is not a child to the root	Invalid directory
cd wp	Valid	Makes WP the current directory	A:\WP>
cd wpdocs	Valid	Makes WPDOCS the current directory	A:\WP\WPDOCS>
cd \	Valid	Makes the root directory the current directory	A:\>

▼ INDICATING A PATH IN A FILE SPECIFICATION

Suppose you want to work on a spreadsheet you have already created and placed into a subdirectory. You would instruct DOS to find the file and display it on the screen. To do this, you must specify the path to the file. A complete path specifies the route DOS must take from the root directory through the subdirectories leading to the file. Recall from Project 1 that a file specification consists of up to four components: a drive, a path, a filename, and an extension. The path identifies the name of the directory and, if applicable, directories above it, each separated by a backslash (\). For example, the file specification A:\WP\DOSNOTES.DOC indicates the file DOSNOTES.DOC is located in the WP subdirectory on the A drive. The first backslash represents the root directory; the WP indicates the WP subdirectory; and the final backslash separates the subdirectory from the filename.

One way to specify a path is to include it in the command you are issuing. For example, you can indicate a path when copying a file. Follow these steps to copy the file DOSNOTES.DOC from the root directory to the WP subdirectory.

TO SPECIFY A PATH IN THE COPY COMMAND AND VERIFY THE RESULTS

STEP 1: Type `copy \dosnotes.doc \wp` **and press the ENTER key.**

DOS copies the file DOSNOTES.DOC from the root directory to the WP subdirectory. In the copy command, the \dosnotes.doc is the source specification, *which indicates where the file is being copied from and its name. The \wp is the target specification, which indicates where the file is being copied to. The file DOSNOTES.DOC is now in both the root and WP directories.*

STEP 2: Type `dir wp` **and press the ENTER key.**

DOS displays the list of files in the WP subdirectory (Figure 2-15). The WP subdirectory now has four files, one of which is DOSNOTES.DOC.

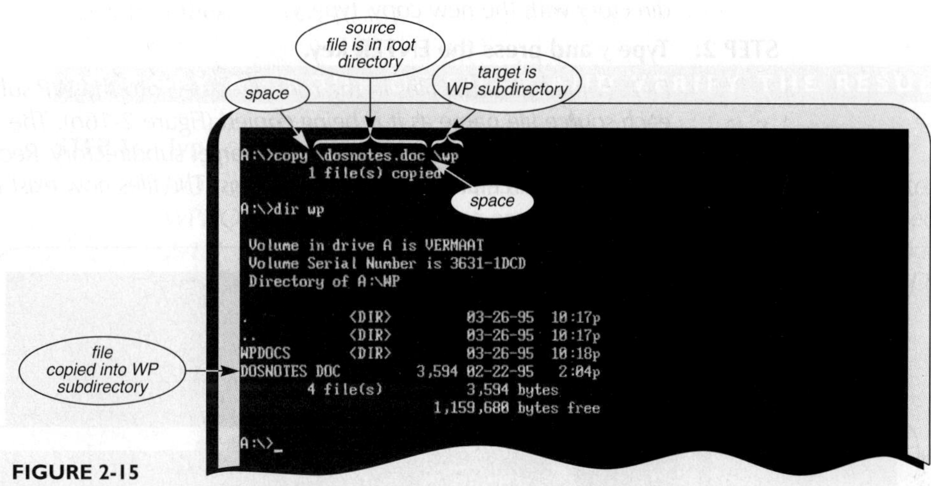

FIGURE 2-15

Because you omitted the filename and extension from the target in the copy command, the target file has the same name as the source file. You can have two files on a disk with the same name, as long as they reside in different directories. The complete path for the file in the WP subdirectory is A:\WP\DOSNOTES.DOC. The first backslash indicates the root directory, and the second backslash separates the WP subdirectory from the filename.

WILDCARD CHARACTERS

Using DOS commands such as copy, rename, and erase, you can access more than one file at a time. For example, you might want to copy all the files from one subdirectory to another subdirectory. To do this, you use a **wildcard character** in the file specification of a DOS command as a substitute for other characters. DOS recognizes two wildcard characters: the asterisk (*) and the question mark (?). The asterisk represents one or more characters, whereas the question mark represents a single character.

The Asterisk (*) Wildcard Character

To represent one or more characters in a file's name or extension, you use the **asterisk (*) wildcard character**. You can use the asterisk once in a filename and once in an extension. Wherever the asterisk appears, any character can occupy that position and all the remaining positions in the filename or the extension. To represent all filenames and all extensions, use the notation *.* — where the first * represents all filenames; the second * represents all extensions; and the period separates the filename portion from the extension portion. Follow the steps on the next page to copy all files from the root directory into the WP subdirectory using a single copy command.

A to the WP subdirectory on drive C, you enter the command copy \wp*.* c:\wp at the A:\> prompt. In this case, \wp*.* is the source location of the files to be copied, and c:\wp is the target location.

If you have multiple subdirectories on a diskette and want to make a **backup copy**, or duplicate, of the entire diskette, you could use the *.* wildcard notation to copy all the files, one directory at a time. The problem is you have to reissue the copy command for each subdirectory on your diskette. A more efficient way to backup a diskette, with a single command, is discussed at the end of this project.

Wildcard characters can be used with any DOS command that uses file specifications. For example, you may want to erase all files in the WP subdirectory that begin with the letter s. First, you display these files; then you erase them as shown in the steps.

TO DISPLAY A GROUP OF FILES

STEP 1: Type `dir \wp\s*.*` **and press the ENTER key.**

DOS displays the names of the files in the WP subdirectory that begin with the letter s (Figure 2-20). Four files display. The first s refers to the filename portion of the file specification, and the second * refers to the extension portion. Thus, all filenames and extensions beginning with the letter s display.*

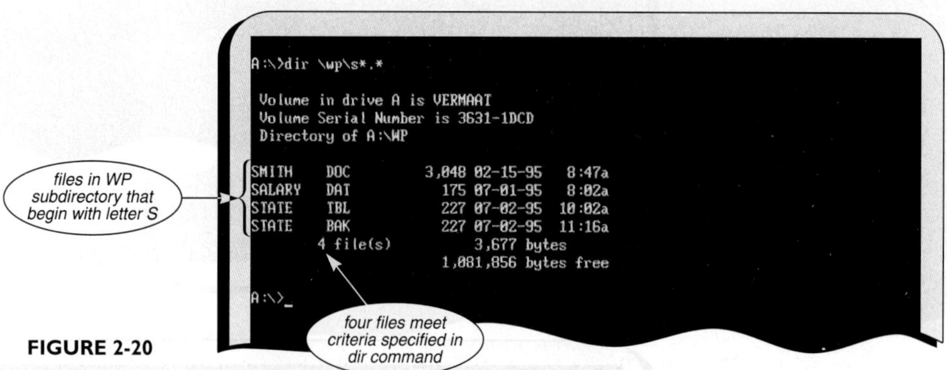

FIGURE 2-20

TO ERASE A GROUP OF FILES AND VERIFY THE RESULTS

STEP 1: Type `del \wp\s*.*` **and press the ENTER key.**

DOS erases files in the WP subdirectory that begin with the letter s. DOS does not display a confirmation indicating the deletion was successful. Thus, you must view a directory listing to verify the results of the del command.

STEP 2: Type `dir \wp\*.*` **and press the ENTER key.**

DOS displays the files in the WP subdirectory (Figure 2-21). The four files that began with the letter s were removed from the WP subdirectory. The other twelve files that do not begin with the letter s remain in the subdirectory.

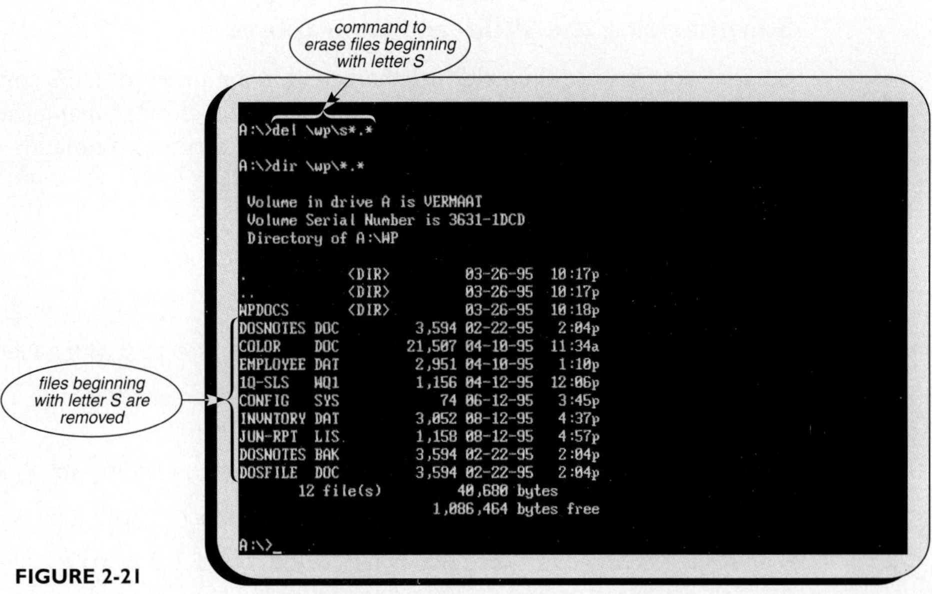

FIGURE 2-21

The Question Mark (?) Wildcard Character

To represent any character occupying one position in a filename or extension, you use the **question mark (?) wildcard character**. That is, the question mark wildcard character represents only a single character replacement, as opposed to the asterisk, which represents one or more characters. As with the asterisk wildcard character, you can use the question mark in any DOS command that uses file specifications. For example, you may know that a quarterly report is on your disk that you created with a spreadsheet package, but you do not remember the first two characters in its filename. In this case, you can use two question marks in the filename: one to represent the first position and one to represent the second position as shown below.

TO DISPLAY A DIRECTORY USING THE ? WILDCARD CHARACTER

STEP 1: Type `dir ??-sls.wq1` **and press the ENTER key.**

DOS displays the entry for the file 1Q-SLS.WQ1 (Figure 2-22). The ?? in the filename indicates that any character could exist in the first two positions of the filename, as long as the remaining characters are -sls and the extension is wq1. Recall that a file's extension indicates the type of file it is; thus 1Q-SLS is a worksheet file.

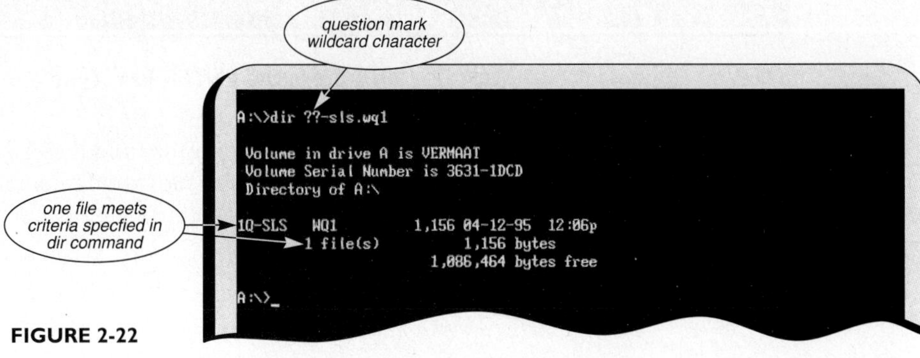

FIGURE 2-22

Summarizing the Wildcard Characters

Because you can use the wildcard characters in a number of DOS commands, Table 2-2 lists a variety of commands entered at the A:\> prompt using the wildcard characters. The results of the command are listed next to the command.

TABLE 2-2

Assume you are at the A:\> prompt when you first enter the command.	
Command	***Result***
dir state.*	Displays all files in the root directory with a filename of STATE.
copy state.* \ss	Copies files from the root directory that have a filename of STATE into the SS subdirectory.
dir \ss\state.*	Displays all files in the SS subdirectory with a filename of STATE.
del state.*	Erases all files in the root directory with a filename of STATE.
undelete state.*	Recovers all files in the root directory with a filename of STATE.
dir ?????.doc	Displays all files in the root directory that have five characters or less in their filename and an extension of DOC.
copy \wp*.* c:	Copies all files in the WP subdirectory on the current drive to the root directory on drive C.
copy \wp*.* c:\wp	Copies all files in the WP subdirectory on the current drive into the WP subdirectory on drive C.

▼ MOVING FILES

If you accidentally place files into the wrong directory, you can use the **move command** to transfer your files from one subdirectory to another subdirectory or from one drive to another drive. Moving files is different than copying files. When you copy files, they exist in both the source and target locations; when you move files, they are removed from the source location and exist only in the target location. Your disk, for example, has several files in the WPDOCS subdirectory. You can move all of the files in this subdirectory to the SS subdirectory as shown in the following steps. (In earlier versions of DOS, the move command is unavailable.)

TO MOVE ALL FILES FROM ONE DIRECTORY TO ANOTHER AND VERIFY THE RESULTS

STEP 1: Type `dir \wp\wpdocs` **and press the ENTER key. Type** `dir ss` **and press the ENTER key.**

DOS displays all files in the WPDOCS subdirectory and then all files in the SS subdirectory (Figure 2-23). WPDOCS contains six files and SS contains two files.

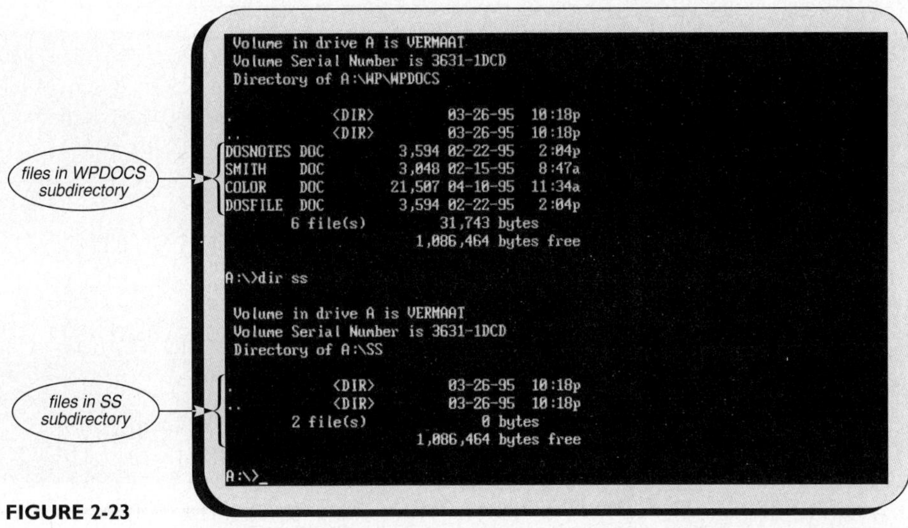

FIGURE 2-23

STEP 2: **Type** `move \wp\wpdocs\*.* \ss` **and press the ENTER key.**

DOS moves all of the files from the WPDOCS subdirectory into the SS subdirectory, listing each source file name as it is being moved (Figure 2-24). Notice, you must place a space before the source and target specifications. The files no longer exist in the WPDOCS subdirectory.

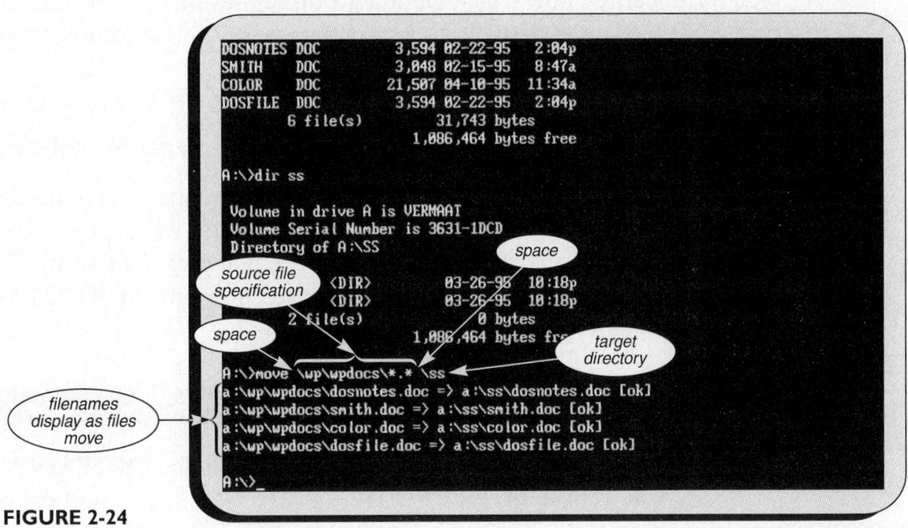

FIGURE 2-24

STEP 3: **Type** `dir \wp\wpdocs` **and press the ENTER key. Type** `dir ss` **and press the ENTER key.**

DOS displays all files in the WPDOCS subdirectory and then all files in the SS subdirectory (Figure 2-25 on the next page). Compare Figure 2-23 to Figure 2-25. Notice the files originally in the WPDOCS subdirectory are now in the SS subdirectory.

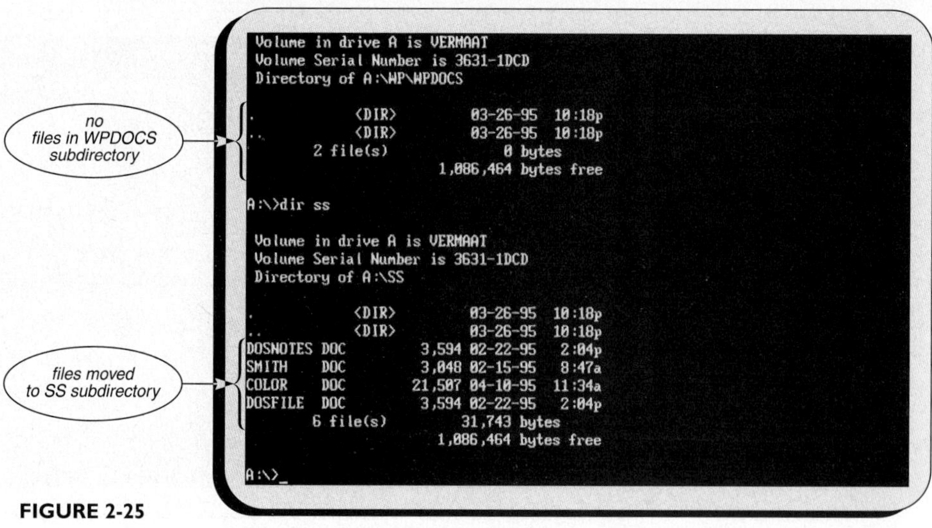

FIGURE 2-25

▼ DISPLAYING AND PRINTING LARGE DIRECTORIES

In Project 1, you learned to use the dir command to list files on a disk. In this project, you have learned how to list all or a group of files in a specific directory. Additionally, you can specify a variety of other parameters for the dir command as shown on the following pages.

Using the Directory Command with a Large Number of Files

Many directories contain more files than can fit in one screen display with the standard dir command. To illustrate this limitation, you will make a copy of the files in the WP subdirectory into the root directory. You will give the backup files the same filename as the original files, but they will have an extension of DUP. Then, you will display the directory listing of the root directory.

TO DISPLAY A LONG DIRECTORY LIST

STEP 1: Type `copy \wp\*.* \*.dup` **and press the ENTER key. When DOS asks if you want to overwrite A:\DOSNOTES.DUP, type** `y` **and press the ENTER key.**

DOS makes a duplicate copy of each file in the WP subdirectory, giving each target file the same filename with the extension of DUP and placing them in the root directory. Each source file lists as it is being copied (Figure 2-26).

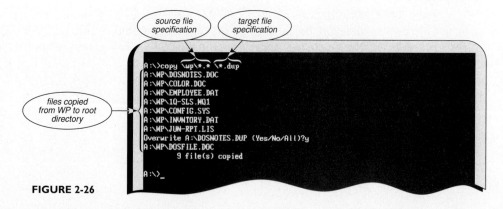

source file specification

target file specification

```
A:\>copy \wp\*.* \*.dup
A:\WP\DOSNOTES.DOC
A:\WP\COLOR.DOC
A:\WP\EMPLOYEE.DAT
A:\WP\1Q-SLS.WQ1
A:\WP\CONFIG.SYS
A:\WP\INVNTORY.DAT
A:\WP\JUN-RPT.LIS
Overwrite A:\DOSNOTES.DUP (Yes/No/All)?y
A:\WP\DOSFILE.DOC
        9 file(s) copied

A:\>_
```

files copied from WP to root directory

FIGURE 2-26

STEP 2: Type `dir` **and press the ENTER key.**

DOS displays the filenames in the root directory (Figure 2-27). The list is too long to fit on the screen. Thus, the first two files scroll off the top of the screen to make room for the bottom files, and you can view only the last screenful of files.

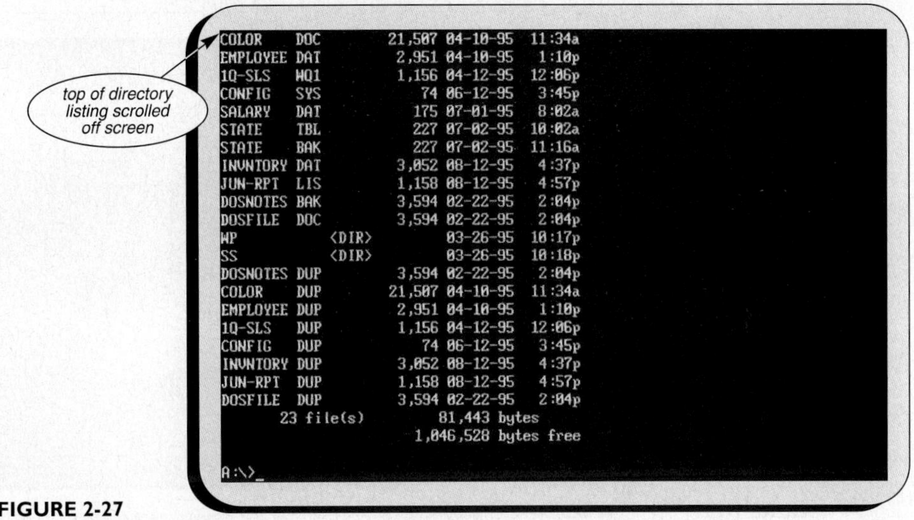

FIGURE 2-27

Because you may want to see the first screenful of files, DOS provides you with qualifiers for the dir command. A **qualifier**, which consists of a slash (/) followed by a single letter, changes the way a DOS command behaves. For example, you use the /p qualifier to pause your display as shown in the following steps.

TO PAUSE A DIRECTORY LISTING

STEP 1: Type `dir /p` **and press the ENTER key.**

DOS displays the first screenful of files in the directory listing and pauses after displaying the message Press any key to continue . . . at the bottom of the screen (Figure 2-28). At this point, DOS waits for you to press a key on the keyboard, giving you a chance to read the first screenful of files in the directory listing.

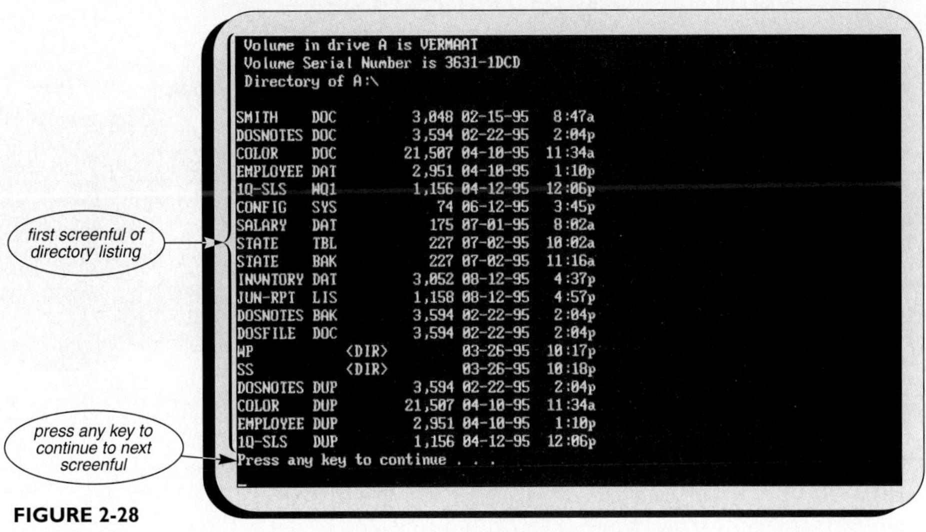

FIGURE 2-28

STEP 2: Press the ENTER key. (You could actually press any key.)

DOS displays the next screenful of files in the directory listing (Figure 2-29). Because this screenful concludes the directory listing, the DOS prompt displays beneath the directory.

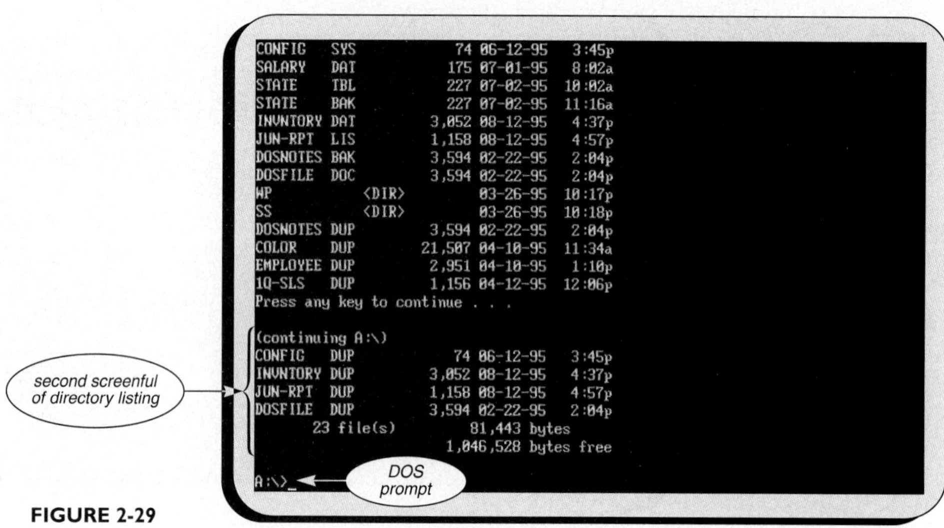

FIGURE 2-29

Another option of displaying a large directory listing is to use the /w qualifier to widen the display. The wide display allows more files to fit on the screen at a time as shown in the steps below.

TO WIDEN A DIRECTORY LISTING

STEP 1: Type `dir /w` **and press the ENTER key.**

DOS displays the root directory files in a wide format (Figure 2-30). Notice that only the filename and extension display in a wide directory listing. That is, the size of the files and time and date the files were created are not listed. Also, the filenames are separated from the extensions with a period, and subdirectory names are enclosed in brackets ([ ]).

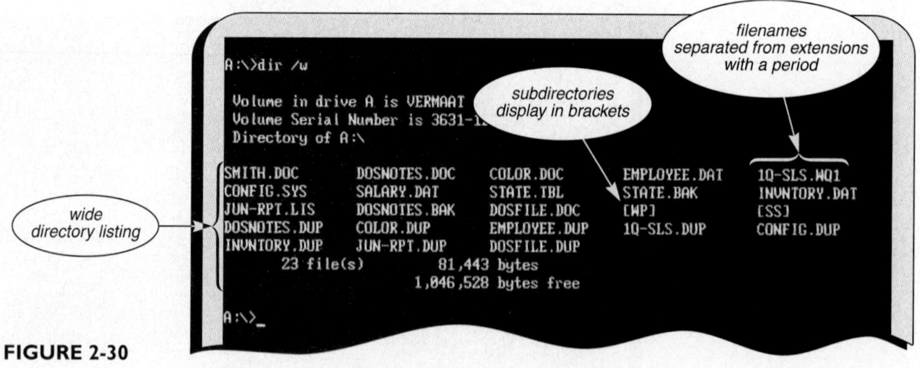

FIGURE 2-30

Printing a Directory Listing

At times, you might like a hardcopy, or printout, of a directory listing. To obtain this printout, you must redirect the default output of the dir command. The default output is the screen. Thus, you want to redirect the screen output to the printer. The **redirect output symbol** is the greater than sign (>), and the code for the printer is PRN. Follow these steps to print a directory listing.

TO PRINT A DIRECTORY LISTING

STEP 1: Ready your printer.

STEP 2: Type `dir > prn` **and press the ENTER key.**

Because DOS is sending the directory to the printer, your screen does not display the directory listing (Figure 2-31).

directory listing does not display on screen
A:\>dir > prn
A:\>_

FIGURE 2-31

STEP 3: Remove the hardcopy directory listing from the printer (Figure 2-32).

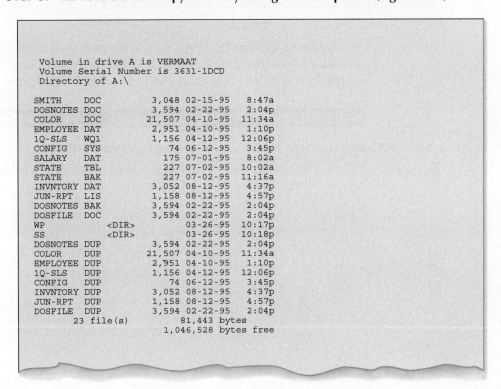

```
 Volume in drive A is VERMAAT
 Volume Serial Number is 3631-1DCD
 Directory of A:\

SMITH    DOC         3,048 02-15-95   8:47a
DOSNOTES DOC         3,594 02-22-95   2:04p
COLOR    DOC        21,507 04-10-95  11:34a
EMPLOYEE DAT         2,951 04-10-95   1:10p
1Q-SLS   WQ1         1,156 04-12-95  12:06p
CONFIG   SYS            74 06-12-95   3:45p
SALARY   DAT           175 07-01-95   8:02a
STATE    TBL           227 07-02-95  10:02a
STATE    BAK           227 07-02-95  11:16a
INVNTORY DAT         3,052 08-12-95   4:37p
JUN-RPT  LIS         1,158 08-12-95   4:57p
DOSNOTES BAK         3,594 02-22-95   2:04p
DOSFILE  DOC         3,594 02-22-95   2:04p
WP           <DIR>         03-26-95  10:17p
SS           <DIR>         03-26-95  10:18p
DOSNOTES DUP         3,594 02-22-95   2:04p
COLOR    DUP        21,507 04-10-95  11:34a
EMPLOYEE DUP         2,951 04-10-95   1:10p
1Q-SLS   DUP         1,156 04-12-95  12:06p
CONFIG   DUP            74 06-12-95   3:45p
INVNTORY DUP         3,052 08-12-95   4:37p
JUN-RPT  DUP         1,158 08-12-95   4:57p
DOSFILE  DUP         3,594 02-22-95   2:04p
       23 file(s)          81,443 bytes
                        1,046,528 bytes free
```

FIGURE 2-32

Other Qualifiers for the Directory Command

Several other qualifiers may be placed in the directory command to change the way it displays the directory listing. Table 2-3 lists several useful qualifiers available for the dir command.

TABLE 2-3

DIR Command with Parameter	*Function*
dir /p	Displays one screen of the listing at a time.
dir /w	Displays the listing in a wide format.
dir /a:d	Displays the listing of subdirectory names only.
dir /a:-d	Displays the listing of filenames only.
dir /o	Displays the listing in alphabetical order by name.
dir /o:e	Displays the listing in alphabetical order by extension.
dir /o:d	Displays the listing in alphabetical order by date and time.
dir /o:s	Displays the listing in alphabetical order by size, smallest first.
dir /o:-s	Displays the listing in alphabetical order by size, largest first.
dir /s	Displays the listing of the current directory and all of its subdirectories.

You can use as many qualifiers on one dir command as you like. For example, you may want a hardcopy directory listing of the root, as well as all of its subdirectories, in alphabetical order. Follow these steps to print this directory.

TO USE MULTIPLE QUALIFIERS WITH A COMMAND

STEP 1: Type `dir /s/o > prn` **and press the ENTER key.**

DOS prints the listing of the files in all subdirectories in the A drive in alphabetical order (Figure 2-33).

```
 Volume in drive A is VERMAAT
 Volume Serial Number is 3631-1DCD

Directory of A:\

SS           <DIR>          03-26-95  10:18p
WP           <DIR>          03-26-95  10:17p
1Q-SLS   DUP          1,156 04-12-95  12:06p
1Q-SLS   WQ1          1,156 04-12-95  12:06p
COLOR    DOC         21,507 04-10-95  11:34a
COLOR    DUP         21,507 04-10-95  11:34a
CONFIG   DUP             74 06-12-95   3:45p
CONFIG   SYS             74 06-12-95   3:45p
DOSFILE  DOC          3,594 02-22-95   2:04p
DOSFILE  DUP          3,594 02-22-95   2:04p
DOSNOTES BAK          3,594 02-22-95   2:04p
DOSNOTES DOC          3,594 02-22-95   2:04p
DOSNOTES DUP          3,594 02-22-95   2:04p
EMPLOYEE DAT          2,951 04-10-95   1:10p
EMPLOYEE DUP          2,951 04-10-95   1:10p
INVNTORY DAT          3,052 08-12-95   4:37p
INVNTORY DUP          3,052 08-12-95   4:37p
JUN-RPT  DUP          1,158 08-12-95   4:57p
JUN-RPT  LIS          1,158 08-12-95   4:57p
SALARY   DAT            175 07-01-95   8:02a
SMITH    DOC          3,048 02-15-95   8:47a
STATE    BAK            227 07-02-95  11:16a
STATE    TBL            227 07-02-95  10:02a
       23 file(s)         81,443 bytes

Directory of A:\SS

.            <DIR>          03-26-95  10:18p
..           <DIR>          03-26-95  10:18p
COLOR    DOC         21,507 04-10-95  11:34a
DOSFILE  DOC          3,594 02-22-95   2:04p
DOSNOTES DOC          3,594 02-22-95   2:04p
SMITH    DOC          3,048 02-15-95   8:47a
        6 file(s)         31,743 bytes

Directory of A:\WP

.            <DIR>          03-26-95  10:17p
..           <DIR>          03-26-95  10:17p
WPDOCS       <DIR>          03-26-95  10:18p
1Q-SLS   WQ1          1,156 04-12-95  12:06p
COLOR    DOC         21,507 04-10-95  11:34a
CONFIG   SYS             74 06-12-95   3:45p
DOSFILE  DOC          3,594 02-22-95   2:04p
DOSNOTES BAK          3,594 02-22-95   2:04p
DOSNOTES DOC          3,594 02-22-95   2:04p
EMPLOYEE DAT          2,951 04-10-95   1:10p
INVNTORY DAT          3,052 08-12-95   4:37p
JUN-RPT  LIS          1,158 08-12-95   4:57p
       12 file(s)         40,680 bytes

Directory of A:\WP\WPDOCS

.            <DIR>          03-26-95  10:18p
```

```
..           <DIR>          03-26-95  10:18p
        2 file(s)              0 bytes

Total files listed:
       43 file(s)        153,866 bytes
                       1,046,528 bytes free
```

FIGURE 2-33

Displaying the Directory Tree

Although you can use the /s qualifier on the dir command to list files in all subdirectories on a disk, you can display a neater representation of all subdirectories on a disk with the tree command. The **tree command** graphically lists the directory structure of a disk. With the tree command, you can list only directory names or both directory and filenames as shown in the steps on the next page.

TO GRAPHICALLY LIST THE DIRECTORY STRUCTURE OF A DISK

STEP 1: Type `tree` **and press the ENTER key.**

DOS displays the names of all of the directories on the default drive, beginning with the current directory (Figure 2-34). Because the current directory is the root, all subdirectories on the disk are displayed. Notice each child directory displays indented beneath its parent.

FIGURE 2-34

STEP 2: Type `tree /f /a > prn` **and press the ENTER key.**

DOS prints the files in all of the directories on the default drive beginning with the current directory (Figure 2-35). The /f qualifier instructs DOS to also list files with the directories. Because many printers cannot print the graphic lines, the /a qualifier instructs DOS to use text characters rather than the graphic characters in the tree output.

```
Directory PATH listing for Volume VERMAAT
Volume Serial Number is 3631-1DCD
A:.
|   SMITH.DOC
|   DOSNOTES.DOC
|   COLOR.DOC
|   EMPLOYEE.DAT
|   1Q-SLS.WQ1
|   CONFIG.SYS
|   SALARY.DAT
|   STATE.TBL
|   STATE.BAK
|   INVNTORY.DAT
|   JUN-RPT.LIS
|   DOSNOTES.BAK
|   DOSFILE.DOC
|   DOSNOTES.DUP
|   COLOR.DUP
|   EMPLOYEE.DUP
|   1Q-SLS.DUP
|   CONFIG.DUP
|   INVNTORY.DUP
|   JUN-RPT.DUP
|   DOSFILE.DUP
|
+---WP
|   |   DOSNOTES.DOC
|   |   COLOR.DOC
|   |   EMPLOYEE.DAT
|   |   1Q-SLS.WQ1
|   |   CONFIG.SYS
|   |   INVNTORY.DAT
|   |   JUN-RPT.LIS
|   |   DOSNOTES.BAK
|   |   DOSFILE.DOC
|   |
|   \---WPDOCS
\---SS
        DOSNOTES.DOC
        SMITH.DOC
        COLOR.DOC
        DOSFILE.DOC
```

FIGURE 2-35

To view the directory structure of a different disk, add the drive name followed by a colon as a parameter on the tree command. For example, the command tree c: /f displays the directory structure of drive C.

REMOVING SUBDIRECTORIES

When you no longer need a subdirectory, you can remove, or delete, it. You use the **rmdir command**, abbreviated **rd**, to remove a subdirectory from a disk. You must be in another directory before you can remove a subdirectory, and you must first move or remove all the files stored within it. DOS takes this precaution to prevent you from accidentally removing a subdirectory containing files you need to keep. Follow these steps to remove the SS subdirectory from the disk in drive A.

TO REMOVE A SUBDIRECTORY AND VERIFY THE RESULTS

STEP 1: Type `del ss` **and press the ENTER key.**

DOS responds with the prompt, All files in directory will be deleted! Are you sure (Y/N)? (Figure 2-36). When you place a subdirectory name after the del command, you instruct DOS to erase all files in that subdirectory.

FIGURE 2-36

STEP 2: Type the letter `y` **and press the ENTER key.**

DOS deletes all the files in the SS subdirectory.

STEP 3: Type `dir ss` **and press the ENTER key.**

DOS displays the directory of SS (Figure 2-37). Notice it contains just two files: the dot and dot dot entries. A subdirectory with just these entries may be removed.

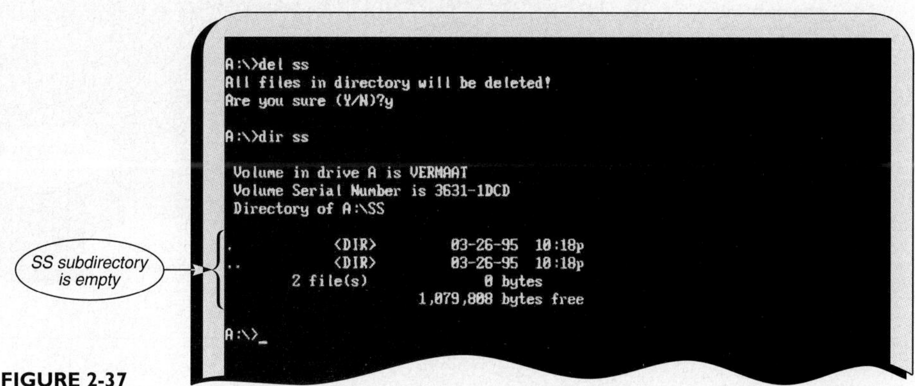

FIGURE 2-37

STEP 4: Type `cls` **and press the ENTER key. Type** `rd ss` **and press the ENTER key.**

DOS removes the SS subdirectory from the disk in drive A.

STEP 5: Type `tree` **and press the ENTER key.**

DOS displays the directory structure of the disk in drive A (Figure 2-38). Notice the SS subdirectory is not in the list.

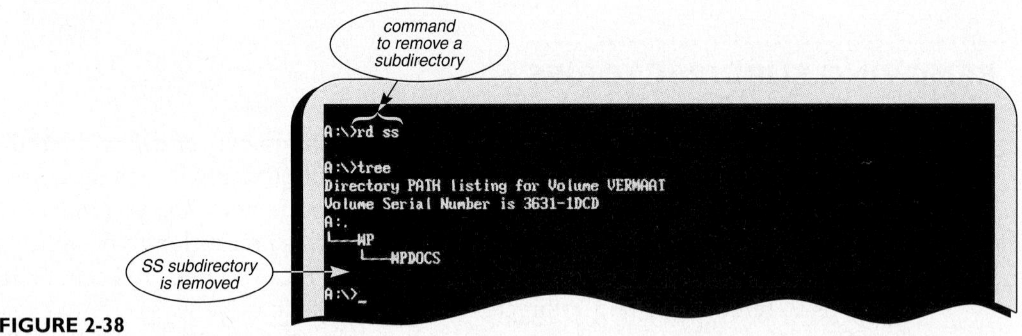

FIGURE 2-38

CHECKING THE STATUS OF A DISK

You may want to know the number of directories and files you have on a disk. The **chkdsk command** checks the condition of your disk and reports disk statistics to you as shown in these steps.

TO CHECK THE STATUS OF A DISK

STEP 1: Type `chkdsk` **and press the ENTER key.**

DOS displays several lines of summary information (Figure 2-39). These lines indicate how many bytes (characters) can be stored on the disk; how much of this disk space is used by how many directories; how much of this disk space is used by how many files; and how much disk space is available for future storage. This command also reports allocation unit statistics and how much base memory you have on your computer and how much of the base memory is available for use.

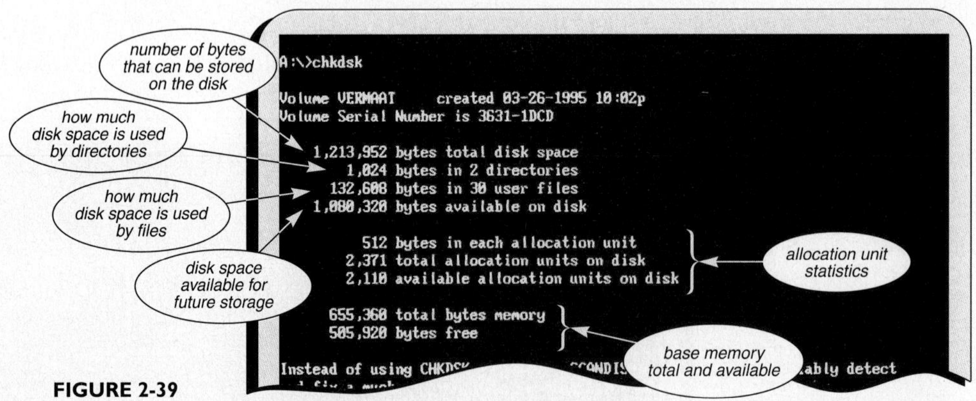

FIGURE 2-39

You should issue the chkdsk command periodically to determine if your disk has a problem. If the chkdsk command checks your disk and detects a problem(s), it displays diagnostic messages. If these messages display, ask your instructor for assistance.

▼ COPYING AN ENTIRE DISKETTE

With the copy command and wildcard characters, you can copy all of the files in a specific subdirectory to another subdirectory or disk. However, if you want to backup an entire disk (all subdirectories and all files), you should use the **diskcopy command.** The source and destination disks will be identical at the conclusion of the diskcopy; therefore, DOS destroys the existing contents of the destination disk as it copies the new information to it. Additionally, the source and target must be the same. That is, if the source is a 5 1/4 inch high-density disk, the target also must be a 5 1/4 inch high-density disk. Because most computer configurations today have drive A and B as different sizes or densities, you must specify the source and target drive as the same drive as shown in these steps.

TO COPY AN ENTIRE DISKETTE

STEP 1: Type `diskcopy a: a:` **and press the ENTER key.**

DOS prompts you to insert the source diskette into drive A (Figure 2-40).

FIGURE 2-40

STEP 2: Insert the disk you want to copy from into drive A.

STEP 3: Press the ENTER key (you can actually press any key).

DOS begins reading the contents of the source disk into memory and then prompts you to insert the target diskette into drive A (Figure 2-41).

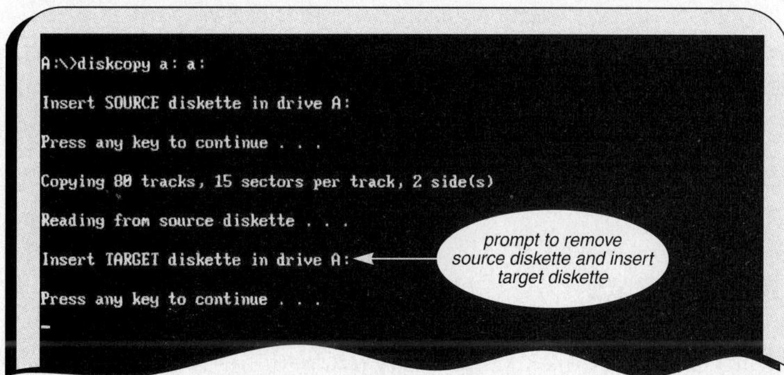

FIGURE 2-41

STEP 4: Remove the source disk from drive A. Insert the disk you want the files copied to into drive A. Remember, any existing files on the target diskette will be erased.

STEP 5: Press the ENTER key (you can actually press any key).

DOS begins writing the files from memory to the target diskette. Depending on the size and density of your disks and the DOS version you are using, DOS may prompt you to insert your source and target diskettes one or more times to swap data. After copying, DOS asks if you want to write another duplicate of this disk.

STEP 6: Type the letter n for No.

DOS assigns a volume serial number to the destination disk and asks if you want to copy another diskette (Figure 2-42).

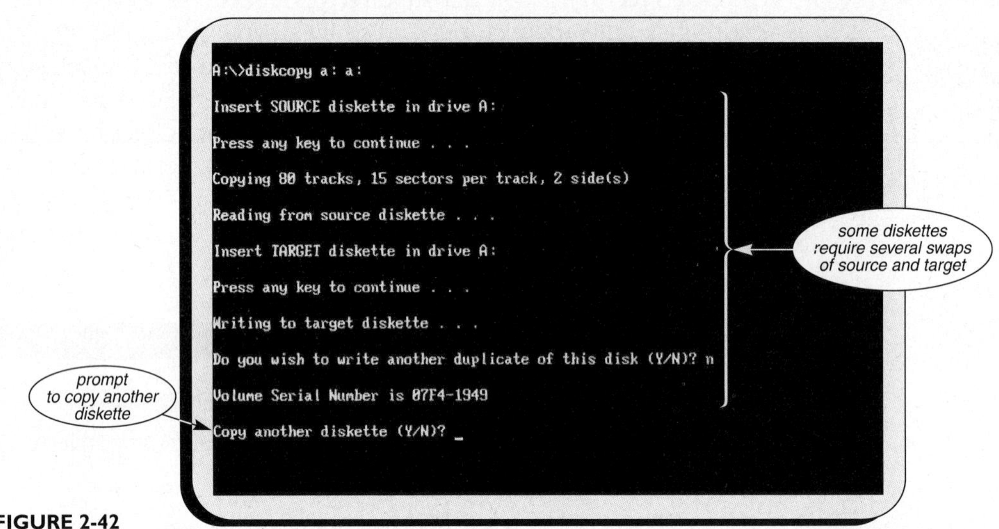

FIGURE 2-42

STEP 7: Type the letter n for No.

You return to the DOS prompt. Both the source and target diskettes are now duplicates of each other.

The diskcopy command only works with diskettes; therefore, you cannot use the diskcopy command to backup a hard disk.

▼ PROJECT SUMMARY

In Project 2, you learned how to make, change, and remove subdirectories; change the current directory and specify the path; use wildcard characters in commands; use qualifiers on the dir command; redirect output to the printer; and use the chkdsk and diskcopy commands. All the activities you learned in this project are summarized in the Quick Reference.

▼ KEY TERMS

asterisk (*) wildcard character *(DOS53)*
backup copy *(DOS56)*
chdir command (cd) *(DOS48)*
child directory *(DOS43)*
chkdsk command *(DOS68)*
current directory *(DOS49)*
diskcopy command *(DOS69)*
dot entry *(DOS46)*
dot dot entry *(DOS46)*
mkdir command (md) *(DOS44)*
move command *(DOS58)*
parent directory *(DOS43)*
path *(DOS46)*
qualifier *(DOS61)*
question mark (?) wildcard character *(DOS57)*
redirect output symbol (>) *(DOS63)*
rmdir command (rd) *(DOS67)*
root directory *(DOS42)*
subdirectories *(DOS43)*
tree command *(DOS65)*
wildcard characters *(DOS53)*

QUICK REFERENCE

The following table provides a quick reference to each task presented in the project.

Task	Command Syntax	Description
Change Directory	cd directory-path	Changes the current directory on a disk
Check Disk Status	chkdsk	Verifies and reports a disk's condition
Make Subdirectory	md directory-name	Creates a new subdirectory
Move Files	move source target	Transfers the source file specification to the target file specification
Remove	rd directory-path	Removes a subdirectory from a disk
Tree	tree /f	Displays the directory structure of a disk

SHORT ANSWER ASSIGNMENTS

SHORT ANSWER ASSIGNMENT 1

True/False

Instructions: Circle T if the statement is true or F if the statement is false.

T F 1. Every disk has at least two root directories.

T F 2. A root directory has room to keep track of an unlimited number of files.

T F 3. The root directory can also be a parent directory.

T F 4. A subdirectory can have subdirectories.

T F 5. A subdirectory name cannot have an extension.

T F 6. The dir a: command always produces a directory listing of the files in the root directory of drive A.

T F 7. To move from one subdirectory to another, use the move command.

T F 8. The delete command can be used to remove a subdirectory and all of its files.

T F 9. You can only use one wildcard question mark character in a command to identify a file's name.

T F 10. Use the tree command to display the directory structure of a disk.

T F 11. The chkdsk command displays the names of the subdirectories on a disk.

T F 12. Both the source and target drive must be the same type when you use the diskcopy command.

T F 13. Use the cd command to create a new subdirectory.

T F 14. The redirect output symbol is an equal sign (=).

T F 15. The command dir /o prints a directory.

T F 16. A subdirectory can be both a parent and a child.

T F 17. The dot entry refers to the subdirectory, and the dot dot entry refers to its parent.

T F 18. The command cd.. always returns you to the root directory.

T F 19. The asterisk wildcard character is used to represent one or more characters in a file's name or extension.

T F 20. The command del wp removes the wp subdirectory from the default drive.

SHORT ANSWER ASSIGNMENT 2

Multiple Choice

Instructions: Circle the correct response.

1. To make a new subdirectory, use the ________ command.
   a. cd
   b. md
   c. rd
   d. td
2. The ________ is the first entry in a path.
   a. backslash
   b. filename
   c. subdirectory name
   d. drive name
3. Filenames are grouped on disks into ________.
   a. current directories
   b. source and target filename entries
   c. internally labeled entries
   d. directories and subdirectories
4. The ________ command is used to transfer files from one location to another.
   a. del
   b. move
   c. copy
   d. tree
5. The ________ qualifier tells the dir command to display one screenful of files at a time.
   a. /a
   b. /p
   c. /w
   d. /o
6. The ________ command is used to duplicate the contents of a disk.
   a. chkdsk
   b. rd
   c. tree
   d. diskcopy
7. Which wildcard character means match all characters that follow?
   a. asterisk (*)
   b. ampersand (&)
   c. percent sign (%)
   d. question mark (?)

8. Which command returns you to the parent directory?
   a. cd .
   b. cd ..
   c. cd >
   d. cd <
9. To print a directory listing, enter the ________ command.
   a. print dir
   b. print > dir
   c. dir < prn
   d. dir > prn
10. The ________ command is used to check the status of a disk.
    a. chkdsk
    b. status
    c. checkdisk
    d. diskcheck

SHORT ANSWER ASSIGNMENT 3

Fill in the Blanks

1. The special file directory created when a disk is formatted is called the ________ directory.
2. A ________ is a directory that you make on a disk.
3. Use the ________ command to make a subdirectory.
4. The ________ character is used to represent the root directory.
5. Use the ________ command to delete a subdirectory.
6. Use the ________ command to move files from one subdirectory to another.
7. The ________ command enables you to change from one subdirectory to another.
8. Use the ________ command to display the number of directories on a disk.

SHORT ANSWER ASSIGNMENT 4

Using DOS Commands

Instructions: Explain how to accomplish each of the following tasks using DOS.

Problem 1: Copy all of the files from the root directory on the disk in drive A to the root directory of the disk in drive A.

Explanation: ____

____

____

Problem 2: Make a subdirectory named SUB1 on your disk in drive A.

Explanation: ____

____

____

Problem 3: Transfer all files from the SUB1 subdirectory to the SUB2 subdirectory.

Explanation: ____

____

____

Problem 4: Erase the files in subdirectory SUB1 and remove subdirectory SUB1.

Explanation: ____

____

____

SHORT ANSWER ASSIGNMENT 5

Understanding DOS Commands

Instructions: Explain what will happen after you perform each of the following DOS commands.

Problem 1: Type `copy g*.* c:` at the A:\> prompt and press the ENTER key.

Explanation: ____

____

____

Problem 2: Type `erase d?s.*` at the C:\> prompt and press the ENTER key.

Explanation: ____

____

____

Problem 3: Type `diskcopy a: a:` at the A:\> prompt and press the ENTER key.

Explanation: ____

____

____

Problem 4: Type `dir \dos` at the C:\> prompt and press the ENTER key.

Explanation: ____

____

____

SHORT ANSWER ASSIGNMENT 6

Recovering from Problems

Instructions: In each of the following situations, a problem occurred. Explain the cause of the problem and how it can be corrected.

Problem 1: You type cd .. and press the ENTER key. DOS responds with the message Invalid directory.

Cause of problem: ______________________________

____

Method of correction: ______________________________

____

Problem 2: The current drive is A, and the current directory is DIRA. You attempt to delete subdirectory DIRA and DOS responds with the message, Invalid path, not directory, or directory not empty.

Cause of problem: ______________________________

____

Method of correction: ______________________________

____

Problem 3: Your computer has a hard disk, and the root directory contains 512 files. Even though you know you have enough room for the file, when you attempt to store another file in the root directory, DOS prevents you from doing it.

Cause of problem: ______________________________

____

Method of correction: ______________________________

____

Problem 4: You want to display a directory one screenful at a time, and type the command `dir p` and press the ENTER key. DOS displays the message, File not found.

Cause of problem: ______________________________

____

Method of correction: ______________________________

____

SHORT ANSWER ASSIGNMENT 7

Directories on a Hard Drive or LAN

Instructions: If you used a hard disk or LAN to complete Project 2, perform the following tasks on the computer you used to complete Project 2.

1. Determine which directories you have on drive C, if you are using a hard disk, or on drive F, if you are using a LAN.
2. Draw a diagram of this directory structure.

HANDS-ON EXERCISES

HANDS-ON EXERCISE 1

Working with Directories

Instructions: At the DOS prompt, perform the following tasks to create the subdirectories specified below. Each printout should be on a separate page and properly labeled.

1. Place a newly formatted disk into drive A and make these subdirectories in the root directory: SPSHEET, WORDPROC, GAMES, HOUSE, and MODEM.
2. Make two subdirectories in the SPSHEET subdirectory: FINANCES and EXPENSES.
3. Make three subdirectories in the WORDPROC subdirectory: WORKMEMO, PERSONAL, and WORDLIST.
4. Use the tree command to print the directory structure.
5. Make the HOUSE subdirectory the current directory.
6. Copy two or more files into the HOUSE subdirectory. You can use the files from either your data diskette or Student Diskette.
7. Copy all the files in the HOUSE subdirectory to the FINANCES subdirectory.
8. Use the tree command to print the directory structure with files.
9. Move the files from the HOUSE subdirectory to the EXPENSES subdirectory.
10. Remove the GAMES subdirectory from your disk.
11. Remove the EXPENSES subdirectory from your disk.
12. Use the tree command to print the directory structure with files.

HANDS-ON EXERCISE 2

Working with Directories

Instructions: At the DOS prompt, perform the following tasks to print the directory listings specified below. Each printout should be on a separate page. Handwrite the task number on the printout.

1. Insert your data diskette into drive A.
2. Print the directory listing for the root directory.
3. Print the directory listing for the WP subdirectory.
4. Print a wide directory listing for the root directory.
5. Print an alphabetical directory listing of all directories on the disk.
6. Print a directory listing of files in the root that begin with the letter s.

7. Print a directory listing of files in the WP subdirectory that have an extension of DOC.
8. Print a directory listing of files in the root directory that have five characters or less in their filename.
9. Print a directory listing of just directory names on the disk.

HANDS-ON EXERCISE 3

Working with Disks

Instructions: At the DOS prompt, perform the following tasks to work with your disks.

1. Make a duplicate copy of your data diskette.
2. Verify that both disks are identical by doing a chkdsk on both disks. Print the output from each chkdsk.
3. Verify that both disks are identical by doing a tree command with files on both disks. Print the output from each tree command.

INDEX

Programming in QuickBASIC

PROJECT 1

An Introduction to Programming in QuickBASIC

In Project 1 we provide an introduction to the principles of program design and computer programming using the QuickBASIC programming language. QuickBASIC was developed for the personal computer (PC) by Microsoft Corporation, one of the largest microcomputer software companies in the world. Today, QuickBASIC is one of the most widely used programming languages on PCs.

Our approach in illustrating QuickBASIC is to present a series of applications that can be processed using a PC. We carefully explain the input data, the output to be produced, and the processing. Through the use of a flowchart, we illustrate the program design and logic. The flowchart is followed by an explanation of the QuickBASIC statements required to implement the logic. We then present the complete QuickBASIC program. The program solution, when entered into the PC and executed, will produce the output from the specified input.

THE PROGRAMMING PROCESS

Computer programs can vary significantly in size and complexity. A simple program may contain only a few statements. A complex program can contain hundreds and even thousands of statements. Regardless of the size of the program, it is extremely important that the task of computer programming be approached in a professional manner, as computer programming is one of the most precise of all activities.

Learning computer programming should not be approached as a trial-and-error-type of activity. By carefully reviewing the sample problems, the program design, and the QuickBASIC code we present within these projects, you should be able to write well-designed programs that produce correct output when executed on a PC.

Computer programming is not *naturally* an error-prone activity. Errors enter into the design and coding of the computer program only through carelessness or lack of understanding of the programming process. With careful study and attention to detail, you can avoid errors. Just as it is the job of the accountant, the mathematician, the engineer, and the scientist to produce correct results, so too it is the job of the computer programmer to produce a program that is reliable, easy to read, and produces accurate results.

The actual programming process involves the activities described in Figure 1-1. When you use this careful approach to program design and coding, you can develop programs that are easy to read, efficient, reliable, and execute properly.

STEP	DESCRIPTION
1	Define the problem to be solved precisely in terms of input, processing, and output.
2	Design a detailed logic plan using flowcharts or some other logic tool.
3	Desk check the logic plan as if you are the computer.
4	Code the program.
5	Desk check the code as if you are the computer.
6	Enter the program into the computer.
7	Test the program until it is error free.
8	Run the program using the input data to generate the output results.

FIGURE 1-1 The program development cycle

SAMPLE PROGRAM 1 — PATIENT LISTING

n this first sample program we generate a patient listing on the screen. The input data consists of the series of patient records shown in Figure 1-2. Each record contains a patient name, a doctor name, and a room number.

PATIENT NAME	DOCTOR NAME	ROOM NUMBER
Tim Krel	Nance	112
Mary Lepo	Gold	102
Tom Pep	King	245
Joe Ruiz	Ward	213
EOF	End	0

FIGURE 1-2 The patient records

The data taken as a group is called a **file**. The data about a single individual is called a **record**. Each unit of data within the record is called a **field**, or **data item**. Thus, the input data consists of a file of patient records. Each record contains a patient name field, a doctor name field, and a room number field.

In the list of records in Figure 1-2, the last record contains the patient name `EOF`, the doctor name `End`, and the room number `0`. This record is called a trailer record, or sentinel record. A **trailer record** is added to the end of the file to indicate when all the valid records have been processed.

The output for this sample program is a listing on the PC screen of each record in the patient file. The output listing is shown in Figure 1-3.

```
          Patient Listing

Room           Patient        Doctor

 112           Tim Krel       Nance
 102           Mary Lepo      Gold
 245           Tom Pep        King
 213           Joe Ruiz       Ward

End of Patient List
```

FIGURE 1-3 The required output for Sample Program 1

The patient list includes the room number, the patient name, and the doctor name for each record. Notice that the sequence of the fields displayed on the screen is different from the sequence of the fields in the input record. Column headings identify each field. After all records have been processed, the message `End of Patient List` displays.

Program Flowchart

The flowchart, QuickBASIC program, and output for Sample Program 1 are shown in Figure 1-4. The flowchart illustrates a simple looping structure. After the headings are displayed, a record is read. This read statement, prior to the loop, is called a **primary read**, or **lead read**.

A. PROGRAM FLOWCHART

Start
Print Headings
Read a Record
End of File?
Yes
Print End of Listing Message
End
No
Print a Line
Read a Record

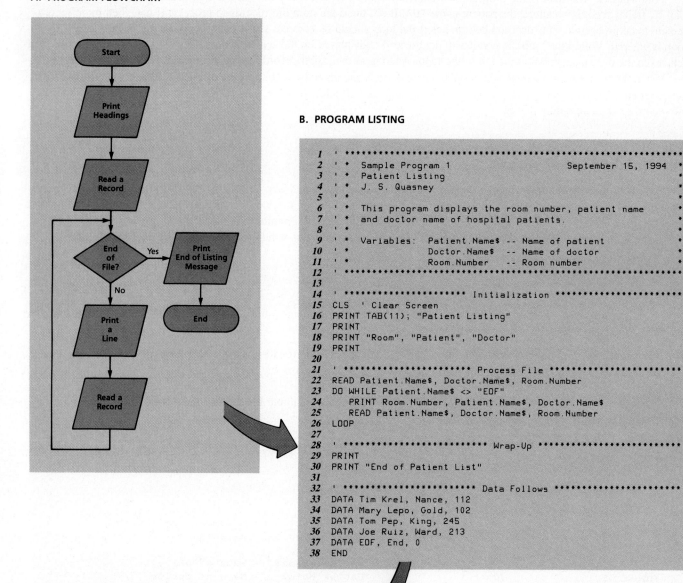

B. PROGRAM LISTING

```
' ****************************************************************
' *  Sample Program 1                            September 15, 1994  *
' *  Patient Listing                                                 *
' *  J. S. Quasney                                                   *
' *                                                                  *
' *  This program displays the room number, patient name             *
' *  and doctor name of hospital patients.                           *
' *                                                                  *
' *  Variables:  Patient.Name$ -- Name of patient                    *
' *              Doctor.Name$  -- Name of doctor                     *
' *              Room.Number   -- Room number                        *
' ****************************************************************

' ********************** Initialization **********************
CLS  ' Clear Screen
PRINT TAB(11); "Patient Listing"
PRINT
PRINT "Room", "Patient", "Doctor"
PRINT

' *********************** Process File ***********************
READ Patient.Name$, Doctor.Name$, Room.Number
DO WHILE Patient.Name$ <> "EOF"
   PRINT Room.Number, Patient.Name$, Doctor.Name$
   READ Patient.Name$, Doctor.Name$, Room.Number
LOOP

' ************************* Wrap-Up *************************
PRINT
PRINT "End of Patient List"

' *********************** Data Follows ***********************
DATA Tim Krel, Nance, 112
DATA Mary Lepo, Gold, 102
DATA Tom Pep, King, 245
DATA Joe Ruiz, Ward, 213
DATA EOF, End, 0
END
```

C. OUTPUT RESULTS

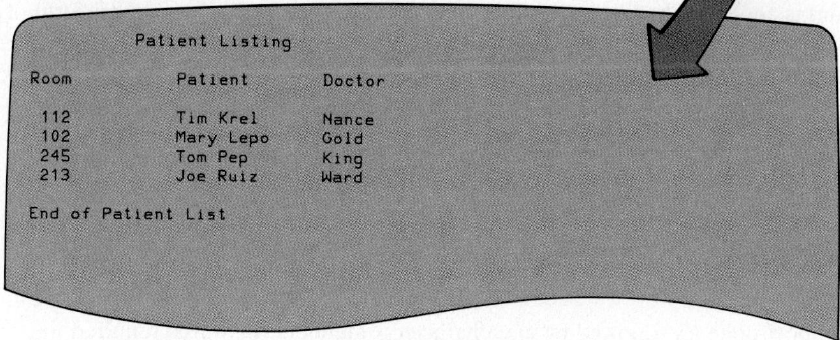

FIGURE 1-4 The program flowchart (A), program listing (B), and output results (C) for Sample Program 1

Following the lead read in the program flowchart in Figure 1-4, a test is performed to determine if the record just read was the trailer record containing the patient name EOF. If so, there are no more records to process. If not, then more records remain to be processed. This decision determines if the loop should be entered. If the end-of-file has not been reached, the loop is entered. Within the loop the previously read record is displayed on the screen and another record is read. Control then returns to the decision symbol at the top of the loop. As long as the trailer record has not been read, the looping continues.

When the trailer record is read, the looping process stops and an end-of-job message displays followed by termination of the program. This basic logic is appropriate for all applications which involve reading records and displaying the fields from the record read on an output device.

The QuickBASIC Program

Programs should be well documented, easy to read, easy to understand, and easy to modify and maintain. For these reasons, programming standards have been developed to guide the beginning programmer in the task of writing programs. We illustrate and explain these standards in all sample programs we present in these programming projects.

A program written using QuickBASIC consists of a series of statements which serve one of three functions:

1. Document the program
2. Cause processing to occur
3. Define data

A quality program is well documented. This means the program contains information which helps a reader understand the program. Documentation within the program should include the following:

- A prologue, including the program name, program title, an author identification, the date the program was written, a brief description of the program, and a description of the variable names used in the program. The first 12 lines of Sample Program 1 (Figure 1-5) contain the prologue.
- Remark lines should come before any major module in a program. In Sample Program 1, lines 14, 21, 28, and 32 are remark lines that precede major modules.

```
1  ' ****************************************************************
2  ' *  Sample Program 1                          September 15, 1994  *
3  ' *  Patient Listing                                               *
4  ' *  J. S. Quasney                                                 *
5  ' *                                                                *
6  ' *  This program displays the room number, patient name,          *
7  ' *  and doctor name of hospital patients.                         *
8  ' *                                                                *
9  ' *  Variables:  Patient.Name$ -- Name of patient                  *
10 ' *              Doctor.Name$  -- Name of doctor                   *
11 ' *              Room.Number   -- Room number                      *
12 ' ****************************************************************
```

FIGURE 1-5
The prologue for Sample Program 1

Documentation within a QuickBASIC program is accomplished through the use of the REM statement. The general form of the REM statement is shown in Figure 1-6.

```
REM comment

  or

' comment
```

FIGURE 1-6
The general form of the REM statement

The remark statement begins with REM or an apostrophe (') followed by any characters, numbers, or words required to document the program. Notice that in these programming projects, we use the apostrophe (') rather than the keyword REM to initiate a remark line. Asterisks (*) are used in the remark lines to highlight the documentation.

Blank lines, such as lines 13, 20, 27, and 31 of Sample Program 1 (Figure 1-4), are used to end any major module. For example, the Initialization module (Figure 1-7) begins with a remark line and ends with a blank line. The proper use of remark lines, blank lines, and indentations can substantially improve the readability of a program. We suggest that you follow the format illustrated in Sample Program 1 when coding all QuickBASIC programs.

The apostrophe (') can also be used to include in-line remarks as shown following the `CLS` statement in line 15 of Figure 1-7. All characters that follows the apostrophe in an in-line remark are considered to be part of the documentation.

Remember that remark lines and blank lines can be added before or after any line in a program. In addition, they are strictly for human comprehension and have no effect on the outcome of the program.

```
14  ' ********************** Initialization **********************
15  CLS    ' Clear Screen
16  PRINT TAB(11); "Patient Listing"
17  PRINT
18  PRINT "Room", "Patient", "Doctor"
19  PRINT
20
```

FIGURE 1-7
The Initialization module of Sample Program 1

THE DATA STATEMENT

Sample Program 1 employs `DATA` statements to define the data. The `DATA` statements for Sample Program 1 are shown in Figure 1-8.

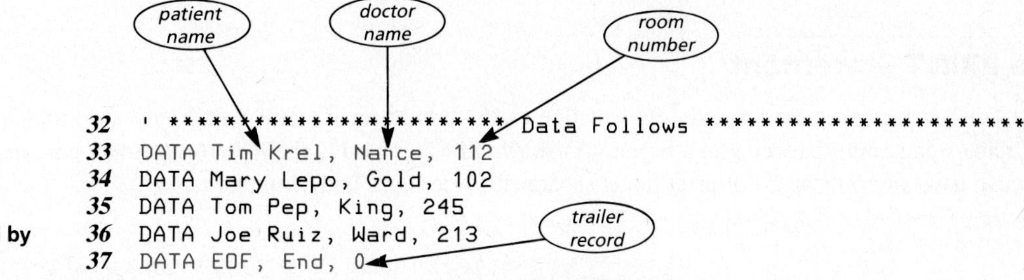


```
32  ' ********************** Data Follows **********************
33  DATA Tim Krel, Nance, 112
34  DATA Mary Lepo, Gold, 102
35  DATA Tom Pep, King, 245
36  DATA Joe Ruiz, Ward, 213
37  DATA EOF, End, 0
```

FIGURE 1-8
The data to be processed by Sample Program 1

In Figure 1-8, line 33 defines the first patient record. Line 34 defines the second patient record, and so on. `DATA` statements begin with the keyword `DATA` followed by a space and the data. The `DATA` statement in line 33 contains the patient name (Tim Krel), the doctor name (Nance), and the room number (112). As shown in Figure 1-8, each of the data items must be separated by a comma.

The last `DATA` statement is the trailer record, when a trailer record is used in this manner, you must include an entry for each field. In line 37, the phrase `EOF` is included for the patient name, the word `End` is included in place of the doctor name, and the numeric value `0` is included for the room number. These values, of course, will not be included in the listing generated by the program.

The general form of the `DATA` statement is shown in Figure 1-9.

`DATA` data item, data item, ..., data item
where each data item is a numeric or string value

FIGURE 1-9
The general form of the DATA statement

THE CLS, PRINT, AND END STATEMENTS

Up to this point, we have talked about REM and DATA statements. Both of these statements are classified as nonexecutable. Neither type of statement has anything to do with the logic shown in the flowchart in Figure 1-4. For example, the DATA statements can be moved from the bottom of the program to the top of the program with no effect on the logic of the program.

In this section we discuss the CLS, PRINT, and END statements.

The CLS Statement

The first executable statement in Sample Program 1 is the CLS statement in line 15 (Figure 1-10). The function of this statement is to clear the output screen and move the cursor to the upper left corner. The **output screen** is the one that shows the results due to the execution of a program.

```
14  ' ********************** Initialization **********************
15  CLS   ' Clear Screen
16  PRINT TAB(11); "Patient Listing"
17  PRINT
18  PRINT "Room", "Patient", "Doctor"
19  PRINT
20
```

FIGURE 1-10
The Initialization module of Sample Program 1

The PRINT Statement

The PRINT statement is used to write information on the output screen. It is commonly used to display headings and the values of variables and control spacing in a report. As shown in Figure 1-11, the PRINT statement consists of the keyword PRINT. It may also have an optional list of print items separated by commas and semicolons.

FIGURE 1-11
The general form of the PRINT statement

> PRINT list
>
> where **list** is the items to display separated by semicolons or commas

The list in a PRINT statement includes print items. The **print items** can be any of the following:

- Variables, such as Doctor.Name$, Patient.Name$, and Room.Number
- Constants, such as numeric and string values—string values must be enclosed in quotation marks (")
- Function references, such as the TAB function—the TAB function allows you to move the cursor to the right to a specified column position

Lines 16 through 19 of Sample Program 1 (Figure 1-10) display the report title and column headings. Line 16 displays the report title on line 1. The first print item in line 16 is the TAB function. It causes the cursor to move to column 11. The semicolon following the TAB function instructs the PC to display the next print item (Patient Listing) at the current cursor location (column 11). Hence, the report title Patient Listing displays beginning in column 11 on line 1. After line 16 is executed, the cursor moves down one line on the output screen to line 2.

The PRINT statement in line 17 contains no print items. A PRINT statement with no print items causes the PC to skip a line. Thus, line 2 on the output screen is left blank.

Line 18 displays the three column headings. Each column heading is surrounded by the required quotation marks. Notice that the column headings also are separated by commas. When the print items are separated by commas, the fields are displayed in predefined columns called print zones. There are five print zones per line. Each **print zone** has 14 positions for a total of 70 positions per line as shown in Figure 1-12.

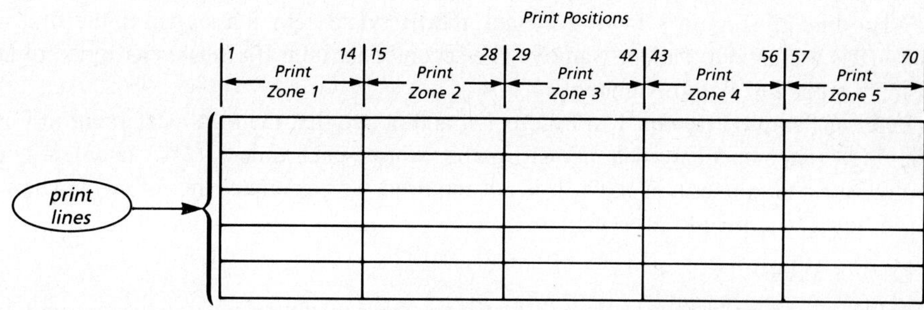

FIGURE 1-12
There are five print zones of 14 positions each for a total of 70 positions

When line 18 in Sample Program 1 executes, `Room` displays beginning in column 1, `Patient` displays beginning in column 15, and `Doctor` displays beginning in column 29. Like line 17, line 19 causes the PC to skip a line on the output screen.

The END Statement

The last line in Sample Program 1 is the `END` statement. When executed, the `END` statement instructs the PC to stop executing the program. Although the `END` statement is not required, it is recommended that you always include one.

VARIABLES

In programming, a **variable** is a location in main memory whose value can change as the program executes. There are two major categories of variables—numeric and string. A **numeric variable** can only be assigned a numeric value. A **string variable** may be assigned a string of characters such as a word, name, phrase, or sentence.

A **variable name** is used to define and reference a variable in main memory. Variable names must conform to certain rules. In QuickBASIC, a variable name begins with a letter and may be followed by up to 39 letters, digits, and decimal points. You may not use a QuickBASIC keyword, such as `CLS` or `PRINT`, as a variable name. For a complete list of the QuickBASIC keywords, refer to the last page of the reference card at the back of this book.

String variable names always end with a dollar sign ($). Numeric variable names never end with a dollar sign. For example, in Sample Program 1, Room.Number is a numeric variable and Patient.Name$ and Doctor.Name$ are string variables.

With respect to the variable names used in Sample Program 1, notice how we use the decimal point (.) to better describe what the variables will hold during the execution of the program.

THE READ STATEMENT

To assign the data in the `DATA` statements to variables, we use the `READ` statement. As shown in Figure 1-13, the `READ` statement consists of the keyword `READ` followed by one or more variable names separated from each other by commas. The variable names must be specified in the `READ` statement in the order in which the data is recorded in the `DATA` statements.

FIGURE 1-13
The general form of the READ statement

`READ` variable$_1$, variable$_2$, ..., variable$_n$

where each variable is a numeric variable or string variable

When line 22 (Figure 1-14) is executed, the first data item is assigned to the first variable in the `READ` statement. Thus, `Tim Krel` is assigned to Patient.Name$. The second data item (`Nance`) is assigned to Doctor.Name$ and the third data item (`112`) is assigned to Room.Number.

Refer to Sample Program 1 in Figure 1-4 and notice that the `READ` statement in line 22 has the same number of variables as the `DATA` statements have data items. In other words, each time a `READ` statement is executed, one `DATA` statement is used. Although we recommend this style, it is not required. For example, the following shows that it is valid to write the `READ` statement in line 22 as three `READ` statements:

```
READ Patient.Name$
READ Doctor.Name$
READ Room.Number
DATA Tim Krel, Nance, 112
```

We could have also placed one data item per `DATA` statement as follows:

```
READ Patient.Name$, Doctor.Name$, Room.Number
DATA Tim Krel
DATA Nance
DATA 112
```

THE DO WHILE AND LOOP STATEMENTS

Following the first `READ` statement in line 22, lines 23 through 26 establish a **Do loop** (Figure 1-14). The `DO WHILE` statement in line 23 and the `LOOP` statement in line 26 cause the range of statements between them to be executed repeatedly as long as Patient.Name$ does not equal the string value `EOF`. The expression `Patient.Name$ <> "EOF"` following `DO WHILE` in line 23 is called a **condition**. A condition can be true or false. In the case of the `DO WHILE`, the statements within the loop are executed while the condition is true.

```
21  ' ************************ Process File ************************
22  READ Patient.Name$, Doctor.Name$, Room.Number
23  DO WHILE Patient.Name$ <> "EOF"
24     PRINT Room.Number, Patient.Name$, Doctor.Name$
25     READ Patient.Name$, Doctor.Name$, Room.Number
26  LOOP
27
28  ' ************************* Wrap-Up ***************************
29  PRINT
30  PRINT "End of Patient List"
31
```

FIGURE 1-14
The Process File and Wrap-Up modules of Sample Program 1

When Patient.Name$ does equal `EOF`, the condition in line 23 is false. Therefore, the PC skips the statements within the loop and continues execution at the first executable statement following the corresponding `LOOP` statement. The first executable statement following the `LOOP` statement is the `PRINT` statement in line 29.

One execution of a Do loop is called a **pass**. The statements within the loop, lines 24 and 25, are indented by three spaces for the purpose of readability. Collectively, lines 24 and 25 are called the **range** of statements in the Do loop.

Following execution of the lead read in line 22, Patient.Name$ is equal to `Tim Krel`. Hence, control passes into the Do loop and the first patient record is displayed due to the `PRINT` statement in line 24. Next, the `READ` statement in line 25 assigns the variables Patient.Name$, Doctor.Name$, and Room.Number the data items found in the second `DATA` statement. The `LOOP` statement in line 26 automatically returns control to the `DO WHILE` statement in line 23. This process continues while Patient.Name$ does not equal `EOF`.

The general forms of the `DO WHILE` and `LOOP` statements are shown in Figure 1-15.

```
DO WHILE condition
    [range of statements]
LOOP
```

FIGURE 1-15
The general forms of the DO WHILE and LOOP statements

Testing for the End-of-File

Lines 33 through 36 in Sample Program 1 (Figure 1-4) contain data for only four patients. The fifth patient in line 37 is the **trailer record**. It represents the end-of-file and is used to determine when all the valid data has been processed. To incorporate an end-of-file test, a variable must be selected and a trailer record added to the data. We selected the patient name as the test for end-of-file and the data value EOF. Since it guards against reading past end-of-file, the trailer record is also called the **sentinel record**. The value EOF is called the **sentinel value**. The value EOF is clearly distinguishable from all the rest of the data assigned to Patient.Name$. This sentinel value is the same as the string constant found in the condition in line 23.

After the READ statement in line 25 assigns Patient.Name$ the value EOF, the LOOP statement returns control to the DO WHILE statement. Since Patient.Name$ is equal to the value EOF, the DO WHILE statement causes the PC to pass control to line 29 which follows the corresponding LOOP statement. Line 29 skips a line and line 30 displays an end-of-job message. Lines 29 and 30 are referred to as an **end-of-file routine**.

Three other worthy points to consider about establishing a test for end-of-file in a Do loop are:

1. It is important that the trailer record contain enough values for all the variables in the READ statement. In Sample Program 1, if we only added the sentinel value EOF to line 37, there would not be enough data to fulfill the requirements of the three variables in the READ statement. We arbitrarily assigned End and 0 to the second and third variables in the READ statement.
2. The Do loop requires the use of two READ statements. The first READ statement (line 22) reads the first patient record before the PC enters the Do loop. The second READ statement, found at the bottom of the Do loop (line 25), causes the PC to read the next data record. This READ statement reads the remaining data records, one at a time, until there are no more data records left. If the first record contains the patient name EOF, the DO WHILE statement will immediately transfer control to the statement below the corresponding LOOP statement.
3. Sample Program 1 can process any number of patients by placing each in a DATA statement prior to the trailer record.

Conditions

The DO WHILE statement in line 23 (Figure 1-14) contains the condition

```
Patient.Name$ <> "EOF"
```

The condition is made up of two expressions and a **relational operator**. The condition specifies a relationship between expressions that is either true or false. If the condition is true, execution continues with the line following the DO WHILE statement. If the condition is false, then control is transferred to the line following the corresponding LOOP statement.

The PC makes a comparison between the two operators based on the relational operator. Figure 1-16 lists the six valid relational operators.

RELATION	MATH SYMBOL	QuickBASIC SYMBOL	EXAMPLE
Equal To	$=$	=	Educ$ = "12"
Less Than	$<$	<	Total < 25
Greater Than	$>$	>	Disc > .15
Less Than Or Equal To	$\leq$	<= or =<	Deduc < = 10
Greater Than Or Equal To	$\geq$	>= or =>	Code$ > = "A"
Not Equal To	$\neq$	<> or ><	State$ < > "TX"

FIGURE 1-16
Relational operators used in conditions

There are several important points to watch for in the application of conditions. For example, it is invalid to compare a numeric variable to a string value as in the following:

```
DO WHILE Cents > "10"
```

this condition Cents > "10" is invalid

Furthermore, the condition should ensure termination of the loop. For example, look at the following logical error:

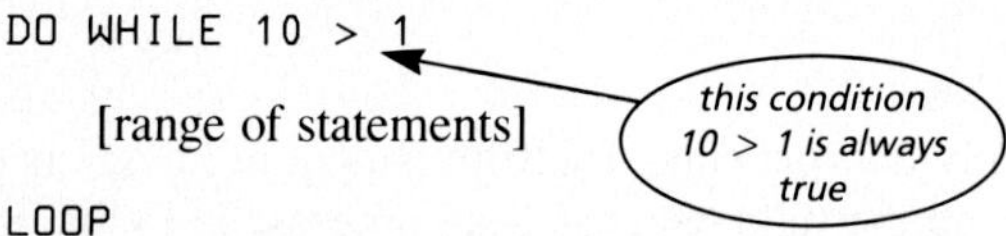

```
DO WHILE 10 > 1
     [range of statements]
LOOP
```

this condition 10 > 1 is always true

If such an error is not detected, a never-ending loop develops. There is no way to stop the endless program execution except by manual intervention, such as pressing **Ctrl + Break** on your PC keyboard. (The plus sign between two keys means hold down the first key and press the second key, and then release both keys.)

The complete QuickBASIC program and the output results are again illustrated in Figures 1-17 and 1-18.

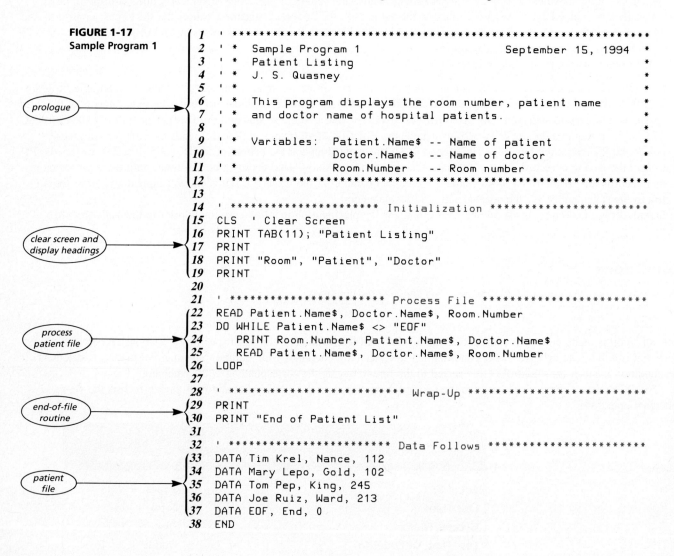

FIGURE 1-17
Sample Program 1

```
' ***********************************************************************
' *   Sample Program 1                                September 15, 1994  *
' *   Patient Listing                                                     *
' *   J. S. Quasney                                                       *
' *                                                                       *
' *   This program displays the room number, patient name                 *
' *   and doctor name of hospital patients.                               *
' *                                                                       *
' *   Variables:  Patient.Name$ -- Name of patient                        *
' *               Doctor.Name$  -- Name of doctor                         *
' *               Room.Number   -- Room number                            *
' ***********************************************************************

' ********************** Initialization **********************
CLS   ' Clear Screen
PRINT TAB(11); "Patient Listing"
PRINT
PRINT "Room", "Patient", "Doctor"
PRINT

' ********************** Process File ************************
READ Patient.Name$, Doctor.Name$, Room.Number
DO WHILE Patient.Name$ <> "EOF"
   PRINT Room.Number, Patient.Name$, Doctor.Name$
   READ Patient.Name$, Doctor.Name$, Room.Number
LOOP

' ************************ Wrap-Up ***************************
PRINT
PRINT "End of Patient List"

' ********************** Data Follows ************************
DATA Tim Krel, Nance, 112
DATA Mary Lepo, Gold, 102
DATA Tom Pep, King, 245
DATA Joe Ruiz, Ward, 213
DATA EOF, End, 0
END
```

prologue
clear screen and display headings
process patient file
end-of-file routine
patient file

FIGURE 1-18
The output results due to the execution of Sample Program 1

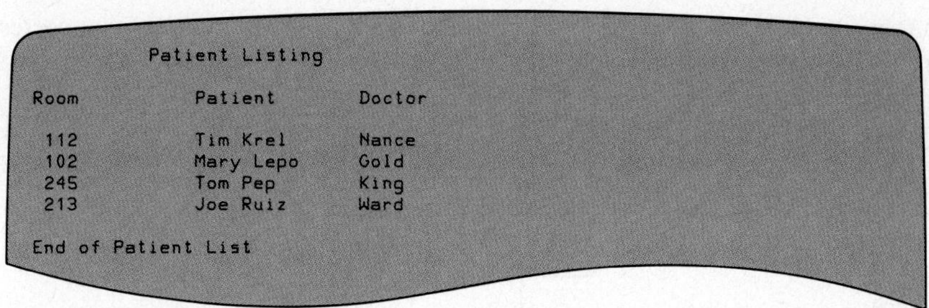

Patient Listing
Room Patient Doctor
112 Tim Krel Nance
102 Mary Lepo Gold
245 Tom Pep King
213 Joe Ruiz Ward
End of Patient List

TRY IT YOURSELF EXERCISES

1. Which of the following are valid numeric variables in QuickBASIC?
   a. X$
   b. Account
   c. 8T
   d. Inventory.No

2. Write a `CLS` statement and a series of `PRINT` statements that display the value `LINE 1` beginning in column 1 of line 1, `LINE 3` in column 1 of line 3, and `LINE 5` in column 1 of line 5.
3. Write a `PRINT` statement that displays the string values `Name, Account, Balance, Date` in print zones 1 through 4 of the current line.
4. Use the `TAB` function in a `PRINT` statement to display the string value `The answer is` beginning in column 42 of the current line.
5. Given the following `DATA` statement:

   ```
   DATA 16723, 12, 56
   ```

   Use the variables Inventory.Number, On.Order, and On.Hand to write a `READ` statement that assigns Inventory.Number the value `16723`, On.Order the value `12`, and On.Hand the value `56`.
6. State the purpose of the `LOOP` statement.
7. List and describe the six relational operators.
8. Which of the following are invalid `DO WHILE` statements? Why?
   a. DO WHILE X = 10
   b. DOWHILE Acct$ <> "End"
   c. DO WHILE 5 < Tax
   d. DO WHILE On.Hand LT 25
   e. DO WHILE Volts Equals 37

9. Determine whether the conditions below are true or false, given the following: Hours = 6, Tonnage = 12.5, and Bonus = 1.75
   a. Hours >= 10
   b. Tonnage >= 12
   c. Bonus <> 2
   d. Hours <> 6
   e. Tonnage < 12.5
   f. Bonus = 1.75

10. Write the QuickBASIC code for the Process File and Wrap-Up modules that correspond to the following program flowchart. Use the variable names specified in the Read and Print symbols. Do not include any `DATA` statements. Start each module with a remark line and end each module with a blank line. For the end-of-file test, assume the trailer record includes the following data items: `EOF, 0, 0`.

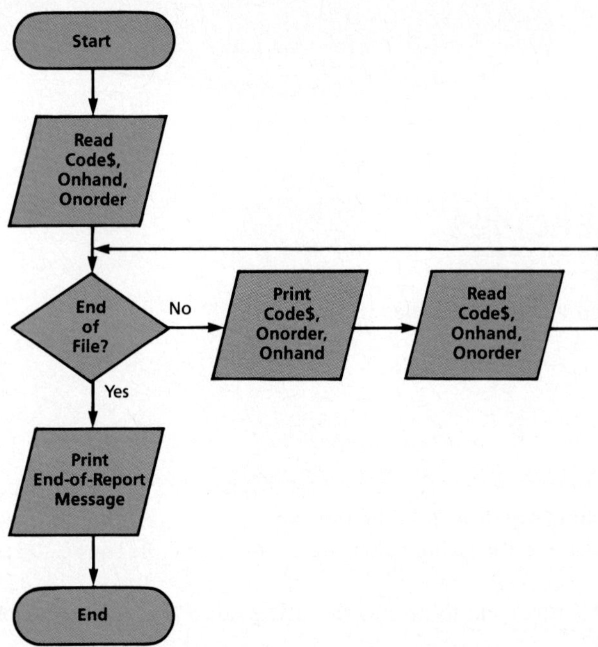

THE QB OPERATING ENVIRONMENT

To enter a program such as Sample Program 1 into the PC and execute it, you must familiarize yourself with the QB operating environment.

Starting a Session

Boot the PC using the steps outlined by your instructor, or those found in the PC's Operations manual. Once the PC is operational, do the following:

1. Place the QuickBASIC program disk in the default drive and your data disk in the other drive.
2. At the DOS prompt, enter `QBI` if you are using the textbook version of QuickBASIC or `QB` if you are using the commercial version of QuickBASIC.

Several seconds will elapse while the QuickBASIC program is loaded from the disk into main memory. The red light on the disk drive turns on during this loading process. After the QuickBASIC program is loaded into main storage, it is automatically executed.

The first screen displayed by QuickBASIC includes a Welcome message in the middle of the screen. In the Welcome message, QuickBASIC directs you to press the **Esc key** to begin entering a program or press the **Enter key** to obtain help from the QB Advisor. The **QB Advisor** is an on-line help system that answers your questions about QuickBASIC as fast as you can click the mouse or press the **F1 key**. The QB Advisor is discussed in more detail later in this section.

The QB Screen

There are four parts to the QB screen—the view window, menu bar, immediate window, and the status line. These are shown in Figure 1-19.

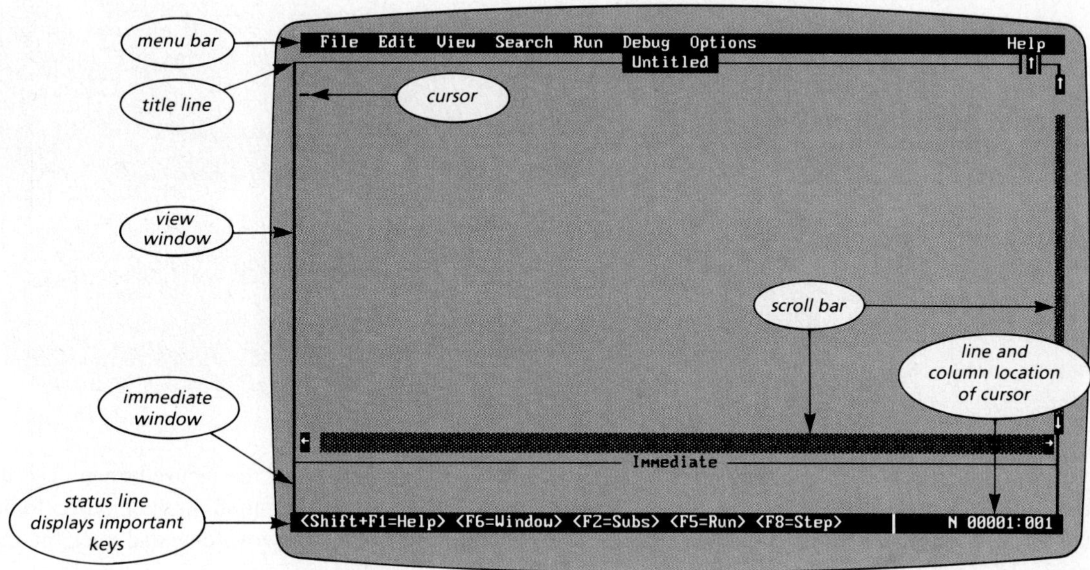

FIGURE 1-19 The QB (QuickBASIC) screen

View Window The **view window** is the largest part of the screen and the one that contains the cursor (Figure 1-19). In the view window you can enter, modify, and display programs. When the QuickBASIC program first executes, the view window is active. That is, if you start typing characters, they will appear on the first line of the view window. At the top of the view window is the title line. The **title line** displays the name of the current program. The program title is highlighted when the view window is active. The program is called "Untitled" until it is given a name. Program names will be discussed shortly.

Along the bottom and the right side of the view window are the **scroll bars**. If you have a mouse, you can move the pointer along the scroll bars and move the window in any direction to see code that does not appear in the view window.

Menu Bar The **menu bar**, the line at the very top of the QB screen (Figure 1-19), displays a list of menu names. Each menu name has a corresponding menu of commands. These commands are useful when entering and modifying programs.

To activate the menu bar, press the **Alt key**. Next, type the first letter of the name of the menu you want to open. You can also select a menu by using the **Right Arrow key** or the **Left Arrow key** to highlight the menu name. With the menu name highlighted, press the **Enter key**. QuickBASIC immediately displays a *pull-down menu* that lists a series of commands. Figure 1-20 shows the **File menu**, which is superimposed over the display of Sample Program 1. To deactivate the menu bar or any menu and activate the view window, press the **Esc key**.

FIGURE 1-20
The File menu

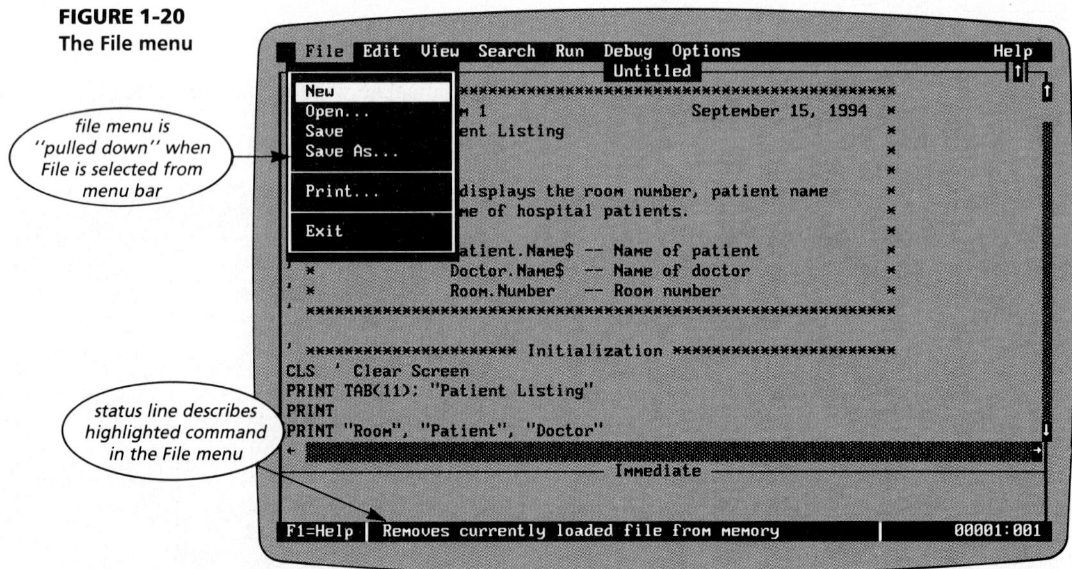

If your PC has a mouse, move the mouse pointer to the desired menu name and click the mouse button. The **mouse pointer** is a character-size, rectangular box on the screen. The **mouse button** is the left button on the mouse. To deactivate the menu bar and reactivate the view window, move the mouse pointer to any part of the view window and click the mouse button.

Immediate Window The narrow window below the view window is called the **immediate window**. The immediate window is used to execute statements as soon as they are entered. Statements entered in the immediate window are not part of the current program.

At any time, you can activate the immediate window by pressing the function key **F6**. This moves the cursor from the view window to the immediate window. QuickBASIC highlights the word Immediate. The function key **F6** is like a **toggle switch**. Press it once, and the cursor moves from the view window to the immediate window. Press it again, and the cursor moves back to the view window. You may use the immediate window as a calculator and debugging tool. For more information on the use of the immediate window, refer to the section titled Debugging Techniques in the Appendix.

If you have a mouse, move the pointer to the inactive window and click the mouse button.

Status Line The line at the very bottom of the QB screen (Figure 1-19) is the **status line**. This line contains a list of the most often used function keys and the line and column location of the cursor on the screen. Keyboard indicators, such as C for Caps Lock and N for Num Lock, display immediately to the left of the cursor line and column location counter when these keys are engaged.

If the menu bar is active and one of the menus is selected, then the status line displays the function of the highlighted command in the menu (Figure 1-20).

Dialog Boxes

QuickBASIC uses **dialog boxes** to display messages and request information from you. For example, if you use a keyword for a variable name, such as PRINT LET instead of PRINT BET, QuickBASIC displays a dialog box when you move the cursor off the line containing the invalid variable name LET. You move the cursor off the line by pressing the **Enter key** or the **Up Arrow key** or **Down Arrow key**.

The dialog box shown in Figure 1-21 displays if you attempt to end the QuickBASIC session and return control to DOS without saving the latest changes made to the current program. Dialog boxes list acceptable user responses in buttons and text boxes. **Buttons** are labeled to indicate what they represent. **Text boxes** are used to enter information such as a file name.

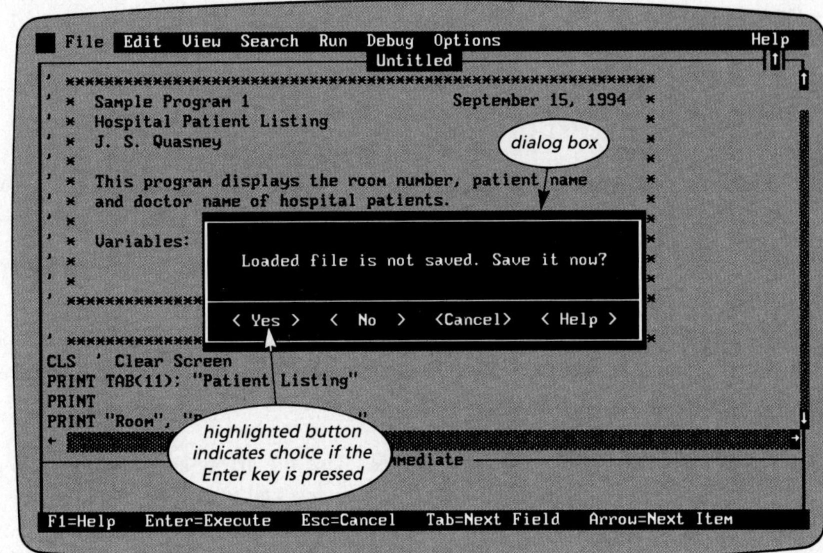

FIGURE 1-21
QuickBASIC displays a dialog box in the middle of the view window when it requires a response from the user before it can continue

In response to the message in the dialog box in Figure 1-21, you can use the **Tab key** or mouse pointer to select one of four buttons—Yes, No, Cancel, or Help. When you press the **Enter key**, the highlighted button, the one with the cursor, is selected. If your PC has a mouse, move the mouse pointer to the desired button or text box and click the mouse button.

Cursor Movement Keys

Several keys on the keyboard are used to move the cursor on the screen. These keys are called the **cursor movement keys**. The arrow keys are used to move the cursor in the windows, menu bar, or menu, one position at a time. Other keys such as the **Home key** and **End key** are used to move the cursor more than one position at a time. The cursor movement keys are summarized on the last page of the reference card at the back of this book.

Function Keys

IBM-type keyboards include a set of ten or twelve **function keys**, which are located to the far left side of the keyboard or along the top of the typewriter keys. The function keys are labeled **F1** through **F10** or **F12**. Pressing these keys instructs QuickBASIC to carry out various tasks. For example, if you press function key **F1** with the cursor in a keyword, QuickBASIC displays a help screen. If you press **Shift + F5**, QuickBASIC executes the current program in the view window. For a complete list of the function keys, refer to the last page of the reference card at the back of this book.

Terminating a QuickBASIC Session

To terminate your QuickBASIC session, press the **Alt key** to activate the menu bar. With the cursor on the word **File**, type the letter **F** or press the **Enter key** to display the **File menu** (Figure 1-20). Next, type the letter **X** for **Exit** or use the arrow keys to move the cursor to the word `Exit` and press the **Enter key**. Thus, the sequence of keystrokes **Alt**, **F**, **X** instructs the PC to return control to DOS. To quit QuickBASIC using a mouse, click on **File** in the menu bar and click on **Exit** in the **File menu**. The term *click on* means move the mouse pointer to the specified word and click the mouse button.

If you did not save the latest version of the current program, then the dialog box shown earlier in Figure 1-21 appears. QuickBASIC requests that you select one of the buttons before continuing. An alternative to selecting a button is to press the **Esc key**, which cancels the command and returns control to the view window.

When the DOS prompt appears, remove your diskettes from the disk drives. Turn the PC's power switch to Off. Turn the monitor power switch to Off. Finally, if you are using a printer, turn the power switch to Off.

Editing QuickBASIC Programs

QuickBASIC programs are entered one line at a time into the view window. The **Enter key** signals QuickBASIC that a line is complete. During the process of entering a program, you will quickly learn that it is easy to make keyboard errors and grammatical errors because of your inexperience with the QuickBASIC language and your unfamiliarity with the keyboard. Logical errors can also occur in a program if you have not considered all the details associated with the problem.

You can eliminate some of the errors if you carefully review your design and program before you enter it into the view window. Any remaining errors are resolved by editing the program. **Editing** is the process of entering and altering a program.

This section describes the most common types of editing. You will find the editing features of QuickBASIC to be both powerful and easy to use.

Deleting Previously Typed Characters Use the arrow keys or mouse to position the cursor. Press the **Delete key** to delete the character under the cursor and the **Backspace key** to delete the character to the left of the cursor. To delete a series of adjacent characters in a line, position the cursor on the leftmost character to be deleted. Hold down one of the **Shift keys** and press the **Right Arrow key** until the characters to delete are highlighted. Press the **Delete key**.

If you have a mouse, select the adjacent characters to delete by moving the pointer from the first character to the last while holding down the mouse button.

Changing or Replacing Previously Typed Lines Move the cursor to the character position where you want to make a change. Begin typing the new characters. QuickBASIC is by default in the insert mode. In the **insert mode**, the cursor is a blinking underline, and the character under the cursor and those to the right are *pushed* to the right as you enter new characters in the line. In the **overtype mode**, the cursor is a blinking box, and the character under the cursor is replaced by the one you type. Use the **Insert key** to toggle between the insert and overtype modes. As you enter new characters in this mode, they replace the old characters.

Adding New Lines Press the **Enter key** to add a new or blank line. To add a new line above the current line, move the cursor to the first character and press the **Enter key**. To add a new line below the current line, move the cursor immediately to the right of the last character and press the **Enter key**.

You should only press the **Enter key** with the cursor at the beginning or end of a line. If you press the **Enter key** in the middle of a line, it is split. To join the split lines, press the **Backspace key** with the cursor on the first character of the second line.

Deleting A Series of Lines Position the cursor at the beginning or end of the series of lines to delete. Hold down one of the **Shift keys** and press the **Up Arrow key** or **Down Arrow key** to highlight the series of lines. Press the **Delete key**.

If you have a mouse, highlight the lines to be deleted by holding down the mouse button and moving the pointer from the first character to the last in the series of lines. With the lines highlighted, press the **Delete key**.

Moving Text Moving text from one location to another in a program is called **cut and paste**. To cut and paste text, follow these steps:

1. Use the arrow keys or mouse to move to the beginning of the text you want.
2. Hold down one of the **Shift keys** and use the arrow keys to select the text. If you are using a mouse, click the mouse button and move the pointer to select the text.
3. Hold down one of the **Shift keys** and press the **Delete key** to *cut* the text. The deleted text is placed in the clipboard. The **clipboard** is a temporary storage area that contains the last text deleted through the use of the **Shift key** and **Delete key**.
4. Move the cursor to the new location using the arrow keys or the mouse. Hold down one of the **Shift keys** and press the **Insert key** to *paste* the text.

Copying Lines Copying text from one location to another in a program is called **pasting**. To paste text, follow these steps:

1. Use the arrow keys or mouse to move the cursor to the beginning of the text you want to paste.
2. Hold down one of the **Shift keys** and use the arrow keys to select the text. If you are using a mouse, hold down the mouse button and move the pointer to select the text.
3. Hold down the **Ctrl key** and press the **Insert key** to copy the text into the clipboard.
4. Move the cursor to the new location using the arrow keys or the mouse. Hold down one of the **Shift keys** and press the **Insert key** to *paste* the text.

You will find a summary of the editing keys on the last page of the reference card at the back of this book.

EXECUTING PROGRAMS AND HARD-COPY OUTPUT

The menu bar at the top of the screen contains eight menu names (Figure 1-19). Each menu name has a menu of commands. As we indicated earlier, to activate the menu bar, press the **Alt key**. Next, open a menu in one of two ways: (1) type the first letter in the menu name; or (2) use the **Left Arrow key** or **Right Arrow key** to move the cursor to the menu name and press the **Enter key**.

If you have a mouse, you can activate the menu bar and pull down a menu by moving the pointer to the menu name and clicking the mouse button.

The two most important menu names are Run and File. The **Run menu** is primarily used to execute the current program. The **File menu** contains several important commands. One in particular, the **Print** command, is used to print all or part of the current program.

Executing the Current Program

You execute (run) the current program by selecting the **Start** command in the **Run menu** (Figure 1-22 on the next page). The **Start** command can be selected in any one of the following three ways:

1. Press the **Alt key**, **R** for **Run**, and **S** for **Start**.

   or

2. Press **Shift + F5**.

   or

3. If you have a mouse, click on **Run** in the menu bar and click on **Start** in the Run menu.

If an error message displays within a dialog box when you execute the program, carefully read the message and then press the Enter key or click the OK button in the dialog box. QuickBASIC responds by highlighting the line with the error. Correct the line and execute the program again.

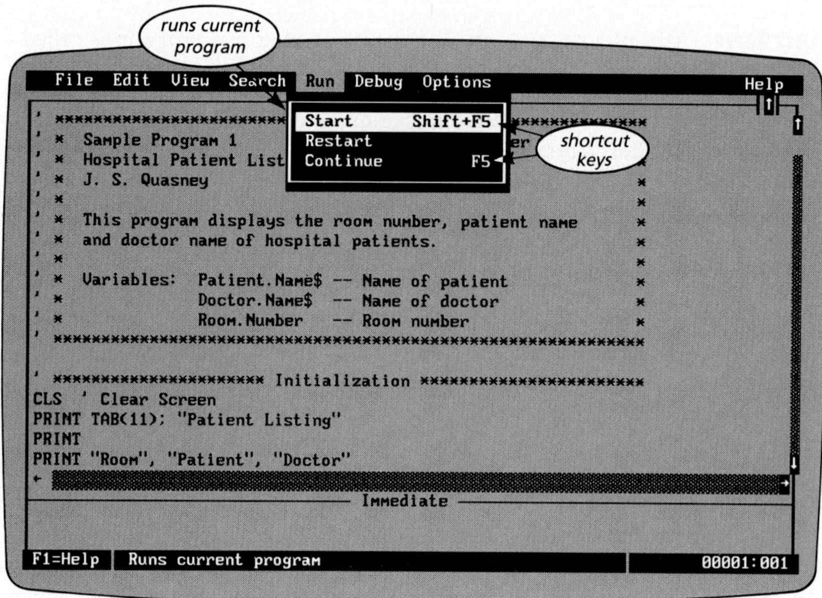

FIGURE 1-22
The Run menu

When the program first executes, QuickBASIC replaces the QB screen with the output screen. As we indicated earlier, the output screen shows the results due to the execution of the current program. Figure 1-23 shows the output screen for Sample Program 1. After you read the output results, you can redisplay the QB screen by pressing any key on the keyboard. This is indicated at the bottom of the output screen. To redisplay the output results, press the function key **F4**.

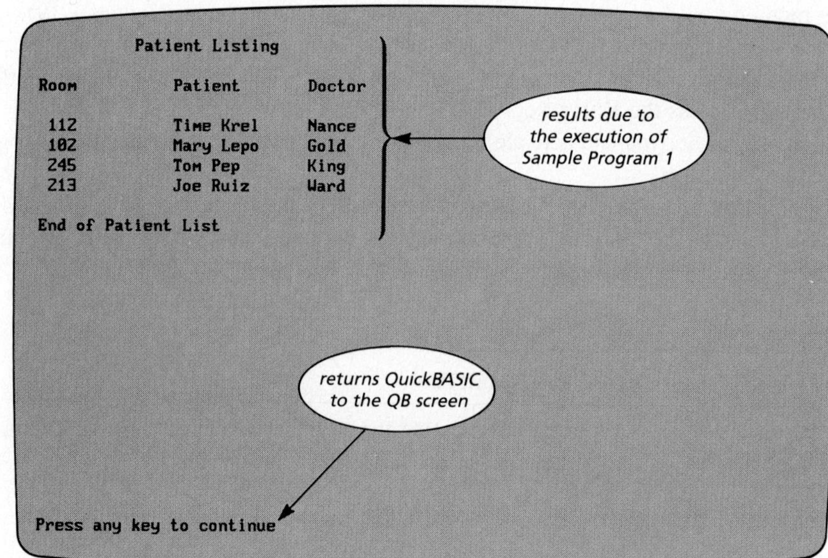

FIGURE 1-23
The output screen

Listing Program Lines to the Printer

Most programmers use a keyboard for input and a monitor (screen) for output. In many instances, it is desirable to list the program and the results on a printer. A listing of this type is called **hard-copy output**.

You can list all or part of the current program to the printer by using the **Print** command in the **File menu**. With the printer in the Ready mode, press the **Alt key** to activate the menu bar and type the letter **F** to pull down the **File menu** (Figure 1-24). Next, type the letter **P** for **Print** to print the current program. The three periods following the **Print** command mean a dialog box will appear requesting additional information. When the Print dialog box appears (Figure 1-25), make sure the bullet is next to the selection Current Module (Entire Program or Document if you are using the textbook version). Finally, press the **Enter key**.

If you have a mouse, click on **File**, click on **Print**, and click on **OK** when the Print dialog box appears.

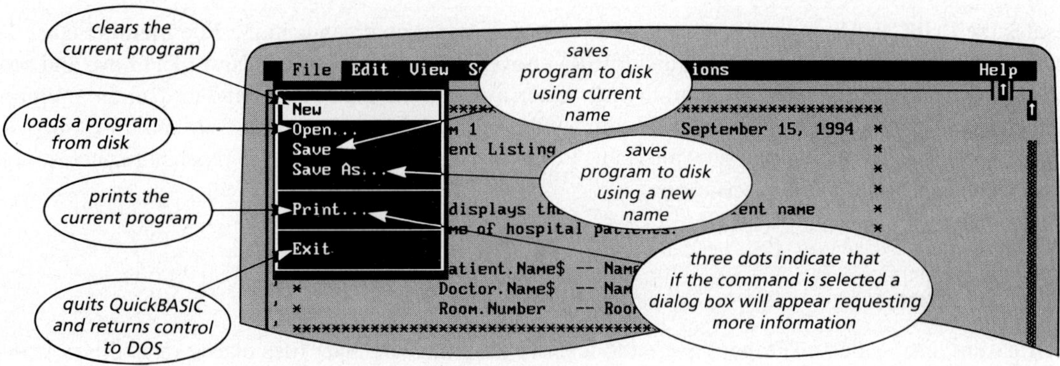

FIGURE 1-24 The File menu

Listing a Portion of the Program to the Printer

To print a portion of the current program, use the **Shift key** and arrow keys (or the mouse) to highlight the lines in the program you want to print. Next, follow the steps outlined in the previous paragraphs for printing the program. When the Print dialog box appears on the screen, the bullet should be in front of Selected Text (Figure 1-25). QuickBASIC automatically assigns the bullet to Selected Text when a series of lines is selected prior to issuing the **Print** command.

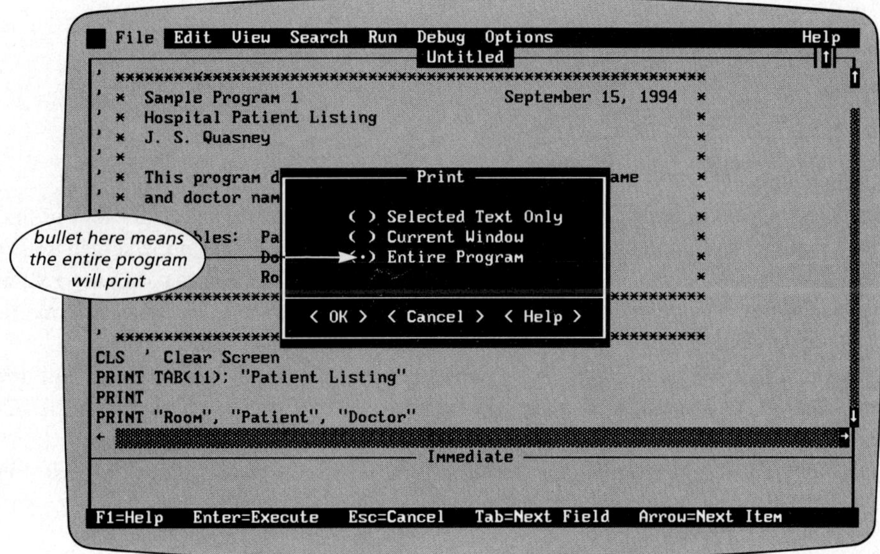

FIGURE 1-25 The dialog box for the Print command

Printing the Results on the Output Screen

To print a copy of the output screen, press **Print Screen** (**Shift + Prt Sc** on older PCs) while the output screen displays on the monitor. Later we discuss the `LPRINT` statement as an alternative means to generating hard-copy output.

SAVING, LOADING, AND ERASING PROGRAMS

Besides the **Print** and **Exit** commands, there are four additional commands in the **File menu** (Figure 1-24) that are essential for your first session with QuickBASIC—**Save**, **Save As**, **Open**, and **New**. The **Save** and **Save As** commands allow you to store the current program to disk. Later, you use the **Open** command to load the program from disk into main storage to make it the current one. The **New** command erases the current program from main memory. It clears the view window and indicates the beginning of a new program. Before we discuss these three commands further, it is important that you understand the concept of a file specification.

File Specifications

A **file specification**, also called a **filespec**, is used to identify programs and data files placed in auxiliary storage. A filespec is made up of a device name, file name, and extension.

filespec

device name:file name.extension

The **device name** refers to the disk drive. If no device is specified, then the filespec refers to the default drive of the PC. If a device name is included in the filespec, then it must be followed by a colon.

File names can be from 1 to 8 characters in length. Valid characters are uppercase or lowercase A–Z, 0–9, and certain special characters ($ & # @ ! % " ( ) – { } _ / \). If an extension is used, then the file name must be followed by a period.

An **extension** that is up to three characters in length may be used to classify a file. Valid characters are the same as for a file name. With QuickBASIC, the default extension is `bas`. That is, when you use a command that requires a filespec, QuickBASIC will automatically append an extension of `bas` if one is not included.

Examples of valid filespecs include `b:payroll`, `b:lab2-1`, `PAYROLL.BAS`, `Accounts`, and `S123`. The first two examples reference files on drive B. The latter three examples reference files on the default drive.

Saving the Current Program to Disk

When you enter a program through the keyboard, it is stored in main memory (RAM), and it displays in the view window. When you quit QuickBASIC or turn the computer off, the current program disappears from the screen and, more importantly, from main memory. To save a program to disk for later use, use the **Save** or **Save As** command in the **File menu**. Use the **Save** command to save the program under the same name. Use the **Save As** command to save the program under a new name. Because this is the first time we are saving the program, we will use the **Save As** command.

To select the **Save As** command, press the **Alt key** to activate the menu bar. Type the letter **F** to pull down the **File menu** (Figure 1-24). Type **A** for **Save As**. Here again, the three periods following the **Save As** command in the File menu mean QuickBASIC requires additional information. In this case QuickBASIC needs to know the filespec.

When the Save As dialog box appears (Figure 1-25), enter the file name and press the **Enter key**. In Figure 1-26, we entered the file name `prg-1`. QuickBASIC stores the current program using the filespec `a:prg-1.bas`. Notice in Figure 1-26 that the default drive (A:\) is specified below the file name box.

The **dirs/drives box** in the Save As dialog box includes a list of the disk drives and any subdirectories that are part of the current default drive. You may use the **Tab key** or mouse to activate this box and select a different default drive.

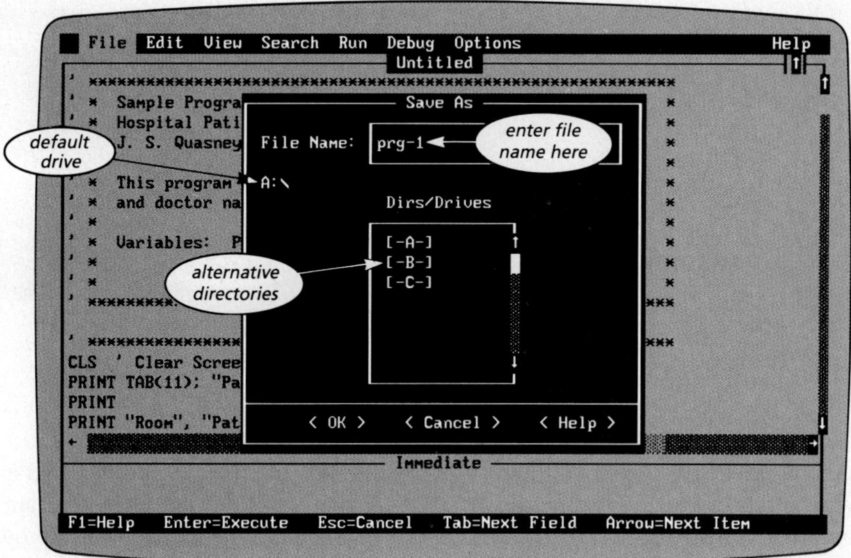

FIGURE 1-26 The dialog box for the Save As command

If you loaded the current program from disk or saved the program earlier, use the **Save** command to save the program under its current name.

To save the current program using a mouse, click on **File** and click on **Save** or **Save As**. If you click on **Save As**, enter the name in the file name box and click on the **OK** button.

Loading a Program from Disk

To load a program stored on disk into main storage, use the **Open** command in the **File menu** (Figure 1-24). This command causes the dialog box shown on the next page in Figure 1-27 to display. In the middle of the dialog box, QuickBASIC displays the files box. The **files box** lists the file names on the default drive that have an extension of `bas`. The current default drive displays just above the files box. To display any other directory on your PC, enter the disk drive (or path) in the file name box or select one from the dirs/drive box and press the **Enter key**.

In the file name box, enter the name of the program you want to load from auxiliary storage into main storage. In Figure 1-27 we entered the file name `prg-1`. Enter the file name by typing it on the keyboard or use the **Tab key** and arrow keys to select the file name from the file names box. Each time you press an arrow key, the name of the program under the cursor displays in the file names box. To complete the command, press the **Enter key**.

If you did not save the current program before attempting to load a new one, QuickBASIC will give you the opportunity to save it before it loads the new program into main storage.

To load a program from disk using the mouse, click on **File** and click on **Open**. Double-click on the name of the program in the files box.

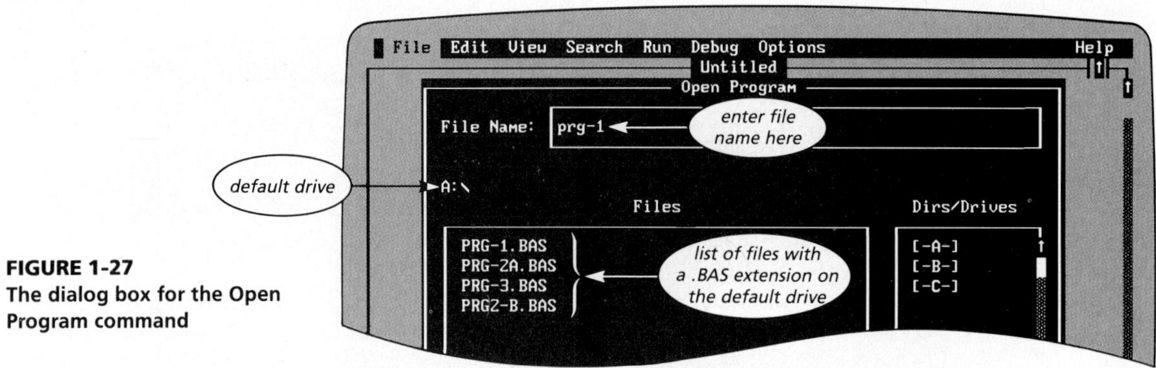

FIGURE 1-27
The dialog box for the Open Program command

Starting a New Program

The **New** command in the **File menu** (Figure 1-24) instructs QuickBASIC to erase the current program from main storage. This also clears the view window. Use this command when you are finished with the current program and wish to start a new one from scratch. Notice that it is not necessary to clear the current program if you are loading a program from disk. The **Open** command clears main storage before it loads the new program.

THE QB ADVISOR ON-LINE HELP SYSTEM

The QB Advisor is a fully integrated, on-line help system with instant access to any QuickBASIC question. You can request immediate help when you first enter QuickBASIC by pressing the **Enter key** rather than the **Esc key**. Thereafter, at any time while you are using QuickBASIC, you can interact with the QB Advisor and display help screens on any QuickBASIC topic using the keys described on the last page of the reference card at the back of this book. For example, if you press **Shift + F1**, the initial help screen shown in Figure 1-28 displays. To return to the view window, press the **Esc key**. If you press **F1**, QuickBASIC displays help for the topic in which the cursor is positioned. The QB Advisor is literally a complete reference manual at your fingertips. The best way to familiarize yourself with the QB Advisor is to use it.

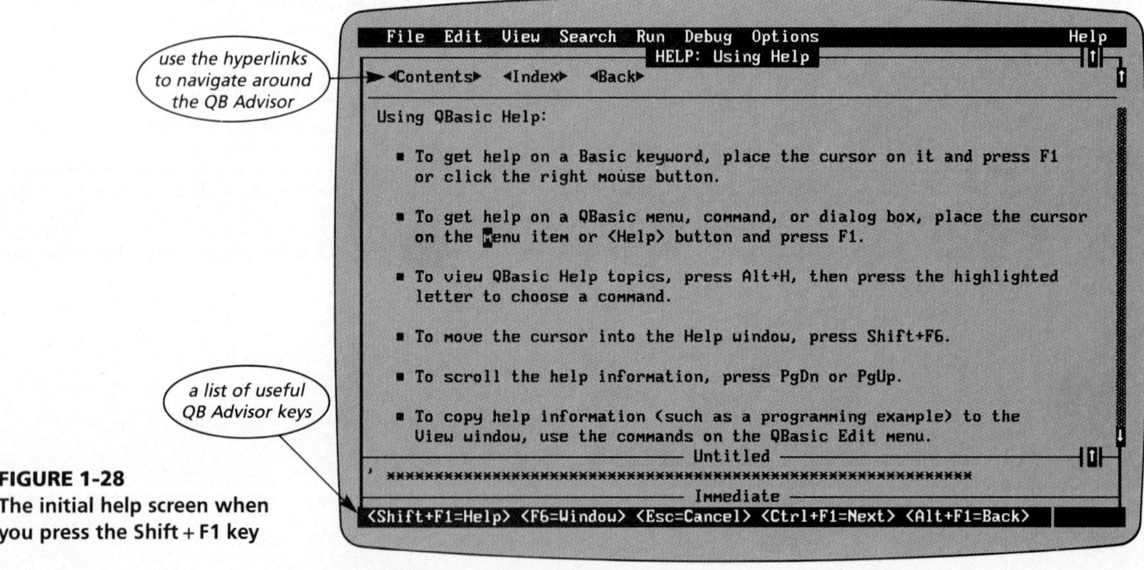

FIGURE 1-28
The initial help screen when you press the Shift + F1 key

TRY IT YOURSELF EXERCISES

1. Identify the 8 major components of the QB screen shown below.

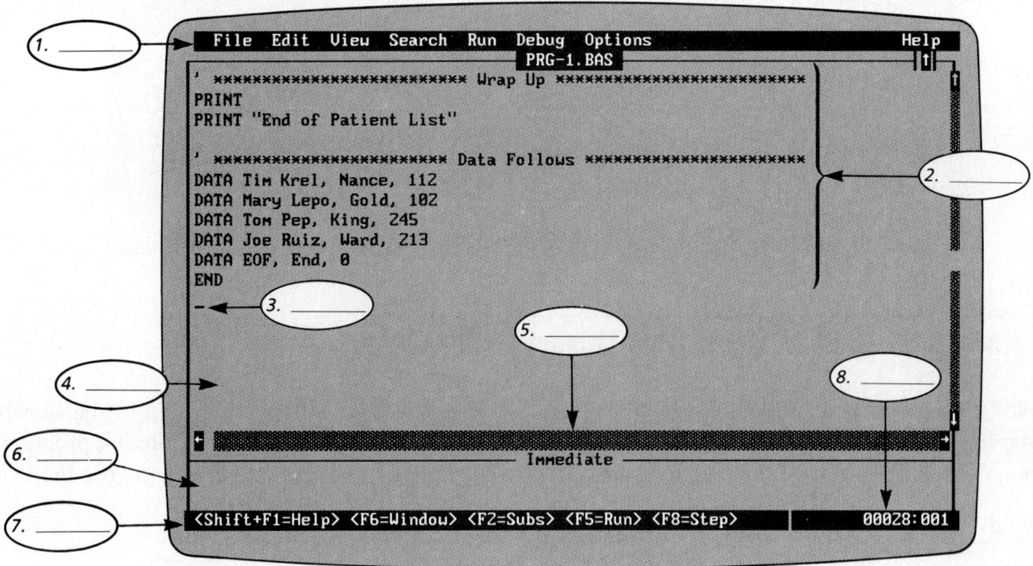

2. List the function of the following keys when a dialog box is active.
   a. Esc b. Tab c. Enter

3. List the function of the following keys when the view window is active.
   a. Alt b. Shift + Delete c. Enter
   d. Home e. End f. Ctrl + Home
   g. Ctrl + Q, X h. Shift + F5 i. F4
   j. F6 k. Backspace l. Delete
   m. Insert n. Shift + Insert o. Page Up

STUDENT ASSIGNMENTS

STUDENT ASSIGNMENT 1: Personnel Report

Instructions: Design and code a program using QuickBASIC to produce the personnel listing as shown on the next page under OUTPUT. The listing includes the employee name, department number, and pay rate for each employee shown under INPUT. Submit a program flowchart, listing of the program, and a listing of the output results. To obtain a hard copy of the output results, use the Print Screen key.

INPUT: Use the following sample data:

NAME	DEPT. NO.	PAY RATE
Sue Long	10	4.25
Chin Song	12	5.15
Mary Lopez	14	4.75
Jan Honig	14	3.85
EOF	99	9.99

Student Assignment 1 (continued)

OUTPUT: The following results are displayed:

```
            Personnel Report

Dept.            Name             Pay Rate

 10              Sue Long          4.25
 12              Chin Song         5.15
 14              Mary Lopez        4.75
 14              Jan Honig         3.85

End of Personnel Report
```

STUDENT ASSIGNMENT 2: Club Membership Report

Instructions: Design and code a program using QuickBASIC to produce the club membership listing shown under OUTPUT. The listing includes a name, birth date, and age for each member shown under INPUT. Submit a program flowchart, listing of the program, and a listing of the output results. To obtain a hard copy of the output results, use the Print Screen key.

INPUT: Use the following sample data:

BIRTH DATE	AGE	NAME
December 7	41	John Sutherlin
March 16	38	Jim Wachtel
June 9	27	Mary Hathaway
August 6	25	Louise Scott
EOF	99	End

OUTPUT: The following results are displayed:

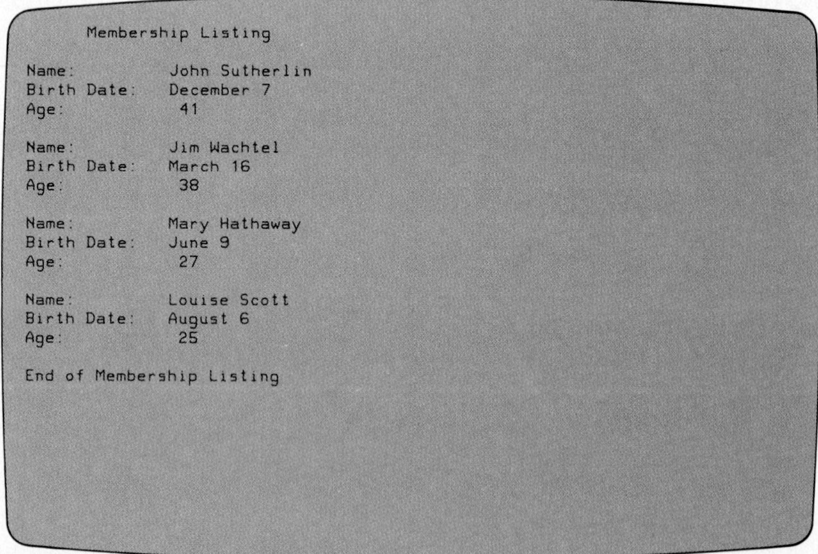

```
        Membership Listing

Name:          John Sutherlin
Birth Date:    December 7
Age:            41

Name:          Jim Wachtel
Birth Date:    March 16
Age:            38

Name:          Mary Hathaway
Birth Date:    June 9
Age:            27

Name:          Louise Scott
Birth Date:    August 6
Age:            25

End of Membership Listing
```

PROJECT 2

Basic Arithmetic Operations and Accumulating Totals

Many applications require that arithmetic operations be performed on the input data to produce the required output. QuickBASIC includes the following basic arithmetic operators: addition (+), subtraction (–), multiplication (*), division (/), and raising a value to a power (^). These operators are similar to those used in ordinary mathematics. The operators and an example of their use in a LET statement are illustrated in Figure 2-1.

MATHEMATICAL OPERATION	BASIC ARITHMETIC OPERATOR	EXAMPLE
Addition	+	LET Total = Sub1 + Sub2
Subtraction	–	LET Profit = Price - 5.95
Multiplication	*	LET Gross = Hours * Rate
Division	/	LET Amount = Cost / 5
Raising to a Power	^	LET Discount = Rate ^ 2

FIGURE 2-1 QuickBASIC arithmetic operators

THE LET STATEMENT

The LET statement is used to assign a variable a value. As shown in Figure 2-2, the first entry in a LET statement is the keyword LET. The keyword LET is followed by a variable name, an equal sign, and an expression.

```
LET numeric variable = numeric expression
  or
LET string variable = string expression
```

FIGURE 2-2 The general form of the LET statement

Expressions

An **expression** can be numeric or string. A **numeric expression** consists of one or more numeric constants, numeric variables, and numeric function references, all of which are separated from each other by parentheses and arithmetic operators. A **string expression** consists of one or more string constants, string variables, and string functions separated by the concatenation operator (+), which combines two strings into one. A numeric expression can only be assigned to a numeric variable. A string expression can only be assigned to a string variable.

Figure 2-3 illustrates numeric expressions in LET statements. Figure 2-4 illustrates string expressions in LET statements.

VALUE OF	LET STATEMENT	RESULTS IN
A = 15 B = 10	LET F = A + B - 10	F = 15
J = 32 H = 16	LET L = J * 2 - H	L = 48
P = 14 Y = 7	LET Q = P / Y	Q = 2
W = 4 S = 6	LET T = 6 * (S - W)	T = 12

FIGURE 2-3 Numeric expressions in LET statements

VALUE OF	LET STATEMENT	RESULTS IN
X$ = ABC	LET W$ = "DEF" + X$	W$ = DEFABC
F$ = WATER G$ = WINE	LET A$ = F$ + " INTO " + G$	A$ = WATER INTO WINE
S$ = "TOP"	LET S$ = S$ + "IT"	S$ = TOPIT

FIGURE 2-4 String expressions in LET statements

From the examples in Figures 2-3 and 2-4 you can see that when performing arithmetic operations, the calculations are specified to the right of the equal sign. The variable assigned the result of the expression is placed to the left side of the equal sign.

Order of Operations

When multiple arithmetic operations are included in a LET statement, the **order of operations** follows the normal algebraic rules. That is, the operations are completed in the following order:

- First, exponentiation is performed from left to right.
- Next, multiplication and division are performed from left to right.
- Finally, addition and subtraction are performed from left to right.

For example, the expression 27 / 3 ^ 2 + 4 * 3 is evaluated as follows:

```
27 / 3 ^ 2 + 4 * 3 = 27 / 9 + 4 * 3
                   = 3      + 4 * 3
                   = 3      + 12
                   = 15
```

If you had trouble following the logic behind this evaluation, use the following technique. Whenever a numeric expression is to be evaluated, *scan* from left to right three different times. On the first scan, every time you encounter an ^ operator, you perform exponentiation. In this example, 3 is raised to the power of 2, yielding 9.

On the second scan, moving from left to right again, every time you encounter the operators * and /, perform multiplication and division. Hence, 27 is divided by 9, yielding 3, and 4 and 3 are multiplied, yielding 12.

On the third scan, moving again from left to right, every time you detect the operators + and –, perform addition and subtraction. In this example, 3 and 12 are added to form 15. Thus, the following `LET` statement

```
LET Amount = 27 / 3 ^ 2 + 4 * 3
```

assigns 15 to the variable Amount.

The expression below yields the value of –19.37, as follows:

$$
\begin{aligned}
4 - 3 * 4 / 10 ^\wedge 2 + 5 / 4 * 3 - 3 ^\wedge 3 &= 4 - 3 * 4 / 100 + 5 / 4 * 3 - 27 \\
&= 4 - 0.12 + 3.75 - 27 \\
&= -19.37
\end{aligned}
$$

Hence, the following `LET` statement

```
LET Total = 4 - 3 * 4 / 10 ^ 2 + 5 / 4 * 3 - 3 ^ 3
```

assigns –19.37 to the variable Total.

The Use of Parentheses in an Expression

Parentheses may be used to change the order of operations. In QuickBASIC, parentheses are normally used to avoid ambiguity and to group terms in a numeric expression; they do not imply multiplication. When parentheses are inserted into an expression, the part of the expression within the parentheses is evaluated first, and then the remaining expression is evaluated according to the order of operations.

If the first example contained parentheses, as does (27 / 3) ^ 2 + 4 * 3, then it would be evaluated in the following manner:

$$
\begin{aligned}
(27 / 3) ^\wedge 2 + 4 * 3 &= 9 ^\wedge 2 + 4 * 3 \\
&= 81 + 4 * 3 \\
&= 81 + 12 \\
&= 93
\end{aligned}
$$

Use parentheses freely when you are in doubt as to the formation and evaluation of a numeric expression. For example, if you want to have the PC divide `9 * Tax` by `3 ^ Payment`, the expression may correctly be written as `9 * Tax / 3 ^ Payment`, but you may also write it as `(9 * Tax) / (3 ^ Payment)` and feel more certain of the result.

For more complex expressions, QuickBASIC allows parentheses to be contained within other parentheses. When this occurs, the parentheses are said to be **nested**. In this case, QuickBASIC evaluates the innermost parenthetical expression first and then goes on to the outermost parenthetical expression. Thus, (27 / 3) ^ 2 + (5 * (7 + 3)) is broken down in the following manner:

$$
\begin{aligned}
(27 / 3) ^\wedge 2 + (5 * (7 + 3)) &= 9 ^\wedge 2 + (5 * (7 + 3)) \\
&= 81 + (5 * 10) \\
&= 81 + 50 \\
&= 131
\end{aligned}
$$

SAMPLE PROGRAM 2 — AUTO EXPENSE REPORT

The following sample program generates an auto expense report. The program performs calculations and accumulates totals using `LET` statements. Input consists of auto expense records that contain an employee name, the license number of the employee's car, the beginning mileage for the employee's car, and the ending mileage for the car.

The auto expense file that will be processed by the sample program is shown in Figure 2-5.

NAME	LICENSE	BEGINNING MILEAGE	ENDING MILEAGE
T. Rowe	HRT-111	19,100	19,224
R. Lopez	GLD-913	21,221	21,332
C. Deck	LIV-193	10,001	10,206
B. Alek	ZRT-904	15,957	16,419
EOF	End	0	0

FIGURE 2-5 The employee auto expense file for Sample Program 2

The output generated by Sample Program 2 is a report displayed on the screen. The report contains the employee name, the automobile license number, the total mileage, and the expense. The total mileage is calculated by subtracting the beginning mileage from the ending mileage. The expense is calculated by multiplying the mileage by twenty-five cents.

The report contains both report headings and column headings. After all records have been processed, the total number of employees and total auto expenses are displayed. In addition, the average expense per employee is calculated by dividing the total auto expense by the total number of employees. The average expense per employee is then displayed followed by an end-of-report message. The format of the output is shown in Figure 2-6.

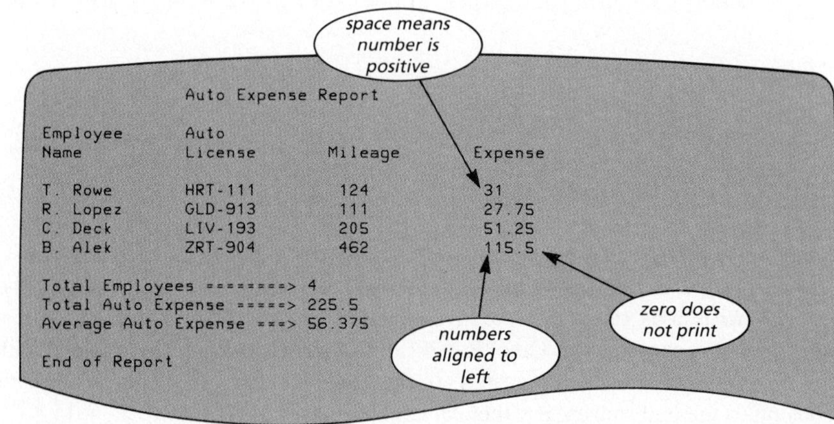

FIGURE 2-6
The report for Sample Program 2

When using the `PRINT` statement, nonsignificant zeros to the right of a decimal point are not printed. For example, Alek's expense displays as 115.5 rather than 115.50. In addition, when printing decimal numbers, the numbers are left aligned under the column heading rather than right aligned. The single space displayed to the left of each number means that the number is positive. These factors are illustrated in the output in Figure 2-6. Later in this section, we discuss the `PRINT USING` statement, which allows you to adjust the values displayed to include nonsignificant zeros and right-align numeric values under the column headings.

Accumulators

Most programs require **accumulators**, which are used to develop totals. Accumulators are initialized to a value of zero in the Initialization module, then incremented within the loop in the Process File module, and finally manipulated or displayed in the Wrap-Up module. Although QuickBASIC automatically initializes numeric variables to zero, good programming practice demands that this be done in the program. There are two types of accumulators: counters and running totals.

A **counter** is an accumulator that is used to count the number of times some action or event is performed. For example, appropriately placed within a loop, the statement

```
LET Total.Employees = Total.Employees + 1
```

causes the counter Total.Employees to increment by 1 each time a record is read. Associated with a counter is a statement placed in the Initialization module which initializes the counter to some value. In most cases the counter is initialized to zero.

A **running total** is an accumulator that is used to sum the different values that a variable is assigned during the execution of a program. For example, appropriately placed within a loop, the statement

```
LET Total.Expense = Total.Expense + Auto.Expense
```

causes Total.Expense to increase by the value of Auto.Expense. Total.Expense is called a running total. If a program is processing an employee file and the variable Auto.Expense is assigned the employee's auto expense each time a record is read, then variable Total.Expense represents the running total of the auto expense of all the employees in the file. As with a counter, a running total must be initialized to some predetermined value, such as zero, in the Initialization module.

Program Flowchart

The flowchart for the sample program, which produces an auto expense report and accumulates and prints final totals, is illustrated in Figure 2-7.

Prior to the loop in the flowchart, the accumulators are initialized, the headings are displayed, and the first employee record is read. Within the loop, the employee counter is incremented, the beginning mileage is subtracted from the ending mileage, giving the mileage driven by the employee. The auto expense is then calculated by multiplying the mileage driven times the auto cost per mile (.25). The auto expense is then added to the total auto expense accumulator. Next, a line of information is displayed. At the bottom of the loop another record is read. Control then returns to the top of the loop to determine if the trailer record was read. This looping process continues until there are no more auto expense records.

When the trailer record is read, the total number of employees and total auto expenses are displayed. Next, the total auto expense is divided by the total number of employees to give the average auto expense. Finally, the average and an end-of-report message are displayed.

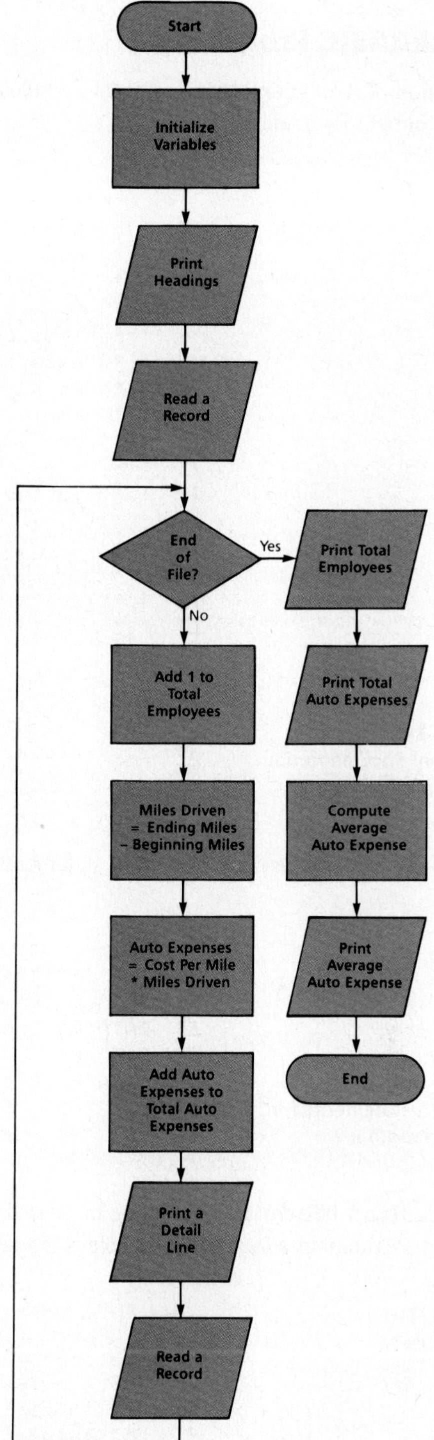

FIGURE 2-7 The flowchart for Sample Program 2

The QuickBASIC Program

The first section of the QuickBASIC program includes the initial documentation. As shown in Figure 2-8, the documentation is similar to Sample Program 1.

```
' ******************************************************************
' *   Sample Program 2                            September 15, 1994  *
' *   Auto Expense Report                                          *
' *   J. S. Quasney                                                *
' *                                                                *
' *   This program displays an auto expense report.  Mileage       *
' *   expense is calculated on the basis of 25 cents per mile.     *
' *   As part of the Wrap-Up module, the total number of           *
' *   employees, total auto expense, and the average expense       *
' *   per employee are displayed.                                  *
' *                                                                *
' *   Variables:  Emp.Name$         -- Name of employee            *
' *               License$          -- Auto license number         *
' *               Begin.Mileage     -- Beginning mileage           *
' *               End.Mileage       -- Ending mileage              *
' *               Miles.Driven      -- Miles driven                *
' *               Cost.Per.Mile     -- Auto cost per mile          *
' *               Auto.Expense      -- Auto expense                *
' *               Total.Employees   -- Number of employees         *
' *               Total.Expense     -- Total auto expense          *
' *               Average.Expense   -- Average auto expense        *
' ******************************************************************
```

FIGURE 2-8
The initial documentation for Sample Program 2

The DATA Statements The DATA statements in Figure 2-9 correspond to the employee auto expense file described in Figure 2-5.

```
' *********************** Data Follows ***********************
DATA T. Rowe, HRT-111, 19100, 19224
DATA R. Lopez, GLD-913, 21221, 21332
DATA C. Deck, LIV-193, 10001, 10206
DATA B. Alek, ZRT-904, 15957, 16419
DATA EOF, End, 0, 0
END
```

FIGURE 2-9
The DATA statements for Sample Program 2

Initialization Module Following the initial program documentation shown in Figure 2-8, the Initialization module initializes the accumulators to zero and displays the report title and column headings. The Initialization module is shown in Figure 2-10.

```
' ********************** Initialization **********************
CLS  ' Clear Screen
LET Total.Employees = 0
LET Total.Expense = 0
LET Cost.Per.Mile = .25
PRINT TAB(15); "Auto Expense Report"
PRINT
PRINT "Employee", "Auto"
PRINT "Name", "License", "Mileage", "Expense"
PRINT
```

FIGURE 2-10
The Initialization module for Sample Program 2

Lines 26 and 27 initialize the employee counter (Total.Employees) and total expense running total (Total.Expense) to zero. When these two LET statements are executed, the zeros on the right side of the equal sign are assigned to the variables Total.Employee and Total.Expense. Counters and running totals should always be set to zero at the beginning of a program.

When the LET statement in line 28 is executed, the constant 0.25 on the right side of the equal sign is assigned to Cost.Per.Mile. This variable can then be used later to compute the auto expense. The purpose of assigning 0.25 to a variable is to facilitate future changes to the program. For example, if the auto cost per mile were changed from 0.25 to 0.28, the constant value in line 28 could be changed to 0.28.

Lines 29 through 33 display the report title and column headings. The PRINT statement in line 29 displays the report title beginning in column 15. Line 30 skips a line in the report. Lines 31 and 32 display the column headings. Finally, line 33 skips a line in the report to leave space between the column headings and the first record displayed.

The Process File Module The statements that make up the Process File module for Sample Program 2 are illustrated in Figure 2-11.

```
35  ' ************************ Process File ************************
36  READ Emp.Name$, License$, Begin.Mileage, End.Mileage
37  DO WHILE Emp.Name$ <> "EOF"
38     LET Total.Employees = Total.Employees + 1
39     LET Miles.Driven = End.Mileage - Begin.Mileage
40     LET Auto.Expense = Cost.Per.Mile * Miles.Driven
41     LET Total.Expense = Total.Expense + Auto.Expense
42     PRINT Emp.Name$, License$, Miles.Driven, Auto.Expense
43     READ Emp.Name$, License$, Begin.Mileage, End.Mileage
44  LOOP
45
```

FIGURE 2-11
The Process File module for Sample Program 2

The READ statement in line 36 assigns the data in the first DATA statement (line 56 in Figure 2-9) to Emp.Name$, License$, Begin.Mileage, and End.Mileage. Next, the DO WHILE statement in line 37 tests to see if Emp.Name$ is not equal to EOF. Since Emp.Name$ does not equal EOF, control enters the loop.

The LET statement in line 38 increments the employee counter (Total.Employees). Each time this statement is executed, Total.Employees is incremented by 1. Since Total.Employees was initially set to zero (line 26 in Figure 2-10), it is equal to 1 after line 38 is executed the first time. After the statement is executed a second time, the value of Total.Employees is equal to 2. This counting continues each time through the loop. When the end-of-file is detected, the value of Total.Employees is equal to the number of records processed.

The LET statement in line 39 calculates the mileage the automobile was driven (Miles.Driven) by the employee being processed by subtracting the beginning mileage (Begin.Mileage) from the ending mileage (End.Mileage). Line 40 computes the auto expense (Auto.Expense) by multiplying the miles the automobile was driven (Miles.Driven) by the cost per mile (Cost.Per.Mile). The value 0.25 was assigned to Cost.Per.Mile in line 28 of the Initialization module (Figure 2-10).

The LET statement in line 41 adds the auto expense (Auto.Expense) to the accumulator Total.Expense. Here again, the variable Total.Expense was initialized to zero. When line 41 is executed the first time, the auto expense is added to the value zero. Hence, Auto.Expense is equal to the T. Rowe's auto expense after the first pass on the loop. When line 41 is executed the second time, the auto expense for R. Lopez is added to the auto expense for T. Rowe. Thus, the effect of this LET statement is to accumulate the auto expenses for all the employees.

The PRINT statement in line 42 displays the employee name, license number, miles driven, and the auto expense. Next, the READ statement in line 43 assigns the data for the second employee to Emp.Name$, License$, Begin.Mileage, and End.Mileage. The LOOP statement in line 44 transfers control back up to the DO WHILE statement in line 37. Notice that statements 38 through 43 are indented three spaces to illuminate the statements within the Do loop. The looping process continues until the trailer record is read, at which time control is transferred to the Wrap-Up module (line 47).

End-of-File Processing After all the records are processed, control transfers to the `PRINT` statement in line 47 (Figure 2-12), which causes the PC to skip a line in the report. The next `PRINT` statement displays the total number of employees (Total.Employees). Notice the manner in which the `PRINT` statement is written to display both a constant and a variable. The phrase `Total Employees ========>` is enclosed within quotation marks ("). The right quotation is followed by a semicolon (;). A semicolon causes the PC to display the value of Total.Employees immediately after the phrase rather than in the next print zone. Recall that if the numeric value is positive, a blank space appears before the numeric value.

After line 49 displays the total expenses, line 50 computes the average expense which is displayed by line 51. Line 52 skips a line and line 53 displays an end-of-report message. Finally, line 61 (Figure 2-9) terminates execution of the program.

```
46  ' ************************** Wrap-Up **************************
47  PRINT
48  PRINT "Total Employees ========>"; Total.Employees
49  PRINT "Total Auto Expense =====>"; Total.Expense
50  LET Average.Expense = Total.Expense / Total.Employees
51  PRINT "Average Auto Expense ===>"; Average.Expense
52  PRINT
53  PRINT "End of Report"
54
```

FIGURE 2-12
The Wrap-Up module for Sample Program 2

The Complete QuickBASIC Program The complete Sample Program 2 is illustrated in Figure 2-13. The report generated by Sample Program 2 is shown in Figure 2-14.

```
 1  ' ***************************************************************
 2  ' *  Sample Program 2                          September 15, 1994 *
 3  ' *  Auto Expense Report                                          *
 4  ' *  J. S. Quasney                                                *
 5  ' *                                                               *
 6  ' *  This program displays an auto expense report.  Mileage       *
 7  ' *  expense is calculated on the basis of 25 cents per mile.     *
 8  ' *  As part of the Wrap-Up module, the total number of           *
 9  ' *  employees, total auto expense, and the average expense       *
10  ' *  per employee are displayed.                                  *
11  ' *                                                               *
12  ' *  Variables: Emp.Name$         -- Name of employee             *
13  ' *             License$          -- Auto license number          *
14  ' *             Begin.Mileage     -- Beginning mileage            *
15  ' *             End.Mileage       -- Ending mileage               *
16  ' *             Miles.Driven      -- Miles driven                 *
17  ' *             Cost.Per.Mile     -- Auto cost per mile           *
18  ' *             Auto.Expense      -- Auto expense                 *
19  ' *             Total.Employees   -- Number of employees          *
20  ' *             Total.Expense     -- Total auto expense           *
21  ' *             Average.Expense   -- Average auto expense         *
22  ' ***************************************************************
23
24  ' ********************** Initialization ***********************
25  CLS  ' Clear Screen
26  LET Total.Employees = 0
27  LET Total.Expense = 0
28  LET Cost.Per.Mile = .25
29  PRINT TAB(15); "Auto Expense Report"
30  PRINT
31  PRINT "Employee", "Auto"
32  PRINT "Name", "License", "Mileage", "Expense"
33  PRINT
34
```

FIGURE 2-13
Sample Program 2

FIGURE 2-13 (continued)

```
' ************************ Process File ************************
READ Emp.Name$, License$, Begin.Mileage, End.Mileage
DO WHILE Emp.Name$ <> "EOF"
   LET Total.Employees = Total.Employees + 1
   LET Miles.Driven = End.Mileage - Begin.Mileage
   LET Auto.Expense = Cost.Per.Mile * Miles.Driven
   LET Total.Expense = Total.Expense + Auto.Expense
   PRINT Emp.Name$, License$, Miles.Driven, Auto.Expense
   READ Emp.Name$, License$, Begin.Mileage, End.Mileage
LOOP

' ************************** Wrap-Up *************************
PRINT
PRINT "Total Employees ========>"; Total.Employees
PRINT "Total Auto Expense =====>"; Total.Expense
LET Average.Expense = Total.Expense / Total.Employees
PRINT "Average Auto Expense ===>"; Average.Expense
PRINT
PRINT "End of Report"

' ************************ Data Follows **********************
DATA T. Rowe, HRT-111, 19100, 19224
DATA R. Lopez, GLD-913, 21221, 21332
DATA C. Deck, LIV-193, 10001, 10206
DATA B. Alek, ZRT-904, 15957, 16419
DATA EOF, End, 0, 0
END
```

```
                 Auto Expense Report

Employee         Auto
Name             License         Mileage        Expense

T. Rowe          HRT-111          124           31
R. Lopez         GLD-913          111           27.75
C. Deck          LIV-193          205           51.25
B. Alek          ZRT-904          462           115.5

Total Employees ========> 4
Total Auto Expense =====> 225.5
Average Auto Expense ===> 56.375

End of Report
```

FIGURE 2-14 **The output results due to the execution of Sample Program 2**

REPORT EDITING

Although the output in Figure 2-14 is readable, it does not conform to the format used by business and industry. For example, a column of numeric values usually has the decimal points aligned and is right-justified under the column heading. Numeric values that represent dollars and cents should include two digits to the right of the decimal point. Placing information in a format such as this is called **report editing**.

QuickBASIC provides for report editing through the use of the `PRINT USING` statement. This statement allows you to do the following:

- Specify the exact image of a line of output.
- Force decimal-point alignment when displaying numeric tables in columnar format.
- Control the number of digits displayed for a numeric result.

- Specify that commas be inserted into a number. (Starting from the units position of a number and progressing toward the left, digits are separated into groups of 3 by a comma.)
- Specify that the sign status of the number be displayed along with the number (+ or blank if positive, – if negative).
- Assign a fixed or floating dollar sign ($) to the number displayed.
- Force a numeric result to be displayed in exponential form.
- **Left-** or **right-justify** string values in a formatted field (that is, align the leftmost or rightmost characters, respectively).
- Specify that only the first character of a string be displayed.
- Round a value automatically to a specified number of decimal digits.

The general form of the `PRINT USING` statement is shown in Figure 2-15.

> `PRINT USING` "format field"; list
>
> or
>
> `PRINT USING` string variable; list
>
> where **format field** or **string variable** indicates the format and **list** is a variable or a group of variables separted by semicolons.

FIGURE 2-15
The general form of the PRINT USING statement

Report editing with the `PRINT USING` statement is accomplished using special characters to format the values to be displayed. When grouped together, these special characters form a **format field**. A format field is incorporated in a program as a string constant in the `PRINT USING` statement or as a string constant assigned to a string variable.

To illustrate the use of the `PRINT USING` statement, we will modify Sample Program 2. The new, formatted report is illustrated in Figure 2-16.

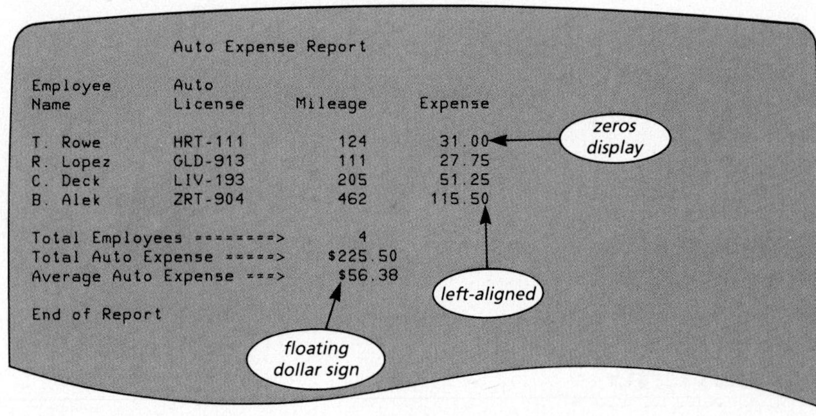

FIGURE 2-16
The formatted auto expense report

Compare the report in Figure 2-16 to the one in Figure 2-14. Notice that the mileage in the third column in Figure 2-16 is right-justified under the column heading. Also, the dollar and cents values in the expense field are right-justified under the column heading, and the decimal points are aligned. In addition, the total auto expense and the average expense per employee values are displayed with the dollar sign immediately adjacent to the leftmost digit in the number. This is known as a **floating dollar sign**.

To control the format of the displayed values, the `PRINT USING` statement is used in conjunction with a string expression that specifies exactly the image to which the output must conform. The string expression is placed immediately after the words `PRINT USING` in the form of a string constant or string variable. If the format is described by a string variable, then the string variable must be assigned the format by a `LET` statement before the `PRINT USING` statement is executed in the program. In either case, the items to display follow the string constant or string variable in the `PRINT USING` statement separated by semicolons or commas. The two methods for specifying the format for the `PRINT USING` statement are shown in Figure 2-17.

Method 1:

```
' Format Specified as a String in the PRINT USING Statement
PRINT USING "Item ### costs $$,###.##"; Item; Cost
```

Method 2:

```
' Format Specified Earlier and Assigned to a String Variable
D1$ = "Item ### cost $$,###.##"
      .
      .
      .
PRINT USING D1$; Item; Cost
```

FIGURE 2-17
The two methods for defining the format for a PRINT USING statement

In Method 1 of Figure 2-17, the string following the keywords `PRINT USING` instructs the PC to display the values of Item and Cost using the format found in the accompanying string constant. In Method 2, the string constant has been replaced by the string variable D1$ which was assigned the desired format in a previous statement. If Item is equal to 314 and Cost is equal to 2145.50, then the results displayed from the execution of either `PRINT USING` statement in Method 1 or Method 2 are as follows:

```
Item 314 costs $2,145.50
```

In Method 2 of Figure 2-17, notice that the keyword `LET` is not part of the `LET` statement. QuickBASIC considers any statement with an equal sign to be a `LET` statement. Hence, the keyword `LET` is optional. When defining format fields, we will not use the keyword `LET`.

Figure 2-18 illustrates how a `LET` statement and a `PRINT USING` statement are used to display the detail line in the report in Figure 2-16.

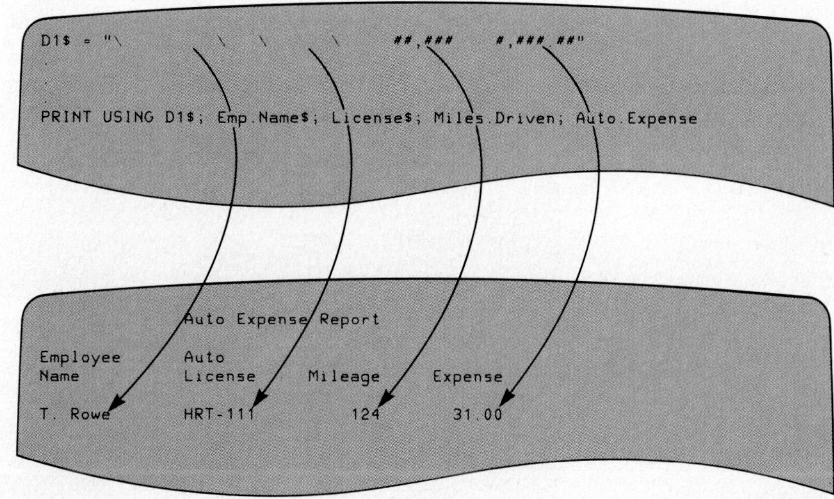

FIGURE 2-18
Using LET and PRINT USING statements to format the output

The backward slash (\) is used to create a format for string fields. The first backward slash indicates the first character position in the string field, and the second backward slash indicates the last character position in the field. Therefore, in the format field for Emp.Name$, eleven characters positions are defined—the two backward slashes and the nine spaces between them.

License$ is also a string variable. It is defined as eight characters in length by the two backward slashes and the six spaces between them. Numeric fields are defined through the use of the number sign (#). Each occurrence of a number sign corresponds to a numeric digit position. Punctuation, such as the comma and decimal point, is placed in the format field where it is to occur in the actual output. The format field for Miles.Driven includes a comma in case the value exceeds 999. Since Miles.Driven in the first line of the report is less than 1,000, the comma does not display. Similarly, a decimal point is placed in the format where it is supposed to print. For Auto.Expense, the format field `###.##` specifies three digits to the left of the decimal point and two digits to the right of the decimal point. Thus, the value displays in dollars and cents form.

Notice in Figure 2-18, following the keyword `PRINT USING`, D1$ identifies the format. This variable name is then followed by a semicolon, and the names of the fields to display are separated by semicolons. The table in Figure 2-19 illustrates additional examples of format fields.

EXAMPLE	DATA	FORMAT FIELD	RESULTS IN
1	125.62	###.##	125.62
2	005.76	###.##	bb5.76
3	.65	###.##	bb0.65
4	1208.78	#,###.##	1,208.78
5	986.05	#,###.##	bb986.05
6	34.87	$$#,###.##	bbbb$34.87
7	3579.75	$$#,###.##	b$3,579.75
8	561.93	$##,###.##	$bbb561.93
9	SALLY	\ \	SALLY
10	EDWARD	\\	ED

FIGURE 2-19 Examples of format fields (b represents a blank character)

You can include constants in a format field. The `LET` statement in Figure 2-20 illustrates this point.

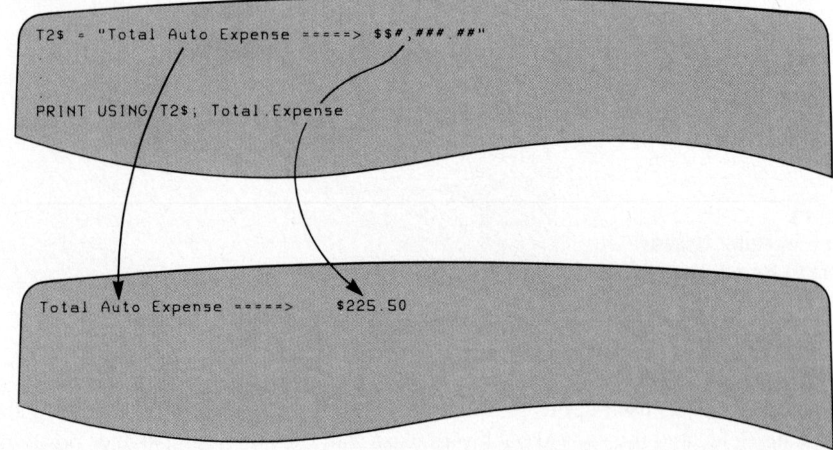

FIGURE 2-20
An example of including a constant in a format field

In Figure 2-20, the constant `Total Auto Expense =====>` is part of the string expression that includes the format field. When the variable T2$ is referenced by the `PRINT USING` statement, the constant is displayed exactly as it appears in the string expression. There are additional format symbols available with QuickBASIC. Those we present here, however, are the most widely used.

The coding in Figure 2-21 illustrates the complete program which produces the auto expense report shown on the next page in Figure 2-22. Particular attention should be paid to lines 30 through 39. These lines, when grouped together, show exactly what the report will look like when the program executes. Notice that this group of lines includes `PRINT` statements that display the report title and column headings and `LET` statements that define format fields. The column headings are within one string constant, rather than separated by commas, to better control the spacing. The format fields for the detail line (D1$) are immediately below the column headings in line 35.

We did not use the keyword `LET` in lines 35 through 39 so that all the string constants would begin in the same column in the program.

```
1  ' ***************************************************************
2  ' *  Sample Program 2 Modified                September 15, 1994  *
3  ' *  Auto Expense Report                                          *
4  ' *  J. S. Quasney                                                *
5  ' *                                                               *
6  ' *  This program displays an auto expense report.  Mileage       *
7  ' *  expense is calculated on the basis of 25 cents per mile.     *
8  ' *  As part of the Wrap-Up module, the total number of           *
9  ' *  employees, total auto expense, and the average expense       *
10 ' *  per employee are displayed.                                  *
11 ' *                                                               *
12 ' *  Variables:  Emp.Name$         -- Name of employee            *
13 ' *              License$          -- Auto license number         *
14 ' *              Begin.Mileage     -- Beginning mileage           *
15 ' *              End.Mileage       -- Ending mileage              *
16 ' *              Miles.Driven      -- Miles driven                *
17 ' *              Cost.Per.Mile     -- Auto cost per mile          *
18 ' *              Auto.Expense      -- Auto expense                *
19 ' *              Total.Employees   -- Number of employees         *
20 ' *              Total.Expense     -- Total auto expense          *
21 ' *              Average.Expense   -- Average auto expense        *
22 ' *              D1$, T1$, T2$, T3$, T4$  --  Print images        *
23 ' ***************************************************************
24
25 ' ********************** Initialization **********************
26 CLS   ' Clear Screen
27 LET Total.Employees = 0
28 LET Total.Expense = 0
29 LET Cost.Per.Mile = .25
30 PRINT "              Auto Expense Report"
31 PRINT
32 PRINT "Employee      Auto"
33 PRINT "Name          License     Mileage     Expense"
34 PRINT
35 D1$ = "\         \   \      \    ##,###     #,###.##"
36 T1$ = "Total Employees ========>    ###"
37 T2$ = "Total Auto Expense =====> $$#,###.##"
38 T3$ = "Average Auto Expense ===>  $$,###.##"
39 T4$ = "End of Report"
40
41 ' *********************** Process File ***********************
42 READ Emp.Name$, License$, Begin.Mileage, End.Mileage
43 DO WHILE Emp.Name$ <> "EOF"
44    LET Total.Employees = Total.Employees + 1
45    LET Miles.Driven = End.Mileage - Begin.Mileage
46    LET Auto.Expense = Cost.Per.Mile * Miles.Driven
47    LET Total.Expense = Total.Expense + Auto.Expense
48    PRINT USING D1$; Emp.Name$; License$; Miles.Driven; Auto.Expense
49    READ Emp.Name$, License$, Begin.Mileage, End.Mileage
50 LOOP
51
```

image of report

FIGURE 2-21
Sample Program 2 modified to include report editing

(continued)

FIGURE 2-21 (continued)

```
' ************************** Wrap Up **************************
PRINT
PRINT USING T1$; Total.Employees
PRINT USING T2$; Total.Expense
LET Average.Expense = Total.Expense / Total.Employees
PRINT USING T3$; Average.Expense
PRINT
PRINT T4$

' ************************ Data Follows ***********************
DATA T. Rowe, HRT-111, 19100, 19224
DATA R. Lopez, GLD-913, 21221, 21332
DATA C. Deck, LIV-193, 10001, 10206
DATA B. Alek, ZRT-904, 15957, 16419
DATA EOF, End, 0, 0
END
```

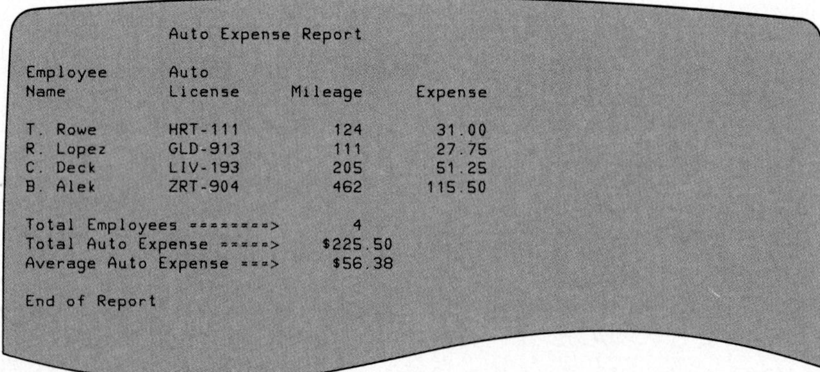

```
              Auto Expense Report

Employee      Auto
Name          License      Mileage      Expense

T. Rowe       HRT-111          124        31.00
R. Lopez      GLD-913          111        27.75
C. Deck       LIV-193          205        51.25
B. Alek       ZRT-904          462       115.50

Total Employees ========>        4
Total Auto Expense =====>  $225.50
Average Auto Expense ===>   $56.38

End of Report
```

FIGURE 2-22
The formatted auto expense report due to the execution of the modified Sample Program 2

PRINTING A REPORT ON THE PRINTER

While the PRINT and PRINT USING statements display results on the screen, the LPRINT and LPRINT USING statements print results on the printer. Everything that has been presented with respect to the PRINT and PRINT USING statements in this section applies to the LPRINT and LPRINT USING statements. Obviously, to use these statements, you must have a printer attached to your PC and it must be in the Ready mode.

Figure 2-23 illustrates the results of the modified Sample Program 2 printed on a printer. To obtain the hard-copy results as shown in Figure 2-23, change all the PRINT and PRINT USING statements in Sample Program 2 (Figure 2-21) to LPRINT and LPRINT USING statements.

```
              Auto Expense Report

Employee      Auto
Name          License      Mileage      Expense

T. Rowe       HRT-111          124        31.00
R. Lopez      GLD-913          111        27.75
C. Deck       LIV-193          205        51.25
B. Alek       ZRT-904          462       115.50

Total Employees ========>        4
Total Auto Expense =====>  $225.50
Average Auto Expense ===>   $56.38
```

FIGURE 2-23
A printed version of the auto expense report

TRY IT YOURSELF EXERCISES

1. Which arithmetic operation is performed first in the following numeric expressions?
   a. `5 * (Amt + 8)`
   b. `Cost - Sale + Discount`
   c. `8 / 3 * 5`
   d. `(X * (2 + Y)) ^ 2 + Z ^ (2 ^ 2)`
   e. `X + Y / Z`

2. Evaluate each of the following:
   a. `2 * 10 * 6 / 12 - 7 ^ 2 / 7`
   b. `(6 - 8) + 5 ^ 3`
   c. `12 / 6 / 2 + 7 * 3 + 5`

3. Calculate the numeric value for each of the following valid numeric expressions if Amt = 3, Sale = 4, Cost = 5, Discount = 3, S1 = 4, S2 = 1 and S3 = 2.
   a. `(Amt + Sale / 2) + 6.2`
   b. `3 * (Amt ^ Sale) / Cost`
   c. `(Amt / (Cost + 1) * 4 - 5) / 2`
   d. `S2 + 2 * S3 * Discount / 3 - 7 / (S1 - S2 / S3) - Discount ^ S1`

4. Determine the output results for each of the following programs.

   a.
```
' Exercise 4.a
X = 2.5
Y = 4 * X / 2 * X + 10
PRINT Y
Y = 4 * X / (2 * X + 10)
PRINT Y
X = -X
PRINT X
X = -X
PRINT X
END
```

   b.
```
' Exercise 4.b
C = 4
D = 1
S = C + D
PRINT S
T = D - C
PRINT T
C = S + T - C
PRINT C
D = 2 * (S + T + C) / 4
PRINT D
END
```

5. Calculate the numeric value for each of the following numeric expressions if X = 2, Y = 3, and Z = 6.
   a. `X + Y ^ 2`
   b. `Z / Y / X`
   c. `12 / (3 + Z) - X`
   d. `X ^ Y ^ Z`
   e. `X * Y + 2.5 * X + Z`
   f. `(X ^ (2 + Y)) ^ 2 + Z ^ (2 ^ 2)`

6. Insert parentheses so that each of the following results in the value indicated on the right-hand side of the arrow.
   a. `10 / 3 + 2 + 12 ----> 14`
   b. `3 ^ 2 - 1 ----> 3`
   c. `6 / 2 + 1 + 3 * 4 ----> 4`

7. For each of the following format fields and corresponding data, indicate what the PC displays. Use the letter b to indicate the space character. Notice that if a format field does not include enough positions to the left of the decimal point, the PC displays the result preceded by a percent (%) sign. If the format field does not include enough positions to the right of the decimal point, the PC rounds the result to fit the format field.

Format Field	*Data*	*Result*
a. ####	15	
b. #,###	345	
c. $$,###.##	1395.54	
d. ###.##	12.5675	
e. ##,###.###	19412.5	
f. ##.##	576.3	
g. ###.#####	32.2	
h. #.##	.234	

STUDENT ASSIGNMENTS

STUDENT ASSIGNMENT 1: Payroll Report

Instructions: Design and code a QuickBASIC program to generate the formatted payroll report shown under OUTPUT. The weekly pay is calculated by multiplying the hourly pay by the number of hours. All hours are paid at straight time. As part of the Wrap-Up module, display the total number of employees and the total weekly pay of all employees. Submit a program flowchart, listing of the program, and a listing of the output results.

INPUT: Use the following sample data:

EMPLOYEE NAME	HOURLY PAY RATE	HOURS WORKED
Joe Lomax	7.70	40
Ed Mann	6.05	38.5
Louis Orr	8.10	45
Ted Simms	9.50	39.5
Joan Zang	12.00	92
EOF	0	0

OUTPUT: The following results are displayed:

```
                 Payroll Report

Employee        Hourly        Hours        Weekly
Name            Rate          Worked       Pay

Joe Lomax        7.70          40.0        308.00
Ed Mann          6.05          38.5        232.93
Louis Orr        8.10          45.0        364.50
Ted Simms        9.50          39.5        375.25
Joan Zang       12.00          92.0      1,104.00

Total Employees ========>         5
Total Weekly Pay =======>  $2,384.68

End of Report
```

STUDENT ASSIGNMENT 2: Test Score Report

Instructions: Design and code a QuickBASIC program that prints the student test report shown under OUTPUT. In each detail line, include the student's name, test scores, and average test score. The average test score is calculated by adding the score for test 1 and the score for test 2 and dividing by 2. After all records for all students have been processed, print the total number of students and the class average for all tests. To obtain a class average, add all test scores and divide by twice the number of students. Use the `LPRINT` and `LPRINT USING` statements to generate the report on the printer.

INPUT: Use the following sample data:

STUDENT NAME	TEST 1 SCORE	TEST 2 SCORE
Julie Banks	70	78
John Davis	92	93
Joe Gomez	88	84
Sally Katz	78	83
EOF	0	0

OUTPUT: The following results are printed:

```
                 Test Score Report

Student
Name             Test 1         Test 2      Average

Julie Banks        70             78          74.0
John Davis         92             93          92.5
Joe Gomez          88             84          86.0
Sally Katz         78             83          80.5

Total Students ===========>    4
Class Average  ===========>   83.25

End of Report
```

PROJECT 3

Decisions

QuickBASIC includes the `IF` and `SELECT CASE` statements to instruct the PC to select one action or another on the basis of a comparison of numbers or strings. You use the `IF` statement to implement the **If-Then-Else structure** shown in Figure 3-1. When the structure in a flowchart has more than two alternative paths, you use the `SELECT CASE` statement. This type of structure is called a **case structure** and is shown in Figure 3-2.

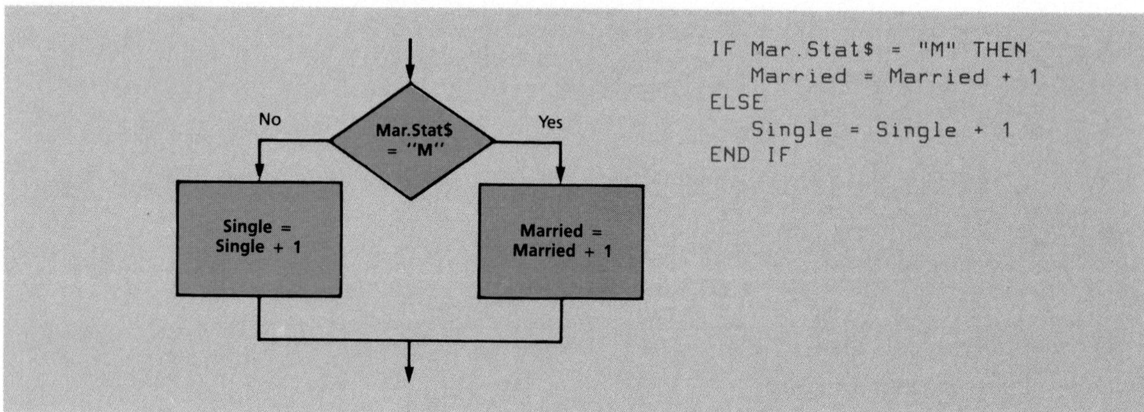

No
Mar.Stat$ = "M"
Yes
Single = Single + 1
Married = Married + 1
IF Mar.Stat$ = "M" THEN
Married = Married + 1
ELSE
Single = Single + 1
END IF

FIGURE 3-1 For the If-Then-Else structure, use the IF statement

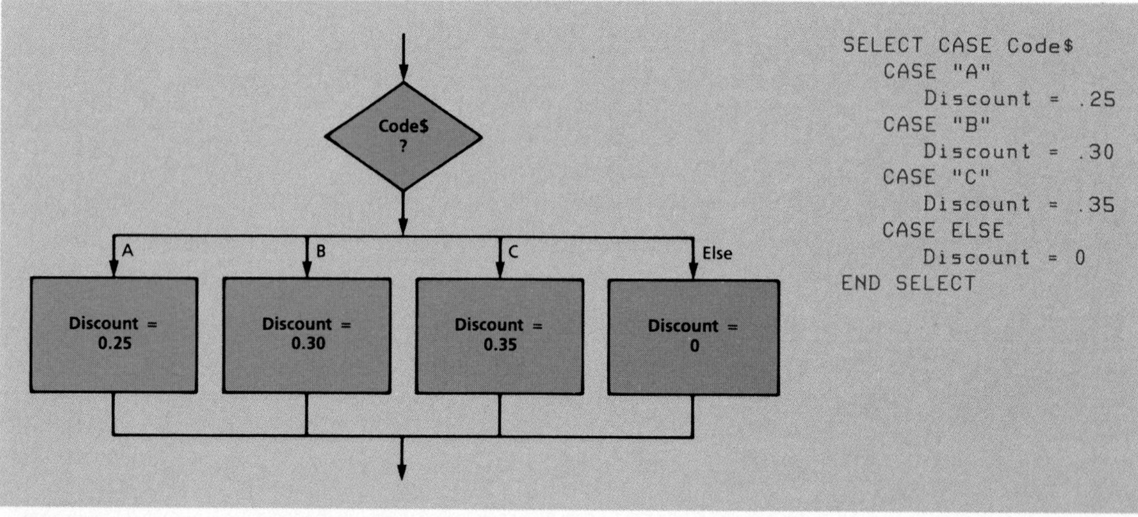

Code$?
A
B
C
Else
Discount = 0.25
Discount = 0.30
Discount = 0.35
Discount = 0
SELECT CASE Code$
CASE "A"
Discount = .25
CASE "B"
Discount = .30
CASE "C"
Discount = .35
CASE ELSE
Discount = 0
END SELECT

FIGURE 3-2 For a Case structure, use the SELECT CASE statement

THE IF STATEMENT

The `IF` statement is commonly regarded as the most powerful statement in QuickBASIC. The major function of this statement is to choose between two alternative paths. The `IF` statement has two general forms as shown in Figure 3-3.

Single-Line IF

```
IF condition THEN true task ELSE false task
```

Block IF

```
IF condition THEN
   true task
ELSE
   false task
END IF
```

FIGURE 3-3 The general form of the IF statement

In Figure 3-3, **condition** is a comparison between two expressions that is either true or false. **True task** and **false task** are statements or series of statements. If the condition is true, the PC executes the true task, also called the `THEN` clause, or **true case**. If the condition is false and an `ELSE` clause is included, the PC executes the false task, also called the `ELSE` clause, or **false case**. After either task is executed, control passes to the statement following the single-line `IF` statement or to the statement following the `END IF` for a block `IF`.

Figure 3-4 illustrates several examples of `IF` statements with conditions made up of numeric and string expressions. For numeric conditions, the PC evaluates not only the magnitude of each resultant expression but also its sign. For string expressions, the PC evaluates the two strings from left to right, one character at a time. With the block `IF` statement, the true and false tasks are indented by three spaces to improve the readability of the code.

Examples 1 through 3 in Figure 3-4 include conditions made up of numeric expressions. Examples 4 and 5 show `IF` statements with conditions made up of string expressions.

EXAMPLE	STATEMENT	VALUE OF VARIABLES	RESULT
1	`IF Amt = 0 THEN Dis = 4`	Amt = 0	The variable Dis is assigned the value 4, and control passes to the line following the IF statement.

2	`IF A < B THEN`
	`   PRINT X`
	`   T = T + 10`
	`ELSE`
	`   PRINT Y`
	`   Tax = Tax + 5`
	`END IF`
		A = 3
		B = 5
			The value of X is displayed; T is incremented by 10, and control passes to the line following the END IF.

3	`IF F < X - Y - 6 THEN`
	`   PRINT S`
	`END IF`
		F = 23
		X = 7
		Y = –8
			Control passes to the line following the END IF.

4	`IF C$ < D$ + E$ THEN`
	`   READ A, B, C`
	`   PRINT Y`
	`END IF`
		C$ = "JIM"
		D$ = "JA"
		E$ = "MES"
			Control passes to the line following the END IF.

5	`IF X$ = "YES" THEN`
	`   PRINT A$`
	`END IF`
		X$ = "yes"	Control passes to the line following the END IF. "YES" and "yes" are not the same string.

FIGURE 3-4 Examples of IF statements

Six types of relations can be used in a condition within an `IF` statement. These relations include determining if:

1. One value is equal to another (=)
2. One value is less than another (<)
3. One value is greater than another (>)
4. One value is less than or equal to another (< =)
5. One value is greater than or equal to another (> =)
6. One value is not equal to another (< >)

Recall that these are the same six relational operators we discussed earlier with the `DO WHILE` statement in Project 1 on page QB 9 in Figure 1-16.

CODING IF-THEN-ELSE STRUCTURES

This section describes various forms of the If-Then-Else structure and the use of `IF` statements to implement them in QuickBASIC.

Simple If-Then-Else Structures

Consider the If-Then-Else structure in Figure 3-5 and the corresponding methods of implementing the logic in QuickBASIC. Assume that the variable Age represents a person's age. If Age is greater than or equal to 18, the person is an adult. If Age is less than 18, the person is a minor. Adult and Minor are counters that are incremented as specified in the flowchart.

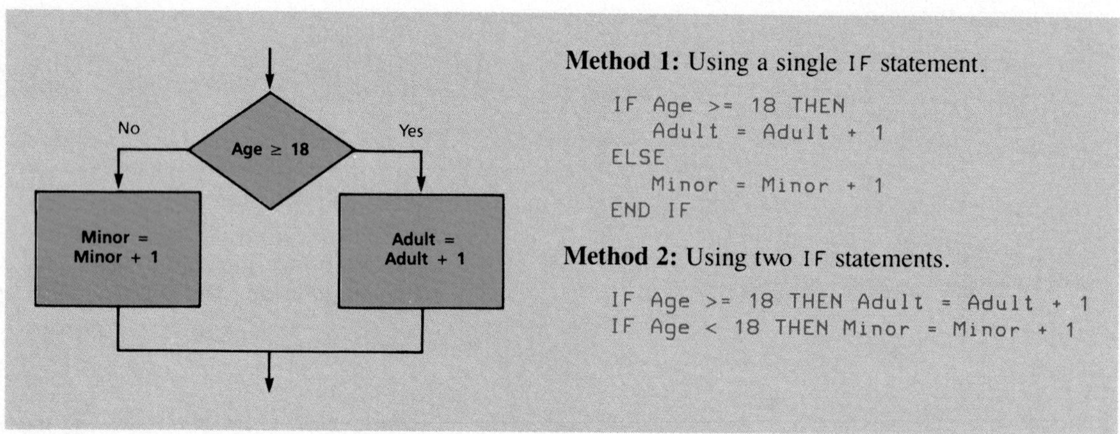

No
Age ≥ 18
Yes
Minor = Minor + 1
Adult = Adult + 1
Method 1: Using a single IF statement.
IF Age >= 18 THEN
   Adult = Adult + 1
ELSE
   Minor = Minor + 1
END IF
Method 2: Using two IF statements.
IF Age >= 18 THEN Adult = Adult + 1
IF Age < 18 THEN Minor = Minor + 1

FIGURE 3-5 Coding an If-Then-Else structure with alternative processing for the true and false cases

In the first method shown in Figure 3-5, an `IF` statement resolves the logic indicated in the partial flowchart. The first line compares Age to 18. If Age is greater than or equal to 18, then Adult is incremented by 1. If Age is less than 18, the false task is carried out and Minor is incremented by 1. Regardless of the counter incremented, control passes to the statement following the `END IF`.

In Method 2, two single-line `IF` statements are used. Age is compared to the value 18 twice. In the first `IF` statement, the counter Adult is incremented by 1 if Age is greater than or equal to 18. In the second `IF` statement, the counter Minor is incremented by 1 if Age is less than 18.

Although both methods are valid and both satisfy the If-Then-Else structure, the first method is more efficient, as it involves fewer lines of code and less execution time. Therefore, the first method is recommended over the second.

Notice that the first method in Figure 3-5 could have been written as a single-line `IF` statement without the `END IF`. However, for readability purposes we recommend that you use the block `IF` statement as shown in Method 1.

As shown in Figures 3-6, 3-7, and 3-8, the If-Then-Else structure can take on a variety of appearances. In Figure 3-6, there is a task only if the condition is true.

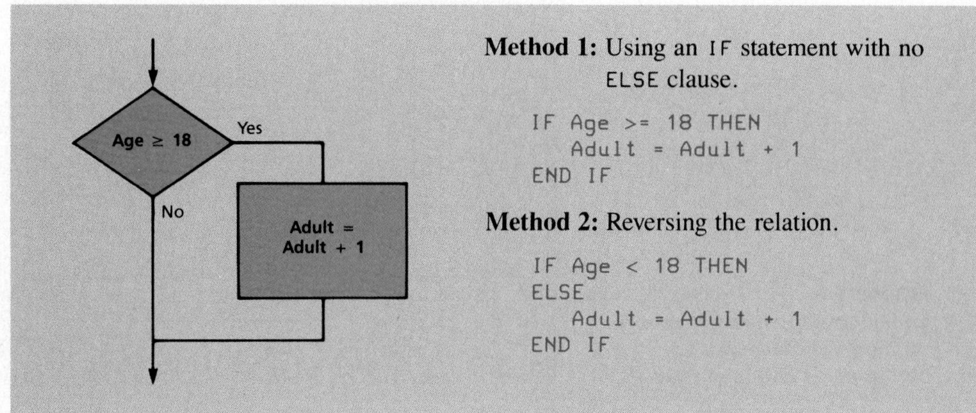

FIGURE 3-6
Coding an If-Then-Else structure with alternative processing for the true case

In Figure 3-6, the first method is preferred over the second since it is more straightforward and less confusing. In Method 2 of Figure 3-6, we reversed the relation. Although this method satisfies the If-Then-Else structure, it is also more difficult to understand. The second method shows that it is valid to have a null `THEN` clause.

The If-Then-Else structure in Figure 3-7 illustrates the incrementation of the counter Minor when the condition is false.

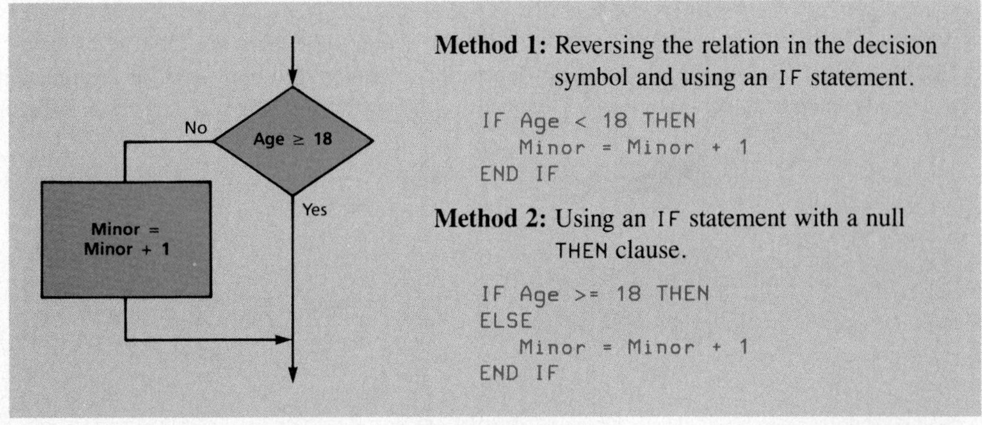

FIGURE 3-7
Coding an If-Then-Else structure with alternative processing for the false case

In Method 1, the relation in the condition that is found in the partial flowchart has been reversed. The condition `Age >= 18` has been modified to read `Age < 18` in the QuickBASIC code. Reversing the relation is usually preferred when additional tasks must be done as a result of the condition being false. In Method 2, the relation is the same as in the decision symbol. When the condition `Age >= 18` is true, the null `THEN` clause simply passes control to the statement following the `END IF`. Either method is acceptable. Some programmers prefer always to include both a `THEN` and an `ELSE` clause, even when one of them is null. On the other hand, some prefer to reverse the relation rather than include a null clause.

On the next page in Figure 3-8, each task in the If-Then-Else structure is made up of multiple statements. We have included a suggested method of implementation.

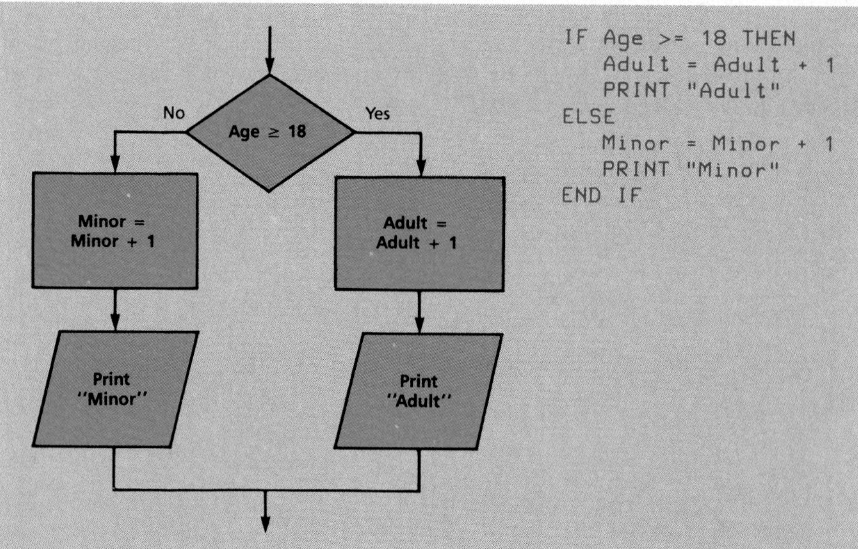

FIGURE 3-8
Coding an If-Then-Else structure with several statements for both the true and false cases

In the code in Figure 3-8, if the condition `Age >= 18` is true, the two statements in the `THEN` clause are executed. If the condition is false, the two statements in the `ELSE` clause are executed.

Although there are alternative methods for implementing the If-Then-Else structure, the method we have presented is more straightforward and involves fewer lines of code.

Nested If-Then-Else Structures

A nested If-Then-Else structure is one in which the action to be taken for the true or false case includes yet another If-Then-Else structure. The second If-Then-Else structure is considered to be nested, or layered, within the first.

Study the partial program that corresponds to the nested If-Then-Else structure in Figure 3-9.

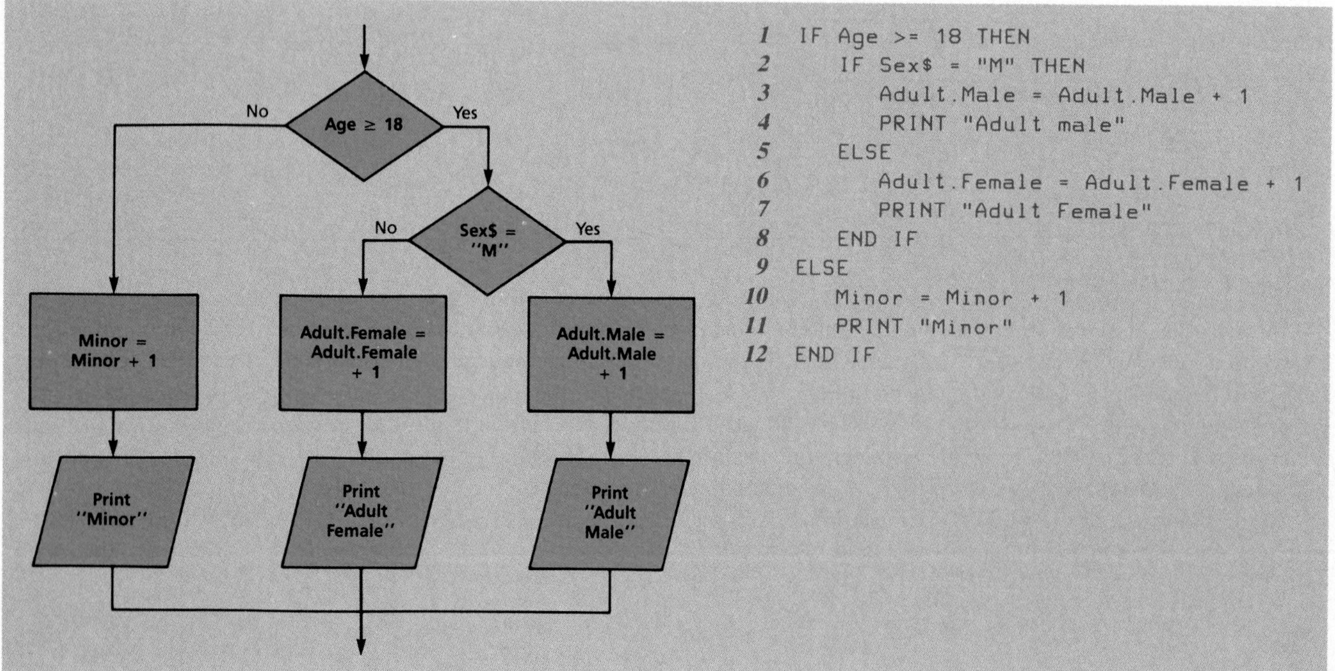

FIGURE 3-9 Coding a nested If-Then-Else structure

In the partial program in Figure 3-9, if the condition `Age >= 18` is true, control passes to the `THEN` clause beginning with line 2. If the condition is false, the `ELSE` clause beginning in line 10 is executed. If control does pass to line 2, then a second `IF` tests to determine if Sex$ equals the value M. If the condition in line 2 is true, lines 3 and 4 are executed. If the condition is false, then the PC executes lines 6 and 7.

QuickBASIC requires that you end each block `IF` statement with an `END IF`. Hence, the block `IF` in line 1 has a corresponding `END IF` in line 12, and the block `IF` in line 2 has a corresponding `END IF` in line 8.

Notice in Figure 3-9 that only one of the three alternative tasks is executed for each record processed. Regardless of the path taken, control eventually passes to the statement immediately following the last `END IF` in line 12.

SAMPLE PROGRAM 3 — VIDEO RENTAL REPORT

To illustrate a program that uses an `IF` statement, consider the following video rental problem. In this application, if the video tape is rented for three days or less, the charge is $2.49 per day. There is a one dollar per day discount for each of the first three days for customers who are at least 65 years old. If the video tape is rented for more than three days, the charge is $3.49 per day for each day over three days.

The video records consist of the customer's name, age, video title, and the number of days rented as shown in Figure 3-10.

CUSTOMER NAME	AGE	VIDEO TITLE	DAYS RENTED
Helen Moore	47	Lost in Space	1
Hank Fisher	67	Together Again	3
Joe Frank	34	Three Lives	7
Al Jones	64	The Last Day	5
Shirley Star	65	Monday Morning	4
EOF	0	End	0

FIGURE 3-10 The video rental file for Sample Program 3

The output is a printed video rental summary report that lists the customer name, customer age, title of the video tape rented, the number of days the tape was rented, and the charge for the rental. After all records have been processed, the number of senior citizen customers, the number of tapes rented, and the total charges are printed. The format of the output is illustrated in Figure 3-11.

```
                              Video Rental Report

Customer                      Video                  Days
Name                 Age      Title                  Rented     Charge

Helen Moore           47      Lost in Space             1         2.49
Hank Fisher           67      Together Again            3         4.47
Joe Frank             34      Three Lives               7        21.43
Al Jones              64      The Last Day              5        14.45
Shirley Star          65      Monday Morning            4         7.96

Senior Citizens ==========>          2
Videos Rented ============>          5
Total Charges ============>     $50.80

End of Report
```

FIGURE 3-11 The report for Sample Program 3

Program Flowchart

The flowchart in Figure 3-12 illustrates the logic required to produce the video rental report.

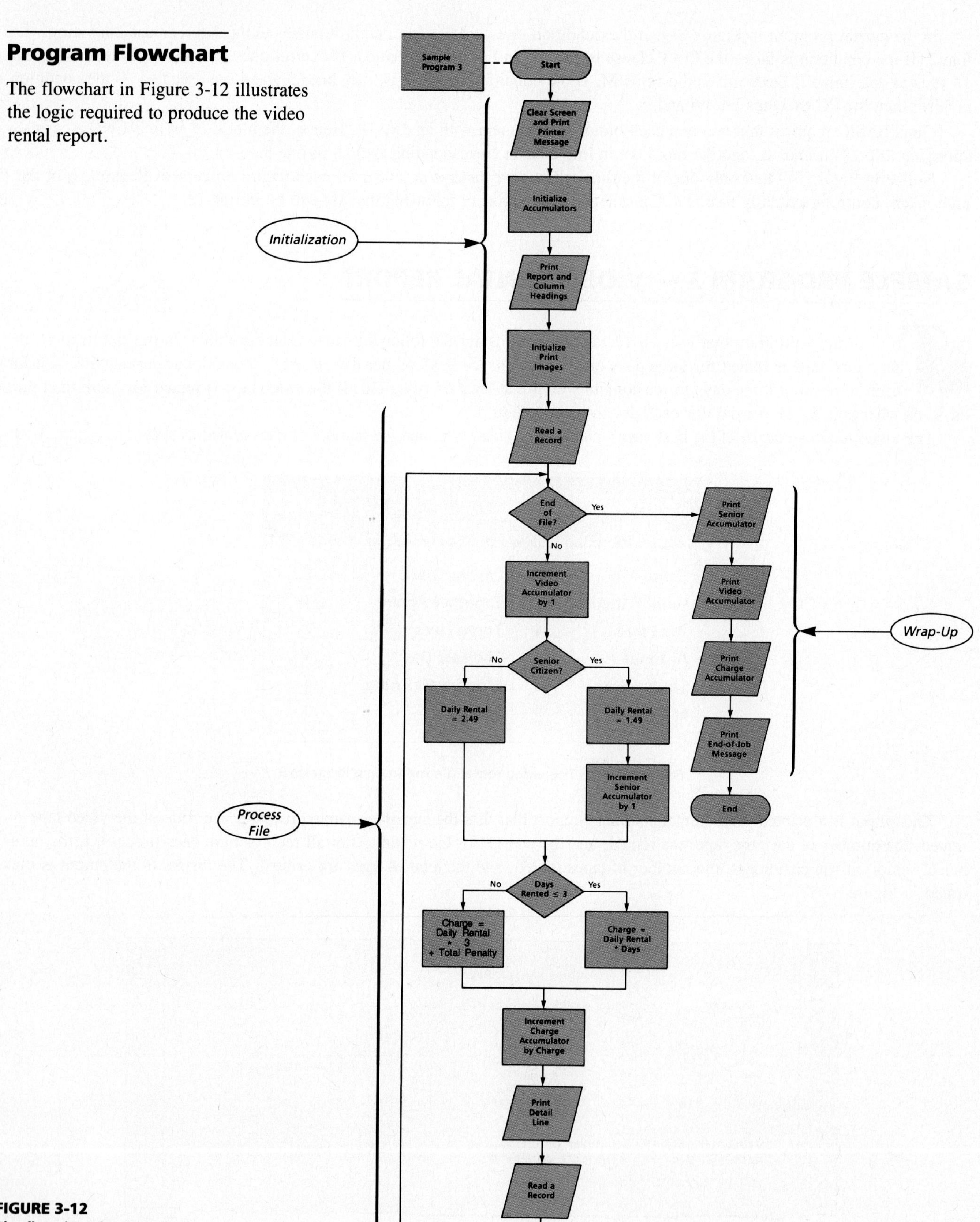

FIGURE 3-12
The flowchart for Sample Program 3

The QuickBASIC Program

The program in Figure 3-13 corresponds to the program flowchart in Figure 3-12.

FIGURE 3-13
Sample Program 3

```
'*************************************************************
' *  Sample Program 3                     September 15, 1994    *
' *  Video Rental Report                                        *
' *  J. S. Quasney                                              *
' *                                                             *
' *  This program prints a video rental report.  The charge     *
' *  is based on the number of days the video is rented and     *
' *  the age of the customer.                                   *
' *       As part of the Wrap-Up module, the total number       *
' *  of videos, senior customers, and charges are printed.      *
' *                                                             *
' *  Variables:  Cus.Name$        -- Name of customer           *
' *              Cus.Age          -- Customer age               *
' *              Video.Title$     -- Title of video             *
' *              Days.Rented      -- Days rented                *
' *              Daily.Rental     -- Cost per day               *
' *              Charge           -- Cost of renting video      *
' *              Penalty          -- Cost per day after 3 days  *
' *              Total.Videos     -- Number of videos rented    *
' *              Total.Seniors    -- Number of senior rentals   *
' *              Total.Charges    -- Total charges              *
' *              DL1$, TL1$, TL2$, TL3$, TL4$ -- Print images   *
'*************************************************************

' ********************** Initialization **********************
CLS  ' Clear Screen
PRINT "****** Video Rental Report Printing on Printer ******"
LET Total.Videos = 0
LET Total.Seniors = 0
LET Total.Charges = 0
LET Penalty = 3.49
LPRINT "                          Video Rental Report"
LPRINT
LPRINT "Customer                  Video              Days"
LPRINT "Name            Age       Title              Rented    Charge"
LPRINT
DL1$ = "\            \  ###   \              \    ###       ###.##"
TL1$ = "Senior Citizens ==========>     ###"
TL2$ = "Videos Rented ============>     ###"
TL3$ = "Total Charges ============> $$,###.##"
TL4$ = "End of Report"

```

(continued)

FIGURE 3-13 (continued)

```
43  ' ************************ Process File ************************
44  READ Cus.Name$, Cus.Age, Video.Title$, Days.Rented
45  DO WHILE Cus.Name$ <> "EOF"
46     LET Total.Videos = Total.Videos + 1
47     IF Cus.Age >= 65 THEN
48        LET Daily.Rental = 1.49
49        LET Total.Seniors = Total.Seniors + 1
50     ELSE
51        LET Daily.Rental = 2.49
52     END IF
53     IF Days.Rented <= 3 THEN
54        LET Charge = Daily.Rental * Days.Rented
55     ELSE
56        LET Charge = (Daily.Rental * 3) + Penalty * (Days.Rented - 3)
57     END IF
58     LET Total.Charges = Total.Charges + Charge
59     LPRINT USING DL1$; Cus.Name$; Cus.Age; Video.Title$; Days.Rented; Charge
60     READ Cus.Name$, Cus.Age, Video.Title$, Days.Rented
61  LOOP
62
63  ' ************************** Wrap-Up *************************
64  LPRINT
65  LPRINT USING TL1$; Total.Seniors
66  LPRINT USING TL2$; Total.Videos
67  LPRINT USING TL3$; Total.Charges
68  LPRINT
69  LPRINT TL4$
70
71  ' ************************ Data Follows **********************
72  DATA Helen Moore, 47, Lost in Space, 1
73  DATA Hank Fisher, 67, Together Again, 3
74  DATA Joe Frank, 34, Three Lives, 7
75  DATA Al Jones, 64, The Last Day, 5
76  DATA Shirley Star, 65, Monday Morning, 4
77  DATA EOF, 0, End, 0
78  END
```

Discussion of Sample Program 3

When Sample Program 3 is executed, the report shown in Figure 3-14 prints on the printer. Sample Program 3 includes a few significant points that did not appear in previous programs. They are as follows:

- When executed, line 26 clears the screen and line 27 displays a friendly message informing the user that the report is being printed on the printer.
- `LPRINT` and `LPRINT USING` statements are used throughout the program to print the report on the printer rather than display the report on the monitor.
- There are two `IF` statements that select alternative paths on the basis of the data in the video record being processed. The block `IF` in lines 47 through 52 determines whether the customer is a senior citizen. If the customer is a senior citizen, the daily rental (Daily.Rental) is set to $1.49 and the senior citizen counter is incremented. If the customer is not a senior citizen, then the daily rental is set to $2.49.

  The second block `IF` statement (lines 53 through 57) determines how much to charge the customer being processed. If the video is rented for three days or less, the charge is determined from the following `LET` statement:

  ```
  LET Charge = Daily.Rental * Days.Rented
  ```

  If the video is rented for more than three days, the charge is determined from the following `LET` statement:

  ```
  LET Charge = (Daily.Rental * 3) + Penalty * (Days.Rented - 3)
  ```

```
                         Video Rental Report

Customer                    Video                  Days
Name               Age      Title                  Rented    Charge

Helen Moore         47      Lost in Space            1         2.49
Hank Fisher         67      Together Again           3         4.47
Joe Frank           34      Three Lives              7        21.43
Al Jones            64      The Last Day             5        14.45
Shirley Star        65      Monday Morning           4         7.96

Senior Citizens ==========>          2
Videos Rented ============>          5
Total Charges ============>     $50.80

End of Report
```

FIGURE 3-14
The report printed when Sample Program 3 is executed

LOGICAL OPERATORS

In many instances, a decision to execute a true task or false task is based upon two or more conditions. In previous examples that involved two or more conditions, we tested each condition in a separate IF statement. In this section, we discuss combining conditions within one IF statement by means of the logical operators AND and OR. When two or more conditions are combined by these logical operators, the expression is called a **compound condition**. The logical operator NOT allows you to write a compound condition in which the truth value of the simple condition following NOT is **complemented**, or reversed.

The NOT Logical Operator

A simple condition that is preceded by the logical operator NOT forms a compound condition that is false when the simple condition is true. If the simple condition is false, then the compound condition is true. Consider the two IF statements in Figure 3-15. Both print the value of Discount if Margin is less than or equal to Cost.

Method 1: Using the NOT logical operator.

```
IF NOT Margin > Cost THEN
   PRINT Discount
END IF
```

Method 2: Reversing the relational operator.

```
IF Margin <= Cost THEN
   PRINT Discount
END IF
```

FIGURE 3-15
Use of the NOT logical operator

In Method 1 of Figure 3-15, if Margin is greater than Cost (the simple condition is true), then the compound condition NOT Margin > Cost is false. If Margin is less than or equal to Cost (the simple condition is false), then the NOT makes the compound condition true. In Method 2, the relational operator is reversed and, therefore, the NOT is eliminated. Both methods are equivalent.

Because the logical operator NOT can increase the complexity of the decision statement significantly, use it sparingly. As shown in Figure 3-15, you can always reverse the relational operator in a condition to eliminate the logical operator NOT.

The AND Logical Operator

The AND operator requires that both conditions be true for the compound condition to be true. Consider the two IF statements in Figure 3-16. Both methods read a value for Selling.Price if Margin is greater than 10 and Cost is less than 8.

Method 1: Using the AND logical operator.

```
IF Margin > 10 AND Cost < 8 THEN
   READ Selling.Price
END IF
```

Method 2: Using nested IF statements.

```
IF Margin > 10 THEN
   IF Cost < 8 THEN
      READ Selling.Price
   END IF
END IF
```

FIGURE 3-16 Use of the AND operator

In Method 1 of Figure 3-16, if Margin is greater than 10 and Cost is less than 8, the READ statement assigns a value to Selling.Price before control passes to the line following the END IF. If either one of the conditions is false, then the compound condition is false, and control passes to the line following the END IF without a value being read for Selling.Price. Although both methods are equivalent, Method 1 is more efficient, more compact, and more straightforward than Method 2.

Like a single condition, a compound condition can be only true or false. To determine the truth value of the compound condition, the PC must evaluate and assign a truth value to each individual condition. Then the truth value is determined for the compound condition.

For example, if A equals 4 and C$ equals "X", the PC evaluates the following compound condition in the manner shown:

```
IF A = 3 AND C$ = "X" THEN LET F = F + 1
```

1. false (A = 3)
2. true (C$ = "X")
3. false

The PC first determines the truth value for each condition, then concludes that the compound condition is false because of the AND operator.

The OR Logical Operator

The OR operator requires that only one of the two conditions be true for the compound condition to be true. If both conditions are true, the compound condition is also true. Likewise, if both conditions are false, the compound condition is false. The use of the OR operator is illustrated in Figure 3-17.

Method 1: Using the OR logical operator.

```
IF Code$ = "A" OR Marital.Status$ = "M" THEN
   END
END IF
```

Method 2: Using two IF statements.

```
IF Code$ = "A" THEN
   END
END IF
IF Marital.Status$ = "M" THEN
   END
END IF
```

FIGURE 3-17 Use of the OR operator

In Method 1 of Figure 3-17, if either Code$ equals the value A or Marital.Status$ equals the value M, the THEN clause is executed and the program halts execution. If both conditions are true, the THEN clause is also executed. If both conditions are false, the THEN clause is bypassed, and control passes to the line following the END IF. Method 2 employs two IF statements to resolve the same If-Then-Else structure. Again, both methods are equivalent, but, Method 1 is easier to read and understand than Method 2.

As with the logical operator AND, the truth values of the individual conditions in the IF statement are first determined, then the truth values for the conditions containing the logical operator OR are evaluated. For example, if F equals 4 and H equals 5, the following condition is true:

```
IF F = 3 OR H = 5 THEN PRINT "Yes"
```

1. false 2. true

3. true

Combining Logical Operators

Logical operators can be combined in a decision statement to form a compound condition. The formation of compound statements that involve more than one type of logical operator can create problems unless you fully understand the order in which the PC evaluates the entire condition. Unless parentheses dictate otherwise, reading from left to right, conditions containing arithmetic operators are evaluated first; then those containing relational operators; then those containing NOT operators; then those containing AND operators; then those containing OR operators. Refer to the last page of the Reference Card at the back of this book for a summary listing of the order of both arithmetic and logical operators.

For the following compound condition assume, that D = 3, P = 5, R = 3, T = 5, S = 6, and Y = 3:

```
IF S > Y OR T = D AND P < 5 OR NOT Y = R THEN READ L
```

1. true 2. false 3. false 4. true

6. false 5. false

7. true

8. true

The Use of Parentheses in Compound Conditions

Parentheses may be used to change the order of precedence. When there are parentheses in a compound condition, the PC evaluates that part of the compound condition within the parentheses first, then continues to evaluate the remaining compound condition according to the order of logical operations. For example, suppose variable J has a value of 2, and E has a value of 6. Consider the following compound condition:

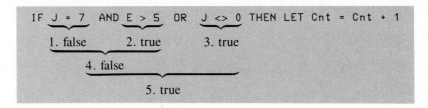

```
IF J = 7  AND E > 5  OR  J <> 0 THEN LET Cnt = Cnt + 1
   1. false   2. true    3. true
        4. false
                5. true
```

Following the order of logical operations, the compound condition yields a truth value of true. If parentheses surround the last two conditions, then the `OR` operator is evaluated before the `AND` condition, and the compound condition yields a truth value of false, as shown:

```
IF J = 7  AND (E > 5  OR  J <> 0) THEN LET Cnt = Cnt + 1
   4. false    1. true    2. true
                   3. true
            5. false
```

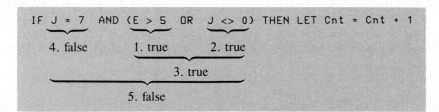

Parentheses may be used freely when the evaluation of a compound condition is in doubt. For example, if you wish to evaluate the compound condition

```
IF C > D AND S = 4 OR X < Y AND T = 5 THEN READ F
```

you may incorporate it into a decision statement as it stands. You may also write in the following way:

```
IF (C > D AND S = 4) OR (X < Y AND T = 5) THEN READ F
```

and feel more certain of the outcome of the decision statement.

THE SELECT CASE STATEMENT

The `SELECT CASE` statement is used to implement the case structure. Figure 3-18 illustrates the implementation of a case structure, which determines a letter grade (Letter.Grade$) from a grade point average (GPA) using the following grading scale:

GRADE POINT AVERAGE	LETTER GRADE
GPA ≥ 90	A
80 ≤ GPA < 90	B
70 ≤ GPA < 80	C
60 ≤ GPA < 70	D
0 ≤ GPA < 60	F
GPA < 0	Error

For example, if your GPA is 79.6, your letter grade is a C.

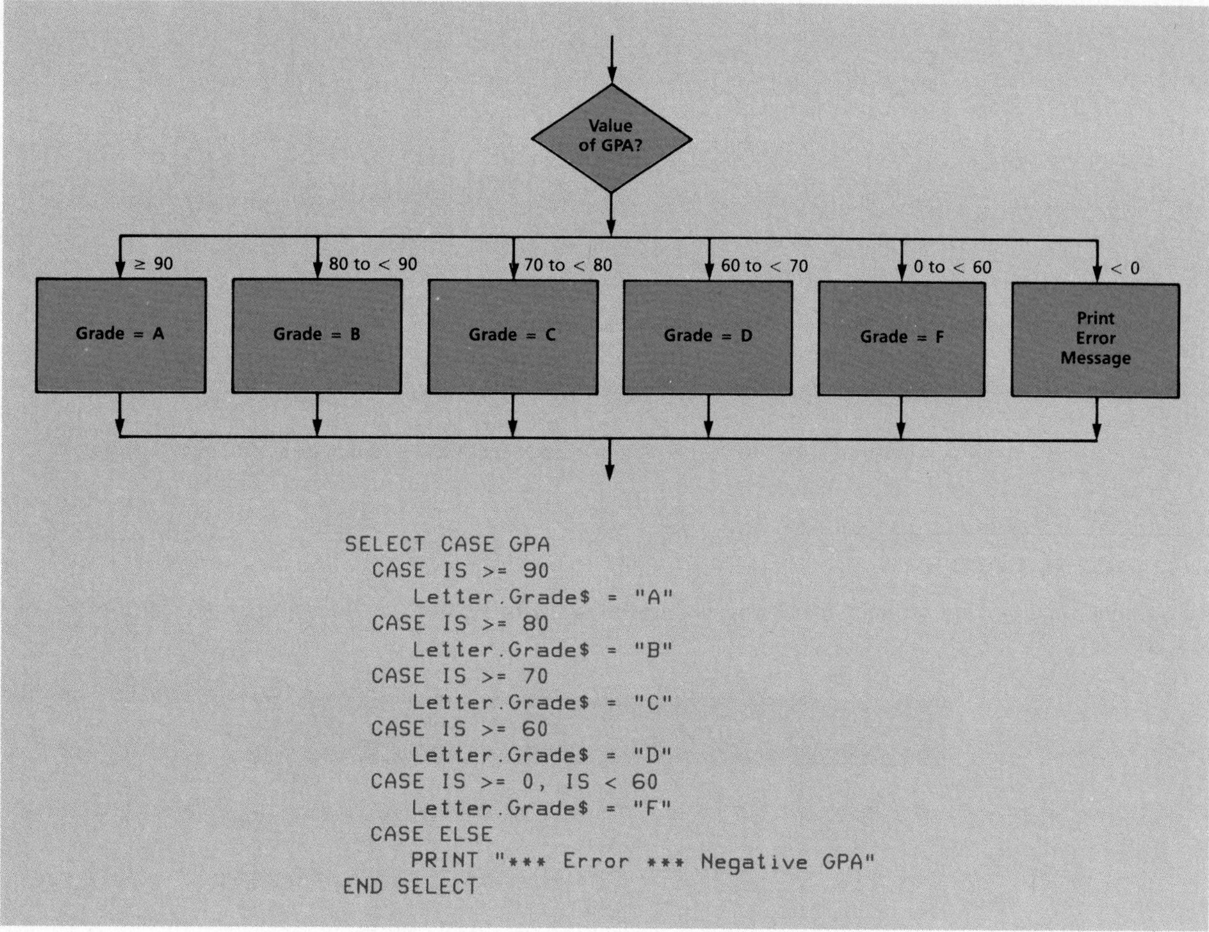


```
SELECT CASE GPA
  CASE IS >= 90
     Letter.Grade$ = "A"
  CASE IS >= 80
     Letter.Grade$ = "B"
  CASE IS >= 70
     Letter.Grade$ = "C"
  CASE IS >= 60
     Letter.Grade$ = "D"
  CASE IS >= 0, IS < 60
     Letter.Grade$ = "F"
  CASE ELSE
     PRINT "*** Error *** Negative GPA"
END SELECT
```

FIGURE 3-18 Implementation of a case structure

The SELECT CASE statement in Figure 3-18 is used to implement the grading scale. When the PC executes the SELECT CASE statement, it compares the variable GPA, which follows the keywords SELECT CASE, to the expressions following the keyword CASE in each CASE clause, also called a **case**. The PC begins the comparison with the first case and continues through the remaining ones until it finds a match. When a match is found, the range of statements immediately following the keyword CASE is executed. Following execution of the case, control immediately transfers to the statement following the END SELECT. The PC does not search for additional matches in the remaining cases.

For example, if GPA is equal to 79.6, then the PC finds a match in the third case. Therefore, it assigns Letter.Grade$ the value C and passes control to the statement following the END SELECT. If GPA equals a negative value, then no match is found, and the PRINT statement following the CASE ELSE is executed.

The CASE ELSE just prior to the END SELECT in Figure 3-18 instructs the PC to use this case if there is no match with any of the previous CASE clauses.

In a SELECT CASE, you place the variable, or expression, also called the **test-expression**, to test after the keywords SELECT CASE. Next, you assign the group of values, also called the **match-expression**, that make each alternative case true after the keyword CASE. Each case contains the range of statements to execute, and you may have as many cases as required. After the last case, end the SELECT CASE with an END SELECT.

The general form of the SELECT CASE statement is shown in Figure 3-19.

```
SELECT CASE test-expression
  CASE match-expression
     [range of statements]
  CASE match-expression
     [range of statements]
     .
     .
     .
  CASE ELSE
     [range of statements]
END SELECT
```

where **test-expression** is a numeric or string expression and **match-expression** indicates the values for which the case is selected.

FIGURE 3-19 The general form of the SELECT CASE statement

Valid Match-Expressions

There are several ways to construct valid match-expressions following the keyword CASE. Consider the match-expressions in Figure 3-20.

EXAMPLE	MATCH-EXPRESSION
1	`CASE "F" TO "H", "S", Code$`
2	`CASE IS = Salary, IS = Max.Salary - 5000`
3	`CASE IS < 12, 20 TO 30, 48.6, IS > 100`

FIGURE 3-20 Valid match-expressions in a SELECT CASE statement

In Example 1 in Figure 3-20, the match-expression is a list made up of the letters F to H, the letter S, and the value of the variable Code$. In Example 2, the match-expression includes Salary and the expression Max.Salary – 5000. If a relational operator is used, then the keyword IS is required. The second value in the list of Example 2 shows that expressions with arithmetic operators are allowed. The third example includes a list that requires the use of the keywords IS and TO. Use the keyword IS before any relational operator, such as = or >. Use the keyword TO to define a range of values.

TRY IT YOURSELF EXERCISES

1. Determine the value of Amt that will cause the condition in the following IF statements to be true:

a.
```
IF Amt > 8 OR Amt = 3 THEN
   Z = Z / 10
END IF
```

b.
```
IF Amt + 10 >= 7 AND NOT Amt < 0 THEN
   PRINT "The answer is"; A
END IF
```

2. Construct partial programs for each of these structures.

a.

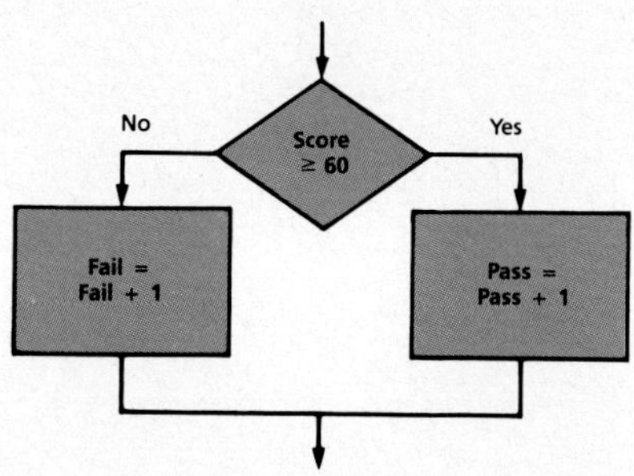

b.

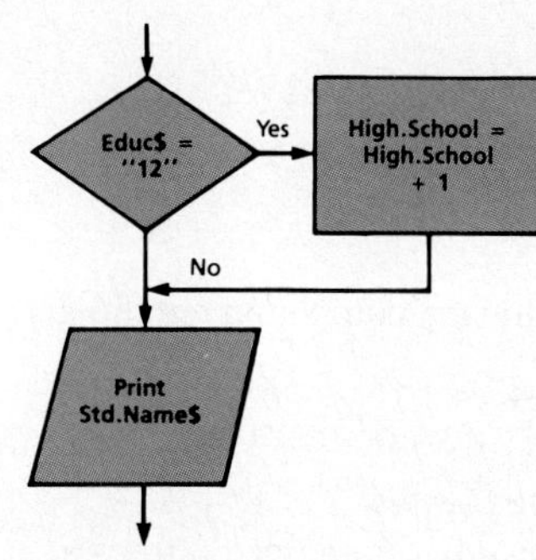

3. Construct partial programs for each of these logic structures.

a.

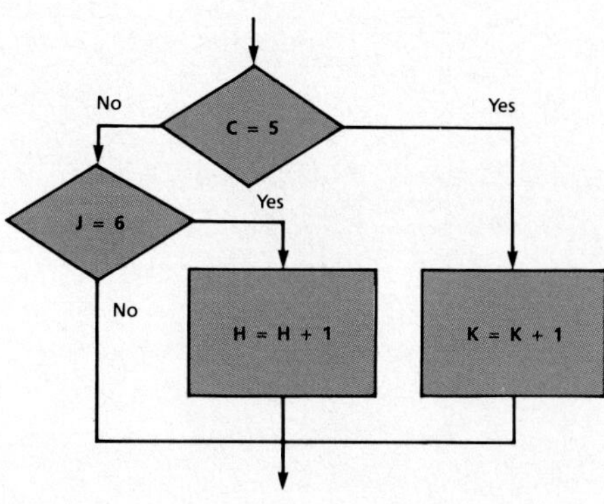

b.

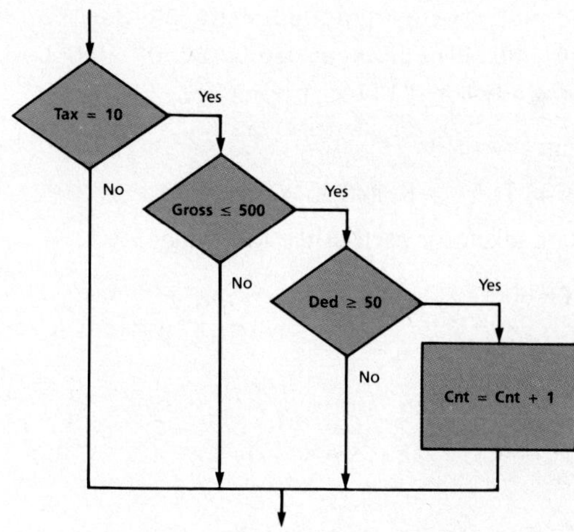

4. What is displayed if the following program is executed?

```
' Exercise 4
READ I
DO WHILE I <> -99
   SELECT CASE I
      CASE 1, 4, 7
         PRINT I, "Case 1"
      CASE IS < 8
         PRINT I, "Case 2"
      CASE 14 TO 21
         PRINT I, "Case 3"
      CASE ELSE
         PRINT I, "Case 4"
   END SELECT
   READ I
LOOP
DATA 1, 4, 7, 2, 21, 20, -99
END
```

5. Given the following:

   Emp.Num = 500
   Salary = $700
   Job.Code$ = “1”
   Tax = $60
   Insurance.Ded = $40

   Determine the truth value of the following compound conditions:

   a. `Emp.Num < 400 OR Job.Code$ = "1"`
   b. `Salary = 700 AND Tax = 50`
   c. `Salary - Tax = 640 AND Job.Code$ = "1"`
   d. `Tax + Insurance.Ded = Salary - 500 OR Job.Code$ = "0"`
   e. `NOT Job.Code$ < "0"`
   f. `NOT (Job.Code$ = "1" OR Tax = 60)`
   g. `Salary < 300 AND Insurance.Ded < 50 OR Job.Code$ = "1"`
   h. `Salary < 300 AND (Insurance.Ded < 50 OR Job.Code$ = "1")`
   i. `NOT (NOT Job.Code$ = "1")`

6. Given the following:

   T = 0, V = 4, B = 7, Y = 8, and X = 3

   Determine the action taken for each of the following:

   a.
   ```
   IF T > 0 THEN
       READ A
   END IF
   ```
   b.
   ```
   IF B = 4 OR T > 7 THEN
       IF X > 1 THEN
           READ A
       END IF
   END IF
   ```
   c.
   ```
   IF X = 3 OR T > 2 THEN
       IF Y > 7 THEN
           READ A
       END IF
   END IF
   ```
   d.
   ```
   IF X + 2 < 5 THEN
       IF B < V + X THEN
           READ A
       END IF
   END IF
   ```

7. Write a program that determines the number of negative values (Negative), number of zero values (Zero) and number of positive values (Positive) in the following data set: 4, 2, 3, –9, 0, 0, –4, –6, –8, 3, 2, 0, 0, 8, –3, 4. Use the –999999 to test for the end-of-file.
8. The values of three variables Num1, Num2, and Num3 are positive and not equal to each other. Using `IF` statements, determine which has the smallest value and assign this value to Little.
9. The IOU National Bank computes its monthly service charge on checking accounts by adding $0.50 to a value computed from the following:
   $0.21 per check for the first ten checks
   $0.19 per check for the next ten checks
   $0.17 per check for the next ten checks
   $0.15 per check for the remaining checks

   Write a sequence of statements that includes a `SELECT CASE` statement and a `PRINT` statement to display the account number (Account), the number of checks cashed (Checks), and the computed monthly charge (Charge). Assume the account number and the number of checks cashed are in `DATA` statements.

STUDENT ASSIGNMENTS

STUDENT ASSIGNMENT 1: Student Registration Report

Instructions: Design and code a QuickBASIC program to process the data shown under INPUT. Generate the student registration report shown under OUTPUT. A student with less than 12 hours is defined as part-time. The registration fee is determined from the following:

Credits Hours	Fee
Less than 12	$400.00
12 or more	$400.00 plus $30.00 per credit hour in excess of 11 hours

As part of the end-of-job routine, print the total number of part-time students, full-time students, students, and fees.

INPUT: Use the following sample data:

STUDENT NAME	CREDIT HOURS
Joe Franks	14
Ed Crane	9
Susan Lewis	18
Fred Smith	12
Jack North	10
Nikole Hiegh	17
EOF	0

OUTPUT: The following results are printed:

```
                 Student Registration

Student        Credit
Name           Hours        Fee     Status

Joe Franks       14      490.00     Full-Time
Ed Crane          9      400.00     Part-Time
Susan Lewis      18      610.00     Full-Time
Fred Smith       12      430.00     Full-Time
Jack North       10      400.00     Part-Time
Nikole Hiegh     17      580.00     Full-Time

Total Part-Time ====>         2
Total Full-Time ====>         4
Total Students =====>         6
Total Fees =========>  $2,910.00

End of Report
```

STUDENT ASSIGNMENT 2: Employee Salary Increase Report

Instructions: Design and code a QuickBASIC program to process the data shown under INPUT. Use `IF` statements with compound conditions to display on the screen the employee salary increase report shown under OUTPUT.

Determine the employee salary increase from the following:

1. All employees get a 4% salary increase
2. All employees get a 0.025% times the number of annual merits salary increase.
3. Employees with more than three annual merits and 10 or more years of service get an additional 2.5% salary increase
4. Employees with four or more annual merits and less than 10 years of service get an additional 1.5% salary increase

INPUT: Use the following sample data. Make sure you enclose the employee names within quotation marks, since each name includes a comma.

EMPLOYEE NAME	ANNUAL MERITS	SERVICE	CURRENT SALARY
Babjack, Bill	9	3	$19,500
Knopf, Louis	0	19	29,200
Taylor, Jane	8	12	26,000
Droopey, Joe	8	4	28,000
Lane, Lyn	2	9	19,800
Lis, Frank	6	1	21,000
Lopez, Hector	10	1	15,000
Braion, Jim	8	19	26,500
EOF	0	0	0

OUTPUT: The following results are displayed:

```
                  Employee Salary Increase Report

Employee          Annual      Current                          New
Name              Merits      Salary         Raise            Salary

Babjack, Bill       9       19,500.00     1,116.38        20,616.38
Knopf, Louis        0       29,200.00     1,168.00        30,368.00
Taylor, Jane        8       26,000.00     1,742.00        27,742.00
Droopey, Joe        8       28,000.00     1,596.00        29,596.00
Lane, Lyn           2       19,800.00       801.90        20,601.90
Lis, Frank          6       21,000.00     1,186.50        22,186.50
Lopez, Hector      10       15,000.00       862.50        15,862.50
Braion, Jim         8       26,500.00     1,775.50        28,275.50
                           ==========     ========       ==========
                           185,000.00    10,248.78       195,248.78

Total Employees =============>        8
Average Employee Raise =====>  $1,281.10

End of Report
```

STUDENT ASSIGNMENT 3: Computer Usage Report

Instructions: Design and code a QuickBASIC program to process the data shown under INPUT and prints the report shown under OUTPUT. Use the SELECT CASE statement to determine the computer charges. At the end-of-job, print the total customers, total hours in decimal, and the total charges. The monthly charges can be determined from the following:

1. $165.00 for one hour or less usage
2. $240.00 for usage greater than one hour and less than or equal to two hours
3. $300.00 for usage greater than two hours and less than or equal to three hours
4. $330.00 for usage greater than three hours and less than or equal to four hours
5. $375.00 for usage greater than four hours and less than or equal to five hours
6. $1.25 per minute if the usage is greater than five hours

INPUT: Use the following sample data:

CUSTOMER NAME	HOURS	MINUTES
Acme Inc.	2	0
Hitek	2	50
Floline	5	10
Niki's Food	1	14
Amanda Inc.	6	22
EOF	0	0

OUTPUT: The following results are printed:

```
                 Computer Usage Report

Customer
Name              Hours      Minutes      Charges

Acme Inc.           2            0         240.00
Hitek               2           50         300.00
Floline             5           10         387.50
Niki's Food         1           14         240.00
Amanda Inc.         6           22         477.50

Total Customers =======>         5
Total Hours ===========>     17.60
Total Charges =========> $1,645.00

End of Report
```

PROJECT 4

Interactive Programming, For Loops, and an Introduction to the Top-Down Approach

One of the major tasks of any program is to integrate the data that is to be processed into the program. In the first three projects, the READ and DATA statements were used to integrate the data into the program. This project introduces you to another method of data integration through the use of the INPUT statement. The INPUT statement is different than the READ and DATA statements, because with the INPUT statement the data is entered *during* execution rather than as *part of the program*.

A second topic covered in this project is alternative methods for implementing loops in QuickBASIC. Through the first three projects, we have consistently created loops using the DO WHILE and LOOP statements. In this project we discuss the creation of loops using the DO and LOOP UNTIL statements and the FOR and NEXT statements. The DO and LOOP UNTIL statements allow you to create loops that test for termination at the bottom of the loop rather than at the top of the loop. The FOR and NEXT statements allow you to more efficiently establish counter-controlled loops. A **counter-controlled loop** is one that exits the loop when a counter has reached a specified number.

Finally, this project presents the top-down approach to solving problems. The top-down approach is a useful methodology for solving large and complex problems. This approach breaks the problem into smaller parts and allows you to solve each part independent of the others.

THE INPUT STATEMENT

The INPUT statement causes a program to temporarily halt execution and accept data through the keyboard as shown in Figure 4-1. After the user enters the required data (1.25 in Figure 4-1) through the keyboard, the program continues to execute.

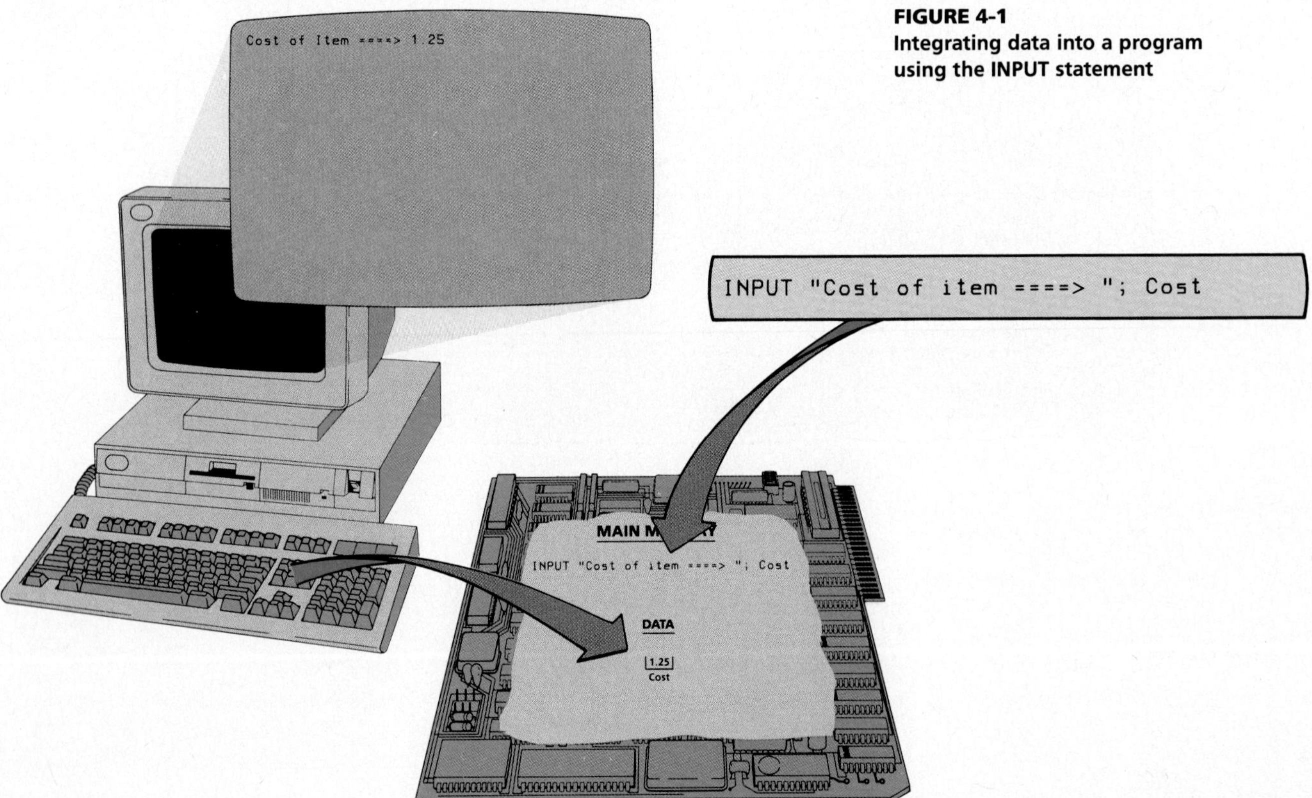

FIGURE 4-1
Integrating data into a program using the INPUT statement

The INPUT statement has two general forms, shown in Figure 4-2. With the first general form, the keyword INPUT is immediately followed by one or more variables separated by commas. When executed, this first form displays a question mark on the screen to indicate that it is waiting for the user to enter data.

The second general form of the INPUT statement shows that the programmer may enter a **prompt message** to inform the user of the required data. In this second and most often used form, the keyword INPUT is followed by the prompt message in quotation marks, a comma or semicolon after the prompt message, and a list of variables separated by commas. A semicolon after a prompt message tells the PC to display a question mark immediately after the prompt message. A comma instructs the PC not to display the question mark. Although this statement may include more than one variable, most programmers place one variable per INPUT statement.

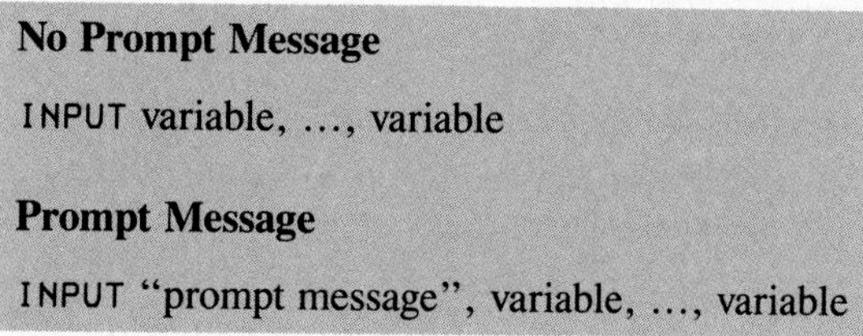
No Prompt Message

INPUT variable, ..., variable

Prompt Message

INPUT "prompt message", variable, ..., variable

FIGURE 4-2 The general form of the INPUT statement

Figure 4-3 illustrates several examples of INPUT statements.

EXAMPLE	INPUT STATEMENT	DATA ENTERED THROUGH KEYBOARD
1	`INPUT Amount, Cost`	`125.56, 75`
2	`INPUT Cus.Name$, Age, Deduction`	`Joe Dac, 57, 25`
3	`INPUT "Discount =====>", Disc`	`.25`
4	`INPUT "What is your name"; User.Name$`	`Marci Jean`
5	`PRINT "Do you want to continue?"` `INPUT "Enter Y for Yes, else N", Control$`	`Y`

FIGURE 4-3 Examples of the INPUT statement

Examples 1 and 2 in Figure 4-3 show that it is not necessary to include a prompt message. When either INPUT statement is executed, a question mark displays on the screen. Examples 3 through 5 include prompt messages. In Example 3, the prompt message

```
Discount =====>
```

displays on the screen at the location of the cursor. Following the display of the prompt, the PC halts execution until the user enters the data (.25) and presses the Enter key.

In Example 4 of Figure 4-3, the following prompt displays:

```
What is your name?
```

Because we ended the prompt message with a semicolon, the PC displays the question mark after the prompt. Example 5 shows how you can utilize the PRINT statement along with the INPUT statement to display prompt messages made up of more than one line.

THE BEEP AND LOCATE STATEMENTS

Two QuickBASIC statements that are often used in tandem with the `INPUT` statement are the `BEEP` and `LOCATE` statements.

The BEEP Statement

When executed, the `BEEP` statement causes the PC's speaker to beep for a fraction of a second. Several `BEEP` statements in a row cause the PC to beep for a longer duration. The following line causes the PC to beep for approximately a second:

```
BEEP : BEEP : BEEP : BEEP
```

Notice the colons between the `BEEP` statements. In QuickBASIC, the colon allows you to place more than one statement per line. The `BEEP` statement is often used to alert the user that there is a problem with the program or data.

The LOCATE Statement

QuickBASIC defines the output screen as having 25 rows and 80 columns. The `LOCATE` statement can be used to position the cursor precisely on any one of the two thousand display positions on the screen. For example, the following line causes the PC to move the cursor to row 4, column 15:

```
LOCATE 4, 15
```

It makes no difference whether the cursor is above or below row 4 or to the right or left of column 15. The general form of the `LOCATE` statement is shown in Figure 4-4.

FIGURE 4-4
The general form of the LOCATE statement

```
LOCATE row, column
```

When executed, the partial program in Figure 4-5 displays the prompt message in the `INPUT` statement in row 6, column 12.

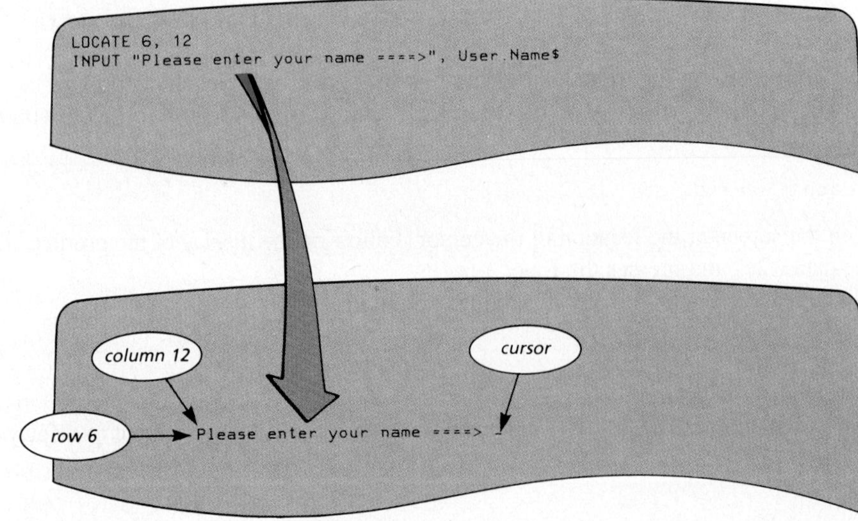

FIGURE 4-5
Use of the LOCATE statement to position the cursor

EDITING DATA ENTERED THROUGH THE KEYBOARD

In most interactive applications it is required that you check the incoming data to be sure that it is reasonable. A **reasonableness check** ensures that the data is legitimate, that is, the data is within a range of acceptable values. If the data is not validated before being used, then the PC can very well generate incorrect information.

The partial program in Figure 4-6 requests that the user enter a value for the variable Item.Cost. Assume that the program specifications state that the value of Cost must be greater than zero and less than 1,000.00.

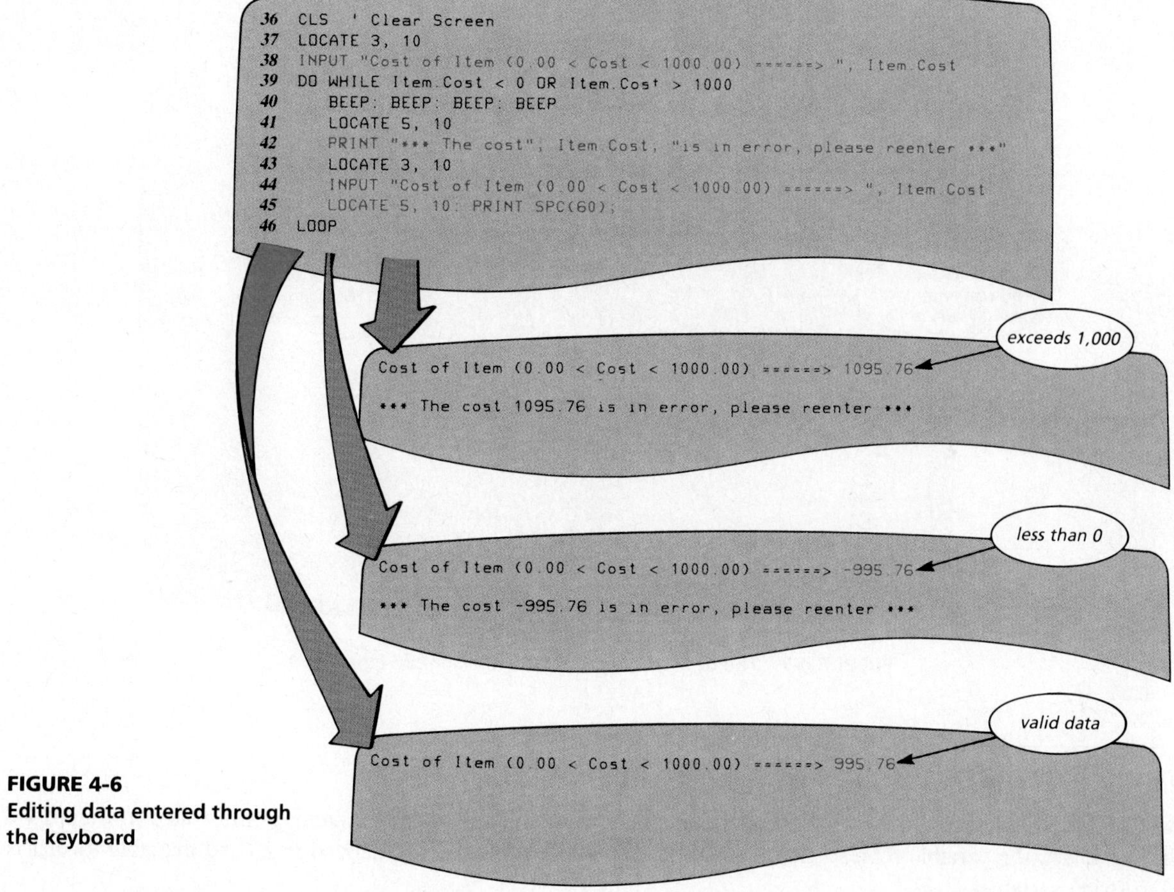

FIGURE 4-6
Editing data entered through the keyboard

When the PC executes the partial program in Figure 4-6, the `CLS` statement in line 36 clears the output screen. Line 37 moves the cursor to column 10 in row 3. The `INPUT` statement in line 38 displays the prompt message and halts execution of the program. After the user enters the value `1095.76` and presses the Enter key, the `DO WHILE` statement in line 39 tests the value of Item.Cost. Since it is greater than 1,000.00, control enters the loop. Line 40 causes the PC speaker to beep for a second. Due to lines 41 and 42, the PC displays an error message beginning at column 10 in row 5.

Lines 43 and 44 again cause the prompt message to display beginning at column 10 in row 3. After the user enters `-995.76`, the error message in row 5 is erased by the `SPC` function in the `PRINT` statement in line 45. The `SPC` function displays as many spaces as indicated in the parentheses. Thus, `SPC(60)` displays 60 spaces and in doing so erases the error message in row 5. Since `-995.76` is still outside the limits, the PC reexecutes the loop and displays the error message due to line 42. Finally, when the user enters `995.76`, the PC exits the loop and continues execution at the line following the `LOOP` statement.

Data validation is an important part of the programming process. It should be apparent that the information produced by a computer is only as accurate as the data it processes. The term **GIGO** (Garbage In—Garbage Out, pronounced GEE-GOH) is used to describe the generation of inaccurate information from the input of invalid data. Data validation should be incorporated into all programs, especially when the `INPUT` statement is used.

SAMPLE PROGRAM 4 — ITEM COST REPORT

The sample program in this project illustrates the preparation of an item cost table that contains the cost of one to ten items. The program begins by asking the user to enter the cost of an item. The cost must be greater than zero and less than 1,000.00. After validating the entry, the sample program displays the cost table. Once the table displays, the user is asked if another table should be prepared. The user must enter a Y for yes or an N for no.

If the user enters the letter Y, the loop is executed again and the user is asked to enter the cost of the next item. If the user enters the letter N, the program displays an end-of-job message followed by termination of execution. Figure 4-7 shows the desired output results for Sample Program 4.

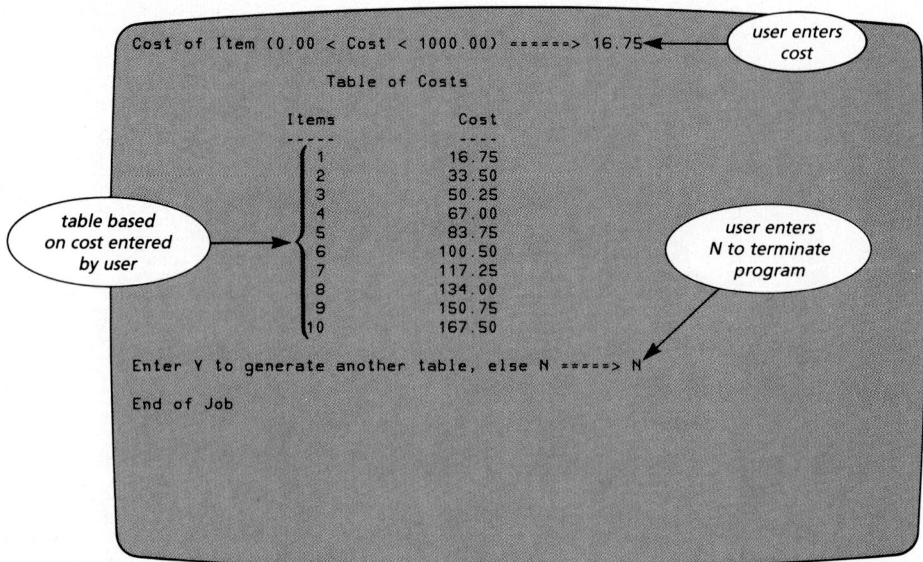

FIGURE 4-7 The desired output results for Sample Program 4

Program Flowchart

The flowchart for Sample Program 4 which produces the item cost table for one to ten items is illustrated in Figure 4-8. At the top of the flowchart, the variable representing the maximum number of items is initialized to 10 and the table format is assigned to string variables.

Control then enters the loop. Notice that this is the first time in this book that a decision symbol is not at the top of the loop. In this flowchart, the decision to terminate the loop is at the bottom. Loops that have the decision to terminate at the top are called **Do-While loops**. Loops that have the decision to terminate at the bottom are called **Do-Until loops**.

Within the major loop, the output screen is cleared and the user is requested to enter the cost of an item. Next, the cost is validated, the table headings are displayed, and a counter is initialized to one. The table is then generated by a looping process that continues while the counter is less than or equal to 10. After the table displays, the user is asked if another is desired. The decision symbol at the bottom of the Do-Until loop determines whether to continue or terminate processing on the basis of the value (Y or N) entered by the user.

Before we can code the logic shown in Figure 4-8 we need to discuss the FOR and NEXT statements.

FIGURE 4-8
The flowchart for Sample Program 4

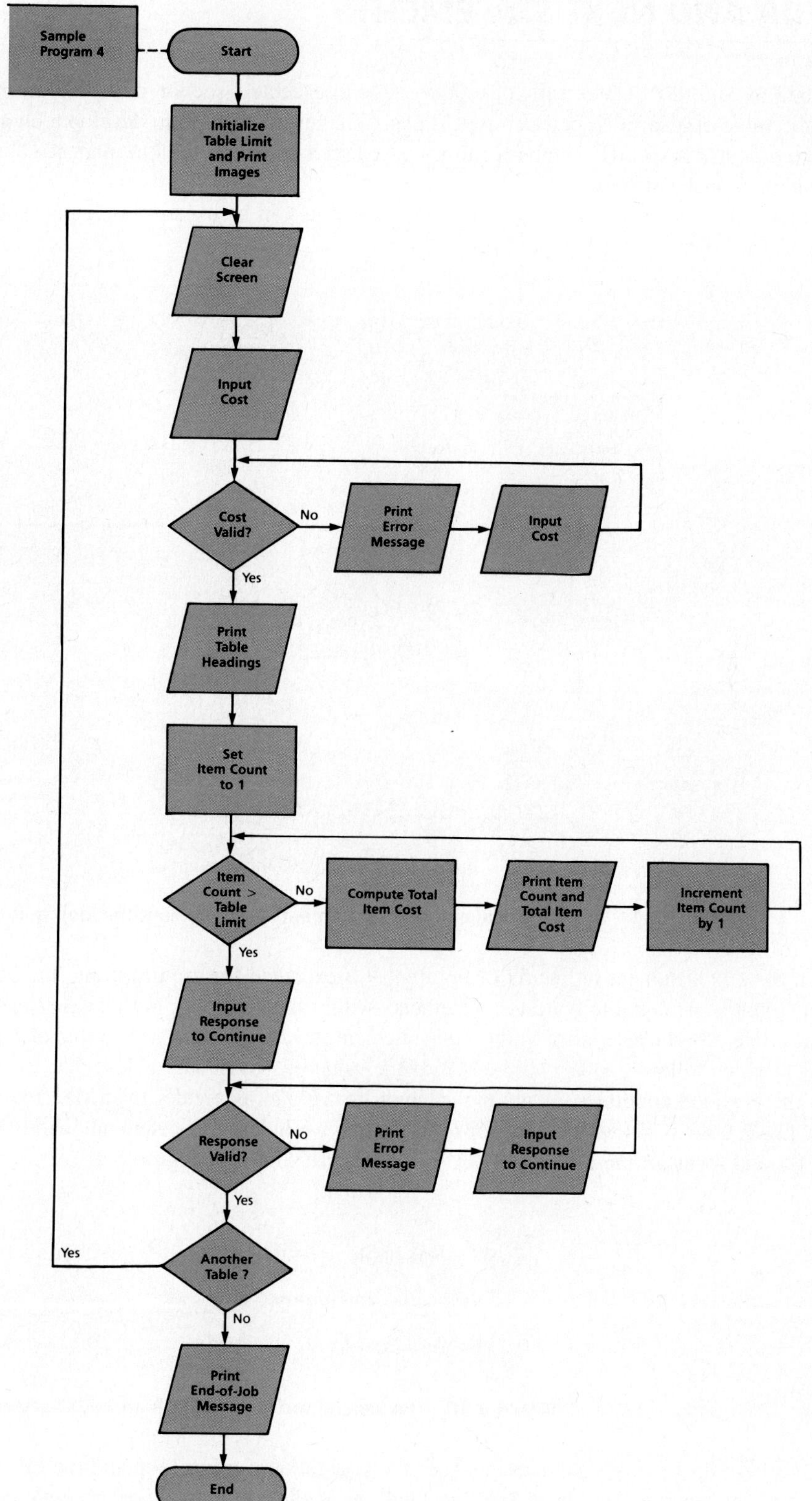

THE FOR AND NEXT STATEMENTS

The `FOR` and `NEXT` statements make it possible to execute a section of a program repeatedly, with automatic changes in the value of a variable between repetitions. Whenever you have to develop a counter-controlled loop (a loop that is to be executed a specific number of times based on a counter), the `FOR` and `NEXT` statements can be used to develop it. We call such a loop a **For loop**.

Figure 4-9 illustrates how the `FOR` and `NEXT` statements can be used to implement the loop that generates the cost table described in the flowchart for Sample Program 4.

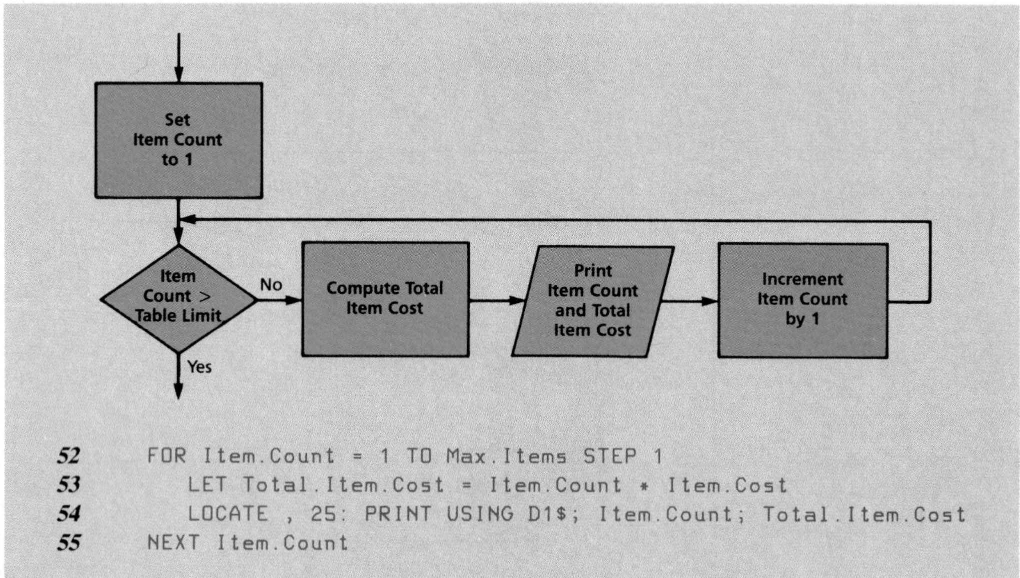


```
52     FOR Item.Count = 1 TO Max.Items STEP 1
53        LET Total.Item.Cost = Item.Count * Item.Cost
54        LOCATE , 25: PRINT USING D1$; Item.Count; Total.Item.Cost
55     NEXT Item.Count
```

FIGURE 4-9 **Using the FOR and NEXT statements to implement the loop that generates the cost table**

When the `FOR` statement in line 52 of Figure 4-9 is executed for the first time, the For loop becomes active and the variable Item.Count is set equal to one. The statements within the For loop, in this case lines 53 and 54, are executed. The `NEXT` statement in line 55 returns control to the `FOR` statement in line 52, where the value of Item.Count is incremented by the amount (1), which follows the keyword `STEP`. If the value of Item.Count is less than or equal to Max.Items (table limit), execution of the For loop continues. When the value of Item.Count is greater than Max.Items, control transfers to the line following `NEXT Item.Count`. As with other loops, notice that we indent the statements within the loop by three spaces.

The general forms of the `FOR` and `NEXT` statements are shown in Figure 4-10.

```
FOR loop-variable = initial TO limit STEP increment
     [range of statements]
NEXT loop-variable
```

FIGURE 4-10 **The general forms of the FOR and NEXT statements**

In Figure 4-10, the `FOR` statement indicates the beginning of a For loop and the `NEXT` statement indicates the end. The range of statements within the For loop is executed repeatedly as long as *loop-variable* is not greater than *limit*. *Loop-variable* is initially assigned the value of *initial*. Each time the range of statements is executed, *loop-variable* is increased by the value of *increment*. When *loop-variable* is greater than *limit*, control passes to the line following the corresponding `NEXT` statement.

If *increment* is negative, the test to terminate the For loop is reversed. The value of *loop-variable* is decremented each time through the For loop, and the For loop is executed while *loop-variable* is greater than or equal to *limit*. If the keyword `STEP` is not included in a `FOR` statement, then the increment value is automatically set to one.

Figure 4-11 illustrates several valid FOR statements.

EXAMPLE	FOR STATEMENT
1	FOR Count = 1 TO 100 STEP 1
2	FOR X = 5 TO Y STEP 3
3	FOR Amount = 1.25 TO 7.35 STEP .05
4	FOR Tax = A TO B STEP C
5	FOR S = 0 TO -35 STEP -3
6	FOR X = 1 TO 10

FIGURE 4-11 Examples of valid FOR statements

In Example 1 of Figure 4-11, the For loop is executed 100 times. Example 2 points out that the initial and increment values can be values other than one. Example 3 initializes Amount to 1.25 for the first pass. Thereafter, the value .05 is added to Amount each time the range of statements is executed. Hence, Amount takes on the values 1.25, 1.30, 1.35, 1.40, and so on, until Amount exceeds 7.35.

Example 4 shows that the initial, limit, and increment values can be variables. Example 5 includes a negative increment (–3). Thus, the test is reversed and S must be less than –35 before the For loop terminates. Finally, Example 6 illustrates a FOR statement without the keyword STEP. In this case, the increment value is automatically set to one.

The QuickBASIC Program

The program in Figure 4-12 corresponds to the program flowchart in Figure 4-8.

FIGURE 4-12
Sample Program 4

```
' ****************************************************************
' *  Sample Program 4                          September 15, 1994  *
' *  Item Cost Report                                             *
' *  J. S. Quasney                                                *
' *                                                               *
' *  This program displays a table of costs of 1 to 10 items.     *
' *  The user enters the cost per item and the program            *
' *  displays the table of costs.                                 *
' *       The cost per item entered by the user is validated      *
' *  (greater than zero and less than 1000.00).   After the       *
' *  table is displayed the user is asked if another table        *
' *  should be generated.                                         *
' *       This activity continues until the user indicates        *
' *  that no more tables are to be generated.                     *
' *                                                               *
' *  Variables:   Item.Cost         -- Cost of item               *
' *               Item.Count        -- Item count                 *
' *               Max.Items         -- Maximum number of items    *
' *                                    in table                   *
' *               Total.Item.Cost  -- Cost of items               *
' *               Control$          -- Response to continue       *
' *               H1$, H2$, H3$, D1$, T1$ -- Print images         *
' ****************************************************************

```

(continued)

FIGURE 4-12 (continued)

```
' *********************** Initialization ***********************
LET Max.Items = 10
LET H1$ = "     Table of Costs"
LET H2$ = "Items              Cost"
LET H3$ = "-----              ----"
LET D1$ = "  ##           ##,###.##"
LET T1$ = "End of Job"

' ****************** Generate Cost Table *********************
DO
   ' ************ Accept and Validate Cost of Item ************
   CLS  ' Clear Screen
   LOCATE 3, 10
   INPUT "Cost of Item (0.00 < Cost < 1000.00) ======> ", Item.Cost
   DO WHILE Item.Cost < 0 OR Item.Cost > 1000
      BEEP: BEEP: BEEP: BEEP
      LOCATE 5, 10
      PRINT "*** The cost"; Item.Cost; "is in error, please reenter ***"
      LOCATE 3, 10
      INPUT "Cost of Item (0.00 < Cost < 1000.00) ======> ", Item.Cost
      LOCATE 5, 10: PRINT SPC(60);
   LOOP

   ' **************** Generate Table of Costs *****************
   LOCATE 5, 25: PRINT H1$
   LOCATE 7, 25: PRINT H2$
   LOCATE 8, 25: PRINT H3$
   FOR Item.Count = 1 TO Max.Items STEP 1
      LET Total.Item.Cost = Item.Count * Item.Cost
      LOCATE , 25: PRINT USING D1$; Item.Count; Total.Item.Cost
   NEXT Item.Count

   ' ******** Accept and Validate Response to Continue ********
   LOCATE 20, 10
   INPUT "Enter Y to generate another table, else N =====> ", Control$
   DO WHILE Control$ <> "N" AND Control$ <> "Y"
      BEEP: BEEP: BEEP: BEEP
      LOCATE 22, 10
      PRINT "*** Response in error, please reenter ***"
      LOCATE 20, 10
      INPUT "Enter Y to generate another table, else N =====> ", Control$
      LOCATE 22, 10: PRINT SPC(50);
   LOOP

LOOP UNTIL Control$ = "N"

' ************************* Wrap-Up *************************
LOCATE 22, 10
PRINT T1$
END
```

Discussion of Sample Program 4

When Sample Program 4 is executed, the variables in lines 26 through 31 are initialized. Line 26 initializes Max.Items (table limit) to 10. Lines 27 through 31 define the table format. The variables are used later in the PRINT statements in lines 49 through 51, 54, and 73.

The DO statement in line 34 indicates the beginning of a Do-Until loop. With a Do-Until loop, the condition that determines whether the loop should continue is in the LOOP statement (line 69). As shown in Figure 4-13, there are two basic types of loops. The Do-While loop has the decision symbol at the top of the loop. The Do-Until loop has the decision symbol at the bottom of the loop. If the decision is at the top (Figure 4-13A), use the DO WHILE and LOOP statements. If the decision is at the bottom (Figure 4-13B), use the DO and LOOP UNTIL statements.

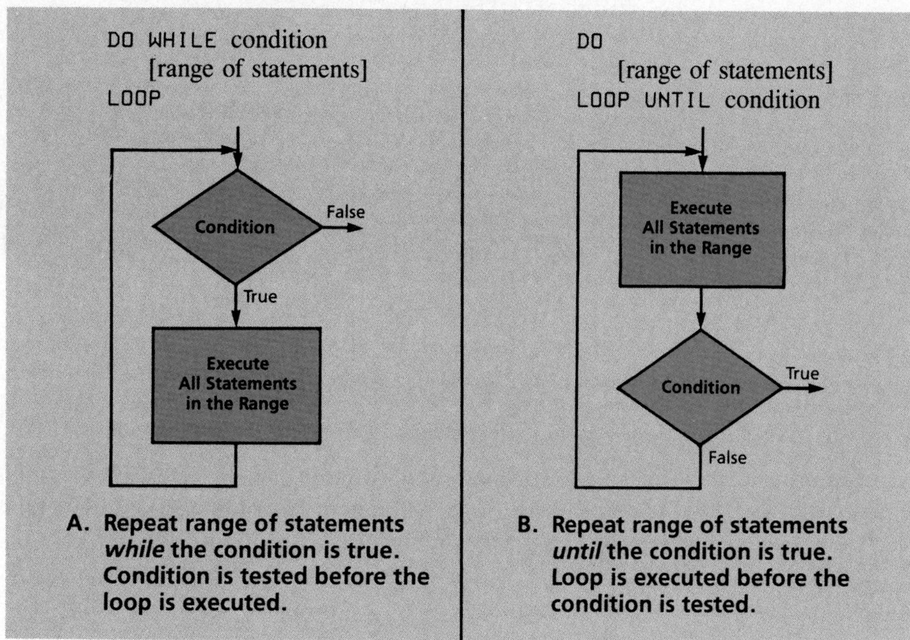

FIGURE 4-13 The two basic types of loops and the statements in QuickBASIC which should be used to implement them

Upon entering the Do-Until loop, the screen is cleared by line 36. Lines 37 through 46 accept and validate the cost of the item entered by the user. Lines 49 through 51 display the table title and column headings. Lines 52 through 55 compute and display the rows of the table. Notice in line 54 that the LOCATE statement does not include a row number. When the LOCATE statement is written in this fashion, it references the current row, which is one greater than the one referenced by the previously executed PRINT or PRINT USING statement. Hence, each time line 54 is executed in the For loop, the PRINT USING statement begins printing in column 25 of the next row. Notice in lines 49 through 51 and 54 that it is common practice to incorporate both the LOCATE and PRINT statements on the same line. Of course, it is important that you separate the two statements with the colon.

After the table is displayed on the screen, lines 58 through 67 accept and validate a response from the user that indicates whether the Do-Until loop should continue. In this case, only two values, Y and N, are acceptable (line 60). If the user enters a Y, line 69 causes the PC to continue execution at the top of the loop (line 34). If the user enters the value N, the condition in line 69 is false. Thus, control passes to line 72 and an end-of-job message is displayed followed by termination of execution of the program.

Figure 4-14 shows the display of Sample Program 4 when the value 579.46 is entered as the cost of an item.

```
Cost of Item (0.00 < Cost < 1000.00) ======> 579.46

                 Table of Costs

            Items             Cost
            -----             ----
              1             579.46
              2           1,158.92
              3           1,738.38
              4           2,317.84
              5           2,897.30
              6           3,476.76
              7           4,056.22
              8           4,635.68
              9           5,215.14
             10           5,794.60

Enter Y to generate another table, else N =====> N

End of Job
```

FIGURE 4-14
The results displayed due to the execution of Sample Program 4 and a cost per item of $579.46

AN INTRODUCTION TO THE TOP-DOWN APPROACH

Top-down programming is a divide and conquer strategy used by programmers to solve large problems. The first step in top-down programming is to divide the task into smaller, more manageable subtasks through the use of a top-down chart. Figure 4-15 illustrates a top-down chart for the problem solved by Sample Program 4.

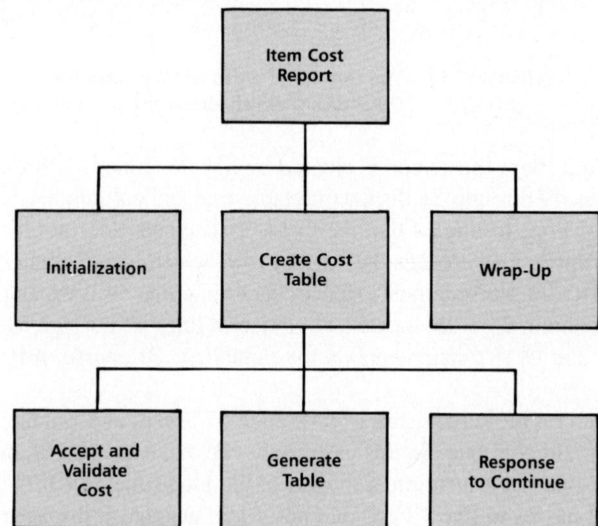

FIGURE 4-15
A top-down chart for the problem solved by Sample Program 4

A top-down chart differs from a program flowchart in that it does not show decision-making logic or flow of control. A program flowchart shows *how* to solve the problem. A top-down chart shows *what* has to be done.

A top-down chart is very similar to a company's organization chart where each lower level subtask carries out a function for its superior task. In Figure 4-15, the top box (Item Cost Report) represents the complete task. The next level of boxes (Initialization, Create Cost Table, and Wrap-Up) shows the subtasks that are required to solve the task of the top box. The lowest level of boxes (Accept and Validate Cost Item, Generate Table, and Response to Continue) indicates the subtasks required to create a table. Usually, a task is divided into lower level subtasks whenever it appears to be too complicated or lengthy to stand by itself.

Implementing the Top-Down Approach

Once the larger, more complex problem has been decomposed into smaller pieces, a solution to each subtask can be designed and coded. We call the group of statements that are associated with a single programming task a **subroutine**, or **module**.

The subroutines that formulate a program solution begin with a name, followed immediately by a colon (:), and end with a `RETURN` statement. Subroutines are *called* by their superior modules using the `GOSUB` statement. When a subroutine has completed its task, control returns to the superior module via a `RETURN` statement. The rules regarding a subroutine name are the same as for a variable name.

THE GOSUB AND RETURN STATEMENTS

The `GOSUB` statement is used to call a subroutine. As shown in Figure 4-16, the keyword `GOSUB` is immediately followed by the subroutine name to which control is transferred. Once control transfers, the instructions in the subroutine are executed.

FIGURE 4-16
The general form of the GOSUB statement

```
GOSUB subroutine-name
```

The `RETURN` statement (Figure 4-17) at the bottom of the subroutine returns control to the statement following the corresponding `GOSUB` in the superior module.

FIGURE 4-17
The general form of the RETURN statement

```
RETURN
```

Consider the partial program on the next page in Figure 4-18 and the following important points regarding the implementation of the top-down approach:

- The `END` statement is the last statement in the Main module. Control returns to DOS through this statement.
- Indent by three spaces the statements within modules.
- So that lower level modules can easily be located, they should be placed below their superior module and in the order in which they are called.

FIGURE 4-18
Implementing the top-down chart in Figure 4-15

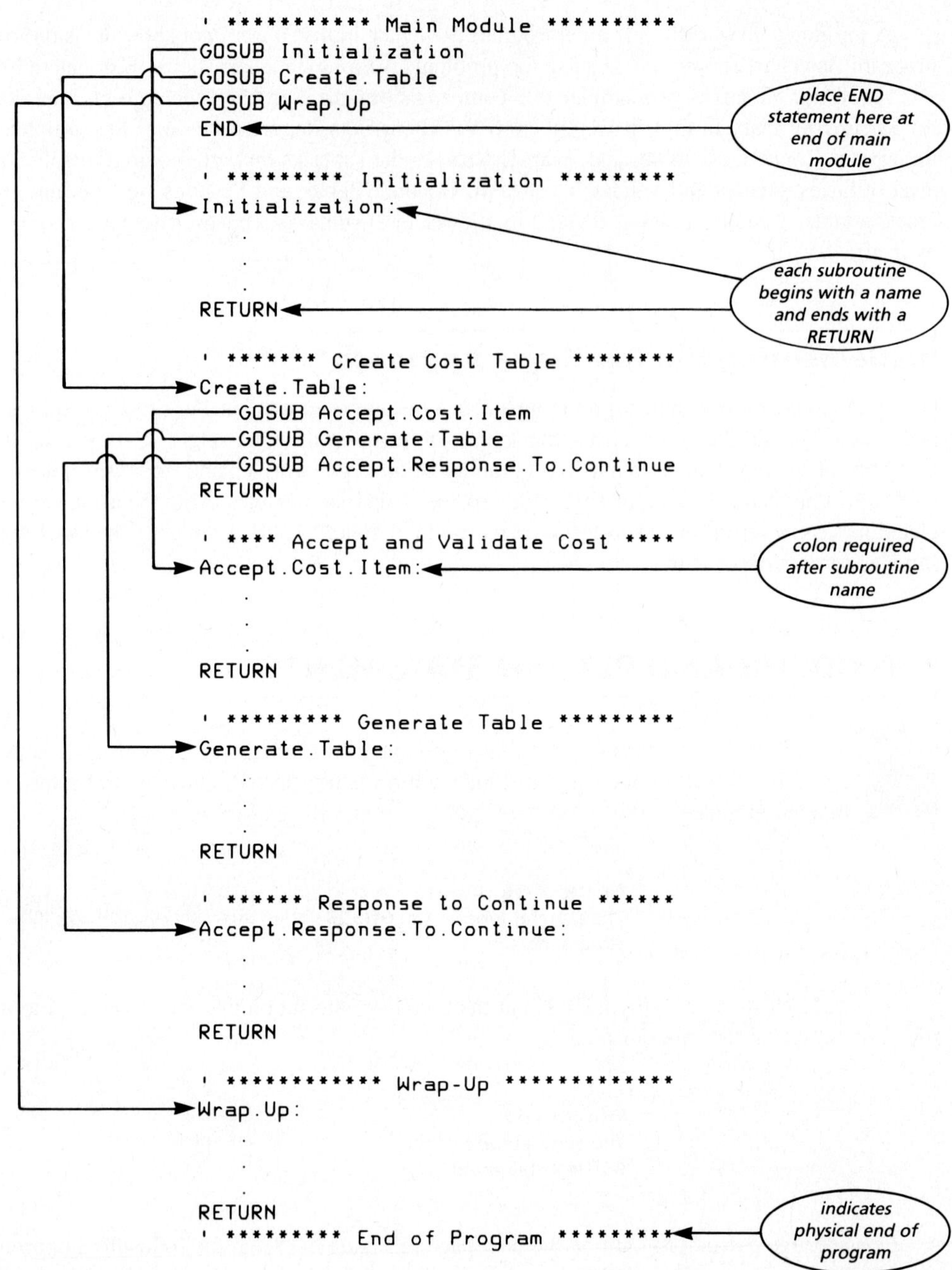

A modified version of Sample Program 4 which utilizes the top-down approach is shown in Figure 4-19. The coding corresponds to the top-down chart in Figure 4-15.

FIGURE 4-19
A top-down version of Sample Program 4

```
' ***************************************************************
' *  Sample Program 4 Modified              September 15, 1994  *
' *  Item Cost Report                                           *
' *  J. S. Quasney                                              *
' *                                                             *
' *  This program displays a table of costs of 1 to 10 items.  *
' *  The user enters the cost per item and the program          *
' *  displays the table of costs.                               *
' *       The cost per item entered by the user is validated    *
' *  (greater than zero and less than 1000.00).  After the      *
' *  table is displayed the user is asked if another table      *
' *  should be generated.                                       *
' *       This activity continues until the user indicates      *
' *  that no more tables are to be generated.                   *
' *                                                             *
' *  Variables:  Item.Cost        -- Cost of item               *
' *              Item.Count       -- Item count                 *
' *              Max.Items        -- Maximum number of items    *
' *                                  in table                   *
' *              Total.Item.Cost  -- Cost of items              *
' *              Control$         -- Response to continue       *
' *              H1$, H2$, H3$, D1$, T1$ -- Print images        *
' ***************************************************************

' ***************************************************************
' *                         Main Module                         *
' ***************************************************************
GOSUB Initialization
GOSUB Create.Table
GOSUB Wrap.Up
END

' ***************************************************************
' *                       Initialization                        *
' ***************************************************************
Initialization:
   LET Max.Items = 10
   LET H1$ = "    Table of Costs"
   LET H2$ = "Items              Cost"
   LET H3$ = "-----              ----"
   LET D1$ = "  ##          ##,###.##"
   LET T1$ = "End of Job"
RETURN

' ***************************************************************
' *                      Create Cost Table                      *
' ***************************************************************
Create.Table:
   DO
      GOSUB Accept.Cost.Item
      GOSUB Generate.Table
      GOSUB Accept.Response.To.Continue
   LOOP UNTIL Control$ = "N"
RETURN

```

(continued)

FIGURE 4-19 (continued)

```
' ****************************************************************
' *               Accept and Validate Cost of Item               *
' ****************************************************************
Accept.Cost.Item:
   CLS   ' Clear Screen
   LOCATE 3, 10
   INPUT "Cost of Item (0.00 < Cost < 1000.00) ======> ", Item.Cost
   DO WHILE Item.Cost < 0 OR Item.Cost > 1000
      BEEP: BEEP: BEEP: BEEP
      LOCATE 5, 10
      PRINT "*** The cost"; Item.Cost; "is in error, please reenter ***"
      LOCATE 3, 10
      INPUT "Cost of Item (0.00 < Cost < 1000.00) ======> ", Item.Cost
      LOCATE 5, 10: PRINT SPC(60);
   LOOP
RETURN

' ****************************************************************
' *                   Generate Table of Costs                    *
' ****************************************************************
Generate.Table:
   LOCATE 5, 25: PRINT H1$
   LOCATE 7, 25: PRINT H2$
   LOCATE 8, 25: PRINT H3$
   FOR Item.Count = 1 TO Max.Items STEP 1
      LET Total.Item.Cost = Item.Count * Item.Cost
      LOCATE , 25: PRINT USING D1$; Item.Count; Total.Item.Cost
   NEXT Item.Count
RETURN

' ****************************************************************
' *           Accept and Validate Response to Continue           *
' ****************************************************************
Accept.Response.To.Continue:
   LOCATE 20, 10
   INPUT "Enter Y to generate another table, else N =====> ", Control$
   DO WHILE Control$ <> "N" AND Control$ <> "Y"
      BEEP: BEEP: BEEP: BEEP
      LOCATE 22, 10
      PRINT "*** Response in error, please reenter ***"
      LOCATE 20, 10
      INPUT "Enter Y to generate another table, else N =====> ", Control$
      LOCATE 22, 10: PRINT SPC(50);
   LOOP
RETURN

' ****************************************************************
' *                           Wrap-Up                            *
' ****************************************************************
Wrap.Up:
   LOCATE 22, 10
   PRINT T1$
RETURN
' ********************** End of Program **********************
```

Discussion of Sample Program 4 Modified

When the modified version of Sample Program 4 in Figure 4-19 executes, line 28 in the Main module transfers control to the Initialization module which begins at line 36. After lines 37 through 42 are executed, the RETURN statement in line 43 transfers control back to line 29 in the Main module. Next, line 29 transfers control to the Create.Table module (lines 48 through 54). In this module, the Do-Until loop includes three GOSUB statements. Each time through this loop, a cost table such as the one in Figure 4-20 is generated.

When the user enters the letter N in response to the INPUT statement in line 97, control passes back to line 53. Since the condition in line 53 is true, control passes to the RETURN statement in line 54. Line 54 returns control to line 30. Next, line 30 transfers control to the Wrap.Up module which begins at line 105. After the end-of-job message is displayed, control returns to line 31 in the Main module and the program terminates execution.

```
Cost of Item (0.00 < Cost < 1000.00) ======> 67.50

                 Table of Costs

             Items            Cost
             -----            ----
                 1           67.50
                 2          135.00
                 3          202.50
                 4          270.00
                 5          337.50
                 6          405.00
                 7          472.50
                 8          540.00
                 9          607.50
                10          675.00

Enter Y to generate another table, else N =====> N

End of Job
```

FIGURE 4-20 **The results displayed due to the execution of the modified Sample Program 4 and a cost per item of $67.50**

TRY IT YOURSELF EXERCISES

1. What is displayed if each of the following programs are executed?
   a. X is assigned the value 2, and Y is assigned the value 4.

```
' Exercise 1.a
INPUT "Enter values for X and Y ===> ", X, Y
Sum = X + Y
Diff = Y - X
Prod = X * Y
Quot = X / Y
PRINT Sum, Diff
PRINT Prod, Quot
END
```

b.

```
' Exercise 1.b
Total = 0
GOSUB Increment.Total
PRINT Total
GOSUB Increment.Total
PRINT Total
GOSUB Increment.Total
PRINT Total
Total = Total - 6
PRINT Total
END
' Increment Total
Increment.Total:
   Total = Total + 2
RETURN
```

c. Selling.Price and Discount.Rate are assigned $30.00 and 25%, respectively.

```
' Exercise 1.c
' ***********************************
' *            Main Module          *
' ***********************************
GOSUB Accept.Data
GOSUB Compute.Discount
GOSUB Display.Discount
END

' ***********************************
' *      Accept Operator Data       *
' ***********************************
Accept.Data:
   CLS  ' Clear Screen
   INPUT "Selling Price ===>", Selling.Price
   INPUT "Discount Rate in % ===>", Discount.Rate
RETURN

' ***********************************
' *         Compute Discount        *
' ***********************************
Compute.Discount:
   Discount.Rate = Discount.Rate / 100
   Discount = Discount.Rate * Selling.Price
RETURN

' ***********************************
' *          Discount Amount        *
' ***********************************
Display.Discount:
   PRINT "Discount ======>"; Discount
RETURN

' *********** End of Program *******
```

2. Is the following partial program invalid? If it is invalid, indicate why.

```
' Exercise 2
' Main Module
  .
  .
  .
GOSUB Calculate
' Calculate Square
Calculate:
   X = X * X
RETURN
END
```

3. Write a sequence of `LOCATE` and `PRINT` statements that will display the word `Retail` beginning in column 12 of row 15.
4. Write a series of statements that will display the number 22 in column 22 of row 22.
5. Consider the two following types of loops:
   a. `DO WHILE ... LOOP`
   b. `DO ... LOOP UNTIL`

   Answer the following questions for each type of loop:

   (1) Does the loop terminate when the condition is true or false?
   (2) What is the minimum number of times the range of statements in the loop is executed?
   (3) Is the test to terminate the loop made before or after the range of statements is executed?
6. At what column and row is the cursor after the following two statements are executed?

```
LOCATE 15, 34
LOCATE 17
```

7. Identify the syntax and logic error(s), if any, in each of the following:
   a. `FOR X = 1 TO 6 STEP -1`
   b. `FOR Amt = 1 TO Sq`
   c. `FOR T$ = 0 TO 7`
   d. `FOR Value = 10 TO 1`
   e. `FOR H = A TO B STEP -B`
8. How many times does the `PRINT` statement execute when the following program is executed?

```
' Exercise 8
FOR J = 1 TO 30
   FOR N = 1 TO 20
      FOR I = 1 TO 3
         PRINT J, N, I
      NEXT I
   NEXT N
NEXT J
END
```

9. Explain the purpose of the following statement. What are the colons used for?

```
BEEP : BEEP : BEEP : BEEP
```

STUDENT ASSIGNMENTS

STUDENT ASSIGNMENT 1: Weekly Pay Rate Table

Instructions: Design and code a top-down QuickBASIC program, such as the one in Figure 4-19, to generate the weekly pay rate table shown under OUTPUT. Request that the user enter through the keyboard an hourly rate between $3.35 and $30.00, inclusive. Validate the entry. Use a For loop to generate a table of 10 hourly rates in increments of $0.50 and the corresponding weekly rates. A weekly rate is equal to 40 times the hourly rate. After the table displays, request the user to enter the letter Y to generate another table or the letter N to terminate the program. Use the following top-down chart as a guide to solving this problem:

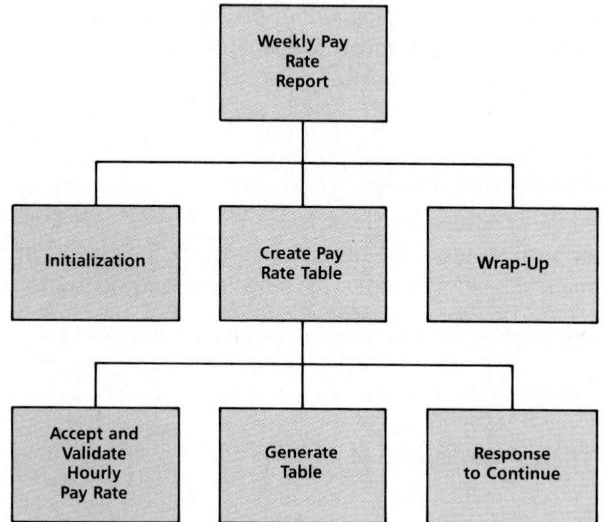

INPUT: Use the following sample data:

Table 1 – Hourly rate $6.75
Table 2 – Hourly rate $22.50

OUTPUT: The following results are displayed for the first table:

```
Initial Pay Rate (3.35 <= Cost <= 30.00) ======> 6.75

            Table of Hourly and Weekly Rates

              Hourly                    Weekly
              Rate                      Rate
              ------                    ------
                6.75                    270.00
                7.25                    290.00
                7.75                    310.00
                8.25                    330.00
                8.75                    350.00
                9.25                    370.00
                9.75                    390.00
               10.25                    410.00
               10.75                    430.00
               11.25                    450.00

Enter Y to generate another table, else N =====> Y
```

STUDENT ASSIGNMENT 2: Metric Conversion Table

Instructions: Design and code a top-down QuickBASIC program, such as the one in Figure 4-19, to generate a metric conversion table as shown on the next page in the printout. Request that the user enter through the keyboard an initial metric value, a limit metric value, and an increment metric value. Validate each entry. The initial metric value must be between 1 and 1,500, inclusive. The limit metric value must be greater than the initial metric value and less than 2,000. The increment metric value must be greater than zero and less than or equal to 100.

Use a For loop to generate a table of the metric values between the initial metric value and limit metric value. For each metric value, print the equivalent yards, feet, and inches. There are 39.37 inches in a meter, 12 inches in a foot, and 3 feet in a yard. After the table prints, request the user to enter the letter Y to generate another table or the letter N to terminate the program. Use the following top-down chart as a guide to solving this problem:

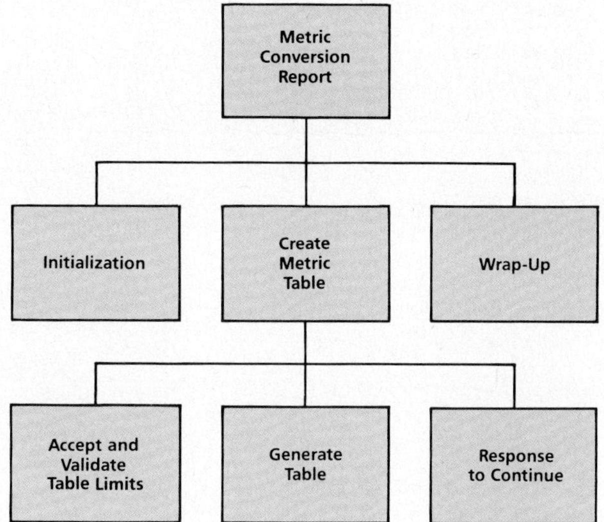

Before you print each table, use the following statement to move the paper in the printer to the top of the next page:

```
LPRINT CHR$(12);
```

This `LPRINT` statement prints the value of the function `CHR$(12)`, which is the form feed character.

INPUT: Use the following sample data:

Table 1 – Initial meters 100, Limit meters 200, Increment meters 10
Table 2 – Initial meters 140, Limit meters 160, Increment meters 2

OUTPUT: The following results display on the screen for the Table 1 data:

```
Initial Meter Value (1 <= Initial Meter <= 1500) ==> 100

Limit Meter Value (Initial Meter < Limit Meter < 2,000) ======> 200

Increment Meter Value (0 < Increment Meter <= 100) ======> 10

********* Report Being Printed On Printer *********

Enter Y to generate another table, else N =====> Y
```

Student Assignment 2 (continued)

The following results are printed on the printer for the Table 1 data:

```
        Metric Conversion Table

Meters        Yards        Feet      Inches
------        -----        ----      ------
100.00       109.36      328.08    3,937.00
110.00       120.30      360.89    4,330.70
120.00       131.23      393.70    4,724.40
130.00       142.17      426.51    5,118.10
140.00       153.11      459.32    5,511.80
150.00       164.04      492.13    5,905.50
160.00       174.98      524.93    6,299.20
170.00       185.91      557.74    6,692.90
180.00       196.85      590.55    7,086.60
190.00       207.79      623.36    7,480.30
200.00       218.72      656.17    7,874.00

End of Table
```

PROJECT 5

Sequential File Processing

In the first four projects we emphasized the importance of integrating data into the program. You learned that data may be entered into a program through the use of the INPUT statement or the READ and DATA statements. This project presents a third method for entering data—the use of data files. With data files, the data is stored in auxiliary storage rather than in the program itself. This technique is used primarily for dealing with large amounts of data.

QuickBASIC includes a set of file-handling statements that allow a user to do the following:

- Open a file
- Read data from a file
- Write data to a file
- Test for the end-of-file
- Close a file

FILE ORGANIZATION

QuickBASIC provides for two types of file organization: sequential and random. A file that is organized sequentially is called a **sequential file** and is limited to sequential processing. This means that the records can be processed only in the order in which they are placed in the file. Conceptually, a sequential file is identical to the use of DATA statements within a QuickBASIC program.

The second type of file organization, **random files**, allows you to process the records in the file in any order. If the fifth record is required and it is stored in a random file, then the program may access it without reading the first four records. Random files are not discussed in this project.

CREATING A SEQUENTIAL DATA FILE

This section presents the OPEN, WRITE #n, and CLOSE statements. These statements are used to create a sequential data file. The OPEN statement is used to activate the file. The WRITE #n statement is used to write a record to the file. And the CLOSE statement is used to deactivate the file.

Opening Sequential Files

Before any file can be read from or written to, it must be opened by the OPEN statement. The OPEN statement identifies by name the file to be processed. It indicates whether the file is to be read from or written to. It also assigns the file a filenumber that can be used by statements that need to reference the file in question.

The general form of the OPEN statement is shown in Figure 5-1.

OPEN filespec FOR mode AS #filenumber

where **filespec** is the name of the file;
mode is one of the following:
APPEND opens file so that records can be added to the end of the file;
INPUT opens file to read beginning with the first record;
OUTPUT opens file to write records; and
filenumber is a numeric expression whose value is between 1 and 255.

FIGURE 5-1
The general form of the OPEN statement

As described in Figure 5-1, a sequential data file may be opened for input, output, or append. If a file is opened for input, the program can only read records from it. If a file is opened for output, the program can only write records to it. The Append mode allows you to write records to the end of a file that already has records in it. Figure 5-2 illustrates several OPEN statements.

EXAMPLE	STATEMENT
1	`OPEN "B:PAYROLL.DAT" FOR OUTPUT AS #4`
2	`OPEN "ACCOUNT.DAT" FOR APPEND AS #2`
3	`OPEN Filename$ FOR OUTPUT AS #1`
4	`OPEN "PART.DAT" FOR INPUT AS #1`

FIGURE 5-2
Examples of OPEN statements

The OPEN statement in Example 1 in Figure 5-2 opens PAYROLL.DAT on the B drive for output as filenumber 4. Since it is opened for output, you can only write records to PAYROLL.DAT. If you attempt to read a record, the PC will display a diagnostic message.

Example 2 opens the data file ACCOUNT.DAT for append as filenumber 2. Records can only be written to a data file opened for append. If ACCOUNT.DAT exists, records are written in sequence after the last record. If ACCOUNT.DAT does not exist, the PC creates it and the data file is treated as if it were open for output.

Example 3 in Figure 5-2 shows that in an OPEN statement you can use a string variable as the data file name. The assumption is that you will assign a file name to the string variable before the OPEN statement is executed.

Example 4 opens the data file PART.DAT on the default drive for input as filenumber 1. A file opened for input means we plan to read data from it. Later in this project we will show how data can be read from a data file.

Closing Sequential Files

When a program is finished reading or writing to a file, it must close the file with the CLOSE statement. The CLOSE statement terminates the association between the file and the filenumber assigned in the OPEN statement. If a file is being written to, the CLOSE statement ensures that the last record is written to the data file.

The general form of the CLOSE statement is shown in Figure 5-3.

CLOSE

or

CLOSE #filenumber_1, ..., #filenumber_n

FIGURE 5-3
The general form of the CLOSE statement

The CLOSE statement terminates access to a data file. For example, CLOSE #1 causes the data file assigned to filenumber 1 to be closed. Any other files previously opened by the program remain open. Following the close of a specified file, the filenumber may be assigned again to the same file or to a different file by an OPEN statement. The keyword CLOSE without any filenumber, closes all opened data files.

Note that when executed, the END statement closes all opened files before terminating execution of the program.

Writing Data to a Sequential File

To write data to a sequential file, we use the WRITE #n statement. The WRITE #n statement writes data in a format required by the INPUT #n statement. The format requirement is similar to that of the READ and DATA statements—all data items are separated by commas. The WRITE #n statement even goes one step further by surrounding all string data items written to the file with quotation marks.

The general form of the `WRITE #n` statement is shown in Figure 5-4.

FIGURE 5-4
The general form of the WRITE #n statement

```
WRITE #filenumber, variable1, variable2, ..., variablen
```

Consider the `WRITE #n` statement in Figure 5-5. Assume that Part.No$ = 129, Description$ = Hex Bolt, On.Hand = 200, and Wholesale = 1.26. The `WRITE #n` statement transmits the record shown to the sequential file assigned to filenumber 1. The `WRITE #n` statement causes a comma to be placed between the data items in the record. Quotation marks are placed around the values of the string variables Part.No$ and Description$, and a carriage return character ↵ is appended to the last data item written to form the record.

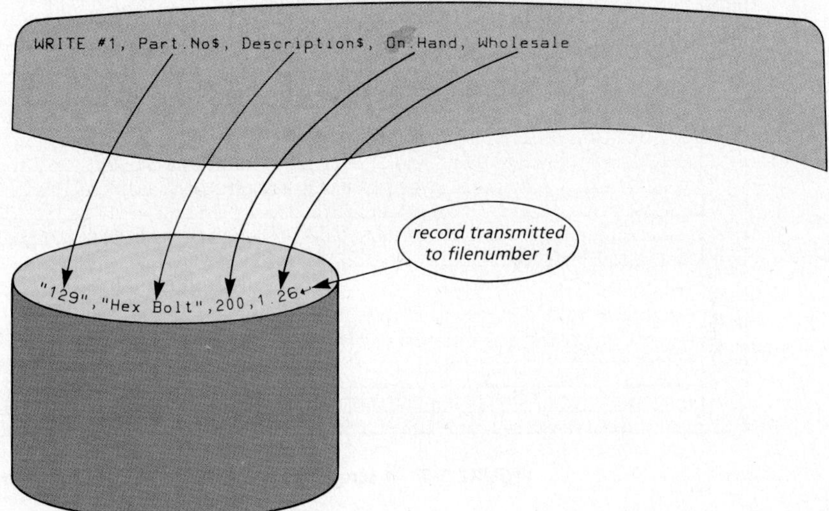

FIGURE 5-5
Writing data to a data file

SAMPLE PROGRAM 5A — CREATING A SEQUENTIAL DATA FILE

In this sample program, we create a sequential data file (PART.DAT) on the B drive from the part data shown in Figure 5-6. The data must be written in a format that is consistent with the `INPUT #n` statement. We use a series of `LOCATE`, `PRINT`, and `INPUT` statements to display the screen on the screen layout form shown on the next page in Figure 5-7. As part of the Wrap-Up module, the number of records written to PART.DAT is displayed.

PART NUMBER	DESCRIPTION	ON HAND	WHOLESALE PRICE
323	Canon PC-25	12	$799.92
432	Timex Watch	53	27.95
567	12 Inch Monitor	34	50.30
578	Epson Printer	23	179.95
745	6 Inch Frying Pan	17	9.71
812	Mr. Coffee	39	21.90
923	4-Piece Toaster	7	17.57

FIGURE 5-6 The data to be written to the sequential file PART.DAT

Notice that we are not validating the data entered through the keyboard in this sample program so that we can present a clear-cut example of how to create a sequential file. In a production environment, reasonableness checks are always considered for the part number, description, on hand, and wholesale price. Data should always be validated before it is written to a file.

```
Part File Build
---------------

Part Number ==========> XXX

Description =========> XXXXXXXXXXXXXXXXX

On Hand ==============> 999

Wholesale Price =====> 999.99

Enter Y to add record, else N ===> X

Enter Y to add another record, else N ===> X
```

FIGURE 5-7 A screen layout form for Sample Program 5A

A top-down chart, a program flowchart for each module, a program solution, and a discussion of the program solution follow.

Top-Down Chart and Program Flowcharts

Figure 5-8 illustrates the top-down chart and corresponding program flowcharts for each module in Sample Program 5A. In the Initialization module, the record counter is initialized to zero and the data file PART.DAT is opened. The Do-Until loop in the Build File module executes until the user indicates that there are no more records to enter. Within the Do-Until loop, a part record is accepted through the keyboard. After each record is entered, the user must enter the letter Y to add the record. This entry gives the user the opportunity to cancel the record while it is displayed on the screen, but before it is added to PART.DAT. After all the records are entered, the Wrap-Up module displays the number of records written to PART.DAT.

In the program flowcharts, notice that the `OPEN`, `WRITE #n`, and `CLOSE` statements are represented by the Input/Output symbol (parallelogram).

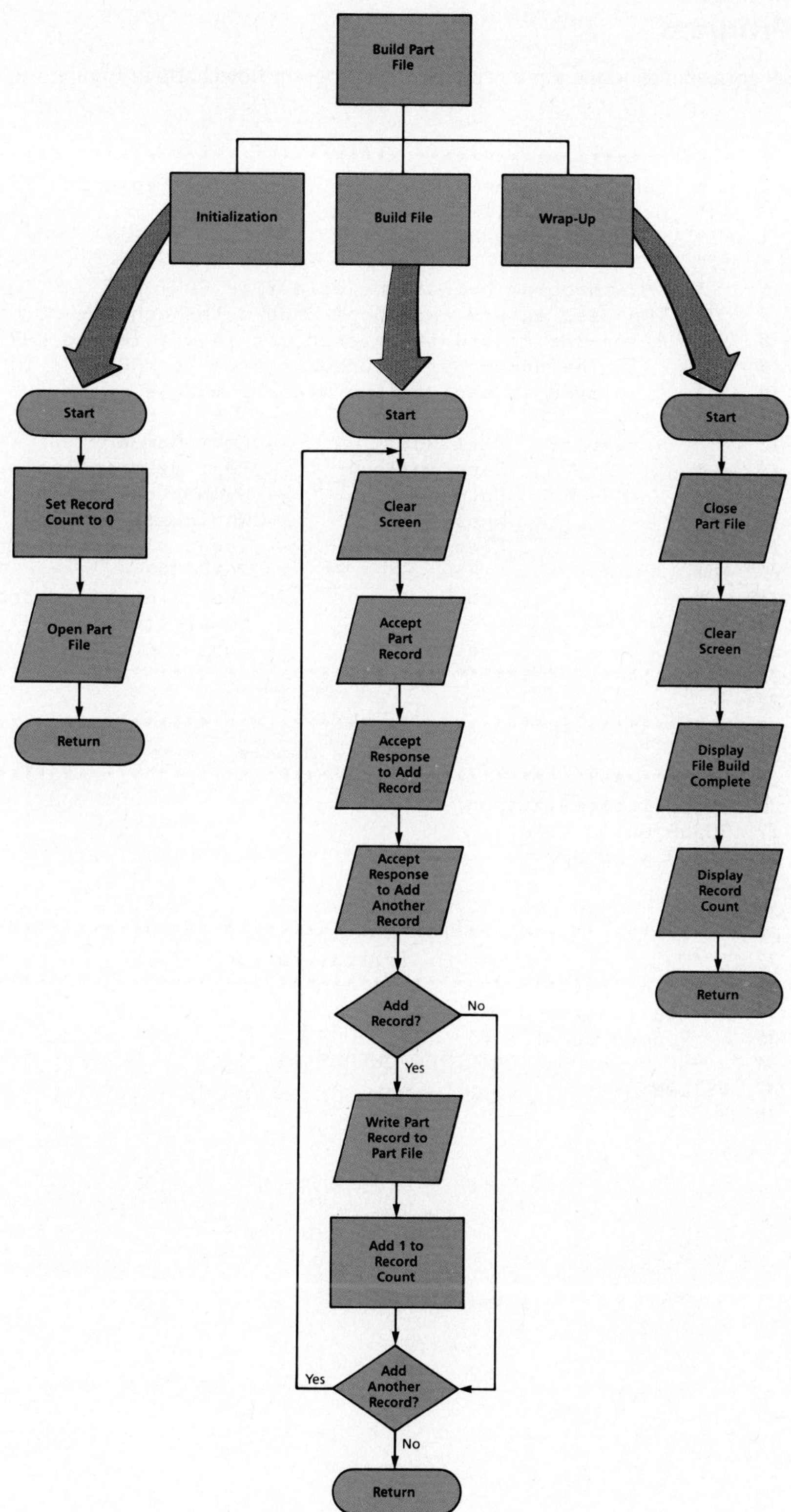

FIGURE 5-8 A top-down chart and corresponding program flowc
for Sample Program 5A

The QuickBASIC Program

The program in Figure 5-9 corresponds to the top-down chart and program flowcharts in Figure 5-8.

FIGURE 5-9
Sample Program 5A

```
' ****************************************************************
' *  Sample Program 5A                          September 15, 1994  *
' *  Build Part File                                                *
' *  J. S. Quasney                                                  *
' *                                                                 *
' *  This program builds the data file PART.DAT.                   *
' *  The user enters each part record through the keyboard.        *
' *  After the record is entered, it is written to PART.DAT.       *
' *       The number of records written to PART.DAT is              *
' *  displayed as part of the Wrap-Up module.                       *
' *                                                                 *
' *  Variables:  Part.No$          -- Part number                   *
' *              Description$      -- Part description              *
' *              On.Hand           -- Number on hand                *
' *              Wholesale         -- Wholesale price of part       *
' *              Record.Count      -- Count of records added to     *
' *                                   PART.DAT                      *
' *              Add.Rec$          -- Indicates if record is to     *
' *                                   be written to PART.DAT        *
' *              Control$          -- Controls Do-Until loop        *
' ****************************************************************

' ****************************************************************
' *                          Main Module                            *
' ****************************************************************
GOSUB Initialization
GOSUB Build.File
GOSUB Wrap.Up
END

' ****************************************************************
' *                        Initialization                           *
' ****************************************************************
Initialization:
   Record.Count = 0
   OPEN "B:PART.DAT" FOR OUTPUT AS #1
RETURN
```

FIGURE 5-9
(continued)

```
39 ' ***************************************************************
40 ' *                         Build File                          *
41 ' ***************************************************************
42 Build.File:
43    DO
44       CLS   ' Clear Screen
45       LOCATE 5, 25: PRINT "Part File Build"
46       LOCATE 6, 25: PRINT "---------------"
47       LOCATE 8, 25: INPUT "Part Number =======> ", Part.No$
48       LOCATE 10, 25: INPUT "Description =======> ", Description$
49       LOCATE 12, 25: INPUT "On Hand ===========> ", On.Hand
50       LOCATE 14, 25: INPUT "Wholesale Price ===> ", Wholesale
51       LOCATE 16, 25: INPUT "Enter Y to add record, else N ===> ", Add.Rec$
52       LOCATE 18, 25
53       INPUT "Enter Y to add another record, else N ===> ", Control$
54       IF Add.Rec$ = "Y" OR Add.Rec$ = "y" THEN
55          WRITE #1, Part.No$, Description$, On.Hand, Wholesale
56          Record.Count = Record.Count + 1
57       END IF
58    LOOP UNTIL Control$ = "N" OR Control$ = "n"
59 RETURN
60
61 ' ***************************************************************
62 ' *                          Wrap-Up                            *
63 ' ***************************************************************
64 Wrap.Up:
65    CLOSE #1
66    CLS   ' Clear Screen
67    LOCATE 10, 15: PRINT "Creation of PART.DAT is Complete"
68    LOCATE 14, 15
69    PRINT "Total Number of Records in PART.DAT ===>"; Record.Count
70 RETURN
71
72 ' ********************** End of Program **********************
```

Discussion of the Program Solution

When Sample Program 5A is executed, line 36 of the Initialization module opens PART.DAT for output on the B drive as filenumber 1. In the Build File module, lines 45 through 53 of the Do-Until loop accepts data values through the keyboard. The display due to the execution of these lines for the first record entered by the operator is shown on the next page in Figure 5-10. Notice the two messages at the bottom of the screen. The first message (displayed due to line 51) gives the operator the opportunity to reject the transaction by assigning Add.Rec$ a value other than Y (or y). The second message (displayed due to line 53) requests that the operator enter a Y (or y) to add another record to the part file.

Owing to line 54, the part record is added by the `WRITE #n` statement if Add.Rec$ is equal to Y (or y). Line 58 controls the Do-Until loop. If Control$ equals N (or n), then the loop terminates, and control returns to line 28 of the Main module. If Control$ is equal to any other value, then the loop continues.

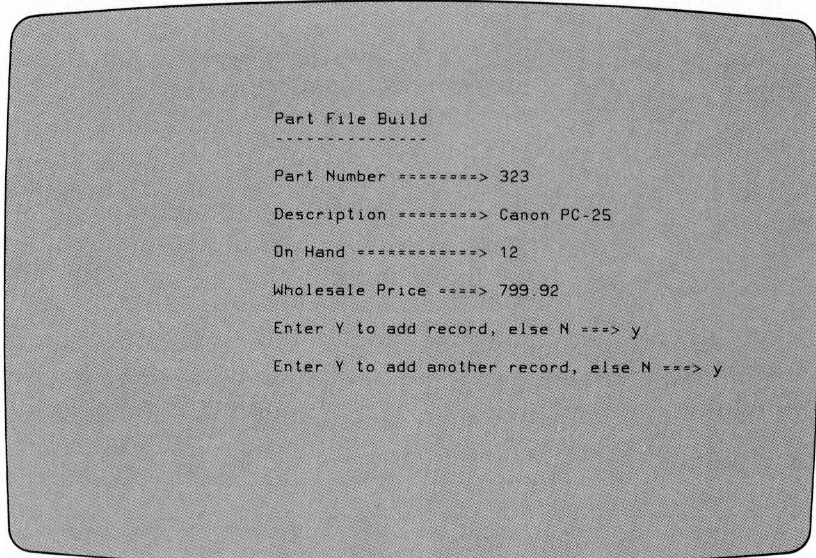

Part File Build

Part Number ========> 323
Description ========> Canon PC-25
On Hand ============> 12
Wholesale Price ====> 799.92
Enter Y to add record, else N ===> y
Enter Y to add another record, else N ===> y

FIGURE 5-10
The display after the first part record is entered due to the execution of Sample Program 5A

The `WRITE #n` statement in line 55 writes the record to the sequential file PART.DAT in a format that is consistent with the `INPUT #n` statement. Figure 5-11 shows the format of the data written to PART.DAT by Sample Program 5A.

```
"323","Canon PC-25",12,799.92
"432","Timex Watch",53,27.95
"567","12 Inch Monitor",34,50.3
"578","Epson Printer",23,179.95
"745","6 Inch Frying Pan",17,9.71
"812","Mr. Coffee",39,21.9
"923","4-Piece Toaster",7,17.57
```

FIGURE 5-11
A listing of PART.DAT created by Sample Program 5A

In the Wrap-Up module, line 65 closes PART.DAT. This ensures that the last record entered by the operator is physically written to the data file on auxiliary storage. Figure 5-12 shows the display due to lines 66 through 69 of the Wrap-Up module.

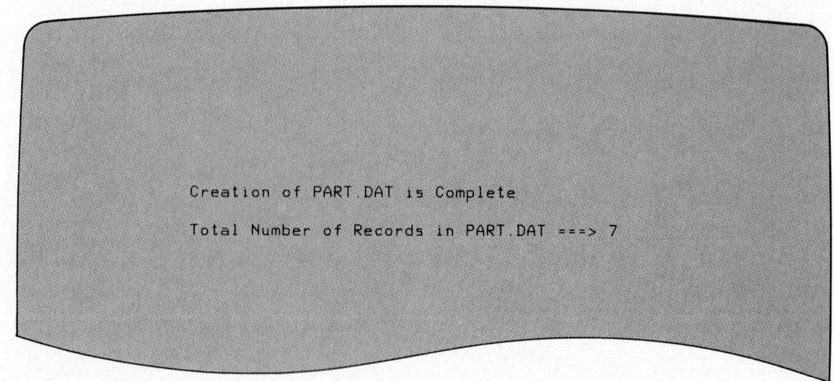

FIGURE 5-12
The display due to the execution of the Wrap-Up module in Sample Program 5A

READING DATA FROM A SEQUENTIAL DATA FILE

The INPUT #n statement is used to read data from a data file that has been created by using the WRITE #n statement. The EOF function is used to determine when all the records have been processed. The following sections describe how the INPUT #n statement and EOF function work.

The INPUT #n Statement

The INPUT #n statement is similar to the READ statement except that it reads data from a data file instead of from DATA statements. In the following partial program,

```
OPEN "PART.DAT" FOR INPUT AS #1
  .
  .
  .
INPUT #1, Part.No$, Description$, On.Hand, Wholesale
```

the PC reads four data items from the sequential file PART.DAT.

The general form of the INPUT #n statement is shown in Figure 5-13.

```
INPUT #filenumber, variable₁, variable₂, ..., variableₙ
```

FIGURE 5-13 The general form of the INPUT #n statement

The EOF Function

When a sequential data file that was opened for output is closed, the PC automatically adds an end-of-file mark after the last record written to the file. Later, when the same sequential file is opened for input, you can use the EOF(n) function to test for the end-of-file mark. The n indicates the filenumber assigned to the file in the OPEN statement.

If the EOF function senses the end-of-file mark, it returns a value of –1 (true). Otherwise, it returns a value of 0 (false). Hence, the EOF function can be used in a DO WHILE statement to control the loop. For example, consider the partial program in Figure 5-14. In the DO WHILE statement, the EOF(1) function is used to control the Do loop. Each time the DO WHILE statement is executed, the PC checks to see whether the data pointer is pointing to the end-of-file mark in PART.DAT.

```
OPEN "PART.DAT" FOR INPUT AS #1
  .
  .
  .
DO WHILE NOT EOF(1)
   INPUT #1, Part.No$, Description$, On.Hand, Wholesale
   LET Record.Count = Record.Count + 1
   LET Total.On.Hand = Total.On.Hand + On.Hand
   LET Part.Cost = On.Hand * Wholesale
   LET Total.Part.Cost = Total.Part.Cost + Part.Cost
   LPRINT USING DL1$; Part.No$; Description$; On.Hand; Wholesale; Part.Cost
LOOP
```

FIGURE 5-14 Using the EOF function to test for end-of-file

When using the EOF function, it is important to organize your program so that the test for the end-of-file precedes the execution of the INPUT #n statement. In Figure 5-14, notice that only one INPUT #n statement is employed, and that this statement is placed inside at the top of the Do loop. This is different from our previous programs which employed two READ statements—one prior to the Do-While loop and one at the bottom of the Do-While loop.

The logic in Figure 5-14 also works when the file is empty (that is, when the file contains no records). If the PART.DAT file is empty, the `OPEN` statement in the partial program still opens the file for input. However, when the `DO WHILE` statement is executed, the `EOF` function immediately detects the end-of-file mark on the empty file, thereby causing control to pass to the statement following the corresponding `LOOP` statement.

SAMPLE PROGRAM 5B — PROCESSING A SEQUENTIAL DATA FILE

In this sample program we will show how to read data and generate a report using the part file (PART.DAT) built by Sample Program 5A. The display shown in Figure 5-15A instructs the user to prepare the printer to receive the report. The report shown in Figure 5-15B contains a detail line for each part number. The total cost for each part is determined by multiplying the number of on hand by the wholesale price.

As part of the end-of-job routine, the sample program prints the number of part records processed, total number of parts in inventory, and the total cost of all the parts.

A. SCREEN DISPLAY

```
Set the paper in the printer to the top of page.

Press the Enter key when the printer is ready...

End of Job
```

B. PRINTED REPORT

```
                Part Cost Report

Part                                Wholesale       Part
No.    Description       On Hand    Price           Cost
----   -----------       -------    ---------       ----
323    Canon PC-25            12       799.92   9,599.04
432    Timex Watch            53        27.95   1,481.35
567    12 Inch Monitor        34        50.30   1,710.20
578    Epson Printer          23       179.95   4,138.85
745    6 Inch Frying P        17         9.71     165.07
812    Mr. Coffee             39        21.90     854.10
923    4-Piece Toaster         7        17.57     122.99
                         -------              ---------
                             185              18,071.60

Total Number of Parts =====>   7

End of Job
```

FIGURE 5-15 The screen display (A) and printed report (B) generated by Sample Program 5B

A top-down chart, a program flowchart for each module, a program solution, and a discussion of the program solution follow.

Top-Down Chart and Program Flowcharts

Figure 5-16 illustrates the top-down chart and corresponding program flowcharts for each module in Sample Program 5B.

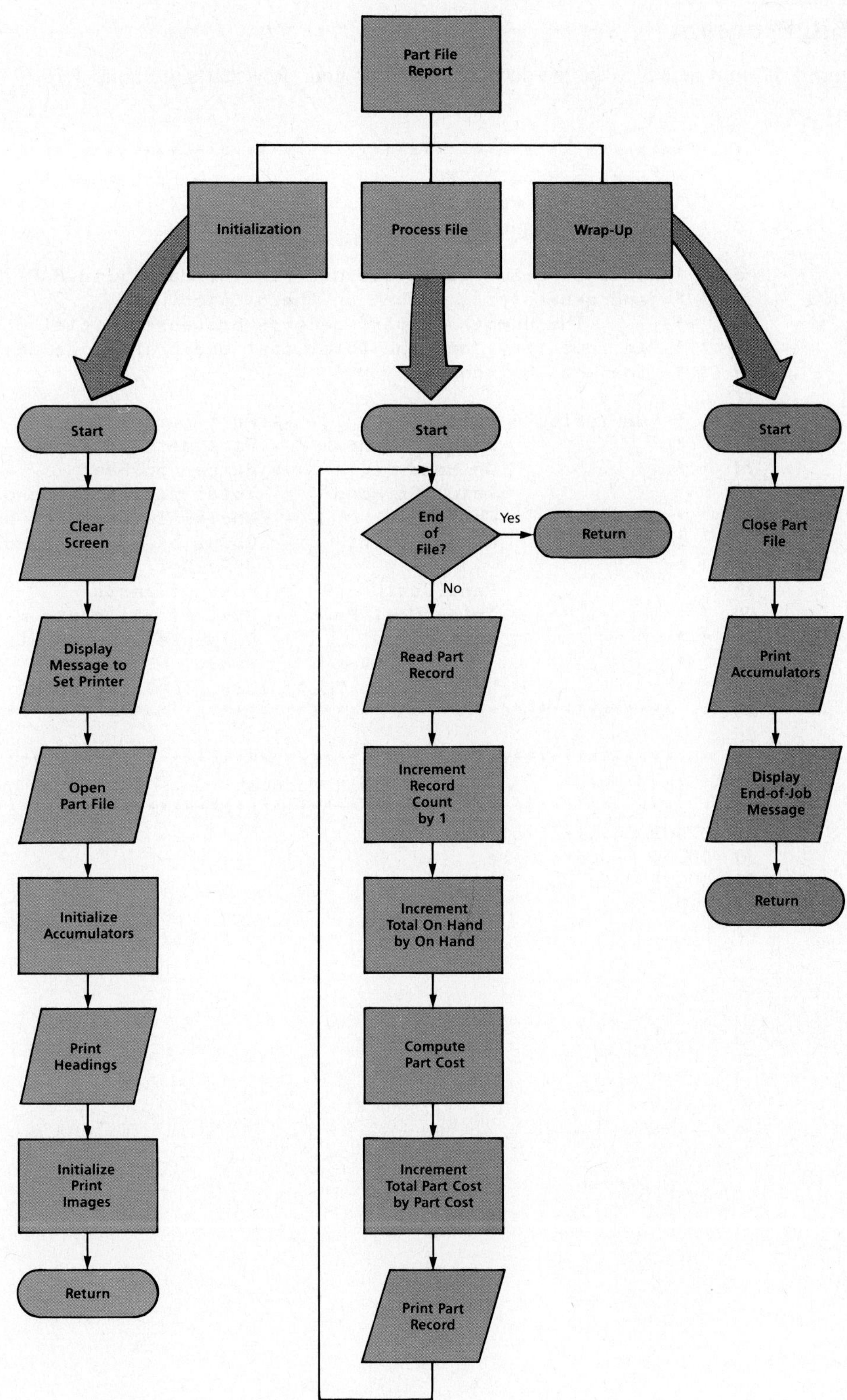

FIGURE 5-16 A top-down chart and corresponding program flowcharts for Sample Program 5B

The QuickBASIC Program

The program in Figure 5-17 corresponds to the top-down chart and program flowcharts in Figure 5-16.

FIGURE 5-17
Sample Program 5B

```
' *****************************************************************
' *  Sample Program 5B                           September 15, 1994  *
' *  Part File Report                                                *
' *  J. S. Quasney                                                   *
' *                                                                  *
' *  This program reads records from the data file PART.DAT         *
' *  and generates a report on the printer.                          *
' *       The number of part records processed, total pieces         *
' *  in inventory, and the total cost are printed as part of         *
' *  the Wrap-Up module.                                             *
' *                                                                  *
' *  Variables:  Part.No$          -- Part number                    *
' *              Description$      -- Part description               *
' *              On.Hand           -- Number on hand                 *
' *              Total.On.Hand     -- Total pieces on hand           *
' *              Wholesale         -- Wholesale price of part        *
' *              Record.Count      -- Count of records added to     *
' *                                   PART.DAT                       *
' *              Part.Cost         -- Cost of parts                  *
' *              Total.Cost.Part   -- Cost of all parts              *
' *              Control$          -- Response when printer is      *
' *                                   ready                          *
' *              DL1$, TL1$, TL2$, TL3$, TL4$  -- Print Images*
' *****************************************************************

' *****************************************************************
' *                          Main Module                             *
' *****************************************************************
GOSUB Initialization
GOSUB Process.File
GOSUB Wrap.Up
END
```

FIGURE 5-17 (continued)

```
' ****************************************************************
' *                       Initialization                         *
' ****************************************************************
Initialization:
   CLS  ' Clear Screen
   LOCATE 10, 20
   PRINT "Set the paper in the printer to the top of page."
   LOCATE 12, 20
   INPUT "Press the Enter key when the printer is ready...", Control$
   OPEN "B:PART.DAT" FOR INPUT AS #1
   Record.Count = 0
   Total.On.Hand = 0
   Total.Part.Cost = 0
   LPRINT "                          Part Cost Report"
   LPRINT
   LPRINT "Part                                      Wholesale        Part"
   LPRINT "No.     Description          On Hand      Price            Cost"
   LPRINT "----    -----------          -------      ---------        ----"
   DL1$ = "\ \     \           \         #,###     #,###.## ##,###.##"
   TL1$ = "                              -------               ---------"
   TL2$ = "                              ##,###               ###,###.##"
   TL3$ = "Total Number of Parts ====>#,###"
   TL4$ = "End of Job"
RETURN

' ****************************************************************
' *                        Process File                          *
' ****************************************************************
Process.File:
   DO WHILE NOT EOF(1)
      INPUT #1, Part.No$, Description$, On.Hand, Wholesale
      LET Record.Count = Record.Count + 1
      LET Total.On.Hand = Total.On.Hand + On.Hand
      LET Part.Cost = On.Hand * Wholesale
      LET Total.Part.Cost = Total.Part.Cost + Part.Cost
      LPRINT USING DL1$; Part.No$; Description$; On.Hand; Wholesale; Part.Cost
   LOOP
RETURN

' ****************************************************************
' *                          Wrap-Up                             *
' ****************************************************************
Wrap.Up:
   CLOSE #1
   LPRINT TL1$
   LPRINT USING TL2$; Total.On.Hand; Total.Part.Cost
   LPRINT
   LPRINT USING TL3$; Record.Count
   LPRINT
   LPRINT TL4$
   LOCATE 14, 20
   PRINT "End of Job"
RETURN

' ********************** End of Program **********************
```

Discussion of the Program Solution

When Sample Program 5B is executed, the screen display and printed report shown earlier in Figure 5-15 on page QB 92 are generated. The following points should be considered in the program solution represented by Sample Program 5B in Figure 5-17.

- Lines 39 through 42 in the Initialization module display on the screen instructions to the user to set the paper in the printer and press the Enter key when ready. Notice how the `INPUT` statement in line 42 temporarily halts the program until the user has prepared the printer to receive the report.
- Line 43 opens the data file PART.DAT on the B drive for input as filenumber 1. Hence, the program can read records from B:PART.DAT.
- The `DO WHILE` statement in line 63 controls the Do-While loop using a condition made up of the `EOF` function. The loop continues to execute while it is not end-of-file.
- Within the Do-While loop, the `INPUT #n` statement in line 64 reads a PART.DAT record by referencing filenumber 1 which was specified in the `OPEN` statement (line 43). After lines 65 through 68 manipulate the data and accumulate totals, line 69 prints the detail line. Line 70 returns control to the `DO WHILE` statement in line 63 which tests for the end-of-file mark.
- When the end-of-file mark is sensed in line 63, control passes to the `RETURN` statement in line 71. Line 71 returns control to line 31 in the Main module. Line 31 calls the Wrap-Up module, which prints the accumulators and displays an end-of-job message on the screen. Finally, control returns to the `END` statement in line 32 and the program terminates execution.

TRY IT YOURSELF EXERCISES

1. Fill in the blanks in the following sentences:
   a. The ____________ statement with a mode of ____________ must be executed before an `INPUT #n` statement is executed.
   b. The ____________ statement must be executed before a `WRITE #n` statement is executed.
   c. The ____________ function is used to test for the end-of-file mark with a sequential data file.
   d. When records are to be added to the end of a sequential data file, the ____________ mode is used in the `OPEN` statement.
2. Assume Cost = 15, Desc$ = Keyboard, and Code = 4. Using commas, quotation marks, and ↵ for end of record, indicate the makeup of the record written to auxiliary storage by the following `WRITE #n` statement:

```
WRITE #1, Cost, Desc$, Code
```

3. Explain why the `EOF` function should be used in a condition controlling the loop before the `INPUT #n` statement is executed.
4. A program is to read records from one of three sequential data files: PART1.DAT, PART2.DAT, and PART3.DAT. The three files are stored on the diskette in the A drive. Write three `OPEN` statements that would allow the program to read records from any of the three sequential files.
5. Which of the following are invalid file-handling statements? Why?
   a. `OPEN Seq$ FOR OUTPUT AS #1`
   b. `INPUT #1, Cost,`
   c. `DO WHILE NOT EOF(#2)`
   d. `CLOSE #1`
   e. `WRITE #2, A,`
   f. `OPEN FOR INPUT "INV.DAT" AS #2`
   g. `WRITE #1, USING "####.##"; Cost`

STUDENT ASSIGNMENTS

STUDENT ASSIGNMENT 1: Payroll File Build

Instructions: Design and code a top-down QuickBASIC program to build the payroll file PAYROLL.DAT. Use the sample data shown under INPUT. Generate a screen to receive the data similar to the one under OUTPUT. At the end-of-job, display the number of records written to the data file.

INPUT: Use the following sample data:

EMPLOYEE NUMBER	EMPLOYEE NAME	DEPENDENTS	PAY RATE	HOURS WORKED
23A5	Linda Frat	3	6.75	40
45K8	Joe Smit	1	12.50	38.5
56T1	Lisa Ann	1	16.25	48
65R4	Jeff Max	5	17.75	42
73E6	Susan Dex	2	13.50	40
87Q2	Jeff Web	0	22.45	50
91W2	Marci Jean	3	13.45	40
92R4	Jodi Lin	9	11.50	56
94Y2	Amanda Jo	12	12.75	20
96Y7	Niki Rai	3	16.00	42.5

OUTPUT: The sequential data file PAYROLL.DAT is created in auxiliary storage. The results for the first payroll record are shown below on the left. The results below on the right are displayed prior to termination of the program.

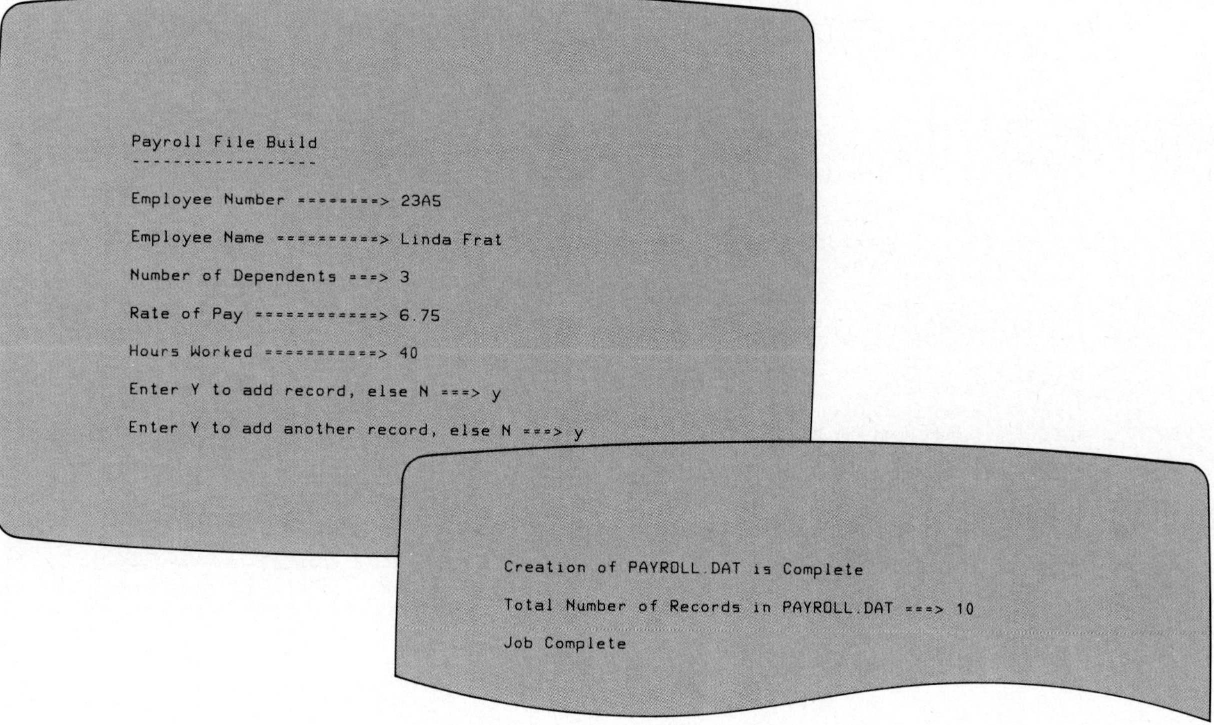

Payroll File Build

Employee Number ========> 23A5
Employee Name ==========> Linda Frat
Number of Dependents ===> 3
Rate of Pay ============> 6.75
Hours Worked ===========> 40
Enter Y to add record, else N ===> y
Enter Y to add another record, else N ===> y
Creation of PAYROLL.DAT is Complete
Total Number of Records in PAYROLL.DAT ===> 10
Job Complete

STUDENT ASSIGNMENT 2: Processing a Payroll File

Instructions: Design and code a top-down QuickBASIC program that generates the messages shown on the screen display under OUTPUT and prints the payroll report under OUTPUT. Apply the following conditions:

1. Gross pay = hours worked × hourly rate.
   Overtime (hours worked > 40) are paid at 1.5 times the hourly rate.
2. Federal withholding tax = 0.2 × (gross pay – dependents × 38.46). Assign federal withholding tax a value of zero if the gross pay less the product of the number of dependents and $38.46 is negative.
3. Net pay = gross pay – federal withholding tax.
4. At the end-of-job, print the number of employees processed, total gross pay, total federal withholding tax, and total net pay.
5. Print the report on the printer.

INPUT: Use the sequential data file PAYROLL.DAT created in Student Assignment 1. If you did not do Student Assignment 1, ask your instructor for a copy of PAYROLL.DAT.

OUTPUT: The following screen with messages and prompts is displayed:

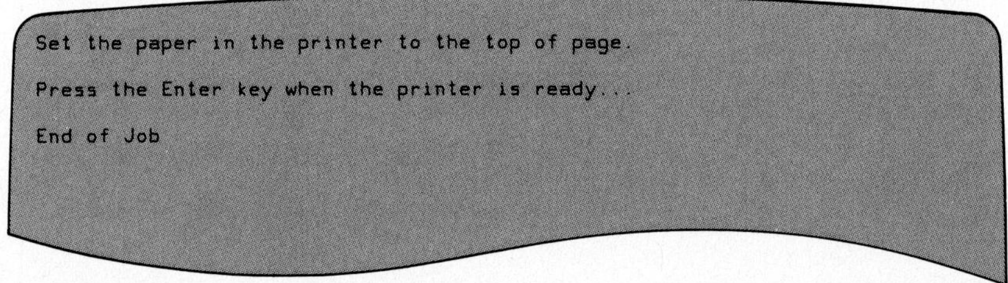

Set the paper in the printer to the top of page.
Press the Enter key when the printer is ready...
End of Job

The following report prints on the printer:

Payroll File List

Emp. No.	Name	Dep.	Hours	Pay Rate	Gross Pay	With. Tax	Net Pay
23A5	Linda Frat	3	40.0	6.75	270.00	30.92	239.08
45K8	Joe Smit	1	38.5	12.50	481.25	88.56	392.69
56T1	Lisa Ann	1	48.0	16.25	845.00	161.31	683.69
65R4	Jeff Max	5	42.0	17.75	763.25	114.19	649.06
73E6	Susan Dex	2	40.0	13.50	540.00	92.62	447.38
87Q2	Jeff Web	0	50.0	22.45	1,234.75	246.95	987.80
91W2	Marci Jean	3	40.0	13.45	538.00	84.52	453.48
92R4	Jodi Lin	9	56.0	11.50	736.00	77.97	658.03
94Y2	Amanda Jo	12	20.0	12.75	255.00	0.00	255.00
96Y7	Niki Rai	3	42.5	16.00	700.00	116.92	583.08

```
Total Employees =======>      10
Total Gross Pay =======>   6,363.25
Total Tax =============>   1,013.97
Total Net Pay =========>   5,349.28

End of Payroll Report
```

PROJECT 6

Arrays and Functions

In the previous projects we used simple variables such as Count, Emp.Name$, and Balance to store and access data in a program. In this project we discuss variables that can store more than one value under the same name. Variables that can hold more than one value at a time are called **arrays**.

An array is often used to store a **table** of organized data. Income tax tables, insurance tables, or sales tax tables are examples of tables that can be stored in an array for processing purposes. Once the table elements are assigned to an array, the array can be searched to extract the proper values.

Functions are used to handle common mathematical and string operations. For example, it is often necessary in programming to obtain the square root of a number or extract a substring from a string of characters. Without functions, these types of operations would require that you write sophisticated routines in your program. Functions clearly simplify the programming task.

Although we discuss only the most frequently used functions, you should be aware that QuickBASIC has over 70 built-in functions to aid you in your programming. For a summary of all the functions available in QuickBASIC, refer to pages R.4 and R.5 of the reference card in the back of this book.

ARRAYS

The banking application in Figure 6-1 illustrates an example of table processing. The account number, name of the account holder, and account balance of individuals who have savings are stored in arrays. When the teller enters account number 20013, the program searches the account number array to find an equal account number.

When the equal account number is found, the corresponding name (Darla Simmons) and the corresponding balance (932.49) are *pulled* from the table and displayed on the screen.

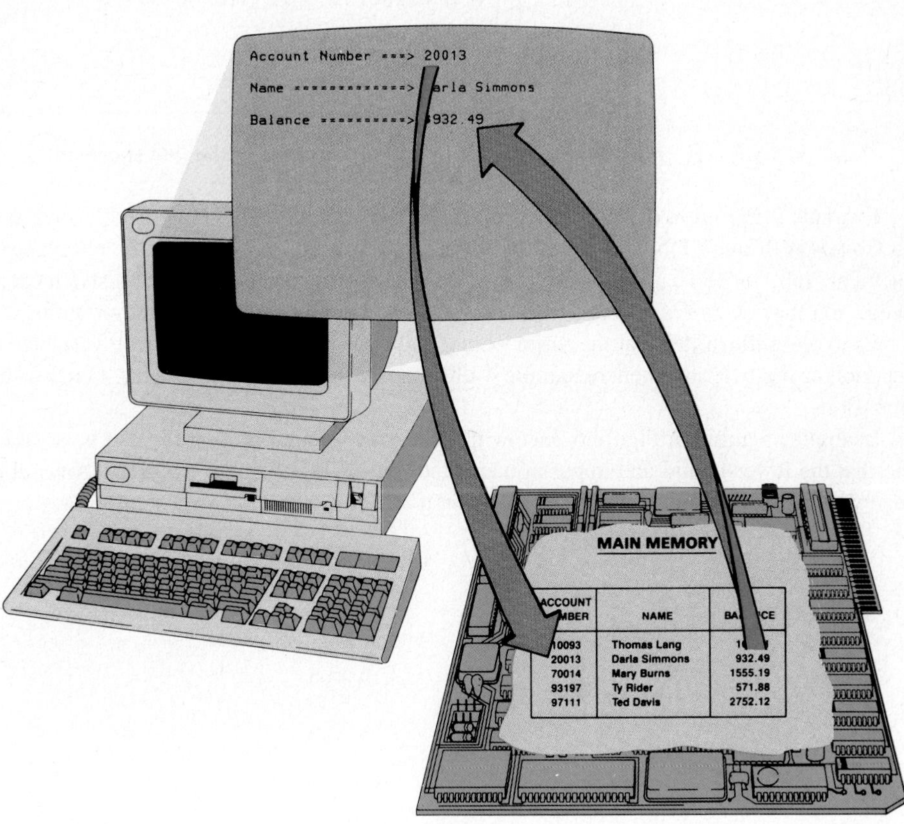

FIGURE 6-1
An example of table processing

THE DIM STATEMENT

Before arrays can be used, they must be declared in a program. This is the purpose of the DIM statement, also called the dimension statement. The general form of the DIM statement is shown in Figure 6-2.

DIM array-name(lb_1 TO ub_1), ..., array-name(lb_1 TO ub_n)

where **array-name** is a variable name, **lb_1** is a positive or negative integer or numeric variable that serves as the lower-bound value of the array, and **ub_n** is a positive or negative integer or numeric variable that serves as the upper-bound value of the array.

FIGURE 6-2 The general form of the DIM statement

Figure 6-3 illustrates several examples of declaring arrays. Example 1 reserves storage for a one-dimensional numeric array Tax, which consists of 5 elements, or storage locations. These elements—Tax(1), Tax(2), Tax(3), Tax(4), and Tax(5)—can be used in a program the same way in which a simple variable can be used. Notice that the elements of an array are distinguished from one another by **subscripts** that follow the array name within parentheses.

EXAMPLE	DIM STATEMENT
1	`DIM Tax(1 TO 5)`
2	`DIM Job.Code$(1 TO 15), Bonus(1 TO 15)`
3	`DIM Part.No$(Begin TO Fin), Des(Begin TO Fin)`
4	`DIM Function.Tax(1 TO 50, 1 TO 25)`
5	`DIM Inventory.No$(15 TO 35)`
6	`DIM X(-5 TO 10)`

FIGURE 6-3 Examples of the DIM statement

Example 2 in Figure 6-3 declares two arrays—Job.Code$ and Bonus. Both arrays are declared to have 15 elements. Thus, Job.Code$(1) through Job.Code$(15) and Bonus(1) through Bonus(15) can be referenced in the program containing the DIM statement. Job.Code$(0) and Job.Code$(16) do not exist according to the DIM statement, and therefore, should not be referenced. You may declare as many arrays in a DIM statement as required by the program.

Example 3 illustrates that the lower-bound and upper-bound values can be variables that are assigned a value prior to the execution of the DIM statement. Example 4 illustrates a two-dimensional array. QuickBASIC allows an array to have up to 60 dimensions.

Examples 5 and 6 in Figure 6-3 show that the lower-bound of an array can be a value different from 1. It is important to note that the lower-bound and upper-bound values define the range of the array. Any subscript reference that is outside the range will cause a diagnostic message to display.

SAMPLE PROGRAM 6 — CUSTOMER ACCOUNT TABLE LOOKUP

In this sample program we implement the banking application shown on page QB 99 in Figure 6-1. The account number, name of the account holder, and account balance of customers who have savings accounts are shown in Figure 6-4. The table data is stored in the sequential data file ACCOUNTS.DAT. ACCOUNTS.DAT includes a data item (5) prior to the first account record that is equal to the number of records in the data file.

ACCOUNT NUMBER	CUSTOMER NAME	BALANCE
10093	Thomas Lang	$ 100.51
20013	Darla Simmons	932.49
70014	Mary Burns	1,555.19
93197	Ty Rider	571.88
97111	Ted Davis	2,752.12

FIGURE 6-4 **The table data stored in ACCOUNTS.DAT**

The screen display in Figure 6-5 illustrates the output results when the user enters account number 70014. When the user enters the account number, the program should direct the PC to *look up* and display the corresponding customer name and balance. The message at the bottom of the screen in Figure 6-5 asks the user to enter the letter Y to look up another account or the letter N to terminate the program.

If the account number is not found in the table, a diagnostic error displays.

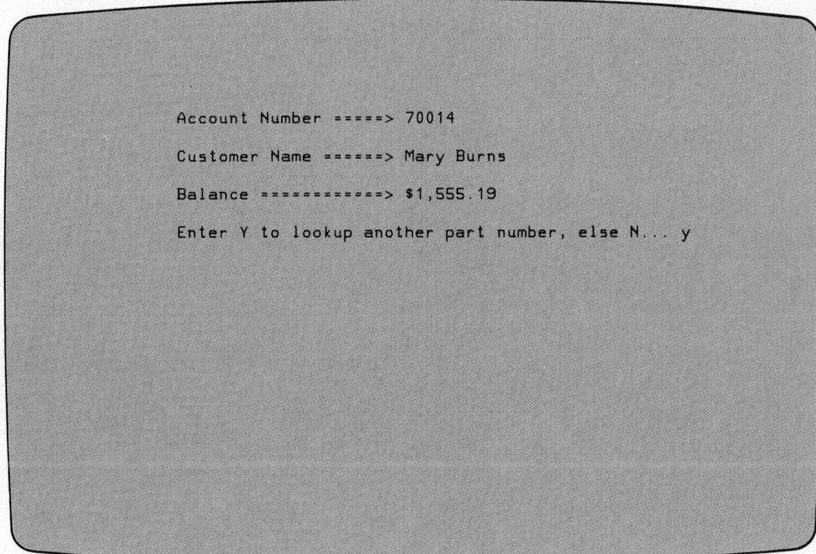

Account Number =====> 70014
Customer Name ======> Mary Burns
Balance ============> $1,555.19
Enter Y to lookup another part number, else N... y

FIGURE 6-5
The display due to the execution of Sample Program 6 and the entering of account number 70014

A top-down chart, a program flowchart for each module, a program solution, and a discussion of the program solution follow.

Top-Down Chart and Program Flowcharts

The top-down chart and corresponding program flowcharts that illustrate the logic for the Sample Program 6 are shown in Figure 6-6.

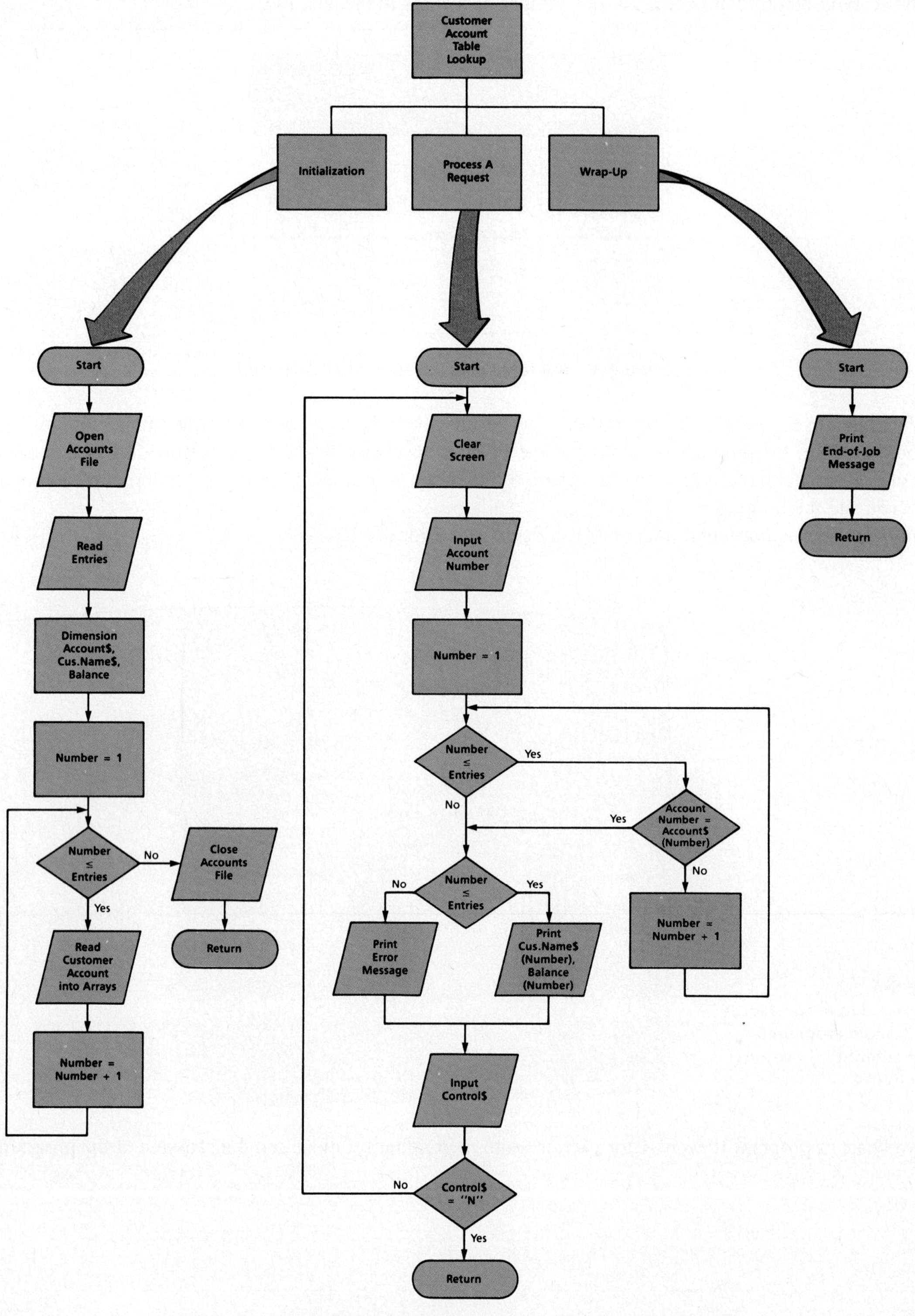

FIGURE 6-6 A top-down chart and corresponding program flowcharts for Sample Program 6

In the Initialization module in Figure 6-6, ACCOUNTS.DAT is opened and the number of records in the account file is read. This value is used to dimension the three arrays that will hold the account information. Next, the same value is used to control a Do-While loop that assigns the account information to the three arrays. After the Do-While loop is finished, ACCOUNTS.DAT is closed.

In the Process A Request module, the program accepts the account number from the user. A Do-While loop is then used to search the array that contains the account numbers. If the search is successful, the customer name and balance display. If the search is unsuccessful, a diagnostic message displays. Finally, the user is asked if he or she wants to enter another account number.

When the user enters the letter N (or n), control returns to the Main module and the Wrap-Up module displays an end-of-job message.

The QuickBASIC Program

The QuickBASIC code in Figure 6-7 corresponds to the top box in the top-down chart in Figure 6-6. The GOSUB statements call the subordinate modules. Following the return of control from the Wrap-Up module, the END statement terminates execution of the program.

```
' ***************************************************************
' *                        Main Module                          *
' ***************************************************************
GOSUB Initialization
GOSUB Process.Request
GOSUB Wrap.Up
END
```

FIGURE 6-7 The Main module for Sample Program 6

Initialization Module The Initialization module for Sample Program 6 is shown in Figure 6-8. The primary objective of this module is to load the data in ACCOUNTS.DAT into the arrays. Line 35 opens ACCOUNTS.DAT on the B drive. Line 36 assigns the first data item in ACCOUNTS.DAT to the variable Entries. Entries is then assigned the value 5. Line 37 dimensions the three arrays with an upper-bound value equal to Entries. The For loop in lines 38 through 40 reads the data in ACCOUNTS.DAT into the three arrays. Arrays Account$, Cus.Name$, and Balance, therefore contain the data in ACCOUNTS.DAT. Since each array contains data that corresponds to the other arrays, we call them **parallel arrays**. Line 41 closes ACCOUNTS.DAT before control is returned to the Main module.

```
31  ' ****************************************************************
32  ' *                          Initialization                     *
33  ' ****************************************************************
34  Initialization:
35     OPEN "B:ACCOUNTS.DAT" FOR INPUT AS #1
36     INPUT #1, Entries
37     DIM Account$(1 TO Entries), Cus.Name$(1 TO Entries), Balance(1 TO Entries)
38     FOR Number = 1 TO Entries
39        INPUT #1, Account$(Number), Cus.Name$(Number), Balance(Number)
40     NEXT Number
41     CLOSE #1
42  RETURN
```

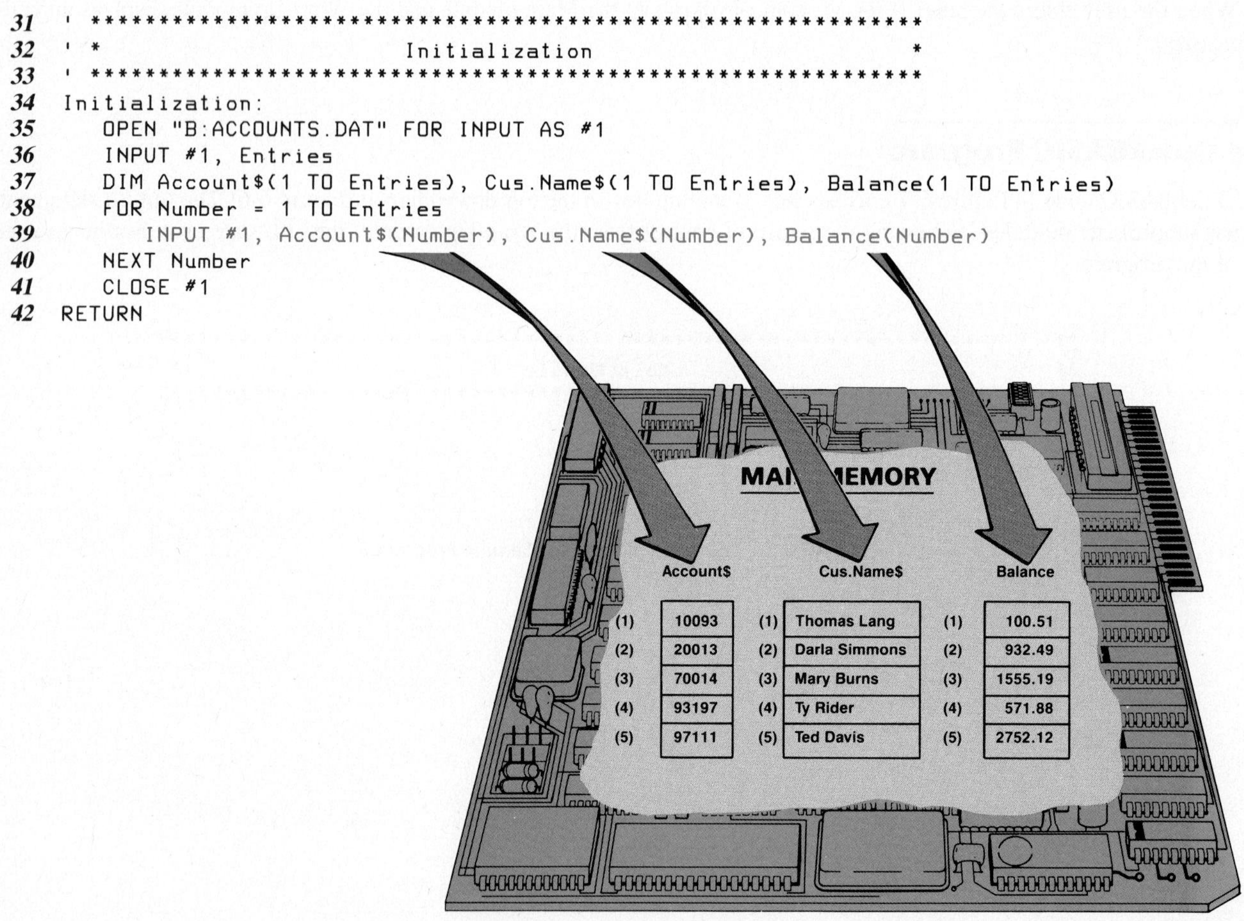

FIGURE 6-8 The Initialization module for Sample Program 6

Process A Request Module After the data in ACCOUNTS.DAT is loaded into the arrays and control passes back to the Main module, line 27 transfers control to the Process A Request module (Figure 6-9). This module begins by clearing the screen and accepting the account number from the user. The account number is assigned to the variable Search.Argument$ (line 51).

```
44 ' ***************************************************************
45 ' *                    Process A Request                        *
46 ' ***************************************************************
47 Process.Request:
48    DO
49       CLS  ' Clear Screen
50       LOCATE 5, 15
51       INPUT "Account Number =====> ", Search.Argument$
52       FOR Number = 1 TO Entries
53          IF Search.Argument$ = Account$(Number) THEN
54             EXIT FOR    ' Process a Table Hit
55          END IF
56       NEXT Number
57       IF Number <= Entries THEN
58          LOCATE 7, 15
59          PRINT "Customer Name ======> "; Cus.Name$(Number)
60          LOCATE 9, 15
61          PRINT USING "Balance ============> $$,###.##"; Balance(Number)
62       ELSE
63          LOCATE 7, 15
64          PRINT "Account Number "; Search.Argument$; " NOT FOUND"
65       END IF
66       LOCATE 11, 15
67       INPUT "Enter Y to lookup another part number, else N... ", Control$
68    LOOP UNTIL Control$ = "N" OR Control$ = "n"
69 RETURN
```

FIGURE 6-9 The Process A Request module for Sample Program 6

The For loop in lines 52 through 56 of Figure 6-9 searches the Account$ array for a match with Search.Argument$. Each time through the loop, the `IF` statement (line 53) compares Search.Argument$ to the next element in Account$ until a *hit* is made. When a *hit* occurs, the `EXIT FOR` statement in line 54 causes a premature exit from the For loop and control passes to line 57. If no *hit* occurs, a normal exit from the For loop also passes control to line 57.

Line 57 determines if the search for the account number in Account$ was successful. If the search was successful, then Number is less than or equal to Entries. In this case, the customer number and balance from the two corresponding arrays are displayed using the value of Number for the subscript. Figure 6-10 shows the display due to a successful search.

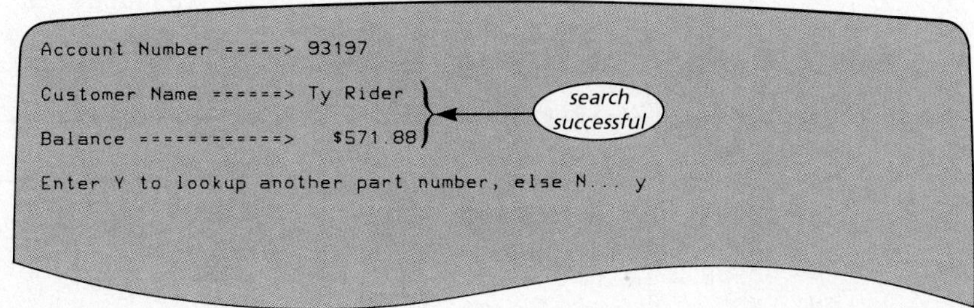

FIGURE 6-10 The display from Sample Program 6 due to entering the account number 93197

If the search is unsuccessful, then Number is greater than Entries and the diagnostic message in line 64 displays as shown in Figure 6-11. Note that if there is a premature exit from the For loop, the search is successful. If the For loop ends normally, the search is unsuccessful.

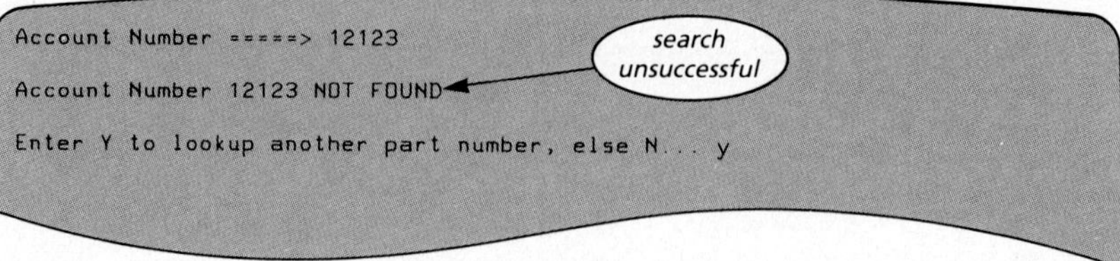
Account Number =====> 12123
Account Number 12123 NOT FOUND
Enter Y to lookup another part number, else N... y
search unsuccessful

FIGURE 6-11
The display from Sample Program 6 due to entering the invalid account number 12123

After the true or false task in the `IF` statement (lines 57 through 65) is executed, line 67 requests that the user enter the letter `Y` to process another account number or the letter `N` to terminate execution of the program.

The complete QuickBASIC program is shown in Figure 6-12.

FIGURE 6-12
Sample Program 6

```
1   ' ****************************************************************
2   ' *   Sample Program 6                            September 15, 1994  *
3   ' *   Customer Account Table Lookup                                   *
4   ' *   J. S. Quasney                                                   *
5   ' *                                                                   *
6   ' *   This program loads the data in ACCOUNTS.DAT into arrays.        *
7   ' *   The user enters the account number and the program looks      *
8   ' *   up and displays the customer number and account balance.       *
9   ' *        If the account number is not found, then a                 *
10  ' *   diagnostic message is displayed.  After processing a           *
11  ' *   request, the user is asked if he or she wishes to              *
12  ' *   display information of another account or terminate the       *
13  ' *   program.                                                        *
14  ' *                                                                   *
15  ' *   Variables: Account$          -- Account number array            *
16  ' *              Cus.Name$         -- Customer name array             *
17  ' *              Balance           -- Customer balance array          *
18  ' *              Search.Argument$  -- Account number requested        *
19  ' *              Control$          -- Response to continue            *
20  ' *              Entries           -- Number of customers             *
21  ' ****************************************************************
22
23  ' ****************************************************************
24  ' *                        Main Module                                *
25  ' ****************************************************************
26  GOSUB Initialization
27  GOSUB Process.Request
28  GOSUB Wrap.Up
29  END
30
```

FIGURE 6-12 (continued)

```
' ***************************************************************
' *                       Initialization                        *
' ***************************************************************
Initialization:
   OPEN "B:ACCOUNTS.DAT" FOR INPUT AS #1
   INPUT #1, Entries
   DIM Account$(1 TO Entries), Cus.Name$(1 TO Entries), Balance(1 TO Entries)
   FOR Number = 1 TO Entries
      INPUT #1, Account$(Number), Cus.Name$(Number), Balance(Number)
   NEXT Number
   CLOSE #1
RETURN

' ***************************************************************
' *                      Process A Request                      *
' ***************************************************************
Process.Request:
   DO
      CLS  ' Clear Screen
      LOCATE 5, 15
      INPUT "Account Number =====> ", Search.Argument$
      FOR Number = 1 TO Entries
         IF Search.Argument$ = Account$(Number) THEN
            EXIT FOR   ' Process a Table Hit
         END IF
      NEXT Number
      IF Number <= Entries THEN
         LOCATE 7, 15
         PRINT "Customer Name ======> "; Cus.Name$(Number)
         LOCATE 9, 15
         PRINT USING "Balance ============> $$,###.##"; Balance(Number)
      ELSE
         LOCATE 7, 15
         PRINT "Account Number "; Search.Argument$; " NOT FOUND"
      END IF
      LOCATE 11, 15
      INPUT "Enter Y to lookup another part number, else N... ", Control$
   LOOP UNTIL Control$ = "N" OR Control$ = "n"
RETURN

' ***************************************************************
' *                           Wrap-Up                           *
' ***************************************************************
Wrap.Up:
   LOCATE 13, 15
   PRINT "Job Complete"
RETURN
' *********************** End of Program ********************
```

FUNCTIONS

QuickBASIC includes over 70 numeric and string functions. Numeric functions are used to handle common mathematical calculations. String functions are used to manipulate strings of characters.

Numeric Functions

Three of the most frequently used numeric functions are the INT, SQR, and RND functions. The purpose of these functions is summarized in Figure 6-13.

FUNCTION	FUNCTION VALUE
INT(X)	**Returns the largest integer that is less than or equal to the argument X.**
SQR(X)	**Returns the square root of the argument X.**
RND	**Returns a random number greater than or equal to zero and less than 1.**

FIGURE 6-13 Frequently used numeric functions

INT Function The INT function returns a whole number that is less than or equal to the argument. Figure 6-14 shows several examples of the INT function.

VALUE OF VARIABLE	QuickBASIC STATEMENT	RESULT
X = 12.45	LET Y = INT(X)	Y = 12
H = 27.89	LET G = INT(H + 10)	G = 37
J = -15.67	LET K = INT(J)	K = -16

FIGURE 6-14 Examples of the INT function

SQR Function The SQR function computes the square root of the argument. Figure 6-15 illustrates several examples of the SQR function. Note that the argument for the SQR function must be a non-negative value.

VALUE OF VARIABLE	QuickBASIC STATEMENT	RESULT
Y = 4	LET X = SQR(Y)	X = 2
D = 27	LET P = SQR(D * 3)	P = 9
E = -16	LET U = SQR(E)	Illegal Function Call

FIGURE 6-15 Examples of the SQR function

RND Function The `RND` function returns an unpredictable number that is greater than or equal to zero and less than 1. The partial program in Figure 6-16 uses a For loop and the `RND` function to generate three random numbers — .7132002, .6291881, and .3409873.

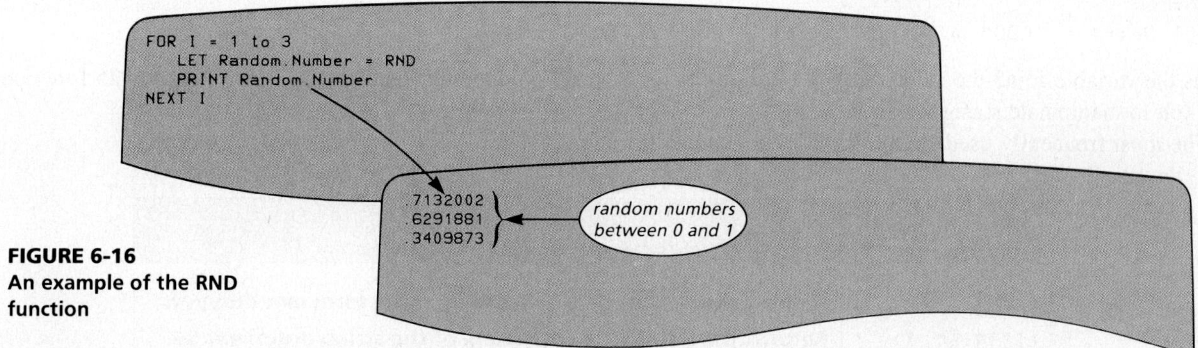

FIGURE 6-16
An example of the RND function

The `INT` and `RND` functions can be used to generate random digits over any range. The following expression generates random numbers between L and U:

```
INT((U - L + 1) * RND + L)
```

For example, to simulate the roll of a six-sided die, we can write the following:

```
LET Die = INT((6 - 1 + 1) * RND + 1)
```

or

```
LET Die = INT(6 * RND + 1)
```

In Figure 6-17, the For loop generates five rolls of two dice. The first `LET` statement represents the roll of one die and the second `LET` statement represents the roll of the second die.

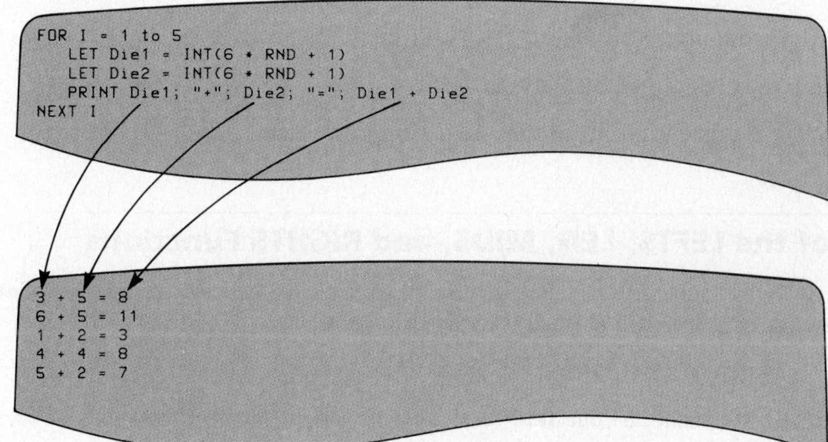

FIGURE 6-17
An example of a partial program that simulates five rolls of two dice

Each time you run the program in Figure 6-17, it generates the same sequence of random numbers. To generate a new sequence of random numbers each time you execute the program, insert the `RANDOMIZE` statement at the top of the program. When executed, the `RANDOMIZE` statement requests that you enter a number between –32768 and 32767. The value you enter is used by the PC to develop a new set of random numbers.

String Functions

The capability to process strings is important in business applications. In QuickBASIC, you can join two strings together through the use of the concatenation operator (+). For example, the following LET statement:

```
LET Join$ = "ABC" + "DEF"
```

assigns the variable Join$ the value ABCDEF. Besides the concatenation operator, QuickBASIC includes over 25 functions that allow you to manipulate string values.

The most frequently used string functions are shown in Figure 6-18.

FUNCTION	FUNCTION VALUE
DATE$	Returns the system date as a string in the form mm-dd-yyyy.
LEFT$(S$, X)	Returns the leftmost X characters of the string argument S$.
LEN(S$)	Returns the number of characters in the string argument S$.
MID$(S$, P, X)	Returns X characters from the string argument S$ beginning at position P.
RIGHT$(S$, X)	Returns the rightmost X characters of the string argument S$.
TIME$	Returns the system time of day as a string in the form HH:MM:SS.

FIGURE 6-18 Frequently used string functions

The DATE$ and TIME$ Functions The DATE$ and TIME$ functions return the DOS system date and time. For example, if the system date is initialized to September 15, 1994, then the statement PRINT "The date is "; DATE$ displays the following result:

```
The date is 09-15-1994
```

If the system time is equal to 11:44:42, then the statement PRINT "The time is "; TIME$ displays the following result:

```
The time is 11:44:42
```

The system time is maintained in 24-hour notation. That is, 1:30 P.M. displays as 13:30:00.

Use of the LEFT$, LEN, MID$, and RIGHT$ Functions

The LEN(S$) function returns the number of characters in S$. For example, the following LET statement assigns Length the value 5 because there are 5 characters in the string BASIC:

```
LET Length = LEN("BASIC")
```

The LET statement LET Number = LEN(DATE$) assigns Number the value 10 because there are 10 characters in the system date (mm/dd/yyyy).

The LEFT$, MID$, and RIGHT$ functions are used to extract substrings from a string. Figure 6-19 illustrates several examples of these functions.

VALUE OF VARIABLE	QuickBASIC STATEMENT	RESULT
Assume S$ is equal to `GOTO is a four-letter word`		
1	`LET Q$ = LEFT$(S$, 7)`	`Q$ = GOTO is`
2	`LET W$ = LEFT$(S$, 4)`	`W$ = GOTO`
3	`LET D$ = RIGHT$(S$, 11)`	`D$ = letter word`
4	`LET K$ = RIGHT$(S$, 1)`	`K$ = d`
5	`LET M$ = MID$(S$, 6, 2)`	`M$ = is`
6	`LET T$ = MID$(S$, 16, 6)`	`T$ = letter`

FIGURE 6-19 Examples of the LEFT$, RIGHT$, and MID$ functions

QuickBASIC also allows the argument to include a function. For example, if the system date is 9/15/94, then the `LET` statement `LET Day$ = MID$(DATE$, 4, 2)` assigns Day$ the string value `15`. If the system time is equal to 10:32:52, then the `LET` statement `LET Second$ = MID$(Time$, 7, 2)` assigns Second$ the string value `52`.

Consider the partial program in Figure 6-20 and the corresponding output results. Lines 1 and 2 display the system date and time. Lines 4 through 6 display on separate lines the substrings month, day, and year. Lines 8 through 10 display on separate lines the substrings hour, minute, and second.

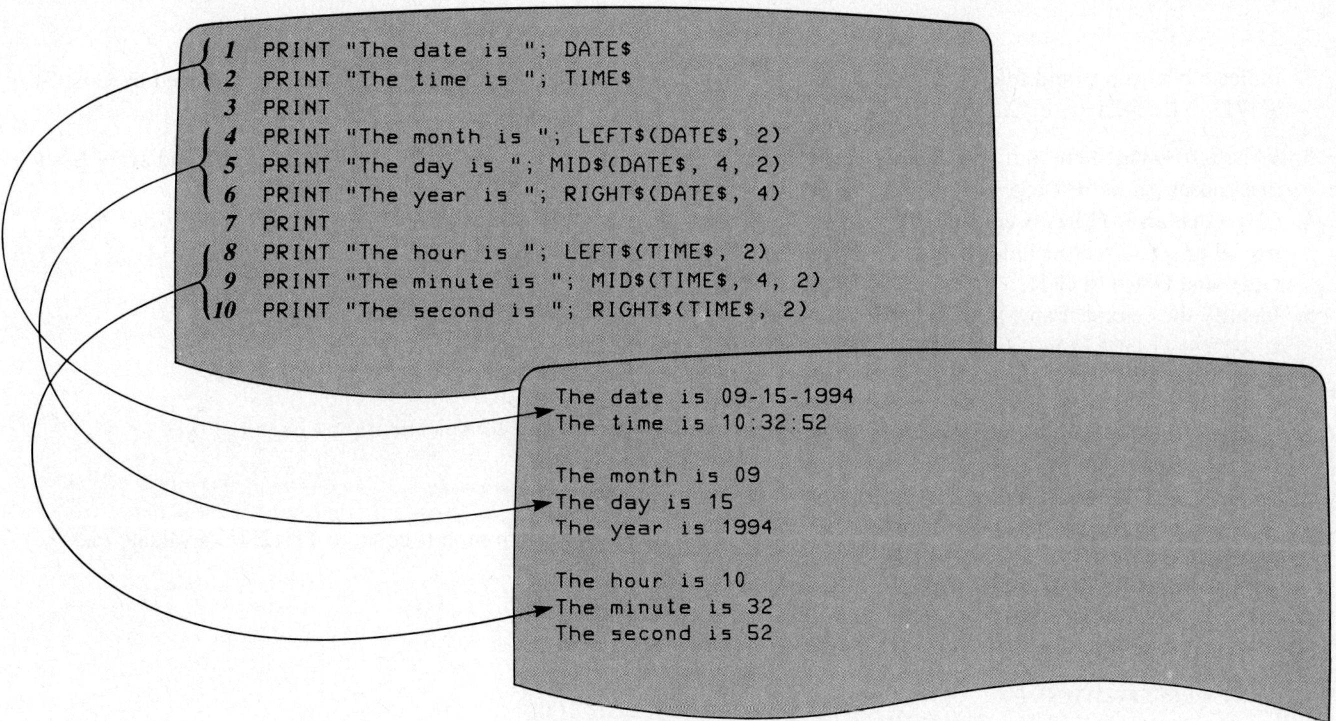

1 PRINT "The date is "; DATE$
2 PRINT "The time is "; TIME$
3 PRINT
4 PRINT "The month is "; LEFT$(DATE$, 2)
5 PRINT "The day is "; MID$(DATE$, 4, 2)
6 PRINT "The year is "; RIGHT$(DATE$, 4)
7 PRINT
8 PRINT "The hour is "; LEFT$(TIME$, 2)
9 PRINT "The minute is "; MID$(TIME$, 4, 2)
10 PRINT "The second is "; RIGHT$(TIME$, 2)
The date is 09-15-1994
The time is 10:32:52
The month is 09
The day is 15
The year is 1994
The hour is 10
The minute is 32
The second is 52

FIGURE 6-20 An example of a partial program that uses string functions. Assume system date is 9/15/94 and system time is 10:32:52

TRY IT YOURSELF EXERCISES

1. What is displayed when the following programs are executed?

a.
```
' Exercise 1.a
City$ = "Los Angeles"
PRINT LEFT$(City$, 1) + MID$(City$, 5, 1) + " LAW"
END
```

b.
```
' Exercise 1.b
PRINT "Number", "Square", "Square Root"
FOR I = 1 TO 10
   PRINT I, I ^ 2, SQR(I)
NEXT I
END
```

2. Assume arrays Part and Cost are dimensioned by the statement `DIM Part(1 TO 5), Cost(1 TO 5)`. Assume that the two arrays were loaded with the following values:

ARRAY PART	ARRAY COST
15	1.23
71	2.34
92	.25
94	1.37
99	5.25

Indicate how you would reference the following values using subscripts. For example, .25 can be referenced by Cost(3).
a. 71 b. 5.25 c. 2.34 d. 15 e. 1.37 f. 1.23 g. 99

3. Write a `DIM` statement to minimally dimension array X so that subscripts in the range 1 to 900 are valid and array Y so that subscripts in the range –5 to 22 are valid.
4. Given that array G has been declared to have 10 elements (1 to 10), assume that each element of G has a value. Write a partial program that includes a `DIM` statement to shift all the values up one location. That is, assign G(1) to G(2), G(2) to G(3), and G(10) to G(1).
5. Identify the errors, if any, in each of the following:

a. `DIM Amt(1 TO -1)`
b. `DIM Bal (1 TOO 10)`
c. `DIM Sales`
d. `DIM (1 TO 35)X`

6. Indicate what each of the following are equal to. Assume Phrase$ is equal to `Aim the arrow carefully.`

a. `LEN(Phrase$)`
b. `MID$(Phrase$, 4, 3)`
c. `LEFT$(Phrase$, 13)`
d. `RIGHT$(Phrase$, 5)`

7. Assume that the system date is equal to December 25, 1994 and the system time is equal to 11:12:15. Evaluate the following:

a. `X$ = TIME$`
b. `X$ = MID$(TIME$, 4, 1)`
c. `X$ = RIGHT$(DATE$, 2)`
d. `X$ = LEFT$(DATE$, 2)`

8. Write a `LET` statement that assigns Number a random value between 1 and 52.
9. Explain the purpose of the `RANDOMIZE` statement.
10. What does each of the following equal?

a. `INT(23.46)`	b. `SQR(121)`
c. `LEN("ABC")`	d. `INT(-12.43)`
e. `SQR(SQR(81))`	f. `SQR(INT(36.57))`

STUDENT ASSIGNMENTS

STUDENT ASSIGNMENT 1: Phone Number Lookup

Instructions: Design and code a top-down QuickBASIC program that requests a person's last name and displays the person's telephone number.

Read the data shown in the phone number table under INPUT into parallel arrays from a sequential data file or `DATA` statements. If you plan to use a sequential data file, ask your instructor for a copy of PHONE.DAT.

Accept a person's last name in lowercase from the user. Search the last name array. If the search is successful, display the corresponding telephone number. If the search is unsuccessful, display a diagnostic message. After the search, ask the user if he or she wants to look up another telephone number. The output results should be similar to the displayed results shown under OUTPUT.

INPUT: Use the following phone number table data. Include a value at the beginning of the file which indicates the number of elements required in the parallel arrays that will hold the names and phone numbers.

Look up the phone numbers of the following individuals: fuqua, bingle, smith, and course.

NAME	PHONE NUMBER
miller	(213) 430-2865
flaming	(213) 866-9082
fuqua	(714) 925-3391
bingle	(805) 402-3376
course	(213) 423-7765

OUTPUT: The following results are displayed for bingle and smith:

```
Person's Name =====> bingle
Phone Number ======> (805) 402-3376
Enter Y to lookup another phone number, Else N... y
```

```
Person's Name =====> smith
The Name smith NOT FOUND
Enter Y to lookup another phone number, Else N... y
```

STUDENT ASSIGNMENT 2: Weight Table Lookup

Instructions: Design and code a top-down QuickBASIC program that accepts a male or female height and displays the average weight ranges for a small-framed, medium-framed, and large-framed person. If the search is unsuccessful, display an error message. The table entries are shown in the height and weight table data under INPUT. The output results are shown under OUTPUT.

INPUT: Use the following height and weight table data. Read the table data into two separate sets of parallel arrays, one for the male weights and one for the female weights, by means of a data file or DATA statements. If you plan to use a sequential data file, ask your instructor for a copy of WEIGHT.DAT. Initialize a variable to nine (the number of different heights for males and for females prior to the DIM statement). Use this variable to dimension the arrays and control any loops that search for heights. Look up the following:

Sex – Male, Height – 72
Sex – Female, Height – 64
Sex – Male, Height – 76
Sex – Female, Height – 72
Sex – Male, Height – 70

MEN

HEIGHT	SMALL FRAME	MEDIUM FRAME	LARGE FRAME
66	124–133	130–143	138–156
67	128–136	134–147	142–161
68	132–141	138–152	147–168
69	136–145	142–156	151–170
70	140–150	146–160	155–174
71	144–154	150–165	159–179
72	148–158	154–170	164–184
73	152–162	158–175	168–189
74	156–167	162–180	173–194

WOMEN

HEIGHT	SMALL FRAME	MEDIUM FRAME	LARGE FRAME
62	102–110	107–119	115–131
63	105–113	110–122	118–134
64	108–116	113–126	121–138
65	111–119	116–130	125–142
66	114–123	120–135	129–148
67	118–127	124–139	133–150
68	122–131	128–43	137–154
69	126–135	132–147	141–158
70	130–140	136–151	145–163

OUTPUT: The following screen displays for the first set of data under INPUT:

```
Person's Sex (M or F) ========> M

Person's Height in Inches
Male 66-74, Female 62-70) ====> 72

Small Frame Weight Range =====> 148-158

Medium Frame Weight Range ====> 154-170

Large Frame Weight Range =====> 164-184

Enter a Y to lookup another weight range, else N... Y
```

APPENDIX

QuickBASIC Debugging Techniques

Although the top-down approach and structured programming techniques help minimize errors, they by no means guarantee error-free programs. Owing to carelessness or insufficient thought, program portions can be constructed which do not work as anticipated and give erroneous results. When such problems occur, you need techniques to isolate the errors and correct the erroneous program statements.

QuickBASIC can detect many different **grammatical errors** and display appropriate diagnostic messages. However, there is no BASIC system that can detect all errors. Some of these errors can go undetected by QuickBASIC until either an abnormal end occurs during execution or the program terminates with the results in error.

There are several techniques you can use for attempting to discover the portion of the program that is in error. These methods are **debugging techniques**. The errors themselves are **bugs**, and the activity involved in their detection is **debugging**. QuickBASIC has a fully integrated debugger which pinpoints errors by tracing, or highlighting, through the QuickBASIC source code. The QuickBASIC debugging features include the following:

- Examining values through the immediate window
- Executing one statement at a time
- Breakpoints
- Tracing
- Set next statement
- Recording
- Watch variables and watchpoints

EXAMINING VALUES THROUGH THE IMMEDIATE WINDOW

Following the termination of execution of a program, the program's variables remain equal to the latest values assigned. Through the immediate window, you can examine their values. This is an easy-to-use, and yet, powerful debugging tool.

To activate the immediate window, press F6. You may then display the value of any variables in the program by using the `PRINT` statement and the names of the variables. Recall that when a statement is entered in the immediate window, it is executed immediately. After viewing the values, press F6 to deactivate the immediate window and activate the view window.

If you have a mouse, move the pointer to the inactive window and click the mouse button.

EXECUTING ONE STATEMENT AT A TIME

Another debugging tool is the Step mode. In the **Step mode**, the PC executes the program one statement at a time. To activate this mode, press the F8 key. The first time you press the F8 key, the PC displays the first executable statement in reverse video. Thereafter, each time you press the F8 key, the PC executes the statement in reverse video and displays the next executable statement in reverse video. Hence, the PC steps through the program one statement at a time as you press the F8 key.

While the PC is in the Step mode and before you press the F8 key again, you can do any of the following to better understand what the program is doing:

- Activate the immediate window and use the `PRINT` statement to display the values of variables.
- Use the F4 key to toggle between displaying the program and the output screen.
- Modify any statement in the program. If you modify the statement in reverse video, the reverse video disappears. It reappears as soon as you move the cursor off the line.

To exit the Step mode, press the F5 key. The F5 key continues normal execution of the program. If you want to halt the program again, press Ctrl + Break. To continue execution after pressing Ctrl + Break, you can do one of the following:

- Press F5 to continue normal execution
- Press Shift + F5 to start execution from the beginning of the program
- Press F8 to activate the Step mode

BREAKPOINTS

A **breakpoint** is a line in the program where you want execution to halt. Breakpoints are established by moving the cursor to the line in question, followed by pressing the F9 key or selecting the Toggle Breakpoint command in the Debug menu. When you execute the program after setting one or more breakpoints, the PC halts execution at the next breakpoint and displays it in reverse video. Once the program halts at a breakpoint, you can do one of the following:

- Press the F8 key to enter the Step mode and execute from the one statement at a time to the next breakpoint
- Display the values of variables in the immediate window
- Edit the program
- Delete or add new breakpoints
- Press F5 to continue execution of the program

To toggle off a breakpoint, move the cursor to the breakpoint and press the F9 key. An alternative method for clearing breakpoints is to select the command Clear All Breakpoints in the Debug menu. This latter method can be useful, especially when you have set a number of breakpoints and cannot remember where they are located in the program. A breakpoint only displays in reverse video when it halts execution of the program.

To save time, you should carefully select breakpoints. Commonly used breakpoints include lines immediately following input, calculations, and decision statements.

TRACING

The Trace On command in the Debug menu causes the PC to trace the program. **Tracing** means that the program will execute in slow motion. As the program executes in slow motion, the PC highlights each statement as it executes it. With the Trace On command you can quickly get an idea as to flow of control in your program. This activity must be observed to be appreciated.

The Trace On command works like a toggle switch. Select it once and the PC will trace the flow of control. Select it again, and you turn tracing off. You know that tracing is on when there is a bullet in front of the command in the Debug menu. If you are using the commercial version of QuickBASIC, note that you must toggle on Full Menus in the Option menu for the Trace On command to display in the Debug menu.

Two QuickBASIC statements that carry out the same function as the Trace On command are `TRON` and `TROFF`. The `TRON` statement turns on tracing for all future statements executed. The `TROFF` statement turns tracing off. Although most QuickBASIC programmers use the Trace On command to trace a program, some find the `TRON` and `TROFF` statements useful for tracing small sections of a program.

SET NEXT STATEMENT

The Set Next Statement command in the Debug menu allows you to establish with the cursor where execution will continue following a program halt. For example, assume that you have set a breakpoint in a program. When the PC halts execution at the statement, you can move the cursor to any line in the program and select the Set Next Statement command. When execution resumes, it will begin at the cursor rather than at the statement in reverse video. The Set Next Statement command works much like the infamous `GOTO` statement. Use caution when evaluating the program results following the use of this command since skipping over code can produce unexpected results. If you are using the commercial version of QuickBASIC, note that you must toggle on Full Menus in the Option menu for the Trace On command to display in the Debug menu.

RECORDING

The History On command in the Debug menu is often used in conjunction with breakpoints. When you select the History On command, the PC records the last 20 lines executed by the program. When the program halts at a breakpoint, you can use the Shift + F8 to go back through the last 20 lines executed. You can use the Shift + F10 to go forward through the last 20 lines executed.

Stepping through the last 20 lines can also be useful when your program halts due to a logic error. If you select History On prior to execution, then you can step through the last 20 lines executed before the program's premature termination.

To stop recording the last 20 lines, select History On. This command acts like a toggle switch. Select it once and it's on. Select it again and it's off. You know that the History On command is active when there is a bullet in front of the command in the Debug menu. (Full Menus in the Option menu must be active for the History On command to display in the Debug menu.)

WATCH VARIABLES AND WATCHPOINTS

The Add Watch command in the Debug menu allows you to enter the names of variables or expressions that you want displayed in the watch window. The **watch window** (Figure A-1) displays above the view window whenever watch variables are active. Watching a variable is often combined with the Step mode (F8) or breakpoints to track its value, thus avoiding repeated use of the `PRINT` statement in the immediate window.

FIGURE A-1
The watch window displays above the view window. Program halts on LOOP statement when Emp.Number$ = "128". Value of Emp.Hours is 38. Value of Emp.Rate is 4.6.

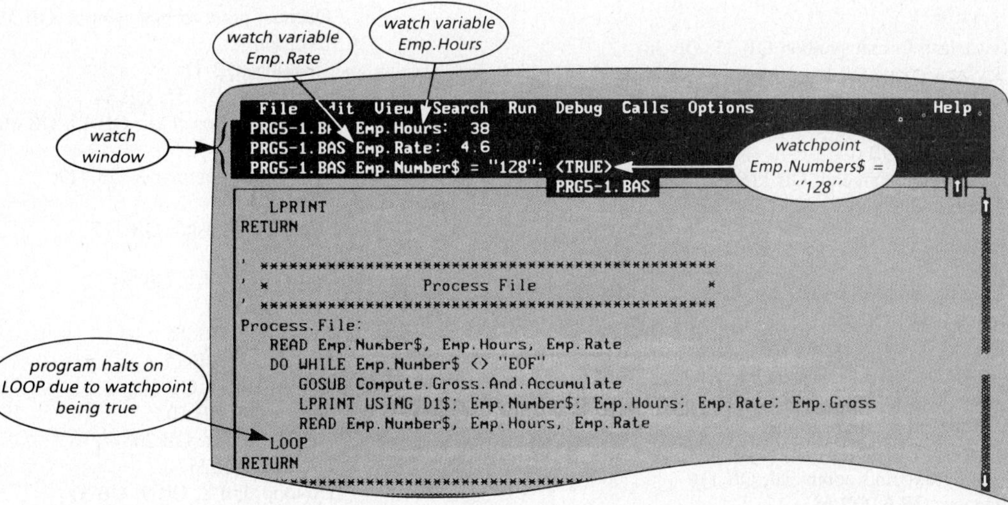

With the commercial version of QuickBASIC, you can add watch variables or conditions to the watch window by pressing Shift + F9 or selecting the Instant Watch command. The main difference between the Instant Watch and Add Watch commands is that with Instant Watch you do not have to type the variable name or condition. You simply select a watch variable by moving the cursor within the variable name in the program. To select a condition, you must use the Shift and arrow keys to highlight it before pressing Shift + F9.

The Watchpoint command in the Debug menu allows you to enter a watchpoint in the watch window. A **watchpoint** (Figure A-1) is a condition that halts program execution when it becomes true.

To delete individual watch variables or watchpoints, select the Delete Watch command in the Debug menu. To delete all watch variables and watch points, select the Delete All Watch command.

QuickBASIC Index

MICROSOFT QuickBASIC REFERENCE CARD

Legend: Uppercase letters are required keywords. You must supply items within < >'s. You must select one of the entries within { }'s. Items within [ ]'s are optional. Three ellipsis points (...) indicate that an item may be repeated as many times as you wish. The symbol ƀ represents a blank character.

Summary of BASIC Statements

STATEMENT

BEEP
Causes the speaker on the PC to beep for a fraction of a second.

CALL <name> [(argumentlist)]
Transfers control to a subprogram.

CHAIN <"filespec">
Instructs the PC to stop executing the current program, load another program from auxiliary storage and start executing it.

CHDIR <pathspecification>
Changes the current directory for the specified drive.

CIRCLE <(x, y), radius> [,color [,start,end [,shape]]]
Causes the PC to draw an ellipse, circle, arc, or wedge with center at (x, y).

CLEAR [,,stack]
Reinitializes all program variables, closes files, and sets the stack size.

CLOSE [#] [filenumber] [,[#] [filenumber]]...
Closes specified files.

CLS
Erases the information on the screen and places the cursor in the upper left corner of the screen.

COLOR [background] [,palette]
In medium-resolution graphics mode, sets the color for the background and palette of colors.

COLOR [foreground] [,background] [,border]
In the text mode, defines the color of the foreground characters, background, and border around the screen.

COM(n) {ON | OFF | STOP} Enables or disables trapping of communications activity on adaptor n.

COMMON [SHARED] <variable> [,variable]...
Passes specified variables to a chained program.

CONST <constantname> = <expression> [, constantname = expression]...
Declares symbolic constants that can be used in place of numeric or string expressions.

STATEMENT

DATA <data item> [,data item]...
Provides for the creation of a sequence of data items for use by the READ statement.

DATE$ = mm {/ | -} dd {/ | -} yy[yy] Sets the system date, where mm = month, dd = day, yy = year, yyyy = 4-digit year.

DECLARE {FUNCTION | SUB} name [(parameterlist)]
Declares references to QuickBASIC procedures and invokes argument-type checking.

DEF FN<name> [(variable, [, variable]...)] = <expression>
Defines and names a function that can be referenced in a program as often as needed. Multiline functions end with an END DEF statement.

DEFtype <letterrange> [,letterrange]...
Sets the data type for variables and functions.

DIM [SHARED] <arrayname(size)> [AS type], [arrayname(size) [AS type]]...
Reserves storage locations for arrays and declares the array type.

DO
Causes the statements between DO and LOOP to be executed repeatedly. The loop is controlled by a condition in the corresponding LOOP statement.

DO UNTIL <condition>
Causes the statements between DO UNTIL and LOOP to be executed repeatedly until the condition is true.

DO WHILE <condition>
Causes the statements between DO WHILE and LOOP to be executed repeatedly while the condition is true.

DRAW <string expression>
Causes the PC to draw the object that is defined by the value of the string expression.

END [{DEF | FUNCTION | IF | SELECT | SUB | TYPE}] Ends a QuickBASIC program, procedure, or block of code.

ERASE <arrayname> [,arrayname]...
Eliminates previously defined arrays.

ERROR <integerexpression>
Simulates the occurrence of a QuickBASIC error or allows the user to define error codes.

EXIT <statement>
Exits statement, where statement is equal to FOR, DO, DEF, FUNCTION, or SUB.

STATEMENT

FIELD <#filenumber, width AS string variable> [,width AS string variable]...
Allocates space for variables in a random file buffer.

FILES [filespecification]
Lists the names of all programs and data files in auxiliary storage on the default drive or the drive specified by file specification.

FOR <loopvariable> = <initial> TO <limit> [STEP increment]
Causes the statements between the FOR and NEXT statements to be executed until the value of loopvariable exceeds the value of the limit.

FUNCTION <name> [(parameterlist)] [STATIC]
Declares the name, the parameters, and initiates a function procedure that ends with an END FUNCTION.

GET <(x_1, y_1) – (x_2, y_2), arrayname>
Reads the colors of the points in the specified area on the screen into an array.

GET <[#]filenumber> [,record number]
Reads the specified record from a random file and transfers it to the buffer that is defined by the corresponding FIELD statement.

GOSUB {linelabel | linenumber} Causes control to transfer to a subroutine beginning at the specified line. Also retains the location of the next statement following the GOSUB statement.

GOTO {linelabel | linenumber} Transfers control to the specified line.

IF <condition> THEN [clause] [ELSE [clause]]
The single line IF statement causes execution of the THEN clause if the condition is true. If the ELSE clause is included, it causes execution of the ELSE clause if the condition is false.

IF <condition> THEN
[statementblock$_1$]
[ELSE
[statementblock$_2$]]
END IF
The block IF statement allows for multiple lines in the THEN and ELSE clauses. Causes execution of the THEN clause if the condition is true. Causes execution of the ELSE clause if the condition is false. The ELSE IF <condition> THEN clause may be used in place of the ELSE clause.

INPUT [;]["prompt message" {, | ;}] <variable> [,variable]...
Provides for the assignment of values to variables from a source external to the program, such as the keyboard.

INPUT <#filenumber, variable> [,variable]...
Provides for the assignment of values to variables from a sequential file in auxiliary storage.

(***BASIC Statements*** *continued on page R.2 in left column*)

MICROSOFT QuickBASIC REFERENCE CARD

STATEMENT

KEY {**n, string value** / **ON** / **OFF** / **LIST**} Assigns a string value to a function key. Also used to display the values and enable or disable the function key display line.

KEY(n) {**ON** / **OFF** / **STOP**} Activates or deactivates trapping of the specified key n.

KILL <filespecification>
Deletes a file from disk.

[LET] <variable> = <expression>
Causes the evaluation of the expression, followed by the assignment of the resulting value to the variable to the left of the equal sign.

LINE [(x1, y1)] <-(x2, y2)> [,color] [,B[F]][,Style]
Draws a line or a box on the screen.

LINE INPUT [;]["prompt message";] <string variable> or
LINE INPUT <#filenumber,> <string variable>
Provides for the assignment of a line up to 255 characters from a source external to the program, such as the keyboard or a sequential file.

LOCATE [row] [,column] [,cursor] [,start] [,stop]
Positions the cursor on the screen. Can also be used to make the cursor visible or invisible and to control the size of the cursor.

LOCK <[#]filenumber>, {record / [start] TO end}
Locks all or some of the records in a file.

LOOP {**WHILE** / **UNTIL** / **b̸**} **[condition]** Identifies the end of a loop.

LPRINT [item] [{, / ; / b̸} item]... Provides for the generation of output to the printer.

LPRINT USING <string expression;> <item> [{, / ; / b̸} item]...
Provides for the generation of formatted output to the printer.

LSET <string variable> = <string expression>
Moves string data left-justified into an area of a random file buffer that is defined by the string variable.

MID$ <(string var, start position [,number]> = <substring>
Replaces a substring within a string.

MKDIR <pathname>
Creates a new directory.

NAME <oldfilespecification> AS <newfilespecification>
Renames a file on disk.

STATEMENT

NEXT [numeric variable] [,numeric variable]...
Identifies the end of the For loop(s).

ON COM(n) GOSUB {linelabel / linenumber}
Causes control to transfer to the specified line when data is filling the communications buffer (n).

ON ERROR GOTO {linelabel / linenumber}
Enables error trapping and specifies the first line of an error-handling routine that the PC is to branch to in the event of an error. If linenumber is zero, error trapping is disabled.

ON <numeric expression> GOSUB {linelabel-list / linenumber-list}
Causes control to transfer to the subroutine represented by the selected line. Also retains the location of the next statement following the ON-GOSUB statement.

ON <numeric expression> GOTO {linelabel-list / linenumber-list}
Causes control to transfer to one of several lines according to the value of the numeric expression.

ON KEY(n) GOSUB {linelabel / linenumber}
Causes control to transfer to the specified line when the function key or cursor control key (n) is pressed.

ON PEN GOSUB {linelabel / linenumber}
Causes control to transfer to the specified line when the light pen is activated.

ON PLAY(n) GOSUB {linelabel / linenumber}
Plays continuous background music. Transfers control to the specified line when a note (n) is sensed.

ON STRIG(n) GOSUB {linelabel / linenumber}
Causes control to transfer to the specified line when one of the joystick buttons (n) is pressed.

ON TIMER(n) GOSUB {linelabel / linenumber}
Causes control to transfer to the specified line when the specified period of time (n) in seconds has elapsed.

ON UEVENT GOSUB {linelabel / linenumber}
Defines the event-handler for a user-defined event.

OPEN <filespec> FOR <mode> AS <[#]filenumber>
[LEN = record length]
Allows a program to read or write records to a file. If record length is specified, then the file is opened as a random file. If the record length is not specified, then the file is opened as a sequential file.

STATEMENT

OPTION BASE {0 / 1}
Assigns a lower bound of 0 or 1 to all arrays declared with only an upper-bound value.

OUT <port>, <data>
Sends a byte to a machine I/O port.

PAINT <(x, y)> [[,paint] [,boundary]]
Paints an area on the screen with the selected color.

PALETTE [attribute, color] or
PALETTE USING <arrayname> [(arrayindex)]
Changes one or more of the colors in the palette.

PCOPY <sourcepage>, <destinationpage>
Copies one screen page to another.

PEN(n) {**ON** / **OFF** / **STOP**} Enables or disables the PEN read function used to analyze light pen activity.

PLAY <string expression>
Causes the PC to play music according to the value of the string expression.

PLAY {**ON** / **OFF** / **STOP**} Enables, disables, or suspends play event trapping.

POKE <address>, <byte>
Writes a byte into a storage location.

PRESET <(x, y)> [,color]
Draws a point in the color specified at (x, y). If no color is specified, it erases the point.

{PRINT / ?} [item] [{, / ; / b̸} item]... Provides for the generation of output to the screen.

{PRINT / ?} <#filenumber,> [item] [{, / ; / b̸} item]...
Provides for the generation of output to a sequential file.

PRINT USING <string expression;> <item> [{, / ; / b̸} item]...
Provides for the generation of formatted output to the screen.

PRINT <#filenumber,> USING <string expression;>

<item> [{, / ; / b̸} item]... Provides for the generation of formatted output to a sequential file.

(***BASIC Statements*** *continued on page R.3 in left column*)

MICROSOFT QuickBASIC REFERENCE CARD

STATEMENT

PSET <(x, y)> [,color]
Draws a point in the color specified at (x, y).

PUT <(x_1, y_1), arrayname> [,action]
Writes the colors of the points in the array onto an area of the screen.

PUT <[#]filenumber> [,record number]
Writes a record to a random file from a buffer defined by the corresponding FIELD statement.

RANDOMIZE [numeric expression]
Reseeds the random number generator.

READ <variable> [,variable]...
Provides for the assignment of values to variables from a sequence of data items created from DATA statements.

REDIM [SHARED]<arrayname(size)> [AS type] [arrayname(size) [AS type]]...
Changes the space allocated to an array declared $DYNAMIC.

{REM | '} [comment] Provides for the insertion of comments in a program.

RESET
Closes all disk files.

RESTORE {linelabel | linenumber}
Allows the data items in DATA statements to be reread.

RESUME {linelabel | NEXT | 0 | ƀ} Continues program execution at the linelabel, or the line following that which caused the error, after an error-recovery procedure.

RETURN {linelabel | linenumber}
Causes control to transfer from a subroutine back to the statement that follows the corresponding GOSUB or ON-GOSUB statement.

RMDIR <pathname>
Removes a directory from disk after all files and subdirectories have been removed.

RSET <string variable> = <string expression>
Moves string data right-justified into an area of a random file buffer that is defined by string variable.

RUN {linenumber | linelabel | ƀ} Restarts the program in main storage.

SCREEN [mode] [,color switch] [,active page] [,visual page]
Sets the screen attributes for text mode, medium-resolution graphics, or high-resolution graphics.

SEEK <[#]filenumber>, <position>
Sets the position in a file for the next read or write.

STATEMENT

SELECT CASE <testexpression>
CASE <matchexpression$_1$>
[range of statements$_1$]
[CASE <matchexpression$_2$>
[range of statements$_2$]
.
.
.
[CASE ELSE
[range of statements$_n$]
END SELECT
Causes execution of one of several ranges of statements depending on the value of testexpression.

SHARED <variable> [AS type] [,variable [AS type]]...
Gives a SUB or FUNCTION procedure access to variables declared at the module level without passing them as parameters.

SHELL [commandstring]
Places the current QB session in a temporary wait state and returns control to MS-DOS. Can also execute another program or MS-DOS command as specified in commandstring.

SLEEP [seconds]
Suspends execution of the calling program.

SOUND <frequency>, <duration>
Causes the generation of sound through the PC speaker.

STATIC <variablelist>
Causes variables and arrays to be local to either a DEF FN, a FUNCTION, or a SUB, and maintains values between calls.

STOP
Stops execution of a program. Unlike the END statement, files are left open.

STRIG(n) {ON | OFF | STOP} Enables or disables trapping of the joystick buttons.

SUB <globalname> [(parameterlist)] [STATIC]
Establishes the beginning of a subprogram. The end of the subprogram is identified by the END SUB statement.

SWAP <variable$_1$>, <variable$_2$>
Exchanges the values of two variables or two elements of an array.

SYSTEM
Closes all open files and returns control to MS-DOS.

TIME$ = hh[:mm[:ss]]
Sets the system time, where
hh = hours, mm = minutes, and ss = seconds.

TIMER {ON | OFF | STOP} Enables or disables trapping of timed events.

STATEMENT

TROFF
Disables statement tracing.

TRON
Causes the PC to trace execution of program statements.

TYPE <labelname>
<fieldname$_1$> AS <fieldtype>
.
.
.
<fieldname$_n$> AS <fieldtype>
END TYPE
Creates user-defined data types containing one or more elements.

UEVENT {ON | OFF | STOP} Enables, disables, or suspends user-defined event trapping.

UNLOCK <[#]filenumber>, {record | [start] TO end}
Unlocks records in a file.

VIEW [[SCREEN] (x_1, y_1) – (x_2, y_2)] [,color] [,boundary]
Defines a viewport.

VIEW PRINT [topline TO bottomline]
Establishes boundaries for the screen text viewport.

WEND
Identifies the end of a While loop.

WHILE <condition>
Identifies the beginning of a While loop. Causes the statements between WHILE and WEND to be executed repeatedly while the condition is true.

WIDTH {40 | 80} Erases the information on the screen, sets the width of the line on the screen to 40 or 80 characters, and places the cursor in the upper left corner of the screen.

WIDTH LPRINT <width>
Sets the printer column width.

WINDOW <[SCREEN] (x_1, y_1) – (x_2, y_2)>
Redefines the coordinates of the viewport. Allows you to draw objects in space and not be bounded by the limits of the screen.

WRITE [expression list]
Writes data to the screen.

WRITE <#filenumber,> [item] [{, | ; | ƀ} item]...
Writes data to a sequential file. Causes the PC to insert commas between the items written to the sequential file.

MICROSOFT QuickBASIC REFERENCE CARD

Summary of BASIC Functions

FUNCTION

ABS(N)
Returns the absolute value of the argument N.

ASC(X$)
Returns a two-digit numeric value that is equivalent in ASCII code to the first character of the string argument X$.

ATN(N)
Returns the angle in radians whose tangent is the value of the argument N.

CDBL(N)
Returns N converted to a double-precision value.

CHR$(N)
Returns a single string character that is equivalent in ASCII code to the numeric argument N.

CINT(N)
Returns N converted to an integer after rounding the fractional part of N.

CLNG(N)
Returns N converted to a long integer after rounding the fractional part of N.

COMMAND$
Returns the command line used to start the program.

COS(N)
Returns the cosine of the argument N where N is in radians.

CSNG(N)
Returns N converted to a single-precision value.

CSRLIN
Returns the vertical (row) coordinate of the cursor.

CVI(X$), CVL(X$), CVS(X$), CVD(X$)
Returns the integer, long integer, single-precision, or double-precision numeric value equivalent to the string X$. Used with random files.

DATE$
Returns the current date (mm-dd-yyyy).

EOF(filenumber)
Returns −1 (true) if the end-of-file has been sensed on the sequential file associated with filenumber. Returns 0 (false) if the end-of-file has not been sensed.

ERDEV
Returns an error code from the last device that caused an error.

FUNCTION

ERDEV$
Returns a string expression containing the name of the device that generated a vital error.

ERL
Returns the line number preceding the line that caused the error. If no line numbers are used, then ERL returns a zero.

ERR
Returns the error code for the last error that occurred.

EXP(N)
Returns e(2.718281...) raised to the argument N.

FILEATTR
Returns the file mode for an open file.

FIX(N)
Returns the value of N truncated to an integer.

FRE(N)
Returns the amount of available stack space (N = −2), string space (N not equal to −1 or −2), or size in bytes of the largest array you can create (N = −1).

FREEFILE
Returns the next free QuickBASIC file number.

HEX$(N)
Returns the hexadecimal equivalent of N.

INKEY$
Returns the last character entered from the keyboard.

INP(N)
Returns the byte read from an I/O port N.

INPUT$(N)
Suspends execution of the program until a string of N characters is received from the keyboard.

INPUT$(N, [#]filenumber)
Returns a string of characters from the specified file.

INSTR(P, X$, S$)
Returns the beginning position of the substring S$ in string X$. P indicates the position at which the search begins in the string X$.

INT(N)
Returns the largest integer that is less than or equal to the argument N.

LBOUND(arrayname[,dimension])
Returns the lower-bound value for the specified dimension of arrayname.

FUNCTION

LCASE$(X$)
Returns X$ in all lowercase letters.

LEFT$(X$, N)
Returns the leftmost N characters of the string argument X$.

LEN(X$)
Returns the length of the string argument X$.

LOC(#filenumber)
With a random file, it returns the number of the last record read or written. With a sequential file, it returns the number of records read from or written to the file.

LOF(#filenumber)
Returns the number of bytes allocated to a file.

LOG(N)
Returns the natural log of the argument N where N is greater than 0.

LPOS(N)
Returns the current position of the line printer's print head within the printer buffer where N is equal to 1 for LPT1, 2 for LPT2, and so on.

LTRIM$(X$)
Returns X$ with leading spaces removed.

MID$(X$, P, N)
Returns N characters of the string argument X$ beginning at position P.

MKI$(N), MKL$(N), MKS$(N), MKD$(N)
Returns the string equivalent of an integer, long integer, single-precision, or double-precision value. Used with random files.

OCT$(N)
Returns the octal equivalent of N.

PEEK(N)
Returns the value of the byte stored at the specified storage location N.

PEN(N)
Returns light pen coordinate information. The information is dependent on the value assigned to N.

PLAY(n)
Returns the number of notes currently in the music background buffer.

PMAP (c, n)
Returns the world coordinate of the physical coordinate c or vice versa. The parameter n varies between 0 and 3, and determines whether c is an x or y coordinate, and whether the coordinate is to be mapped from the physical to the world coordinate or vice versa.

(***BASIC Functions*** *continued on page R.5 in left column*)

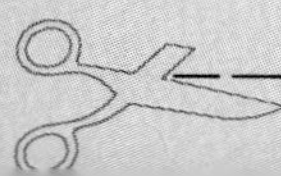